Computers
for Twenty-First
Century Educators

sixth edition

COMPUTERS
for Twenty-First
Century Educators

James Lockard
Northern Illinois University

Peter D. Abrams
Northern Illinois University

PEARSON

Boston | New York | San Francisco
Mexico City | Montreal | Toronto | London | Madrid | Munich | Paris
Hong Kong | Singapore | Tokyo | Cape Town | Sydney

Senior Editor: Arnis E. Burvikovs
Editorial Assistant: Christine Lyons
Development Editor: Sonny Regelman
Marketing Manager: Tara Whorf
Production Administrator: Michael Granger
Editorial-Production Service: Omegatype Typography, Inc.
Composition and Prepress Buyer: Linda Cox
Manufacturing Buyer: Andrew Turso
Cover Administrator: Kristina Mose-Libon
Interior Design: Carol Somberg
Electronic Composition: Omegatype Typography, Inc.

For related titles and support materials, visit our online catalog at www.ablongman.com.

Between the time website information is gathered and then published, it is not unusual for some sites to have closed. Also, the transcription of URLs can result in typographical errors. The publishers would appreciate notification where these errors occur so that they may be corrected in subsequent editions.

Many of the designations used by manufacturers and sellers to distinguish their products are claimed as trademarks. Where those designations appear in this book, and Allyn and Bacon was aware of a trademark claim, the designations have been printed in initial or all caps.

Library of Congress Cataloging-in-Publication Data

Lockard, James.
    Computers for twenty-first century educators / James Lockard, Peter D. Abrams.—6th ed.
      p. cm.
    Includes bibliographical references and index.
    ISBN 0-205-38089-1 (alk. paper)
    1. Computer-assisted instruction—United States.   2. Microcomputers—United States.   I. Abrams, Peter D. II. Title.

LB1028.5.L58 2004
371.33'4—dc22

2003057964

Photo credits appear on page 438, which constitutes an extension of the copyright page.

Printed in the United States of America

10 9 8 7 6 5 4 3 2 1   RRD-IN   08 07 06 05 04 03

Brief Contents

Contents

chapter 3

The Internet, Computer Networks, and Distance Learning: Communication Tools of the Twenty-First Century 38

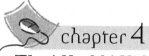

chapter 4

The World Wide Web: Bringing the World into the Classroom   64

chapter 5

Word Processing and Publishing:
Managing Text   99

chapter 6
Databases: Managing Information, Creating Knowledge   134

chapter 7

Spreadsheets: Managing and Analyzing Numeric Data   163

chapter 8

Graphics Tools: Communicating Visually   190

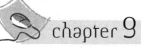

chapter 9
Additional Software and Hardware Tools:
Enhancing Teaching and Learning Efficiently   221

chapter 10

Computer-Assisted Instruction Fundamentals 244

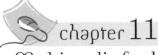

chapter 11

Multimedia for Learning 275

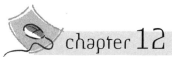

chapter 12

Courseware Evaluation   309

chapter 13

Beyond Computer Literacy: Technology Integration and Curriculum Transformation   337

chapter 14

Technology Implementation   348

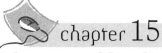

chapter 15
Issues and Implications   372

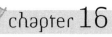

chapter 16
Today and Tomorrow: What May Lie Ahead   391

Preface

C*omputers for Twenty-First Century Educators* is a response to and reflection of the ever-growing role of electronic technologies in education. Most such technologies are now computer based, and computers are found in virtually every K–12 school across the United States—public and private—as well as in countless preschools and throughout higher education. The total amount of money spent by U.S. schools annually for technology is enormous. One might appropriately ask what *students* are getting from all that money. After all, it is the impact on learning that justifies educational expenditures.

Schools have always been a reflection of the society in which they exist. Technology is the driving force in the economies of developed nations worldwide, with developing nations working hard to attain a comparable position. Yet technology can be costly, which leads to concerns over a possible "digital divide" that could separate our population into two new groups of "haves" and "have nots," largely along economic lines. More than half the homes in the United States have personal computers, but that means a very large number still lack this tool for knowledge. Technology is very much a social issue as well as a critical educational concern.

Whatever the concerns, we must recognize that schools already have embraced technology, a fact that carries significant consequences for teachers as well as students. Our concern in writing this book was to address the challenges posed by technology for current and future teachers.

Whom Is This Book For?

This book will benefit any current educator or potential educator who wishes to become computer competent in order to provide leadership in educational institutions of the twenty-first century. It evolved from our own experiences teaching an introductory instructional computing course, one that we first designed in the early 1980s. Today we have multiple courses that continue to serve both pre-service and in-service teachers, as well as students from other disciplines throughout our university, including even computer science. An introductory course is available to both undergraduate and graduate students. We have attempted to write on a level appropriate to the former, yet suitable for the latter.

What Is the Premise of This Book?

In our view the cornerstone of technology in education is the ability to use the World Wide Web effectively and to create concrete products using applications (including word processing, databases, spreadsheets, and multimedia software tools). These products integrate the vital task of demonstrating what one has learned with development of increasingly important life skills that use technology. The National Educational Technology Standards (NETS), developed in recent years by the International Society for Technology in Education and widely adopted across the United States, have validated our long-established view. They are clearly identified throughout the book as a basis for its content.

In addition to product development tools, the computer can and should serve as a tutor, a method of instruction most commonly referred to as *computer-assisted instruction*. Furthermore, specific concepts and issues related to society, educational computing, and technology implementation are important to any computer educator, as also recognized in NETS. This book provides solid coverage of all these areas.

Because no one computer type now dominates in education, we chose not to emphasize one over the others, which makes this book equally usable with any available hardware. It is also software independent, focusing on principles and concepts, not the details of any specific program.

How Is the Book Organized?

We have organized this sixth edition of *Computers for Twenty-First Century Educators* into a total of 16 chapters. The first chapter sets the educational context, presenting both the potential benefits and acknowledging the problems surrounding schools and technology. It presents the landmark National Educational Technology Standards for students, teachers, and administrators. The content of each succeeding chapter is identified by the standards that it addresses. Chapter 2 puts computer technology into perspective with a brief history of computers and computing, followed by an overview of hardware and software, including terminology fundamental to computing.

Chapter 3 begins extensive treatment of the computer as a tool, both personally and practically in education. That chapter explores computer networks, the Internet, and distance learning—tools that offer both incredible opportunities as well as major new challenges for educators. Chapter 4 takes you on a journey into how the World Wide Web works, how to get the best educational value from it using tools such as WebQuests, and even how to develop web pages on a basic level.

Effective written communication using word processing and desktop publishing is the focus of Chapter 5, while Chapter 6 addresses information organization and management with databases. Chapter 7 explores spreadsheet applications for working with and presenting data.

In Chapter 8, attention turns to graphics software, including presentation tools such as *PowerPoint* as well as graphical organizers such as *Inspiration* and other visualization tools. It also provides guidance on hardware graphics production tools ranging from scanners to digital cameras as well as related presentation tools (video data projectors and document cameras). Chapter 9 delves into a broad range of "utility" software tools that can enhance both teaching and learning—materials generators, puzzle software, test creators, and PDF generators for making documents portable. It also leads you to explore some of the more promising new hardware tools for learning, namely personal digital assistants, GPS/GIS systems, and digital camcorders for the easiest video production ever.

Our treatment of the computer as tutor and an instructional tool covers computer-assisted instruction (Chapter 10), interactive multimedia for learning (Chapter 11), and courseware evaluation (Chapter 12).

To round out consideration of using computer technology in education, you will explore the concepts of computer literacy, curriculum integration, and computer competence in Chapter 13. Chapter 14 presents concrete suggestions for successful implementation of educational computing, while Chapter 15 examines technology issues and implications such as computer viruses and equity. Chapter 16 completes the book with thoughts on the future of computer technology and its educational applications. Concluding the book are an extensive glossary, including terms italicized in the text, and a comprehensive index.

What's New in This Edition?

This sixth edition reflects the comprehensive updating essential to any book in so volatile a field as educational computing and technology. All chapters were revised thoroughly. Ample, updated illustrations attempt to show concepts concretely to support and enhance the written text. Chapter bibliographies document sources and provide rich opportunities for further learning.

The near universality of Internet connections in schools led to further enhancement of our treatment of the Internet and World Wide Web and justifies a position at the beginning of the applications chapters. This reflects the major role the Web now plays in most schools as well as our daily lives. Most chapters also now include URLs of related, supportive websites. However, we have purposely limited URLs printed in the chapters to those that have remained accessible for a significant period of time or that we deemed the most significant among newer sites. A much wider range of useful, correlated web resources is provided on the companion website, where it can be updated regularly to maintain the links.

In response to suggestions from users, we merged desktop publishing into our treatment of text-based communications and expanded treatment of web page creation and graphics software and hardware. We split graphics from other kinds of software and hardware tools to create two chapters. Treatment of software creation was revamped and enhanced to reflect the increasingly dominant constructivist orientation to student multimedia projects and the creation of web pages. Chapters on integrated software and desktop publishing, computer managed instruction, programming, and artificial intelligence in education were deleted to make room for more extensive treatment of other topics. We retained chapters on the practical aspects of putting computers to work in our schools and revised them to reflect current themes and issues.

A comprehensive companion website for students and instructors is new to this edition. The student section contains:

- Complete chapter summaries.
- Full chapter bibliographies.
- An extended Appendix that includes a glossary, content from earlier editions of the text, and links to websites of producers and distributors of software products mentioned in the text.
- *PowerPoint* slides for students to use as guides to each chapter.
- Links to related articles from the *New York Times* website through the eThemes of the Times feature.
- Other helpful references and resources.

A hallmark of websites is that they are dynamic, changing in response to forces around us. Thus, additional sections may be added for some chapters as appropriate, and all sections of the companion website will be reviewed regularly and updated appropriately. We trust these web resources will draw you and your students back on a regular basis.

Instructor resources are now offered in electronic format and can be accessed by instructors through our companion website. These resources—including teaching tips, a test bank, and *PowerPoint* presentations for each chapter—are fully downloadable. **Please contact your Allyn & Bacon sales representative for access to these resources.** For help finding the representative in your area, visit <www.ablongman.com/replocator>.

How to Use This Book

We strongly urge you to use this book to support a hands-on approach to learning. Like bicycle riding, educational computing must be a practical, "let's do it" activity, not one about which you merely read, think, and discuss—important as those activities are. We recommend that students read the relevant material from this book *prior* to each session in the course, with minimal time spent in lecture and discussion and as much time as possible devoted to hands-on work at the computer where the most important learning will occur. Whether you use Windows or a Macintosh is irrelevant. It is critical that you *use* electronic technologies, and use them a lot.

Because this book is intended to support hands-on learning, you may want to consider one of the many available software guide books that integrate well with this text. Select one appropriate to your hardware and software. In our courses, we use *Microsoft Office* and a companion "how-to" manual.

Beginning with the very first edition, our goal has been to provide a truly comprehensive resource on educational computing technologies. In so doing, we have written a volume that includes far more material than most one-term courses can possibly cover. Throughout, we have tried to maintain maximum independence among the chapters. Feel free to use only those chapters that are appropriate to your focus and time frame, and use them in the order that you prefer. (We do not cover all chapters in our own course, either!) We believe this flexibility—combined with its comprehensiveness, technical accuracy, and machine-independence—makes this book one of the most broadly suitable text resources on the market today.

We acknowledge that some chapters or sections are more difficult for novice computer educators than others. For example, networking and telecommunications concepts are elements of contemporary computing that are apt to be new to many users or possibly misunderstood, as are many aspects of digital media. However difficult they may seem, these topics represent key aspects of future educational computer use. We have presented them as simply as we know how.

In sum, this is your book; use it as best fits your course, goals, and students. There is no one right way to go about the business of developing the technology competence of educators and future educators, but we are certain that an hour of hands-on lab time following brief development of conceptual understanding of the tools and their applications is the most valuable approach to a course of this nature.

Acknowledgments

Writing a book is an awesome adventure: often an exhilarating roller coaster ride, sometimes a swim through crocodile-infested waters, occasionally a peaceful sail across the smooth waters of a placid lake. Frequently, a blizzard rages around you, threatening to bury your computer under tons of snow; sometimes there's a hurricane blowing away everything in its path; and every now and then, the weather is perfect. Through it all, you trudge on in the belief that you are doing something of importance, something that will benefit others. It is that belief that sustains us.

Our families have now stood by us through six editions of this book, something we never imagined would happen in our wildest dreams, nor did they in theirs. We are eternally grateful to them for their love, support, and understanding. Most of the time spent writing this book was "borrowed" from them in the end, as all authors and their families are only too aware. We hope to make it up to them somehow.

As with previous editions, we are indebted to those who use this book across the United States and the world, for it is you who have given this text its uncommon endurance. We know of no other book in this field that has achieved so many editions and we appreciate the loyalty of our adopters, many of whom have been with us from the first edition. Your support makes the effort worthwhile.

As with each previous edition, the suggestions we received from current adopters of the book, our own students, and our reviewers were instrumental in significant changes made throughout this edition. We extend a sincere thank you to the following colleagues who offered excellent suggestions for modifications to the fifth edition: Lorena Jinkerson, Northern Michigan University; Jeremy Dickerson, The University of North Carolina at Wilmington; Jane Danielson, University of Southern Maine; and Steven Builta, Northern Illinois University. We have struggled to incorporate every new idea as best we could, to be current and comprehensive, and above all to be accurate. We also thank the following reviewers of this sixth edition: Jeremy Dickerson, The University of North Carolina at Wilmington; Lorena Jinkerson, Northern Michigan University; and Desi Larson, University of Southern Maine.

This edition reflects the contributions, guidance, support, and resolute encouragement of several key individuals at Allyn & Bacon. We extend our deepest thanks to Senior Editor, Arnis Burvikovs; Development Editor, Sonny Regelman; and Editorial Assistant, Christine Lyons. They never lost faith in our work and were always there when we needed them. We are also grateful for the excellent work of their many colleagues at Allyn & Bacon with whom we have not had direct contact, but whose contributions are obvious in the finished product. In addition, we deeply appreciate the excellent work of Karla Walsh and her associates at Omegatype Typography, Inc.

You, the users of this book—students and instructors alike—are the key to future editions. We need to know what works for you and what does not. We welcome and encourage your comments, questions, suggestions, and tips at any time and will gladly respond to email from you. Use the address below, or use the email link on the companion website, which you may access at <www.ablongman.com/lockard6e>. Since the website is a new feature in this format, we are especially keen to know what you like and dislike about it. We will consider all comments and suggestions carefully.

Jim Lockard
College of Education—ETRA
Northern Illinois University
DeKalb, IL 60115
Email: jlockard@niu.edu

Computers
for Twenty-First
Century Educators

Computers and Technology in Education

CHAPTER 1

OBJECTIVES

*After completing this chapter,
you will be familiar with and able to discuss:*

■ The need for twenty-first century teachers to be technology competent.

■ The state of computers in education in the United States.

■ The views of education and learning that are the foundations of this book, including the movement from behaviorism to constructivism.

■ The national standards for technology in education that apply to teachers, students, and administrators.

In addition, you will be able to:

■ Assess whether your educational beliefs are compatible with those that support this book.

C*omputers for Twenty-First Century Educators* reflects the belief that computers are an essential part of the "basics" of education in the twenty-first century, both in the United States and worldwide. As Moursund (1995) observed nearly a decade ago, the basics and the societal standards that shape them do change over time and can no longer be defined solely by the three Rs. He suggested this goal for education (p. 6):

> All students should gain a working knowledge of speaking and listening, observing (which includes visual literacy), reading and writing, arithmetic, logic, and storing and retrieving information. All students should learn to solve problems, accomplish tasks, and carry out other higher order cognitive activities that make use of these basic skills.

More recently, Jason Ohler (2002), director of the Educational Technology Program at the University of Alaska Southeast, has begun a campaign to recognize art as the fourth area of literacy, the fourth R. He bases his effort on the dramatic impact on student learning options of multimedia and multimedia creation tools, which essentially are bringing art into classrooms regardless of the ostensible subject being taught. In his article, Ohler writes:

> In a multimedia world, art is a literacy as basic as reading, 'riting, and 'rithmetic. . . . The age of art has arrived, leaving behind the text-centric world that has guided us for so long. The language of art has become the next literacy—the fourth R. We need not linger any longer over whether art should have a permanent and central place in our curriculum. It should. And we need to move quickly to prepare students to be literate in the world that they are inheriting and shaping.

The pioneering National Educational Technology Standards for Students project (ISTE, 2002d) is based on the conviction that "all kids must be ready for a different world" and that "our educational system must produce technology capable kids." Computer technology is critical to attaining many elements of these goals.

Computers offer no panacea for the issues confronting education, but they can improve learning and teaching, *if* they are used appropriately. The challenge is to employ an extremely powerful tool to its greatest advantage. To do so, students and teachers alike must become *technology competent.* Technology competent means being able to take full advantage of computers and other technologies to expand and enhance learning opportunities, teaching methods, and ultimately, daily living. To develop such competence takes time, more time than any single course entails. This book provides the foundation for personal growth toward a high level of computer competence.

Few developments in human history have had an impact on individuals and society comparable to that of computers and related technologies. In the twenty-first century, the computer is our all-purpose tool—our hammer, our pencil, our printing press, our rocket, our servant. It is what *we* make of it. Educators must help to focus and guide the impact of computer technology, or its forces surely will sweep us along, perhaps in directions not in the best interests of students and learning.

The State of Computers in Education

Very early in the computer era, many observers predicted a rapid expansion of computer use in K–12 education. It would sweep teachers along with it and send on to higher education students who were already comfortable computer users, individuals who had experienced the power of technology for learning. This has happened to a lesser extent than predicted. Even today, the need for introductory courses on computers in education continues.

Did something go wrong in the "computer revolution"? Is the computer just a fad, as some have maintained all along? The answer to both questions is no. Rather, projections of the speed with which change would occur were naive. Kozma and Johnston (1991) noted that the steam engine took 150 years to achieve a pervasive impact on society. In 50 years the computer had such an impact on business, producing the so-called Information Age, but education still lags behind in technology integration. Neither teacher preparation nor in-service education thus far has "kept pace with the rapid changes in the quality and quantity of information technology" (Moursund & Bielefeldt, 1999, p. 1).

Statistics on computers in American education show progress in getting computers into schools. Looking at the historical record in 1983, K–12 schools in the United States had only one computer per 125 students on average (Moursund & Bielefeldt, 1999, p. 7). The number of computers in schools increased 600 percent from 1983–84 to 1991–92, and the average number of students per computer nationwide fell from 125 to 19 (Kinnaman, 1992). The National Center for Educational Statistics (NCES, September 2002) reported that as of fall 2001, the national average was 5.4 students per computer with Internet access, the latter being a new qualifier (compared to previous NCES reports) that confirms the widespread adoption of the Internet in U.S. schools. This is a major improvement from the 12.1 to 1 ratio reported in 1998. (The report shows some intriguing differences by school size and location, if you care to look it up.) One presidential commission declared that a ratio of four to five students per computer was reasonable for effective use of computers (President's Committee, 1997). That level has been met according to these NCES data, given that many school computers do not have Internet access.

Even with Internet access, numbers of computers do not tell the whole story. Many of the computers in our schools are too old and underpowered to support current software and lack significant hardware components such as DVD drives and CD burners. Obsolete technology remains a problem, despite substantial technology spending over the years. According to market research firm Quality Education Data (2002), 2002–2003 expenditure projections for technology in K–12 public schools ranged from $6.1–8.22 billion, depending on the extent to which funds from the No Child Left Behind federal initiative <www.nclb.gov> would be used for technology purchases (Figure 1.1). However, as the figure also shows, district technology expenditures have fallen annually since peaking in 1998–1999, with federal programs holding total spending above the 1997–1998 level. The question of what has been achieved with the billions invested in technology remains.

Underused or improperly used technology is rarely a matter of choice or conscious decision. Few educators are resisting computer technology; instead, many are totally overwhelmed by it. The question is not *whether* to use computers but rather how *best* to use them. Many teachers are still in a position of having had computers thrust upon them, with little or no assistance in learning to use them. According to one government

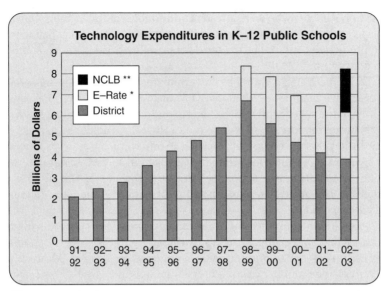

Figure 1.1 TECHNOLOGY EXPENDITURES IN K–12 PUBLIC SCHOOLS (QED, 2002)

*E-Rate funds telecommunications equipment and service costs

**No Child Left Behind federal legislation

study (NCES, December 1998, p. iii), 79 percent of teachers "identified innovative technologies as one of the three areas for which they most needed information." Another federal study of teachers found that only about 20 percent "reported feeling very well prepared to integrate educational technology into classroom instruction" (NCES, January 1999, p. iii).

Schools have responded with wide-ranging staff development programs to address these needs. In another NCES study (September 2000), 88 percent of surveyed teachers reported professional development activities helped to prepare them to use technology, whereas yet another study (NCES, June 2001) found that 74 percent reported participation in such activities during the previous 12 months. Still, there is a long way to go. For example, a 2001 National Assessment of Educational Progress study (NCES, September 2002) reported that 74 percent of fourth graders, 64 percent of eighth graders, and 42 percent of twelfth graders said that they never or hardly ever used a computer in school to study (history or social studies). Is this because there are no appropriate uses in those fields, or does it reflect lack of teacher preparation to integrate technology into meaningful learning experiences? We believe it is the latter.

But what about persons just preparing to become the next generation of teachers? *Electronic Learning* featured as its March/April 1996 cover story an article with the subtitle, "Why schools of education are still sending you staff you'll have to train in technology" (Barksdale, 1996). In April 1999 the cover of *Technology & Learning* asked, "New

Teachers and Technology: Are They Prepared?" The answer given, of course, was no. The CEO Forum (2000) termed the preparation of a new generation of teachers "a national crisis" because of the relative lack of training in technology use and integration.

Pre-service teachers often complete their preparation with little or no technology exposure and few role models who teach with computer technology, either in their coursework or their field experiences. Moursund & Bielefeldt (1999) concluded that neither faculty nor field supervisors demonstrate effective use of technology to their students. Nearly one-third of campuses participating in the Campus Computing Project <www.pt3.org/technology> reported the largest challenge they faced with technology was assisting faculty to integrate technology into instruction. The problem is compounded by the acknowledgment that fewer than 17 percent of campuses recognize use of technology in the faculty reward and promotion process.

Few educators at any level will ever make effective use of computers with their students unless they first become competent computer users on a personal level. This requires ready access to computers, time, training, modeling, and support on a level that relatively few educational institutions have provided. The federal government has responded to the challenges of preparing new teachers to use technology with the PT3 program—Preparing Tomorrow's Teachers to Use Technology <www.ed.gov/teachtech> and also <www.pt3.org>. Universities across the country have revamped their teacher education programs with the aid of grants under PT3. One of the most influential PT3 efforts has been the National Educational Technology Standards projects, which are presented in some detail later in this chapter.

Access to computers in K–12 schools continues to improve steadily amid interesting changes. In 1997 according to one available national study (QED, 1997), 17 percent of the computers in schools still were obsolete Apple IIs, down from 46 percent just two years earlier. The remaining distribution was 31 percent Windows systems, 36 percent Macintosh, and 16 percent other types. The latest QED survey (QED, 2002) found that Windows systems (combining all brands) account for more than two-thirds of all school computers, whereas the Macintosh is the single most common brand. The survey also found that 21 percent of planned purchases for 2002–2003 were Macintoshes, the remaining being primarily Windows systems. Such data support the authors' decision not to link this book to any particular type of computer. The principles of educational computing are independent of the specific computer available. Today's teachers need to be comfortable with both Macintosh and Windows computers.

However much educator access to computers has increased, in-service computer education is spotty at best (NCES, January 1999, p. v). Our experience confirms that many schools adopted a quick-fix approach. When the first computers were purchased, most schools provided limited in-service training. But just as computers are often seen as one-time investments, so too may be teacher training. Schools, of all organizations, have not always recognized the need for ongoing learning! Practicing teachers need support and regular opportunities to enhance their technology skills.

Although schools may have failed to recognize the critical importance of teacher training, fund-granting agencies often have not. Grants to support technology in schools are vital to the efforts of many districts, and their requirements are leading to change. For example, major technology grants in the state of Illinois now require that the budget devote a significant amount, often 30 percent of the grant total, to training. Federal programs often have similar requirements. For example, the now-ended Department of Education's Technology Innovation Challenge Grant program <www.ed.gov/Technology/challenge> specifies as a key selection criterion that the project would "ensure continuous professional development for teachers, administrators, and other individuals" (DOE, 1999).

Pre-service teacher education in technology often appears to be too little, too late. Many colleges and universities lack current hardware and software, and the time available in the curriculum for technology is often woefully inadequate. For maximum impact, teacher education students must become fluent computer users very early in their college education and then work with the technologies of learning in every phase of their teacher preparation. Technology must be integrated throughout their professional education courses.

Computers and Learning

Among the numerous changes that have occurred concurrently with the growth of technology applications in schools has been an evolution in views of the nature of learning. It is beyond the scope of this book to deal with these changes in detail, but their impact requires acknowledgment. For a brief overview of learning theories and their influence on teaching, see Roblyer (2003, pp. 52–72) or Tiene and Ingram (2001).

For several decades much of educational practice had rested on the concepts of behaviorism. Behaviorists explain learning as stimulus-response, harking back to the experiments of Pavlov and Skinner. However, "the core of behaviorism—the reinforcement principle—did not adequately explain the complexity of thinking, memory, problem solving, and decision-making" (Mueller & Mueller, 1997, p. 1). The rather mechanical view of learning that is behaviorism began to decline by the 1970s as cognitive psychology asserted more compelling views, notably from the work of Piaget and Gagné. Cognitive perspectives are now yielding to *constructivism*. Constructivists see learning not as events but as a process by which individuals make (i.e., *construct*) their own meaning from their experiences. The focus shifts from the role of the teacher to the learner's own actions and initiative, which technology can support in ways never before possible. Suffice it to say, your view of how learning occurs will significantly affect your approach to computers as a part of the learning process.

Closely related to constructivism is a renewed focus on learning by doing, which can be associated with the practices and teachings of John Dewey a century ago. Some related terms and concepts that you probably already have encountered include *engaged learning*, *active learning*, *authentic learning*, and *problem-based learning*. Each has its own unique elements, but at the most basic, all share the view that learning is an active, hands-on process. A passive learner is not an effective learner. Tinzmann et al. (1997, pp. 5–12) described indicators of engaged learning in several areas. First, students' roles are much more active as they become "explorers, teachers, cognitive apprentices, producers of knowledge, and self-directors and managers of their own learning. . . . Teachers act as facilitators, guides, and co-learners who seek professional growth and who design curriculum and their own research. . . . Learning tasks are authentic, challenging, and multidisciplinary. . . . Assessment is authentic, based on performance, generates new learning, and is seamless and ongoing." The authors note that engaged learning is not new, not a result of the technology explosion. "(T)echnology does offer some rich opportunities to enhance learning and assessment and to promote new student and teacher roles. . . . Computer technologies especially offer greatly increased opportunities for students to learn."

Computers have been used to support both behavioral and cognitive approaches to learning, a mark of their flexibility as tools, but they offer special potential for constructivist learning. Your own evolving philosophy of learning will determine just how you choose to use these versatile devices.

National Standards for Technology in Education

Although efforts to incorporate technology into classrooms have proceeded at differing paces throughout the world, and the phenomenon is truly worldwide, influential U.S. groups in the area of teacher education have made development of standards a key issue. Although most other countries have centralized educational systems in which change can be effectively mandated, the U.S. system is highly decentralized. The federal government can seek to influence policies and procedures by such means as fairly general laws and more specific regulations, such as those that determine a school's ability to compete for grant funds. However, these means have somewhat limited reach.

Professional organizations promote standards in the belief that such specifications, even when voluntary, provide an indispensable baseline against which professionals in the field can measure their own status. Where the current reality falls short, standards offer a goal for which to strive. Several major standards projects have established an extremely useful basis for your efforts to master varied applications of technology for the benefit of your students. We'll reference these standards throughout this book to show you just what each chapter addresses. For now, let's look at these standards.

National Council for Accreditation of Teacher Education

NCATE is the National Council for Accreditation of Teacher Education, the official agency for accrediting teacher preparation programs. Programs that have sought and received NCATE accreditation are widely recognized as having demonstrated particularly high standards of excellence. However, not all teacher preparation programs choose to participate in the accreditation process.

In its Vision of the Professional Teacher for the 21st Century, NCATE (2002) listed seven key expectations of accredited programs, one of which stated that programs should "prepare candidates who can integrate technology into instruction to enhance student learning." Among the six expected outcomes of such a program is that its graduates will "be able to integrate technology into instruction effectively." NCATE accreditation rests on the development of a Conceptual Framework by each institution that "reflects the unit's commitment to preparing candidates who are able to use educational technology to help all students learn; it also provides a conceptual understanding of how knowledge, skills, and dispositions related to educational and information technology are integrated throughout the curriculum, instruction, field experiences, clinical practice, assessments, and evaluations." In short, technology must be pervasive throughout an accredited program of teacher preparation.

NCATE establishes standards for each aspect of the curriculum by soliciting guidelines from the leading professional organization for each field or area. For technology, the primary organization has been ISTE, the International Society for Technology in Education. ISTE has developed for NCATE specific standards for programs in the areas of educational computing and technology facilitation, educational computing and technology leadership, and secondary computer science education (ISTE, 2002f). These are specialty certification programs, not teacher preparation in general. However, in addition to them, the Recommended Foundations in Technology for All Teachers are applicable to anyone pursuing a degree or certification in any area of teaching. The complete standards have become a part of ISTE's National Educational Standards project, which is presented next.

National Educational Technology Standards (NETS)

NETS (ISTE, 2002d) is an ongoing initiative of the International Society for Technology in Education, funded initially by the National Aeronautics and Space Administration (NASA) in consultation with the U.S. Department of Education, the Milken Exchange on Education Technology, and Apple Computer. NETS later received major funding through a PT3 grant from the Department of Education <www.ed.gov/pt3>. A long list of professional partner organizations includes the American Federation of Teachers and the National Education Association, administrator organizations such as the National Association of Elementary School Principals and the secondary school counterpart, and most major curriculum organizations, including the International Reading Association, National Council for the Social Studies, National Council of Teachers of English, and National Science Teachers Association.

NETS is predicated on the belief that "(t)raditional educational practices no longer provide students with all the necessary skills" and that new learning environments are essential to do so. The new environments should prepare students to:

- Communicate using a variety of media and formats
- Access and exchange information in a variety of ways
- Compile, organize, analyze, and synthesize information
- Draw conclusions and make generalizations based on information gathered
- Use information and select appropriate tools to solve problems
- Know content and be able to locate additional information as needed

- Become self-directed learners
- Collaborate and cooperate in team efforts
- Interact with others in ethical and appropriate ways (ISTE, 2002a)

Figure 1.2 contrasts traditional and new environments. If your view of learning is consistent with the new environments described, then this book was meant for you! Technology plays a vital role in achieving these enhanced environments.

Technology Foundation Standards for All Students (NETS-S)

The first product of the NETS initiative is NETS-S. NETS-S are standards that define six broad technology foundation categories, which then are elaborated in profiles of technology-literate K–12 students. Profiles are given for these groupings: pre-kindergarten–grade 2, grades 3–5, grades 6–8, and grades 9–12. Within each, very specific performance indicators are listed along with actual curriculum examples and classroom scenarios. Although we can't cover them here, we encourage you to review them yourself at <http://cnets.iste.org/students/s_stands.html>. We also highly recommend the ISTE book *Connecting Curriculum and Technology* <http://cnets.iste.org/students/s_book.html>, which is a treasure trove of detail on how to assist students in mastering the standards through lessons that integrate technology into the curriculum.

The general NETS-S are listed on the inside back cover of this book, and the applicable NETS-S standards for each chapter will be noted by NETS-S number in the

Traditional vs. New Learning Environments

Traditional Learning Environments	New Learning Environments
■ Teacher-centered instruction	■ Student-centered learning
■ Single sense stimulation	■ Multisensory stimulation
■ Single path progression	■ Multipath progression
■ Single media	■ Multimedia
■ Isolated work	■ Collaborative work
■ Information delivery	■ Information exchange
■ Passive learning	■ Active/exploratory/inquiry-based learning
■ Factual, knowledge-based/ learning	■ Critical thinking and informed decision making
■ Reactive response	■ Proactive/planned action
■ Isolated, artificial context	■ Authentic, real-world context

Figure 1.2 TRADITIONAL VS. NEW LEARNING ENVIRONMENTS (ISTE, 2002A)

NETS Notes in the margins. This will help to clarify the links between national standards and the content of this book.

National Educational Technology Standards for Teachers (NETS-T)

Following completion of NETS-S and *Connecting Curriculum and Technology*, the NETS team turned to development of NETS-T, National Educational Technology Standards for Teachers. NETS-T was the first outcome of the PT3 funding for the NETS project and represents "a national consensus on what teachers should know about and be able to do with technology" (ISTE, 2002c). NETS-T standards are organized into six categories and have become the basic standards for teacher preparation that are expected by NCATE. These standards are listed on the inside front cover of this book and by number in the NETS Notes in the margins of the following chapters.

The initial item in NETS-T (Technology Operations and Concepts, A) notes that teachers must demonstrate introductory knowledge, skills, and understanding of the student standards laid out in NETS-S. This is clearly necessary because one can hardly expect teachers to assist students to learn things they are themselves unable to do. Item B of that section expresses the expectation that teachers will continue to enhance their technology knowledge and skills throughout their teaching careers. These two items alone involve a substantial, but reasonable, expectation of teachers and the programs that prepare them. They are your initial challenge as a teacher, and this book will assist you in attaining them.

The remaining 21 elements of NETS-T are organized under the following headings: Planning and Designing Learning Environments and Experiences; Teaching, Learning and the Curriculum; Assessment and Evaluation; Productivity and Professional Practice; and Social, Ethical, Legal, Human Issues. It is far beyond the scope of this book or any single course to address so many complex matters. However, the remaining chapters of this book should help you acquire at least some of the knowledge involved in the five areas, whereas much more should be among the performance outcomes of your methodology courses, field and clinical experiences, on-the-job learning, and so on. We can only alert you to them at this point.

Technology Standards for School Administrators (TSSA)

Both pre-service and in-service teachers are the intended audience for this book. However, your introduction to NETS would be incomplete without mention of the third major phase of the project, NETS for Administrators, or TSSA (ISTE, 2002e). TSSA recognizes that the best efforts of teachers may fail without the support of school administrators, many of whom are woefully lacking in technology knowledge. Administrators who do not understand the educational applications of technology are in no position to provide the support needed by teachers as they endeavor to help students become technology competent. The details of TSSA are not appropriate for this book, but we suggest you take a short time to familiarize yourself with them on the Web. You will readily see the connections to NETS-S and NETS-T.

Acceptance of the National Educational Technology Standards

As previously indicated, the U.S. system of education does not provide for federally mandated changes, as is true of most other countries. However, the level of support for enhancing technology skills among teachers is so great that, as of the end of 2002, nearly all states in the United States had in some way adopted or adapted the NETS standards to their own expectations of teachers (ISTE, 2002g). The list is changing constantly, so check the ISTE reference for the very latest information.

For more specific details on the expectations of states for teachers and teacher preparation, we suggest Maryland at <www.smcm.edu/msde-pt3>, Texas at <www.tea.state.tx.us/technology/ta/ed_standards.html>, Kentucky at <www.kde.state.ky.us/oet/customer/leadership.asp>, and also Illinois at <www.isbe.state.il.us/profprep/PDFs/tecstandards.pdf>. For additional national data, check out <www.thejournal.com/magazine/stateofthestates>.

SUMMARY

In this first chapter you've explored the rationale for technology in today's schools. Education in the twenty-first century must differ greatly from what it was even 20 years ago. The most basic purpose of schools is to prepare students to contribute to society through productive lives. This has always been the goal of education, but society itself has changed enormously and will continue to do so. We can no longer know just what our students' futures will be, and there will be multiple futures for us all. To live successfully in a rapidly changing world, we need different skills than our parents and grandparents.

Forward-looking educators have long worked to apply the power of evolving technologies to the needs and challenges of education. We reviewed briefly some of the key data regarding computers in U.S. schools. However impressive the statistics, ultimately, it is what you as a teacher do with technology that matters. It is up to you to create the kind of new learning environment that is the foundation of the NETS project. To be able to do so, you will need to develop the skills prescribed for students, and more. The National Educational Technology Standards provide the framework for the remainder of this book. You won't learn everything you could use right away, but by the time you finish your studies, you will be well on your way toward the goal of being ready for teaching in the twenty-first century.

The challenges teachers face are enormous, but we view them with great optimism. We believe computer technology is an inescapable component of the changes now confronting education in the United States, indeed throughout the world. *You* will contribute to these essential changes in education. Continue with us now on a journey through the challenging, exciting world of computer technology in education!

Companion Website

Visit the companion website at <www.ablongman.com/lockard6e> for more information about the topics discussed in this chapter.

expect the world®

The New York Times
nytimes.com

Themes of the Times

Expand your knowledge of the concepts discussed in this chapter by reading current and historical articles from the *New York Times* by visiting the Themes of the Times section of the companion website <www.ablongman.com/lockard6e>.

References

Barksdale, J. M. "New Teachers: Unplugged." *Electronic Learning*, March/April 1996, pp. 38–45.

CEO Forum. *Teacher Preparation Star Chart*. Washington, DC: CEO Forum on Education and Technology, January 2000. Retrieved December 20, 2002, from <www.ceoforum.org/downloads/tpreport.pdf>

DOE (Department of Education). Technology Innovation Challenge Grants. 1999. Retrieved December 27, 2002 from <www.ed.gov/Technology/challenge/99ticg.doc>. See also <www.ed.gov/Technology/challenge>

ISTE (International Society for Technology in Education). Establishing new Learning Environments. 2002a. Retrieved December 20, 2002, from <http://cnets.iste.org/intro2.html>

ISTE (International Society for Technology in Education). National Educational Technology Standards for Students. 2002b. Retrieved December 20, 2002, from <http://cnets.iste.org/students/s_stands.html> or <http://cnets.iste.org/students/pdf/NETSS_standards.pdf>

ISTE (International Society for Technology in Education). National Educational Technology Standards for Teachers. 2002c. Retrieved December

20, 2002, from <http://cnets.iste.org/teachers/t_stands.html>

ISTE (International Society for Technology in Education). National Educational Technology Standards Project. 2002d. Retrieved December 20, 2002, from <http://cnets.iste.org/intro.html>

ISTE (International Society for Technology in Education). Technology Standards for School Administrators. 2002e. Retrieved December 27, 2002, from <http://cnets.iste.org/tssa>

ISTE (International Society for Technology in Education). U.S. National Accreditation. 2002f. Retrieved December 20, 2002, from <http://cnets.iste.org/ncate/n_overview.html>

ISTE (International Society for Technology in Education). Use of NETS by States. 2002g. Retrieved December 27, 2002, from <http://cnets.iste.org/docs/States_using_NETS.pdf>

Kinnaman, D. E. "Newsline: 2.5 Million Strong—and Growing." *Technology & Learning*, September 1992, *13*(1), p. 67.

Kozma, R. B., and Johnston, J. "The Technological Revolution Comes to the Classroom." *Change*, January/February 1991, *23*(1), pp. 10–23.

Moursund, D. "The Basics Do Change." *Learning and Leading with Technology*, September 1995, *23*(1), p. 6.

Moursund, D., and Bielefeldt, T. *Will New Teachers Be Prepared to Teach in a Digital Age?* Santa Monica, CA: Milken Exchange on Education Technology, 1999.

Mueller, R. J., and Mueller, C. L. *The Cognitive Revolution and the Computer.* DeKalb, IL: Author, 1997.

NCATE. National Council for Accreditation of Teacher Education. *Professional Standards for the Accreditation of Schools, Colleges, and Departments of Education, 2002 Edition.* Washington, DC: NCATE, 2002. Retrieved December 20, 2002, from <www.ncate.org/2000/unit_stnds_2002.pdf>

NCES. U.S. Department of Education, National Center for Educational Statistics. *Status of Education Reform in Public Elementary and Secondary Schools: Teachers' Perspective.* Washington, DC: December 1998. NCES 1999-045. Retrieved December 20, 2002, from <http://nces.ed.gov/pubs99/1999045.pdf>

NCES. U.S. Department of Education, National Center for Educational Statistics. *Teacher Quality: A Report on the Preparation and Qualifications of Public School Teachers.* Washington, DC: January 1999. NCES 1999-080. Retrieved December 20, 2002, from <http://nces.ed.gov/pubs99/1999080.pdf>

NCES. U.S. Department of Education, National Center for Education Statistics. *Teachers' Tools for the 21st Century.* Washington, DC: September 2000. NCES 2000-102. Retrieved December 20, 2002, from <http://nces.ed.gov/pubs2000/2000102.pdf>

NCES. U.S. Department of Education, National Center for Education Statistics. *Teacher Preparation and Professional Development: 2000.* Washington, DC: June 2001. NCES 2001-088. Retrieved December 20, 2002, from <http://nces.ed.gov/pubs2001/2001088.pdf>

NCES. U.S. Department of Education, National Center for Education Statistics. *Internet Access in U.S. Public Schools and Classrooms: 1994–2001.* Washington, DC: September 2002. NCES 2002-018. Retrieved December 20, 2002, from <http://nces.ed.gov/pubs2002/2002018.pdf>

Newburger, E. (2001). *Home Computers and Internet Use in the United States: August 2000.* U.S. Census Bureau, Current Population Reports, September 2001. Retrieved December 28, 2002, from <www.census.govprod/2001pubs/p23-207.pdf>

Ohler, J. "Art: The Fourth R." 2002. Retrieved December 20, 2002, from <http://teacher.scholastic.com/professional/teachtech/art_the4thr.htm>. See also Ohler's website at <www.uas.alaska.edu/edtech/fourthr>

President's Committee of Advisors on Science and Technology, panel on Educational Technology. "Report to the President on the Use of Technology to Strengthen K–12 Education in the United States." 1997. <www.whitehouse.gov/WH/EOP/OSTP/NSTC/PCAST/k-12ed.html>

QED (Quality Education Data). *QED's Educational Technology Trends,* 10th ed. Denver, CO: Quality Education Data, 1997.

QED (Quality Education Data). Press Release 15 November 2002. "Technology Spending in U.S. School Districts Holds at $7 Billion." Retrieved December 20, 2002, from <www.qeddata.com/combo_pr.htm>

Roblyer, M. *Integrating Educational Technology into Teaching,* 3rd ed. Columbus, OH: Merrill Prentice Hall, 2003.

Tiene, D., and Ingram, A. *Exploring Current Issues in Educational Technology.* Boston: McGraw-Hill, 2001.

Tinzmann, M. B., Rasmussen, C., Foertsch, M., McNabb, M., Valdez, G., and Houm, A. *Learning with Technology.* Oak Brook, IL: North Central Regional Educational Laboratory, 1997. <www.ncrel.org>

Computer Systems in Perspective

CHAPTER 2

OBJECTIVES

After completing this chapter, you will be familiar with and able to discuss:

- Basic computer terminology and concepts, such as data, RAM, ROM, mainframe, microcomputer, CPU, hardware, and software.
- The contributions to the development of computing of such major figures as Blaise Pascal, Charles Babbage, Ada Lovelace, Hermann Hollerith, and John Von Neumann.

- The four generations of mainframe computers and their underlying technologies.
- The basic components of any computer system.
- Common input, output, and storage devices.
- The main characteristics of monitors and printers.
- The concept of programs and their importance.
- Key functions of operating systems.

The late 1970s brought to educators a powerful new tool—the personal computer (PC), or microcomputer. How to achieve the enormous potential of the microcomputer was, however, not obvious. Microcomputers were fundamentally different from earlier educational technologies. Learning to use a microcomputer was far more demanding than, say, an overhead projector. Appropriate uses in education also were not always intuitive. Few educators were prepared to adopt microcomputers immediately. The need for pre-service and in-service teacher education in computer applications grew through the 1980s and 1990s and continues today. That need is the reason for this book's existence. It will provide you with a comprehensive introduction to educational computing.

This chapter begins with a short history of computer development, followed by basic concepts of microcomputer technology and terminology. A conceptual introduction to software concludes the chapter.

Early Data Processing Devices

NETS NOTES
NETS **S** 1
NETS **T** I-A

Today's computers are the culmination of a long search for better and more efficient ways of getting things done (Figure 2.1). Humans have always sought more efficient ways of meeting challenges. Just as we have created machines to ease our physical labors, we have also searched for ways to make mental work easier. The resulting tools have been called *data processing machines.*

Data are meaningful pieces of information. Examples of data are names, numbers, addresses, ages, and similar descriptive information about individuals. *Processing* is doing something with data. Examples of simple *data processing* are alphabetizing names, sorting addresses, or calculating the average age of a group of people. Although all these processing tasks can be performed manually, as either the amount of data or the complexity of the processing increases, a more efficient way of performing such tasks is not only desirable but often necessary—thus, the need for data processing machines.

The Abacus

The abacus was invented and used by the Chinese centuries ago to speed up simple mathematical calculations. By moving small beads on wires, the process of addition and subtraction is facilitated. The abacus is arguably the world's oldest data processing device.

The First Machines

Around 1650, the French mathematician and philosopher Blaise Pascal constructed the tooth-and-gear adding machine, which consisted of a series of interlocking wheels with ten teeth around their outside rims. When one wheel made a complete revolution, its gearing caused the next wheel to turn a single notch. The teeth on each wheel represented the digits 0 through 9. As each wheel was turned forward to represent the numbers to be summed, this device functioned as a mechanical adding machine. If one turned the wheels in the reverse direction, it served as a mechanical subtracting machine.

Twenty years later, Gottfried Leibniz enhanced Pascal's device, giving it the ability to multiply and divide. Thus, by the end of the seventeenth century, a machine existed that could mechanically perform the basic operations of mathematics. The concept

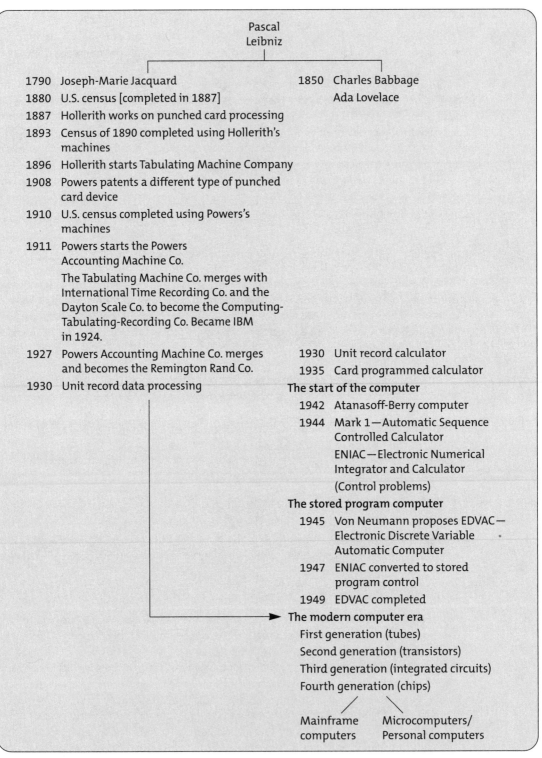

Pascal
Leibniz

1790	Joseph-Marie Jacquard	1850 Charles Babbage
1880	U.S. census [completed in 1887]	Ada Lovelace
1887	Hollerith works on punched card processing	
1893	Census of 1890 completed using Hollerith's machines	
1896	Hollerith starts Tabulating Machine Company	
1908	Powers patents a different type of punched card device	
1910	U.S. census completed using Powers's machines	
1911	Powers starts the Powers Accounting Machine Co.	

The Tabulating Machine Co. merges with International Time Recording Co. and the Dayton Scale Co. to become the Computing-Tabulating-Recording Co. Became IBM in 1924.

1927 Powers Accounting Machine Co. merges and becomes the Remington Rand Co.

1930 Unit record data processing

1930 Unit record calculator

1935 Card programmed calculator

The start of the computer

1942 Atanasoff-Berry computer

1944 Mark 1—Automatic Sequence Controlled Calculator

ENIAC—Electronic Numerical Integrator and Calculator

(Control problems)

The stored program computer

1945 Von Neumann proposes EDVAC—Electronic Discrete Variable Automatic Computer

1947 ENIAC converted to stored program control

1949 EDVAC completed

The modern computer era

First generation (tubes)

Second generation (transistors)

Third generation (integrated circuits)

Fourth generation (chips)

Mainframe computers

Microcomputers/Personal computers

Figure 2.1 COMPUTER HISTORY OUTLINE, SHOWING TWO LINES OF DEVELOPMENT

behind Pascal's machine was still the basis for the adding machines and calculators of the early twentieth century.

Automated Manufacturing and Jacquard

The next developmental step for data processing machines stems from the work of Joseph-Marie Jacquard in 1790. Realizing the repetitive and time-consuming nature of hand weaving cloth, Jacquard designed and constructed an automated loom. This loom was controlled by a series of cards with holes punched into them. A single card directed the automated loom in constructing one row of the fabric. A set of such cards then directed construction of a series of rows of the fabric, eventually resulting in the desired pattern.

There were many advantages to such a process. First, the procedure was automatic. Once the cards had been prepared, they controlled the loom in making the desired fabric. Second, when a given fabric had been completed, the cards could be reinserted into the loom and used again to make an identical fabric. Third, by changing some of the cards, the operator of the loom could make material with variations in the original pattern. Finally, an entirely new deck of punched cards could be inserted and used to create a totally different patterned cloth on the same machine.

Jacquard's concept, the use of a series of cards punched with holes that could be processed by machine, established one of the two paths that data processing machines would follow in the next 150 years. The other path developed from the ideas of Charles Babbage.

The Analytical Engine, Babbage, and Lady Ada

About the middle of the nineteenth century, an Englishman named Charles Babbage approached the processing of data from a different perspective. Living in the midst of the Industrial Revolution and aware of advances being made in motors and related devices, Babbage proposed a new concept for a data processing machine. His machine would be capable of accepting a large amount of information. Once that information was stored internally, the machine would perform all the desired processing and produce the results. Jacquard's processing was accomplished in small steps, each controlled by a punched card. Babbage's processing was to be accomplished only after all information was entered into the system.

Babbage called his machine the Analytical Engine, and although he drew plans for it, the engine never became fully operational. The concept was sound, but the technology of his time was inadequate to construct it. About 100 years later, with much greater mechanical sophistication and the use of electricity, Babbage's concept served as the starting point in the development of modern data processing devices. It is for this reason that Babbage is often referred to as the "father of modern data processing."

Ada Lovelace, the daughter of the poet Lord Byron and a gifted mathematician, assisted Babbage in his work. In fact, much of what is known about the Analytical Engine's potential comes from an article written by Lady Ada in which she presented a fascinating analysis of the machine and Babbage's ideas. Her contributions to the development of computing were acknowledged when a computer language—*Ada*—was named in her honor.

Two Lines of Development

The conceptual directions established by Jacquard and Babbage continued to evolve for about a century. Unit record data processing followed Jacquard's approach, whereas modern computers are derived from Babbage's concepts.

|NETS
|NOTES
NETS **S** 1
NETS **T** I-A

Unit Record Data Processing

The next advance occurred in the United States in the late 1800s and returned to the work of Jacquard. With the beginning of the great immigration period in the United States, the taking of the census every ten years became an increasingly difficult task. Officials noted that the 1880 census had taken nearly seven years to complete and projected that the 1890 census would require more than ten years to complete if performed in the same manner. Clearly, something had to be done!

The Census Bureau hired Hermann Hollerith to develop procedures for speeding up the processing of census data. To perform many of the data processing tasks, Hollerith designed a series of machines. They used a card punched with holes to represent the census information of one person. Other cards were punched to represent the census information of other people, one card per person. These cards became known as *unit records*, because they contained the data record of one person, or unit. A group of these unit records was referred to as a *file*.

Hollerith's machines processed these cards automatically and completed the necessary census tasks faster and more efficiently than by hand. The machine that prepared the punched cards eventually became known as the keypunch. Examples of other machines that Hollerith produced were the reproducer (which made copies of cards), the sorter (which rearranged cards in a file), and the tabulator (which counted the data on cards in files).

Commercial Applications

Using his unit record processing machines, Hollerith was able to complete the 1890 census in approximately three years rather than the previously estimated ten years. This procedure for processing data clearly worked. In fact, it worked so well that in 1896 Hollerith left the Census Bureau and founded the Hollerith Tabulating Machine Company. Hollerith reasoned that if such machines could process census data efficiently, they would also find applicability in the general business community.

In the early 1900s, the Census Bureau discontinued using the Hollerith machines and hired another engineer, James Powers, to develop other ways to process census data. By 1910, Powers developed and put into use a series of machines that, although functioning on concepts similar to Hollerith's, were different enough to qualify for patents. The 1910 census was run using these machines and was completed efficiently and speedily. Powers also saw the benefit of these machines for the business community, and in 1911 he founded the Powers Accounting Machine Company.

The history of data processing for a good part of the twentieth century is the history of these two companies. In 1911, the Hollerith Tabulating Machine Company merged with the International Time Recording Company and the Dayton Scale Company to become the Computing-Tabulating-Recording Company. In 1924, its name was changed to International Business Machines (IBM).

The Powers Accounting Machine Company merged with several office supply companies to become the Remington Rand Company. Through mergers, the Remington Rand Company became Sperry Rand and later Unisys.

The similar machines that these two companies produced served the data processing needs of the business community for many years. Their machines were continually upgraded to reflect technological advances and finally became the full-fledged unit record data processing equipment that was available into the 1960s.

Although unit record processing met the needs of the business community, it did not serve the somewhat different needs of the scientific community. In an oversimplified comparison, business often required relatively straightforward and noncomplex processing of a large amount of individual data (such as payroll or billing), whereas scientific needs often focused on complex processing of a relatively small amount of data (as in statistics or engineering). There were many attempts to modify unit record machines to meet the demands of the scientific community. Examples include the upgraded unit record calculator and the card-programmed calculator. Neither was completely successful. A scientific data processing machine had to be conceptualized differently from business data processing machines.

The Start of the Computer

Machines suited to scientific applications began to appear in the mid-1930s. They were developed from the concepts of Babbage's Analytical Engine rather than from the concepts of Jacquard's automatic loom. The first electronic digital computer was designed and built by John Atanasoff and Clifford Berry at Iowa State College in 1942. In 1944, with funding from IBM, engineers and scientists at Harvard University designed and built the Mark I (the Automatic Sequence Controlled Calculator). These machines worked on the principle of data being input into a central processing unit, where all processing was sequentially controlled until completed. The results were then output to the user.

With the harnessing of electricity into vacuum tubes and electrical circuits, not only could such a machine be built, but also it indeed worked as Babbage had envisioned. For example, the Mark I could complete in approximately two minutes what had previously required more than 20 hours of manual processing. These were the types of machines that the scientific community needed.

About the same time, the University of Pennsylvania was also developing and building a data processing machine following Babbage's ideas and geared to scientific processing. This machine was called the ENIAC (Electronic Numerical Integrator and Calculator), and it also worked successfully. Scientific data processing machines were becoming a reality.

The Control Problem

These early machines also had problems, the most serious of which was control. Setting up data processing machines to perform a specific job often required many hours of actual rewiring. Once rewired, the machines could perform quickly and accurately, but after completing a specific task, extensive rewiring was again necessary to perform a different processing task. Researchers had demonstrated that machines could be built that were capable of doing scientific processing. What was missing was a method of efficiently controlling them.

The Stored Program Computer

The control problem was addressed eventually by John Von Neumann, a mathematician and physicist. In 1945, Von Neumann published an article proposing a solution and outlining a machine that incorporated his new control concepts. This machine he called the EDVAC (Electronic Discrete Variable Automatic Computer). The age of the unit record machine was ending; the age of the computer was about to begin.

Von Neumann's concept was termed *stored program control*. The idea was to build control capabilities into the machine and not view control as something external to the processing unit. The internal control unit would understand and use an instruction to direct the rest of the system to perform a desired operation. A series of instructions would make up a program that, when entered into the system, would be executed one instruction at a time to perform a complex processing task. Such computer systems were known as stored program computer systems to differentiate them from earlier machines.

Work was begun on Von Neumann's EDVAC. While his machine was being built, the ENIAC at the University of Pennsylvania was converted to stored program control. In 1947, the redesigned ENIAC became one of the first functioning stored program computer systems. By 1950, the EDVAC was completed, as were other stored program computers.

The Modern Computer Era

Although the paths from Jacquard and Babbage existed in parallel for many years, they converged in the modern computer era, which is identified by four generations of technology.

NETS
NOTES

NETS **S** 1
NETS **T** I-A

First Generation: Tubes

Although a few stored program computers existed before 1950, they were still not widely available to the general scientific community. At that time, however, the Remington Rand Corporation hired some of the personnel who had worked on the ENIAC computer at the University of Pennsylvania. In 1951, Remington Rand introduced the first commercially available computer system, the UNIVAC I. The IBM 650 soon followed. By the mid-1950s, both of the large unit record machine companies built and distributed stored program computers.

The computers of this period are called the first generation of modern computer systems. They were constructed using vacuum tubes, were very large and expensive, and were prone to break down, often from their own heat.

Second Generation: Transistors

The mid-1950s saw development of the transistor, which made vacuum tubes obsolete. Transistors were cheaper, faster, more reliable, and easier to incorporate into complex electrical circuits. As a result, computers were reengineered using transistors. The new computers were faster and more complex than their predecessors. At the same time, costs were held down by advances in technology. Transistor-based computers are called the second generation of computer systems.

The introduction of business-oriented computers also marked a significant change in direction. Although first-generation computers were oriented toward scientific processing, computer manufacturers soon realized that their machines could also perform the functions of unit record equipment more quickly, more efficiently, and at lower cost. The new computers eventually took over all of the business data processing that had been performed for more than 50 years by unit record machines.

Third Generation: Integrated Circuits

The early 1960s saw the development of solid logic technology and solid state integrated circuits (ICs), which allowed many single-function electronic components of a computer to be combined into one device. Computers were redesigned to take advantage of these advances in technology, and the third generation of computers was born.

Similar to the advances of the second generation, third-generation machines were more complex and faster, and their costs did not appreciably increase. Because of greater capabilities, the distinction between business and scientific computers slowly disappeared. There was simply a range of small to large computers that could perform business or scientific processing with comparable ease. Computers had become an integral part of both the business and scientific communities.

Fourth Generation: Microelectronics

The early 1970s saw another technological leap, the introduction of the *microprocessor*, a tiny device that combined the functions of numerous integrated circuits on a single chip. The fourth generation of computers was upon us. Again machines were redesigned to make use of the new technology and became even faster and more complex at stable or falling cost.

For an online history of computing science, complete with many illustrations and photos, visit <www.eingang.org/Lecture>.

The Personal Computer

NETS
NOTES
NETS **S** 1
NETS **T** I–B

While computers were becoming increasingly complex, several individuals conceived of using microprocessors to build small computers for individual use. The first of these machines appeared in the mid-1970s. They became known as *microcomputers* to differentiate them from the much larger, multiuser computers, which became known as *mainframe* computers. Microcomputers steadily have become more powerful and more readily available and are now often referred to simply as computers. In this book we use the terms *computer, microcomputer,* and *personal computer* (PC) interchangeably. Today's highly popular lightweight portable computers are called *laptop* or *notebook* computers.

Remarkable Power

Today's PCs are not toys or scaled-down mainframe computers with limited power and applicability. In the early years, typical first- and second-generation mainframe computers cost over $250,000, and in terms of their processing capabilities, they were worth it. Today, you can buy a much more powerful PC for a fraction of 1 percent of that price.

Flexible Applications

Personal computers are capable of doing more than just many of the same things that mainframe computers can. Many applications have been developed for PCs that are either inefficient or impractical on a mainframe, yet are extremely useful. Examples include word processing, spreadsheets, and computer-based learning, applications that are more individual in nature and, thus, better suited to personal computers than to mainframes.

Far More Users

Low-cost, remarkable processing power and new applications have seen the movement of computers and computer power into areas with little or no initial access to computer capabilities. Such areas include K–12 education, small businesses, and the home. PCs have extended computing power to a much wider audience than mainframe computers. Mainframe use had been limited to persons who had access to such large computers. This excluded a great majority of individuals who, therefore, could not take advantage of the computer to satisfy their individual data processing needs. PCs have changed this and have made computer power accessible to nearly everyone.

This book will acquaint you with this widely available tool of the Information Age, the personal computer. You will explore what it is, how it can be controlled, specific applications for education, and some of the implications as computers increasingly find their way into our daily lives.

Hardware: The Physical System

NETS
NOTES

NETS **S** 1
NETS **S** 4
NETS **T** I-A
NETS **T** I-B

Although the word *computer* suggests a single machine, a computer is really a system of interconnected components, not just one piece of equipment. These components are collectively referred to as *hardware*. Figure 2.2 illustrates the basic hardware components of a computer system. The key component is the *central processing unit (CPU)*, which includes the control unit and the arithmetic/logic unit circuits. In addition, the CPU contains circuits that connect to other internal and external units (memory, input devices, output devices, and storage devices). Let's consider these types of mechanical/electrical devices individually as they apply to a computer system.

Central Processing Unit

The CPU is the key component, the "brain" of the system. This is where most of the work of the system actually takes place. Major makers of CPUs include Intel, Motorola,

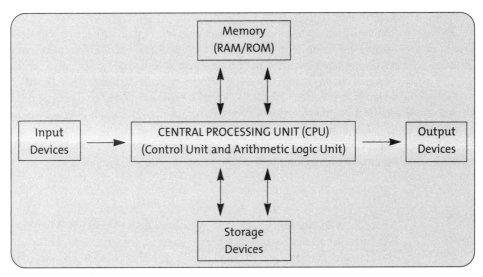

Figure 2.2 COMPONENTS OF A COMPUTER SYSTEM

IBM, and AMD. A CPU features a microprocessor that consists of two principal parts, the *control unit* and the *arithmetic/logic unit (ALU)*. See Figure 2.3.

Control Unit

Because a computer system consists of many components, something has to assure that they work together properly. The control unit of the CPU is the manager of all the other pieces of the system. It can be likened to a police officer directing traffic.

Figure 2.3

INSIDE A PC: CPU AND RAM

Arithmetic/Logic Unit

The power of a computer rests ultimately on its ability to perform arithmetic and logical operations. Computer arithmetic is carried out in a series of steps by circuitry within the ALU. In early PCs, arithmetic processing speeds could be greatly increased by the addition of a special math chip that performs arithmetic operations directly rather than as a series of steps. Such chips, called *math coprocessors*, added to the basic math capabilities of the CPU. CPUs now incorporate the equivalent of a math coprocessor in their circuitry.

The logic circuitry of the ALU handles the decision-making capabilities of the computer. The seemingly complex functioning of a computer system is actually just the combination of many simple logic steps into a lengthy sequence.

Memory

In order to do anything, the CPU must have data to process. Memory consists of microchips that accept data from external sources, retain data for some time, send data to and accept data from the CPU, and finally, provide processing results to the user through external devices. Memory has a capacity; that is, chips can accept and retain only a certain amount of data. The basic unit of memory capacity is termed a *byte*, the space required to hold one character. Because a computer must be able to hold and manipulate millions of characters at once, memory size is specified as a number followed by the letters MB, the symbol for *megabyte* (1,000,000 bytes). A personal computer has two types of memory: RAM and ROM.

Random-Access Memory

Random-access memory (RAM) is a series of chips that can accept, retain, and have their data erased when the data are no longer needed. A simple analogy for RAM is safety deposit boxes into which you can place items for storage until retrieved. RAM is termed *volatile* because all data in RAM are erased and lost when the computer is turned off.

RAM is critical in any computer system. The amount needed depends on the programs the computer is to run. Personal computers typically have at least 128MB–256MB of RAM. Additional RAM can be installed in most systems as needed to maintain or improve performance.

Read-Only Memory

The second type of memory in a PC is *read-only memory (ROM)*. ROM chips are programmed during manufacturing to contain information that the computer needs to function properly. ROM contains data that cannot be erased, altered, or expanded by the user. It is termed *nonvolatile* because the data are retained regardless of whether the computer is on or off.

Input Devices

The CPU of a computer system is capable of performing a wide variety of tasks, but for most things to occur, it must be given data. Data are entered into the system through input devices. Most systems include two primary input devices, a keyboard and a pointing device. Various other input devices also are available.

Keyboard

A computer keyboard resembles a typewriter, often with the addition of a calculator-like set of numeric keys, directional arrow keys for movement about the screen, and other special-purpose keys. Curved *ergonomic* keyboards are designed to lessen strain on the wrist and arm caused by continual keyboard use, which can lead to debilitating carpal tunnel syndrome.

Pointing Device

A pointing device is used to move a marker, or *cursor* (such as an arrow), around the video screen. The most common device is a *mouse*, a hand-sized device with buttons that the user moves around on a flat surface. Rotation of a ball on the underside of the mouse signals the movement of the onscreen cursor. An *optical mouse* uses light beams instead. The user can then select a screen area or object as input to the computer by simply pressing a button on the mouse. One variation of the mouse is a *trackball*, an inverted, stationary mouse; the user rotates the ball to move the cursor. Trackballs were once popular in laptop computers but have been largely replaced by a *touchpad* that responds to finger movements on its surface. Some notebook computers provide a small pointer stick nestled between the keys. Whatever the style, all such input devices simplify interaction with the computer.

Scanners

A *mark sense scanner* reacts to pencil marks made in designated spaces on preprinted forms. The scanner senses these markings and transmits the information to the computer. The most common use of these devices is to "read" test answer sheets, a function of growing interest to schools implementing competency-based educational programs.

An *optical scanner* is capable of "reading" typed or printed pages and graphic images into the computer system. *Optical character recognition (OCR)* software converts the scanned image into normal text, just as if you actually had typed the material. This eliminates the need to retype existing material. Most popular scanners work equally well with black-and-white or color originals.

Voice and Handwriting Recognition

One major area of continuing research and development is *voice recognition*. Voice recognition has obvious benefits for special needs individuals with motor control impairments, but the ability to speak to a computer to control it and to input data promises to affect all computer users dramatically. The state of the art appears to be the voice systems in use by major airlines to provide automated flight information. However, the current capabilities of PC-based software such as IBM's *ViaVoice* and ScanSoft's *Dragon Naturally Speaking* impress us far less, though they continue to improve. One major difficulty is the need to train the software to recognize individual voices, a process requiring hours in most cases.

Another area of R&D that has achieved success and is in wide use is *handwriting recognition*. The most common application appears to be Graffiti, the stylized system used to write on personal digital assistants (PDAs) that use the Palm operating system. Graffiti requires learning to write characters in the shape that it recognizes rather than recognizing the way you write. The system is functional but noticeably slower than keyboard input. Very promising is the radically different approach of the Tablet PC, introduced in late 2002 (Figure 2.4). Using an approach called *bezier splines*, built into the Windows XP Tablet PC Edition operating system, these computers do a remarkable job of recognizing natural handwriting without training. See <www.microsoft.com/windows xp/tabletpc> for a product overview.

Other Input Devices

A *joystick* is a small box with a movable stick and one or two buttons. Moving the stick moves a cursor on the screen, and pressing a button sends signals to the system. A joystick is most often used to play computer games.

A *graphics pad* or *tablet* (Figure 2.5) is a board that the user touches and draws on to communicate with the computer system. These pads have gained wide popularity in art and computer-aided design (CAD).

In some systems, a *touchscreen* allows the user to input information by simply touching the video screen with a finger or other pointer. This is especially useful for non-readers and individuals with special needs that make other input devices impractical.

Output Devices

When the computer has performed its processing tasks, the results must be communicated back to the user. Information from the CPU is converted into an understandable form through output devices. The primary output devices are display screens and printers.

Figure 2.4
A TABLET PC
Courtesy of Acer.

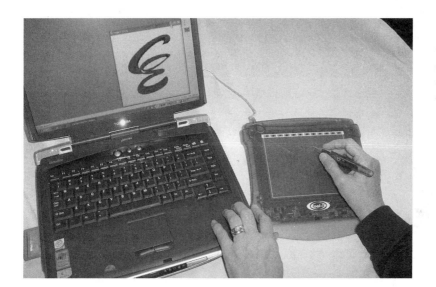

Figure 2.5
Graphics tablets are essential tools for artists and graphic designers.

Displays

The most common way to receive information from a computer system is through a *monitor*. A *CRT* monitor displays high-quality images (text and graphics) on a video screen that resembles a television set. Portable computers use a built-in flat display screen called a *liquid crystal display (LCD)*. Freestanding LCD monitors have become very popular for desktop computers as well because they weigh much less, take up much less desktop space, and display a clearer image (to most users) that is free of the flicker inherent in CRTs and TVs (Figure 2.6, left). Although you may not notice the flicker on a CRT, if you work long hours at a computer, as secretaries do, changing to an LCD monitor will frequently relieve previous eyestrain. In our view the end of CRT monitors for most uses is approaching. Several manufacturers now offer all-in-one desktop PCs that are built around an LCD monitor (Figure 2.6, right).

Resolution refers to the sharpness or clarity of an image on the screen. For monitors it means the number of independently controlled dots (called *pixels*) that show on the screen at once and is given as the number of horizontal dots by the number of vertical dots. Common resolutions range from 640 × 480 (called *VGA*) to 1,600 × 1,200 (called *UXGA*). The computer's software control panel can change the resolution setting within the range of resolutions available for the specific monitor and the display circuitry of the computer itself. Because the physical size of the monitor does not change, higher resolutions make each image element smaller, so users need to adjust their systems to suit their own preferences for clarity and readability. LCD screens may have a specific optimal resolution and may not produce sharp images at other settings. Many web pages are now designed for resolution settings of 1,024 × 768 (*XGA*) or even higher, so that horizontal scrolling may be necessary on a system set to a lower resolution.

Common screen sizes are 14 inches to 21 inches, whereas notebook computer displays vary from about 12 to 16 inches. For comfortable viewing by groups of more than

Figure 2.6 LCD monitors will replace CRTs as the norm.

four or five, the video output of a computer should be connected to a *video projector* to display large images on a movie screen or wall. Because projectors are costly, some schools use *scan converters* to display computer output on a regular television, but this is less desirable because the image is much smaller and often fuzzy.

Printers

Printers produce paper output or *hardcopy*. Printers differ from one another in print method, range of capabilities, speed, print quality, and interface method.

Two quite different methods of printing are widely used. *Ink jet* printers form characters by spraying droplets of ink onto paper. Ink jet printers are relatively fast and are very reasonable in price. They can also print in full color, even on transparency plastic! Some are very small and operate on batteries for use with battery-powered notebook computers. Many ink jets produce excellent print quality, including photo-quality pictures.

Laser printers have become increasingly popular as prices have declined dramatically. Laser printers use technology similar to photocopy machines. Their high print quality and speed make laser printers desirable. They are rapidly becoming the norm, although color models are still rather expensive.

Printers differ greatly in speed. The speed of ink jet and laser printers is measured in pages printed per minute. Inexpensive ink jet printers output fewer than 10 pages of text per minute and may need several minutes to print one 8 × 10 color picture, whereas laser printers commonly print 10 to 20 pages per minute.

Ink jet printers produce high quality output because of the size and uniform color of the dots they produce. Laser printers offer the finest print quality available, almost identical to professional typesetting, but may not reproduce photos well in monochrome.

The *interface method* is the type of connection used between the computer and the printer. The computer, the connecting cable, and the printer must all use the same method. The standard interface for early Macintosh computers was serial (one signal at a time), whereas early DOS and Windows systems used a *parallel* interface (multiple signals at once). This meant that printers were either unique to one computer type or the other, or they had to have two interface connections. Today both platforms use the *USB (universal serial bus)* interface and schools no longer need unique printers for each. Parallel printers are still common, but newer Windows PCs, especially notebooks, no longer have parallel connectors (Figure 2.7), thus requiring a USB printer or a special adapter.

Storage Devices

Storage devices are another vital component of any computer system. A storage device is always accessible to the CPU. The CPU may send data to the device to store. The device can read stored data and send it to the CPU. In this way, storage devices serve both input and output functions. Because the data are stored until explicitly erased, storage devices constitute an auxiliary memory whose capacity is far greater than the RAM of the computer. These capabilities make some combination of storage devices indispensable for computer systems. Diskettes and cartridges, hard disks, and optical discs comprise this category.

Diskettes and Cartridges

Diskette drives use a high-density (HD) 3.5" diskette in a hard plastic case to store information magnetically. The data storage capacity of such a diskette is 1440K, or 1.44MB. Older computers used a double-density (DD) 3.5" diskette that held 700K to 800K of data. Early microcomputers used a 5.25" "floppy" diskette with a capacity ranging from 100K to 1.2MB of data (1K = 1000 bytes).

A diskette can be removed from the drive and stored until the data are needed again; the diskette is then inserted back into the drive to make its contents accessible. Diskettes are also used to move files from one computer to another. Diskettes are very inexpensive and can be erased and reused. They remain useful in schools, especially for student

Figure 2.7

PARALLEL PRINTER PORT
ON DESKTOP PC, ABSENT
ON NOTEBOOK

work that tends not to produce large files. Students can carry files between school and home easily and inexpensively.

Because diskettes hold relatively little data, higher-capacity cartridge systems evolved. The most common is the Zip drive, which uses cartridges that hold 100MB (nearly 70 floppies!), 250MB, or 750MB (roughly equal to 500 floppies!). A Zip cartridge is similar in size to a diskette, only thicker. Zip drives may be built-in, like diskette drives, or portable, connected to the back of the computer as needed. External drives can be shared among many computers, both standard and notebooks.

Hard Disks

All computers today have at least one hard disk drive. A hard disk's rigid magnetic recording surfaces are permanently sealed inside a container and cannot be removed. Hard disk drives store very large quantities of data, commonly tens of *gigabytes* (1GB = 1000MB, or 1 billion characters). Such drives greatly increase the performance capabilities of computers because they operate much faster than diskettes and cartridges. They eliminate diskette handling, store and retrieve data much more quickly, and can handle much larger programs and data sets.

Optical Discs

Optical discs also provide high-volume storage. The most common type is the *CD-ROM* (compact disc–read-only memory), which is quite similar to an audio CD and is now the minimum optical drive on most computers, including notebooks. A laser beam reads the data on a CD, not magnetic heads. CD-ROMs now provide a means of inexpensively distributing large volumes of data, such as electronic encyclopedias and software programs. A CD-ROM can store about 700MB. CD-ROM drives also play audio CDs, making your computer into a sound system as well.

A CD-ROM drive can only read prerecorded discs. Much more popular is the slightly more expensive *CD-RW* drive, or *CD burner*, which also records CDs by "burning" the data onto the disc with a laser beam. Blank CDs come in two types: CD-R and CD-RW, both of which work in the same burner. A CD-R disc can be recorded on just once, although that does not have to be done all at one time, and read or "played" as often as desired on any CD-ROM or CD-RW drive. Data can even be erased from a CD-R, but the space used cannot be recovered and reused. The more costly CD-RW discs can be erased and the space reused, much like other storage systems, but the discs tend to be readable only in a CD-RW drive. Because blank CD-Rs are so inexpensive, we prefer them to avoid the compatibility issues of CD-RWs. CD-Rs can even be used to create audio CDs that will play in home and car stereo systems.

DVD discs are rapidly replacing videotapes for home movie viewing because of better picture and sound quality in less space. Similarly, DVD-ROM drives have virtually replaced CD-ROM drives in newer computers because they can play standard audio CDs and CD-ROMs as well as DVDs. One DVD can store up to 4.7GB of data in the most common format, nearly the equivalent of seven CD-ROMS, with capacities to 17GB possible, all on a disc physically the same size as a CD. This huge capacity makes DVDs appealing for any large storage need, including making *backup* copies of data on a hard disk, an important task largely ignored by most computer owners, at least until their hard disk crashes and they lose all their files. We anticipate a growing market for educational materials on DVD, as suggested by products such as the *Encarta Reference Library* on DVD, which features far more video and audio resources as well as additional reference tools compared to the CD encyclopedia version, and all on a single disc.

DVD use in education will increase rapidly as DVD recorders become more common. Prices have become quite reasonable and many computers now feature DVD burners. Blank DVDs are inexpensive as well. See Figure 2.8. It should not be long before students can begin to save samples of their work in an *electronic portfolio* on DVD, starting in the early grades and adding to it each year. Similar to their paper records, the DVD will be a cumulative record of their work over an extended period of time.

Modems

A *modem* (*mo*dulator-*dem*odulator) is a device that allows one computer to communicate with another through phone lines. In this way, a modem provides for both input and output, much like storage devices.

The single most important characteristic of modems is their speed or *baud rate*, which indicates how fast they transmit data through the lines. The most common modem speed is 56K. Still higher speeds are possible with special hardware such as *cable modems* that use the cable TV wiring rather than phone lines. Most telephone modems include send and receive fax capabilities as well. Some can even function as voice mail systems. Modems and high speeds have dramatically increased in importance with the growth of the Internet as an educational tool, the subject of the next chapter.

Inside a PC

Now that you know about the various components of a typical computer, you may wonder how they all fit together. This is a topic that is most easily learned hands-on, so we've limited the discussion to general concepts and supplemented it with photographs on the companion website for this book, which should help you identify what you can

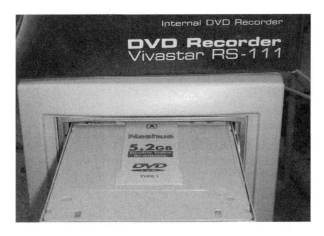

Figure 2.8
A DVD RECORDER
(BURNER) AND
BLANK DVD

Figure 2.9
INSIDE VIEW OF A TYPICAL COMPUTER

see inside an actual computer, if you have the opportunity to look at one that is open. The following discussion is based on such an open PC (Figure 2.9).

Every computer requires a *power supply* to convert electricity to the voltages required by electronic components. In most cases, the power cord plugs directly into the power supply, making it easy to locate.

At the front of the computer case are *drive bays*, the mounting locations for drives you can access from the outside, for example, floppy drives, CD/DVD drives, Zip drives, and so on. The number varies with the physical size of the case. The hard drive also mounts in a bay, but because it does not need to be accessible, the bay may be in the back of the case. If you see a front bay that is not accessible from the outside, it's for a hard drive. Many computers come with unused bays to allow for installing additional hardware, if desired.

The main component of a PC is the *motherboard*, which is the major electronic circuitry of the computer. The motherboard holds the CPU, the ROM and RAM, and many other less familiar components. It also usually has a series of *slots*, connectors into which expansion cards containing circuitry not included on the motherboard can be inserted. Among the most common cards are video adapters, to which the monitor connects; modems; NICs; and sound cards, all of which have external connectors called *ports*. However, these functions may also be integrated into the electronics of the motherboard, as are the standard ports for the keyboard, mouse, parallel printer, USB, and so on. You should have no trouble identifying connectors on cards versus those that are integrated just by examining the computer case, even without opening it.

Now let's turn to software, without which a computer is little more than a mass of useless electronics.

Software: Making the System Work

The physical elements of a computer system are actually isolated components. While connected, they do not work as an integrated unit unless directed to do so by the con-

NETS
NOTES

NETS **S** 1
NETS **T** I-A
NETS **T** I-B

trol section of the CPU. The obvious question then is, how do you control the control section?

Programs

Getting a computer system to perform a desired task is a matter of giving to the CPU individual instructions concerning what should be done. The control section then directs and coordinates the rest of the system in executing the instructions. A *program* is a series of instructions designed to cause the system to perform a logical sequence of steps that will produce the desired result. The process of writing these instructions is called *programming*. Programming is vital, even if *you* do no programming personally. Without programs, a computer can do little more than decorate your desk.

The programs that cause a computer system to perform desired tasks are called *software* to distinguish them from the physical components of the computer system, or *hardware*. Programs come from two basic sources: A user can write them, or they can be purchased (Figure 2.10). We will look at both ways of obtaining computer programs, but not just yet. You first need to understand how to get the computer system "up and running" before you can be concerned with programs of direct interest to educators.

Operating Systems

Before a computer system can perform tasks, it must be prepared to accept and execute instructions. Initial preparation of the system is the task of a very special program called an *operating system*. An operating system is supplied with a computer or is purchased for it. The control section of the CPU uses the operating system both to set itself up and to get information on how to perform various system-related tasks.

Figure 2.10
SOFTWARE MAKES COMPUTERS USEFUL

The computer manufacturer normally installs an operating system on the hard disk. A backup copy is supplied to the user on a CD-ROM. The system programs needed to get the computer started are read from the hard disk (or a system diskette) when the computer is turned on. This is called *booting* the system.

Early IBM-compatible PCs used MS-DOS from Microsoft, which was a text-based operating system that responded primarily to typed commands. The Macintosh operating system (Mac OS) popularized the *graphical user interface (GUI),* which uses graphics or *icons* to represent the system's devices and software. The user "points" to an icon or menu with a pointing device and clicks to select a drive, program, data file, or operation. *Microsoft Windows* uses a similar visual interface. New versions of the Mac OS and Windows appear regularly (Figure 2.11). Finally, some computers use UNIX, an operating system developed for mainframe computers. Starting with OS X, the Mac OS uses UNIX as its core.

Data files, such as documents, can generally be exchanged between Macintosh and PC systems with little difficulty. However, software written for each platform must be unique and will not run on the other. Thus, major software products tend to be available in both Windows and Mac versions.

Each operating system has its own unique aspects and even terminology, but Windows and the Mac OS are increasingly similar, which benefits all users. Our discussion of operating system functions is necessarily general, but you will gain a basic understanding of the principles. Mastering the essential parts of the particular operating system for a specific computer should not be difficult.

There are two general categories of tasks that an operating system performs: *system operation tasks* and *system utility tasks.*

Figure 2.11

Today's operating systems use a graphical user interface (GUI).

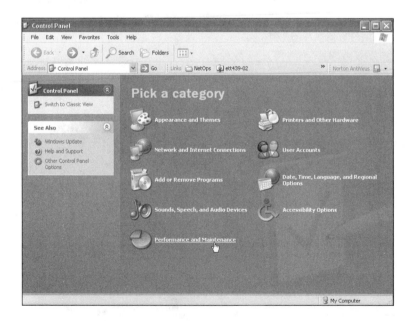

System Operation Tasks

System operation tasks are those that guide the most basic functioning of the computer. They occur through the operating system as needed, without direct requests from the user. Three examples illustrate the concept.

- *Screen control.* The system must be able to display characters and images on the video screen.
- *Keyboard and pointer input.* The system must be able to accept and interpret input from the keyboard and pointing device.
- *Interfacing.* The system must be able to control its various components and allow them to communicate with each other.

System Utility Tasks

System utility tasks are functions that are often needed in the course of normal system use. These tasks are performed at the specific request of the user. Three basic system utility tasks illustrate the concept (Figure 2.12):

- *Format.* The system prepares a disk to accept information.
- *Copy.* The system makes duplicate copies of files, programs, or entire diskettes.
- *Erase/Delete.* The system erases data from a disk.

Other operating system functions in both categories are too numerous to cover here. Refer to your operating system manual to become familiar with those most commonly needed. Booting the system and performing various system tasks are important jobs of

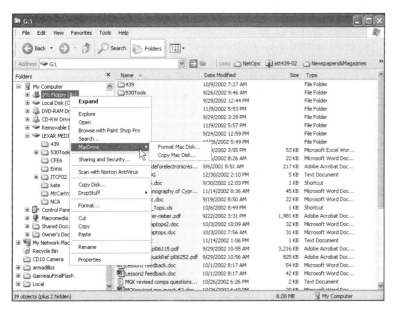

Figure 2.12
SYSTEM UTILITY TASKS IN A POP-UP MENU

any operating system. Without them, a computer could not function and run the programs that direct it to perform an almost unlimited variety of tasks. Turning the computer on initiates system boot up automatically and prepares the computer for user control.

SUMMARY

The human search for easier ways to accomplish necessary tasks has produced many useful devices. Efforts to assist with mental tasks began with the abacus. Pascal and Leibniz produced the first mechanical calculating devices in the seventeenth century. In the nineteenth century, the automation of weaving looms by Jacquard established one of two paths that led to the modern computer era. The other path stemmed from Babbage, who conceptualized the Analytical Engine.

Jacquard's concepts for automated looms guided the development of unit record data processing, which progressed rapidly from the work of Hollerith and Powers for the U.S. Census Bureau. From their government experience, both went on to form private firms that are known today as IBM and Unisys, respectively.

Unit record data processing satisfied the needs of business, but it was less appropriate for scientific needs. Scientific requirements led to the development of the stored program computer, an outgrowth of the work of Babbage. The paths from Jacquard and Babbage converged at the start of the modern computer era in the 1950s.

The modern era is divided into generations of computers based on the underlying technology. The first generation relied on vacuum tubes. Transistors marked the second generation. In the third generation, solid state technology and integrated circuits were the key features. Microelectronics, specifically the chip and microprocessors, created the fourth generation.

These four generations bring developments to our focal point, the personal computer. These computers have placed computing power into the hands of millions who before the late 1970s could never have dreamed of it. In addition, significant new applications have become available that hold special interest for educators.

A computer system consists of several physical components called hardware. The basic elements of a system are the CPU, memory, input and output devices, and storage devices. The CPU handles such critical aspects of the system's operation as arithmetic, logic, and control. RAM and ROM are vital memory components of the computer system. Input and output devices are essential to communication between the user and the computer. They exist in many different forms. In addition, to be useful, computers require storage devices, which also provide input and output capabilities.

Making all the system components function as a unit is a control task. The heart of control is a series of instructions to the system called a program, or software. One highly specialized program essential to any computer is the operating system. Major functions of an operating system include system operation tasks of which the user is largely unaware and system utility tasks that are at the user's direct command. While the trend has been to make computers more compatible, there is a need for complete standardization of operating systems across manufacturers to ease the problems of exchanging programs and data among computer makes and models.

chapter 2
activities

1. Using whatever computer system is available, identify the input and output devices.
2. Remove the cover(s) on any available computer, even one that no longer works. Be sure it is not plugged in! Examine the inside and try to identify as many components as possible, including the power supply, drive bays and drives (floppy, optical, and hard disk—are there any that are not filled?), the CPU, RAM (are there unused RAM slots to allow adding memory?), card slots, and connection ports for the monitor, keyboard, and so on. Are the latter integrated or on cards?
3. Try out a variety of input devices. If alternative input devices are unavailable in your school, visit a computer store. How do the devices differ? Which ones appeal most to you? Why?
4. Compare sample output from ink jet and laser printers. Research the cost of each printer as well as its operating cost per page for ink or toner. Discuss the merits and applications of each, keeping their relative costs in mind.
5. What types of monitors and printers are available in your school? If they are not ideal, what should you have access to? Why?

6. Make a side-by-side visual comparison of different monitors. How noticeable are the differences? How significant are they?
7. If you have access to computers using different operating systems, familiarize yourself with their differences. Make a wall chart for the computer room or area that lists common tasks and the corresponding procedure for each system.
8. Visit the online store of at least two major computer vendors (the companion website provides links). Look at the various models that each offers and the choices available to you to customize a computer, such as memory, monitor type and size, hard drive capacity, and so on. What would you choose for your "ideal" system? You should be able to print out your final specifications after you make your choices. If not, write down all the specifications. Be prepared to justify the choices you made based on how each option addresses a specific need or potential use.
9. Interview at least one teacher who uses computers in his or her teaching, whether in a lab or in the classroom. Ask the teacher how he or she uses the computers. Also ask about the specifications of the available computers and what hardware and/or software, if any, the teacher would change or add to make them more useful as learning tools.

Companion Website

Visit the companion website at <www.ablongman.com/lockard6e> for more information about the topics discussed in this chapter.

expect the world®

The New York Times
nytimes.com

Themes of the Times

Expand your knowledge of the concepts discussed in this chapter by reading current and historical articles from the *New York Times* by visiting the Themes of the Times section of the companion website <www.ablongman.com/lockard6e>.

The Internet, Computer Networks, and Distance Learning: *Communication Tools*

of the Twenty-First Century

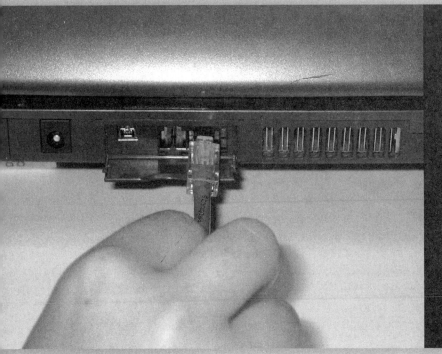

OBJECTIVES

After completing this chapter, you will be able to:

- Explain the basic concepts of computer networks.
- Compare and contrast different ways to get Internet access.
- Decipher an Internet address and explain its components.
- Discuss personal communication uses of the Internet, including email and computer conferencing.

- Discuss the educational potential of discussion groups (listservs) and Usenet, comparing the two formats.
- Briefly compare and contrast telnet and FTP.
- Distinguish among peer networks, local area networks, and wide area networks.
- Explain the Internet as a network and how it is organized.

- Explain three method of connecting to the Internet: NICs, modems, and broadband.
- Define distance learning and briefly recount its forms prior to the Internet.
- Discuss several key issues related to distance learning.
- Assess whether distance learning may be appropriate for you personally.
- Develop lesson plans that incorporate email, newsgroups, or other computer communication tools.

NETS
NOTES

NETS **S** 1
NETS **S** 3
NETS **S** 4
NETS **T** I-A
NETS **T** I-B
NETS **T** II-B
NETS **T** III-B
NETS **T** V-A

For all its warmth and rich potential, the typical classroom is actually a relatively isolated place. This isolation has benefits, as it affords us a great deal of freedom to interact with our students as we deem best. The classroom walls help to close out the countless distractions around us. But isolation can also be undesirable. The classroom limits student and teacher access to others and to information resources beyond those physically housed in the room. How many classrooms have so much as a telephone?

Since the mid-1990s, the Internet has stimulated explosive growth of interest in reaching out beyond the classroom for numerous purposes. More and more teachers are becoming aware of the vast resources that exist beyond their own rooms, schools, and districts. Information of every type and in every format abounds for those who know how to find and use it. Colleagues are available for advice, counsel, and sharing around the world, if you know how to reach them.

This chapter introduces you to the Internet and computer networks, which have become vital tools for the educator in the global village of the twenty-first century. You will learn about the technical aspects of computer communications that make it all work, and explore distance learning, an increasingly popular use of the Internet.

The Internet

The Internet is a worldwide network of interconnected computer networks with millions of users. It reaches virtually all types of organizations, schools and institutions of higher education, research centers, military installations, commercial businesses, public service organizations, and of course, individuals—including teachers and students! Growth in the number of Internet users is so rapid that it is pointless to cite numbers in a book. They would be hopelessly outdated before you read them.

No doubt you can already relate to this statement: "The Internet has made such a difference in our society that it is difficult to remember when we did not depend on it for communications, instruction, and even entertainment" (Roblyer, 2003, p. 196). However, it seems likely that, for most students, entertainment has a much higher priority than third place and instruction may not even be on the list!

Since our concern is educational applications of technology, let's jump right in to the Internet as an educational resource.

What Can I Do on the Internet?

The Internet has become the all-purpose information and communications tool of the twenty-first century. Virtually any information need you might have you can potentially satisfy via the Internet. Increasingly, the Internet is also taking on communications functions that once were the domains of the postal system and the telephone system. Even shopping has moved in significant volume from bricks-and-mortar stores to online versions of traditional retailers, as well as uniquely Internet-based approaches to merchandising such as eBay. The real question may be to ask what you can't do on the Internet.

Most Internet activities or functions fall into one of several basic categories. Most familiar are the communications methods: electronic mail (email), conferencing, discussion forums, and newsgroups. Telnet and FTP, although less well known, are extremely useful in specific situations. Distance learning has become a popular alternative to the traditional classroom. Finally, the World Wide Web (WWW or just the Web) is such a vast topic that it requires a full chapter of its own, which follows this one.

Internet activities obviously require Internet access and some understanding of Internet addresses, so let's look first at those topics. Then we'll explore each type of activity individually.

Getting Access to the Internet

To use the Internet you must have access to a computer that is connected to the Internet. Such access varies depending on whether you own the computer in question. There are two major ways to access the Internet without your own hardware. First, virtually all educational institutions provide Internet access to their students in computer labs or classrooms with computers and to their staff with office computers. Some uses of the Internet require no more than sitting down at an available computer, whereas others may be open only to those individuals, including students, with accounts specific to the institution or site.

Second, and closely related, is Internet access in public locations, especially public libraries, which offer it as a service to patrons. In communities throughout the world you can find students and adults using computers in their nearest library for the same tasks they might do at school, work, or home. In fact, although you might not realize it, even the homeless are benefiting from such public Internet access. The communication potential and the rich resources to address nearly any issue are very useful to individuals who have no permanent address or telephone number. Dabu (2002) termed this the "emerging wave of digital access for the homeless." The Homeless People's Network <http://aspin.asu.edu/hpn> is one specific example of resources for this group.

If you own a computer with the proper components (as explained later in the chapter), you need a means to connect it to the Internet. You have at least three options. First, your school or employer may provide remote dialup access to its computer systems, including Internet access, typically for the cost of a local phone call.

Anyone can purchase Internet access through an *information service*. Major services include America Online, CompuServe, and Prodigy (Figure 3.1). Such services began

Figure 3.1
Many exclusive resources are available through information services.

as general-purpose information utilities and continue to offer a vast range of resources only to subscribers. For many, though, the key attraction is the link provided to the Internet, although it may not include all possible Internet functions.

If you simply want unlimited full-service Internet access, *Internet service providers* (ISPs) are comparable to long-distance telephone companies. For a monthly fee, you can access their Internet host computer. You do not get all the special information resources of an America Online, just maximum Internet capabilities. How you actually connect to any Internet host is explained in the technical section of this chapter.

Internet Addresses

Every computer on the Internet must have a unique address, just as every phone line has a unique number. These computer addresses consist of two or more levels, separated by periods, which become more specific from right to left. For example, one computer at our university has the address <wpo.cso.niu.edu>. Looking at the levels from the right, *edu* identifies the broad education domain, *niu* is our specific university (Northern Illinois University), *cso* is Computer Systems and Operations within NIU, and *wpo* is the specific computer itself. (All addresses will be shown within angle brackets, < >, to make them clear. The angle brackets are *not* part of any address.)

In addition to *edu*, common top-level domains (TLDs) include *gov* for government computers (e.g., <lcweb.loc.gov>, Library of Congress Information System), *com* for commercial businesses (e.g., <aol.com>, America Online), and *org* for nonprofit organizations (e.g., <npr.org>, National Public Radio). Newer TLDs include *biz* for businesses, *info* for information sites, *name* for individuals, *pro* for professionals offering services, *coop* for use only by cooperatives and cooperative service organizations, *aero* for the aviation industry, and *museum*. Following the top-level domain may come a country code, such as *uk* for the United Kingdom, for example, <leicester.ac.uk>, and *de* for Germany. The *us* code exists but is not used for most U.S. addresses.

Pay attention to the exact spellings in Internet addresses. An address on the Internet may be case-sensitive, meaning *Sam* is not the same as *sam*. Copy the spelling exactly as you find it to avoid problems.

Organizing the Internet's Resources

Computers throughout the world have long stored vast amounts of information. Think just of the electronic card catalogs of the world's libraries, one small electronic application. However, virtually none of that information was readily available to most people, because users had to be where the computer was located to access its data.

Once even a few computer networks were connected to the Internet, unprecedented volumes of information potentially became available to users, subject to the willingness of the information's owners to share. Far more information is publicly accessible than you can imagine. The trick is locating what you need. What good are vast information resources if they are as accessible as the contents of a library for which there is no index, catalog, or organization? Imagine that all the books in the library were just there, randomly stored on shelves with no system of organization. Everything is there, but how can you find what you need? How might you ever learn of things that you could use but are unaware of? Today's answer is primarily the World Wide Web.

The World Wide Web

Research scientists at CERN, the European center for nuclear particle research, created the World Wide Web (WWW or just the Web) to expedite the process of locating information. A web *page* consisted of text with highlighted "hot" words (*hyperlinks*) within it. Users selected a highlighted word to connect to the related information. It could be within the same document or a page on a computer halfway around the world!

The WWW remained a specialist's tool until software developers at the National Center for Supercomputing Applications (NCSA) at the University of Illinois–Urbana Champaign recognized that the Web need not be limited to text. Because the Internet could carry computer files of all kinds, graphics, sound, or even movies could also become part of nonlinear or *hypermedia* Internet documents. To allow you to reach and view these multimedia documents stored at websites, the developers created a web *browser*, the NCSA *Mosaic* software.

Mosaic became available in 1993. Practically overnight, it revolutionized the Web and popularized the Internet as a tool for everyone, not just scientists and academics. Creating web *home pages*, the initial point of connection to a website, became a new international pastime! *Mosaic* was the first complete set of Internet hypermedia information tools, both *server* software to store and deliver information at a website and *client* software to allow users to access that information. *Netscape* and Microsoft *Internet Explorer* followed to extend Mosaic and now dominate the browser market (Figure 3.2).

Website addresses can be any valid Internet address, but many are readily identifiable because they include *www*, such as <www.niu.edu>. To access a site or even a specific page at that site through your browser, you must specify its uniform resource locator, or URL. A complete URL gives the type of site (*http* for hypertext is most common, but others are possible) and its address with a colon and two slashes between. The ad-

Figure 3.2

TYPICAL WEB PAGE
SHOWING HYPERLINKS

dress may be just the computer, or it may include detailed location information for a specific page. To reach the home page for our university, for example, the URL is <http://www.niu.edu>. The NETS-S standards are located at <http://cnets.iste.org/students/s_stands.html>, which identifies the host computer (cnets.iste.org), a folder stored on that computer (/students), and finally a specific page within that folder (/s_stands.html). Because so many URLs begin with *http://www*, most browsers now accept entering just the remainder of the URL, filling in the initial part automatically behind the scenes for you.

At this point, it is important to note that new websites appear daily, and existing ones are moved, removed, or closed to public access. Throughout this book, you will find many URLs given, but some are certain not to be valid when you look for them. That is the nature of the Web. If you are lucky, the address we provide may lead to a page that gives a new address for the site. If not, try deleting parts of the URL one by one, starting with the last element. That is, delete from the end back to the first slash. Enter that part of the address, and if it doesn't work, remove another element. At some level you may find a page that will guide you to what you are seeking. You can repeat this process until you reach just the TLD or country code. Typically, that much of the URL will still be valid, but the exact path may have changed. With a little detective work, you may locate the resource anyhow. However, sometimes resources simply are no longer available.

Electronic Mail

One of the oldest and still most-used Internet services is electronic mail (*email*). Email is sending and receiving messages electronically, something like fax without the paper. Email generally reaches its recipient in a very short time, regardless of location around the world. It is quick and easy to use and generally costs nothing.

Email is not real-time communication like a phone call but rather *asynchronous*, meaning that the sender and recipient do not have to be at their computers at the same time. The receiving computer stores the message in the recipient's electronic inbox until that person retrieves it (Figure 3.3). This is "time shifting," much like recording a program on your VCR for later viewing. Email works equally well between any two points in the world, regardless of time zone, when one party is on vacation, or when one is simply too busy to attend to it immediately. It is much the same as regular mail in that regard. Email also avoids telephone tag; barring computer problems, electronic messages are always received.

To send and receive email, you must have an email account. Your college or university probably provides you with an email account, as many businesses and organizations do for their employees. If you purchase Internet access from a service provider, you probably have an email account through that service. However, such accounts may be inconvenient to access away from your school or home, such as when traveling on breaks or vacations. Also, the account is linked to your association with the provider, so what happens to your email address when you graduate, change jobs, or switch ISPs? To maintain a more permanent email address, millions of users use free email services provided by such enterprises as Yahoo! and HotMail. Many individuals maintain multiple email accounts with different providers, but keeping up with reading them all can be a challenge.

Regardless of the provider, email addresses take the form of <userID@host-computer>, for example, <president@whitehouse.gov>, which is a real address although responses to mail are likely to be written by a staff member, not the president. Your own email address, then, is <your-ID@your-host>, for example, <JaneDoe@hotmail.com>.

Many email systems offer far more communication and organizational assistance than just email. Figure 3.3 shows additional features of one system that include an electronic calendar and a task or "to do" list. In this system the calendar feature even allows for automatic meeting scheduling by searching for common available times on the calendars of a specified list of users.

Figure 3.3
EMAIL SOFTWARE WITH ADDITIONAL FEATURES

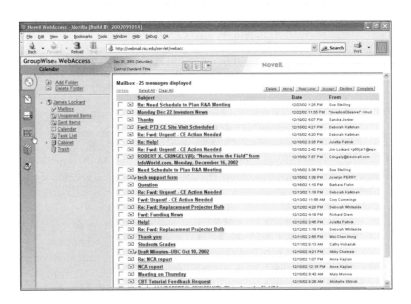

Chat and Other Conferencing

Although time shifting is a great advantage of email for many users, real-time communication is also possible. For group interaction, *computer conferencing* or "chat" mode is much like a telephone conference call, except that you "speak" with your keyboard and "listen" with your monitor. Since 1988 *Internet Relay Chat (IRC)* has supported conferencing between two or more sites that are online simultaneously <www.irc.org/history. html>. Many websites now incorporate some form of chat among users. *AOL Instant Messenger* is a very popular means of instant communication among users, and it's free!

Verbal and even visual communication over the Internet is also possible as computer communication and telecommunications join together. Cornell University developed Internet videoconferencing software called *CU-SeeMe*, which requires only a very fast Internet connection (explained in the technical section later) and video input capability in your computer. The latter is now available for $100 or less, making desktop videoconferencing feasible, although image size tends to be small, movement jerky, and picture quality somewhat poor.

Microsoft's *NetMeeting* is an integral part of the Windows operating system. It includes audio and video conferencing, an electronic whiteboard for visual collaboration, chat capabilities, file transfer from one computer to another, even operation of a computer from a remote location <www.microsoft.com/windows/NetMeeting/Features>. See Figure 3.4. The major deterrent to much greater use of conferencing software is ready access to a sufficiently fast Internet connection.

Real-time Internet voice communication—long-distance calling without a phone!—is also available. Like videoconferencing, it works and has attracted attention as a growing challenge to the phone companies. Many phone companies are investing heavily in the Internet as an unavoidable part of their future.

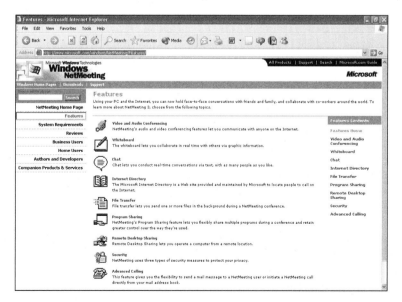

Figure 3.4

MANY COMMUNICATION FEATURES OF NETMEETING

Discussion Groups (Lists) and Newsgroups (Usenet)

Literally millions of individuals worldwide have Internet access. A powerful educational application of the Internet is communication with knowledgeable individuals, even experts. But how do you locate and contact others who may share your interests?

Many educators participate in Internet discussion groups called *lists*. A list comes into being when someone interested in a particular area of discussion, say authentic assessment, establishes a central electronic address through which others may communicate. There is no cost to "subscribe" to such a list, and lists of lists are readily available (e.g., <www.lsoft.com/catalist.html>). Popular software that automates management of a discussion list is called *listserv* software, for *list server*. It handles both the database of subscribers and the processing of messages.

List addresses are like personal email addresses, except that the user ID is the name of the list, for example, <edtech@h-net.msu.edu>, a popular forum on educational technology. When you subscribe to a list, you soon receive in your email a copy of each message sent to the list by all subscribers. The volume of email you receive varies with the list. Some produce only a few messages each week. Very active lists can bury you in daily email and make message management a daunting task.

As a list subscriber, you decide what your level of participation will be. Kibitz, or express your own views at every opportunity. Even if initially you only read (called *lurking*), sooner or later someone will write something that you wish to know more about or pose a question that you can answer. You can then join in the discussion, or if it is more appropriate, contact the person directly at his or her personal electronic address.

Somewhat similar to lists is *Usenet*, a collection of discussion forums called *newsgroups*. However, the communication model is more like a bulletin board than email. Messages are "posted" to a particular Usenet group. Instead of subscribing and receiving an email copy of each message personally, an Internet host system subscribes to specific newsgroups. The host then receives and stores one copy of each group's distributed messages, and users all access that one copy. One of the easiest ways to access newsgroups is through Google <www.google.com>. On the main Google page, click on the Groups tab. Then select one of the listed forums, or click on the link "Browse complete list of groups" (Figure 3.5). Other access methods may require special *newsreader* software to access the forums. Information about Usenet is available at <www.usenet.org>.

Newsgroups are organized by categories, then subgroups. Among the major categories are *alt* (alternative, often unsuitable for children), *comp* (computer related), *k12* (K–12 education), *misc* (miscellaneous), *news* (Usenet news), *rec* (recreation and arts), *sci* (science and technology), and *soc* (social issues). Specific groups include *k12.chat.elementary*, *k12.ed.health-pe*, *k12.lang.art*, *k12.news*, and *misc.kids.computer*. Remember, what you can actually access depends on your host system. You may have to ask your system administrator to subscribe to a group of special interest. For an index to existing newsgroups, point your browser to <http://tile.net>.

Within newsgroups, *threads* are subtopics of the general discussion, such as multimedia within alternative assessment approaches. Threads organize related messages into subgroups that you can read independently of the rest. In contrast, if you subscribe to a list on alternative assessment, you'll have to sort through the complete set of email messages you receive to find the ones dealing with just multimedia.

Telnet

Telnet is software that enables you to log on to a remote computer and use it as if your computer were a terminal connected directly to that system. What you can do depends on the computer you connect to. Many, such as the Library of Congress, provide public access facilities to Internet users. When you connect to them, you see a menu or other directions concerning what you may do. Others are open only to individuals with specific system accounts, who can then run software on the remote computer, such as simulation and modeling programs available only on supercomputers. Telnet also may offer access to your email from any available computer when you are traveling. Ask your system administrator for instructions if this would be useful to you.

FTP (File Transfer Protocol)

The final Internet tool to consider is file transfer protocol (FTP). FTP is a method for logging on to a remote computer. However, once connected, you may only search certain directories and then transfer files from them to your own computer (called *downloading*). FTP sites are popular means of distributing software that is either a demo or trial version, free to anyone who wants it (called *public domain* or *freeware*) or offered for a test period, after which you are asked to pay a modest registration fee to the author (called *shareware*).

You may think you have little use for FTP, but perhaps a concrete example will suggest otherwise. Assume that you become a real fan of the World Wide Web. Browsers for the Web (e.g., Netscape and Internet Explorer) are available at no cost to individual users. However, the developers are continually improving their browsers and want you to have the latest version. If you connect to the Netscape website <www.netscape.com>,

Figure 3.6

Just click the Free Download button to get the latest software version by FTP.

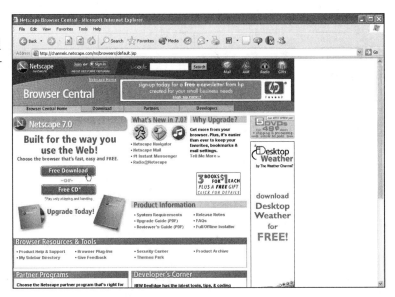

for example, you will find a link under tools labeled "Browser Central." That will take you to another page that will allow you to download the latest version of the Netscape browser to your computer (Figure 3.6). Although you only need to click the button provided, you are actually using FTP to obtain the software. This use of the Internet is growing as a new software distribution method, including for commercial software products for which you do pay but that you can get "instantly" via the Internet. Downloading purchased music and videos from the Internet has begun and may ultimately become the preferred commercial method of distribution.

The Technical Side of Computer Communications

The Internet enables communication among computers at a distance, irrespective of their physical locations. Let's look at the technical basics of computer communication that support our routine technology applications today. We will deal briefly with computer networks and remote access connections. For more detailed treatment of telecommunications and networks, see *Networking for Dummies* (Lowe, 2002).

Computer Networks

You realize that the Internet is a worldwide network of computer networks. But what exactly is a network in the first place? A *computer network* is two or more computers (and their users) linked together to exchange information and share resources. Peer networks, local area networks or LANs, and wide area networks or WANs are the most common types.

Peer Networks (Workgroups)

Imagine that you are part of a work team preparing a complex report jointly, perhaps a new social studies curriculum. Each team member has a specific writing assignment, but the pieces of the report are highly interdependent. Team members work on their parts during planning periods scattered throughout the day, before or after school, or even at home. Group meetings occur only at critical points. Relatively few printouts are ever made. Yet each member has constant access to the latest draft of each part of the report, because the school computers at which the team members work are interconnected as part of a peer network or workgroup (Figure 3.7).

A *workgroup* is a group of computers that are connected by cables or wirelessly to enable group members to share files and peripheral hardware, even an Internet connection. Members of the workgroup decide which file directories or *folders* on their computers are to be accessible to other members of the group. (This might be just one common folder.) All other folders on that machine remain private. Each group member can access whatever has been made "public" on each machine in the group. There is no central computer that all users share, hence, the term *peer network* (Lowe, 2002). Recent versions of Windows include a network setup wizard to create a peer network (Figure 3.8).

In our curriculum development example, team members are responsible to always keep a copy of the latest version of their individual work in a public directory, from which any other member can then retrieve, read, annotate, revise, and resave it as needed. The advantages of this system over sharing printouts should be obvious. If team members are diligent about maintaining their own parts of the document and placing a copy in the public directory, all members will be up to date at all times. The team can work as

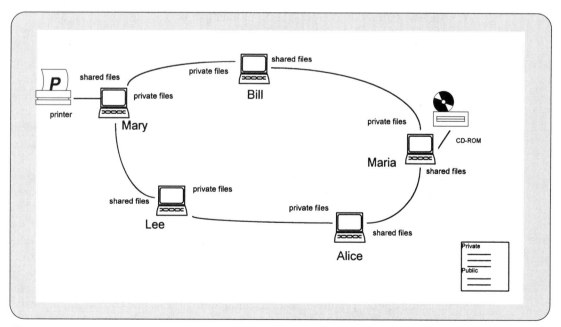

Figure 3.7 COMPUTERS CONNECTED IN A WORKGROUP OR PEER NETWORK

Figure 3.8
PEER NETWORK
SETUP WIZARD

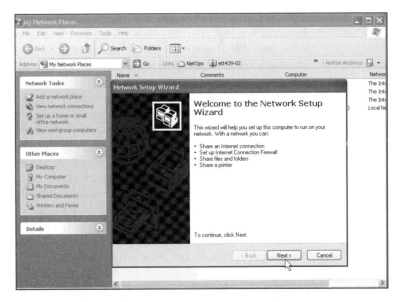

a group without regard to individual schedules. Face-to-face meetings, which can be difficult to schedule, are minimized, and progress toward the common goal occurs faster.

Local Area Networks

A *local area network (LAN)* is a computer network that involves only a limited physical area, such as within one classroom, school building, or perhaps a campus. Each computer on a LAN can operate independently, but all are connected to permit sharing of data and hardware, especially more expensive items such as color laser printers. Although this may sound much the same as a peer network, there are important distinctions.

First, a LAN has as a major function the sharing of common *hardware* resources. For example, each workstation on a LAN can access a central tower of CD-ROM drives, as in a library, or print directly to a shared high-speed printer, thus replacing the *sneaker net* (walking with a diskette to a printing station). In addition, a LAN can link together different types of computers (e.g., Macintosh and Windows) to share files, hardware, and Internet access.

Second, file sharing normally occurs between individual stations and a common master computer called the *file server,* or simply *server,* not among the individual computers directly. The server is dedicated to the operation and management of the LAN, including safeguarding files through regular backups. All communication occurs through the server, as Figure 3.9 illustrates. In a peer network, all connected computers are essentially equal; there is no server.

Third, a LAN can store a master copy of a software application (like your word processor) and provide it on request to any workstation on the LAN. The workstations do not need their own copies. However, this does not mean that you can simply install your one copy of whatever software you have on a server for all to use. You need legal licenses for all users, and special network versions of the software are often necessary.

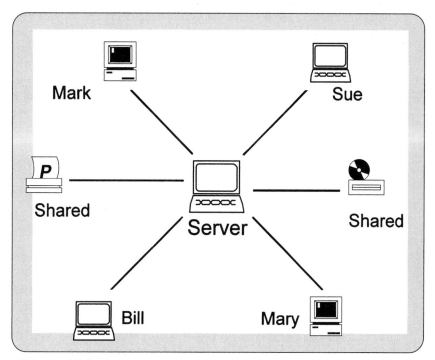

Figure 3.9 COMPUTERS CONNECTED IN A LOCAL AREA NETWORK (LAN)

Many schools have installed LANs in their computer labs to simplify operations (as well as to provide Internet access). New software is installed on just the server rather than on each computer in the lab. Updates of software are handled similarly, which means that all computers on the LAN always use the exact same version of the software.

Finally, although the advantages of a LAN are substantial, there is also a negative side. LANs have earned a reputation for being difficult to install, configure, and maintain. Common wisdom is that organizations virtually must have a trained network manager to set up and maintain a LAN. Peer networks are easier to set up than a LAN and less costly but also less versatile.

Wide Area Networks

A *wide area network (WAN)* is conceptually similar to a LAN, but the components may be entire LANs. Within a single school building, a LAN is appropriate. If the district consists of many buildings scattered over a community, a WAN can connect them to a common server called a *host*. For a company, a WAN could be a worldwide network of in-house computers.

Technically, a WAN differs in the method of connecting the workstations as well. Within a physical location, direct connection using cables is possible. To connect locations beyond your physical property, where cable installation is not feasible, dedicated telephone lines are often leased from the phone company. Within a school district or other relatively small area, LANs may be connected into WANs wirelessly using radio waves and, for larger geographic areas, connections via satellite are possible.

From this discussion, you realize that the Internet is itself a WAN—the ultimate one! At any given site, if a LAN server is connected to the Internet, all computers on the LAN have access to the Internet. If the LAN supports off-site users through dial-in connections, they, too, can access the Internet. If a LAN or WAN is completely private, available only to authorized users within the organization, it is called an *intranet*.

Making the Connection: NICs, Modems, and Broadband

There are three primary ways to connect to a network: a network interface, a telephone modem, and higher speed broadband.

Network Interface

Computers on a LAN are connected to the network through a network interface. This may be an installed *network interface card (NIC)* or an integrated network connection. Both use special network cables to connect to a network outlet similar to a telephone jack or to a *hub*, a device that allows multiple computers to share one outlet. Increasingly, networks are using *wireless* NICs to minimize the cost of wiring a building, although they generally provide somewhat slower connections. Wireless NICs (Figure 3.10) are available to install in both desktop and notebook computers; many notebooks now have integrated wireless networking.

Ethernet is a networking standard of detailed hardware and software specifications that permits devices to communicate at speeds up to 10 million or 100 million bits (*megabits*) per second (*Mbps*), with 1 *gigabit* per second (*Gbps* or 1,000 megabits) speeds beginning to appear. Because Ethernet was adopted as a standard by the Institute of Electrical and Electronic Engineers (IEEE), virtually any computer, from

Figure 3.10
WIRELESS NETWORKING
HARDWARE FOR DESKTOP
AND NOTEBOOK COMPUTERS

supercomputer to the most basic Macintosh or PC, can be connected to an Ethernet network.

Modems

You need not be connected directly to a LAN to enter the world of computer communication. Rather, you can use a phone line and a modem. Assuming you have a typical, single-line telephone, the cable that now leads from the wall to your phone connects instead to the modem, and a new cable runs from the modem to your telephone. A modem is required because most telephones are currently *analog*, whereas computers are *digital* (as are growing numbers of cell phones). Analog means the signal is in the form of waves, whereas a digital signal consists only of "off" or "on" states. The modem converts between the two signal formats (see Figure 3.11). Modems generally also have fax capability, and many can function as voicemail systems.

The most important characteristic of a modem is its speed, originally referred to as *baud rate*. Modem speed is now given in bits per second (bps), with 56Kbps the fastest and most common. Speed determines how quickly information transfers between computers, and faster is clearly better. Even a 56K modem is noticeably slower than an Ethernet network connection, however.

Broadband Connections: DSL and Cable Internet

In most communities, off-site (remote) access to any computer network requires use of a regular telephone line and a modem to bridge between analog and digital data formats. However, this combination lacks the *bandwidth*, meaning data-carrying capacity, necessary for speedy Internet access. Think of using a drinking straw to provide water to firefighters. Two primary competitors are seeking to address the bandwidth problem, especially for home users.

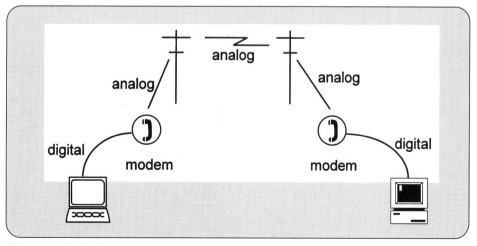

Figure 3.11 COMPUTER COMMUNICATION USING MODEMS AND TELEPHONE LINES

Telephone companies are promoting DSL (*digital subscriber line*) service as a *broadband* alternative to normal phone service. Broadband describes any single-wire system that can carry multiple channels of information at once <www.webopedia.com/TERM/b/broadband_transmission.html>. In addition to high-speed data service, DSL supports simultaneous voice use on the same line, eliminating the need for a second phone line that many individuals install just for modem use. DSL requires a special DSL modem connected to an existing telephone jack and then to the NIC on a computer, much like an Ethernet connection on a LAN. Speeds may also compare favorably with an office LAN. Monthly charges are higher for DSL than for ordinary phone service, of course.

The other competitors in broadband Internet service are the cable TV companies. Cable companies already provide a high-capacity, broadband connection into millions of homes. Cable-based Internet service requires a *cable modem* (Figure 3.12), which can deliver access at speeds comparable to or greater than DSL. Because cable service is separate from your phone system, like DSL it does not tie up the telephone.

Because DSL and cable Internet do not require dialing over the phone lines, both are connected continuously whenever the computer is operating. In this regard, as well as speed of access, they compare well to office networks. However, both services are available only in certain areas, and many people have no access to either or perhaps to only one or the other. Both provide faster speeds for downloads than uploads, presumably reflecting the fact that Internet activity normally involves far more downloading than uploading. Costs may be similar or favor one over the other. Neither is yet pervasive, and it is unclear whether one will dominate the broadband market eventually. Regardless, we can look forward to greatly enhanced access to the world's information resources as more areas are served by these or other broadband connection options.

How the Internet Works

As our last technical topic, let's take a simplified look at how the Internet actually works. The Internet was developed in the late 1960s when several existing research networks joined together to facilitate communication among their users. As the perceived ben-

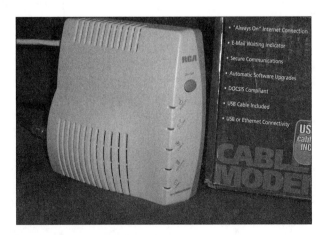

Figure 3.12
CABLE MODEM FOR BROADBAND INTERNET CONNECTION

efits of such interconnections grew, more and more networks joined together, growing into today's Internet.

In some ways, the Internet resembles the telephone system in that it provides point-to-point (or person-to-person) communication around the world. You must have an access point to use it (compare to a telephone number) and a computer with necessary hardware and software (compare to a phone, phone line, and wall jack). The phone system does not need an individual line from your phone to every other phone in the world. Instead, calls are routed from one phone to another over a web of land lines and satellite links. Similarly, computers connect to the Internet with only a link to the nearest other computer that is already connected.

Assume the Internet started with two networks that leased phone lines to link themselves together. When a third decided to join, it needed only to connect to the nearer of the existing two, through which it gained access to the other. This process has continued to create the network of millions of computers that make up the Internet today. Organizations that are large enough to afford to connect directly to the Internet, such as universities, government agencies, and corporations, do so through leased high-speed telephone lines. This provides an on-site Internet connection point for the organization's LANs and stand-alone computers, as well as dial-in access for modem users (Figure 3.13). Individuals not affiliated with such an organization and smaller organizations

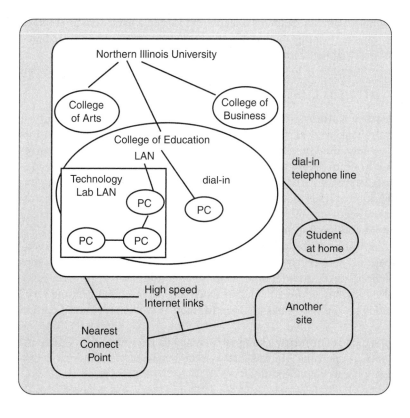

Figure 3.13

HOW THE INTERNET
WORKS (CONCEPTUALLY)

turn to information services such as America Online or to Internet service providers to establish an account with dial-in access.

In addition to such connection details, the Internet relies on a common "language" that allows diverse computer types to communicate with one another. This is known as *TCP/IP*, the acronym for Transmission Control Protocol/Internet Protocol. TCP/IP is conceptually similar to the pattern of tones that each telephone key produces to allow worldwide communication.

Finally, just as the telephone system requires a unique number for each phone line, the Internet requires a unique *IP address* for each connected computer. Although IP addresses are really four-part numbers, such as 111.222.33.4, you generally see only alphanumeric equivalents because they are much easier to remember (e.g., <apple.com>).

Distance Learning

In the Internet age, *distance learning* has become a buzzword in very little time. The United States Distance Learning Association (USDLA, 2003) defines distance learning as "the acquisition of knowledge and skills through mediated information and instruction. Distance learning encompasses all technologies and supports the pursuit of lifelong learning for all. Distance learning is used in all areas of education including pre-K through grade 12, higher education, home school education, continuing education, corporate training, military and government training, and telemedicine." At the heart of the concept of distance learning lie two key elements: a learner physically separated in time and/or distance from the means of learning and learning methods that are necessarily mediated through technology, normally including two-way communication.

Brief Background on Distance Learning

The concept of distance learning is hardly new. Until late in the nineteenth century, education was rarely conceived as something for the masses. Seeking to extend its resources to new learners, the University of Chicago established the first major correspondence learning program before the turn of the twentieth century (McIsaac & Gunawardena, 1996). Learners and teachers were physically separated and the learning was mediated through print materials that were mailed back and forth. By today's standards, correspondence study seems primitive, but it started a movement to extend learning opportunities to more and more individuals.

Distance learning took on new forms in the twentieth century as radio and eventually television became delivery systems for instruction. Print materials were supplemented with audiocassettes or videotapes as these technologies became prevalent. The concepts evolved and spread worldwide, until distance learning has become a tool in developing nations to address issues of basic literacy as well as higher education needs.

Distance learning has continually changed to adapt to new ways to mediate instruction. It is no surprise that the Internet has sparked a massive new interest in distance learning, again on a worldwide scale.

Distance Learning and the Internet

Previously in this chapter you learned about the communication possibilities on the Internet. Just as early correspondence courses provided learning at a distance, so too have educators applied email and discussion lists to assist others to learn. More sophisticated methods are appearing constantly and changing frequently. The buzzword of the late 1990s became *web-based instruction* as electronic messaging merged with the Web to create new learning environments. In conjunction with learning we will use the terms *distance*, *online*, and *web-based* interchangeably, though distinctions can be made.

Forces fueling the explosive growth of distance learning have been the desire of institutions of higher education to extend their services to new segments of the population, in some cases creating *virtual universities*, and the needs of businesses to train and retrain employees in large numbers at many locations. Corporate virtual universities have arisen to make training more timely (it's available at any time, just in time) and less costly (no need to bring people together into a classroom). Countless online courses and even degrees are now available from a vast array of providers, including for-profit businesses whose only product is distance learning. The range of applications extends to the K–12 world as well, as *virtual high schools* have come into existence across America. See <www.govhs.org> and <www.ivhs.org> as examples. The former is open to any student, whereas the latter is limited to students in Illinois whose schools have elected to participate in the Illinois Virtual High School.

If you have not already experienced some form of online learning, imagine taking a course with few or no group meetings. Instead, your instructor conducts the course via the Web. You and other students worldwide must have Internet access. To begin the course, you register and receive directions to access the course website. The syllabus includes any pertinent details of the course, how to use the system, and so on. Instead of group lectures and demonstrations, the instructor creates and organizes course materials on web pages, often in conjunction with required textbooks. Links to key Internet resources are also provided.

Among the course resources is an electronic messaging system. The instructor may begin a discussion by posting a message concerning course content in some way and requesting learner input into an electronic discussion. Learners respond to both the instructor and each other in threaded discussions. The teacher monitors the discussion and, at certain intervals, posts new points, say, every Monday. In between, class members read assigned materials, complete activities and assignments found at the website, read discussion messages and add their responses, hopefully asking questions, contesting or analyzing points made, offering insights from experience or readings, and so forth. Students learn from and react to each other's comments, as well as the instructor's prepared materials and message contributions. Anyone, including the instructor, may contribute at any time and as often as desired.

Creating a Distance Learning Course

In the next chapter you will learn about the process of creating and publishing your own web pages. Online learning materials are sometimes created in that way. However, course creation is simplified when online instructors obtain access to a web-based course development system that provides essential services (such as communication tools) and a framework into which course content may be entered. There are many such systems in existence; among the most popular ones are WebCT <webct.com> and Blackboard <http://blackboard.com>. Figure 3.14 gives you some sense of the typical layout of a course developed using Blackboard.

We chose to include distance learning in the Internet chapter rather than the Web chapter that follows because systems such as Blackboard were designed to minimize the web knowledge needed to create courses. Most of the work occurs within the system itself and does not require that the creator of a course have skill with common web development tools at all. Figures 3.15 and 3.16 illustrate a small part of the means by which Blackboard courses are created, which stand in marked contrast to most web page development, a point sure to become clearer as you progress through the next chapter.

Issues with Online Learning

The prospect of being able to learn something that you need on your own schedule, even if there is no local opportunity to do so, obviously has great appeal to many learners. Let's look at some of the issues that are prominent in the literature about online learning. If this topic is of special interest to you, we suggest you regularly read the online publication, *Journal of Computer-Mediated Communication*, available at <www.ascusc. org/jcmc> and the *Journal of Asynchronous Learning Networks* at <www.aln.org>.

Research on Effectiveness
In educational research, a common outcome when comparing a new means of learning to a familiar one is "no significant difference," which can be interpreted positively

Figure 3.14

AN ONLINE COURSE IN
BLACKBOARD

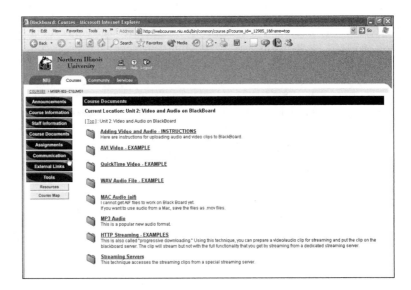

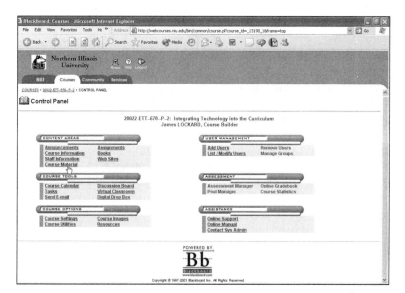

Figure 3.15
INSTRUCTOR OPTIONS FOR A BLACKBOARD COURSE

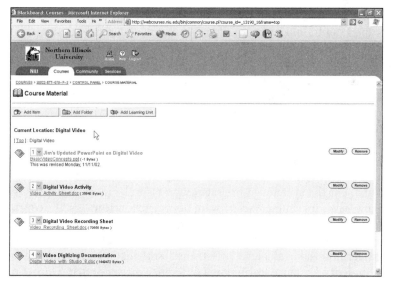

Figure 3.16
ADDING CONTENT TO A BLACKBOARD COURSE

(it's just as good, so why not use it?) or negatively (it's no better, so why bother?). In a nutshell, that's the story of years of research comparing distance learning to traditional, face-to-face learning. The U.S. Distance Learning Association (2003) and Roblyer (2003) both note that studies have consistently shown comparable effectiveness across methods. See also <www.aln.org/alnweb/journal/jaln-vol4issue2-3.htm> and the No Significant Difference website at <http://teleeducation.nb.ca/nosignificantdifference/index.cfm>. Thus, research evidence neither encourages nor discourages use of distance learning approaches in general, leaving the choice to be made on other grounds. Those range from altruistic desires to reach new learners to a hope to earn profits from the sale of online courses to saving training costs in business.

Lack of Community

This area of concern is difficult to title, as it encompasses several related matters. When a group of learners meets together physically in a classroom on some schedule, there is the likelihood that the learners may, in fact, come to see themselves as a unit and may develop a sense of cohesiveness among themselves. This can be vital to the learning dynamics, as is the instructor's ability to monitor nonverbal communication and react or adjust the instruction accordingly. Distance learning inherently operates in a much more isolated realm. Instructors preparing distance courses commonly spend a great deal of time seeking ways to build this "community" among individuals who may well never meet in person and whose only means of communication may be electronic. It is not our purpose to try to address this issue but rather to alert you to the fact that isolation is a significant concern in distance learning and contributes to high dropout rates in such courses (Schilke, 2001).

Course Design and Delivery

Any course, regardless of means of delivery, may be good or bad, as you have no doubt experienced. The unique and comparatively unfamiliar nature of distance learning adds elements to issues of course design and delivery that can play a major role in learning outcomes. Again, we can only point you to some of the issues.

First, technical problems can overwhelm would-be distance learners. If the delivery system is not dependable or is frequently unavailable, if the learner has trouble connecting to the Internet or the connection downloads materials too slowly, if the learner's computer crashes in the middle of taking a course and isn't repaired for several weeks—in circumstances such as these some number of learners will give up in frustration. We have experienced all of these problems firsthand.

Second, "live" courses are not inherently interactive (consider the lecture hall with hundreds of students), but the absence of interaction seems to be more noticeable in online courses when you are less immediately aware of your fellow learners. If a course involves primarily reading materials on a computer display with little or no interaction with the instructor and/or fellow students, it can be difficult to maintain motivation to continue. Distance learning requires a level of self-discipline that makes it unsuitable for many potential students. Distance learning is a different experience that requires of the learner new skills and new approaches. It is necessary to relearn how to learn.

Third, online learners lack the ready support structure that a regular classroom provides in classmates and a physically present instructor. To whom does the online learner turn with problems accessing the course or obtaining materials, or most importantly, understanding the content and completing assignments? Online courses need to provide adequate support for learners at all times, both technical and academic.

Fourth, it can be difficult to achieve a balance between the flexibility that online learning can offer and the goals of creating community. For example, chat sessions are one means of bringing scattered students together, yet they also mean everyone must be available and online at the same time, which runs counter to the goal of "learn when you can." This can be a particular problem when learners live across time zones even within the United States, to say nothing of international learners.

It takes a lot of time and effort to create an online course. Educators who choose to do so need to be aware of this, especially when the preparation must be done in addition to all other responsibilities. Online course development should be a compensated activity, but frequently in universities it is not. If you want to explore the topic more fully, a comprehensive faculty training program on distance learning is offered online free by the University of Florida at <http://training.ifas.ufl.edu/deft>.

Countless resources deal with these and other issues in far greater detail. For example, the July 2002 issue of the *Journal of Asynchronous Learning Networks* has articles addressing many of them all in one place <www.aln.org/alnweb/journal/jaln-vol6 issue1.htm>. See also Eaton (2001). The companion website contains links to a variety of resources to further your understanding of distance learning. Whatever the challenges, it seems clear that education must make the effort to find potential solutions and test them until we truly know how best to harness the power of the Internet to bring learning opportunities to individuals otherwise unable to participate in them.

SUMMARY

The Internet has the potential to be the single most significant influence on early twenty-first century education, as schools and teachers increase access to it and learn to use it effectively. This chapter contributed to that goal by introducing you to the Internet and many of its functions, including the World Wide Web, various applications that ultimately rest on electronic mail services, and the remote log-on functions of Telnet and FTP. You should now have a broad understanding of what the Internet is, how you can access it, and what you can do with it to benefit yourself as well as your students.

Effective and efficient use of the Internet demands a rudimentary understanding of the technical aspects of computer communication. You learned about networks in general, how computers can connect to them directly or through a modem, and the essential features of communications software. You also have a general idea of how the Internet actually works and how increased communication speeds should become available soon.

Distance learning has evolved from the correspondence courses of the nineteenth century to online courses at all educational levels. Virtual high schools and universities, as well as corporate and profit-oriented business, offer new learning opportunities worldwide to countless individuals. There are even full degree programs intended to serve persons who for various reasons are unable to participate in traditional education. Online courses may be created in different ways, but most commonly use special web course development systems such as Blackboard and WebCT. Research has shown distance learning outcomes to be comparable to those of traditional instruction, but much work remains to determine best practices in providing learning at a distance. Students may lack a sense of community and feel lost and alone. Technical difficulties may seem overwhelming. Remaining motivated when there is no tangible group to face on a regular basis can be problematic. As with any new technology, there are many challenges in distance learning, but the benefits in extending educational opportunity to individuals not otherwise served require us to find and test solutions.

Communications is perhaps the most rapidly changing area within educational computing today. The ride may be harried, perhaps even frightening at times, but the potential benefits are so enormous as to demand that educators get on board immediately. You'll be very glad you did.

chapter 3 activities

1. Obtain a school account for Internet access. Learn to use the available email software, and set up a group among your classmates to communicate regularly in this way.

2. Join an Internet discussion group. Monitor the messages carefully for at least one month. When you are comfortable, join in the discussion. Keep a log of your interaction with the group. One particularly good group to join is called EDTECH. You can join it by sending the message "SUB EDTECH (your full name) [e.g., SUB EDTECH John Doe]" to the address <listserv@h-net.msu.edu>. Your first reply will provide instructions on how the list works. Be sure to save that message, as it also tells you how to unsubscribe.

3. Sign up for a free email account with Yahoo!, HotMail, or another service that is different from your school email account. Send messages from your current account to your new account and vice versa. How are the systems similar and how are they different? Which do you prefer? Why?

4. What would you have to do if you decided to change to a new email account? Think about the email you now receive and what you should do to assure that you continue to receive messages when you switch to the new service.

5. What are your options currently for participating in a chat or other conferencing activity? If you have no other option, sign up for free access to AOL Instant Messenger <www.aim.com> with at least one fellow student or family member. Try out the system on several different occasions and record your experiences and impressions in a journal.

6. Interview the administrator of the network in your school. Ask how the network is organized and maintained. If wireless access is available, what is required to use it? What is the size of the network staff and how many computers and users are served by it? What are the major challenges for this administrator?

7. Investigate the Internet services available in your area, both dialup and broadband. Prepare a comparison of what each offers and their costs. Which is the "best deal?" Why?

8. Visit your nearest public library to determine whether it offers public access to the Internet. If so, what are the policies for using public computers? If not, ask the library staff about plans to offer this service in the future.

9. Explore the newsgroups to which you have access. (Use Google groups if you don't have another means to access Usenet.) Identify several that could be of value to you.

10. Explore the online offerings of your school, or choose another institution in your area or state, if your own school is not yet involved. Prepare a report on what is available, to whom, at what cost, and so on. You may want to compare two or more sources of distance learning opportunities.

11. Prepare a position paper on the issue of access to information through telecommunications, including the gaps between "haves" and "have nots" and the proper role of schools in providing access.

Companion Website

Visit the companion website at <www.ablongman.com/lockard6e> for more information about the topics discussed in this chapter.

expect the world®

The New York Times
nytimes.com

Themes of the Times

Expand your knowledge of the concepts discussed in this chapter by reading current and historical articles from the *New York Times* by visiting the Themes of the Times section of the companion website <www.ablongman.com/lockard6e>.

References

Dabu, C. "Bridging the Digital Divide." *Digital Journal.com.* Retrieved December 28, 2002, from <www.digitaljournal.com/news/?articleID=2083>

Eaton, J. *Distance Learning: Academic and Political Challenges for Higher Education Accreditation.* Washinton, DC: Council for Higher Education Accreditation, 2001. Retrieved January 1, 2003, from <www.chea.org/Commentary/distance-learning/chea_dis_learning.pdf>

Killmer, K., and Koppel, N. "So Much Information, So Little Time. Evaluating Web Resources with Search Engines." *T.H.E. Journal,* August 2002. Retrieved December 29, 2002, from <www.thejournal.com/magazine/vault/A4101.cfm>

Lowe, D. *Networking for Dummies,* 6th ed. New York: Wiley, 2002.

McIsaac, M., and Gunawardena, C. "Distance Education." In Jonassen, D., ed. *Handbook of Research for Educational Communications and Technology.* New York: Simon & Schuster Macmillan, 1996, pp. 403–437.

Roblyer, M. *Integrating Educational Technology into Teaching,* 3rd ed. Columbus, OH: Merrill Prentice Hall, 2003.

Russell, T. L. *The No Significant Difference Phenomenon.* Raleigh, NC: North Carolina State University, 1999.

Schilke, R. *A Case Study of Attrition in Web-Based Instruction: Updating Garland's Model of Barriers to Persistence in Distance Education.* Unpublished doctoral dissertation. Northern Illinois University, 2001.

Tennant, R. "Internet Basics." *ERIC DIGEST,* September 1992. (ERIC Clearinghouse on Information Resources, EDO-IR-92-7.

USDLA (United States Distance Learning Association). "Research Info & Statistics." 2003. Retrieved January 1, 2003, from <www.usdla.org/html/aboutUs/researchInfo.htm>

The World Wide Web:

Bringing the World
into the Classroom

OBJECTIVES

After completing this chapter, you will be able to:

- Explain the background and basic functioning of the Web.
- Use your browser more effectively by tailoring it to your needs.
- Locate appropriate resources on the Web using indexes and search tools.
- Explore Internet and web curriculum applications and identify specific ones that you could include in your teaching.
- Explain the concepts behind WebQuests and outline the content and process for creating one.
- Describe what a website is, how to plan one, and two different ways to create and publish a site.
- Identify potential issues in using the Web in schools and propose solutions to them.
- Develop lesson plans that utilize web resources, including interdisciplinary units.

$\mathcal{F}$ollowing its initial development in Switzerland, the evolution of the World Wide Web (WWW or the Web) has proceeded at a pace remarkable even for "new" technologies. In about a decade the Web has transformed the Internet from a tool for a limited circle of specialists to a worldwide daily activity of ordinary people. Businesses virtually must have a website to succeed, and that reality has given rise to the new business form called *e-commerce*. Individuals proudly share the address of their personal web pages, where they display the latest family or vacation photos and videos. Teachers are creating their own web pages for many purposes. Education has taken to the Web like few other technologies, so it is vital to explore the educational applications of this remarkable entity.

First, you'll learn briefly about the Web and how it works as well as key points in using browser software effectively. Effective educational use of the Web typically starts with locating useful and appropriate sites, which is the next topic, followed by some specific resource recommendations. To help students to make efficient use of the Web, you'll learn about a popular approach to including web resources in lessons on virtually any topic, namely *WebQuests*. We'll also explore the increasingly common educational activity of creating new web pages. Finally, it is important to consider some of the issues that arise in using the Internet and the Web in education.

Understanding the Web

To learn to use the World Wide Web effectively as a tool for learning, it is important to understand conceptually what the Web is and how it works. This discussion reviews and builds on the brief introduction to the Web in the previous chapter.

NETS
NOTES

NETS **S** 1
NETS **S** 4
NETS **S** 6
NETS **T** I-A
NETS **T** I-B
NETS **T** V-C

Background of the Internet and the Web

In the relatively short time that most educators have had access to the Internet, many have become users of the Web without a clear understanding of what it is. The Internet, as you learned previously, is the ultimate wide area network, a worldwide network of other networks. The original Internet (and smaller networks that preceded it) were tools of specialists—primarily researchers, both academic and military, scattered around the world. For their initial purposes, the network did not have to be particularly easy to use, as they assumed users would be technologically sophisticated.

Fortunately, Tim Berners-Lee, a scientist at the European particle physics laboratory CERN <http://public.web.cern.ch/public>, had a better idea (Berners-Lee, 2003). In the early 1980s he had written a program for storing information, but it was for his private use. He was familiar with *hypertext*, which means that within text certain words are identified as links that can be clicked to jump to other text in the same document or in a different one. In 1989 he proposed a global hypertext system that would allow individuals to link their documents together into a web of documents. Berners-Lee's *WorldWideWeb* software became available within CERN in late 1990 and on the Internet in 1991, giving us a descriptive name for the system. By 1993 the concepts of web servers and browsers, URLs, the http communication protocol, and the language used to prepare web documents were all in place.

The Web was clearly useful from its beginning, but it was not destined to have broad impact until an undergraduate student programmer at the National Center for Supercomputing Applications at the University of Illinois, Marc Andreesen, recognized the vast public potential of the Web, provided it could be made easy enough to use and the content expanded beyond text to include multimedia, creating *hypermedia*. The result of Andreesen's vision was the first graphical web browser, NCSA *Mosaic* (Jones, 2003), which he developed with his fellow student Eric Bina. Andreesen went on to co-found Netscape Communications, and the Internet was changed forever from a tool for the few to a tool for all.

Web Terminology

It is important to understand the terminology that you encounter routinely, so let's quickly look at web terms. The Internet is a global network comprised of millions of servers. Technically, the World Wide Web itself is that subset of Internet servers that support documents formatted to web specifications (Webopedia, 2003). However, most users understand the Web as the resources—the documents, graphics, audio and video files—that are found on those servers. Web *pages* are documents formatted using HyperText Markup Language (HTML), the web programming language. You'll learn about HTML in a later section of this chapter. *Websites* are collections of web pages. *Home page* refers to the first page of a website (which could also be the only page). A home page is intended to serve as the starting point for access to the site, something like a menu or table of contents.

The address of any page on the Web is called a uniform resource locator, or URL. To access web pages, you must use a *browser*, which is a program that can locate web pages on the Internet by their URL and then display them based on their formatting information. *Internet Explorer* and *Netscape* dominate the browser market, although *Mozilla* has achieved some popularity. Unfortunately, browsers do not interpret the formatting information identically. Consequently, they may not display pages identically; in fact, the differences can be astounding. Some web pages indicate that they are best viewed with a particular browser, which often means they look somewhat different with any other one.

Navigating Effectively

Using HTML, web page developers create *hyperlinks*, clickable items on a page, which can be words or objects such as buttons. Clicking on a hyperlink takes the user to the page or file specified by the link. The destination could be another web page, or it could be a specific image, a video file, or any accessible resource.

Text hyperlinks normally appear as blue underlined words, which turn purple when they have been activated. This helps remind you of which links you have followed and which you have not. Other link types can be nearly anything on a page and usually don't indicate when they have been followed. Back and Forward buttons enable you to retrace your steps in either direction, should you need to do so.

You also can retrace your steps or review sites you have previously visited using the *history* feature of your browser (Figure 4.1). In *Internet Explorer*, click the History but-

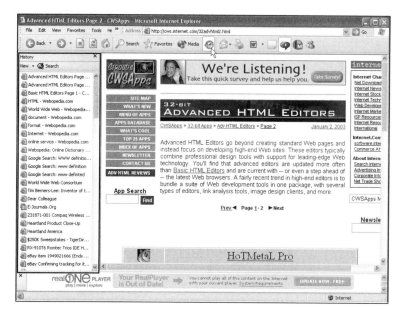

Figure 4.1
Retrace your steps with
your browser's history list.

ton on the toolbar as shown in the figure. The history list (column on the left) will open, showing your navigation "history." In *Netscape*, the history list is found in the Communicator menu under Tools, and in *Mozilla*, it's in the Go menu. Each browser allows you to set the number of days over which the history is maintained and also to clear current entries in the history at any time.

When you find a page that you anticipate wanting to visit again in the future, your browser will keep a record of it for you. *Netscape* and *Mozilla* call these records *bookmarks; Internet Explorer* calls them *favorites*. To add a bookmark in *Mozilla*, click the Bookmark menu and then choose from the options in the menu that appears (Figure 4.2). Your list of useful websites will grow and become increasingly valuable to you over time. Be sure to think about the organization of your list so that you can find sites of interest easily at a future time.

Records of useful sites are wonderful, but what if you aren't working on your own computer, perhaps in a computer lab or at a friend's home? Probably the easiest way to save URLs as you find them and then take them to a different computer is to copy and paste them into a simple text document. Use your word processor or *SimpleText* on a Macintosh or *Notepad* in any version of Windows. If you click on the URL in the address window of your browser, it should turn to light text against dark, which means it has been selected. Click Edit in the menu bar and then select copy (or use keyboard shortcuts Control-C in Windows, Command-C on a Mac). Switch to your document file, position the cursor on a new line, and select paste from the Edit menu (or keys Control/Command-V). Depending on the software you are using, the URL may even appear as a functional link, (i.e., blue and underlined and clickable to activate) as if it were on a web page (Figure 4.3).

Figure 4.2
Keep track of useful websites by bookmarking them.

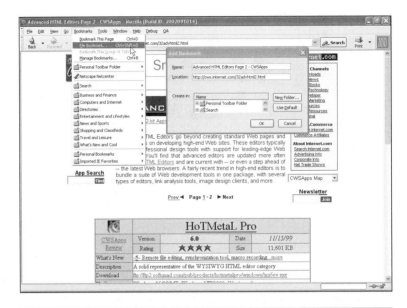

Figure 4.3
SAVING URLS IN A WORD PROCESSOR TO MOVE TO ANOTHER COMPUTER

.

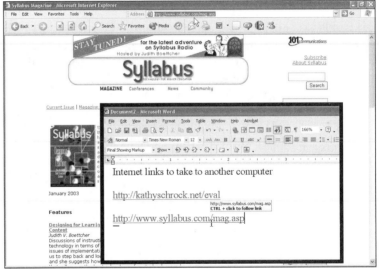

Finding and Evaluating Web Resources

NETS
NOTES

NETS **S** 1
NETS **S** 5
NETS **S** 6

So far, we have concentrated on conceptual and technical aspects of the Internet and the Web. In the preceding chapters you read that the question is not what you can do with the Internet, but what you can't do. You also learned that organization is not the Internet's strongest point. So just how do you find things out there? This is vitally important because of the extremely rapid rate of change on the Web. Vast new resources will exist by the time you read this, and specific things we mention may no longer exist,

NETS
NOTES

or the URLs may have changed. You need tools to find resources over time, which is our theme in this section.

Basic Sources

The professional literature relevant to your teaching interests is sure to have articles or notices concerning the Internet that are closely related to your needs. Among general publications, there are countless pointers to resources in *Learning and Leading with Technology* (<www.iste.org>, click on L&L) and *Technology & Learning* (<www.techlearning.com>, click on Resources). See Figure 4.4. Look also for the most recent edition of

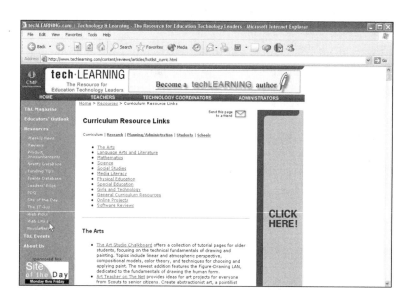

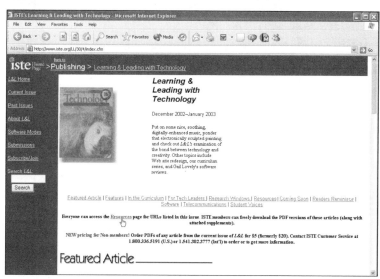

Figure 4.4
KEY MAGAZINES FOR WEB RESOURCES

Sharp, Levine, and Sharp (2002), which is updated regularly. We also recommend regular monitoring of the Classroom Connect website <www.classroom.net>, an invaluable resource (see Figure 4.5). Give strong consideration to subscribing to the *Classroom Connect Newsletter* <www.classroom.net/store/storehome.jhtml>. You'll find a wealth of how-to guidance, immediately useful URLs, lesson plans that integrate the Internet into learning activities, announcements and guidance on grants and other funding opportunities, and more.

Of course, you can always use the Internet itself to help you find what you need. Let's look at some of the most popular indexes and search tools for the World Wide Web, as well as specific resources to help you locate existing lesson plans and discussion groups.

Indexes, Directories, and Portals

Some websites are themselves indexes to other websites. Their indexes resemble menus, in that they offer categories of potential links that may have many levels before you reach actual sites to which you can connect. Some include descriptions of the sites to help you decide whether they really are what you want before you follow a link. Once you find a promising site, a click on its entry makes the connection.

Indexes are useful because they may quickly guide you to the material you need. If they are well organized and reasonably comprehensive, indexes can be invaluable. On the other hand, an index includes only those things its creators knew about and then chose to list. Just because you do not find what you want using an index does not mean it does not exist. You may have looked in a category other than where the information was placed in the index, or the index may not contain a link to something that does exist. One potential solution is to check more than one index before giving up a search. They do not all contain the same things because each was created manually by different individuals.

Figure 4.5

CLASSROOM CONNECT— A WEALTH OF TEACHING RESOURCES

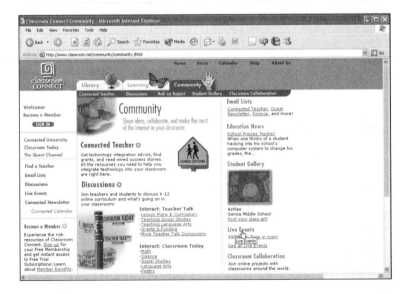

Among the indexes, we suggest two general sites to get you started. Yahoo! started out as a directory but has changed much in recent years. You can still access the index view directly at <dir.yahoo.com>. Look Smart <www.looksmart.com> identifies sites within its categorical listings that have been reviewed by its editors.

Less well known but very useful are the Librarians' Index to the Internet <http://lii.org>, a project of the Library of California, and the Galaxy directory <www.galaxy.com>, which claims to be the first searchable directory on the Internet. Finally, unlike the previous commercial tools, the Virtual Library <http://vlib.org> is maintained by volunteers. The Virtual Library was started by Tim Berners-Lee, the creator of the Web <http://vlib.org/AboutVL.html>.

Many Internet users turn to *portals* as their starting point for locating information. Portals are websites that offer far more than just listings of links to other locations, including much actual content (e.g., news, online stores, and even services like chat and email accounts). In fact, they are generally customizable sites that are intended to be your first point of entry to the Internet, regardless of your task. Portal operators hope you will set your browser to open their site whenever you start it, that is, to make it your home page. Advertising from sponsors, however, annoys many users.

Yahoo! was started by two Stanford University students and quickly became a commercial site and then a portal <www.yahoo.com>. You can customize Yahoo! to speed access to areas of personal interest by clicking on My Yahoo!. Take another look at Yahoo! and compare it to the Virtual Library. You'll immediately recognize the difference. AOL began primarily as a way to gain dialup access to the Internet, but its wealth of services and links qualifies it as a portal as well. Netscape.com has evolved into a portal, as has the home page of Comcast High Speed Internet <www.comcast.net>.

Web Search Tools

Web search tools build automated indexes of websites by periodically scanning the contents of web pages worldwide using "crawler" or "spider" software. You enter keywords of interest, and the search engine looks for your words in its index. They could be from any context, so there are likely to be many misses along with some hits any time you search. Still, the potential is even greater than with prepared indexes, because theoretically more of the Web is regularly checked. Nonetheless, experience shows that different search engines produce different results.

Looking for information on the Web can become a bottomless pit into which your time pours as you *surf* aimlessly around. Don't surf when you can *search*. Successful searches begin with the right tool and an understanding of search methods. The Florida Instructional Technology Resource Center, in conjunction with the Southeast and Islands Regional Technology in Education Consortium (SEIR*TEC), compiled experiences with a wide range of search tools onto a small quick reference card, which you can obtain from <www.itrc.ucf.edu/iqr>. We highly recommend that you download and print this resource for your own use.

You can access various search tools using the Search box on many websites, especially portals such as netscape.com and Internet Sleuth <www.isleuth.com>, which offer a choice of search engines (see Figure 4.6). *Meta search engines,* such as Ixquick <www.

Figure 4.6
SEARCH ENGINE CHOICES
FROM A PORTAL

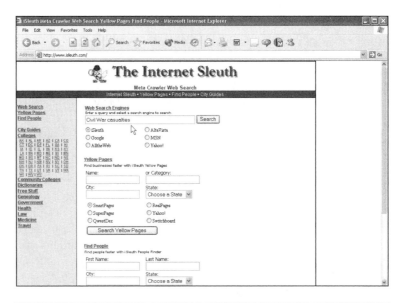

ixquick.com>, Metacrawler <www.metacrawler.com>, or Vivísimo <http://vivisimo.com/form?form=Advanced>, simultaneously search a set of other search engines, which may yield more information but also tends to take longer to complete. For a list of meta search tools, including reviews of their strengths and weaknesses, see <www.searchenginewatch.com/links/metacrawlers.html>.

The search engine Google <www.google.com> offers tabs to focus a search on multimedia elements (images, audio, video) as well as the typical topic or word searches. Other favorites include All The Web <www.alltheweb.com>, which claimed to index over 2 billion web documents as of December 2002, and Teoma <www.teoma.com>. Useful search tools, especially for students, include Kids Search Tools <www.rcls.org/ksearch.htm>, which links to such popular individual sites as Ask Jeeves <www.ask.com>, its special version for younger users called Ask Jeeves for Kids <www.ajkids.com>, Ask An Expert <www.askanexpert.com> (or access multiple expert resources from <http://njnie.dl.stevens-tech.edu/askanexpert.html>), and Yahooligans <www.yahooligans.com>, "the web guide for kids" from Yahoo!. See Figure 4.7. Another great site for kids that is the work of librarians is <http://sunsite.berkeley.edu/KidsClick!>. For a listing of websites and search tools that are filtered or otherwise made "kid safe," see <http://searchenginewatch.com/links/kids.html>. Safety on the Web is a topic we treat separately later in this chapter.

For a quick comparison of major search engines, see <www.infopeople.org/search/guide.html>. If you are interested in how web searching has reached its current state, you can read about the history of search engines at <www.galaxy.com/info/history2.html>.

Effective Web Searching

Newcomers to web searching tend to make very simple requests of a search engine and, in turn, the engine produces hundreds or thousands of "hits," most of which are not what you wanted. According to Killmer and Koppel (2002), developing an effective search strategy requires understanding the search logic of the engine you are using and also Boolean logic. When you enter, say, three words into a search box, the underlying engine has its own logic for handling those words. It may be to look for and return to you all indexed sites with any one of the words, sites with all three regardless of where or how they occur, or only sites containing the words together as a phrase. The results

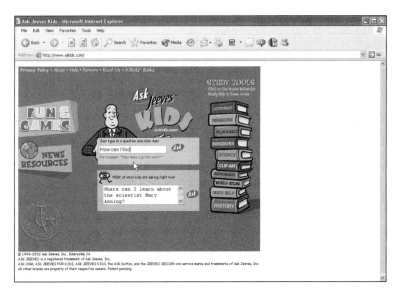

Figure 4.7 ASK JEEVES FOR KIDS—A RESEARCH TOOL FOR YOUNGER USERS

from these approaches will obviously differ greatly, so it helps to know how your chosen tool works.

Most search tools allow you to be more explicit in your search request by using *Boolean logic operators*, which should return a higher percentage of useful hits. For instance, to be certain that your search terms are treated as a phrase and not as individual words, most engines allow you to connect multiple terms with a plus sign or the word AND (or you can usually put the phrase in quotation marks). This is also typically the default for search engines. To specify equivalent terms, try using OR (e.g., computer OR microcomputer) and to eliminate sites with specific words use NOT (e.g., automobile NOT Yugo). Some sites make this quite easy in their "advanced search" interface, for instance, <www.allthe web.com/advanced>. Always look on the basic page of any search tool for an "advanced" option and check out what it offers to enhance the results of your search. For a tutorial on search logic, see <www.netstrider.com/tutorials/Boolean>. Detailed web searching tips and guidance are provided at <http://searchenginewatch.com/facts>.

Another factor in effective searching is presentation of results. Some search tools simply provide a listing of everything they found. Others rank the results by estimated relevance to your request and may offer links to similar or related sites, which can be very useful. Some engines clearly indicate that certain site owners have paid to be included in search outcomes, but many don't differentiate. How might these differences among search tools affect your view of their value or even their validity?

If you expect students to do any significant amount of searching, especially middle school and older students, take the time to teach them about engine logic and Boolean logic. Then guide them to explore a range of search tools before they begin their actual projects (Killmer & Koppel, 2002). Provide links to a select set of search tools and a specific goal, say, to find speeches of former President Clinton on the topic of education. Have students record minimally the exact search term(s) they used and, separately for each engine or index used, the number of results they found, their judgment of the relevance of the results, differences in results based on search logic, and their observations about the presentation of results. Have them try different search strategies as well as different engines. The investment in time will pay off in better searches as students experience for themselves the differences among a variety of tools.

Tutorials on many aspects of Internet use, including searching, are available at <http://library.albany.edu/internet> and at <www.virtualsalt.com>, among others.

Evaluating Websites

Before you go too far in exploring the Web, it is critical to recognize that there are no controls on who can post web pages. Students have typically had little concern for the validity of the resources that they use in school, because teachers have preselected those resources for acceptability, accuracy, and value. No such criteria apply universally to materials on the Web. In fact, many websites contain content that is dubious at best, and completely unacceptable in schools at worst. Unfortunately, some of the latter (e.g., sites denying the Holocaust, white supremacy sites, etc.) may present their message in ways that carefully conceal their intent or provide a cover of legitimacy. Students (and teachers!) must learn critical evaluation skills to cope with the materials they are likely to encounter.

See, for example, a true account of a student misled by Internet information on the holocaust <www.anovember.com/articles/zack.html>.

Education World suggests the COCOA P principle for website evaluation:

- Coverage (Is coverage appropriate to the topic?)
- Objectivity (Avoid bias, prejudice, inappropriate language.)
- Currency (Check the "last updated" information at the bottom of the page but realize that recent changes could be trivial, not substantive.)
- Origin [author] (Is the author an authority or a respected organization?)
- Accuracy (Grammar and spelling errors may indicate deeper problems.)
- Purpose (Does the site aim to inform, persuade, or entertain?)

Details on using this approach are at <www.educationworld.com/a_tech/techtorial/tech torial002.shtml>.

Schrock (2002) offers even more suggestions, 26 in all, in her "ABCs of Web Site Evaluation." We can only highlight a few of the 26 criteria listed.

- Who is the *author* of the material and what is that person's *authority*? Is the author well known and well regarded? Is there a biography of the author? Did a trusted site provide the link that you followed to find the site you are evaluating?
- Can you identify *bias* in the site? Is it trying to inform you or persuade you of a point of view? What organization sponsors the page, or can't you tell? Is that organization an appropriate source of this information?
- Are there full *citations* to support the information present and to allow cross-checking?
- Credible sites include the *date* of creation and last update, which may help to establish whether the information is current.
- What other sites *link* to this site? You can find out by using AltaVista. In the search box, enter *link:URL*—for example, link:www.creator.org (try that one for a lesson on hate groups).

Read her entire article at <http://school.discovery.com/schrockguide/pdf/weval_02.pdf>. Schrock also provides links to specific sites illustrating various evaluation points at <http://kathyschrock.net/abceval>.

Website evaluation is time-consuming, but it is essential to appropriate use of web resources. The following websites provide much greater detail on site evaluation:

- Evaluating Internet-Based Information: A Goals-Based Approach <www2.ncsu.edu/ unity/lockers/project/meridian/jun98/feat2-6/feat2-6.html>
- WWW Cyberguides <www.cyberbee.com/guides.html>
- Evaluation Criteria (New Mexico State University) <http://lib.nmsu.edu/instruction/ evalcrit.html>
- Evaluating Internet Research Sources <www.virtualsalt.com/evalu8it.htm>
- Critical Evaluation Information <http://school.discovery.com/schrockguide/eval.html>

To help students learn to be critical consumers of web information, consider using some of the pages at <http://zapatopi.net>, home of the "save the northwest tree octopus" movement among other farces, or the site of the Dihydrogen Monoxide Research Division <www.dhmo.org>. A wide range of sites selected for various specific evaluation lessons is posted at <www2.widener.edu/Wolfgram-Memorial-Library/webevaluation/examples.htm>. Kathy Schrock's detailed lesson plan with many resources for teaching critical evaluation of websites is available at <http://kathyschrock.net/eval>.

Lesson Plans

Education is a process of sharing, not only between teacher and students, but also among teachers. When good ideas are shared, everyone benefits by not reinventing the wheel. Most teachers regularly wonder how others have organized a particular lesson, what creative approaches have worked well, and so on. Traditionally, we have relied on our colleagues in the building or district, occasional professional conferences, and publications in the field as sources of sharing. The Internet today offers many such opportunities that may be more extensive, varied, and up-to-date.

One popular online source of lesson plans is the ERIC system. You probably know it already, because most education students quickly become dependent on ERIC to locate information for research reports. You can access the entire ERIC database on the Internet at <http://ericir.syr.edu>. Once you connect to that website, you can search the ERIC database for articles and resources, just as in the past. You can also check out the lesson plan repository at <http://ericir.syr.edu/Virtual/Lessons/> (Figure 4.8).

Scholastic maintains a collection of lesson plans at <http://teacher.scholastic.com/resources> and also provides links to many other lesson plan sites at <http://teacher.scholastic.com/products/instructor/lesson_plans.htm>. Check out resources collected

Figure 4.8

LESSON PLANS AT THE
ASK ERIC SITE

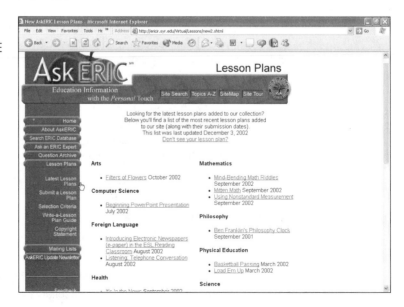

for educators in North Carolina at Learn NC, the North Carolina Teachers' Network <www.learnnc.org/learnnc/lessonp.nsf>. Another useful site is The Lesson Plans Page <www.lessonplanspage.com>. A web search will produce countless other lesson plan sites. Just use good search techniques to get results most focused on your areas of interest.

Finding Other Schools

Schools around the world are putting their own home pages on the Web. You can use a website index or directory to find links to many of them. Typically, you start at the main page of the index site, then look under Education, and then K12. Using Yahoo!, the direct link is <http://dir.yahoo.com/Education/K_12/Schools>, which had entries for nearly 10,000 elementary schools, about 5,000 middle schools, and over 12,000 high schools around the world on our last visit there. Another resource is the Web66 International School Web Site Registry <http://web66.coled.umn.edu/schools.html>. Figure 4.9 is an example.

Finding Free Teaching Materials

To assist in the endless quest for educational materials, we suggest some excellent resources. FREE (Federal Resources for Educational Excellence) is a compilation of online teaching and learning resources from 40 different federal agencies <www.ed.gov/free>. As a teacher you can simplify your own search for educational materials by visiting the Gateway to Educational Materials <www.geminfo.org>, a one-stop searchable clearinghouse that provides content summaries and links to the referenced sites. Sites for Teachers <www.sitesforteachers.com> claims to be the best resource for teachers on the Web. Its links are arranged by popularity, meaning the number of visitors they

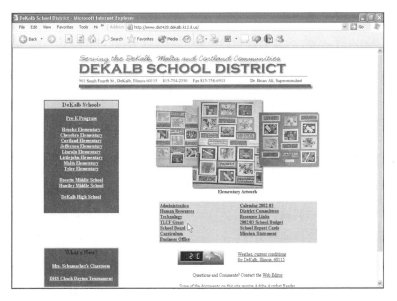

Figure 4.9

HOME PAGE OF DEKALB, ILLINOIS, SCHOOLS

receive, which is updated hourly and reset to start over weekly. For a rather different range of free materials, check out Free Stuff for Canadian Teachers at <www.thecanadian teacher.com/links>.

Internet and Web Curriculum Applications

NETS
NOTES

NETS **T** II-A
NETS **T** II-C
NETS **T** III-A
NETS **T** III-D
NETS **T** V-B

Before there was a Web, Maddux, Johnson, and Willis (1992) suggested that computer communications applications in education have unique potential to go beyond Type I activities (i.e., doing differently something we already do) to the more innovative, more powerful, more desirable Type II activities that create learning experiences that would be otherwise impossible.

As an illustration, they projected a futuristic scenario (p. 122) of sixth-grade students working on an acid rain research project with peers throughout the United States and around the world. Students gather reference material worldwide. Locally they gather pertinent data, which they compare with that of other participants via the electronic network. A joint report is prepared using group writing techniques on the network. The final version reaches all students electronically, and each location downloads it and submits it to local newspapers for publication. This type of activity was merely hypothetical in 1992, but it is now happening in many schools, thanks to Internet access and the Web.

The scope of potential curriculum applications is far too great for comprehensive treatment. Let's briefly explore primary source materials, email, and collaborative projects.

Primary Sources

Until recently, students rarely had the opportunity to study original source materials before college and then perhaps only in graduate school. Now anyone can access primary sources via the Web. Social studies classes at any level can come alive as students learn to conduct research as historians do, delving into original materials and drawing their own conclusions. The opportunities to develop critical thinking skills have never been greater. The textbook need no longer determine the scope of any class!

The federal government maintains many extensive sites. The Library of Congress <http://lcweb.loc.gov> is the national depository for countless materials. An excellent starting point in this vast collection is the American Treasures exhibit. The exhibit uses the categories by which Thomas Jefferson organized his own library into sections, namely Memory (history), Reason (philosophy), and Imagination (fine arts). The American Memory collections include presidential papers, products of the Federal Writers Project and the Federal Theater Project, early movies and audio recordings, maps, photographs, and much more. The potential for curriculum support is enormous. For help in using this site, check out the resources, including lesson plans prepared by other teachers, at <http://memory.loc.gov/ammem/ndlpedu>. Other outstanding collections are available from the National Archives <www.nara.gov>; click on Digital Classroom for lesson plans and other curriculum aids.

Did you ever wonder what the CIA and FBI actually do? Their websites offer access to their documents that have been requested most frequently under the Freedom of Information Act. Visit them at <www.foia.ucia.gov> and <www.fbi.gov>. The World Factbook, also from the CIA, is a treasure store of geopolitical data located at <www.odci.gov/cia/publications/factbook>. The Factbook can be downloaded at no cost, in its entirety or in parts, which include many files of high-quality maps of the world by region.

Many universities have rich collections of primary documents that you may access freely. Here are several examples.

- The Abraham Lincoln Historical Digitization Project <http://lincoln.lib.niu.edu> covers Lincoln's years in Illinois, 1831–1860, and includes lesson plans for using these materials.

- The Writings of Henry D. Thoreau <www.niulib.niu.edu/thoreau> is an ongoing project to preserve nearly half of Thoreau's writing that might otherwise never appear in print. The site has received several awards as a valuable Internet resource.

- The Douglass Archives of American Public Address <http://douglassarchives.org> support the study of American rhetorical history through speeches and related documents. It is named after Frederick Douglass, the former slave who became one of America's greatest orators.

- The University of Virginia maintains an electronic text collection <http://etext.lib.virginia.edu> that includes the writings of George Washington and Thomas Jefferson as well as materials on countless topics such as African American and Native American history and the Civil War. In addition to English, original resources in 14 other languages are available, including Apache and Icelandic.

- The Avalon Project <www.yale.edu/lawweb/avalon/avalon.htm> contains historical documents from around the world, organized by century. Of particular note are collections concerning the Nuremberg War Crimes Trials after World War II and Native American Treaties.

- Carrie electronic library at <www.ku.edu/carrie>, a full text electronic library, features a collection of constitutions from around the world, translated into English, as well as UN and other international documents in its Document Room.

Teaching using primary resources may involve materials that can be highly controversial; think of such topics as slavery or race relations. As a teacher, you must prepare students for the possibility of offensive materials. Also remember that contemporary English differs from the language of earlier centuries, which may cause problems. Interest in teaching with Internet primary sources has led to many books on the topic, among them Shiveley and VanFossen (2001), Glazer (2001), Shiroma (2000), and Kobrin (1996).

Electronic Mail

At the most obvious, routine communication may be facilitated via email. For example, parents often want more contact with school, but work schedules interfere. Teachers across the country use email to increase their accessibility to their students, to parents, and to colleagues. School websites often include teacher and/or administrator email addresses, or teachers provide them directly to families of their students.

A fun student use of email is today's version of penpals. Because email uses a keyboard, not a pen, the activity is called *keypals*. Students enjoy corresponding with others of similar age and comparing notes on school, family, pets, hobbies, and so forth. This can be especially beneficial when the keypal lives in a different part of the country or world, as it can foster understanding through experience. Keypals can be a highly effective element of multicultural education.

How do you set up keypals? Obviously, students first must have email access. Then you can obtain help in locating keypals from Intercultural Email Classroom Connections or the KeyPals Club, both accessible at <www.teaching.com> or through ePALS, a multilingual website at <www.epals.com>. The latter has particular potential for students learning other languages.

Electronic Journals, Magazines, and News

So powerful is the potential and so appealing the immediacy of electronic communication that there are now many electronic journals—journals that exist only on the Internet. When authors complete an article, they submit it to the journal electronically. The editor shares it by email with reviewers, who critique it electronically. If it is accepted, it becomes part of an issue of the journal, which is sent electronically to the subscriber list or posted on the journal's website. Some *e-journals* publish articles individually when they are ready rather than waiting to compile an issue. The whole process from time of submission may take only a few weeks, compared with the many months often required to get an article in print in a paper journal. For individuals in fast-changing fields, the appeal is enormous. In fact, the meaning of the term *journal* is changing in academia.

To identify scholarly publications, visit E-Journals <www.e-journal.org>, a part of the WWW Virtual Library, the Internet Public Library <www.ipl.org>, or New Jour <http://gort.ucsd.edu/newjour>, which listed and described over 12,000 publications in December 2002 with corresponding URLs. A well-maintained list of online publications in educational technology and culture is available at <http://carbon.cudenver.edu/~mryder/itc_data/ejournals.html>. Most academic libraries now offer their patrons access to electronic journals, so be sure to check your local resources. The University of Waterloo (Canada), among others, offers unrestricted access to some of its collection as well <http://webdev.uwaterloo.ca/ejournals>.

Newslink <http://newslink.org/mag.html> reported in late 2002 that 23 of the 50 top circulation U.S. magazines and 7 of the top 25 Canadian publications were online and provided links to each of them, along with a wide range of other publications, including newspapers internationally. You can search for specific online magazines at <www.searchmagazines.com> or newspapers around the world at <www.newspapers.com>. For links to the multiple units of Time, Inc., visit <www.pathfinder.com>. Among the best sources for news are the many television news organizations, to which Newslink provides links as well.

What could you do in current events with easy access to both current and historical events of the day? The History Channel <www.historychannel.com/thisday> offers extensive resources and Yahoo! <http://dir.yahoo.com/arts/humanities/history/this_day_

in_history> lists many other sites with similar information, including ones with a specific focus such as Asian or black history. Daily items are compiled by the folks at *Classroom Connect* into the Connected Calendar at <www.classroom.com/community/connection/ calendar.jhtml>, a still easier to use resource. Each day has a question about the subject and has a link to relevant information. There are also links to the History Channel and Yahoo! sites mentioned previously.

Collaborative Projects

One of the greatest benefits of the Internet is the ability to collaborate with others at a distance. We can only highlight a few exemplary collaborative projects, which should stimulate your thinking about the potential. The Annenberg/CPB Journey North Project <www.learner.org/jnorth> enables global collaboration in the study of wildlife migration (Figure 4.10). Nearly 400,000 students from over 8,000 schools participated in the spring 2002 session, producing the latest available data. The Annenberg Foundation supports Journey North as a model for reform in math and science education.

The Global Schoolhouse <www.globalschoolhouse.org> is a project of the Global SchoolNet Foundation. Over 700 collaborative projects around the world are cataloged at this site, which can be searched by curriculum area, grade level, and even technologies used in the project. It also offers links to online expeditions and videoconferencing opportunities among schools. Other excellent resources for interschool collaboration can be found at iEARN <www.iearn.org>, whose projects seek to "enhance learning and make a difference in the world."

Among the most popular international collaborative projects are the various "quests" that create virtual adventures around the globe. Well-known early adventures included

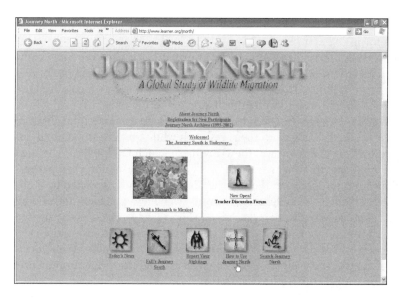

Figure 4.10

JOURNEY NORTH, A COLLABORATIVE WEB ACTIVITY

MayaQuest and AfricaQuest. Two different quests now take place each year, operating within the Classroom Connect family of learning projects as the Quest Channel <http://quest.classroom.com>. All quest activities are keyed to both state and national standards. The Quest Channel is a subscription service, but a free trial is available.

Specific Curriculum Area Resources

Each year the online resources support for all content areas grows by leaps and bounds. Although it is tempting to try to list examples here, as did previous editions, they change frequently, so a more useful resource is the companion website for this book. At that site is listed a wide range of resources by area, including the fine arts, interdisciplinary units, language arts, math, science, and social studies. Please visit the site for the most current links, including resources specifically for special needs learners.

WebQuests

Of the countless applications that teachers are making of the Web and its resources, one stands out as such a phenomenon that we highlight it as a major topic, namely, WebQuests.

NETS
NOTES

NETS **S** 5
NETS **T** II-A
NETS **T** II-D
NETS **T** II-E
NETS **T** III-A
NETS **T** III-B
NETS **T** III-C

What Is a WebQuest?

As previously mentioned, many web users delight in "surfing," which tends to mean somewhat aimless or poorly focused wandering about on the Web. Such activity can be fun, of course, but the school curriculum has precious little room for such time-consuming activity, especially when no particular outcome can be assured. At its worst, surfers may become lost and disoriented, unable to get back where they came from (since many don't know how to use the browser history, unlike you) and perhaps uncertain of what it was they were looking for in the first place.

Anyone who has spent much time looking for information on the Web must know firsthand how easy it is to lose focus, only to discover that significant time has passed without the desired result. Bernie Dodge of San Diego State University recognized the negative impact that this approach to web information gathering could have on school acceptance of a valuable resource (the Web itself) and set out to do something about it. Starting in 1995 he worked on a way to focus research while guiding students to appropriate, useful resources. The result was the WebQuest, which Dodge (1995) defined as "an inquiry-oriented activity in which some or all of the information that learners interact with comes from resources on the Internet." Major resources related to WebQuests can be found at Dodge's WebQuest Page <http://webquest.sdsu.edu> and at Tom March's Australian site <www.ozline.com/learning> (Figure 4.11). (Don't be surprised if many links at both sites no longer work. Even individuals devoted to using the Web find it difficult to keep every link listed up-to-date.) From that beginning, WebQuests have become one of the true hot topics in educational technology, featuring prominently in national and international conferences each year.

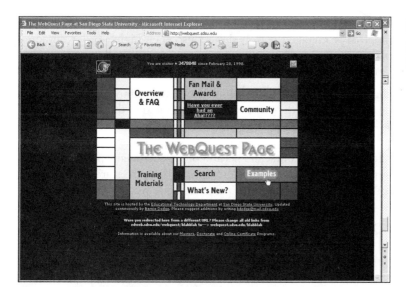

Figure 4.11
MAJOR RESOURCE SITES
RELATED TO WEBQUESTS

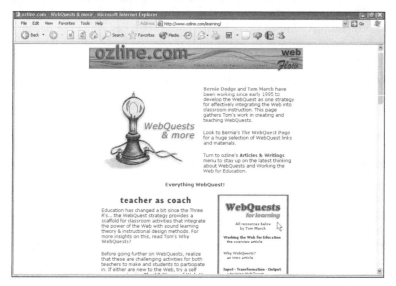

Structure of a WebQuest

Although there can be no hard-and-fast rules about the form of a WebQuest, Dodge recommended a basic structure that indeed has been followed by many of the multitude of teacher-developers of WebQuests. The six-element model is:

- An *introduction* to set the stage and provide background information on the task. The introduction serves to motivate the learner by showing the benefit to be gained from the effort.

- A **task** that is doable and interesting, which should motivate learners and draw them into the activity, that is, engage them. It should also elicit higher-order thinking, not just simple question answering (from an interview with Bernie Dodge at <www.education-world.com/a_tech/tech020.shtml>).

- A set of carefully selected **resources** (information sources) to complete the task. Many (though not necessarily all) of the resources are embedded in the WebQuest document itself as links to information on websites. Information sources may include web documents, experts available via email or real-time conferencing, searchable databases on the Net, and, of course, books and other documents physically available in the learner's setting. Because links to specific resources are provided, the learner's time is not spent searching or, worse, surfing to find information.

- A description of the **process** the learners should go through to complete the task. A typical WebQuest process consists of three activities, but the content of the lesson determines how many are appropriate, more or fewer. Each activity is broken out into clearly described steps with links to resources repeated within the relevant part of the process.

- An **evaluation** section that explains or summarizes the assignments that the learners are required to complete in the WebQuest. These activities guide the organization and presentation of the learning and provide the means by which the learners' work will be evaluated, including self-evaluation along the way.

- A **conclusion** that brings closure to the WebQuest, reminds the learners of what they've achieved, and encourages them to extend the experience into other domains.

Example WebQuests

A search for the term *WebQuest* on the Web produced nearly 113,000 results using Teoma, nearly 300,000 with Google, and over 360,000 from All The Web. These results suggest the scope and impact of the WebQuest concept. (Dodge's own page came up as the first entry in all three!) We encourage you to seek out existing WebQuests that you can use with little or no modification before deciding to create your own. This is a great way to try this web application without a major time investment. In the spirit of a WebQuest, here are some key resources that should lead you to useful examples.

- The WebQuest Page <http://webquest.sdsu.edu/matrix.html>
- San Diego Schools <http://projects.edtech.sandi.net/projects/index.html>
- A WebQuest to Learn About WebQuests <www.cedu.niu.edu/~lockard/wq>
- Kathy Schrock's Guide to WebQuests <http://school.discovery.com/schrockguide/webquest/webquest.html>
- Hewitt's Index of Best WebQuests and Resources <www.davison.k12.mi.us/academic/hewitt14.htm>
- WebQuests (an interesting Canadian site) <http://sesd.sk.ca/teacherresource/webquest/webquest.htm>

Creating a WebQuest

Creating a WebQuest is like preparation of any other sound teaching materials for the classroom—a lot of work that pays off when students achieve their learning goal well and enjoyably. Although the range of WebQuests available on the Web is great, creating new ones may make sense for two primary reasons.

First, there may well not be one that meets your needs as a teacher. Every curriculum has its nuances; every teacher has a personal style. These are among the reasons for the existing range of WebQuests.

Second, don't think you have to do this yourself! Creating a WebQuest can be an excellent student project, a way for your students to demonstrate mastery of a content area while also using their technology skills. Granted, students should have considerable experience using WebQuests before undertaking such a task. You may still need to provide resource links to avoid having students do painstaking searches, which is precisely the reason for WebQuests in the first place.

Assuming the decision is to create a WebQuest, start by clearly understanding that it is just a web page structured in a particular way. As such, it is an application of the next section, which explains basic web page creation. There are many templates that provide the shell of a WebQuest and, thus, speed the development process. The "original" template source is, of course, the Dodge WebQuest Page <http://webquest.sdsu.edu>.

Filamentality <www.filamentality.com/wired/fil/index.html> offers a much different, fill-in-the-blank approach that is very easy to use and that does not require any knowledge of HTML or servers. Everything is done on the website. Filamentality combines the "filaments of the Web" with the "mentality of the learner." It is a free service of SBC, the communications giant, and even provides the server space that makes your activity available on the Web, which is another issue when you create your own. However, there are two key limits. First, storage is only for one year, after which your work goes away or you must move it to a different server. Second, no graphics are allowed on the pages, which need have little impact on their educational value but certainly may affect their appeal. Still, it's a great way to begin with the least knowledge required and lots of guidance along the way. Filamentality projects are not inherently WebQuests, but they can be structured as such.

The creators of Filamentality recognize its limits and offer a more powerful alternative at modest cost ($25 per year at time of writing). It's called Web and Flow, and you can check it out at <www.web-and-flow.com>. A free 30-day trial is available. You could also adapt TrackStar's "track" approach to the WebQuest format <http://trackstar.hprtec.org>.

Creating Web Pages

The release of the original World Wide Web browser *Mosaic* in 1993 unleashed a torrent of Internet interest and activity. As schools plunge into Internet use, it's appropriate to learn how web pages actually are created. At its simplest, this is a three-part task: planning/design, creating/development, and publishing.

Planning a Website

The final quality of any website is proportional to the care that went into planning or designing it. This is not only the logical first step but also one that is not directly linked to the actual means of creating the pages that make up the site, so you can start the process without knowing how to implement the plan. More time spent on this step will result in considerable time saved in development. Beginners often rush to development on the computer too soon!

Planning a website is much like any other project. Start with an idea, a concept, and then flesh out the details. It could be much like the process of planning a research paper. First, create an outline at just the top level, the most fundamental elements of the page. Refine that outline with subpoints at the next level. Then add one or more additional levels until you have a good picture of the content and its relative structure. You'll probably want to use your word processor for this. (If you don't know how to use it to work with outlines, the next chapter will help.)

Once the outline appears to be complete, turn it into *storyboards*, sketches of individual screens. Don't worry about artistic ability. What matters is the idea and the relative positioning of elements on the screen, including consistent placement of things that appear on each screen. What should appear on each screen or page? How will the user move about; that is, what will the navigation structure be? Among the popular and successful storyboarding methods we have used are individual sheets of paper, large index cards (easy to handle and rearrange), sticky notes (work well on a large sheet of butcher paper or an empty wall), and graphics software such as *PowerPoint* or *Inspiration* (see Chapter 8). Make appropriate notations about links among the screen plans. Storyboarding itself is vital; which method is a matter of choice.

A storyboard will help you plan the "look and feel" of your site, but it still lacks the full content. When you are satisfied with your storyboard (or even concurrently with its refinement), gather together the full content, including text, any links on the page, and any multimedia elements desired, from simple lines to animated images to audio and video. If any of the resources are not already in electronic form, they must be converted, for which the next several chapters provide general guidance. Collect all of your digital resources in a project folder on your computer.

Developing the Website

To turn your plan and resources into a website, you must somehow create a plain *ASCII* text file for each page. Such a file is called a web document or source file. A web browser then reads the file and displays the content as directed. Web pages work on all computer types because plain text files are universal. (Many web servers are actually UNIX systems, not Macintosh or Windows.) Only the browser software is platform specific. What is required is a standard for structuring these text files, a "language," so that any browser can interpret them. That standard is called HyperText Markup Language, or HTML, as originally developed by Tim Berners-Lee at CERN. Thus, web pages are actually HTML files.

HyperText Markup Language describes the general structure of a document but not necessarily the precise page layout. The browser determines the exact final appearance, which is why the same web page may look quite different to a *Netscape* user than to an *Internet Explorer* or AOL user. HTML began as a limited language, which was quite easy to learn. As more and more features are added, which is happening constantly, it has become much more complex. You can learn to write your own HTML files or you can use a web page editor to do much of the tedious work for you.

Developing with HTML

A web page is first and foremost a document. HTML files consist of the document text to be displayed augmented with *tags*, special codes in the file that give directions to the browser. Tags specify document elements, structure, formatting, and links to other documents and resources including image, audio, or video files. Because these links can be full URLs, a resource could actually be located *anywhere* on the Internet, not just on the computer with the page you are viewing. Tags are written inside pointed brackets, for example, <TITLE>, and most are used in pairs to mark the beginning and end of that element, for example, <H1> . . . </H1>.

To develop a web page directly with HTML, you need a plain text editor (Windows *Notepad* and Macintosh *SimpleText* work fine). Create or import the desired text; many pages reuse text from documents created for other purposes. Only then are you ready to add the tags to structure the document, display images (including backgrounds), play audio files, create links, and so forth. All multimedia elements are stored as separate files, not as part of the HTML file, which makes it easy to change or update those components of a page.

Save your file often, of course, as with any work you do on a computer. Be sure to name your file with a period, then HTM or HTML at the end, for example, myhomepage.htm. HTM and HTML are interchangeable in most cases. These *extensions* identify the file to the browser as an HTML file.

Figure 4.12 lists and briefly explains the most basic HTML tags.

Tag			Function/Example
`<HEAD>`	`</HEAD>`		Identifies the document's "head" block
`<TITLE>`	`</TITLE>`		Specifies the title bar information
`<BODY>`	`</BODY>`		Everything not part of `<HEAD>`
`<H1>`	`</HI>`		Heading, level 1. For Structure. Also H2-H6.
`<OL>`	`</OL>`	numbered list	Surround list items with this; browser numbers
`<UL>`	`</UL>`	unordered list	Surround list items; browser adds bullets
`<LI>`		List Item	Begins each list entry
`<HR>`			Creates a Horizontal Rule (Line) on the page
LINKS			
`<A>`	`</A>`		Mark an "anchor" or link to a resource
	`HREF = URL to link to`		`<A HREF = "http://www.niu.edu">NIU</A>`
MULTIMEDIA			
`<IMG SRC = "image file">`			`<IMG SRC = "pic1.gif">`
`<A HREF = "sound file">`			`<A HREF = "bravo.au"></A>`
`<A HREF = "video file">`			`<A HREF = "crowd.avi"></A>`

Figure 4.12   BASIC HTML TAGS

One way to start to learn about HTML is to study how others have used it. You can view the HTML source document that creates the current display by clicking View in the menu bar (Figure 4.13), then Page Source in Netscape (or View > Page in Internet Explorer). Study the HTML file (inset in Figure 4.13) and then look again at the display. It may look totally confusing, as virtually any published page contains far more than just the basic tags, but you should recognize the code for parts of the display. This may also serve to convince you that you don't want to create pages directly in HTML!

Developing with a Web Page Editor

You can learn basic HTML tags very quickly and insert them manually, but there are countless HTML editors (e.g., Microsoft *FrontPage*, Macromedia *Dreamweaver*, *Composer*) that make the process easier still. Furthermore, many software applications, including the major components of Microsoft *Office*, can save their own files as HTML files for direct use as web pages. You are never far from the ability to produce web pages today. However, even with the best editors, it is often necessary to manually modify the HTML code to get the exact result desired.

Many educators use *Composer* for two excellent reasons: It's easy to use and it's free! If you have Netscape (or Mozilla) installed on your computer, you already have *Composer*. And if you don't, you learned how to download free software in the previous chapter. *Composer* allows you to create a web page in a WYSIWIG environment (What You See Is What You Get), meaning you see your work as you create it. (When you create directly in HTML, you have to move on to the testing stage to see what you really have.)

Figure 4.13

A WEB PAGE AND ITS
SOURCE CODE

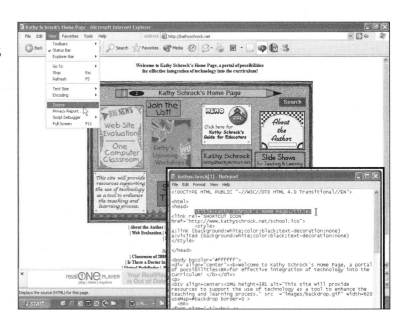

You can format text just by clicking buttons on the toolbar, and inserting images and links is nearly that simple.

Figure 4.14 gives you a look at *Composer*, whereas Figure 4.15 shows you *Dreamweaver*, one of the most popular commercial web page editors. It's far more powerful, of course, but also much more complex and time-consuming to learn to use. Many teachers start with *Composer* and then "move up" as their needs grow.

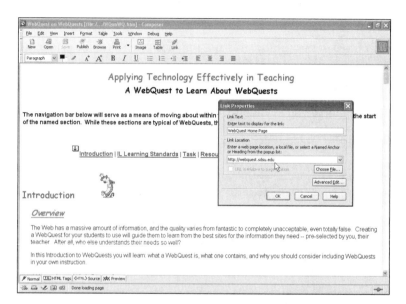

Figure 4.14

MOZILLA *COMPOSER*, A SIMPLE WEB PAGE EDITOR

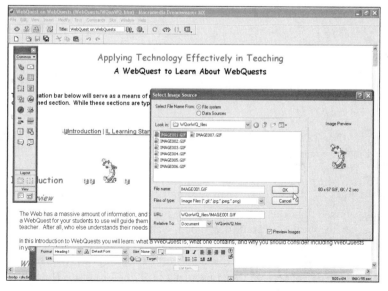

Figure 4.15

MACROMEDIA *DREAMWEAVER MX*, A FULL-STRENGTH WEBSITE TOOL

Testing Your Pages

Once you create an HTML document, you can test it on any computer that has a web browser. Just click File, Open in *Internet Explorer* (File, Open Page in *Netscape*), for example, and you'll be able to load, display, and test your very own web page. (Editors have preview capabilities for this purpose.) Because each browser may display the same page differently, it is wise to test any page you create with at least each major browser to be sure that users of your page see more or less what you intended. You may be able to adjust your page to solve any problems that you discover.

Accessibility

In addition to what you see in this testing, it is also important to strive for maximum accessibility of your pages by individuals with a range of disabilities (Thombs, 2003). A federal law known as Section 508 requires that all federal agencies make their electronic resources accessible to persons with disabilities (see <www.section508.gov>). Although this may not apply to you as an individual teacher, you do have a responsibility to educate all students. The No Child Left Behind law may also have implications for web accessibility. In short, it makes good sense to make pages as accessible as possible.

The intricacies of accessibility go beyond your current understanding of web page design and creation, so we won't try to go into details. You should be aware that there are online tools to help you evaluate the accessibility of web pages. One of the best known is Bobby <http://bobby.watchfire.com>, which has links to many useful resources as well as directions for running a Bobby test. Pages that pass the test are permitted to display a "Bobby approved" logo to indicate their compliance. WebAIM (Web Accessibility in Mind) is another excellent resource on this issue <www.webaim.org>. It offers both general and legal information as well as tutorials on achieving accessibility.

Publishing Your Web Pages

Of course, the web pages you create are not accessible to other users on the Internet unless you place your completed web document files and all required multimedia files on a web server that is connected to the Internet. There are also alternatives if you lack access to a web server.

Publishing on a Web Server

A web server is simply a computer connected to the Internet that runs web server software. That software is able to receive requests for web pages from a browser and deliver the requested files to the browser. Because this happens over the Internet, the server and the user with the browser can be located absolutely anywhere in the world.

To publish your pages so that, theoretically, anyone anywhere can access them, you must have space (i.e., an account) allocated to you on a web server. Many, if not most, educational institutions can provide such space to their teachers and students. If you are not sure about your own situation, ask. You may well have an option you are not aware of. If you don't have a local option, there are many other possibilities. If you pay for Internet access, you almost certainly are entitled to space from your ISP or broadband provider. Services such as AOL provide web space to their subscribers. There are also free sites on which anyone can post web pages, for instance, Yahoo! Geocities <www.geocities.com>. Free sites usually clutter your page with paid advertising but offer paid services that do not. Geocities charges $4.95 per month for its least expensive ad-free service. Geocities also offers basic online web page building tools as an alternative to the methods you just learned about, but you are always free to post pages you have created in other ways. You can learn about other options at <www.free-webhosts.com> or <www.thefreesite.com/Free_Web_Space>.

Any web host will provide instructions on how exactly to upload your web page files from your computer to the server. Ultimately, the process involves FTP, about which you learned in Chapter 3, but the host may provide an upload service that is not obviously FTP. You may be required to follow particular naming conventions for your files and you may have to organize them in a particular folder structure. These details will vary. Your host will also be able to tell you the URL at which anyone can reach your pages once your files are on the web server. It may sound complicated, but it really is not. You can be a web page publisher before you know it.

Using Web Pages without a Server

For many reasons, some educators prefer not to go public with their web pages. They may want to restrict access to just the intended students. Pages may contain content that is perfectly within copyright law if the audience is restricted or controlled but that would not be legal on a public website. Schools may not have their own server and may not allow access to sites such as Geocities because there is no control over the content posted there, an issue to be discussed later in the chapter. Obviously, there must be other ways to utilize one's web creations.

One answer in some schools is a school intranet. An intranet is private and only for the use of individuals associated with the owner of the network (e.g., the school). However, the most common solution is simply to distribute the web page(s) to the intended users in some way. They could be copied onto the hard drive of each computer in the school computer lab. They could be burned onto a CD or DVD, which could then be used wherever one wished. If the site is small and contains little or no multimedia, it may well fit on a floppy disk. Regardless, the user only needs to know which file to open first with a browser. As long as the computer itself is connected to the Internet, the website and all its links will work just as though it were actually published on a server. This may be particularly significant for pages created by students that are usable but not necessarily appropriate for public display.

Students in many schools are developing their own home pages. Creating HTML documents appears to offer many benefits in a constructivist environment, with added motivation potential from "publication" for other users when the documents are placed on a web server or distributed in other ways. There is the added advantage of totally bypassing the issue of computer platform in favor of universally accessible information. The latter point is so important that many software products now provide their help system in HTML files so that both Mac and Windows versions of the software can use the same help files. We believe the Internet and the Web have enormous potential to benefit learners and we encourage educators to explore the constructivist potential of these tools of the twenty-first century.

Issues in Implementation

Networks and the Internet are useful in schools only to the extent that they improve student learning in some way. There are benefits to be attained, but there are also areas of caution and concern. Educators should consider the experience and advice of others.

NETS
NOTES
NETS **S** 2
NETS **T** II-D
NETS **T** II-E
NETS **T** VI-D

Benefits of Computer Communication

The very nature of computer communication is different from other forms of communication. Perhaps most obviously, it is largely independent of distance and time. If you have access to email, you can communicate just as readily with someone in Hong Kong as in New York or Podunk Center. Location is irrelevant as long as each party has suitable network access. Unlike phone calls, worldwide communication poses no problem because of changing time zones or cost. Email moves around the world when it is sent, but the recipient determines when it is actually read. Correspondents generally need not even think about time zones. In addition, the cost of email to the far side of the globe is the same as to the next computer—generally nothing beyond the cost of Internet access itself.

Computer communication enables rapid forming and dissolving of special-interest groups to serve varied purposes. Early in Internet time, discussion groups (lists) came into being in response to significant world events, such as the Tiananmen Square incident in Beijing, the Exxon *Valdez* oil spill disaster in Alaska, and the 1995 earthquake in Kobe, Japan. Much more recently, the Greenpeace Cyberactivist Community <http://act.greenpeace.org> quickly established a targeted discussion forum after the November 2002 oil spill of the tanker *Prestige* off the coast of Spain. Anyone who wishes to follow such situations closely often can get current information that has not been filtered by the media. Just do a search for the topic of interest and include "discussion list" as part of the search term.

Another potential benefit of computer communication is that all participants are essentially equal. Because you typically can't see the other individuals, interaction is only on the level of the ideas expressed. Unless a discussion participant chooses to reveal any of the things that are immediately apparent in face-to-face conversation, such as age, gender, or ethnicity, you will not know these things, nor will they influence you even subtly. Kearsley, Hunter, and Furlong (1992, p. 49) tell the still relevant story of a 10-year-old who engaged in an online discussion of how to design a space station with a college student. The boy was delighted that an older person would interact with him as a peer, possibly because "he doesn't know I'm just a little boy!" Think about the possibility such "blind" communication offers as educators work toward greater understanding among diverse groups of people.

Finally, electronic communication benefits from being digital. You can retrieve, store, modify, and otherwise manipulate your messages, including files. Collaboration on writing projects can take the form of exchanging a copy of the master file. Each par-

ticipant retrieves it, adds annotations and comments, and then returns it to the origi-
nator. The process repeats as needed. By the same token, don't forget that all of your
email, discussion forum postings, and so on are almost certainly being kept in backup
files on a computer somewhere. Erasing a message does not destroy it, as many cases
of government and corporate corruption have demonstrated. Never use computer communication for things you would not want to share publicly.

Planning for Success

Successful projects on the Internet require careful planning, as the discussion of Web-
Quests hopefully made clear. In general, be sure to tie any Internet application to a specific curriculum need or opportunity. Don't use the Web just because it's there. Second,
be sure your planned project promises to be more effective than other approaches to
the same learning goal. It should be a Type II application, something that could not be
achieved as well, as easily, or as completely without the Internet. Third, if the project
involves participants communicating among themselves, whether by email, chat, or discussion forum, be sure to allow adequate time for them to get acquainted. This is essential to meaningful communication and part of creating community.

Research Integrity and Citing Internet Resources

Once students started to use the Internet for research, those aging print encyclopedias
began to gather lots of dust. However, the vast resources of the Internet lead to new
potential for errors and academic dishonesty. Erroneous information abounds on the
Web since no one controls what is posted. Sites that sell term papers are easy to find
and students may already be familiar with them. One that we recently checked claimed
to have over 30,000 papers on file, which cost "only" $7.00 per page. The home page
also duly noted that "all reports are copyrighted by (firm name) and are sold for research and reference purposes only and may not be submitted either in whole or in part
for academic credit." You can judge the likelihood of that for yourself. Furthermore,
students may forget what they should already know about plagiarism. It has never been
easier to plagiarize, whether intentionally or not. Teachers must be alert to problems,
which are not solved by refusing to accept Internet sources for research projects. Rather,
students must be taught to use the resources of the Web effectively and correctly. The
previous chapter dealt with evaluating the content of websites. Here are some resources
on possible dishonesty.

Educators who suspect plagiarism must take time to pursue their concerns. We suggest two possibilities. First, use your favorite search engine to search for a suspect passage. Search terms need not be limited to just a word or two but can be entire phrases,
even sentences. If something was taken directly from a web page, you may well find the
original this way. Second, there are services that assist in identifying plagiarized work.
Plagiarism.org offers much information about the problem and offers as one solution
a user portal called TurnItIn.Com, which can help document plagiarism. Mississippi
State University Libraries provides a large resource on this issue, including links to many
detection services, including TurnItIn.Com.

Assuming students legitimately use the Internet as part of their research, do they know how to prepare citations for information found online? If not, what will you tell your students when they ask? Just as there are multiple citation formats for written materials, so are there for electronic sources. For information located on the Web, a common general citation format is:

Author. Title of item. [Online] Available (give full URL), date viewed or retrieved.

There are also formats for email messages and various multimedia file types. Since writing in education usually follows APA style, one of the most useful resources is the APA Electronic References guide <www.apastyle.org/elecref.html>. For other styles, the Internet Public Library provides links to major guides at <www.ipl.org/div/farq/netcite FARQ.html> and the recommendations of the Library of Congress are available at <http://memory.loc.gov/ammem/ndlpedu/resources/cite>.

Overcoming Obstacles

There are countless potential problems with Internet access in schools. How can schools pay the cost of building infrastructure and Internet connections? The government is helping with the E-Rate plan, which provides up to $2.25 billion per year in subsidies <www.ed.gov/Technology/eratemenu.html>. Look again at Figure 1.1 on national technology expenditures. The top part of each bar is that E-Rate subsidy, which starting in school year 2000–2001 amounted to about one-third of total expenditures.

Is technical support and assistance available in the school or district once infrastructure is in place? First-class infrastructure still cannot operate and maintain itself.

Other commonly perceived problems include the risk of students accessing inappropriate materials (more on this later), uncertain educational value (a short online tour for doubters usually fixes this one—demonstrate a WebQuest, for example), lack of proof that the Internet "works" in schools (consider the links between learning and technology made by the NETS project), and potential for virus infection (it's controllable with antivirus software and not limited to Internet access anyhow; diskettes can easily carry viruses).

Personal Safety

The Internet is itself a growing microcosm of our society. Regrettably, for a few individuals it is a new way to prey on unsuspecting victims. The press has reported a growing number of cases of adolescents who have become involved with predators whom they met on the Internet.

Students who have access to the Internet must be made aware of the importance of privacy and the potential dangers that may await those who ignore it. Caution around strangers is a lesson that applies online as well as on the streets. Here are illustrative URLs for Internet child safety resources:

- University of Oklahoma Department of Public Safety <www.ou.edu/oupd/kidsafe/start.htm>

- SafeSurf <www.safesurf.com>
- National Center for Missing and Exploited Children <www.missingkids.com/cybertip>, which also offers the NetSmartz Workshop at <www.netsmartz.org>

Inappropriate Materials and Acceptable Use Policy

Stories abound of vast Internet storehouses of pornography, hate sites such as those that promote neo-Nazi and antigay views, and other materials inappropriate for K–12 students. These aberrations offer a ready excuse in some schools for not entering the online era or restricting access so severely as to prevent legitimate use. The concerns are valid as they relate to students, but there are ways to address them.

Self-policing may be the most effective answer. Schools that provide students and staff with access to computer communications resources must develop or adapt and then publicize and implement their own Acceptable Use Policy (AUP) concerning these resources. Many schools prepare their policy as a contract that sets out their rules, which all users (and students' parents) must sign to use the Internet at school.

Among many sources, sample policies are available from:

- Southern Regional Education Board at <www.sreb.org/programs/EdTech/seritec/AppropriateUsePolicies.asp>
- Houston Independent School District at <www.rice.edu/armadillo/acceptable.html>
- Virginia Department of Education at <www.pen.k12.va.us/go/VDOE/Technology/AUP/home.shtml>, a particularly rich collection of relevant materials

It is possible to attempt to block access to inappropriate sites using "filter" software that restricts user navigation. Such an approach can be controversial because of cost and limits to its effectiveness, as well as problems created for legitimate uses. Nevertheless, within the federal Consolidated Appropriations Act for fiscal year 2001 was the Children's Internet Protection Act, which mandates filtering in schools and libraries that receive federal funds such as E-Rate money (see <http://ftp.fcc.gov/cgb/consumerfacts/cipa.html> and <www.cybertelecom.org/cda/cipa.htm>). For information on how this legislation affects your organization, see <www.filteringinfo.org/compliance.html>. For a guide to filtering products, see <www.getnetwise.org/tools>.

Public libraries in particular have protested the law out of concern for intellectual freedom and opposition to censorship. In the summer of 2002, the enforcement of the rules was suspended pending review by the U.S. Supreme Court. As we write, that review has yet to occur (see <www.ala.org/cipa>), but we will monitor the situation and post updates on the companion website. In our view, no software solution can be 100 percent effective, so teaching students what is and is not acceptable and how to deal with possible encounters with unacceptable materials will have to be part of any solution to this thorny issue.

For further information, the Consortium for School Networking offers many links and good suggestions about safeguarding wired schools <www.safewiredschools.org> as does the GetNetWise Coalition at <www.getnetwise.org>.

SUMMARY

The Internet, and especially the World Wide Web, has the potential to be the single most significant influence on early twenty-first century education, as schools and teachers increasingly learn to use it effectively. This chapter sought to contribute to that goal by introducing you to the Web in some detail and by providing guidance in navigating its resources effectively.

Next the chapter dealt with finding and evaluating specific web resources. An evolving entity like the Web changes dramatically in very short time frames, and any specific information about resources may well be outdated or no longer correct by the time a book appears in print. Learning to search the Internet for what you want is the best solution to this state of flux, which is unlikely ever to stabilize. The chapter described sources in educational literature that will lead you to web resources and then explained web indexes, directories, and portals. Considerable attention focused on web search tools and how to use them effectively. Once you locate potential web resources, it is essential to evaluate them critically, since there are no controls on the content, no vetting, no assurance of validity or accuracy. Many tips on website evaluation were provided. Because of their unique importance to teachers, locating lesson plans on the Web was given special attention, as were ways to find school sites and free materials for teaching.

The next topic presented was Internet and web curriculum applications, focusing on a few limited areas for which referenced websites are likely to remain active for many years: locating primary source materials, electronic publications, and collaborative projects. Applications for individual content areas are much more volatile and better accessed from the companion website for accurate links.

One particular web application that has gained enormous popularity in a short time is the WebQuest. The chapter guided you through the concepts and typical content structure of this exciting learning tool, as well as options for creating one. Numerous references to the abundant resources concerning WebQuests were provided.

The value of this chapter will be greatly enhanced if you combine it with hands-on experience of the Internet and World Wide Web. To that end, many specific sites have been mentioned, which we hope you will visit and learn from. At the same time, use the advice provided on how to deal with "dead links." Even if an exact URL given in the book is no longer valid, you may well be able to use good problem-solving skills to locate the information or resource, unless it truly no longer exists, which will be true in some cases.

Users of the Web inevitably wonder how websites and pages are created. We have tried to provide a look at those processes, from conceptualization through development and testing to final distribution or "publishing."

Finally, however exciting the Internet may be, it poses many thorny challenges for educators wishing to bring the world into their classrooms. We presented a number of issues and aspects of web use that you must consider, including serious issues related to research integrity, as well as ideas and resources to help address them.

The Web is perhaps the most rapidly changing area within educational computing today. Your ride on the Web may be harried, perhaps even frightening at times, but the potential benefits are so enormous as to demand that educators get on board immediately. You'll be very glad you did.

chapter 4
activities

1. Choose one of the subject areas covered in the Resources and Applications sections. Visit the websites listed for your topic and write a short description of each to share with classmates (electronically, of course!).
2. Use at least three different search tools to investigate hate groups on the Internet. Prepare a report comparing the resources that each tool found for you. What conclusion can you draw about these different tools?
3. Research the opportunities for students to exchange messages with a keypal. Plan a lesson or unit that would involve your students and keypals in another location substantially different from your own.
4. Plan an instructional unit for your students in which collaboration plays a key role. Hypothesize that you are participating in Kids Network, for instance, or that your project includes two schools in South America.

5. Outline the key elements of an Acceptable Use Policy based on online research.
6. Identify, download, and adapt several relevant lesson plans.
7. Identify several existing WebQuests and develop lesson plans that incorporate them.
8. Develop a very simple web page using any of the methods and tools described. Investigate where you might be able to post your work, for example, on a school server or one of the free hosting services.
9. Research issues related to personal security and inappropriate materials on the Internet.
10. How serious is the issue of plagiarism in student research today? Investigate the issue and make recommendations for dealing with it.
11. Develop lesson plans for each area you teach that include use of Internet resources by the students or that are based on materials you have located on the Internet.

Companion Website

Visit the companion website at <www.ablongman.com/lockard6e> for more information about the topics discussed in this chapter.

expect the world®

The New York Times
nytimes.com

Themes of the Times

Expand your knowledge of the concepts discussed in this chapter by reading current and historical articles from the *New York Times* by visiting the Themes of the Times section of the companion website <www.ablongman.com/lockard6e>.

References

Berners-Lee, T. *Long Biography*. 2000. Retrieved January 2, 2003, from <www.w3.org/People/Berners-Lee/Longer.html>

Dabu, C. "Bridging the Digital Divide." *Digital Journal.com*. July 1997. Retrieved December 28, 2002, from <www.digitaljournal.com/news/?articleID=2083>

Dodge, B. "Some Thoughts About WebQuests." 1995, revised 1997. Retrieved January 2, 2003, from <http://edweb.sdsu.edu/courses/edtec596/about_webquests.html>

Glazer, E. *Using Internet Primary Sources to Teach Critical Thinking Skills in Mathematics*. Westport, CT: Greenwood Press, 2001.

Jones Telecommunications & Multimedia Encyclopedia. "Marc Andreesen: Co-Founder of Netscape." Retrieved January 2, 2003, from <www.digitalcentury.com/encyclo/update/andreess.htm>

Kearsley, G., Hunter, B., and Furlong, M. *We Teach with Technology*. Wilsonville, OR: Franklin, Beedle, and Associates, Inc., 1992.

Killmer, K., and Koppel, N. "So Much Information, So Little Time. Evaluating Web Resources with Search Engines." *T.H.E. Journal*, August 2002. Retrieved December 29, 2002, from <www.thejournal.com/magazine/vault/A4101.cfm>

Kobrin, D. *Beyond the Textbook: Teaching History Using Documents and Primary Sources*. Portsmouth, NH: Heinemann, 1996.

Maddux, C. D., Johnson, D. L., and Willis, J. W. *Educational Computing: Learning with Tomorrow's Technologies*. Boston: Allyn & Bacon, 1992.

McCafferty, D. "www.hate Comes to Your Home." *USA Weekend*, March 26–28, 1999, pp. 6–8. (For further information, see, for example, <www.eu.hatewatch.org>.)

Roblyer, M. *Integrating Educational Technology into Teaching*, 3rd ed. Columbus, OH: Merrill Prentice Hall, 2003.

Russell, T. L. *The No Significant Difference Phenomenon*. Raleigh, NC: North Carolina State University, 1999.

Ryder, R. J., and Hughes, T. *Internet for Educators*. Upper Saddle River, NJ: Merrill, 1999.

Schrock, K. "The ABCs of Web Site Evaluation." Retrieved December 29, 2002, from <http://kathyschrock.com/abceval/weval_02.pdf>

Sharp, V., Levine, M., and Sharp, R. *The Best Web Sites for Teachers*, 5th ed. Eugene, OR: International Society for Technology in Education, 2002.

Shiroma, D. *Using Primary Sources on the Internet to Teach and Learn History*. ERIC Document Reproduction Service, ED 442739, 2000.

Shively, J., and VanFossen, P. *Using Internet Primary Sources to Teach Critical Thinking Skills in Government, Economics, and Contemporary World Issues*. Westport, CT: Greenwood Press, 2001.

Thombs, M. "Accessible Web Pages: Advice for Educators." *Syllabus*, January 2003, *16*(6), pp. 26–28. Also available online at <www.syllabus.com/article.asp?id=7095>

Webopedia. World Wide Web (definition). Retrieved January 2, 2003, from <http://webopedia.com/TERM/W/World_Wide_Web.html>

Word Processing and Publishing:

Managing Text

OBJECTIVES

After completing this chapter, you will be able to:

- Explain the basic concepts of word processing.
- List and explain the basic functions of a word processor.
- Discuss additional functions of most word processors and explain why they would or would not be useful to you.
- Define the term *prewriting* and explain how software can contribute to this aspect of writing.
- Discuss the functions, potential usefulness, and limitations of spelling, grammar, and style aids.
- Take a position for or against the process approach to writing instruction.
- Define keyboarding and explain some of the challenges related to teaching keyboarding skills.
- Discuss the outcomes of using word processors as indicated by research, including why the results are mixed.
- Differentiate editing from revision and defend the significance of each.
- Discuss the role of the teacher in implementing word processing in the curriculum.
- Discuss important considerations in teaching students to use a specific word processor.

- Develop lesson plans that include students using word processing in your area of the curriculum.
- Analyze the role of word processing in the curriculum.
- Explain the essential aspects of text publishing, including common elements of page setup (layout).
- Differentiate typeface, type size, and type style.
- Explain the graphics control that is typical of publishing.
- Discuss the potential of visual cueing and marginalia to enhance the communication value of published materials.
- Discuss elements of design needed for effective published materials.
- Suggest possible applications of publishing in your personal or professional life.
- Develop lesson plans that include publishing activities.

This is the first of several chapters that deal with the most widely used computer software applications, namely, *productivity tools*. Productivity software enables any computer user—teacher, student, office worker, bank president—to complete important tasks efficiently. These uses are so important that most computer makers install some kind of productivity software before selling their product, so that a computer is ready to go to work right out of the box. A computer without productivity software is hard to find and likely to be useful only for some very specific limited purpose, say, Internet access.

Although it is possible to purchase individual productivity tools, it is far more common and economical to obtain them in a package. Such a package may be an "all-in-one" *integrated* product such as Microsoft *Works* or *AppleWorks* or separate applications in an "office suite," such as Microsoft *Office*. Either type will typically contain at least four major applications: a word processor, a database, a spreadsheet, and a presentation graphics package. The next four chapters will look individually at each of these applications. Regardless of whether you have an integrated package or an office suite, you will be able to do virtually all of the same things. Integrated products tend to be less powerful in their capabilities but work well even on older computers and are relatively easy to learn. Applications within suites are "industrial strength," meaning only very specialized users are likely to need anything more. They require more computer power, more hard drive space for installation, and more effort to fully exploit their features. However, on the level of the typical user, they are also easy to learn to use.

With that general background, let's turn to the specific topics of this chapter, word processing and its applications in teaching and learning. We also include in this chapter *publishing*, by which we mean the preparation of text materials that closely resemble the work of professional print shops. Examples include newsletters, flyers, even booklets. We consider publishing an extension of word processing because it builds on the basic concepts of word processing. It's not a huge step beyond, but it can be an important one.

Overview of Word Processing

Unless you are totally new to computers, you probably had some experience with both a web browser and a word processor before you started reading this book. Lever-Duffy, McDonald, and Mizell (2003, p. 134) state flatly that word processing is the number one computer application. Although it would be hard to verify that claim, just think about your own computer use and how much of it revolves around creating and manipulating text. Odds are word processing consumes a very significant percentage of your work time at a computer. (We do have to allow time for playing computer games, of course!)

If you are already experienced with word processing, you may be tempted to skip this chapter, and perhaps you can. However, our experience is that even individuals who have used a word processor for some time tend not to understand nearly all of its power and capabilities. We encourage you to skim sections that you believe you already know, but be prepared to slow down and stop as you encounter new ideas that will enhance your life as a student and as a teacher.

To introduce word processing, we will first define it, then explain its basic concepts.

Definitions

Early computers were valued for their "number crunching" abilities, and even today, many people think of computers primarily as numeric devices. Numerous useful applications for teachers and students, however, are related to text management—the control of words by the computer. The earliest efforts toward this goal were *text editors*, crude word manipulators with limited capabilities to ease the mechanical burdens of writing. They did, however, whet the appetite of early users for more powerful ways to control text.

Today's writers manipulate text with a *word processor*, which is computer software for writing, editing, revising, formatting, and printing text. The term *word processing* means using a word processor.

Basic Concepts of Word Processing

Let's compare word processing to its predecessor, typing, a mechanical means of writing largely unknown to today's students. Then we'll briefly review key functions of any word processor and the most important writing aids.

What's Typing?

To review a bit of ancient history, a typewriter produced printed characters on paper by striking small hammers shaped as letters through an inked ribbon. The result was clean printed copy that a good typist could produce much faster than writing by hand, to say nothing of improved legibility. However, mistakes in typed materials were very problematic to correct, since the letters were already printed on the paper. Students writing term papers sometimes faced the horrendous task of retyping an entire paper or large segments of it when they discovered mistakes after the fact. There was no easy way to insert missing words; correct typing errors; move a word, line, or paragraph to a new location; or cleanly delete anything. The ability to type accurately was one of the most vital qualifications of a secretary before computers replaced typewriters for nearly every writing need. See Figure 5.1.

Improvements over Typing

A word processor takes away most of the mechanical problems associated previously with typing. Mistakes are corrected on the screen. Errors in the final printed copy should be a thing of the past. More complicated editing, such as repositioning words or blocks of text, is a matter of a few mouse movements. The days of laboriously retyping an entire document because of a spelling error or changed organization are gone. Once typed, anything that is correct need never be retyped. Any and all changes can be accomplished with relative speed and ease. Teaching materials can be updated each term with ease.

Some things that were not feasible with a typewriter have become commonplace. Boldface printing and straight right margins (called *right alignment*) are examples of these advances. Superscripts and subscripts require little more than a mouse click. Text can be centered on the page with a keystroke or click, eliminating counting of characters to determine the number of spaces to indent. Block indentation of paragraphs is equally simple. It's easy to try something, then undo it instantly.

Control over Page Layout

Word processing differs from conventional typing in another important way. Much of the typical typing process focused on how to achieve the desired page format. Typists had to control margins manually and continually be alert to the approaching end of a line to decide whether to hyphenate a word or move to the next line on the page. A decision to change to double spacing or different margins meant retyping the entire document. Footnotes, headings, and page numbering all required much thought and planning.

The word processor now handles such mechanical matters. Even when entering text, the ENTER key on the keyboard serves only to signal the end of a paragraph or a line that must stand alone. There is no need to watch for the "end" of a line. The

Figure 5.1

AN "EARLY WORD
PROCESSOR," ALSO
KNOWN AS A TYPEWRITER

word processor manages all layout concerns, moving text about as needed. As you write, you can focus on the important things—ideas, organization, and style.

Basic Editing Functions

No matter what word processor you are currently familiar with, at some point you will probably either have to change to a totally different one (e.g., because your new school has something else) or to a new version of the one you "know," and that new version may initially not look like your comfortable old program at all. However, don't let this concern you unduly. All word processors—*AppleWorks*, Microsoft *Word*, or *WordPerfect*, to name a few examples—offer the same basic functions, and usually they are quite obvious. Difficulties seldom arise until you need more advanced capabilities. Figure 5.2 summarizes the basic functions that make word processing an indispensable computer application.

Word wrap allows you to type without attention to the end of each line. As you reach the end of a line, if the final word will not fit within the margin, word wrap automatically moves it to the next line, enabling you to continue with text entry. You press the ENTER key only to begin a new paragraph or to move down to a new line prior to reaching the right margin.

The *insert* function creates space automatically. New material may be inserted anywhere in the document without retyping what follows.

The *cut, erase,* or *delete* function removes unwanted letters, words, phrases, sentences, paragraphs, and even more. Use the mouse to drag the cursor from the beginning to the end of the unwanted text. Then, with just a click or keystroke, the unwanted text disappears immediately and the remaining text is appropriately rearranged so that the layout remains correct.

Cut/Erase/Delete	Removes unwanted text and rearranges remaining characters to fill space.
Cut and Paste/Move/Copy	Relocates/duplicates selected text within a document or from one document to another.
Insert	Adds new material anywhere in a document by "opening" space for it.
Layout	Reformats after changes in margins, tab setting, line spacing, etc., without retyping.
Search/Search and Replace	Locates specified word, phrase, or characters within a document. After locating, optionally replaces with new text.
Word Wrap	Automatically moves any word too long for the current line to the next line of the screen or page. Users need pay no attention to the right margin.

Figure 5.2 BASIC EDITING FUNCTIONS OF ALL WORD PROCESSORS

The *search* and *replace* functions search your document for a specific character, word, or phrase and allow this specific text to be replaced with another. Perhaps you misused or misspelled a word. Assume you used the word *principle* when, in fact, the word should have been *principal*. By using search and replace, you can locate each occurrence of the incorrect word and replace it with the correct word.

The *move* function transfers a portion of your text from one location to another. Typically, you drag the mouse cursor across the desired text to select it, then use the mouse to *drag and drop* the text at its new location. Alternatively, you *cut* the selected text, which puts it in a temporary holding place called a *clipboard*, then *paste* it into the new location. Either way, all text material is rearranged automatically, so that proper spacing and page format are maintained.

Figure 5.3 shows how basic editing functions may be selected from either a standard (drop-down) menu (on the left) or from a context-sensitive pop-up menu (on the right). (This is a composite image, so don't expect to see both menus at once on your own computer!) The latter appears when you right click on the screen and changes, depending on where and when you click. In the figure, the pop-up is in reference to the selected word "students" just behind the menu. Functions such as cut, copy, and paste are also available as buttons on the toolbar, just below the Tools menu choice.

Additional Functions

In addition to basic functions, word processors provide such capabilities as automatic centering of text, underlining, page numbering, and printing boldface characters. Other features produce variations in the document that are similar to typeset material. These include alignment of margins (*left*, *right*, *centered*, or *justified*, which means both left and right margins are straight), proportional spacing of characters (an M takes more space than an I), and changing the size of the text. You can select from a range of fonts and sizes in order to vary headings or just as an aesthetic choice. Word processors also en-

Figure 5.3

Many editing functions are available in either a drop-down menu or a context-sensitive pop-up menu.

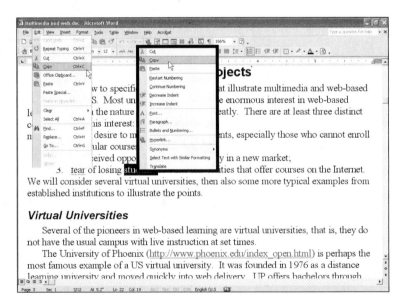

able you to insert graphic images (pictures, charts, etc.) into your documents. The ability to change fonts and place graphics in documents has blurred the distinction between word processing and publishing (a topic yet to come). Commonly used additional word processor functions are outlined in Figure 5.4.

Writing Aids

In addition to the word processing functions previously described, additional functions have been integrated into word processors to facilitate outlining and improve spelling, grammar and usage, and vocabulary. Our experience, however, suggests that many computer users are unaware of these tools or simply fail to use them as a routine part of their writing. Either way, they are not getting the full productivity benefit of their software.

Outlining Assistance

Outlining has become an integral feature of most word processors (Figure 5.5). You can begin to write by creating a multilevel outline, then fill in the subordinate text under each heading. The software helps maintain proper indentation to indicate outline levels. It allows you at any point to display the outline in whatever detail you wish, from only the main headings to all levels and their associated text. You can switch between levels of detail to get a broader or more detailed view of your work.

Although outlining is typically taught as the first step in composition, many students dive right in without first organizing their total plan. Often the result is below the student's capability. All teachers should stress the importance of starting any serious writing project with an outline, and be certain their students know how to use the outline function in their word processing software.

As beneficial as outlining may be for typical students, Bermann and Jerome (2002) note that it has special benefits for students with mild disabilities, who often have difficulty organizing their thoughts. They suggest projecting the outline view of a document to allow a group to collaborate on a writing project.

Spelling Assistance

The spellchecker has become an indispensable word processing aid. A spellchecker compares all words in your document with those in its electronic dictionary. Words that do not match those in the dictionary are then displayed as questionable. Note that all words that do not match words in the electronic dictionary are questioned. When a spellchecker flags such a word, you may correct or ignore it, depending on whether it is actually misspelled or is simply not in the electronic dictionary.

Spellcheckers also suggest alternatives for the possible error (Figure 5.6) and permit you to add new words to the dictionary. If the correct spelling is listed, a simple click corrects the error. Spelling aids cannot, however, tell what you meant to write. If you type "there" instead of "their" or "contact" for "contract," a spellchecker will not find the error because each "misspelled" word is listed in its dictionary.

Early spellcheckers typically were used after a substantial amount of text was written, even an entire draft or document. Now it is more common to set the word processor to check spelling as you type (see the inset in Figure 5.6). As the figure also shows, a suspect word is marked immediately with a squiggly underline (in red on our systems). You can deal with the word whenever it is convenient for you, immediately or

Alignment	Center
(text positioning relative to the margins)	Left
	Right
	Justify means both left and right margins are flush, not ragged, as these lines show if you look carefully.
Chart	Insert data chart into documents
Font/Style	Vary text appearance (font and size). Style variations for a font include **Bold,** *Italic,* ~~Strike through,~~ ^{Super}script, and $_{Sub}$script.
Graphics	Insert images into documents.
Index/Table of Contents	Generated automatically from codes or styles assigned to words or headings in a document.
Merge Printing	Creates personalized documents by inserting name, address, or other material into a basic "template" (e.g., form letters and legal documents).
Page Numbering/Header/Footer	Automatically numbers pages, usually with control over location (e.g., upper right, bottom center), even different for odd and even pages, and whether Roman or Arabic. Typically part of a header or footer, which may contain additional information to appear on each page.
Tables	Allows easy layout of page content in rows and columns, such as this figure.

Figure 5.4 SELECTED ADDITIONAL FUNCTIONS OF WORD PROCESSORS

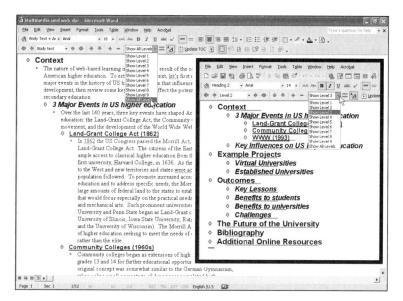

Figure 5.5

OUTLINE VIEW OF A
DOCUMENT AT
DIFFERENT LEVELS

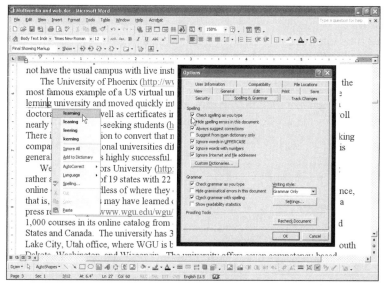

Figure 5.6

SPELLCHECKING FROM
A CONTEXT-SENSITIVE
POP-UP MENU AS WELL
AS SETUP OPTIONS FOR
SPELLING AND GRAMMAR
ASSISTANCE

later, and in either of two ways. There is still a menu option for spelling, but we find it far more convenient to call up the context-sensitive menu for the marked word, also shown in the figure. With one click, you can select the correct word from the choices, add it to the dictionary, or if it's correct but not common enough to add to the dictionary, choose Ignore All. No further occurrences of that word in the document will be marked as misspelled. With such an easy-to-use, on-the-fly system, there is no excuse for misspelled words in any document.

Some educators remain concerned that students will become completely dependent on their electronic spellchecker and unable to spell on their own. That is certainly a point for debate. Martin (2001), for one, argued that it is simply easier (and presumably more productive) to teach students to use the appropriate tools well than to learn to spell every word or learn every grammar rule, which is the topic of the next section.

Grammar and Style Assistance

Proofreading software (also called grammar checkers) is also a feature of more advanced word processors (Figure 5.7). These aids check documents for possible errors in grammar, punctuation, style, sentence and paragraph construction, usage, and so on, often varied as appropriate to the type of writing or intended audience. Analysis is based on the conventions of language usage and specialized dictionaries of troublesome words, including complete phrases. Like spellcheckers, such programs have clear limitations. They tend to emphasize simple mechanical errors and miss many common writing problems. They are, however, much improved today from the early versions that reflected only basic business writing style. A grammar checker can be of value to any writer, but you must always consider each recommendation carefully. See Vernon (2000) for further discussion and suggestions.

Vocabulary Assistance

Frequently, a writer runs into the problem of overuse of a particular word or encounters the need for a word with precisely the right meaning. A thesaurus addresses this need for vocabulary variety and precision. Popular word processors, including Corel *WordPerfect*, Microsoft *Word* and *Works*, and *AppleWorks*, feature an integrated thesaurus (Figure 5.8). It functions much like the other writing aids described previously. Nearly all writers can benefit from using an electronic thesaurus that is so easily available.

Figure 5.7

Grammar checking offers suggestions and explanations of the point.

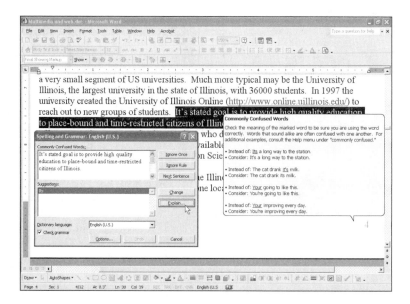

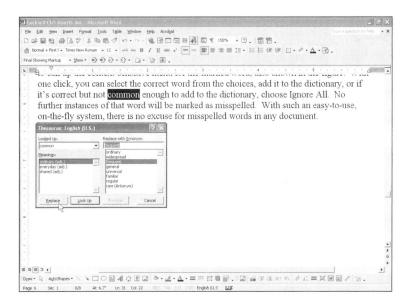

Figure 5.8

Improve your vocabulary and writing style with a thesaurus.

Issues in Word Processing

The Appropriate Age to Begin

NETS
NOTES

NETS **S** 2
NETS **T** I-A
NETS **T** II-A
NETS **T** III-A
NETS **T** VI-B

Teachers often ask, "At what grade level should word processing be introduced?" Proponents of word processing for students tend to argue for use early in their schooling. Many schools do, indeed, start electronic writing early. For instance, Fletcher (2001) presents a case study of second graders that explores when and how they chose to use editing tools in revising their writing.

A more acceptable view for many may be to wait until writing instruction has passed the point of sheer mechanics and at least a short paragraph is required of students from time to time. This timing differentiates the physical act of writing from writing as a visual representation of thoughts or from writing as "art."

Another view is to start a little sooner than just suggested, because word processing may enable more significant writing activities at an early age by removing the physical barriers between thoughts and a visible product.

Ultimately, individual teachers and schools must take into account not only appropriateness for the students but also the school's ability to provide sufficient computer access. Regardless of when it is introduced, word processing should support, enhance, and extend the curriculum, and it should not become an isolated computer activity.

Keyboarding

Keyboarding means learning to use your fingers correctly on the keyboard without looking at them. Keyboarding is basic to most uses of the computer, not just word processing. Persons doing word processing, however, benefit particularly from sound keyboarding skills. A related concern is that students may find it extremely difficult ever to learn to use the keyboard correctly if they do not learn keyboarding before they become two-finger hunt-and-peck typists (Roblyer, 2003, p. 120).

Most educators and advocates of computers in the schools presume the need for keyboarding instruction. The issue again is timing. For the youngest students, you must seriously consider keyboarding from the standpoint of both need and physical ability. It has become common for schools to begin keyboarding instruction in grade 3 or 4 in our experience.

Part of the issue may relate to the goal of keyboarding instruction. In the old days of typing, the standard was being able to type a specified number of words per minute with set accuracy. Although speed with accuracy clearly has merit, perhaps it is most important to achieve a speed that at least equals one's speed of handwriting so that electronic writing minimally does not slow the process. Your own experience no doubt confirms the usefulness of proper keyboard fingering, and we have observed that the most vocal opponents of computer technology in general are often those who are unable to cope with a keyboard. However, we concur with Roblyer (2003, p. 239), who argues that students often arrive in school with experience at the keyboard. Schools should not deny them access to technology because they lack "correct" keyboarding skills.

But who, then, is responsible for keyboarding instruction? Historically, high school business education teachers taught typing. As keyboarding has moved down into the lower elementary grades, the classroom teacher or a specialist technology teacher has assumed that duty. In many cases, keyboarding instruction relies on computer software that guides the learner into correct methods while also slowly working to develop greater speed. One of the most common such programs is *Mavis Beacon Teaches Typing*.

Keyboard instruction is a process of skill development, which is inherently time consuming. For young children, teachers may need to provide rewards (i.e., extrinsic motivation), as their students may not relate to the eventual payoff for their effort. It is also critical to understand that any skill may be lost over time if it is not used regularly. Practice does indeed make perfect in keyboarding. If keyboarding instruction begins early and teachers of all subjects require word processed assignments, the needed practice should occur naturally.

The Process Approach to Writing

For word processing to have maximum value in composition, a particular view of instruction called the *process approach* to writing is recommended. Historically, writing has been viewed as product oriented. The finished document was the crucial element, and most of the emphasis was placed on mechanics. In the 1990s, this view largely gave way to process-oriented writing instruction, which stresses the steps and processes over the finished product.

In an effort to synthesize many models of the writing process, Hunter and Begoray (1990) produced a four-part framework that remains valid today. Writers first *gen-*

erate ideas, whether from memory, external resources, or original research. Next they *organize* the ideas, for example, by sorting and sequencing notecards or creating an outline. *Composing* translates the organized ideas into sentences and paragraphs. *Revision* seeks to improve the composition and may occur repeatedly until the writer is satisfied. Beaver (1992) added a publishing step in which the writing is shared with others, giving more purpose to the task.

Much of the interest in word processing has centered on its ability to facilitate the revision step. With appropriate instruction, word processing can be an integral part of each step in the writing process. The process approach to writing matches well with the power of a word processor to help produce an initial draft quickly, then facilitate mechanical editing and substantive revision, before producing a polished printed copy. A computer, however, is not essential to this approach. Rather, the role of the teacher in guiding the development of writing skills and strategies is the essential feature, as noted in the discussion of research on word processing in the next section.

Limited English Proficiency and Special Needs Students

As U.S. schools become increasingly diverse, issues arise concerning how best to teach limited English proficiency (LEP) students. Reading and writing tend to be more problematic than speaking, as is the case for any second language learner, something you may well have experienced. As you might expect, teachers of LEP students are often enthusiastic about the benefits offered by the features of word processing that you have learned about. The writing aids previously discussed (outlining, spellchecking, grammar and vocabulary assistance) can be of particular benefit if students are taught to use them effectively. This topic is much too broad for us to deal with further, but if it is of interest to you, we recommend the *International Journal of English Studies*, Volume 1, Number 2, 2001. This is a special issue entitled "Writing in the L2 Classroom: Issues in Research and Pedagogy." Of particular interest is the article "Word Processing and Second Language Writing: A Longitudinal Case Study" by Li and Cumming (2001). Depending on the language, a special multilingual word processor may be needed (see Anderson, 2001).

Inclusion of special needs students in the regular classroom has become common. Word processing offers many benefits to students across a full range of disabilities, from mild to severe, but may require adaptive hardware and/or software. As with issues related to LEP students, this vast area is far beyond our scope. However, we refer you to Quenneville (2001) for a succinct overview of such special tools as talking word processors and software that predicts the next word the student will need, allowing users to choose from options to complete their writing—somewhat analogous to the choices offered by spellcheckers. Her reference list is very useful as well. In addition, Walters (2000) explains in some detail how disabled students may be able to keyboard with only one hand when scarce adaptive hardware is unavailable. It's fascinating reading for those who've never thought much about special needs adaptations and includes very concrete suggestions.

Research on Learning with Word Processing

NETS
NOTES

NETS **S** 2
NETS **S** 5
NETS **T** II–B
NETS **T** III–A

What is it that has caused countless computer-phobic teachers at all levels to suppress their high-tech anxieties and plunge into classroom word processing? Clearly, the answer must be a belief that word processing will allow their students to develop writing skills more quickly or to a higher level. Let's look at what educational researchers and users of word processing have reported.

Effects on Quantity and Quality

Anecdotal and research-based reports on the relationship between word processing and the quantity and quality of student writing have long been inconclusive, even contradictory. Godsey's (2000) research found that high school students familiar with keyboarding skills did produce more words in daily journals than those who wrote using pencil and paper. They were also far more agreeable to the assignment than when they were not permitted to use word processing. Padgett (2000) required daily journal writing of her fifth graders. Two student groups switched between word processing and handwriting twice during the experiment so that each student had two sets of data from each approach. Analysis found no significant difference between the groups at the end of the study, but the use of word processing did heighten interest in the activity.

Montague (1990), Dudley-Marling and Oppenheimer (1990), Cochran-Smith (1991), Weisberg (1992), Owston, Murphy, and Wideman (1993), Jones (1994), and Owston and Wideman (1997) all provide evidence that word processing leads to improvements in the quality or quantity of writing. Nichols (1996) found that compositions written by sixth graders using word processors did not differ from those by students using paper and pencil in quality of writing, accuracy of grammar, or reading ease. The word processor group did write more words and sentences than did the paper and pencil group.

One possible explanation for some of these discrepancies is the difficulty of quantifying the assessment of writing. Although most newer studies report using a holistic approach to judge quality, significant subjectivity remains. Other problems with the research are discussed in the conclusion of this chapter.

Editing/Revision

Traditionally, teachers of writing have invested much time in writing comments on student papers, with the goal of helping students to develop their writing skills. However, the next assignment given to the students usually involves a different topic and different circumstances. It is doubtful whether the red marks on a previous assignment have much impact on current work. The real need in learning to write is to revise and polish each assignment through several iterations, based on suggestions and rethinking. Teachers may have been unwilling in the past to require such revision because of the arduous and frustrating nature of the task without a computer.

Ease of text editing (small, mechanical details) and revising (making structural changes) is one of the most obvious benefits of using a computer to write. According to Grejda and Hannafin (1991, p. 89), "Improving the revising skills of young writers . . . is widely regarded as integral to all process writing approaches. . . . Yet, revision is among the least researched, least understood, and, usually, least taught aspects of the writing process." Noting the mixed results of past research, they investigated "the effects of word processing and requisite instruction on the mechanical and structural revisions of fifth graders." They found that their word processing subjects performed the least well of all! They attribute this to insufficient time for the students to learn to use the computer comfortably and to a need for better teaching methods, two critical flaws in research studies.

In Dudley-Marling and Oppenheimer's study (1990), students made changes in their initial text primarily at the word level, which the researchers considered editing, not revision. During direct observation, the researchers never once saw a student actually move text around, despite the ease with which it can be done. In fact, students simply ignored suggestions from the teacher that involved restructuring their work. This study offers evidence of the critical role that the teacher must play. According to the researchers, "it is much more likely that student revision will be affected by such factors as topic choice, ownership (determined often by the teacher's style), audience, purpose, and instruction than the mere presence of microcomputers" (p. 41).

The findings of Owston, Murphy, and Wideman (1991) are especially interesting because their study involved a larger number of subjects than most, and all subjects were already experienced with computers, a situation that addressed the computer skills factor. Although the overall findings were favorable to word processing, student revision from draft to final copy did not vary significantly between word processing and handwriting groups. In a later study involving eighth-grade students experienced with computers, Owston, Murphy, and Wideman (1993) found that while papers written using the computer were rated significantly higher in quality, students tended to make "microstructural rather than macrostructural changes to their work" (p. 249). Beals (1998) noted that the software he used was limited to identifying problems in surface structure and that it sometimes identified "errors" that were not errors while failing to identify legitimate problems. Clearly, the teacher is still an important component in student editing and revision.

Anyone seriously interested in exploring the revision practices of writers should read Lindgren and Sullivan's 2002 article about a method of visualizing revisions called LS Graph. The method uses two special software programs that record all keystrokes made by the writer. The keystrokes are then analyzed to determine just what the writer actually did. The potential for better research into revision strategies and activities is clear.

Effects on Attitudes

The favorable impact of word processing on writers' attitudes is much clearer. Roblyer (2003) concluded that word processing seems to improve both the writing itself and attitudes toward writing, *provided* students actually have time to learn to use their word processor well within a context of good writing instruction. Earlier studies showing improved attitudes include Roblyer (1988), Schramm (1989), Montague (1990), Owston, Murphy, and Wideman (1991), Weisberg (1992), and Synder (1993).

Assessment of Written Work

Unless all writing is done on computers, teachers receive a mixture of handwritten and word processed assignments. This leads to the question of whether assessment of the same assignment is uniform, despite the obvious differences in appearance. Roblyer (1997) reported that word processed compositions tended to receive lower grades, much to her surprise. However, Harrington, Shermis, and Rollins (2000) found no significant differences when college English placement essays were handwritten, word processed, or handwritten but transcribed and word processed before grading. Manalo and Wolfe (2000) analyzed the scores of over 150,000 takers of the Test of English as a Foreign Language (TOEFL) exam after a direct writing assignment was added. Takers had the option to handwrite or word process their essays. Results showed that, when actual English proficiency was controlled for, handwritten essays were graded higher by one-third standard deviation. The researchers attribute the difference to the "double translation" of using a word processor—the language and the technology.

Word Processing and Students with Learning Disabilities

Technology appears to have great potential for helping students with various disabilities, yet researchers who have focused on LD students have produced no consistent findings. Quenneville's (2001) review of research on the impact of word processing on the writing of students with learning disabilities found mixed results. However, she concluded that technologies such as word processing with appropriate adaptations can "ease frustration, increase motivation, foster a sense of peer acceptance, and improve productivity in the classroom and at home . . . (but t)he potential of assistive technology for students has not been realized."

Using technology may increase participation and a greater sense of belonging in general education classrooms for students with LD (Bryant & Bryant, 1998). For instance, using a word processor could enable a student to function as the recorder in a collaborative activity when that individual's disabilities might preclude doing so by handwriting.

Bahr, Nelson, and VanMeter (1996) studied fourth- through eighth-grade students with LD whose task was to write a story. Some students used software with which they first created a graphic scene as a stimulus and then wrote about it, whereas others used text-only software. The students using the graphics approach spent more time on the graphics and less time actually writing than students who planned their writing using just text. The researchers concluded that teachers must manage the writing process carefully to assure that efforts focus on the correct aspects of the task.

Langone et al. (1994–1995), working with a small group of elementary school students with learning disabilities, found that all of the students' story lengths actually decreased under the computer-based conditions. The likely explanation is the added time the students needed to cope with the technology itself.

Teaching/Learning Requirements

Some issues raised by research concern the teaching and learning environment. In her master's thesis, Jackowski-Bartol (2001) reported some intriguing findings. First, she found that students had problems with the hand–thought coordination that enables efficient composing at the computer. In turn, computer composition time was substantially greater than traditional composition time. There is clearly need for further research, particularly into the cognitive differences between traditional composition and writing directly on the computer. New approaches to learning to compose appear to be needed. This study also supports the importance of solid keyboarding skills when word processors are the composition tool.

Goldfine (2001) outlines many potential negative effects of word processing on such key writing skills as planning, organizing, revising, and finding and fixing errors. Yet she acknowledges that the answer is to address the problems, not to avoid word processing. To enhance the potential of word processing to develop the higher-order thinking skills essential to excellent writing, she offers many suggestions for counteracting the negative impacts.

Reed (1990) studied English education undergraduate majors in an 11-week course focused on computers and writing. Some had no computer experience, others had prior word processing experience, and a third group had both word processing and programming experience. On a pretest, students were asked to list potential uses of computers. On the posttest, the list of uses increased by 52 percent and the focus of the uses shifted from isolated skills development or drill and practice to uses that support the writing process. Attention shifted from these education students themselves to concerns about their future students, and ideas for "doing things better" began to surface. "The prospective teachers evidently began to view the computer as a system participant that could provide their prospective student writers with a framework for breaking a writing task into prewriting, writing, and revising stages" (p. 21). In other words, you must learn to use a word processor well yourself before you will see its instructional value. This is your first task as a teacher.

Grejda and Hannafin (1991) concluded that methods of introducing word processing (and computer use in general) are flawed. Competence with the hardware and software is a critical factor, they believe, in obtaining meaningful gains from computer use. "While it is clear that word processing has significant potential to improve young writers' compositions, it is equally clear that methods that optimize both the technological and human aspects of writing have yet to be developed" (p. 100).

Research Conclusions

On the surface, the research evidence fails to support unambiguously the value of word processing and may seem disappointing. Yet virtually anyone who has learned to use a word processor knows intuitively that it is somehow better. Appropriately, Dexter and Watts-Taffe (2000) stress the need to get beyond the mechanics of word processing and move on to critical thinking. It is apparent that, in and of itself, word processing does not improve writing skill. Writers still have to understand the need for and practice the art of editing and revising. Most research studies have paid little or no attention to the role of the teacher in stimulating and demanding the editing and revision that can improve writing. If revision remains a once-over-lightly activity, contrary to the intent of the process approach, there is little reason to expect students to show great benefit from word processing. As Erickson (1992, p. 189) suggested, "students do not possess an innate desire to revise on computers, nor do they have the knowledge to do so." Students need to be taught how to revise on the computer. Supporting fully the process approach with the power of a word processor may be the optimal combination of techniques for improving writing outcomes.

Classroom Applications of Word Processing

NETS NOTES

NETS **S** 1
NETS **S** 3
NETS **S** 4
NETS **T** II-A
NETS **T** II-B
NETS **T** II-D
NETS **T** II-E
NETS **T** III-A
NETS **T** III-B
NETS **T** III-C
NETS **T** V-B
NETS **T** V-C
NETS **T** V-D

The following applications, including many experiences and ideas of classroom teachers, represent but a few possible uses of a word processor for school-age students. The creative mind of the teacher and the desire to apply word processing techniques in the classroom will increase and immeasurably enhance this necessarily limited list of possible activities.

Teaching Word Processing

Few teachers actually receive training in how to teach word processing, even the technology specialists in most schools. However, there are fine resources expressly for teaching specific word processors, some of which are listed in the extended chapter bibliography on the companion website. Space permits only a few general suggestions here. If at all possible, demonstrate your points to your students by using a projector connected to your computer before they attempt to perform the same operations.

How Much to Teach

Most word processors have such a wealth of features that even experienced users may not know or use them all. When working with any but the simplest word processors, teach only the really fundamental things initially, such as loading and saving files, rudimentary editing, and printing. Don't overwhelm your students; they'll learn more as needed.

Cursor Movement

Maneuvering within a document is a critical function. Most word processors have several different ways to move the cursor to a desired location: by clicking the mouse, using the cursor movement (arrow) keys on the keyboard, using function keys, and so forth. Be certain that students master the available techniques for moving about a document quickly, such as how to jump to the end or beginning, rather than relying entirely on the cursor keys or scroll bars, which are relatively slow.

Editing

To develop student proficiency in editing with a word processor, prepare sample documents and give them to students electronically. Provide final printouts, as well as drafts, to read for content and organization. Leave wide margins for hand editing. This technique can be used effectively to stress the finalizing aspects of writing, rather than the initial creating, as well as the mechanics of editing. It's a good way to approach word selection and overuse of subject-verb word order, especially when the same pronoun begins each sentence, as is often the case in student writing.

Revising

The mechanical aspect of effective revision is the ability to move blocks of text around within a document. A "scrambled" file on disk, with accompanying printout and, typically, a correct copy, can provide basic practice in moving blocks. Beaver (1992) suggested using familiar course content that has a definite sequence. Correcting the order will also reinforce the content while teaching word processing.

Locating Words in a Document

A word processor can be used as a crude data storage system. This offers a perfect excuse for mastering the search or find function, which can locate a particular piece of information in the file. Students might enter their own personal list of bothersome spelling words, adding and deleting as their spelling improves and new lessons are begun. Name and address files, lists of belongings, and catalogs of collections all offer potential subjects for this use of a word processor.

Students also can use their word processor as a tool for elementary analysis of writing. Provide a document on disk and guide student analysis with questions. How often does the word *honor* appear in a political speech? In what contexts? How often does the pronoun *I* appear in student writing? How does the author use some specific word?

Word Processing and Website Creation

Bailey and Blythe (1998) presented a detailed process and guidelines for creating quality educational websites. They make a strong argument that educational websites, as distinct from many other types, rest on concepts of information literacy. To create such a site, one must first outline the content to be presented, a process for which a word processor is ideal. In addition, many word processors can save documents in web (HTML) format, which makes it quite easy for students and teachers to place class projects on websites.

Adding to what you learned in the previous chapters, although we believe there are advantages to a dedicated web page editor such as *Composer*, it is quite possible to create web pages using *Word*, by far the most common word processor today. Technically, the process is very simple. Create your document, that is, your web page, so that it looks as you want it to. Then click File in the menu bar, then Save as. In the drop-down box for file type, choose web page (Figure 5.9). The trick is that you must learn the *Word* techniques for inserting graphics and other multimedia as well as links to create even a minimal web page. These are not overly difficult but still somewhat more troublesome than the more obvious methods in most web editors. At least that is what teachers have

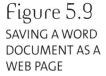

Figure 5.9
SAVING A WORD
DOCUMENT AS A
WEB PAGE

told us based on their course experiences learning to develop web pages both ways. There are also additional issues concerning what you must upload to the server to publish your page when you create one using *Word*. Resources that explain these processes are not common, but you can find guidance on the companion website.

Internet Applications

Word processing can be linked easily to many applications of the Internet. Students can share their opinions on world matters at UNICEF's Voices of Youth at <www.unicef.org/voy/meeting/rig/righome.html>, enjoy words and their fascinating histories at <www.wordfocus.com>, or obtain guidance on all stages of writing from discovering what to write (prewriting stage) to documenting their sources at Paradigm Online Writing Assistance <www.powa.org>. The latter has received many web awards as an excellent site.

How could you use the news as writing prompts? The NY Times Learning Network <www.nytimes.com/learning> offers a daily feature article with classroom activities, historical events that occurred on that day, a crossword puzzle, and a news quiz. The site is worth a daily visit. To improve student writing, Merriam Webster offers an online dictionary and thesaurus at <www.m-w.com>. Keypals provide children of various age groups the opportunity to email penpals, as discussed in Chapter 4. It might be interesting to start from the site of an Australian publisher <www.reedbooks.com.au/keypals>.

Here are some other Internet resources worth exploring, though space does not permit us to describe them.

- Jan Brett's Homepage (a top-rated site by a famous children's author) <www.janbrett.com>
- Purdue's On-line Writing Lab <owl.english.purdue.edu>

- The Children's Literature Web Guide <www.acs.ucalgary.ca/~dkbrown/index.html>
- Gander Academy's Language Arts Page (a Canadian site) <www.stemnet.nf.ca/CITE/language.htm>
- KidPub <www.kidpub.org/kidpub>

All links in this book are live and updated on the companion website, of course.

Prewriting

Getting started is often the most difficult part of writing (as we know only too well from writing this book!). The problem can be especially acute for beginning writers. Although not word processing software, visualization software such as *Kidspiration* (Figure 5.10) and its more familiar sibling *Inspiration* can be great tools for helping students at the prewriting stage. Visual "maps" of your ideas can serve much the same purpose as outlining but are far more concrete. We leave fuller treatment of this software for Chapter 9, where you will meet a whole range of special software products. If you can't wait to know more, skip on ahead!

Digital Plagiarism

In the previous chapters we alerted you to increasing concerns over often unintentional plagiarism stemming from research on the Internet. The best answer to the problem is, of course, education! Krauthamer (2001) offers guidance to writers on how to

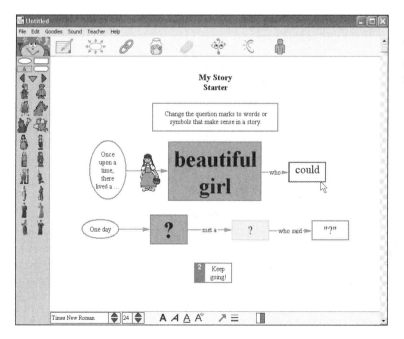

Figure 5.10

Visual mapping software can provide prewriting support.

effectively use the Web for research and then use the results in their writing without plagiarizing. McCullen (2002) also deals with digital plagiarism and how to teach students about it. It is well worth reading and is available online at <www.techlearning.com/db_area/archives/TL/2002/04/viewpoint.html>.

Topic Identification

A major problem for writers is topic selection. Teacher-assigned topics often lack relevance and interest; it is better to help the student identify topics of personal significance.

At the very beginning of the term, have students prepare a list of possible writing topics. This will require prompting in most cases. Try to provide broad guidelines that afford flexibility. Here are some ideas that you can expand upon and adapt to various grade levels:

People	*The Future*
The person(s) I most admire	Careers I am considering
My most unusual relatives	Places I want to visit
Foods	*Activities*
Foods that I love to eat	Jobs I have to do around the house
Foods that I can't stand	My favorite television show
Foods that I'd like to try	The best book that I've ever read

Interdisciplinary Projects

Sosenke (2000) details a seventh-grade interdisciplinary project called World Tour. Under the scenario that your garage band has hit the big time, you have to define the character of the group and design the itinerary, tasks which require word processing. Many other software tools are also used, and we'll return to this project in other chapters. It illustrates a key concept of taking things that most students are keenly interested in (here, rock music) and building a meaningful learning experience around them using technology. That is precisely the idea of technology integration. See how the project was presented to students in the form of a WebQuest at <www.parktudor.pvt.k12.in.us/WorldTour/WTindex.html>.

Letter Writing

Although traditional letter writing has given way to email, which you explored in Chapter 3, some correspondence needs still require paper letters. Beaver (1992) suggested requesting research materials from organizations such as tourism bureaus or preparing invitations to school events as ideal situations for teaching students letter writing as well as how to merge form letters and database addresses, a process called *mail merge* or *merge print*. Every teacher has potential need for this skill personally to maintain contact with parents.

Prompted Writing

Prompted writing guides the learner's writing with questions and instructions placed in a word processing file by the teacher. The student loads the file, then composes a document by responding to the prompts. Can you envision how a website also might be used to prompt or support student writing?

Extend the idea of prompted writing by having students submit their draft documents only electronically. Insert comments right into the file using the revision feature of software such as Microsoft *Word* (Figure 5.11). Students can then revise the work, removing or hiding the comments before printing.

When students are to choose among alternatives, create the full worksheet as a word processing file. Students then load and edit the file, deleting the incorrect choices. This can be especially good for integrating word processing into many content areas. Here are two examples:

1. The twins' teacher *was/were* happy with *they're/their* science project. (Language Arts)
2. *Chicago/Springfield* is the capitol of *Iowa/Illinois*. (Social Studies)

Group Writing Projects

Computers can increase socialization through collaborative or cooperative writing projects. If you have students routinely proofread one another's work, both the writer and the proofreader will benefit.

Give students a topic and time to brainstorm ideas. Ideally, the students would be in a computer lab, and each would begin to draft a document at the computer. After perhaps 15 minutes, direct students to finish their current sentence, then move to a

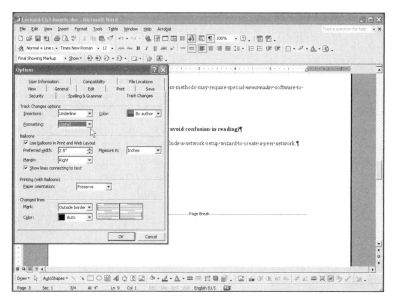

Figure 5.11

Electronic revisions can simplify the editing process.

different computer to read what others have already written and continue the story from there. If you have only one or a few computers, students can still rotate to the computer and continue whatever others have begun. You could also assign parts of a class story for independent development, then load them in sequence into a master file containing the whole story.

A class book based on student research is another good group project. Give each student a specific research assignment to complete, including doing the final write-up on a word processor. Combine all the reports in an appropriate order to create a class reference work.

Word Processing with a Single Classroom Computer

NETS
NOTES

NETS **T** II-D
NETS **T** III-D
NETS **T** III-E

Obviously, word processing is well suited to schools with computer labs that can accommodate many users simultaneously. This does not mean, however, that nothing can be accomplished with only one or a few computers. The concept of rotating learning stations can include the computer.

Ashmus at <www.serve.org/seir-tec/present/onecomptr.html> suggests class magazines, anthologies, and journals as projects that need not require a computer lab. She also provides many links to other resources on teaching with only a few computers.

Although word processing software greatly facilitates editing and revising, both tasks can be completed by hand. You can use a single computer with a projector to display a sample paragraph or document, solicit ideas to improve it, and make the changes as the group observes. This may be more effective than normal paper-based approaches. Handwritten initial drafts are also a way to work around limited numbers of computers.

Weisberg (1992) described in some detail how she used word processing with second graders in a one-computer classroom. Assignments included letters, narratives, and other creative writing. A year-long project involved kids taking a stuffed elephant, named Toby, home for the night or weekend, then writing about the experience on the next school day. The computer was in use all day in Weisberg's class, as students left the regular instruction to take their turns. Individual projects required from six days to one month to complete. Weisberg had been reluctant to try such projects with her class, but she reported that it was exciting for everyone and very productive. Students preferred using the computer, and their writing became more "lucid, creative, and interesting" (p. 28).

For specific lesson ideas that can be done with one or just a few classroom computers, check out the NASA Athena Project's one-computer ideas <http://vathena.arc.nasa.gov/project/teacher/manage/managem1.html> and four computer projects <http://vathena.arc.nasa.gov/project/teacher/manage/managem2.html>.

Writing across the Curriculum

Writing skills are critical to success in life for most individuals. These skills develop slowly and must be nurtured constantly. To teach writing skills in only one curriculum area is to deny their importance. An example of using word processing across curriculum areas begins in math. Brown (1993) had seventh-grade students write arithmetic word problems using a word processor. The problems were then given to the English teacher, who assisted students with editing and revision. Questions were then compiled in book format and distributed to other schools for use.

Once students begin to write with a word processor, they ideally should use it for all writing assignments. This will contribute to maintenance of keyboarding skills, as well as extend the potential benefits of electronic composing to all their writing.

Publishing Your Writing

Now that you have explored the most typical uses of word processing, let's turn to a more advanced application, namely, more formal "publishing" of your written materials. *Publishing* is our term for any processing of written materials that goes beyond the basics to approach the sophisticated appearance of commercially printed products. Think about the visual differences between, say, a term paper you have written and a brochure for a new car or a vacation package. Does your term paper look much different from how a typewritten paper would look? What is different in the layout of this very textbook? As you will see, these differences, however important, still rest on the fundamentals of word processing as you know it. We'll look at the origins of publishing on a computer, the concepts that distinguish publishing from simple word processing, briefly explore the requirements for effective publishing, and finally consider common classroom publishing applications.

NETS NOTES
NETS **S** 1
NETS **S** 4
NETS **T** I-A
NETS **T** I-B
NETS **T** III-A
NETS **T** III-B
NETS **T** III-C
NETS **T** V-C
NETS **T** V-D

Background of Publishing

When word processing was still a new capability of computers, the software itself was relatively simple and unsophisticated. Early word processors lacked many of the tools we now take for granted, such as spellchecking, which created an aftermarket for separate products. Eventually they became integral functions of the word processor itself, resulting in the far more powerful tools we have today.

In those early days, however, the power of the computer was clear, and its potential to take over some of the functions of professional printers led to the development of complex, powerful, costly products called *desktop publishing* software. Its most fundamental capability is *precise* control over placement of each element on each page—text, images, charts, whatever. Pioneering products such as *PageMaker* and *Quark XPress* were not necessarily well suited to the initial writing but rather enabled the final compilation of a wide range of elements, created by and imported from many different programs, into one sophisticated document. They allowed users to do electronically what previously had required physical cut-and-paste techniques. The result was a revolution in businesses such as newspapers and magazines. Furthermore, potentially anyone could be a "publisher." We no longer carefully distinguish *desktop publishing* from *publishing* and use the terms interchangeably, apart from the software used to create any given product.

In all computer applications there is a trade-off between capabilities and complexity, and publishing is no exception. Professional desktop publishing software remains expensive and complex, time consuming to learn much less master. It is primarily a tool of the specialist, someone who will work with the software so regularly and will use so many of its capabilities that the investment in time and money is appropriate. However, unless you are involved with the school newspaper or yearbook, that person probably is not you.

Just as word processors slowly integrated such once-separate tools as spelling and grammar checkers, they have also grown in layout control and sophistication until they now can meet most of our needs as educators without further purchases. The only requirement is the time and effort to learn to use the more powerful features of the software you already know and use. And if that really isn't quite enough for your purpose, there are now products such as Microsoft *Publisher* that are more powerful than a word processor but not as complex or as costly as, say, *PageMaker.*

Concepts of Publishing

The basic concepts of publishing are control over layout, type, and graphics and the ability to add design enhancements.

Layout Control

Precise layout control over every element of every page of a finished document sums up the fundamental concepts of publishing. No doubt you know how to set margins and tabs in a document, and perhaps you have used a two-column layout, but brochures and newspapers may have three or more columns with a full-width "headline" across two or more columns of text. Graphics may appear anywhere within the layout and text may flow around them. One page may use two vertical columns; the next could be a horizontal table with five columns, and then back to two vertical columns. Such a layout is a distinguishing mark of "published" documents versus merely word processed material. *Frames* of varying shapes and sizes may serve as containers for disparate page elements, as shown in Figure 5.12. A word processor is likely to be less flexible in layout control than a desktop publishing program.

Type Control

Prior to word processing, control over type, that is, the form of the characters within a document, was a highly visible difference between professionally published and typewritten materials. Today nearly all computer applications, including word processing and desktop publishing, can draw on a large choice of *fonts* to produce the desired appearance, a font being the design of a set of characters <www.webopedia.com/TERM/f/font.html> (Webopedia, 2003). Type has three main characteristics.

The first is *typeface*, or the actual shape of the letters that comprise the character set. Typefaces may be *serif* or *sans serif*. Serif typefaces have small squiggles called serifs at the ends of the lines of each character. Main body text typically uses a serif font, where the primary concern is easy readability. Examples of serif typefaces are `Courier` and Times Roman. Sans serif typefaces have a plainer appearance. Their lines are straight at the ends; they have no serifs. Headings and other elements that show emphasis may use a sans serif font such as **Helvetica** or Arial.

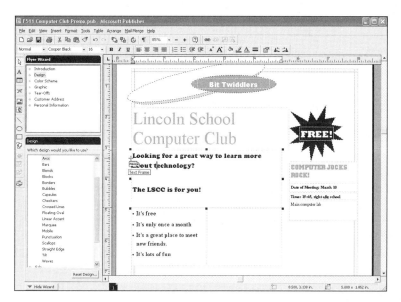

Figure 5.12
PAGE LAYOUT SETUP BASED ON FRAMES

The second characteristic of type is the actual size of the typeface. Height is measured in *points*, a point being about $1/72$ of an inch, whereas width is called *pitch*, meaning the number of characters that fit in 1 inch of line space. A character in any typeface at 12 points is approximately $1/6$ of an inch high when printed. Smaller point sizes (down to about 6 points) are used for special purposes such as footnotes and the "fine print" in insurance policies, whereas larger point sizes up through 72 or even greater can be used for headings and titles. Pitch is meaningful only when all characters are the same width, which is increasingly rare. Most fonts today are proportional, meaning an M is wider than an I, and pitch loses its meaning.

The third type characteristic is *style*, variations created in the appearance of a character while keeping the same form and size of the typeface. Examples of different styles are boldface, italic, and bold italic type. Different styles of the same typeface may be used sparingly for emphasis within a document.

Initially the fonts available on computers were all *bitmaps*, meaning an actual image (called a bitmap) of each size and type of character existed. If you wanted to use, say, 24 point and did not have that size available, you either could not use it at all, or the computer enlarged the nearest size, creating a very jagged appearance. Now nearly all fonts use *scalable* technology, pioneered by Adobe as Adobe *PostScript* and further popularized by *TrueType*. Instead of storing bitmaps, scalable fonts store a set of instructions for drawing the typeface, from which the computer can then render the size required. This approach requires only one file for each typeface and yet provides a virtually unlimited range of sizes that always look smooth and professional when printed.

Graphics Control
Graphics control is the ability of publishing software to import various types of graphics into a document and position them exactly on the final page. The graphics category

includes charts, graphs, and tables as well as clip art, illustrations, and photos. A desktop publishing program may import these from other applications, whereas more advanced word processors allow you to create most of them internally or you can import them as well. You'll learn much more about graphics in a later chapter devoted to that topic. For now, you only need to understand that a desktop publishing package typically offers more precise control over graphics than a word processor.

Design Enhancements

A few additional features tend to distinguish published from word processed material. *Visual cues* help the reader distinguish elements of a document quickly and easily. Publishing software enables you to place lines anywhere in the document, horizontally or vertically, to identify areas, and to enhance the visual appearance of the document. You also can place boxes or borders around page elements including frames containing different forms of data to highlight selected parts of the document and to decrease the potential for confusion when reading a complex document. Within a frame, you might shade the background behind the text, thereby creating an attractive, distinguishing effect.

Marginalia are those elements of a publication that appear in the margins of a page, such as page numbers or perhaps definitions. Page-numbering schemes often vary according to common practice. Roman numerals frequently signify the preliminary pages of a book, whereas Arabic numerals appear throughout the main text. The first page of a section often displays no page number, whereas the page number appears bottom left on even-numbered pages and bottom right on odd-numbered pages. Odd and even page margins (facing pages) may differ to accommodate binding needs. The result is, again, a more professional-looking finished product.

Special effects may include beginning a paragraph with a *drop cap*, an oversized capital letter with a special drop effect. Other text manipulations are also possible, such as fitting text to a specified shape, perhaps a pennant or oval. Effects are possible in most software today, so there is little difference between a word processor and desktop publishing.

Word Processing or Desktop Publishing?

In the previous sections we tried to highlight key elements of publishing as they appear in printed material. We also noted that the issue is mostly one of precision in control over placement on the page. Dedicated desktop publishing software generally has the advantage, but today's best word processors are in fact capable of most of the same things, provided you take time to learn how to do them. Since you surely have access to a word processor but may not have a desktop publisher available, we urge you to explore these more advanced capabilities of your existing software. In many cases there is much help available to you in the form of word processor *templates*, premade designs to enable you to achieve a polished result with minimal effort. Figure 5.13 illustrates the brochure template in MS *Word*, whereas Figure 5.14 shows the vast array of templates offered on the Microsoft website. If your needs exceed the capabilities of a word processor, then turn to more powerful and complex desktop publishing software.

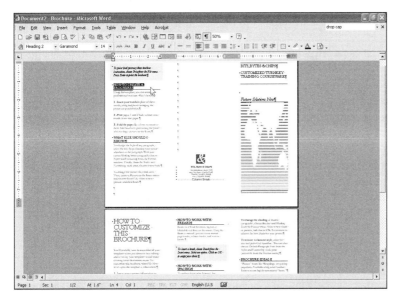

Figure 5.13
Brochure template includes directions for use.

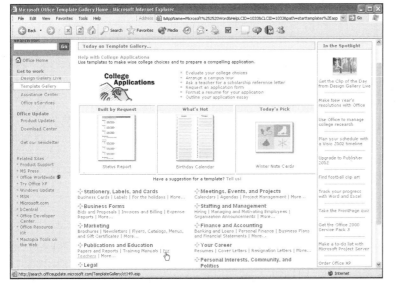

Figure 5.14
Numerous templates are available free on the Web.

Design for Publishing

Effective publishing depends on the creator having basic graphic design skills, that is, the fundamentals of how to produce visually appealing documents. Publishing software, including word processors, will give you the tools to produce such a document, but good design is far from automatic. What type of document will best meet your needs? How can you most effectively arrange the document's elements on its pages? What typeface(s), styles, and sizes are best? How many and what types of illustrations do you need? Should you use photos?

Deciding such issues requires knowledge of good graphic design. All too often, published documents show the technical excellence that the software assures, but they are neither visually appealing nor effective communicators because of poor design. Just as a word processor does not give you writing skills, neither does publishing guarantee good design. To get the most out of desktop publishing, you must not only learn how the software works but also what to do with it. This can be fun and exciting, too, but it takes time and effort.

The chapter reference list includes several good references on graphic design. We can highlight only a few very basic points, which may guide you away from some of the most common errors. Many of these points are equally valid for your next term paper!

- Use a serif typeface for body text; use sans-serif for titles and headings.
- Guide the reader with headings.
- Use type styles and size changes sparingly to maximize their effect.
- Do not use too many typefaces on a page.
- Select easy-to-read typefaces. Avoid ornate, hard-to-read fonts:
  - *ABCD*
  - **ABCD**
  - ABCD
- Don't crowd! White (empty) space is a vital element of good design.
- Consider multiple columns. Short lines can be easier to read.
- Emphasize organization with lines and boxes.
- Think visually! Become familiar with your clip art resources.
- Place captions with illustrations.

Applications of Publishing

To conclude consideration of publishing as a "more advanced" form of text processing, let's explore some common school applications, both for you as the teacher and for your students.

Many forms of single-page documents can benefit from the extra touches that identify desktop published materials. Handouts for your classes, posters for coming events, calendars for a week's or month's activities—the list is limited only by your own imagination.

Brochures and newsletters are among the simpler multipage documents that will look much more professional if given the extra touches of publishing. Students could create travel brochures in social studies, perhaps using commercial ones from a travel agent as a starting point or source of maps, illustrations, and so on. Any class could design and construct their own brochures to explain a unit of instruction (e.g., mammals) or to provide a summary of topics in the course. Students would be reviewing the class content and focusing their thinking as they decide what needs to go into such documents. Your review of their brochures could reveal key misconceptions that you need to address.

School newsletters and newspapers typically cover the entire school or district. However, you could limit coverage to your one grade or class to make an interesting project that involves more students. This is clearly linked to the language arts curriculum, but how could you integrate other parts of the curriculum? One way is to have science reporters, current events columnists, entertainment reviewers, and so on. The possibilities are endless. Think of what fun it would be for the class to plan, write, design, construct, and publish their class news for other students and parents. Or how about creating a newspaper for some noteworthy date in history, a "you were there" project from today's perspective?

Over time, many teachers develop a large number of materials unique to their own way of teaching. These may evolve into manuals, booklets, or even books, which you can prepare using your publishing skills. Who knows? You might even find a market for your materials! As a cross-curricular project, your class could produce instructional materials for use by students the following year, for makeup or review (including their own as they prepare the material), or perhaps for younger students. Consider both textbook-like manuals and student workbooks. This can be an outstanding learning experience for students, because it takes a clear understanding of the material to teach it to someone else. The fun of producing the final product may well entice students into deeper engagement with the subject matter.

Finally, desktop publishing enables you and your students to produce booklets and books. Any class could write their own stories and publish them for other students and classes, perhaps even to sell as fund-raisers. Student literary magazines are now widely produced in-house. Publish outstanding student work for use in other classes. Other ideas include writing oral histories collected from family members or even senior citizens in the community and then creating a booklet from them. How about a guide to the local region and its sights? Or a travel volume based on student experiences on family trips? Travel needn't be to exotic destinations to make a great project and interesting reading. Preparing a booklet or book is an exciting and beneficial activity for the students as well as for the individuals who read them.

SUMMARY

Word processing has significantly changed the writing process in the posttypewriter era. It has greatly reduced the tedium of mechanical editing, eliminated retyping of entire documents, and afforded writers complete flexibility to reorganize their thoughts by moving and changing text at the click of a mouse. Revision is no longer a task to dread, but students are not likely to revise on their own. Teachers must demand and guide revision.

Most word processing software provides the same basic functions. Differences occur in such areas as control of fonts, handling of footers and headers, and specific features such as clip art graphics. To further enhance writing, electronic assistance is available for outlining, spelling and grammar proofing, and even vocabulary word selection with a thesaurus.

There are many benefits to writing with a word processor. The quantity and quality of writing may increase, attitudes toward writing may improve, writer's block may disappear, and even reading skills may improve. Few of these improvements, however, will occur effortlessly. Skillful instruction in composition remains essential. Unresolved are such issues as just when word processing and keyboarding should be introduced. There is also much evidence that stimulating students to revise their work, so necessary to improved writing, is a difficult task. Anyone who uses a word processor knows from experience what a marvel it is. How best to assure its potential with students is not totally clear.

This chapter concluded with publishing, a more advanced application of text management characterized by precise control over any imaginable placement of document elements (text, graphs, illustrations, even photos) on a page. Special software called desktop publishing software has existed since the early days of less sophisticated word processing software. However, today's word processors likely can meet the needs of most educators for documents that closely resemble the work of a professional printer. The key features are present in a typical word processor, but most users have not learned of them or how to use them. They include control over layout, type, and graphics insertions as well as the ability to include visual cues (such as boxed areas) and marginalia (margin notes, flexible page numbering, etc.). Many schools now publish materials in-house that until recently had to be produced commercially. Still more exciting are those publications that were never before feasible, especially student productions. Publishing for an audience lends meaning to writing assignments that is hard to achieve otherwise. You will be well served by taking time to explore more fully the features of your word processor that can make you into your very own print shop.

chapter 5
activities

1. Using whatever word processor you have, write a letter to its publisher explaining what you like and dislike about the program.

2. Investigate the outline feature of your word processor. It probably requires special attention to formatting the headers or elements that constitute the levels of the outline. Take an existing document file that you have created and modify it so that you can view, expand, and collapse the levels in outline view.

3. For your next written assignment in any course, begin your writing by preparing an out-

line only in your word processor. Begin with the main points or headers (probably less than six). Then fill in the next level of points and perhaps a third level. Expand the outline fully and then add the actual text for each point.

4. Determine whether your word processor has the spell check and grammar check turned on as the default. If not, turn them on. Now select a document that you have prepared and direct your word processor to do a full spell and grammar check of the document. What did this show you about your writing?

5. Load an existing document into your word processor and quickly scan it to see if you tend

to use some specific words repeatedly. Select one of these words (or any word if you truly don't see "overuse" in your writing) and use the electronic thesaurus to find alternatives. Replace your starting word with alternatives in several places and then reread the document to see if you like it better.

6. Here is a definition of the term *word processor*: "a program for writing and editing." Notice that it is brief—too brief. Using your word processor, add to the definition to make it more meaningful.

7. How can word processing benefit you as a teacher? List several applications for which you might use word processing in your daily work.

8. Investigate the keyboarding issue as well as available keyboarding/typing instructional software. State and defend a position on when to teach keyboarding skills, who should do so, and at what grade level children should learn to keyboard and use a word processor.

9. Develop a lesson plan that requires students to use word processing in your area(s) of the curriculum.

10. Write a position paper on the role of word processing in the curriculum. Be sure to address several different content areas.

11. Outline a research project to investigate some aspect of word processing's effect on writing skills.

12. Select at least two classroom applications from among those discussed and develop lesson plans that implement these applications.

13. Investigate the templates provided in your word processing software. Examine each to get a sense of what help it actually provides to lay out that kind of document. Assess how easy it would be to use each template.

14. Explore the publishing templates available on the Web. Download any that appear to be useful to you and learn to use them.

15. Using a template, if available, create a newsletter in two-column format to bring your family up-to-date on your activities. Illustrate it with appropriate clip art.

16. Create a flyer, poster, or announcement for a class event.

17. Develop an educationally oriented brochure, perhaps for a local public service agency.

18. Prepare a class newsletter/newspaper based on interviews with classmates.

19. Produce a short classroom manual on some technology equipment that you have.

20. Plan a lesson or activity that incorporates text publishing into your curriculum area.

Companion Website

Visit the companion website at <www.ablongman.com/lockard6e> for more information about the topics discussed in this chapter.

References

Anderson, J. "Web Publishing in Non-Roman Scripts: Effects on the Writing Process." *Language and Education*, 2001, *15*(4), pp. 229–249.

Bahr, C. M., Nelson, N. W., and VanMeter, A. M. "The Effects of Text-Based and Graphics-Based Software Tools on Planning and Organizing of Stories." *Journal of Learning Disabilities*, 1996, *29*, pp. 355–370.

Bailey, G. D., and Blythe, A. "Outlining, Diagramming, and Story Boarding: How to Create Great Educational Websites." *Learning and Leading with Technology*, May 1998, *25*(8), pp. 6–11.

Beals, T. J. "Between Teachers and Computers: Does Text-checking Software Really Improve Student Writing?" *English Journal*, 1998, *87*(1), pp. 67–72.

Beaver, J. F. "Using Computer Power to Improve Your Teaching." *The Computing Teacher*, February 1992, *19*(5), pp. 5–9.

Bermann, M., and Jerome, M. "Assistive Technologies for Students with Mild Disabilities: Update 2002." *ERIC Digest*. (ERIC Document ED 463 595).

Brown, N. M. "Writing Mathematics." *Arithmetic Teacher*, September 1993, *4*(1), pp. 20–21.

Bryant, D., and Bryant, B. "Using Assistive Technology Adaptations to Include Students with Learning Disabilities in Cooperative Learning Activities." *Journal of Learning Disabilities*, 1998, *31*, pp. 41–54.

Cochran-Smith, M. "Word Processing and Writing in Elementary Classrooms: A Critical Review of the Literature." *Review of Educational Research*, 1991, *61*, pp. 107–155.

Dexter, S. L., and Watts-Taffe, S. M. "Processing Ideas: Move Beyond Word Processing into Critical Thinking." *Learning and Leading with Technology*, March 2000, *27*(6), pp. 22–27.

Dudley-Marling, C., and Oppenheimer, J. "The Introduction of Word Processing into a Grade 7/8 Writing Program." *Journal of Research on Computing in Education*, Fall 1990, *23*(1), pp. 28–44.

Erickson, B. J. "A Synthesis of Computer-Supported Composition, Revision, and Quality." *Journal of Research on Computing in Education*, Winter 1992, *25*(2), pp. 172–186.

Fletcher, D. C., "Second Graders Decide When to Use Electronic Editing Tools." *Information Technology in Childhood Education Annual*, 2001, pp. 155–74.

Godsey, S. B. "The Effects of Using Microsoft Word on Journal Word Counts in the High School English Classroom." Unpublished Master's Action Research Project, Johnson Bible College (TN), 2000. (ERIC Document ED 441 254).

Goldfine, R. "Making Word Processing More Effective in the Composition Classroom." *Teaching English in the Two-Year College*, March 2001, *28*(3), pp. 307–315.

Grejda, G. F., and Hannafin, M. J. "The Influence of Word Processing on the Revisions of Fifth Graders." *Computers in the Schools*, 1991, *8*(4), pp. 89–102.

Harrington, S., Shermis, M. D., and Rollins, A. L. "The Influence of Word Processing on English Placement Test Results." *Computers and Composition*, 2000, *17*(2), pp. 197–210.

Hunter, W. J., and Begoray, J. "A Framework for Writing Process Activities." *The Writing Notebook*, January/February 1990, *7*(3), pp. 40–42.

Jackowski-Bartol, T. "The Impact of Word Processing on Middle School Students." Unpublished master's thesis, Chestnut Hill College (PA), 2001. ERIC Document ED 453 825.

Jones, I. "The Effects of a Word Processor on the Written Composition of Second-Grade Pupils." *Computers in the Schools*, 1994, *11*(2), pp. 43–54.

Krauthamer, H. "Electronic Notes." *Teaching English in the Two-Year College*, March 2001, *28*(3), pp. 302–306.

Langone, J., Willis, C., Malone, M., Clees, T., and Koorland, M. "Effects of Computer-Based Word Processing Versus Paper/Pencil Activities on the Paragraph Construction of Elementary Students with Learning Disabilities." *Journal of Research on Computing in Education*, Winter 1994–1995, *27*(2), pp. 171–183.

Lever-Duffy, J., McDonald, J. B., and Mizell, A. P. *Teaching and Learning with Technology*. Boston: Allyn & Bacon, 2003.

Lindren, E., and Sullivan, K. P. H. "The LS Graph: A Methodology for Visualizing Writing Revision."

Language Learning, September 2002, *52*(3), pp. 565–595.

Li, J., and Cumming, A. "Word Processing and Second Language Writing: A Longitudinal Case Study." *International Journal of English Studies, 2001, 1*(2), pp. 127–152.

Manalo, J. R., and Wolfe, E. W. "A Comparison of Word-Processed and Handwritten Essays Written for the Test of English as a Foreign Language." Paper presented at the Annual Meeting of the American Educational Research Association, New Orleans, April 24–28, 2000.

Martin, R. "How Teachers Can Use Grammar to Help Young Writers." Paper presented at the Joint National Conference of the Australian Association for the Teaching of English and the Australian Literacy Educators' Association (Hobart, Tasmania Australia, July 12–15, 2001). (ERIC Document ED 455 532).

McCullen, C. "Prevent Digital Plagiarism." *Technology & Learning*, April 2002, *22*(9), p. 8.

Montague, M. "Computers and Writing Process Instruction." *Computers in the Schools*, 1990, *7*(3), pp. 5–20.

Mumtaz, S. "Children's Enjoyment and Perception of Computer Use in the Home and the School." *Computers & Education*, May 2001, *36*(4), pp. 347–362.

Nichols, L. M. "Pencil and Paper Versus Word Processing: A Comparative Study of Creating Writing in the Elementary School." *Journal of Research on Computing in Education*, Winter 1996, *29*(2), pp. 159–166.

Owston R. D., Murphy, S., and Wideman, H. H. "On and Off Computer Writing of Eighth Grade Students Experienced in Word Processing." *Computers in the Schools*, 1991, *8*(4), pp. 67–87.

Owston, R. D., Murphy, S. and Wideman, H. H. "The Effects of Word Processing on Students' Writing and Revision Strategies." *Research in the Teaching of English*, October 1993, *23*(3), pp. 249–276.

Owston, R. D. and Wideman, H. H. "Word Processors and Children's Writing in a High-Computer-Access Setting." *Journal of Research on Computing in Education*, Winter 1997, *30*(2), pp. 202–220.

Padgett, A. L. "Journal Writing in the Elementary School: Word Processor vs. Paper and Pencil." Unpublished Master's Research Paper, Johnson Bible College (TN), 2000. (ERIC Document ED 441 255).

Quenneville, J. "Tech Tools for Students with Learning Disabilities: Infusion into Inclusive Classrooms." *Preventing School Failure*, Summer 2001, *45*(4), pp. 167–170.

Reed, W. M. "The Effect of Computer-and-Writing Instruction on Prospective English Teachers' Attitudes Toward and Perceived Uses of Computers in Writing Instruction." *Journal of Research on Computing in Education*, Fall 1990, *23*(1), pp. 3–27.

Roblyer, M. D. "Technology and the Oops! Effect: Finding a Bias Against Word Processing." *Learning and Leading with Technology*, April 1997, *24*(7), pp. 14–16.

Roblyer, M. D. "The Effectiveness of Microcomputers in Education: A Review of the Research from 1980–1987." *T.H.E. Journal*, September 1988, *16*(2), pp. 85–89.

Roblyer, M. D. *Integrating Educational Technology into Teaching*, 3rd ed. Columbus, OH: Merrill Prentice Hall, 2003.

Schramm, R. M. "The Effects of Using Word Processing Equipment in Writing Instruction: A Meta-Analysis." Unpublished doctoral dissertation, Northern Illinois University, 1989.

Snyder, I. "Writing with Word Processors: A Research Overview." *Educational Research*, Spring 1993, *35*(1), pp. 49–68.

Sosenke, F. "World Tours: Planning a Fictitious Rock Band's World Tour." *Learning and Leading with Technology*, February 2000, *27*(5), pp. 32–35.

Vernon, A. "Computerized Grammar Checkers 2000: Capabilities, Limitations, and Pedagogical Possibilities." *Computers and Composition*, 2000, *17*(3), pp. 329–349.

Walters, L. "One Hand Typing and Keyboarding for the Disabled Student." 2000. (ERIC Document ED 448 554).

Webopedia. "Definition of Font." Retrieved January 9, 2003 from <www.webopedia.com/TERM/f/font.html>

Weisberg, L. "Beyond Drill & Practice in a One-Computer Classroom." *The Computing Teacher*, August/September 1992, *20*(1), pp. 27–28.

Databases: *Managing*

Information, Creating Knowledge

OBJECTIVES

After you have completed this chapter, you will be able to:

- Explain why information management has become a serious issue.
- Give several examples of data management tasks relevant to teachers and discuss them in terms of appropriate use of the technology.
- Discuss benefits of electronic data management over manual systems.
- Define the terms *field, record, file,* and *database* and identify each in a structure diagram.
- Explain the differences between a database management system (DBMS) and a filing system.

- List and explain the basic functions of a data manager.
- Assess the significance of student use and creation of databases.
- Define teaching and learning with databases in terms of eight stages.
- State and defend a position on database use in education based on research findings.
- Develop lesson plans that include database applications.

This chapter presents the computer as a highly sophisticated tool for data storage and retrieval. You will consider society's growing problems in information management and ways in which computers are assisting with the task. After examining concepts of electronic data storage, you will learn ways to apply computerized data management in your teaching, especially how students may enhance their learning through databases. In addition, you will consider what research shows about databases and learning.

Challenges of the Information Age

Much of the world has moved beyond the Industrial Age into the Information Age. Information is being created at a rate never before imagined, and the Internet has given us access to much of it. While this is a normal evolution, it has the potential to be a mixed blessing. Let's consider problems caused by the information explosion and changes necessitated or enabled by it.

NETS
NOTES

NETS **S** 1
NETS **S** 2
NETS **T** I-A
NETS **T** I-B
NETS **T** V-C
NETS **T** V-D

The Trouble with Information

Among our human faculties, none is more impressive, or at times more exasperating, than our memories. Everyone has many thousands of individual bits and pieces of information stored away in memory. We manage remarkable tasks of retrieving this information, associating it correctly with other items, and even combining pieces into new relationships. Regardless of whether one understands the neurological aspects of the mind, it is truly amazing.

For all its marvels, the human mind is also quite fallible. Just as we achieve great feats of remembering, we also commit great blunders of forgetting. The written word is clearly important as a means of transferring knowledge and information across time and space, but for us individually and daily, it is also an essential aid for our imperfect memories.

As more and more written information has come into existence, problems of storing and retrieving it have led to all manner of devices—drawers in which to place papers, file folders and cabinets, Rolodex cards and containers, even electronic organizers and palm computers. Today we are swimming in a sea of data, and new industries have sprung up to try to handle it.

However, our advances have been less than perfect. How irritating it is to be able to store that valuable document safely in the file cabinet, only to discover later that the labeling on the file folder has slipped your mind! Have you ever forgotten the name you gave a file on your computer? "I know it's here, Carlita, but I can't seem to put my hands on it just now. I'll call you back when it turns up." There goes another valuable hour spent searching through file cabinet drawers or folders on your hard drive.

The Need for Data Management

Data are the raw ingredients of the Information Age. Examples of "raw" data are words and numbers. Such data generally have limited usefulness until they have been processed in some way that adds meaning to them. Processed data may be termed *information*. For example, the raw data of a national census are just words and numbers, but they become information when someone organizes them into a report or a chart with labels that explain and clarify their meaning. Schools and teachers devote much effort to creating information.

However, in the Information Age, it is inadequate merely to create information. As Naisbitt pointed out over 20 years ago in *Megatrends* (1982, p. 24), "We are drowning in information but starved for knowledge." When we analyze and synthesize information to gain insight or form judgments, that information becomes knowledge. When students dig deeply into a topic and then develop ways to share or use their data, their role changes as well. As Dallas teacher Steve Miller (1998) explained the outcome of a project that included student development of a database: "1. Students *applied* research rather than just *did* research. 2. Students were empowered to build their own learning modalities. 3. I became a true coach rather than simply a giver of information." Miller ended his article with an enthusiastic "I'm a believer!" and we hope you will echo that statement as well. Today's educators must guide students in a quest for knowledge. The computer's ability to manipulate those raw ingredients called data may contribute significantly to attaining this goal.

Let's consider briefly a data management problem that is related to the life of teachers and students. Libraries are among our most important repositories of knowledge. In medieval times, keeping track of the collection was no great intellectual challenge. Today, the library of 1 million or more volumes is relatively common, to say nothing of nonbook materials. The task of finding what you need is hardly trivial. For the librarian, tracking what is in the collection, on loan, on order, lost, strayed, or stolen has become formidable.

Although school and public libraries of all sizes have converted to an electronic database, a comparison to the card catalog still serves to illustrate the advantages of electronic data management. (And if your library still uses a card catalog, the presentation should whet your appetite for the inevitable conversion ahead. If you have never used a card catalog, think of what you missed!) The physical card catalog served as the road map to the collection. For many, even most, purposes it was quite adequate, at least in small libraries. But consider its limitations. Books are cataloged in three ways: by author, title, and subject. This necessitates three different cards for each book, differing primarily in the order in which the information is recorded on each. Typically, the three cards are housed in separate sections of the card catalog. Thus, adding a new book to the collection means preparing three cards, then placing each one in the correct location alphabetically in the correct drawer of the card catalog. Hardly an impossible task for a human, but somewhat inefficient and clearly open to error.

Benefits of Electronic Data Management

Although we describe the benefits of electronic data management using the card catalog as our example, the principles are broadly applicable.

A Single Data Set

From the paper-conservation viewpoint, or simply as a labor-saving aid, the use of a computer to replace the physical card catalog is a natural idea. What may be overlooked are other benefits of computerization. Not only are cards unnecessary, but there is also no need for three versions of the same information. The computer stores only one copy of each book's information and can easily retrieve these data based on user-specified criteria. You need only go to the nearest terminal and enter a request.

More Information
Unlike the card catalog, the computer can print the results of your search, eliminating the need to copy down call numbers by hand, an operation open to error, before going to the stacks. The computer may also tell you whether the book is currently on loan, saving a futile search of the shelves. Many systems also can search for materials in other libraries across the region or nation, a feature not available with physical card catalogs. Such a system encourages and facilitates interlibrary loans.

Greater Manipulation Potential
A librarian can produce reports easily on the status of the collection or items on loan. Need an alphabetical list of all titles in the collection? A modest request for the computer; a nearly impossible task otherwise. A list of all authors? Readily available! A library's one set of data on the collection can be rearranged at will with no disruption of service to patrons. In addition, book orders can be tracked and new acquisitions made available to users much more quickly by transferring on-order data electronically to circulation records.

Easier Access to Data
To stay with our example, there is another, less obvious benefit to a computerized card catalog. When searching for materials manually, certain types of requests require sifting through the available data to find just what you are seeking. For instance, suppose you wanted to find all books by Stephen King that have a copyright date no earlier than 1992. You would go to the author section of the catalog, find the Stephen King entries, and then read each one to determine which ones are of interest. Not impossible, but a needless chore. Computerized data can be retrieved readily based on a combination of criteria, such as "Stephen King" and "1992 or newer."

In a file cabinet, each item is placed in a file folder that has only one label, which is used to determine its place in the proper drawer. Locating the file later depends on your recall of the correct drawer *and* folder label. The ability to do so quickly and accurately is a hallmark of an outstanding secretary in most offices. Yet deciding on that label initially is often difficult, because few materials worth filing fit only one possibility. The computer solves this problem by providing the equivalent of multiple labels per item.

Enhanced Human Capacity
Computerized data storage and retrieval are big business and growing in importance. Starting with the capabilities of the human mind, the computer may be seen as a logical, valuable extension of our native abilities. It is not a replacement for mental ability, but an aid, much as other tools help us in everyday living. Computers are not a crutch, as some contend, but merely the latest in an evolutionary chain of tools stretching back to the first stone ax. The major task for early humans was mastery of the environment.

Some of our largest tasks in the Information Age relate to data management and manipulation. The computer is a key to our ability to transform data into information and knowledge.

Data Management in Education

Educational administrators have used computers to manage their data for years. Applications range from scheduling, budgeting, and grade reporting to attendance records and bus routing. But as a teacher, your concern is with your own more direct data management needs and problems. Some of these are obvious. Most teachers maintain various types of student records, such as grade books, anecdotal information for reports to parents, mandated records on exceptional children, or team data in athletics.

What can you add to the list? Think of what is or could be in your file cabinet or desk drawers. Could a computer perhaps help you manage better? Start to think also of how student learning might be enhanced with databases, a topic that you'll look at in considerable detail later in this chapter.

The Issue of Appropriateness

Just because a computer can do something does not mean it is the best or even a better way of doing it. Many early home computer owners were attracted to the idea of storing recipes on their new gadget, only to realize that it really didn't work well unless they intended to place the computer in the kitchen for use while cooking. Personal mailing lists can be computerized, but there is little gain over an address book, unless the list is long and a printer and blank mailing labels are always at hand. Creating a computer file of phone numbers may sound good, but unless you keep your computer turned on at all times, chances are you can look up what you need in a telephone directory more quickly than you can turn on your computer, load and run the software, enter your request, and obtain the response. These are examples of where human judgment must determine appropriate use of the computer's capabilities. In fact, some of those applications are tailor made for today's handheld electronic organizers called personal digital assistants (PDAs), which you will learn about in Chapter 9.

The Technical Side of Data Management

Before turning to educational data management applications, let's look at the technical aspects of data storage and retrieval. Manual filing systems offer useful analogies.

NETS
NOTES

NETS **S** 1
NETS **S** 3
NETS **S** 5
NETS **S** 6

Data File Concepts

Consider the need to manage all the data pertaining to your students. You would probably store these materials in a filing cabinet drawer. The electronic equivalent is called a *file*. A file is all of the information about some (typically) large class of data. Files have names and are stored by name on your diskette or hard disk.

Would you just toss your student data into a file drawer? Of course not, because that would make retrieval virtually impossible. Instead you organize it in some way, such as putting all the data about a single student into one file folder. The electronic equivalent of that folder is called a *record*. Many student records consist of special paper forms that have been completed with the appropriate personal data. Forms are designed to store various data items that pertain to a specific case, one record. The space for an individual item of data, such as first name or phone number, is called a *field*. A field is the smallest meaningful unit of data in a record. Just as you complete a paper form by filling in blanks with items of data, you also enter data into an electronic record one field at a time. When you look on your disk, you see only file names. The fields and records are stored inside the files.

Figure 6.1 illustrates file concepts, while Figure 6.2 shows one record from a specific data file. Can you identify the file name and individual field names? The actual data entries? You are looking at the data entry "form" view. To add a record, you fill in the blank fields of a new copy of the form. Figure 6.3 shows the file of which the record is a part with entries completed for each field of multiple records. You can also add records and modify data in this "list" view.

Database Concepts

Although the term *database* is often used to mean what we have just called a file, the term refers more properly to a collection of related files. Such databases can become very complex. They are usually created and manipulated using software called a *database management system (DBMS)*.

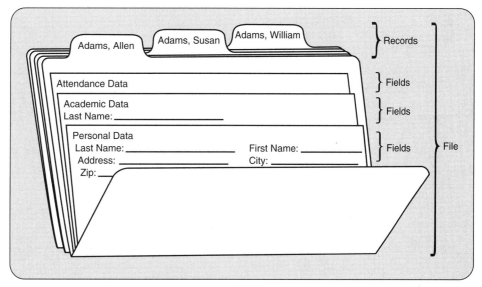

ﬁgure 6.1 STUDENT DATA FILE STRUCTURE

Figure 6.2
A SAMPLE DATABASE
RECORD IN SINGLE
FORM VIEW

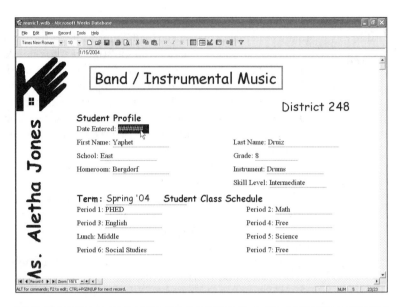

Figure 6.3
STUDENT DATABASE
IN DATA LIST VIEW

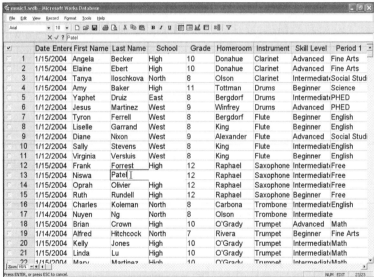

One problem that arises in large applications is *data redundancy.* Consider the central office in a school. Several different files may be needed for each student, such as basic personal data, transcript data, test scores, and so forth. Suppose each were a separate electronic file. How much information would you have to duplicate in each file to be sure that the contents are meaningful and can be correctly identified? Often, the amount is considerable. Such redundancy wastes data entry and updating time as well as storage space.

Relational DBMS software can minimize the redundancy problem. It can link multiple files into a single database or link entire databases together through a common "key" field in the records, for example, student ID number or a product code in business. To retrieve data from any component file, specify the desired record's key field data. District-level applications may require a relational DBMS, but most classroom-level applications involve only individual files and do not require this much power (or complexity).

Data Management Software

Nearly all classroom data management needs are modest enough not to need relational database software; they can use instead much simpler, single-file software, more properly termed a *filing system*. However, we accept common usage and will call these products *data managers* and their files either *databases* or *data files*.

Just as word processing software serves a very general purpose—to manage and manipulate words—products such as Microsoft's *Access* and *Visual FoxPro*, IBM's *Lotus Approach*, and Filemaker Inc's *FileMaker Pro* are also powerful general-purpose data managers. Less powerful (and complex) but highly useful in the classroom is the database component of *AppleWorks* or *Microsoft Works*. The latter products in particular were designed to be simple enough for virtually anyone to use. Your task is to create a specific application to meet your needs. (Spreadsheet software, which you will meet in the next chapter, also supports modest data management tasks.)

Common applications have led producers to create highly specialized data management software for specific purposes. Examples include bibliography managers, electronic grade books, and test construction software. You will meet those tools in Chapter 9.

Data Manager Functions

Regardless of the software you use for data management, certain basic functions are common, just as certain functions are common to word processors. Data are stored and retrieved as complete records, within which you can enter and modify individual data fields. The most basic and essential functions of any data manager are:

1. Create new files
2. Add, change, or delete records and fields
3. Search for specific records
4. Sort (reorder) the records based on the content of one or more fields
5. Print selected records
6. Create reports based on the contents of records that match some criteria

Searching and sorting are the most powerful database functions and are often combined to create reports. Figure 6.4 shows a composite view of accessing these functions from two separate menus. (You would see only one at a time on your computer.) Suppose you want to find the records of all Smiths in the student database. That is a search or *filter* operation. You specify the field to search (e.g., last name), what to look for (e.g., Smith), and your request (e.g., equals, less than, contains, etc.). Most data managers allow

Figure 6.4

DATABASE SEARCH
AND SORT FUNCTIONS
(COMPOSITE IMAGE)

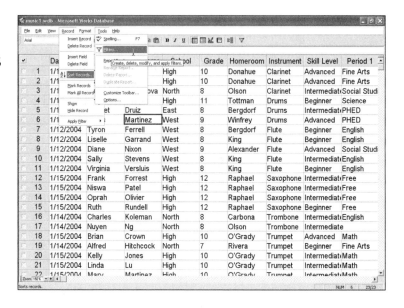

you to specify *multiple criteria* for a search, so that you could locate all Smiths who are in the seventh grade, as one example. Figure 6.5 shows filtering specifications in a composite image.

Sorting is simply a matter of choosing a field and indicating whether to sort in ascending (A–Z) or descending (Z–A) order. Most data managers permit sorting on multiple fields, as shown in Figure 6.6, again in a composite image. This sort first orders

Figure 6.5

SPECIFYING SEARCH
(OR FILTER) CRITERIA
(COMPOSITE IMAGE)

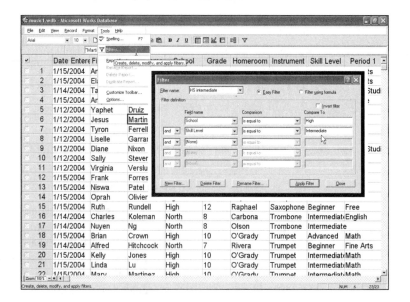

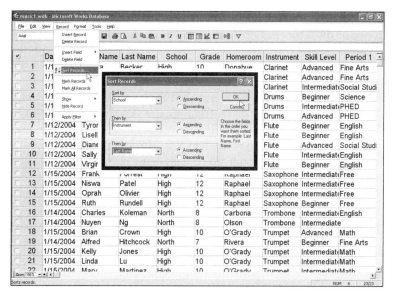

Figure 6.6

DATABASE SORTING
OPTIONS (COMPOSITE
IMAGE)

all records based on the content of the school field; then within each school, it orders the records by instrument, then last name. Thus, Ann Jones will come before Mary Smith or Zach Tong if they all play clarinet at the same school. The real power of manipulating data comes from mastering searching and sorting techniques.

Consider the needs of Aletha Jones, school band director. A typical day is a mixture of working with the entire band, small groups, and individual lessons, perhaps 200 students in all. Ms. Jones travels among different buildings covering many grade levels. Traditionally, she managed student records on file cards, perhaps color-coded by school or instrument family, grade or gender. To schedule lessons, special rehearsals, and events, she spent hours manually sorting and resorting her cards. When Ms. Jones learned about databases, she quickly saw a way to simplify her task. She created a file containing all the pertinent information, including grade level, school building, instrument, skill level, and daily class schedule, including free periods. The file structure became a *template* or model she could reuse from term to term, year to year. Once she entered the current data, she could sort by instrument to group players. Simple reports with multiple criteria almost instantly show which trombone players have fifth hour free or which students play certain instruments well enough to make up a contest ensemble. When she prints her reports, she has instant class lists, attendance sheets, or special dismissal requests for her groups, lessons, and special events.

Setting Up Your Database

To create a new database, first analyze the requirements of the application and determine what fields to include in each record. This task requires a thorough understanding of the system's capabilities and your desired output. For instance, if you need to be able to sort a file by zip code, then zip code probably will have to be a field of its own.

If you are certain this will never matter, you could store in just one field both state and zip code or even more of the address. Similarly, if you anticipate the need for an alphabetical list of the names in the file, then you probably will need separate fields for first and last names. In general, it is better to use many individual fields to avoid the extra work of splitting them later.

Developers commonly create a new database in the form view (Figure 6.2). When you create a field, you typically set its size by creating the text box that will display the data you input. The question is, what size should it be? There will be a default size, which may work fine for last name until a new student named Schwartzendrueber joins the class! You should be able to enlarge (or shrink) a field easily in most database software (Figure 6.7). Similarly, a database layout that meets your needs one year may lack necessary fields another year as school reporting requirements change. It should be easy to add new fields as necessary (Figure 6.8), although software products do differ.

It should be apparent that there are pitfalls in learning to create data files. Experience is clearly the best teacher, but the flexibility of the software you use makes a big difference as well. We suggest you create a file, using your best judgment and intuition, then enter only a few records before thoroughly testing your application. If you have made a major error that the system will not allow you to correct easily, at least you will not have invested a lot of data entry time before going back to redesign the file.

Hypermedia and Data Management

Databases have been primarily means of organizing text. Their storage and retrieval methods are largely linear; that is, one piece of data follows another. You get to what you want by moving sequentially through all that precedes it, or by resorting to access records more directly.

Figure 6.7

MODIFYING THE SIZE OF A
FIELD (COMPOSITE IMAGE)

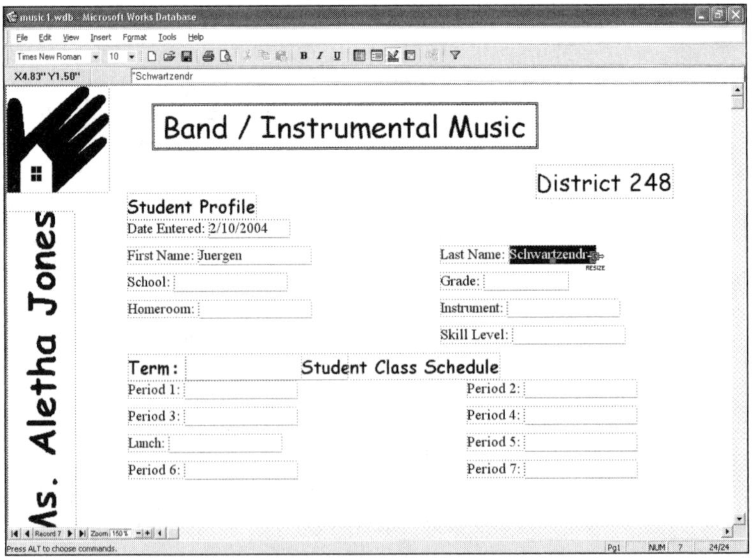

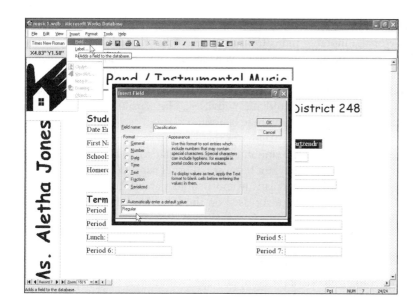

Figure 6.8

ADDING A FIELD
(COMPOSITE IMAGE)

But is that how your mind works? Hardly! You store far more than words in your memory. Did you ever say something such as, "Can you picture that?" You "hear" a familiar song whenever you think of it. Further, your retrieval processes are not linear; that is, you do not need to recall *A* before you can recall *B*. Your mind is a web of associations that are interrelated in a far more complex way than typical databases permit.

Hypermedia is a newer software type that can store and retrieve data nonlinearly in ways that may more nearly resemble those of our minds. In fact, hypermedia software can store not only text but also still images, sound, even movies! The Web, which you explored in Chapter 4, is an example of hypermedia. Look forward to more details about hypermedia in Chapters 8 and 11.

Teaching with Data Managers

Now let's consider general applications of data managers for you as a teacher and especially as learning tools for your students.

Teachers and Data Managers

Data managers can help you work smarter. Possibilities include computerizing any of the data that you now keep in file folders, on index cards, on a Rolodex, or in an address book. It requires some experience with databases to be able to judge whether computerizing any specific set of data is worthwhile. For small data sets needing minimal manipulation, the effort may outweigh the benefit. However, the massive reporting and recordkeeping requirements for special education students, for example, make computerization a sound choice.

NETS
NOTES

NETS **T** III-A
NETS **T** III-C
NETS **T** IV-B
NETS **T** VI-B

Perhaps you have difficulty recalling where you saw an article or other resources for class use. A personal annotated index to journals and other materials might be invaluable. If you work with student organizations, you may deal with mailing lists or membership rosters that are difficult to maintain manually. Advisors for the newspaper or yearbook track slides, negatives, and prints with a database. Recall Ms. Jones, the band teacher, and her need to manage her students' activities. The possibilities are endless; the specific applications of benefit to you may be unique.

There are also numerous available databases that contain resources of great value to teachers. The ERIC database is, no doubt, already familiar to you as an indispensable tool for research projects. You may not be aware of other aspects of the ERIC system, including its collection of lesson plans in most subject areas. You learned about some of these in Chapter 4, as they are accessed on the Internet, but we avoided the term *database* in that chapter.

Students and Data Managers

Jonassen (2000) conceptualized use of the computer as a "Mindtool." He wrote, "Mindtools . . . are computer applications that require students to think in meaningful ways in order to use the application to represent what they know" (p. 4). The key elements are engagement and critical thinking, which are not characteristic of all computer applications. Word processing and the Internet, for instance, tend to fall outside his concept, although that in no way denigrates the important role they play in schools. They are critical means to ends but should not be the center of attention in computer use. Jonassen (2000) continued to stress the role of Mindtools as "intellectual partners with the learner to engage and facilitate critical thinking and higher order learning" (pp. 9, 10).

Recall our earlier discussion of the distinctions among data, information, and knowledge. Clearly, it is the analysis and synthesis, the manipulation of information into knowledge, that qualify database software as a Mindtool for students. In fact, databases are the first tool that Jonassen presented.

To use databases (or any application, for that matter) as a Mindtool, you as a teacher must first master the software yourself. Only then are you ready to assume the five roles that define teaching with applications. The *planner* role consists of learning the software, exploring existing files (databases), and carefully linking database activities to the curriculum. The *facilitator* role includes being competent enough with the software to troubleshoot for the students, posing questions to check understanding, and directing attention in the exercise. As *guide*, you use analogies and questioning strategies to direct learners toward higher-order thinking skills. The *manager* function includes preparing files, diskettes, and so forth, and assuring that the activity reaches closure. As *participant*, perhaps your greatest challenge is to let the learners do it themselves rather than intervening at the first difficulty!

An Eight-Stage Learning Model for Database Use

The most comprehensive treatment of how best to help students develop database skills comes from Jonassen (2000, pp. 49–51). The first five stages are sequential, in our view, whereas students might engage in the remaining ones at varying points in their learning.

Stage 1—Query an Existing Database

As with any software tool, users must first learn the basic concepts and operation of a data manager. You may want to start off-computer. Have students gather simple data on index cards, and then use the cards as a paper database to learn database terminology and simple search strategies. This can also demonstrate how quickly a manual system becomes difficult to use.

Learning to use a computerized data manager begins with existing data files. If the data are relevant to your instruction, this becomes far more than just an exercise in software mechanics. Initially, have students examine the structure of several files to internalize the concepts of fields, records, and files. Direct students to search a file for specific records. For example, if the database contains information about U.S. presidents, ask students to retrieve several specified presidents. Discuss what information is contained in each record, and try to elicit new higher-order questions to investigate.

Gradually extend the assignments toward higher-level goals. Have students retrieve, and perhaps print, all records sharing a common field entry, say, all Democratic presidents. Examine these records for other commonalties. Suggest relationships that might be explored, perhaps party affiliation and serving only one term in office. An example of looking for trends might be to investigate the relationship between age at election and at death. Such ideas involve more complex search strategies, using multiple criteria. Search strategies become crucial when using large databases such as ERIC.

Once students begin work on a problem, consider stopping them after they have examined only some of the appropriate records. Ask what they think the answer to the question is, based on partial data. When they have formulated their hypothesis, guide continued database searching to test or perhaps modify the hypothesis. For example, assume you have a database about the United States in the twentieth century, perhaps a compilation of selected Census Bureau data. (Don't begin with too large or complex a database.) You might start by having students just explore the database to get a sense of its contents as a prelude to determining the kinds of investigations that are possible. Next, ask students to imagine a graph of the birthrate (or unemployment rate or average household income or . . . you get the idea) for the century by some interval, say, decades. Have students sketch a rough graph of their guesses and then devise a search strategy to find the required information in the database. Once found, have students graph the actual data, compare the graph to their guess, and offer possible explanations for the trend shown. This should yield new hypotheses to investigate. This activity is suitable for small-group work; in a large-group session use a data projector to display the graphs for all to see. You will learn how to create graphs easily in the next chapter.

Many database activities require sorting the records for easier examination. Students may not recognize initially that an easy way to examine the pattern of age is to sort the file by age. Simply browsing through the sorted records in order may begin to reveal a pattern. You can encourage organizing and sharing information by assigning specific projects to individuals or groups of students, with guidelines for sharing their results with the class.

Stage 2—Complete Existing Databases

Students also should learn early to modify an existing database. Provide a small file (just a few records) that contains errors to correct. Give specific instructions on what to find and change, or simply a printout of the records with the correct information. Provide the raw data for several new records to add to the database and instructions to delete certain records. Finally, pose several questions that students will be able to answer correctly *only* if their modifications to the file are correct. This is critical to verifying their changes.

Once students understand the data management software, they are ready to extend existing databases or enter data into an empty template created by someone else. The emphasis changes from the mechanics of a specific piece of software to the research required to locate data to be entered into a database. An existing structure limits the research scope to what you, the teacher, find appropriate. Database design is not a factor, and students can move quickly into the actual research.

Your task as a teacher is to obtain or develop suitable databases for your subject areas. Perhaps you can meet your objectives with more advanced assignments using the same databases that you used to introduce students to the data manager software. (Be sure to keep backup copies of any databases that you ask students to modify from their research so that you can reuse the original database with other students.)

At some point you will want empty templates that slowly evolve into useful databases as students complete their research and enter their data. Jonassen (2000, p. 50) noted that the empty structure of just the fields guides the students to purposeful research for specific information. Learning to distinguish important from unimportant or less important information is a critical thinking skill that database activities support.

When students enter research data into a database, accuracy becomes an issue on two levels. First, the data must be accurate. Second, students must enter the data into the database accurately. Some data managers permit you to specify the type of data that a field may contain, for example, text, number, or a date, which may help prevent gross data entry errors. Consider assigning each section of the research to two separate groups of students. Have them compare their findings and resolve any differences before any data entry occurs, then proof or cross-check each other's work during or after data entry. Before any significant exploration of the new database, have students do trial searches and sorts to answer queries for which the correct answer is known; this should serve to validate the database.

Stage 3—Plan a Database

Based on an existing data structure, give students the task to work in small groups to plan a database that will use a similar set or number of fields of which they are not aware. Provide several possibilities from which to choose—collections, favorite sports or teams, popular movies, and so on. Have them determine a purpose for their database, then work through questions that will guide their thinking and lead to a field structure that will organize the data to suit the purpose. Students should share their plans with the whole group and compare multiple "solutions" to the problem with your input to guide their thinking and produce a structure comparable to what you intended. This stage begins to model the organizational skills needed to develop original databases, a later stage.

Stage 4—Adapt Existing Databases

In the previous stage you guided students to think about the structure of a database that would parallel an existing one. Now provide one or more databases that use this structure. There are many possibilities, including the ideas in the previous stage as well as hobbies, TV shows, physical characteristics, even dating patterns. Provide at least one such database, then challenge students to modify it to suit their plan or create a new one based on the same structure. This will help both to develop critical thinking about the structure and to enhance student proficiency with the database software itself.

Stage 5 — Create Original Databases

The next application level is to plan, design, and create a totally original database. Designing a new database is a stimulating process of decision making that helps to develop higher-order thinking skills, according to Truell (1999). Creating an original data structure places students in an active role, determining what to collect and how to organize it for meaning, which depends on its purpose.

What fields are needed? Which potential records are worth including? How should the screen be laid out? What are the questions that we may want to try to answer using this database? The latter is critical to determining the fields of each record, which dictate the data one must collect. There are also many issues surrounding field entries. Suppose a field is labeled "size." What are the possible entries? For some situations, the answer may be numbers, as in shoe sizes. For others, gross categories may suffice, for example, small, medium, large. If one key factor is color, is that a single field, a single attribute, or will it require multiple fields for accurate representation? If the content were to be animals or birds, how do you best describe their sounds?

Jonassen (2000) suggested group work for this stage, with sharing of the design in the class before any development begins. Among questions to consider are whether the proposed structure permits effective and efficient searches and whether it represents the content accurately, appropriately, and with sufficient depth.

Stage 6 — Develop Challenges for Other Students

Once students can create an original database, Jonassen (2000) urged students to develop *difficult* questions based on the data that will require multiple search criteria to answer. This will cause learners to think more fully about both the content and structure of their database and the relationships among the data elements. Some may discover that their structure and/or content does not support answering certain questions, necessitating some redesign of the database.

Once students have developed their difficult questions and verified that their database supports them, let the challenges begin. In small groups let students work to answer the challenges. When they think they have an answer, consider letting them demonstrate their approach and share their answer(s) with the group. Other students, especially the creator(s) of the challenge and database, may offer alternative approaches. This should lead to rich discussion of both the content and the methods employed.

Beaver (1992) suggested that students demonstrate their database projects to the class. Each student group should also prepare questions that other students can answer with each database. Let the groups explore each other's work to the extent that class time and hardware resources permit.

Stage 7—Extrapolate from Databases

At this level, students add new fields to existing databases to expand their usefulness. As an example, Jonassen (2000) suggested extending a geography database by adding fields for a variety of economic and political attributes. Totally new queries become possible, and the students have an opportunity to explore the interrelationships among the attributes.

Stage 8—Reflect on the Activity

Previously we noted that stages 6 through 8 were not necessarily sequential following the first five. Nowhere is this more true than Jonassen's eighth stage of reflection. Reflections start with each individual or group assessing their progress toward their selected goal. It is inherent in various stages when decisions are reached to modify the evolving database to better address the purpose. Reflection also should include assessing what students have learned about working together in groups and, above all, what they have learned about the content itself. Databases are useful to support deep content learning, especially by the creator, and not just as a technology exercise. As Jonassen (2000) wrote, " . . . [C]onstructing databases engages meaningful thinking. Reflection cements the knowledge that learners construct" (p. 51).

Internet Resources

Many educators think of the Internet as the world's largest database. Each time you undertake a search on the Web, you are indeed searching that international database, hopefully using sound search techniques. However, most such activities are limited to Jonassen's lowest-level strategy of querying existing resources (Jonassen, 2000). Also on that level are many online databases that provide information on almost any topic, of which we can highlight only a few. These can be powerful resources for students working with their own databases, as these data "warehouses" provide the raw material for student- or teacher-developed projects, our next section.

For instance, a project might require much basic data about some or all of the U.S. states or perhaps detailed information about one state and its counties. Student researchers might start with the U.S. Census Bureau at <http://quickfacts.census.gov/qfd> (Figure 6.9). This QuickFacts database is a fantastic resource for a database like the partially completed one in Figure 6.10. Imagine the applications of such a database, especially at the higher strategy levels such as extrapolation. As students become familiar with the data source, they can begin to envision new applications of their database through addition of new fields.

Another excellent source of highly accessible U.S. data is the GovStats site, maintained by the Oregon State University Libraries <http://govinfo.kerr.orst.edu>. Very detailed information is available in an easily searchable format. For broader data, consider the potential of Atlapedia <www.atlapedia.com>, a geography database and atlas of countries of the world. Many of its resources are free, but some require an inexpensive subscription. The World Wide Web Virtual Library is a relatively little-known database among educators, but its contents are mind-boggling <http://conbio.net/VL/database>. Start by using the Browse link to get a sense of the wealth of information before using

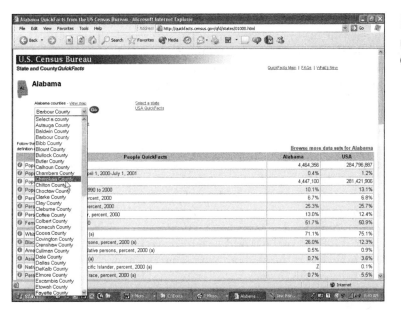

Figure 6.9
U.S. CENSUS BUREAU QUICKFACTS WEBSITE

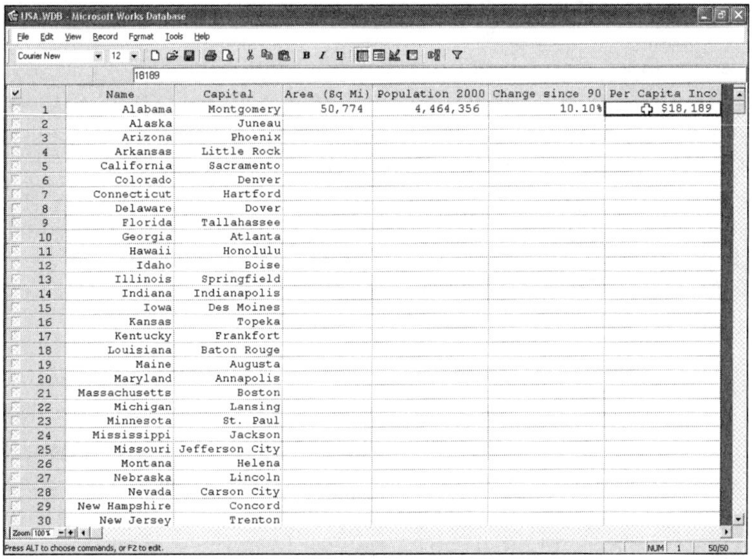

Figure 6.10
SAMPLE U.S. STATES DATABASE

the Search options. You can search just the category titles or the full content of the virtual library. It's even possible to sign up to maintain a section of this international resource.

Most students enjoy the movies. There is virtually no limit to the database activities and projects they could create using such resources as the Internet Movie Database <www.imdb.com>. For a lengthy list of movie-related databases, try <http://classicfilm.about.com/cs/moviedatabases>. A vast wealth of basic curriculum content, some already laid out in a format that parallels a database, is located at Enchanted Learning. The biomes section <www.enchantedlearning.com/biomes> is one example. You may also find the Database of Award-Winning Children's Literature <www.dawcl.com> useful, which contains over 3,500 records from nearly 50 award programs throughout the English-speaking world. The structure of this database is worth looking at for the thought that went into the search categories. The Children's Picture Book Database <www.lib.muohio.edu/pictbks/search> is another good resource for its content and also for practicing search techniques, which you learned for web searching, in a database context. Lamb (2001) provides many additional links to Internet data resources and applications.

There are also Internet database projects that extend to stage 2, which is adding to existing databases. The Global Grocery List <www.landmark-project.com/ggl> lets students add their own local information to a database of grocery prices from around the world, then view information by product and year. It also lists the source location for the data. Students can easily devise challenges for one another from this resource, a stage 5 activity. Another project is Sands of the World, an interactive geology unit that involves hundreds of classes worldwide in the study of sand samples <www.chariho.k12.ri.us/curriculum/MISmart/ocean/sands.htm>.

Classroom Applications

Many teachers have developed methods of teaching with database technology, as well as exciting projects for their students. We can highlight only selected examples (there are more on the companion website), and we urge you to read the entire original sources. Also, be alert for the very latest ideas as they appear in your professional reading. Remember, too, that you are not alone as you implement database activities. Your school library media specialist is almost certain to be knowledgeable about databases and their use and would be happy to assist you in planning and carrying out your lessons.

Now let's look at a range of classroom database applications that have worked well for teachers and students.

Local Data

How about starting each school year with a survey of your students, including typical demographic items about family and most and least "favorites," ranging from food to household jobs to sports to school subjects? Depending on your stage of working with database software, you might create the database yourself from the student information, then guide activities that use it. For all but the youngest students, you could provide only the template as an electronic survey instrument for each student to complete. Having students enter their own data at the beginning of the school term immediately establishes the computer as a basic classroom tool. At higher levels, you might challenge your students to devise the entire survey, planning the appropriate database structure from the very start, then designing and developing the complete file.

Fourth-grade teacher Susan Monahan (1999) used databases and local data to enhance the experience of Travis, a mainstreamed hearing-impaired student. Travis worked with a hearing peer to create a database about the students in their class. They first developed the elements of the database, the fields they would fill in with student data. Some were points of curiosity; others were things they thought they knew about their peers but needed to verify. Monahan explained in detail how she taught the two students about databases and how they developed the structure for theirs. Once they developed the form, they taught their classmates about databases through the process of having each student enter his or her own data into a record. Monahan was enthusiastic about the language goals that Travis reached through this project. He and his partner went on to create a database of book reviews that remained in the school library for students to use and enhance with their latest readings. This is a common language arts application of databases.

As school population diversity increases, more classes have students who are not originally from the community, and most students probably have a relative who lives in some other part of the country, if not the world. Use this as the basis for an ongoing study of weather and factors that influence it. Each student might be responsible for his or her own "home" city or one chosen some other way. The database structure would include fields for the city and whatever factors you wish to include. Possibilities include latitude and longitude, elevation, whether near or on a body of water, high and low temperatures recorded for some specified time period (or records for each), and so on. For an ongoing project, you might do daily or weekly updates of fields for number of days of specific weather patterns (clear, cloudy, sunny, rainy, snowy, etc.). Once there is sufficient data in the database, then students can explore the possible relationships among weather patterns and geographic factors. Such a project could start early in the year, with major use of the evolving database months later, thus sustaining interest over a longer period.

Project-Based Learning (PBL)

In her primer on project-based learning, Gwen Solomon (2003) provided very useful guidance on this increasingly popular approach to learning. She carefully explained the concepts, how they relate to school reform, and the central role of technology in project work. Although the topic of PBL is beyond our scope, we note that Solomon included databases along with word processing and spreadsheets as key tools in working through a project as well as in assessment and evaluation. The article is available online for your convenience. It is well worth reading.

Language Learning

Middle school teacher Pam Lewis (1997) used a database to help students learn verb conjugations in French, but the idea could also be adapted to ESL classes or any English class in which students are learning grammar. Lewis starts the project by having students write out the conjugation of 10 verbs, some regular and some irregular, on note cards, a paper database. Students then sort the cards by various characteristics: alphabetic, verb type, ending for a given pronoun (e.g., first person), pattern if irregular, and so on. Then students create a verb database with fields for the infinitive form, the six person forms (first, second, and third; singular and plural), the past tense form, and other forms that may cause learning challenges. Next they enter the data for a list of verbs, which should grow as they learn new vocabulary. Lewis guides the students in exploring the database by various search and sort tasks. Finally, they answer questions that require manipulation of the database. Complete details are in Lewis's article.

Social Studies

McNally and Etchison (2000) described database use for a unit on the Age of Exploration. Students created a database about the explorers they were studying using fields such as the explorer's name, country of origin, country of sponsorship, century of travels, even a picture (which most database software permits). In addition to the easily imagined manipulations of the database, the authors suggested that students print the records in form view to create a set of trading or study cards.

Holmes (1998) suggested that the three Rs should be replaced by the 6 Cs: compute, communicate, conclude, confirm, categorize, and classify. Her American Presidents database project directly supports these learning needs. Holmes created the template with fields for the president's name, number or order in office, age at election, political party, place and date of birth, name(s) of wife (wives), number of children, religion, previous occupation, number of terms served, vice president, cause and date of death. She also created a visually attractive form view to encourage student engagement (similar in idea to Figure 6.2). She printed blank forms and each student then researched a small number of presidents. The form guided the research; students knew just what data to find. Once students completed the forms by hand and cross-checked them for accuracy, they added their own records to the database. The completed database was then ready for use. Among Holmes's challenges for students was to research the most significant contributions made by each president during his second term (which first necessitated identifying only presidents who served more than one term). Other ideas included to determine what percentage of U.S. presidents first served as vice president, to offer possible conclusions based on observed patterns in the data for all presidents who lived past age 80, and to consider possible patterns in the records of those presidents who shared a common profession, such as law.

Language Arts

For an in-depth study of British Romantic poets, one teacher guided student development of an extensive database as a study guide on individual poems. Beyond basic fields for title, poet, poetic form, and theme, the database categories included tone, sound devices (e.g., alliteration), rhyme pattern and rhythm, symbolism, and room for examples of several different Romantic motifs (Jonassen, 2000, pp. 44–45).

Another language arts database project supported analysis of sentences from works of literature. Fields contained the entire sentence, its author's name, each grammatical part of speech, as well as space for devices such as similes, parallelisms, and rhetorical patterns. After creating records from diverse authors, periods, and/or writing styles, students were able to compare and analyze language use as seldom before (Jonassen, 2000).

Previously you learned about Monahan's use of a database project, which led to a book review database in the library.

Reading teachers long have found great value in building a database of information about books that students read and reactions to them. Initially, there is value just in the recorded information—students may base their reading choices on the experiences of their peers. However, if the database is maintained and extended over time, it can also serve as a means to look at patterns of preferences, changes in interests, differences based on factors such as gender or current events, the rise and fall in popularity of authors or genres, and many other interesting points. Such a project could be part of a multidisciplinary activity, with language arts providing the base and social studies adding elements from history as a possible factor in preferences. Mathematics could also play a role by calculating average ratings of each book, studying volume of student reading (add a field for page count?), and so on.

Math

Mathematics is seldom an obvious area in which to apply databases, but creative teachers have done so. Jonassen (2000, pp. 42–43) illustrated a database created by students in the class of a veteran algebra teacher. The underlying concept is math functions with fields for name, type, graph, inverse, domain, range, and absolute minimum and maximum values. Of course, not all functions have entries for each of the fields, which is one of the key learning points. Once the database was built, even the teacher reached a new understanding of algebra's foundational structure.

Journaling is a popular idea in many subject areas, including math. Management of typical student journals, however, can be overwhelming as you strive to help students find trends or patterns in the data. Gettys (1994) noted that journals are a natural application of database software. After carefully determining appropriate fields, create a template for students to fill in. Sorting on a "topics" field or a "what I learned today" field provides an overview of achievements, as well as the course itself. To explore how daily lessons interrelate, students can search for records that contain the same word in certain fields. Include a field for rating the topic on a 1–10 scale. Later, a two-level sort by rating and topic will provide an outline of the class ordered by the student's reactions to the topics. As a teacher, you could use the student files for feedback on how the lessons have been received, to review what you have covered and to what extent, and to let the student's own words or ideas help you communicate to parents what each child has learned.

Science

Norton and Harvey (1995) devised a high school biology unit based on the story of the Donner party, a group of pioneers heading to California in the 1840s who became trapped by snow in the Sierra Nevada Mountains. Survivors ate their livestock, dogs, hides, and blankets and eventually became cannibals. Students used a database created from information on the Donner party, such as age, gender, whether the individual survived, and when and how each died. Manipulating the database led to many questions, such as average life span at the time, infant mortality rates, and relative aggressiveness of males versus females. (Women were far more likely to have survived than men.) The students prepared papers on survivability for a science conference, where they had to debate and defend their views. Some began a dialog with an expert who had published his conclusions about the Donner incident. The authors stress how students can experience the "entire cycle of information transformation—searching, sorting, creating, and reporting" (p. 25). This unit exemplifies a knowledge-building curriculum.

Multidisciplinary

Creative second-grade teachers developed a multidisciplinary unit anchored in environmental science (Helisek & Pratt, 1994). They began by presenting the word *extinct*, which students quickly connected to a previous unit on dinosaurs. Discussing the fate of dinosaurs led to dangers facing today's animals. Dr. Seuss's *The Lorax* stimulated a discussion of events, consequences, and the role of humans in changes to the earth, from which the key lesson on recycling emerged. After brainstorming what they threw away daily, students selected five common items (e.g., cans and newspapers) and recorded their family discards for a week. The teachers set up a simple database into which students entered their data. They were then able to examine their findings from many perspectives, such as who threw away the most, how quantity might be related to family size or owning pets, and so on. With older students, such questions could lead to Jonassen's extrapolation strategy to extend the existing database to support additional query types. Helisek and Pratt's students also gained experience in data representation by using software to graph their findings, a theme you'll encounter in Chapter 7.

Assessment

A topic of widespread interest among educators is alternative assessment, which typically involves collection of far more student data than previously, in a variety of formats. Barrett (1994) provided an introduction to some of the technologies that can support alternative assessment to "make classroom assessment easier, not more work for everyone" (p. 9). She noted that growing numbers of schools are using database software to store and manage assessment data. Today's more powerful database products can store scanned images, audio, and even video clips as well as the traditional text items, making them flexible enough to use for student portfolios. We'll return to this idea when we explore hypermedia in Chapter 8.

Special Needs Students

Stearns (1992) was concerned that students with learning disabilities (LD) would be left behind as other students became involved in more active forms of learning aimed at higher-order thinking. She believed databases are especially well suited to this group of learners because they are open-ended tools that can be adapted flexibly to virtually any subject. Reporting on three different teachers' experiences, Stearns noted great success in all cases. Many LD students face difficulty separating vital from extraneous material. The outline form of a database helped them find main ideas. One teacher reported that the database research projects produced the best writing of the year. Another teacher found students who rarely would discuss their school activities at home suddenly taking their search printouts home and surprising parents with their questions. The third teacher allowed students to develop their own databases. As work progressed, many noticed common interests, and some voluntary joint projects resulted. This teacher also found that student organizational skills and interests increased away from the computer, such as in their notebooks.

Research on Learning with Databases

Relatively little research has appeared concerning measurable impacts of learning with databases, and so one must be cautious about generalizations.

NETS
NOTES

NETS **T** I-B
NETS **T** II-B
NETS **T** III-A
NETS **T** III-B
NETS **T** V-C
NETS **T** V-D

Summarizing the limited range of available research, Roblyer (2003) noted the common assumption that working with databases will enhance research and problem-solving skills. Research, however, is fairly clear that students require considerable guidance in learning to ask appropriate questions, search available databases, and then analyze their results. "Databases offer the most effective and meaningful help when they are embedded in a structured problem-solving process and when the activity includes class and small-group discussion of search results" (p. 136). Roblyer presents a useful complement to Jonassen's approach to working with databases.

Quinlan (2001) reported on veterinary medicine students' use of a bibliographic database of articles designed to support problem-based learning. Students reported finding value in the database as an aid to solving the problems presented, particularly by helping focus their efforts on a smaller set of resources than their own online searching would likely produce.

A total of 42 teachers and nearly 500 students participated in a study aimed at higher-order thinking skills (Cousins & Ross, 1993). Among four treatments, one involved computer software especially tailored to the correlational problem solving at the heart of the study. Another used general-purpose software that supported such work. Both software products included databases among their tools. Across four skill dimensions, students in each of the treatments were much more successful than were the control-group students. Students using the specialized software "outperformed the control group by 99%" (p. 111). While somewhat less dramatic, students using the general-purpose software were superior to the controls on three dimensions and about equal on one.

Ehman et al. (1992) undertook a highly detailed examination of eight social studies classrooms in which databases were used to teach problem solving. Their review of prior research on databases indicated that gains had been found related to higher-order thinking skills and problem solving, while no impact had been found on recall or lower-level knowledge acquisition. Researchers had also determined that groups of two to four learners are effective. Ehman and associates worked with teachers who were relatively strong computer users and students who were already experienced with computers and databases. Each school had a computer lab. Thus, three of the most common concerns about computer studies (teacher knowledge, student knowledge, and machine access) were addressed at the start. Classes spanned grades 5–12 with ability levels from below average to high. The experimental treatment took ten class days. Several important findings were:

- Problem solving occurs only when users are comfortable with the database tool. Too little time was spent on this preliminary step to the detriment of outcomes.
- Poorly chosen definitions of the fields in a database led to "almost comical" misunderstandings of some concepts. Field labels alone may not suffice to define a field.
- Learners showed little analysis and planning, preferring to jump in and "wade about."
- Large, highly detailed databases overwhelmed learners with information overload.
- At least some students recognized that their database lacked critical information, necessitating a trip to the library. The researchers cite this as evidence of higher-order thinking.
- The most successful teachers were those who functioned as "metacognitive guides." They had a clear plan at the start, gave feedback and reinforcement all along, and used mini-debriefings regularly to identify progress and problems.
- Time was a concern for all. Teaching with databases took more time than conventional instruction. With tight integration of the unit into the curriculum, however, there were fewer teacher concerns than when the unit was an "extra."
- Structure in a database lesson is critical. The introduction to the lesson should stress the problem to be solved, not the computer. Clear expectations are vital, including intermediate milestones for students to attain. Teachers should model key problem-solving elements and guide student practice. A daily five-minute summary of where each group has been, its achievements, and next steps can be very useful. Be sure to allow for final, public sharing of results. Just as student knowledge of the software is important to good results, so too is some knowledge of the content. Where the content was new, less was achieved.
- Small-group work is effective. Members challenge one another's thinking, clarify tasks, and develop more accurate generalizations.

How can teachers help students develop the habit of searching databases as a basic information resource? Perhaps the key is initial experience. A study by Pao (1994) found that medical students who searched the MEDLINE database monthly during their first years of medical school were more likely to continue searching later, to the benefit of their patients. This suggests that regular directed database use may help to implant the use of such a tool in our students.

Inquiry-based science teaching strives for higher-level goals than rote fact recall. Maor (1991) investigated both science understanding and the extent to which students' inquiry skills can be facilitated through the use of a computerized science database on birds of Antarctica and specially designed curriculum materials. Much attention was given in the program to developing both students' inquiry skills and their subject-matter knowledge. Grade 11 and 12 students' knowledge and skills development were assessed as they interacted with the computerized database and the curriculum materials. Overall, the mean score on the Inquiry Skills Test increased significantly, both on the total test and each of three subscales (analysis, interpretation, and application). Maor also found that students' ability to work with the software depended on their ability to envision the structure of the database. Time to attain this visualization varied widely, and those who were never able to do so also never progressed beyond simple interpretation-type questions. Like others, Maor noted the critical need to be able to manipulate the tool comfortably in order to make any skills gains. She also noted that a "constructivist" teacher (a facilitator) was far more effective than a "transmitter" teacher (a lecturer).

Kern (1990) trained students in database searching, using the *Readers' Guide to Periodical Literature* on CD-ROM during the time they were assigned to the library to do research papers for English classes. All students were trained to use the print index, and one group was trained on the computer through group instruction, demonstration, observation, and a hands-on search. The results indicated that the database-search group outperformed the print-index group slightly in the number of articles found, and that the electronic database was generally easy for the students to use. Nearly all students considered their searches successful, and they preferred the database search method to using the print index.

Collis (1990) summarized six database studies. One major concern was the difficulty that students have in formulating "good" questions to ask when querying a database. Many considered their task complete when the computer produced any kind of result, never stopping to analyze what they found for completeness, accuracy, adequacy, relevance, and so forth. In other words, higher-order thinking skills did not develop automatically.

Gaffuri (1991) was concerned that third graders' vocabularies were too limited; their writing tended to be very repetitive and redundant. She developed a practicum to expand written vocabulary through training in using a database and brainstorming strategies. The students' goal was to collect personally unique, distinctive vocabulary words in their personal databases. Brainstorming generated specific words that might be used in lieu of general words (e.g., maple or oak for tree). Students wrote and published individual thesauruses to demonstrate the results of collecting vocabulary and applying it to specific topics. Daily process writing was an integral part of the curriculum. Class time became an ongoing procedure, consisting of reading, writing, editing, presenting, and rewriting. Gaffuri's data indicated the following: (1) brainstorming techniques are easily taught and help children organize for writing; (2) children can use a database for orderly collection of vocabulary; (3) children can write and publish their growing vocabulary studies in a more interesting manner; (4) all students gained confidence in their ability to write; and (5) writing became fun in an environment in which children succeeded.

Rawitsch (1988) sought empirical evidence to support anecdotal claims that database use aids development of higher-order thinking skills. His study of 339 eighth graders examined their work styles and attitudes and had them perform exercises with both paper and computer databases. Rawitsch found that students solved more problems correctly when using the computer, but they took longer to do so. They preferred using the computer. Students with an unstructured work style were less efficient using the computer than those with a structured style. He also found evidence of transfer of learning to more lifelike contexts. Rawitsch stressed that "problem solving with computer data base use . . . cannot effectively be learned as a one-time activity" (p. 3). Rather, the skills should be taught and used repeatedly throughout the curriculum for maximum effect.

Based on 665 subjects, White (1985) found that use of a database in social studies resulted in significantly higher performance on a test involving such tasks as evaluating the relevance of data to a problem, its sufficiency for reaching a conclusion, and ways to organize data to more readily solve a problem.

Although research evidence is limited, observation and anecdotal reports strongly suggest that databases have the potential to be an extremely powerful educational tool when used appropriately.

SUMMARY

Parallel to the explosive growth of raw data and information characteristic of the Information Age is the growth in problems of data management. However, existing computers and inexpensive data management software can ease some common burdens for the teacher. Current paper-and-pencil recordkeeping may be a candidate for computerization. Just because data can be managed electronically, however, does not guarantee a better outcome. Before setting out to use a data manager, consider issues of appropriateness. Common sense comes before mere capability.

Of still greater potential are classroom uses of databases. Projects appropriate for students can be devised readily and may lead students to a clearer understanding of the place and significance of information in society. Students can experience firsthand the ramifications of their decisions about what information to store and how. Class or group research projects may become more exciting as each student benefits individually from the data gathered and entered by all. The massive resources of the Internet bring whole new possibilities to instruction. National census data, for instance, give students access to primary data, something previously reserved for advanced graduate students. Class data files can support activities to develop problem-solving skills. All database projects should be designed carefully to promote higher-order thinking skills to the greatest extent possible. The goal is knowledge building, not mere information gathering.

This chapter described numerous concrete examples of database activities that already have been used successfully by classroom teachers. You should find many ideas among them that you could modify to fit your own teaching situation. Research on demonstrable outcomes of learning with databases is scarce but generally encouraging. The companion website accompanying this book contains still more application ideas and references for anyone seeking further information.

chapter 6 activities

1. Take any common blank form used in your environment for recordkeeping and analyze it using database concepts. Write a brief explanation of it in terms of files, records, and fields.

2. Using the same form, jot down the fields that would be included in a computerized version and estimate the number of characters of space each would require in a computer file. Total the field requirements to determine the approximate size of one record.

3. List three or more data management tasks of your own that you could consider for computerization. Are they appropriate for the computer? Why?

4. Select your most appropriate personal data management task. What sort of information would you need to retrieve from your system for it to help you? This is the information you would minimally put into your database. Can you think of additions that would give you potential for answering questions that you currently cannot (Jonassen's extrapolation stage)?

5. Explain how your selected application would be improved by using a computerized system. What might you lose in the process?

6. Create a small database using any available data manager and one of your own application ideas. Just a few fields and records are necessary to experience databases concretely.

7. Write a proposal to your principal or technology coordinator (real or imagined) to request database software for your classroom. Include your best justification for the purchase based on the most specific plans for its use that you can describe.

8. Design at least one lesson plan that includes database activities for each subject you teach.

9. What further research do you believe is needed concerning databases as Mindtools? Describe what you would like to know and speculate on how one might investigate your questions.

Companion Website

Visit the companion website at <www.ablongman.com/lockard6e> for more information about the topics discussed in this chapter.

expect the world®

The New York Times
nytimes.com

Themes of the Times

Expand your knowledge of the concepts discussed in this chapter by reading current and historical articles from the *New York Times* by visiting the Themes of the Times section of the companion website <www.ablongman.com/lockard6e>.

References

Barrett, H. C. "Technology-Supported Assessment Portfolios." *The Computing Teacher*, March 1994, *21*(6), pp. 9–12.

Beaver, J. F. "Using Computer Power to Improve Your Teaching." *The Computing Teacher*, February 1992, *19*(5), pp. 5–9.

Collis, B. *The Best of Research Windows: Trends and Issues in Educational Computing.* Eugene, OR: International Society for Technology in Education, 1990. (ERIC Document ED 323 993.)

Cousins, J. B., and Ross, J. A. "Improving Higher Order Thinking Skills by Teaching 'With' the

Computer: A Comparative Study." *Journal of Research on Computing in Education*, Fall 1993, *26*(1), pp. 94–115.

Ehman, L., Glenn, A., Johnson, V., and White, C. "Using Computer Databases in Student Problem Solving: A Study of Eight Social Studies Teachers' Classrooms." *Theory and Research in Social Education*, Spring 1992, *20*(2), pp. 179–206.

Gaffuri, A. *Expanding Third Graders' Vocabulary Using a Data Base, Individual Thesauri and Brainstorming Strategies.* Ed.D. Practicum I Report, Early and Middle Childhood Program, Nova University, Ft. Lauderdale, FL, 1991. (ERIC Document ED 331 035.)

Gettys, D. "Journaling with a Database." *The Computing Teacher*, October 1994, *22*(2), pp. 37–40.

Helisek, H., and Pratt, D. "Project Reconstruct." *Science and Children*, April 1994, *31*(7), pp. 25–28.

Holmes, B. "The Database. America's Presidents." *Learning and Leading with Technology*, April 1998, *25*(7), pp. 6–11.

Jonassen, D. H. *Computers as Mindtools for Schools: Engaging Critical Thinking*, 2nd ed. Upper Saddle River, NJ: Merrill, 2000.

Kern, J. F. *Using "Readers' Guide to Periodical Literature" on CD-ROM to Teach Database Searching to High School Students.* Ed.S. Practicum Report, Nova University, Ft. Lauderdale, FL, 1990. (ERIC Document ED 328 291.)

Lamb, A. "Tools for Organizing: Databases." June 2001. Retrieved January 19, 2003, from <http://eduscapes.com/sessions/ptools/data1.htm>

Lewis, P. "Using Productivity Software for Language Learning, Part II. Spreadsheets, Databases, and Mail Merge." *Learning and Leading with Technology*, September 1997, *25*(1), pp. 12–17.

Maor, D. *Development of Student Inquiry Skills: A Constructivist Approach in a Computerized Classroom Environment.* Paper presented at the Annual Meeting of the National Association for Research in Science Teaching (Lake Geneva, WI, April 7–10, 1991). (ERIC Document ED 336 261.)

McNally, L., and Etchison, C. "Strategies of Successful Technology Integrators: Part 2. Software Tools." *Learning and Leading with Technology*, November 2000, *28*(3), pp. 6–9, 17.

Miller, S. "Greece and Rome: A CBT." January 1, 1998. Retrieved January 10, 2003, from <www.techlearning.com/db_area/archives/WCE/archives/smiller.htm>

Monahan, S. "Our Classmates." *Learning and Leading with Technology*, March 1999, *26*(6), pp. 10–13.

Naisbitt, J. *Megatrends.* New York: Warner, 1982.

Norton, P., and Harvey, D. "Information Knowledge: Using Databases to Explore the Tragedy at Donner Pass." *Learning and Leading with Technology*, September 1995, *23*(1), pp. 23–25.

Pao, M. L. "Effect of Search Experience on Sustained MEDLINE Usage by Students." *Academic Medicine*, November 1994, *69*(11), pp. 914–920.

Quinlan, K. M. "Striking the Right Balance: An Evaluation of a Literature Database to Support Problem Based Learning." Paper presented at the Annual Meeting of the American Educational Research Association (Seattle, WA, April 10–14, 2001). (ERIC Document ED 453 705).

Rawitsch, D. "The Effects of Computer Use and Student Work Style on Database Analysis Activities in the Social Studies." In *Improving the Use of Technology in Schools: What Are We Learning.* Research Bulletin #1. St. Paul, MN: MECC/University of Minnesota Center for the Study of Educational Technology, November 1988, pp. 1–3.

Roblyer, M. D. *Integrating Educational Technology into Teaching*, 3rd ed. Columbus, OH: Merrill Prentice Hall, 2003.

Solomon, G. "Project-Based Learning: A Primer." *Technology and Learning*, January 2003, pp. 20–30. Retrieved January 19, 2003, from <www.techlearning.com/db_area/archives/TL/2003/01/project.html>

Stearns, P. H. "Preparing Students with Learning Disabilities for Information Age Success." *The Computing Teacher*, April 1992, *19*(7), pp. 28–30.

Truell, A. D. "Teaching Higher-Order Thinking Skills in Marketing Classes." *Business Education Forum*, October 1999, *54*(1), pp. 39–41.

White, C. S. *The Impact of Structured Activities with a Computer-based File-Management Program on Selected Information Processing Skills.* Unpublished doctoral dissertation, Indiana University, Bloomington, IN, 1985.

Spreadsheets: *Managing and Analyzing Numeric Information*

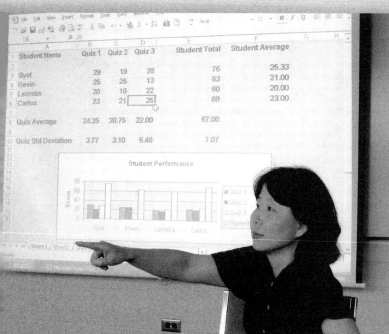

OBJECTIVES

After completing this chapter, you will be able to:

- Briefly discuss the development of application software.
- Discuss basic concepts of spreadsheets.
- List and describe generic functional commands used to construct and manipulate a computer spreadsheet.
- Explain the significance of spreadsheet templates.
- Plan a unit to teach students to use a spreadsheet.

- Describe potential uses of "what if" applications.
- List and evaluate classroom uses of computer spreadsheets.
- Detail at least one spreadsheet application that you would like to try.
- Develop lesson plans that include spreadsheet use by students.

This chapter examines one of the pioneering types of application programs for personal computers, the electronic spreadsheet. This software is first placed in the context of application software, followed by an overview of what a spreadsheet is and what spreadsheet software can do. A sample spreadsheet is developed step-by-step. A wide array of applications of spreadsheets in education concludes this chapter.

Development of Application Software

NETS
NOTES

NETS **S** 1
NETS **T** I-A
NETS **T** I-B

When computers became generally available in the mid-1970s, the first type of software was computer languages that were patterned after the languages then in use on mainframe computers. Computer users were obliged to plan and write their own application programs. At that time, computer usage was viewed largely as a downward extension of mainframe computing; use required expertise in programming and languages. This made it appear that considerable technical knowledge and experience were necessary for anyone to take advantage of the rapidly developing computer technology.

Word processing programs were the first major microcomputer software development to approach usage from a different perspective, namely, that of the computer as a tool. *Tool* or *application* programs allowed users to perform desired tasks without doing the actual programming. Someone else had already created a general-purpose tool for a common need. By learning how to use a specific application program, anyone could benefit from a computer. Rather than devoting weeks, months, or years to mastering programming skills, users could achieve useful results in a matter of hours or, at most, days.

Visible Calculators

The introduction of *VisiCalc* in 1979 continued and accelerated the trend toward application software. The creators of *VisiCalc* recognized that many common tasks entail working with a calculator and a sheet of paper to record and organize information in a row-and-column format. This was especially true in the world of business, finance, accounting, and forecasting. Their new product was a *visible calculator* and much more.

VisiCalc offered users a simple and direct way to construct and manipulate a computer work area of rows and columns called a *spreadsheet*. A wide variety of useful tasks could be performed without knowledge of a complicated computer language. *VisiCalc* was an immediate success and ultimately became a best-seller for use in business, education, and the home.

More Powerful Spreadsheets

Today spreadsheets are a major category of application software, along with word processing and data management programs. Since the creation of *VisiCalc*, various companies have introduced improved versions of spreadsheet programs. Each new version and upgrade has built on previous spreadsheet developments and introduced a wider range of more powerful capabilities. These capabilities represent improvement in two directions. The first adds more manipulation features to the basic spreadsheet, turning it into a "power" spreadsheet. The second integrates tools into the spreadsheet, most commonly the capability to produce graphs and charts directly from the spreadsheet data and the option to clarify spreadsheet data with adjacent narrative introductions, headings, or explanations. Basic spreadsheet uses are the focus of this chapter.

The Technical Side of Spreadsheets

Let's look now at fundamental spreadsheet concepts and basic usage procedures.

NETS
NOTES

NETS **S** 1
NETS **S** 3
NETS **S** 5
NETS **T** I-A
NETS **T** I-B
NETS **T** III-A
NETS **T** IV-B
NETS **T** V-C

Fundamental Concepts

Most spreadsheet programs are similar in their underlying concept and use. What we present here is a generic spreadsheet description. There is enough commonality among spreadsheet software to allow anyone with a conceptual understanding to adapt quickly to the specific characteristics of any particular product.

Electronic Paper

Think of a spreadsheet as a large piece of paper where you store data in rows and columns. Although spreadsheet processing was accomplished by hand for years, using a computer spreadsheet is considerably easier and faster in all but the simplest cases. Many tasks become feasible that simply would be too time consuming or complex to do manually. Full-featured software such as *Excel* can include multiple *worksheets* within a single spreadsheet file.

Cells

Once spreadsheet software is running on your computer, you see a nearly blank screen. A typical empty spreadsheet is illustrated in Figure 7.1. The workspace is organized into columns and rows. Columns are designated by letters (starting with A), and rows are identified by numbers (starting with 1). The intersection of a row and a column is called

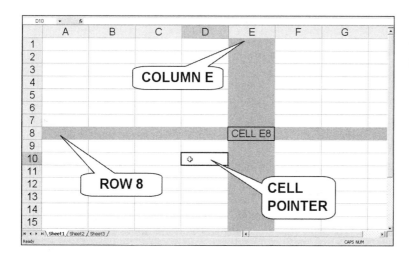

Figure 7.1
TYPICAL SPREADSHEET FORM

a *cell*. A cell is identified by its column and row designation (e.g., A1 or K25), which is its unique "address" within the total spreadsheet.

A cell may contain one of three types of entries:

1. Numbers or *values* (numeric data).
2. *Labels* (alphabetic or alphanumeric data).
3. *Formulas* (expressions of calculations or relationships among cells). Predefined formulas are called *functions*.

Numbers and labels are displayed in the cell just as they are entered. For a formula, the cell displays the result of the calculations.

Cell Pointer

When working within a spreadsheet, the *cell pointer* or cursor keeps you visually informed of your location within the spreadsheet. The cell pointer is usually a highlighted rectangle that identifies the current cell location (see Figure 7.1). The cell pointer moves around the spreadsheet in response to the mouse, the cursor arrow keys, or specific keyboard commands. In the cell currently shown by the cell pointer, you can make a new entry or edit an existing one.

Information Areas

Often there are additional areas above and/or below the worksheet that display useful information. In our illustration from *Excel* (see Figure 7.1), the line above the column labels (called the *formula bar*) displays the current cell pointer location (D10) on the left. The contents of the current cell, formulas, and functions display to the right in the formula bar (here, it's empty); the cell itself displays only the cell value or result of the calculation. At the bottom is the *status bar*, which displays various information (here, "Ready") about the spreadsheet. Pulldown menus and toolbars (rows of small pictures) provide instant, easy access to common operations (see Figure 7.2).

Automatic Updating

In a typical spreadsheet, many cells contain formulas that use the values contained in other cells. Much of the power of a spreadsheet comes from the *automatic updating* of the results of these formulas whenever the value in any related cell changes. For example, if cell B9 contains the price of a box of cereal, cell B10 contains the number of ounces in the box, and cell D9 contains the formula B9/B10, then the value displayed in cell D9 is the cost per ounce. If you change the values in B9 and B10, the unit cost shown in cell D9 changes automatically. You can quickly compare the unit cost of various cereal packages.

The Window

Actually, only a portion of the complete spreadsheet can be seen at any time on the screen. As you move the cursor around the spreadsheet, previously hidden parts become visible and previously visible parts are hidden. Think of the screen as a movable viewing window or frame looking on a much larger spreadsheet (Figure 7.3). Although only a portion can be seen at one time, the entire spreadsheet is nonetheless there and can be examined and manipulated by moving the location of the window on the spreadsheet.

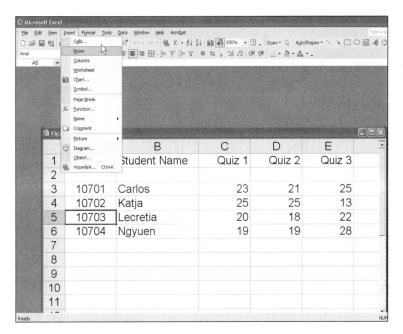

Figure 7.2
PULLDOWN MENUS AND TOOLBARS IN A SPREADSHEET

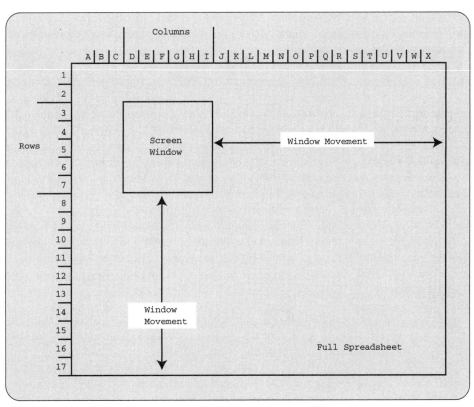

Figure 7.3 THE SPREADSHEET WINDOW

Entering and Generating Data

To understand how a spreadsheet works, first recall the three types of entries that a cell may contain: numbers or values, labels, and formulas.

Entering Data

Two types of data can be entered into a spreadsheet. The first is simple numeric information, placing a specific *number* or *value* in a cell. This is accomplished by moving the cell pointer to the appropriate cell and entering the required digits.

Second, alphabetic information, called *labels,* can also be entered into a cell in the same way. Labels help make a worksheet easy to read and understand.

If the first character of a cell entry is a number, the software interprets the entry as a value; if the first character is not a number, the program interprets the entry as a label. Formula and function entries begin with special coding, such as +, −, =, and @.

Generating Data from Relationships

Information in a cell can be generated by *formulas* that cause a cell to display the result of a calculation. The calculation may involve the contents of other cells in the worksheet or specific values and cell contents. For example, the formula +A2+B7 produces the sum of the values in the indicated cells. The formula +3.1416*Q6*Q6 would yield the area of a circle, if cell Q6 contained the radius value. Remember, the cell contains a formula, which is displayed in the information area, but the worksheet cell shows only the result of the specified calculation.

Analogous to formulas are built-in spreadsheet *functions.* Functions are special commands that allow you to achieve often complex processing without personally creating the necessary formulas. Spreadsheet programs provide an extensive list of functions, including mathematical functions, trigonometric functions, statistical functions, and financial functions. Statistical functions useful to most educators include SUM (add part of a row or column of numbers) and AVERAGE (compute the average of part of a row or column of numbers). Figure 7.4 shows some of the common functions in *Microsoft Works.*

Formulas and functions are powerful features of spreadsheets and will be used in the next section to illustrate a practical example of spreadsheet use. They underlie the concept that the power of a spreadsheet comes from the user's ability to define *relationships* among the many values and cells. Because formulas and functions manipulate values from other cells, any change in those values automatically produces a corresponding change in the value displayed by the formula or function in its cell.

Spreadsheet Commands

Simple data entry and manipulation alone are inadequate to make a spreadsheet powerful and relatively easy to use. There are numerous commands at your disposal that perform manipulation and "housekeeping" tasks, offering enormous flexibility over paper-based methods of work. These commands may be displayed in a menu or as a button on the screen (see Figure 7.2). You select the action needed, supply any necessary information, and the computer executes the command on the spreadsheet. Commonly encountered spreadsheet manipulation and housekeeping commands and brief descriptions of their use are seen in Figure 7.5. Many other commands are available

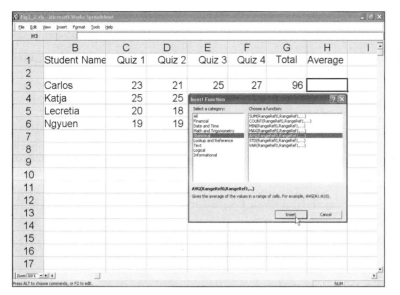

Figure 7.4
FUNCTIONS AVAILABLE
IN A SPREADSHEET

Clear	Erase the contents of one or more cells.
Copy	Duplicate the contents of one or more cells and place them in a holding area called the *clipboard*.
Cut	Remove the contents of one or more cells and place them on the clipboard.
Delete	Delete a selected column or row from a worksheet. Columns to the right move left; the rows below move up to close the gaps.
Format	Specify how the data within a cell will be displayed (e.g., integer value, fixed decimal places, floating decimal point; font, size, and style; alignment in cell [left, right, centered]).
Insert	Insert either a column or a row into a worksheet. The original columns move right and rows move down as necessary to accommodate the inserted column or row.
Open	Load the contents of a worksheet from a disk file and display them.
Paste	Place the contents of the clipboard holding area in the designated cell or cells.
Print	Produce a printed copy of the worksheet currently on the screen. Whereas the screen can display only as much of the worksheet as its window holds, a printout may show the entire worksheet or any specified portion.
Save	Store the current spreadsheet in a disk file for future use.
Width	Widen or narrow columns to meet display requirements. May be done by mouse drag.

Figure 7.5 COMMON SPREADSHEET COMMANDS

within specific spreadsheet programs, but those listed are the most basic and are adequate to develop a concrete illustration in the next section.

Verification of Results

Depending on your needs and skills in developing spreadsheet applications, the result can become very complex. Spreadsheets developed for projecting trends, for instance, may involve hundreds of cells with complex interrelationships expressed in formulas. The possibility of errors in setting up the spreadsheet is very real. It is vital to enter test data into any spreadsheet to verify against *known results* that the spreadsheet has been designed correctly. It is only too easy to believe that any answer produced by the computer is correct.

An Example Spreadsheet: Class Recordkeeping

NETS
NOTES

NETS **S** 1
NETS **S** 3
NETS **S** 6
NETS **T** I-A
NETS **T** I-B
NETS **T** III-D
NETS **T** IV-B
NETS **T** V-C

For a practical introduction to electronic spreadsheets in education, let's stay with the familiar and use a simple class recordkeeping or grade-book example. This example addresses the need to record scores on three quizzes for a group of students. Also desired are the sum of the three quiz scores for each student and the class average on each quiz.

Creating the Spreadsheet

Although this simple example clearly could be done by hand, a computer spreadsheet offers a more flexible and efficient approach to this type of problem. A step-by-step guide to creating it follows, using generic spreadsheet commands. The completed worksheet is shown in Figure 7.6.

1. Create a new worksheet. (Click the new worksheet button or click File, New).

2. Widen column A and column G, using the mouse, to provide enough room for appropriate headings and data.

3. Enter the following headings into the spreadsheet at the specified locations:

Column	*Row*	*Entry*
A	1	Student Name
C	1	Quiz 1
D	1	Quiz 2
E	1	Quiz 3
G	1	Student Total

4. Skip row 2 (for easier reading), and enter in each of the following rows one student's name, score 1, score 2, and score 3. In Figure 7.6, four students have been entered on the worksheet.

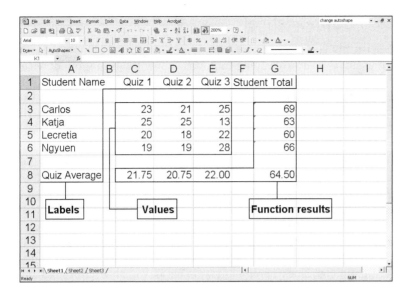

Figure 7.6

CLASS RECORDKEEPING
EXAMPLE

5. Skip another row for readability and enter the label "Quiz Average" in column A, row 8.

6. Use the SUM function in column G, row 3 to cause this cell to display the sum of the data in row 3, columns C, D, and E (i.e., the sum of the three test scores for this student). You have just established the first relationship among cells! You could, of course, have entered your own formula in cell G3, but functions are easier to use and more versatile.

7. For cells G4, G5, and G6, again use the SUM function or comparable formulas. A simpler approach is to COPY the function or formula in G3 [e.g., =SUM (C3:E3)] and PASTE it into G4 through G6. When the COPY and PASTE commands are used, any cell references automatically change to the cells containing the appropriate data [e.g., G4 contains =SUM (C4:E4), etc.]. Cells G4, G5, and G6 then display the sum of the three test scores for each of the students.

8. Enter either a formula or a function in column C, row 8 to calculate the average of all data in column C, rows 3 through 6. Cell C8 will then display the average of the four student scores for test 1, a more complex relationship among cells.

9. Finally, use COPY and PASTE to duplicate the function or formula in cell C8 into row 8, columns D, E, and G. As before, the cell references automatically adjust to reflect the appropriate data cells. The designated cells in row 8 now contain the average student score for each of the tests, as well as the average total score for all three tests.

10. The worksheet is now complete. Click File, Save in the menu or the SAVE button to store a copy of this worksheet on your disk for future use.

11. If desired, PRINT a hard copy of this spreadsheet.

Manipulating the Spreadsheet

Your spreadsheet is basic but complete at this point, much like a grade book at the end of a term. Although useful as a recordkeeping tool, this is only the beginning of what can be done with this computer spreadsheet. Here are some additional activities that you could do easily within this illustration.

Changing Data

If you discover that any of the data entries in this worksheet are incorrect, you only need to reenter the correct data in the appropriate cell. With each new entry, the spreadsheet software recalculates all affected cells automatically to reflect the data change. *Automatic recalculation* is one of the most powerful features of a spreadsheet program. Specifically, changing the score in cell C5 would also automatically alter the result in cells C8, G5, and G8 because each of these is based in part on the contents of C5. Figure 7.7 illustrates this concept. In a manual system, you would have to remember which cells to change and, eraser in hand, make all adjustments yourself. Automatic recalculation becomes increasingly valuable as worksheet size and complexity grow.

Adding a Student

To add a student, use the INSERT ROW command to open up a blank row at the desired location on the spreadsheet, then enter the necessary data. Normally, this would be done so as to insert the student in the proper place alphabetically in the list. (Of course, the software can realphabetize the data at any time!) Functions adjust automatically to include this new student. As scores are entered, the whole spreadsheet is recalculated to include the new data in the sum and average cells. Not only does this

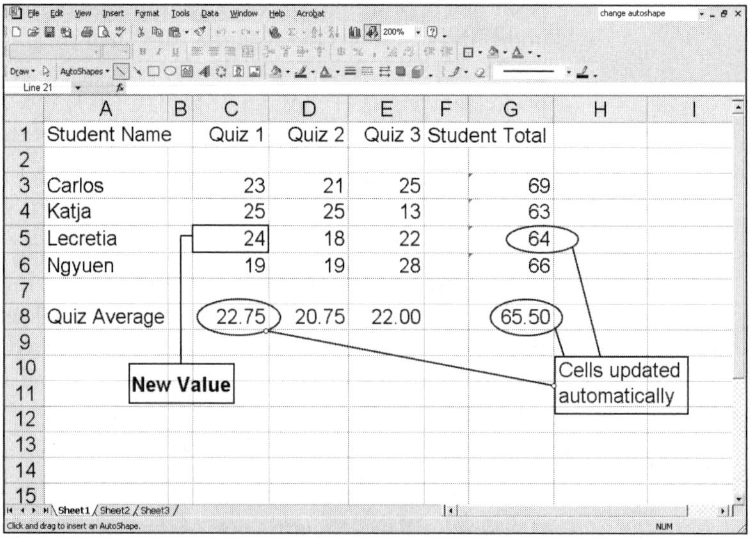

Figure 7.7

Automatic recalculation changed C8, G5, and G8 when C5 changed.

save you a lot of work, but your records are always in the correct order. Additions to a paper grade book normally must be made at the bottom of the list, which can become confusing.

Removing a Student

If a student who is already on the spreadsheet leaves the class, use the DELETE command to remove the row containing that student's data. Functions again adjust automatically to omit this student, and the whole spreadsheet is recalculated to exclude these data in the sum and average cells. This results in a set of records that is easier to read than the typical grade book with lines drawn through students no longer in the class. And your averages and sums are always correct.

Adding a Quiz

To add another quiz, INSERT a blank column at the appropriate location on the spreadsheet. Enter a heading in row 1, and enter the student data for this quiz. Functions will adjust automatically to include the new quiz. The sum and average cells update appropriately.

Adding New Features

Adding more features to this application is also quite easy. Column H could become the student average. Row 10 might be quiz standard deviation or some other statistic. You need only determine and enter the formula or function once, then COPY and PASTE it into all appropriate cells. The flexibility to establish new relationships among cells with very little extra work is a major attraction of spreadsheets.

Among other capabilities of spreadsheet programs, one of the most useful is *data charting* or *graphing* from within the worksheet. For example, in Figure 7.8, the student scores have been used to construct a bar chart that illustrates graphically how the students have performed in class. Other advanced features include simple word processing and database procedures, such as spellchecking, sorting, and selecting.

Wizards and Templates

It is not always necessary to develop an original spreadsheet to meet a need. Many spreadsheet programs have built-in wizards that guide you quickly through setting up a spreadsheet for a variety of common tasks as well as applications you might not think of. Figure 7.9 is a composite image of a *Works* wizard from the scheduling group.

In addition to wizards, the software itself, books and journal articles, and the Web all offer ready-to-use spreadsheet *templates*, including applications for teachers (Figure 7.10). A template is simply a spreadsheet file (or the directions for creating one) with no data provided but necessary formulas and functions in place. Load the template and then enter your own data into the appropriate cells. As you enter data, automatic recalculation occurs, and the calculated results display in cells containing formulas or functions. When you have entered all the data, save the spreadsheet *using a new name* for the file. In this way, the template is available to use again.

Figure 7.8
BAR CHART CONSTRUCTED WITHIN A SPREADSHEET

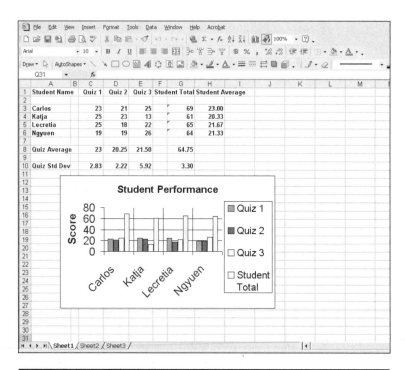

Figure 7.9
Wizards automate spreadsheet creation.

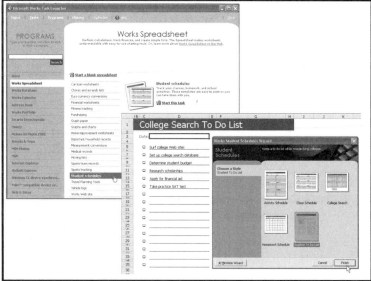

By using templates and wizards, educators who despair of being able to create an original application can still benefit from the power and versatility of a spreadsheet. Sticking with our example, one teacher could develop a template for a grade book and share it with other teachers interested in this approach to student recordkeeping.

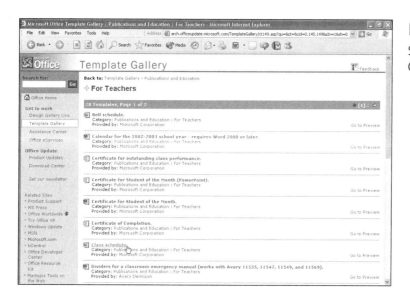

Figure 7.10

SPREADSHEET TEMPLATES
ON THE WEB

Conclusion

It should be apparent that once a spreadsheet has been set up, it can be modified quickly and easily to change, add, delete, or graph data. Our example used only a small data set to illustrate some of the capabilities of a computer spreadsheet. Because spreadsheets can have thousands of rows and hundreds of columns, it is possible to work with rather large data sets. The automatic adjustment of formulas and functions to reflect changes, as well as the automatic recalculation of all cells, makes a computer spreadsheet a very powerful tool.

Categories of Spreadsheet Applications

For simplicity, let's summarize possible uses for spreadsheets under three headings: recordkeeping, complex calculation worksheets, and "what if" applications.

NETS
NOTES

NETS **S** 1

NETS **S** 3

NETS **S** 5

NETS **S** 6

NETS **T** I-A

NETS **T** I-B

NETS **T** III-C

NETS **T** IV-A

NETS **T** IV-B

NETS **T** V-C

Recordkeeping

A computer spreadsheet can be simply a big scratchpad, a place to easily record information that is not manipulated at all. For example, a complete record of your students, relatives, or business associates and any related data could be stored on a spreadsheet. Related data could be anything to which you wished to have easy access. A spreadsheet can manage a mailing list or telephone numbers, or store other routine personal data. Room or department inventories can also be kept on a spreadsheet. The spreadsheet functions as a rudimentary database in such applications.

Advantages of using a spreadsheet in this manner include ease of changing data already on the sheet, adding new data anywhere on the sheet, and deleting unneeded data.

Moving around to view data within this type of computer spreadsheet may be more efficient and easier than working with large amounts of paper. A very large amount of information can be stored even on a single diskette, taking much less storage space than equivalent paper records. A hard copy of all or some of the spreadsheet can then be printed as needed. Even using a computer spreadsheet in this very simple manner can be advantageous, although it would hardly justify purchasing a computer and spreadsheet software. Such applications do not make full use of the inherent power of a spreadsheet.

A computer spreadsheet becomes much more powerful as a "complex" record-keeping system. In addition to storing various amounts of information, include calculations on the data. The student grade-book illustration included three types of calculations: the sum of each student's scores, the average of scores on each quiz and for each student, and the standard deviation for each quiz. Many more calculations based on the data could be added with minimal effort.

Many educators find a spreadsheet grade book much easier, more flexible, and faster to use than special-purpose grade-book programs, which are described in Chapter 9. Inventory records may be more valuable if counts and/or sums of item values are added. In addition to performing the indicated calculations efficiently, the spreadsheet's abilities to allow for data correction, addition, or deletion and to perform automatic recalculation of all formulas and functions after data changes have made the use of computer spreadsheets invaluable to teachers for many diverse applications.

Complex Calculation Worksheets

Computer spreadsheets are not restricted just to simple or complex recordkeeping. They were developed to speed up and simplify many business applications that involve complex calculations. Numerous specialized functions included in most spreadsheet software are useful in particular application areas.

An example is loan-amortization calculation. This involves specifying the principal amount of a loan, the annual interest rate, and the length (term) of the loan. Based on the entered values, a spreadsheet function or series of functions then calculates and displays the amount of each payment, the principal and interest component of each payment, and the remaining balance (Figure 7.11). In addition, other functions can produce the sum of all principal and interest payments to provide a clear picture of the total cost of a loan, as well as the monthly details. Such applications can be very useful when considering whether to borrow money, perhaps in a business math, economics, or family-living class.

"What If" Applications

Being able to answer "what if" questions is another reason that spreadsheets were created and is a major factor in their popularity. Instead of looking at only one possibility, you can have the computer quickly calculate the results for different parameters.

From our loan example, you could direct the computer on the same spreadsheet to generate amortization data to answer many questions. What if the amount of the loan were increased or decreased? What if the interest rate were 2 percent higher or

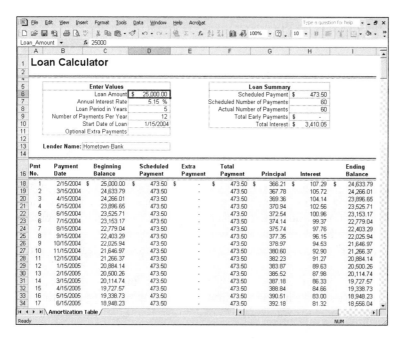

Figure 7.11
LOAN ANALYSIS FOR
INTERACTIVE PROJECTIONS

lower? What if the repayment period were extended or shortened? You can then examine and compare the results, and make appropriate decisions based on this comparison.

There are two different methods for handling "what ifs." If the worksheet is not too large and the number of different parameters of interest is small, you can create multiple worksheets in one by using COPY and PASTE to duplicate the first set of cells into unused areas of the same sheet (or another sheet). For example, if the initial area used was cells A1 through G25, they could be duplicated from H1 through N25 or from A26 through G50.

In a more complex situation, "what if" questions are often explored interactively. Create a worksheet, enter one set of parameters, and print the results. Next, change the parameters and print the result. Do this as many times as necessary, then compare the printouts to see the effects of the changes. For a quick look at alternatives, you may not need printouts.

The popular spreadsheet grade book also has "what if" uses. Suppose you have set up your worksheet to compute total scores and averages. Your students know that their grades will be based on their final averages. With one test remaining, your worksheet shows each student's average to that point. If students ask what score they must achieve on the last test to earn a certain grade, you could very quickly enter different scores for the final exam and watch the resulting average change. Many teachers regularly face such questions but can give an answer only after finding time to do several sets of calculations. A spreadsheet offers almost instantaneous responses.

Can you think of other applications where this type of "what if" comparison would be important, even indispensable? Consider how often you must make decisions based on incomplete data. How could a spreadsheet help you weigh options?

Classroom Applications

The preceding section on application categories may have stimulated your thinking about potential uses for spreadsheets in your teaching. Other concrete examples should further expand your thinking in an area that is admittedly abstract to many teachers.

NETS
NOTES

NETS **S** 3

NETS **S** 5

NETS **S** 6

NETS **T** II–A

NETS **T** II–C

NETS **T** II–E

NETS **T** III–A

NETS **T** III–B

NETS **T** III–C

NETS **T** IV–B

NETS **T** V–C

NETS **T** VI–B

Teaching Spreadsheets

One day, you may find yourself in a situation that requires you to teach others to use spreadsheets. Just as you were probably mystified by the concepts at first, so your students will be. There are numerous tutorials on how to work with spreadsheets on the Web (see, for example, Jackson 2002). Rather than try to list them for you here, we provide links on the companion website. You can also do a simple web search for "spreadsheet tutorials," which produced thousands of hits when we last tried.

Jonassen (2000, pp. 97–99) recommended a six-stage approach to learning to use spreadsheets to achieve higher-order thinking that resembles the model you studied for databases in the previous chapter. Stage 1 is working with existing spreadsheets, both manipulating completed ones and entering data into templates. In stage 2, guide students to begin planning a spreadsheet to explore an area of interest. For stage 3, students adapt current spreadsheets or create new ones that other students will complete. At stage 4, complexity of content increases by relating the content to classroom activities. Students now use their plan and their growing knowledge of the mechanics of spreadsheets to build their own "problem-oriented" spreadsheet. Stage 5 extrapolates from an existing spreadsheet by adding new variables and relationships, whereas stage 6 is a period of reflection, which is interwoven throughout the other stages. Reflection is essential to depth of learning as students truly construct new knowledge from their past and current experiences.

In addition, Jonassen (1996) offered five concrete approaches to maximize learning with spreadsheets while fostering group collaboration:

1. Form teams that assure the distribution of higher-ability math students across the teams, so that no team has an initial advantage.

2. Assist students in clarifying the group goal—identifying the problem and breaking the task into steps.

3. Negotiate tasks and subtasks to assure that the math whizzes don't just solve the problem for their group.

4. Monitor individual and group performance, including coaching of other team members by the math leaders.

5. Assist in reconciling differences within the teams, especially where it is possible to show differing solutions to the same problem.

A fun way to teach anyone about spreadsheets, but especially younger learners and anyone reluctant to explore this tool, starts with small bags of M&Ms. Ask your learners what they already know about the contents of such a bag (colors, descriptions, etc.) and have them guess the total number of candies, number of each color, and so on before opening the bags. You may want to record the guesses for later comparison. Learners then open their bags, count the contents, and record their data on note cards, Post-it notes, or a data collection form. Combine the data into a physical spreadsheet using a large sheet of butcher paper or an overhead transparency marked in rows (bags) and columns (colors and total). Try to reach conclusions about the data. Then use the data from your own bag (yes, you get one, too) to construct a spreadsheet (or enter the data into a template you created previously). Demonstrate a range of spreadsheet operations, including adding bags or colors (just in case something odd appears), correcting errors (if inspection of the data shows an unlikely number), and creating a graph to show the color distributions. Finally, have the learners enter their data into your template and graph their findings. Have them circulate among the computers to view each other's graphs as they reflect on the patterns they see. Finally, have several learners combine their data on a single spreadsheet to graph the results together. This will clearly show the inherent variation among the bags as well as more complex graphs. We first saw this idea in Niess (August/September 1992) and find it still works today, especially among reluctant learners who profess no use for a spreadsheet.

Data Resources

Bull, Bull, and Drier (1999) offered many different spreadsheet activities, but we refer you to their article particularly for the many Internet data sources listed. As the authors noted, data analysis and graphing begin with good data, the location or gathering of which can take significant time. They directed readers to data collections from diverse sources such as the Data and Story Library at Carnegie Mellon University <http://lib. stat.cmu.edu/DASL> to the Education Services Directorate of Queensland, Australia <http://exploringdata.cqu.edu.au/datasets.htm>, from which data can be found on the number of cricket chirps per second at varying temperatures or the 1970 and 1971 U.S. Selective Service (military draft) lotteries. Those two sources alone should keep students in interesting data for a very long time, and many others appear in the article and on our companion website for your convenience.

Budgets

Budgets are an obvious application of spreadsheet software that will work for learners of nearly any age once they have their own money to spend. Children seem to reach that stage at a younger age by the year, yet many have little or no sense of money management. Spreadsheets can help! Begin a budget activity by brainstorming common sources of income and typical spending categories. Settle on a common set, and then create a budget template or have students create their own. Have them track their personal budget over the school year or some specified time period and generate graphs that may demonstrate more clearly their income and spending patterns. For older students, expand the activity to include monthly averages, quarterly figures, even income tax projections. Could you include projecting whether the student will have enough cash to pay anticipated prom expenses?

Fund-Raising and Economics

Although she began by looking for motivating ways to teach middle school students about spreadsheets, Fortunato (2002) ended up with an economics lesson and a modest fund-raising project in the end. She knew concrete, real-life projects motivate students more than typical "schoolwork." The wide range of specialty printing papers and materials now available provided the vehicle. Students chose among magnets, decals, or bumper stickers. They had to design their product and use a spreadsheet to determine the profit under a range of conditions. They quickly learned that they could not use an entire page of blank material for only a couple of products or the selling price would become too high. They learned to balance product characteristics (e.g., size) and profit potential. The project easily evolved into more than just spreadsheet activities as students used graphics software to create parts of the products and a word processor to create marketing materials and order forms. Of course, a spreadsheet maintained the overall accounting for the project. In the end, students learned much about technology and economics in an authentic context. They earned enough money to buy a new color printer for their classroom, a real bonus. See also Fortunato and Humphrey (1996) for ideas about how about to create a middle school technology program.

Zisow (2000/2001) undertook a fund-raising project with her fourth graders. The class had long held a Mother's Day plant sale to raise funds for a field trip on Chesapeake Bay, which was part of an interdisciplinary unit involving art, language arts, math, and science. Zisow enhanced the experience through spreadsheet activities to record sales and forecast profits. There was both a presale phase, when orders were taken, and an open sale phase, when students used presale earnings to purchase more plants for the actual sale date. Zisow ensured that her students engaged in higher-order thinking by posing stimulating questions: Which plant was the most profitable? How much more profitable was the most profitable plant compared to the least profitable? What percentage of each plant type sold in the presale period versus on the sale date? Zisow's lesson is exemplary in its extension of a common school activity into an authentic learning experience.

Indusi (1997) discussed creating a company purchase order using spreadsheets in a unit for middle school students. In developing such a spreadsheet, the concepts of cost, quantity, discounts, tax, and balance due are learned and applied as a lesson in basic economics.

Elementary Grade Applications

Lewis (2001, 2002) strongly advocated use of spreadsheets to support the math curriculum at all levels. Her examples are carefully aligned with the NETS-S standards and also those of the National Council of Teachers of Mathematics. At the lowest grade levels, she suggested teaching counting by inserting clip art into cells and having students duplicate it into adjacent cells the specified number of times. If appropriate, allow students to select the clip art themselves. The activity also teaches concepts of pictographs. She also suggested creating number charts (e.g., a hundreds chart) so that the clear pattern of the numbers that develops in the chart helps students understand key concepts, such as that every number in the tens column ends in zero.

Lewis (2002) offered many other creative ideas for use of spreadsheets at early ages. For instance, addition becomes concrete and visual when students simply fill cells with different colors (e.g., two red next to three blue) and then count the total number of colored cells. She reserved the first column to enter the corresponding addition problem (2 + 3 + 5) as text to link the concrete and the abstract directly. For off-computer work, enlarge the cells and the font to create printable flash cards. Lewis (2001, 2002) is a rich resource of spreadsheet applications throughout the math curriculum.

Jackson (2002, October 9) provided much concrete guidance for using a spreadsheet in the lower grades and in specific subjects in the form of an online "techtorial." Check it out for step-by-step help.

High School Statistics and Research

Suppose you teach talented high school students how to conduct research. Clearly, after students gather their data, they must analyze it, but specialized statistical software is not within most school budgets. Morgan (2001) turned to the statistical functions in his spreadsheet to solve his problem. Students learn about descriptive statistics, inferential statistics, and graphical analysis, or DIG stats. The software does the mathematical work, leaving students free to concentrate on understanding when to use which technique and how to interpret the results, a goal not always achieved in college research courses! One interesting assignment was to analyze eruption data for Old Faithful geyser in Yellowstone National Park (Figure 7.12). You can learn all about DIG stats by visiting Morgan's web site at <www.cvgs.k12.va.us/digstats>.

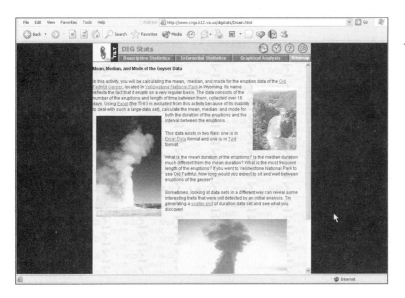

Figure 7.12
THE DIG STATS WEBSITE

Physical and Health Education

The potential of spreadsheets to assist in understanding all manner of human data, including performance on physical tasks, is obvious. Manouchehri and Pagnucco (1999/2000) described a project using graphing calculators and spreadsheets to determine and then draw the graph of a prescribed physical activity, namely, a runner who varies the pace over the time of the run. Although the authors were primarily concerned with the algebra involved, the application can easily be varied to fit any number of training and conditioning activities and, with proper guidance on the underlying issues, could greatly enhance student understanding of the benefits of physical activity.

Students are likely to view themselves as experts on local fast foods, but there is probably much that they still can learn. On a very simple level, students can research costs at various restaurants, enter the data into a spreadsheet, and produce a graph comparing the popular establishments. Popularity rating could be another factor, which would make it interesting to retain and update a group spreadsheet from year to year. A challenging and potentially valuable exercise would be to research the nutritional value of common fast-food meal combinations. A more complex spreadsheet could then reflect cost and health issues, possibly including daily dietary needs and recommended intake of fats, cholesterol, vitamins, and so forth, with accompanying graphs to demonstrate the points visually.

Forecasting—What If . . . ?

You already have read about the power of spreadsheets to allow for hypothesis testing as you vary one or more values within your worksheet. Crisci (1992) applied spreadsheets to a stock market simulation in which students tracked portfolio performance and projected future scenarios. Cashien (1990) and Adams and Kroch (1989) both described applications of spreadsheets to economic models and forecasting. Schlenker and Yoshida (1991) approached the study of levers by using a spreadsheet to calculate the force needed to lift given weights using specified levers. Personal finance issues, such as interest and loan amortization, lend themselves to spreadsheet projection as well.

If students have little interest in common spreadsheet applications (such as budgeting), turn to newspaper data on major sports teams. Activities range from determining which team has the best record in various categories to predicting outcomes of future contests based on past performances. Beaver (1992) illustrated this concept for baseball and also showed how to create onscreen directions to users for entering data.

Earlier in this chapter, you learned to create a grade book that you could also use to project the effects of future test scores on final grades. Why not have students create their own personal grade book, with which they can track and project their own grades at any time? The concept is identical to your class record system, but students would record only their own data. Beaver (1992) suggested using this approach for high schoolers who wish to track or forecast their grade point averages, whether to maintain sports eligibility or project college admission.

Science

Science offers numerous possible applications of spreadsheets. Smith-Gratto and Blackburn (1997) developed the ABCD model for integrating spreadsheets into the elementary science curriculum. Briefly, the four steps are analyze, brainstorm, create connections, and define objectives. Here are a few specific examples of science applications for school use.

Elements in the Body

Albrecht and Davis (2000) challenged science students to think about chemistry and the makeup of the human body in applications suitable for upper elementary grades through high school. Using a Sherlock Holmes theme and many detailed resources from the Internet, students create a spreadsheet of elements, their chemical symbols, and their percentage of the mass of their own body. They next graph the data with the spreadsheet to demonstrate visually and dramatically the preponderance of oxygen, carbon, and hydrogen. Because most occur in compounds, this activity connects to the study of those compounds. They also speculate on the variations that would occur among those who eat and exercise properly compared to those who do not. The same article also details use of spreadsheets to study and compare the atmosphere of the Earth with that of Mars, where again graphs can make the differences easy for even an elementary-age student to comprehend. For older students, the activity can lead to questions such as the probable fertility of Martian soil based on available soil data, which again are entered into a spreadsheet to facilitate the analysis.

The Weather

The weather provides a ready source of data for ongoing science projects. Use a spreadsheet to store daily weather data (temperature at specified times, precipitation, barometer reading, wind conditions, etc.). Design the spreadsheet as a template for a specific time period, such as one month, and include cells for calculating appropriate averages and, perhaps, other statistics. Use the data to produce line or bar graphs and compare them with those published in most newspapers. Categorical data, such as type of cloud cover, can also be collected and used to generate pie or bar charts to illustrate weather patterns.

Niess (March 1992) focused on studying the wind in a variety of geographic locations. The spreadsheet was organized using wind direction for the rows, months for the columns, and days in each month that the wind was from each direction as the data. This provided a basis for pursuing higher-order thinking goals with questions concerning relationships between wind patterns and seasons. When is the wind most stable? Least stable? Calmest? Strongest? Why might such patterns exist when they do?

The Environment

Many teachers at varying grade levels teach units on the environment or aspects of ecology, perhaps in conjunction with Earth Day. A spreadsheet can be used for many relevant activities. To study energy usage, have students inventory their home appliances and record the energy use of each in kilowatts per hour. After estimating hours of use for each appliance over some time period, students can develop an energy-consumption model.

Also related to energy conservation, students can take measurements of their home, recording or calculating square footage of the residence and all windows and doors, as well as thickness of attic insulation. Based on published formulas, students can determine home heating and cooling requirements and estimate the effects of added insulation.

Many environmental activities involve monitoring recycling activities in the home or community, for which a spreadsheet can be very useful. Ramondetta (1992) described a project that focused on lunchroom discards and then projected annual waste. This project could be implemented in most schools.

Density of an Unknown Substance

A simple science experiment suitable from about sixth grade up offers a sound application of spreadsheet capabilities (Albrecht & Firedrake, 1993). Students work collaboratively in groups of three. Each student receives an unidentified lump of the same material and measures its mass and volume, the latter using Archimedes' water displacement method. Data from the three "trials" are entered into a simple spreadsheet template, which calculates the actual measured volume, density, and several averages used to assess confidence in the data. Finally, the results are graphed. Students learn science, data analysis, and spreadsheet skills in a single lesson.

Measurement and Precision

Not all applications of spreadsheets involve fancy mathematics. Albrecht and Firedrake (1994) described a lesson from which students learn key aspects of measurement, error, and precision. Students measure the area of their table tops using locally made meter sticks of varying precision—uncalibrated and calibrated by decimeter, centimeter, and millimeter. The lesson includes lower and upper bounds for each measurement, as well as area for each and the original measurement. Graphing the lower bound, measured length, and upper bound gives dramatic visual demonstration to the effects of the precision of the instrument. Students also consider such questions as how to most accurately report their findings for each stick, given its calibration. Treatment of measurement error, significant digits, and scientific reporting are all part of this creative lesson.

Mathematics

Most spreadsheet applications rely on some element of mathematics, but that does not relegate uses solely to teachers of math. That is why we have taken considerable effort to provide applications from other areas of the curriculum. However, math teachers may well disproportionately understand and apply the power of spreadsheets in their teaching. Examples abound, from which we have selected just a couple to share.

Feicht (2000) acknowledged that his pattern recognition problem can be solved with either a spreadsheet or a graphing calculator. However, he argued that access to computers is often greater than to fancy calculators and, perhaps more important, spreadsheets are easier and more intuitive to use. The problem for this application is to determine the number of blocks in a pyramid with 50 blocks for the base row with the pyramid being 50 rows high. For much smaller numbers, creating a paper table gives the answer easily and quickly, but few students are likely to pursue this approach all the way to 50. If you start with the single top block, the blocks in each row total the number of the previous row plus the current row number. Row 1 totals one block, row 2 totals 1 + 2 or 3, row 3 to-tals 3 + 3 = 6, and so on; the answer is 1,275, by the way. Only a very simple formula is required to make these calculations, and it can be instantly copied to enough cells to solve the problem for any number of rows. Feicht extended the activity into other comparable patterns, such as how many different two-scoop ice-cream cones can be created from the available 31 flavors? He also demonstrated appropriate use of the graphing capabilities of the spreadsheet to further understanding of the patterns involved.

At the elementary level, teachers have used spreadsheets simply as calculators and to demonstrate mathematical relationships. Parker and Widmer (1991) explained how to help children understand the meaning of a million or other large numbers using a spreadsheet to compare such values to everyday things.

Battista and Borrow (1998) recommended using spreadsheets to help primary students think about numerical procedures. Their approach culminated in how students eventually can apply such thinking to algebraic reasoning. Widmer and Sheffield (1998) discussed how using spreadsheets, graphs, and graphing calculators with middle school students can foster a deeper understanding of selected geometric concepts such as diameter and perimeter. Abramovich and Nabors (1997) described how using spreadsheets helped seventh-grade algebra students develop problem-solving skills. Finally, Holmes (1997) presented activities that can aid both the teacher and the student in learning about spreadsheet use for complex math concepts. This application included use of templates.

The Magic Square

A magic square is a 3-cell by 3-cell grid. Each cell contains one of the digits from 1 to 9, without repetition. The challenge is to place the digits so that all row sums and column sums equal 15. Lewis (2002) set up this common puzzle using a spreadsheet (Figure 7.13). Students used a discovery approach (i.e., trial and error) to find a solution. How many unique solutions are there?

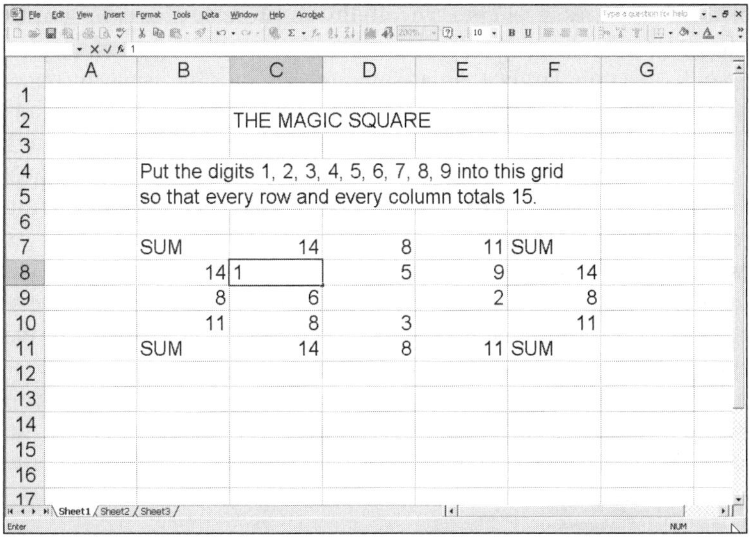

Figure 7.13

THE MAGIC SQUARE IMPLEMENTED WITH A SPREADSHEET (ADAPTED FROM LEWIS, 2002)

Problem Solving beyond Typical Skill Level

South African math teacher J. R. M. Paul (1995) noted that student problem-solving skills are often limited by their developing math skills. When problems require calculations that are too advanced, the teacher modifies the numbers to better suit the students or even completes the calculations personally. Neither is ideal for student learning.

Paul's solution to the dilemma was to let spreadsheet software handle the math involved in problems that students can readily relate to. The "pizza problem" involves assessing the economics of various sizes of pizzas. Is a small pizza cut into four pieces the same amount of food per piece as a large pizza cut into eight? Which represents the best value? What should each pizza cost or what should its diameter be to make them all equal on a unit basis? Another interesting problem was testing the accuracy of a spaghetti measuring stick (the kind with holes labeled for the number of servings). Were the amounts measured truly proportional to the number of servings claimed? Students also explored hypothetical situations, such as appropriate diameters to achieve differing measurements, for example, 1:3:9 for triple portions, rather than the most typical 1:2:4. Paul presented a very solid example of the creative use of spreadsheets in the classroom.

SUMMARY

Spreadsheets are common application software, joining word processing and databases as major productivity tools. They were developed to cope with often difficult and time-consuming financial calculations, but they have found wide usage in other situations as well.

A spreadsheet is simply an arrangement of rows and columns in which data may be stored and manipulated. The intersection of a row and a column is termed a *cell*. Each cell may contain numeric or alphabetic data, or a formula or function that establishes a relationship among cells. Relationships are one key to the power of spreadsheets. Wizards and templates offer this power to users without the need to create original applications. Of special value to many teachers is the ability to produce charts or graphs quickly and easily from spreadsheet data.

Spreadsheets rapidly become larger than a computer screen can display at once. The screen then becomes a window or frame, which you can move about on the spreadsheet as needed. Changing the value in any cell in the spreadsheet automatically alters any other related cell. This is a major advantage of electronic spreadsheets over their manual counterparts. It opens the way to answering "what if" questions to check the results of varying assumptions or projections.

Spreadsheets seem alien to many teachers, who tend not to see applications for a "financial" tool. Yet there are numerous sound classroom applications of spreadsheets. Examples in this chapter described uses across many subject fields and at various grade levels from elementary through high school. The Internet also offers many data resources to support spreadsheet activities. Although it may require more effort for you to become comfortable with a spreadsheet than with word processing or databases, the benefits are worth the effort. The potential of spreadsheets in education is limited only by your creativity as a teacher.

chapter 7
activities

Use any available spreadsheet software to complete the following activities.

1. Compare the specific screen format of your spreadsheet to the general design in Figure 7.1. What are the differences? Determine the maximum size of a worksheet; that is, what is the maximum row and maximum column? How are the columns labeled after Z?

2. Make a list of the actual procedures used with your spreadsheet in place of the generic manipulation and housekeeping commands described in this chapter. Create a wall chart for your computer area or a quick reference handout.

3. Create a functional grade book similar to the illustration given.

4. Expand your basic grade book by investigating the additional functions that your spreadsheet offers and adding those that you consider potentially useful.

5. Develop a personal budget. You'll need both an income and an expenditure section. Divide your expenses into major categories, such as housing, food, automobile, clothing, tuition, books, entertainment, and so forth. Set up a "base" budget and leave space to record your actual expenses for several months. Be sure to include cells that compare actual expenses with your budget each month. Graph your results.

6. Develop a lesson plan for using a spreadsheet with your students.

7. Locate existing lesson plans on the Internet that utilize spreadsheet activities. Modify at least one to suit your own interests.

8. Develop a lesson plan that draws data from the Internet for analysis and graphing with your spreadsheet software.

Companion Website

Visit the companion website at <www.ablongman.com/lockard6e> for more information about the topics discussed in this chapter.

expect the world®

The New York Times
nytimes.com

Themes of the Times

Expand your knowledge of the concepts discussed in this chapter by reading current and historical articles from the *New York Times* by visiting the Themes of the Times section of the companion website <www.ablongman.com/lockard6e>.

References

Abramovich, S., and Nabors, W. "Spreadsheets as Generators of New Meanings in Middle School Algebra." *Computers in the Schools*, 1997, *13*(1–2), pp. 13–25.

Adams, F. G., and Kroch, E. "The Computer in the Teaching of MacroEconomics." *Journal of Economic Education*, Summer 1989, *20*(3), pp. 269–280.

Albrecht, B., and Firedrake, G. "Archimedes, Spreadsheets, and BASIC." *The Computing Teacher*, April 1993, *20*(7), pp. 33–36.

Albrecht, B., and Firedrake, G. "Measurement and Precision." *The Computing Teacher*, September 1994, *21*(1), pp. 46–48.

Albrecht, P., and Davis, P. "Elemental, My Dear Holmes, Elemental." *Learning and Leading with Technology*, May 2000, *27*(8), pp. 22–27.

Battista, M., and Borrow, C. "Using Spreadsheets to Promote Algebraic Thinking." *Teaching Children Mathematics*, April 1998, *4*(8), pp. 470–478.

Beaver, J. "Using Computer Power to Improve Your Teaching. Part II: Spreadsheets and Charting." *The Computing Teacher*, March 1992, *19*(6), pp. 22–24.

Bull, G., Bull, G., and Drier, H. "Exploring Data Warehouses." *Learning and Leading with Technology*, May 1999, *26*(8), pp. 22–27.

Cashien, P. "Spreadsheet Investigations in Economics Teaching." *Economics*, 1990, *26*, pp. 73–84.

Crisci, G. "Play the market!" *Instructor*, January 1992, *101*(5), pp. 68–69.

Feicht, L. "Find the Formula. Using a Spreadsheet to Solve a Pattern." *Learning and Leading with Technology*, March 2000, *27*(6), pp. 36–41.

Fortunato, J. "Selling Your Students on Spreadsheets." *Learning and Leading with Technology*, October 2002, *30*(2), pp. 28–31.

Fortunato, J., and Humphrey, K. *Building Technology Skills: A Middle School Portfolio Program*. Portland, OR: J. Weston Walch, 1996.

Holmes, E. D. "The Spreadsheet—Absolutely Elementary!" *Learning and Leading with Technology*, May 1997, *24*(8), pp. 6–12.

Indusi, J. "Creating a Purchase Order Using Spreadsheets." *Mathematics Teaching in the Middle School*, May 1997, *2*(6), pp. 404–407.

Jackson, L. "Excelling in the K–12 Classroom." An Education World Techtorial. October 9, 2002. Retrieved January 20, 2003 from <www.education world.com/a_tech/techtorial/techtorial010.shtml>

Jonassen, D. H. *Computers in the Classroom: Mindtools for Critical Thinking*. Englewood Cliffs, NJ: Prentice Hall (Merrill), 1996.

Jonassen, D. H. *Computers as Mindtools for Schools: Engaging Critical Thinking*, 2nd ed. Upper Saddle River, NJ: Merrill, 2000.

Lewis, P. *Spreadsheet Magic*. Eugene, OR: ISTE, 2001.

Lewis, P. "Spreadsheet Magic." *Learning and Leading with Technology*, November 2002, *30*(3), pp. 36–41.

Manouchehri, A., and Pagnucco, L. "Julio's Run: Studying Graphs and Functions." *Learning and Leading with Technology*, December/January 1999–2000, *27*(4), pp. 42–45.

Morgan, T. "DIG Stats. A Web Resource for Statistics and Data Analysis." *Learning and Leading with Technology*, September 2001, *29*(1), pp. 32–35.

Niess, M. L. "Winds of Change." *The Computing Teacher*, March 1992, *19*(6), pp. 32–35.

Niess, M. L. "Mathematics and M&Ms." *The Computing Teacher*, August/September 1992, *20*(1), pp. 29–31.

Parker, J., and Widmer, C. C. "Teaching Mathematics with Technology." *Arithmetic Teacher*, September 1991, *39*(1), pp. 38–41.

Paul, J. R. M. "Pizza and Spaghetti. Solving Math Problems in the Primary Classroom." *The Computing Teacher*, April 1995, *22*(7), pp. 65–67.

Ramondetta, J. "Learning from Lunchroom Trash." *Learning*, April–May 1992, *20*(8), p. 59.

Schlenker, R. M., and Yoshida, S. J. "A Clever Lever Endeavor: You Can't Beat the Spreadsheet." *The Science Teacher*, February 1991, *58*(2), pp. 36–39.

Smith-Gratto, K., and Blackburn, M. A. "The Computer as a Scientific Tool: Integrating Spreadsheets into the Elementary Science Curriculum." *Computers in the Schools*, 1997, *13*(1–2), pp. 125–131.

Widmer, C., and Sheffield, L. "Modeling Mathematics Concepts: Using Physical, Calculator, and Computer Models to Teach Area and Perimeter." *Learning and Leading with Technology*, February 1998, *25*(5), pp. 32–35.

Zisow, M. A. "Fundraising with Technology." *Learning and Leading with Technology*, December/January 2000/2001, *28*(4), pp. 36–41.

Graphics Tools:
Communicating Visually

OBJECTIVES

After completing this chapter, you will be able to:

- Describe and explain the use of three different sources of graphics: basic clip art, clip art collections, and the Internet.
- Identify potential applications of draw and paint software in your teaching.
- Explain the fundamental concepts and principles related to scanning, both for images and for optical character recognition.
- Classify digital cameras based on factors such as how images are stored, the camera's resolution, and its lens capabilities.
- Discuss potential uses of scanners and related software in your teaching.
- Discuss possible options for enhancing digital images.
- Explain possible applications of charting or graphing in your field.
- Plan lessons that integrate graphic organizers for concept mapping.
- Brainstorm possible applications of 3-D visualization in your curriculum area.
- Differentiate print graphics from presentation graphics.

- Describe varied applications of print graphics software that are applicable to your teaching situation.
- Identify common mistakes made by creators of electronic slide shows and why they are not appropriate.
- Describe use of graphics software for assessment.
- State and justify a position for or against your use of presentation graphics as a teacher and by your students.
- Discuss basic considerations related to video data projectors and use of document cameras.
- Develop lesson plans that include student use of computer graphics and related technology tools.

Graphics is the term used to mean all forms of visual images. Preceding chapters have shown numerous ways for teachers and students to benefit from use of common, general-purpose computer applications. In this chapter, you will explore tools to help you and your students communicate ideas visually using digital graphics. The importance of "seeing" content is probably obvious, as many students are visual learners, but anyone can benefit from an additional presentation format. You will learn about software and tools to create graphics as well as ways to use or present what you have created. No teacher is apt to find all such tools useful, but every teacher will find something of value among the available resources. In many cases, you can produce results readily of which you could once only dream. None of these tools replaces the more general ones discussed previously; rather, they add important capabilities to a teacher's software skills.

Obtaining and Creating Graphics

Visual communication requires visual materials, which for our purposes mean *digital* resources. Vast quantities of digital graphics are readily available, especially in the form of clip art, but available clip art rarely meets all needs. This section looks first at existing graphics resources and then at a range of tools for creating your own graphics.

NETS
NOTES

NETS **S** 1
NETS **S** 3
NETS **S** 4
NETS **T** I-A
NETS **T** I-B
NETS **T** II-A
NETS **T** II-C
NETS **T** III-A
NETS **T** III-B
NETS **T** III-C
NETS **T** IV-B
NETS **T** V-D

Graphics Sources

Clearly, the quickest way to use graphics is to find existing images that suit your purposes. You already have clip art collections on your computer in nearly every case, but you can also purchase additional materials and download still more from the Internet.

Basic Clip Art

You probably are aware of and already use the large amount of clip art that is provided as part of products like *Microsoft Office* (Figure 8.1) and *Appleworks*, so we'll focus mostly on other sources of graphics. You should be aware of a couple of things about clip art.

First, most clip art is "static," meaning it is made up of traditional still images. However, the Web has popularized a form of animated images, which are a special form of clip art called *animated gifs*. The term *gif* refers to the specific file format of these pieces of art. No doubt you have already seen the downside of using these images as they move endlessly while you are viewing a web page. Used judiciously, animated gifs may add communication value to a message, but they are frequently overused, so consider carefully any use you envision. In the Microsoft Clip Gallery you can tell which graphics are animated by the star icon at the corner of the thumbnail image (see Figure 8.1).

The second thing to understand about clip art is that you can resize most images to fit your need and they still look clear and sharp. However, the nature of animated gifs makes resizing much more problematic. Always view the image at its original size first, so you know just how it should look; then resize as desired if the quality remains acceptable.

Figure 8.1
CLIP ART INTEGRAL TO AN *OFFICE* SOFTWARE SUITE

Clip Media Collections

In addition to the already large amount of clip art that installs automatically with many software packages, options exist to purchase additional clip media from other sources. Typically, a modest price gets you multiple CDs that contain all manner of images and some kind of "browser" for viewing them by categories or searching by content description. Typical collections include both still and animated images, and most recently, audio clips and even video clips. You'll learn more about these multimedia resources later. The amount of material sold in even low-cost clip media collections is enormous, and package titles including words like "millions" are common, even at prices well below $100. However, the quality of the clip media can be uneven.

Internet Resources

Naturally, the Internet is another major source of existing clip art. Many sites offer extensive collections of graphics for the computer user, so we can highlight only a few popular sites that have remained accessible for several years.

The Amazing Picture Machine <www.ncrtec.org/picture.htm> is one of the many services of the North Central Regional Technology in Education Consortium. When you visit, note the cautionary advice given about legal use of the images, noting specifically that the safe approach is to assume everything is copyrighted and ask permission before using. This site links visitors to the source of the images to facilitate requesting permission, although the actual holder of the copyright can be difficult to determine. The site also explains how to cite an image used properly. In addition, the site also offers many lesson plans <www.ncrtec.org/tl/camp/lessons.htm> that illustrate effective use of graphics to support a wide range of learning goals.

The Clip Art Connection <www.clipartconnection.com> is a vast resource of images, as well as a compilation of links to similar sites. We also like the clip art resources at <http://webclipart.about.com>, which provides links to numerous clip art collections. Although most art is noted as being free for your own use on websites, much of it is equally usable in applications not involving the Web that you'll meet shortly. Barrys Clipart Server is another resource that many teachers have found useful <www.barrysclipart.com>.

Finding websites with clip art is as simple as a quick search, but actually downloading the art you find can be confusing. Many sites provide no directions and some, such as Barrys, provide a download link that seems not to work. Click the link and you'll simply see the desired image. To save the image onto your own computer, use one of two approaches. If you are viewing the image, right-click (Windows) or control-click on it and from the pop-up menu, depending on your browser, choose Save image as (*Netscape* and *Mozilla*) or Save picture as (*Internet Explorer*). You can also download the image by right-clicking as noted previously but on the download link; then choose Save link as or Save target as (Figure 8.2). In each case, navigate to the folder in which you wish to store the picture.

Draw and Paint Software

If you have an artistic bent or just can't find a suitable graphic image in available clip art, you may turn to a drawing package to create your own. Computer-based tools have

Figure 8.2

Download clip art using
the pop-up menu.

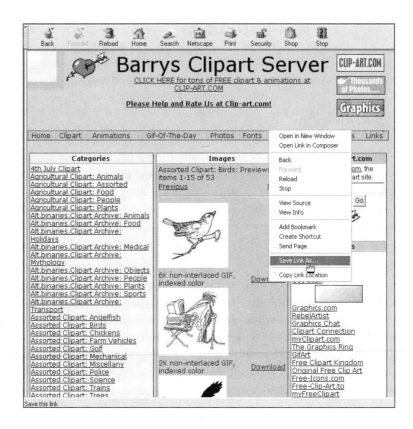

taken the art world by storm, creating whole new classes of artistic work and ways for artists to express themselves.

Among the first drawing programs were *MacDraw* and *MacPaint* (free with early Macintosh computers) and *PaintBrush* for DOS computers. Today, those early products seem quite primitive. Still, they were adequate to stimulate a whole new use for computers.

As with most types of software, enhancements to drawing programs have greatly extended their sophistication but at a price of increased complexity. At the same time, no software seems able to give drawing skills and talent to those not otherwise blessed with them. Although clip art gives us all a chance to incorporate much more imagery into our work than we otherwise would, the nonartists among us are unlikely to become Michelangelos, regardless of the tools we use.

Artistic skill and comprehension are still required when using a drawing package. For the professional graphic artist, software such as *Illustrator*, *Freehand*, *CorelDraw*, or *Canvas* provides complete work environments. Far simpler products such as Windows *Paint* and the built-in drawing tools in *HyperStudio* still offer more capabilities than most nonartists can use effectively but with less complexity. Disney's *Magic Artist* enables the "artistically challenged" to create remarkable products, even 3-D art and animations. The very popular children's paint program *KidPix* may also serve a teacher's needs (Figure 8.3). This product has an extensive teacher's manual filled with classroom applications.

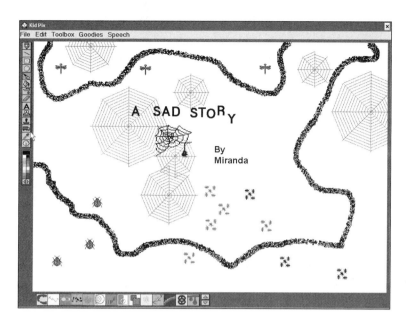

Figure 8.3

KIDPIX—A WIDELY USED DRAWING PROGRAM

The *KidPix* website <www.kidpix.com> offers usage ideas for kids and even has an online paint area where you can draw with a variety of simple tools. There is also a "picture of the month" by a *KidPix* user and a special section of ideas for educators who use the software.

Applications

Because draw and paint software is by definition a generic tool, the applications are essentially unlimited. A few examples will illustrate.

Meltzer (1999–2000) made a strong case that students (and even adults) benefit from creating their own visuals rather than relying on clip art for every need. She contended that learning to draw is as fundamental as other curriculum areas but that clip art inherently sends the message that the user cannot draw well enough. Drawing is important both for learning to communicate your own ideas visually and for the "joys of creation." Meltzer (1999–2000) continued, "Drawing isn't just about eye–hand coordination; it's about expressing what is in our minds and our hearts" (p. 24). The article included many concrete suggestions for creating original art with the basic graphics tools found on nearly all computers.

McCombs (2001) and his colleagues at the American Embassy School in New Delhi faced the common situation of needing more time for technology in the already full curriculum. The solution became enhancing the existing art program with more technology, especially student use of graphics software to express their ideas. Students benefited from the enhancements to both components within the existing curriculum. McCombs explained in some detail how software was used to achieve goals related to design, color, composition, and layout and provided an assessment rubric.

Wiebe (1992) suggested using a drawing program to help students solve math problems involving logical and spatial relationships, which are notoriously difficult for many learners. He illustrated the potential with a problem of who lives in which house. The problem gives varying information, such as the house numbers, who lives where in relationship to the others, and so forth. The visualization provided by creating a computer diagram of the known facts, plus the ability to move the graphics around until they fit in the desired relationships, should aid comprehension.

Eighth graders who had used *KidPix* without knowing it was for "kids" suggested several unusual applications: personal name tags for school field trips, "calling cards" for kids with businesses such as baby-sitting or yard work, and personalized place mats for birthday parties (Nicholson, 1991).

Research

Freedman and Relan (1990) were concerned that many common uses of computers in schools "exclude and even delegitimize certain types of thinking, including . . . aesthetics" (p. 101). They turned to drawing software in an art education course to explore alternatives for working with a computer. As the course progressed, students grew artistically as they came to focus on the formal and conceptual content of their images more than on the technical and manipulative concerns that dominated at the beginning.

The researchers also found a marked shift from preplanned activity (problem solving) to situated actions (problem posing), that is, spontaneous development or change facilitated by the flexible software. The computer became another sketchbook. Interaction was on a much higher level than in noncomputer drawing courses. Students assisted one another in mastering the software, in sharing techniques for using it, and in critiquing each other's achievements. Experimentation was much greater than typical, because changes to a drawing did not destroy the original version. The authors concluded that open-ended software, such as an art package, offers breadth of application missing from typical "instructional" programs.

Scanning Images and Text

Existing printed materials become digital resources when you scan them into computer graphics files. *Page* or *flatbed scanners* are similar to photocopiers in that they scan or "copy" whatever is laid on their glass plate or "bed." Kathy Horan's third graders worked on the Cinderella project, which two teachers in Ohio set up as a worldwide collaborative project (Youtsey & Sare, 2002). The concept was to write a new version of the famous fairy tale but with a different set of characters reflecting the locality of participants. Since their school is in Kansas, Horan's students used a *Wizard of Oz* theme. Mrs. Horan's dog became a main character because it resembled Toto. The children also illustrated their story, in which the dog is featured, with traditional paper drawings. They scanned their drawings so that their work could become part of the online project. You can see the full Cinderella around the World project at <www.northcanton.sparcc.org/~ptk1nc/cinderella>. The article contains many correlations to NETS and other standards.

Beyond purchased clip art, scanning is simply today's means of extending the range of available images. Perhaps you have students with artistic skill. Scan their paper work to include in their electronic portfolio. How many different print materials cross your desk weekly that contain images you might use? You may well be able to "recycle" them for your own purposes. However, just as legal issues surround the use of photocopiers, there are similar issues with scanners. A scanner gives you the potential to copy virtually any flat image, which immediately suggests many popular sources, such as comic strips, newspaper ads, magazine images, and so on. You should be aware that comic strips, in particular, are copyrighted images. Whether you may scan them legally to use for educational purposes seems to fall under the murky "fair use" concept. Just as educators have long appropriated materials from a wide range of sources (not always legally), the same is occurring now with scanners. Copyright issues are a topic in Chapter 15.

In Phoenix, high school students went to an inner-city elementary school to interview first grade students (Braden, 1992). The project was to make a personal book for each first grader. From the interview, the high school students created storyboards using graphics software. Eventually, they completed entire pages of the story they were telling and added text. They also scanned photos of the first graders and added them to the books, which they then printed. Most of these first graders had few books of their own. Their teachers reported that they carried their new personal books around until the school year ended.

Image Basics

The software that controls the scanner, called a *driver*, determines the choices you can make, which affect the result of the scan (Figure 8.4). Some drivers offer a simplified scanning mode that sets these choices, whereas others (as shown) give you more control. One of the most important and often misunderstood options is scanning resolution. Resolution is the number of dots per inch (dpi) that the scanner will produce as it sweeps its light beam over your image. Without getting too technical, even inexpensive scanners are capable of resolutions of 1,200 dpi or more, as shown in the figure. Although

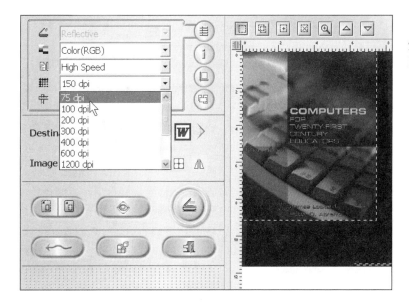

Figure 8.4

SETTING RESOLUTION
IN A SCANNER DRIVER

there are good reasons for wanting such high resolutions, the resulting graphics files are extremely large. Since much of the scanning most teachers and students do is to create digital images to use on web pages or to display within other software, you seldom need more than 75–100 dpi because of the display limitations inherent in computer monitors. At that resolution, the files will be a manageable size.

The other fundamental factor related to scanned images is the graphics file format in which you save the result of your scan. The selected dpi for scanning determines the data content of the image, but the file format will also affect the size of the final file as well as the quality of the image. Available options will vary among scanners (Figure 8.5), but there are certain principles that typically apply. The largest file usually results from choosing the BMP format, as this format stores all the data produced by the scanner. The smallest file is usually the JPG format, which uses complex algorithms in the software to compress the image. The result is frequently a file that is one-tenth or less of the BMP size for the exact same original scan. In general, it is a good idea to save the original scan using a very high quality format such as BMP, so that any further modifications of the image begin with all possible data.

Text and Optical Character Recognition

Of course, you are not limited to graphics when working with a scanner. Scan a page of text materials and the scanner will produce a graphic image of the page. You can read or print it, but that is all unless you have *optical character recognition (OCR)* software, which also comes with most scanners. OCR software tries to match graphic patterns in the image file to characters so that you can save the result as a document file (Figure 8.6). You can then edit that document file as though you had created it yourself at the keyboard.

Figure 8.5
FILE FORMAT CHOICES WHEN SCANNING

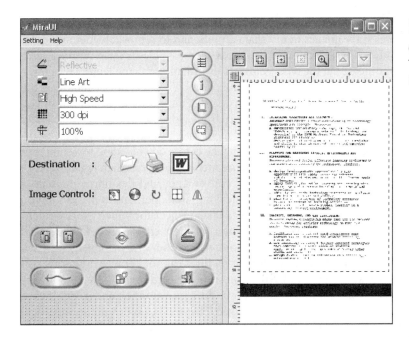

Figure 8.6

CONVERTING SCANNED
TEXT INTO A DOCUMENT
FILE WITH OCR

A scanner with OCR software can be a lifesaver as well as a great work saver. Suppose you have taught before but are just beginning to use a computer for routine teacher duties, such as preparing class materials. You already have handouts from previous years or a teacher colleague that are still usable, but they were not created on a computer. You dread the thought of typing them now into the computer. Instead, let your scanner and OCR create the files for you. Or perhaps you already have computer files but your diskette suddenly goes bad or your hard drive fails. Again, scan an existing paper copy of the documents to recreate the files. To teach writing you might scan sections of an existing document, then print them double- or triple-spaced for students to edit or comment on. Do not, however, expect the results of OCR to be perfect. It's quite normal for the process to be only 90 to 95 percent accurate, so you will have to do some manual correcting in nearly all cases. However, the spellchecker in your word processor will help a lot in the process.

Digital Cameras

No consideration of graphic images would be complete without considering cameras. Photography has moved out of the art department into all areas of the school since digital cameras became widely available. Because there is no cost for film and no waiting time for film processing, the potential for original digital photographs far exceeds what was possible with film cameras both economically and practically.

Although digital cameras differ in many ways, three factors are the most important to understand in our experience. First is how the images are stored, second is image resolution, and third is the lens and its zoom capability.

Image Storage

Most digital cameras store images in internal memory and in removable memory cards (Figure 8.7). The latter come in many different types (Compact Flash, Smart Media, Memory Stick, and many others), but the type seems largely insignificant. You'll probably download the images from the camera to your computer via a USB cable, not by removing the memory card, since few computers have memory card readers. (Some printers allow you to make color prints by inserting the memory card from the camera directly into a reader in the printer.) More significant than the type of memory is the amount, as that factor directly determines the number of pictures you can take before downloading to a computer and erasing the camera memory. Obviously, more memory is better than less.

Beyond capacity, there is also the issue of convenience and flexibility in a school setting. Assume that you have access to multiple computers, perhaps even a lab. If you have a digital camera with sufficient memory, a class project for which every student must take several digital pictures would likely not fill the memory card. However, all the images would be stored in the same memory, which could be inconvenient when some students who are ready to work with their pictures cannot because others are still taking pictures. Even with a simple USB connection, it's still inconvenient to download a few pictures into one computer, then a few more into another, and so on. If each student has personal space on a school server (see Chapter 3), you could download all images to one computer and then distribute them electronically into each student's personal space. It's still needlessly cumbersome.

The solution that many of our partner schools have found ideal is a camera that stores its images on floppy disks, primarily the Sony Mavica camera line (Figure 8.8). These cameras are somewhat more costly than the more typical types, but they earn their value in convenience. Students can have one or more personal floppy disks, which they can then take to any available computer for further work on the digital images.

Camera Resolution

The buzzword for digital cameras is *megapixels*. A *pixel* is a "picture element" in a digital image or, more simply, a dot of color. *Mega* means "million," so a 3-megapixel digital

Figure 8.7
A DIGITAL CAMERA THAT USES
REMOVABLE MEMORY CARDS
TO STORE IMAGES

Figure 8.8

A DIGITAL CAMERA THAT USES FLOPPY DISKS TO STORE IMAGES

camera can produce images containing 3 million individual pixels. The equivalent measurement for a scanned image is the scanning resolution (say, 100 dpi for simplicity) times the physical dimensions of the area scanned (say, a 3″ by 5″ snapshot), which gives 300 by 500 pixels. Multiply those numbers to get 150,000 pixels, far below even 1 megapixel. Practically, you will likely be quite satisfied with the pictures taken with a digital camera of even 1.3 megapixels, and around 2.0 megapixels should meet all your needs. The higher the resolution, the larger the file size and also the larger the image when you try to view it onscreen, often making it necessary to manipulate the image for use on a web page. You can adjust most cameras to lower-than-maximum resolution as well. Higher resolution is more beneficial for printing high-quality images.

Lenses and Zoom Ratio

The zoom factor of any camera (not just digitals) is the extent to which its lens can take in wider areas (called wide-angle) or bring the subject up close (called telephoto). The lens setting is called *focal length*, or the length of its focus. The higher the zoom ratio, the greater the difference is between the two extremes of focal length. However, there are two types of zoom, and they are not equally good. *Optical zoom* means the lens actually can vary its focal length, and the image quality should be relatively consistent. *Digital zoom* means the camera is "faking" the zoom factor by manipulating the pixels. The result can vary from quite acceptable to very poor. Between the two, optical zoom is the better choice.

Image Enhancement

Now that you know how to produce digital images, it's time to consider how to enhance them to get the desired result. Although it would be great to get exactly what you want initially from your scan or digital camera, that is often not the case.

A variety of graphics software, ranging from simple drawing programs such as *Paint-Brush* to highly sophisticated image-manipulation software such as *Adobe Photoshop*, can modify scanned images. Good imaging software offers tools to remove unwanted elements, add others, change colors, and so forth. With the right scanner and software, it is possible to begin with, say, a damaged photograph, scan it, retouch the problems, and then print it again in its original (or even enhanced!) form. Many photo-editing programs automatically remove red-eye as well.

This section can only give you a general idea of the options, which we hope you will explore hands-on. The most common improvements for digital images are *cropping* (removing parts of the image to guide the viewer to the key focal points) and adjustments to brightness, contrast, and color. Your scanner may come with software for these tasks, or you may obtain it separately. Simple improvements are very easy to make, but learning the full power of imaging software is too time-consuming for most educators. Here's a quick look at two of the most common enhancements.

To crop an image (Figure 8.9) using *PaintShopPro*, a popular imaging program, select the area you wish to retain (the dotted rectangle), then click the Image menu, then Crop to Selection. Everything outside the box will disappear.

To lighten or darken an image, experiment with brightness and contrast settings. You can alter the colors in the image as well, perhaps adding or deepening a tan or the green of the grass, but color changes are more challenging to do well. These choices and many more are found in the Color menu under Adjust (Figure 8.10). It's very important to note the Undo feature of your software, as your early attempts at image enhancement are likely to include many undesirable changes. Look in the Edit menu for Undo or locate the Undo button, which is the curved arrow pointing to the left in the toolbar in the figure.

No doubt you realize that it is also possible to use imaging software to do such things as put one person's head on another person's body, although we won't go into those techniques here. Because of this potential to *create* images electronically that never really existed, image manipulation is open to a wide range of abuses as illustrated by the tabloid newspapers at the supermarket checkout lanes. Students who learn to work with graph-

Figure 8.9

CROPPING TO REMOVE
PART OF A DIGITAL IMAGE

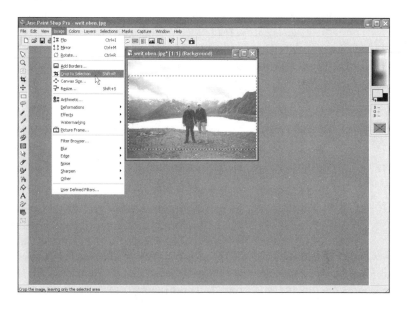

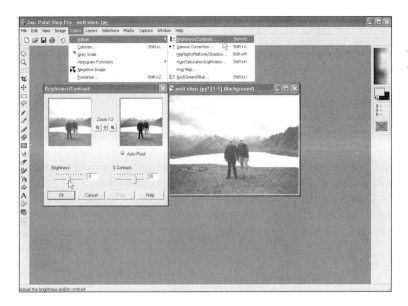

Figure 8.10

ADJUSTING BRIGHTNESS
AND CONTRAST IN A
DIGITAL IMAGE
(COMPOSITE VIEW)

ics software require assistance to recognize and reflect on the ethical issues of what they potentially can do.

Charting and Graphing

You know the value of seeing information presented graphically, yet how many teachers ever produce graphs for their classes? A major deterrent is the time it takes to produce a good graph by hand rather than a lack of appropriate uses for graphs. Today, creating graphs is simple, and you probably already have the necessary tools. Most spreadsheet software can turn numbers instantly into different kinds of graphs. You can also create graphs using most drawing packages, though it is up to you to draw the graph to look as it should.

There are also specialized graphing programs such as Sunburst's *Graphers*, which enables elementary-age children to depict data they collect themselves. Students write up their discoveries in an integrated notebook, then print both the graphs and notes. *Graphers* and Tom Snyder's *Graph Club* also feature spoken directions, widening the range of potential users. Beyond basic data graphing, there are unique programs for graphing mathematical functions and equations, such as *Green Globs* and *Graphing Equations*. For students with access to the powerful *Matlab* software, additional functionality for graphing is available in the free Data Visualization Toolbox <www.datatool.com/Dataviz_home.htm>. Where there's a need, there's no good excuse to avoid graphing.

Applications
To introduce students to charting software, begin by asking them to interpret available graphs, such as those found in the newspaper. To bring greater interest to the lesson, next move to graphs that you have produced based on class projects. Ask students to

complete several graphing activities manually. This should be a good lead-in to the advantages of using software.

How much are we influenced by numbers alone? Suppose a student were to be graded based on five separate assessments, each with a maximum value of 100. Further assume that the student's five scores were 85, 94, 92, 86, and 90. What impression do you obtain from just the values? Now look at just the upper graph in Figure 8.11. Does it appear that this student performs erratically? It does to many observers. Now compare the upper and lower graphs in the figure. The data are unchanged, but the vertical axis divisions have been altered. How does this affect your impression of this student? What could you (and your students) learn about data representation from this exercise? Did you recognize that the graphs were created using a spreadsheet?

How might students learn the effects of extreme values in a set of data? It's particularly easy if you are using a spreadsheet to generate graphs. A single row or column of a few numbers is sufficient to generate a graph. Begin with a data set that lacks ex-

Figure 8.11
STUDENT PERFORMANCE
GRAPHED USING
DIFFERING VERTICAL
AXIS DIVISIONS

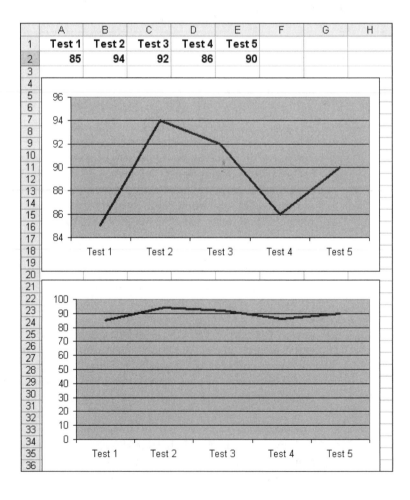

tremes, and graph it as a line or bar chart. Then modify the data, replacing one or more values with numbers well above or below the others. Regraph (some software programs allow you to keep several graphs on screen at once to compare) and guide a discussion of the results. This works particularly well when you can project the computer image in your classroom, so that students instantly see what happens as you vary some values. Of course, it also works well in a lab. Lacking either, you can create and print the graphs, then distribute them as needed for your lesson plan.

Many student projects could benefit from the inclusion of graphs. How about having students track their performance (in class, athletically, or whatever) over some period? If there is a class fund-raising project, track sales or income over time with graphs. What might students in social studies learn by graphing stock market activity? How about trends in voting patterns over some period? Population trends, inflation, unemployment, the national debt—all offer significant learning potential with graphing. Even if similar graphs are already available in newspapers, students will learn more from collecting raw data and developing a representation of it.

Cathy Grant (2000) was concerned that graphing with computers could be mechanical and hide lack of understanding behind high-quality images. Working with second graders in early spring, she had them collect data about clothing fasteners within their class. Vitally important was the step of carefully defining the question(s) to be answered: Is it about how many fasteners there are? Is it about how many kids have which or how many of each kind? Understanding the question is critical to understanding what a graph conveys. Grant first had her students create hand-drawn representations of their data, and then later they used *Graph Club* to depict their findings. In some cases, the computer graph confirmed the students' understanding, whereas in others it helped point out misconceptions. Seeing data in multiple formats (picture graph, bar graph, pie chart) also helped teach and reinforce key mathematical concepts. Grant concluded that neither approach is necessarily complete alone, but when used appropriately together, they can be powerful tools for student discovery of meaning.

Boehm (1997) used that common childhood experience of losing a tooth as the basis for an engaging experience with graphing using real data. The project can extend throughout the year as students collect data monthly and their graphs grow to include the latest data. Although the project will work in a single classroom or one school, Boehm designed it as an Internet project to link schools internationally. The project is hosted at <www.internetschoolhouse.com> under Projects, then Elementary, then August. With other schools participating, the project easily expands beyond math and graphing to include social studies (each participating school submits information about its community) and language arts. (Boehm suggested writing about traditions related to losing baby teeth, which is especially meaningful with international participants.) She also provided guidance on a bulletin board for the project and brought in art with creation of a mural to depict varying tooth fairy traditions.

Because it is inescapable, weather is an ideal topic for graphing that is suitable for science activities at any grade level. Students learn more deeply about weather phenomena by observation than by just reading about them. Minimally, students should gather daily data, including temperature and barometric pressure at specific times, precipitation, and wind velocity and direction. Use these data as appropriate to your lesson plans to generate line, bar, or circle (pie) charts. By displaying precipitation and barometer readings on a common chart, students can discover relationships between pressure changes and weather conditions. Also, have students record nonnumeric data such as cloud cover and type, which can be turned into pie charts showing patterns over a period of time. Consider having students track weather information for cities from diverse parts of the world to compare climates and spark interest in other nations. This can add a social studies element to the project while making good use of Internet resources. You may want to also link the activity to newspaper and television weather information, perhaps a "challenge the weather forecaster" competition.

Niess (1992) provided great detail on a weather project in which students use technology to analyze and interpret U.S. Weather Service data. Among the unique aspects of Niess's project is analysis of wind direction and frequency. She showed how the data can be manipulated in a spreadsheet and ultimately turned into a *wind rose*, a graph that plots the number of days of wind from each compass direction over a certain period. Niess demonstrated clearly a wide range of investigations of weather based on graphing and interpretation.

For science lessons, students might track and graph personal dietary information, weight and height changes, or any data gathered from experiments, as another example.

A final note of caution. In one study (Machmias and Linn, 1987), researchers found that eighth graders accepted graphs generated from data collected by the computer, even when they should have spotted obvious problems such as scaling that failed to show all the data or results that had to stem from errors in equipment usage. Students simply did not question computer-generated graphs as they should have. This study points out the need for explicit teaching of data interpretation (see also Huff, 1954, a classic).

For samples of graphs that communicate extraordinarily well and others that illustrate how not to display data, visit the Gallery of Data Visualization at York University (Canada) <www.math.yorku.ca/SCS/Gallery>.

Concept Mapping and Graphic Organizers

Graphic organizers offer another valuable way for students of all ages to visualize data in the broadest sense. Among the best known software of this type is *Inspiration* and its sibling for younger students, *Kidspiration*. Such programs make it easy to create concept maps, showing the interrelationships of elements of any content. In fact, it works as a kind of visual outline for almost any purpose, including planning stories or even storyboarding for video productions. The key is the ease and flexibility with which units representing various components are created and then linked together. The level of detail can be increased or decreased at will to show more or less of the total "map." Figure 8.12 is adapted from an example diagram provided with the *Inspiration* software. Although maps can be all text, students prefer to take advantage of the graphics provided to illustrate the concepts.

In addition to some basic sample concept maps, Anderson-Inman and Ditson (1999) noted that teachers have become much more willing to use concept maps as learning and teaching tools since computer software became available. Electronic concept maps are easier to create, more flexible, and much faster to revise than paper versions. The

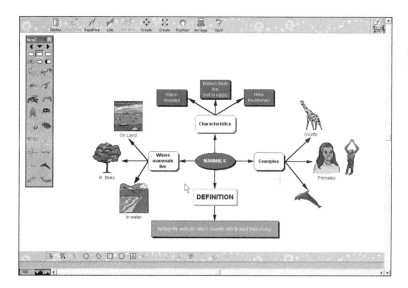

authors argued that concept mapping can help all students understand complex material better and that it is especially effective with students who struggle because of learning disabilities. In their article they explained how teachers can use graphic organizers for brainstorming, curriculum planning, and concept formation tracking. In addition, they noted positive research findings on the benefits of concept mapping.

For an international example, students in South Africa also participated in the Cinderella around the World project mentioned previously. They used a graphic organizer to plan and develop their story. See how they did it at <www.comsewogue.k12.ny.us/cinderella/bruton/bruton.htm>.

3-D Visualization

The final graphics software we include in our discussion provides 3-D visualization. Roblyer (2003, pp. 156–157) noted the use of such software in vocational and art/graphics curricula. However, most teachers are unlikely to think of 3-D imagery as appropriate to their teaching. Steed (2001) provided a lengthy list of applications at the middle and high school levels for areas as obvious as science (air flow patterns, chemistry) and math (geometry, volume) and for far less intuitive applications in the social sciences (recreation of ancient sites, construction of monuments), information technology (how the Internet works), and even teacher professional development (demonstrations, classroom design). Importantly, Steed also made the point that 3-D tools belong in the hands of students, who can use them effectively to "foster their insight, understanding, and new ways of negotiating meaning" (p. 20). Research by Merickel (1992) found that graphic visualization can be beneficial in activating knowledge structures that deal with kinesthetics and visual-spatial orientation, two of Gardner's multiple intelligences. Much additional information is available at Steed's website <www.edu.uleth.ca/faculty/members/steed/3dsplmnt>.

Using Your Visuals

In the first part of this chapter you learned much about the breadth of graphic communication tools. In some cases the output of a specific tool, say, a graph in a spreadsheet, may be the final product. In other cases, you may want or need to integrate a created graphic into some other final product. Let's turn now to additional ways of using graphics in print products, electronic presentations, or electronic portfolios.

NETS
NOTES

NETS **S** 1
NETS **S** 3
NETS **S** 4
NETS **T** I-A
NETS **T** I-B
NETS **T** II-A
NETS **T** III-A
NETS **T** III-B
NETS **T** III-C
NETS **T** IV-B
NETS **T** V-D

Print Graphics

Print graphics software is an inexpensive tool that allows you to create:

- banners to festoon your room and bulletin boards
- signs and posters to announce coming events and dates
- certificates of recognition for some achievement
- greeting cards for all occasions

As of 2003 the original *Print Shop* from Broderbund was in its fifteenth edition, an amazing success story for inexpensive, specialized software. It's a very popular product among teachers. Similar products include *Print Master* (also Broderbund) in several versions, including one on DVD-ROM, to provide the huge resources of the product on a single disc. Scholastic *SuperPrint* can produce banners, posters, storybooks, stickers, and other crafts. Roblyer (2003) reports that some schools hold contests for the best products designed with print graphics software.

Beyond such general-purpose graphics software, there are also many specialized products, such as Broderbund's *Calendar Creator*. American Greetings *CreateACard Gold* produces only greeting cards but puts the maximum creative tools for all occasions in your hands. Over all, general-purpose software offers a range of output types in a single package, whereas specialized products generally have far more flexibility and variety in their one type of output. In other words, *Calendar Creator* may tailor a calendar more to your needs than can *Print Shop*.

Common to all such software is a selection of decorative fonts, border designs, and ready-to-use clip art. There are professional templates for each output format. Clip art and templates are a great benefit to those computer users who have limited artistic skill and little time.

The output of some types of print graphics software is now available in electronic form as well. You may already use electronic greeting card sites such as Hallmark <www.hallmark.com>, Regards.com <www.regards.com>, or Blue Mountain Arts <www.bluemountainarts.com>, some of which offer free services. You can also create a variety of graphics types at the Broderbund Creativity Center <http://expressit.broderbund.com/default.asp>. There are even a few award makers online at <http://teachers.teach-nology.com/web_tools/certificates> where you can create and then print award certificates.

Applications

Beyond the obvious uses of these programs, educational applications abound. How many classroom posters, handouts, even worksheets might be done more attractively and more "professionally" using a graphics program? Figure 8.13 is an example. If you use a camcorder or VCR to document class (or family) activities, use your graphics software to create title boards to videotape at the start of each new segment. Be sure to include the date, because it may be forgotten later.

Fund-raisers have become a way of life, given school budget realities. Graphics software offers a nearly limitless range of sales possibilities. School calendars, special stationery, note pads, custom certificates, and menus for local restaurants are among the more obvious. Because many such ideas have little to do with the curriculum, they may be more appropriate as projects for an after-school computer club. Students might also volunteer to produce salable items for the local PTA/PTO. Although commercialism should not mix with or influence the curriculum inappropriately, students can polish their computer skills with projects such as these. Isn't that more valuable than simply selling purchased candy or other items?

Creative uses of computer graphics abound. Figure 8.14 illustrates a variation on student-created riddles, a fun language arts activity. Using the greeting-card format, the cover gives clues to the graphic answer inside.

Many elementary language arts teachers like to vary reading and writing with an occasional *rebus*, a story in which small graphics replace some words in sentences. Your print graphics software may be suitable for creating a rebus.

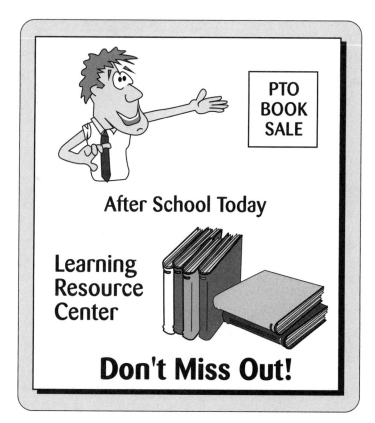

Figure 8.13
A POSTER CREATED WITH A
GRAPHICS PROGRAM

Figure 8.14
A student-created riddle folds into a card format.

A Snowflake

I am icy cold and too
small for you to see
my shape easily.

No two of me are ever alike.

Kids use me to make things.

What am I?

Presentation Graphics

More and more computer users are turning to graphics software to enhance the delivery of presentations they need to make. Some may be before groups, as in a classroom or at a conference; others may be self-running information "kiosks"; still others may be for personal purposes, such as family gatherings. Presentations that use graphics are certain to be more interesting to those who see them than traditional talking head lectures. Most graphical presentations are created using either electronic "slide show" software or simple hypermedia products.

Electronic Slide Shows

Electronic slide show software is typified by the ubiquitous *PowerPoint*, although there are other choices such as Lotus *Freelance* and the slide show component of *Appleworks*. These products simplify the task of preparing presentations by providing:

- professionally designed templates to fill in with your own data
- abundant clip media resources (including audio and video as well as static and animated clip art)
- simple drawing tools to illustrate or enhance your point
- the ability to import existing materials in a wide range of formats, including images you produce with your digital camera or scanner and even your own digital audio and video (see Chapter 9)

You create a presentation one screen at a time, choosing a screen layout from many available options to suit the kind of information you need to present—text with bullet points, text plus graphic, organization chart, even a spreadsheet or table. Add your own text, art work, and so on to complete each slide (Figure 8.15). In delivery mode, a mouse click advances the presentation from one slide to the next in order. Presentations become more visually stimulating when transition effects (fade, dissolve, wipe, etc.) occasionally accompany the change from one slide to the next. You also determine how the content of

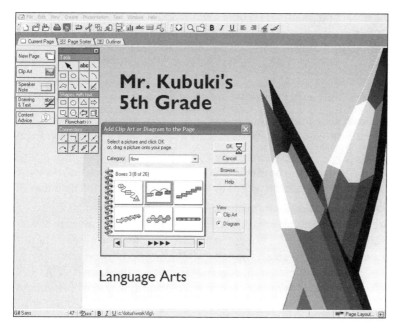

Figure 8.15

CREATING A SLIDE WITH PRESENTATION GRAPHICS SOFTWARE

the slide itself will appear, whether all at once or by some grouping, and what kind of visual effect will be used to display each piece of content.

For experienced teachers and other presenters, presentation graphics have replaced the plastic transparencies of the past and offer many advantages. Because your "slides" are electronic, you can easily and quickly update them from one use to the next. Changes are possible up to the time of the presentation. Unlike transparencies, which were usually monochrome, colors are basic design tools of presentation graphics. You can view your slides in various modes, such as a "slide sorter" that makes it easy to rearrange your slides instantly. You no longer need to store or carry around a large container or notebook full of transparencies.

Because the presentation is simply a computer file, you can easily share it with your audience, perhaps posting it on a class website for students to download and review at will. There is also a handout format in which multiple slides are printed on one sheet of paper to give to audiences. Most products even offer a speaker's notes view where you can annotate your slides with the key points you wish to make about each. This also becomes a part of the file, so you never have to worry about whether the notes and the images are in the same place. It is also common to be able to "package" a finished presentation complete with viewer software so that the presentation can run on a computer that does not have the original graphics software installed. This greatly increases the usability of presentation graphics.

Electronic presentations are impressive, and development is easier than you may imagine. They have become common in many schools as tools for students to share their learning with the class, as well as for teacher presentations. Many teachers create presentations for open house events that simply run on a "kiosk" computer stationed in the classroom. Parents may stop to view a sampler of class activities as they tour the facility. Teachers and administrators use electronic presentations to share information and document needs for the school board. The only real limit is your imagination.

Presentation graphics exist to enhance communication, but their effectiveness depends on the skill of the presenter/creator. Just as other graphics tools do not necessarily turn us all into artists, presentation software cannot guarantee a great presentation. In fact, novices make many common mistakes as they learn to create electronic slide shows and present them. Here are the ones we see most often.

1. Excessive use of flashy slide transitions and animation effects within the slides. What is effective in gaining or focusing attention quickly loses its impact when used again and again.

2. Too much text on a slide. Electronic presentations are not books. That's why the primary layout format is the bullet list. Use key words, not sentences and paragraphs.

3. Difficult-to-read text. Many teachers made useless transparencies by copying typed pages of material onto plastic, which only individuals in the first row of the audience could possibly hope to read. Slide templates try to guide you away from this problem by presetting the font size to one that should work. However, it's easy to change the size. If you do so, plan to increase it rather than decrease it. That will also help avoid too much text per screen. And don't even think about changing to cute fonts like Old English or some other fancy font. They are too hard to read.

4. Only text on slides. If there is little besides text in your entire presentation, it may not be much more interesting to your audience than just talking, perhaps along with a printed handout.

5. Irrelevant multimedia. Clip art is both a blessing and a curse. It's easy to use, so presenters use it. But any graphic or multimedia element is helpful only when it supports the information being presented. A picture may be worth a thousand words, but if the picture is unrelated to the words that are with it, you are delivering conflicting messages. Especially annoying are the animated clip art images that continue to dance, wiggle, wave, or otherwise move throughout the entire time the slide is displayed. Use them with extreme caution! Include audio or video *provided* they add meaning in significant ways, not just "because." A good example is Martin Luther King delivering his famous "I Had a Dream" speech, which is even more powerful when you hear (and see) his delivery than when you just read the text.

6. Reading the slide's content to the audience. Unless your audience consists of pre-readers or illiterate individuals, you should not need to read the text to them. Short bullet points help to minimize this tendency and serve as memory prods for more extemporaneous comments from you, the presenter. If the audience cannot read, try to communicate graphically, since the text points will have little value anyhow.

Hypermedia Software

Beyond specialized presentation software, many schools own hypermedia creation software such as *HyperStudio. Hypermedia* refers to interactive, nonsequential environments that feature multimedia elements—sound, graphics, animations, and video. From the starting screen, the user may freely move about within the environment using navigation buttons the creator has provided. Such software, too, is suitable for electronic presentations. You still create screens one by one, putting on to them whatever content you want, be it text, graphics, or multimedia (Figure 8.16).

One major difference from presentation graphics software is that each screen, typically called a *card*, is completely blank and left to your discretion to complete. There are no templates with professionally drawn graphics and carefully selected color schemes, no slide layouts to help (or constrain) you in designing the look of the screen. There is also no built-in navigation, leaving you to add buttons to each card to connect it to whatever you wish within the set of cards, which is called a *stack*. For linear presentations, this is added work compared to slide show software, but it also encourages nonlinear organization, making it easy to create a "menu" of topics within the presentation to which you can jump in any order. (You can also achieve this with a presentation package, but many users are unaware of how to do so or even that it is possible.)

You'll learn more about hypermedia as a learning tool in Chapter 11.

Applications and Assessment

Electronic presentations can add a whole new dimension to teaching if you take time to explore the possibilities and to master a software package. You could bid farewell to chalk, transparencies, and other traditional tools. With small LCD projectors and notebook computers, you can easily take your show on the road!

Figure 8.16
CREATING A CARD IN HYPERMEDIA SOFTWARE

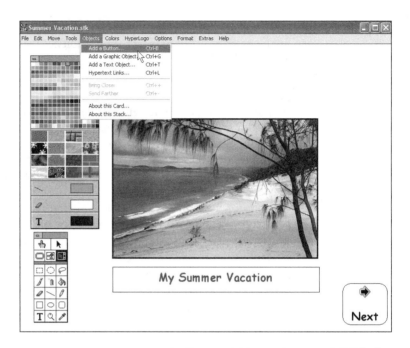

The most common application of presentation graphics is as an electronic replacement for plastic transparencies or 35mm slides to support presentations to any group. Possibilities start with traditional lecture outlines, but consider the potential for prepared discussion questions, graphics alone to stimulate thinking (such as for a creative writing assignment), or any time a large, viewable image would be useful. You can also enter and display comments from class members and then save the new screens for future use.

The broad applicability of electronic presentations across curriculum areas means there is an endless supply of ideas for their use. We can highlight only a few. Bray and Lovely (2002) recommended both slide show and hypermedia software as tools for emergent readers to use to create alphabet books. Tietz (2002) had her fifth graders complete a research project on a U.S. state. Part of the assignment was to create an electronic presentation to accompany the required multiparagraph written report. She found the excitement over the presentation stimulated increased willingness to work hard on the written report. Monahan (1999) used both electronic slide show software and *HyperStudio* to complete a research activity with special needs students. Students gathered data about themselves and compiled their findings using a database. They presented the data to the group by reformatting the database records as slides in an electronic slide show. Then they summarized their hypotheses and findings using a *HyperStudio* stack for which they created original art work. As another example, idioms are common in our language, and learning their nonliteral meaning is essential to their correct use. Lanman-Givens (1991) augmented a fourth-grade unit on idioms by having students illustrate their favorite idioms, using presentation software, and then sharing them with their classmates. Projecting the student work may enhance class interaction in a lesson such as this. (The same lesson concept could be implemented with print graphics.)

As more teachers encourage electronic presentations by students to demonstrate and share learning, they must also develop new means of assessing learning. Our familiarity with tests and written assignments may not be adequate. Garry and Graham (2002) offered many useful suggestions concerning assessment. They noted the potential of technology tools to help students learn the skills of "managing and analyzing data, presenting and evaluating information, and using knowledge and creativity to solve problems." They also cautioned that a slick presentation with no substance is no better than poor performance on more traditional measures. Read their article for a range of tips on developing criteria and the critical need to link assessment to educational standards. Rubrics for assessing an electronic presentation, including several key planning components, are available at <www.uni.edu/profdev/rubrics/pptrubric.html> and <www.asij.ac.jp/middle/ac/lass/6no/discrimination/PowerPoint.htm>.

Projection

Electronic presentations are inherently meant to be delivered electronically. Many schools have attempted to display computer images of all kinds using a *scan converter* to connect the computer to a television set. However, even the largest TVs are too small for this purpose unless the classroom and class size are also small, which is rarely the case. The answer is video data projection.

The most common projection device in schools for years has been the overhead projector (OHP). One of the key features of the OHP long has been the brightness of its image, which makes use possible even in a well-lit classroom or other venue. Data projectors are not new, but they have made their way into schools somewhat slowly, largely because of what appears to be high cost. The early projectors were not only expensive, but also they were large and heavy, which made them difficult to share among classrooms, as is necessary in most schools. They also produced such dim images that a room had to be well darkened to use them at all, even more so than for movie and slide projectors.

Today, a data projector costs less than movie projectors did 30 years ago. They are small and weigh less than early laptop computers, and some even weigh less than many of today's notebook computers. Many models are now bright enough to use in a fully lighted area. Carrying cases often are spacious enough for both a projector and a notebook computer—a complete portable presentation system. Furthermore, all projectors that we have seen also can connect to a VCR and usually to a DVD player. Classes benefit from a large-screen viewing of instructional videos compared to students in the back squinting to watch a smaller TV in the front of the room.

From our experience, most teachers need to know just two things about projectors. First, the brightness of a projector is measured in *lumens* and the higher the lumens value, the brighter the image. If you have any choice in the matter, choose the brightest projector possible. Projectors rated at 2000–3000 lumens are available as we write, with still higher values sure to become available. However, projectors dim over time, so it's not necessarily your eyes if you believe you are not seeing as bright an image this month as last. Somewhere in the onscreen menu of adjustments for the projector is a means to adjust the brightness and contrast. Don't hesitate to experiment with these controls if the image seems dim.

Second, although projectors are getting better by the month, they still don't produce as sharp an image as your own computer monitor. Furthermore, for many reasons, the colors often look somewhat different when projected than they did as you created your presentation. You may find that pale colors disappear entirely on the big screen. If you plan to use a projector frequently to show electronic presentations, expect to experiment some with various slide templates or hypermedia backgrounds to be sure of a good result.

Document Cameras

The theme of this chapter is graphics, but as you learn about projection, it is useful to recall that teachers frequently use real objects or *realia* in their teaching. You can surely remember teachers holding up something in front of the room to make a point, then perhaps passing it around the room. Real objects may become even more useful in the classroom if you connect a *document camera* to your video projector (Figure 8.17). A document camera is a small video camera, typically mounted on a post and aimed down at a platform on which you can place anything you like. Depending on how fancy your camera is, the platform may be lighted from below to help show transparent and translucent objects. There may be lights on the side to illuminate whatever you are showing. The camera probably has a zoom lens to allow extreme close-ups of your realia. You

Figure 8.17

A DOCUMENT CAMERA
FOR PROJECTING REAL
OBJECTS

can also project printed material, such as articles or cartoons from the newspaper. A document camera adds much potential for use of graphical materials in any classroom.

SUMMARY

In this chapter you learned a wide range of techniques related to producing and using graphics to communicate visually. Topics included basic clip art that comes with other software as well as additional clip art resources on discs and the Internet. Draw and Paint software is useful for creating original images, although artistic talent is also necessary for most such products. Scanners are common tools for educators, providing yet another means of producing graphics for use on web pages and with other software. An inexpensive scanner can also turn existing printed materials into editable word processor files using optical character recognition software, which commonly is included with each new scanner. Digital cameras are now common in schools, but available models differ in many ways. You learned about the key factors of image storage method, resolution, and lens capabilities. After you obtain or produce images, you may need to enhance them by cropping, color adjustments, or other means.

Other forms of graphics include charts and graphs, for which there is specialized software as well as the powerful graphing capabilities of most spreadsheets. You read about several interesting curriculum applications of graphing. Next we turned to graphic organizer software, which is widely used to help students visualize their learning by creating concept maps. The final graphics creation tool covered is 3-D visualization, which has much wider applicability than most teachers initially imagine.

Once you have a variety of graphics, the issue turns to ways of using them through other software. You learned about print graphics programs, such as the very popular *PrintShop*, and also specialty software for creating calendars and greeting cards. Some websites allow you to create cards, certificates, and similar products online without purchasing software. Educational applications of print graphics were discussed. The discussion next turned to the hugely popular topic of presentation graphics. Who isn't already familiar with *PowerPoint* presentations? They seem to be everywhere. Electronic slide shows of this sort have become popular in constructivist classrooms as another means of allowing students to demonstrate their learning. However, many electronic presentations suffer from common mistakes by their creators and we highlighted the ones we see most often. You learned that hypermedia software such as *HyperStudio* offers yet another tool for creating electronic presentations. You also read about a variety of educational applications for electronic presentations, including assessment of learning.

Because presentations are usually intended to be shown to more than just a few people at a time, you also learned some basic considerations about video data projection, including the potential for large-screen viewing of instructional videos and for projection of real objects using a document camera.

We live in a visual age and our students are accustomed to high levels of visual stimulation. The tools presented in this chapter offer educators a means of bringing new levels of visual communication into the learning environment.

chapter 8
activities

1. Explore the clip art resources of the software that you use routinely. Inquire about additional software collections that your school may own. Visit a computer store and compare clip art collections available for purchase.

2. Visit several online clip art resources. Identify and download a range of images that you may find useful at some point. Be sure to save them in appropriately labeled folders so that you can find them when you are ready to use them.

3. Explore the features of whatever draw or paint software you have access to. Create an original picture of your choice.

4. Learn to use a scanner to create digital images. Select a photograph and scan it at several different resolutions (dpi). View the resulting files and compare them for usefulness and file size.

5. Select a page of printed material, preferably in a single column. Scan it for OCR, complete the process, and then open the document in your word processor. How accurate was the conversion? Will it be less work to clean up the errors made by the software or would it be easier just to retype the page from scratch?

6. Examine a variety of digital cameras and compare them on their key features: image storage method, resolution, and lens capabilities. Take the same picture with each different camera to which you have access and compare the results. Research the cost of each camera (or the closest available model) and include that in your assessment of the camera.

7. Using any image you have scanned or taken with a digital camera, explore the changes you can make with available image editing software. Try to crop the image to remove extraneous parts of the picture. Adjust the brightness and/or contrast to see whether you can improve the image.

8. Brainstorm ideas for using charting and graphing in your teaching. Learn to create graphs with available software, including your spreadsheet.

9. Create a concept map appropriate to your teaching area using *Inspiration* or comparable graphic organizer software. Develop several possible applications for graphic organizers in your teaching.

10. Brainstorm possible applications of 3-D visualization software in your curriculum area.

11. Review the types of print projects that available software such as *PrintShop* can produce. Make at least three different kinds of products to explore some of the capabilities of the software.

12. Create an electronic slide show with at least five slides. Include both text and graphics; add sound or video if you can. Experiment with different transitions between slides and with animation of the text and graphical elements on the slides.

13. Reflect on electronic slide shows you have already seen in terms of the common mistakes described in the chapter. How many of these errors have you actually seen? Think about them as you create your own slide shows.

14. Create a five-screen presentation using available hypermedia software. Compare the effort required and the results obtained with your experience with electronic slide show software.

15. Compare the video data projectors available in your school in terms of size, weight, and image brightness. Research current projectors on the Internet and develop a proposal for which model(s) offer the best value.

16. Make a presentation using any of the presentation processes you learned about and a video projector. If possible, include projecting images from a document camera to gain experience with this increasingly important technology.

17. Develop multiple lesson plans that integrate visual communications tools, both in what you do as the teacher and in what students do to demonstrate their learning.

Companion Website

Visit the companion website at <www.ablongman.com/lockard6e> for more information about the topics discussed in this chapter.

expect the world®

The New York Times
nytimes.com

Themes of the Times

Expand your knowledge of the concepts discussed in this chapter by reading current and historical articles from the *New York Times* by visiting the Themes of the Times section of the companion website <www.ablongman.com/lockard6e>.

References

Anderson-Inman, L., and Ditson, L. "Computer-Based Concept Mapping: A Tool for Negotiating Meaning." *Learning and Leading with Technology,* May 1999, *26*(8), pp. 6–13.

Boehm, D. "I Lost My Tooth!" *Learning and Leading with Technology,* April 1997, *24*(7), pp. 17–19.

Braden, D. "Storyboards & More." (Kids on Computers.) *The Computing Teacher,* August/September 1992, *20*(1), p. 53.

Bray, B., and Lovely, G. "Technology. It's Primary." November 1, 2002. Retrieved February 1, 2003, from <www.techlearning.com/db_area/archives/WCE/archives/primarbb.html>

Freedman, K., and Relan, A. "The Use of Applications Software in School: Paint System Image Development Processes as a Model for Situated Learning." *Journal of Research on Computing in Education,* Fall 1990, *23*(1), pp. 101–113.

Garry, A., and Graham, P. "Want to Use Technology Effectively? Try Starting with Assessments." December 1, 2002. Retrieved February 1, 2003, from <www.techlearning.com/db_area/archives/WCE/archives/assessap.html>

Grant, C. "Beyond Just Doing It: Making Discerning Decisions About Using Graphing Tools." *Learning and Leading with Technology,* February 2000, *27*(5), pp. 14–17, 49.

Huff, D. *How to Lie with Statistics.* New York: Norton, 1954.

Lanman-Givens, B. "Idiom Graphics." (Kids on Computers.) *The Computing Teacher,* October 1991, *19*(2), p. 55.

Machimas, R., and Linn, M. C. "Evaluations of Science Laboratory Data: The Role of Computer-presented Information." *Journal of Research in Science Teaching,* May 1987, *24*(5), pp. 491–506.

McCombs, J. "Coloring Outside the Lines." *Learning and Leading with Technology,* September 2001, *29*(1), pp. 28–31, 57.

Meltzer, B. "Kiss Clip Art Goodbye." *Learning and Leading with Technology,* December/January 1999–2000, *27*(4), pp. 22–27.

Merickel, M. L. "A Study of the Relationship Between Virtual Reality and the Ability of Children to Create, Manipulate, and Utilize Mental Images for Spatially Related Problem Solving."

Paper presented at the annual convention of the National School Boards Association, October 1992, Orlando.

Monahan, S. "Our Classmates." *Learning and Leading with Technology*, March 1999, *26*(6), pp. 10–13.

Nicholson, M. "*KidPix.*" (Software Reviews.) *The Computing Teacher*, November 1991, *19*(3), pp. 45–47.

Niess, M. L. "Winds of Change." *The Computing Teacher*, March 1992, *19*(6), pp. 32–35.

Roblyer, M. D. *Integrating Educational Technology into Teaching*, 3rd ed. Columbus, OH: Merrill Prentice Hall, 2003.

Steed, M. "3-D Visualization. Using 3-D Software to Represent Curricular Concepts." *Learning and Leading with Technology*, November 2001, *29*(3), pp. 14–20.

Tietz, H. "Savoring Expository Writing Through PowerPoint." September 1, 2000. Retrieved February 1, 2003, from <www.techlearning.com/db_area/archives/WCE/archives/htietz.html>

Wiebe, J. "Word Processing, Desktop Publishing, and Graphics in the Mathematics Classroom." *The Computing Teacher*, February 1992, *19*(5), pp. 39–40.

Youtsey, T., and Sare, S. "The Cinderella Project." *Learning and Leading with Technology*, April 2002, *29*(7), pp. 22–24.

Additional Software and Hardware Tools: *Enhancing*

Teaching and Learning Efficiently

CHAPTER **9**

OBJECTIVES

After completing this chapter,
you will be able to:

- Discuss possible uses of materials generating software in your teaching area with specific examples.
- Develop lesson plans that include software-generated puzzles.
- Analyze and present the advantages and disadvantages of electronic testing and test-generating software.
- Assess your own potential uses of research aids and statistical analysis software.
- Explain the concept of "portable documents" and describe several possible applications for PDF files in your teaching.
- Assess the potential of handheld computing devices as learning tools.
- Prepare a proposal to school administrators for purchase of handheld computing devices with justification.
- Develop lesson plans that incorporate use of PDAs or other handheld devices.
- Analyze and discuss the potential for GPS/GIS systems in schools.
- Identify possible uses of digital video in your content area.

- Research specifications for digital camcorders and use your findings to prepare a purchase recommendation for your school.
- Give several ideas for student use of support tool software.
- Identify and use Internet resources to enhance your teaching.

This chapter looks at types of software and hardware that augment the major tools that you already have studied in previous chapters. These additional support tools are useful across many areas of teaching, offering you means as a teacher to accomplish common, even daily tasks in new ways with greater variety than ever before and in less time. They are important additions to your technology knowledge and skills. Many of these tools are also appropriate for student projects or activities. You'll look first at a range of software tools and then at several types of hardware that are growing rapidly in popularity and applications in U.S. schools.

Software Tools

Worksheet Generators

NETS
NOTES

NETS **S** 1
NETS **S** 3
NETS **S** 4
NETS **T** I-A
NETS **T** I-B
NETS **T** II-A
NETS **T** II-C
NETS **T** III-A
NETS **T** III-B
NETS **T** IV-B

Teachers have long used all manner of worksheets for numerous purposes. However, creating worksheets can be very time consuming due to layouts that are complex compared to normal documents. Abundant software and online resources now make use of the power of the computer to handle the difficult layout work, while letting you, the teacher, concentrate on the content of your worksheet.

There are many different types of worksheets in common use. Let's look first at two of the most popular—word searches and crossword puzzles. Then we'll explore some of the other readily available options.

Word Searches

Using software, you can create a word search puzzle easily by following prompts. First, of course, you must compile your own list of words to be hidden in a rectangular grid of letters. The software may ask you to specify the dimensions of the puzzle in advance, or it may calculate what is necessary as you go. Because words may be positioned vertically, horizontally, diagonally, and going either forward or backward, you must first enter the entire word list. The computer then arranges the words into the puzzle grid and fills the blank spaces with random letters.

Figure 9.1 shows a word search created online at *Puzzlemaker* <www.puzzlemaker. com>, which is part of the Discovery School website. You can also purchase *Puzzlemaker* on CD for offline use. *Teacher's Toolkit* (from teachertools.com) creates word searches and scrambles.

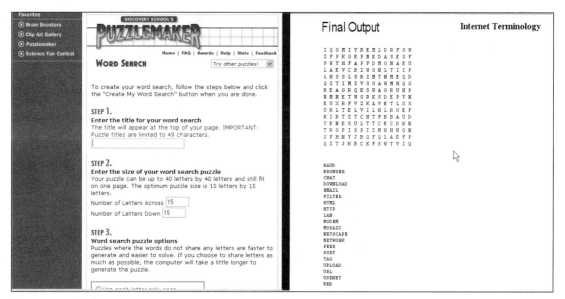

Figure 9.1   SAMPLE WORD SEARCH PUZZLE CREATED ONLINE (COMPOSITE VIEW)

Word search software generates the final layout from your word list and displays the hidden words in a list. You can also request an answer key or solution. Students enjoy word searches, but their instructional value is limited beyond vocabulary list review. Having students create their own word searches from their spelling words may help them achieve the objective while shifting the time burden to the students.

Crossword Puzzles

Teachers use word searches mostly for a change of pace. Crossword puzzles, on the other hand, can serve to reinforce learning by presenting content review in an entertaining, alternative format. It's not hard to come up with words and clues, but fitting them all together and coordinating clues to puzzle locations is a challenge.

Crossword puzzle software requires a little more effort than a word search program. Armed with your items and clues, let the machine prompt you for both. Again, puzzle sizing is often automatic but can usually be specified if there is a reason to do so. The final printout is achieved so easily as to be all but unbelievable to anyone who has ever made such a puzzle by hand (Figure 9.2). Of course, an answer key is also available—not that you need one!

Puzzlemaker <www.puzzlemaker.com> includes crosswords among its many worksheet types, both in the online version and on CD. *Word Cross* <www.teachertools.com> allows you to enhance your puzzles with color and graphics and can handle up to 60 words per puzzle. Text can be imported from existing files or entered directly. Other online puzzle makers are available at <www.varietygames.com/CW> and <www.awesomeclipartforkids.com/crossword/crosswordpuzzlemaker.html>.

Figure 9.2
CROSSWORD PUZZLE
TO REVIEW CONTENT
(COMPOSITE VIEW)

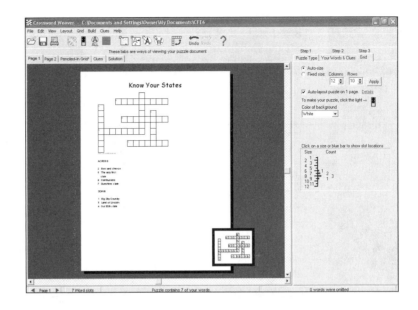

Additional Worksheet Types

Gamco's *Worksheet Magic Plus* software creates 15 different types of worksheets, including word searches and crossword puzzles, as well as secret codes, review sheets, and word and sentence scrambles. Discovery School's *Puzzlemaker* offers mazes, number blocks, math squares, and cryptograms in addition to the more common output types (Figure 9.3).

Figure 9.3
PUZZLE FORMAT OPTIONS
AT PUZZLEMAKER.COM

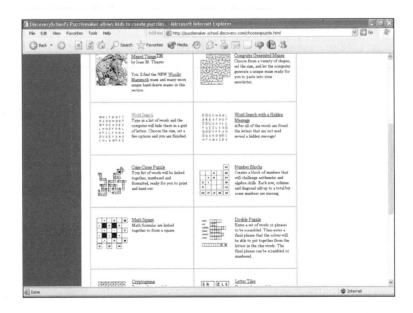

Student Applications

If you have access to puzzle-generating software, do not keep it to yourself! Have your students create puzzles to demonstrate their knowledge and to challenge their classmates. Virtually any field of study and all but the lowest grade levels offer lots of material for puzzles. With some creative guidance from the teacher, preparing a puzzle can be a meaningful learning experience. In fact, even the teacher may find a new challenge in student-created materials!

Test Generators

Many software tools exist to assist you in creating tests in a wide range of formats for both traditional and online delivery.

Capabilities

Software for creating paper tests typically accommodates such formats as multiple choice, matching, true/false, and fill in the blank. Some programs handle short-answer and essay exams, although a word processor may work just as well. Typically, questions first are entered into an item bank. They then may be grouped as a specific test, by objective, by unit, or by subject. Let's look briefly at representative test-making software.

ClassBuilder <www.classbuilder.com> is described as providing complete teacher support for "exam creation, grading, grade book, reports, lesson plans, assignments, calendar, attendance, and lots more." It imports from and exports to Microsoft *Office* applications to make easy use of existing materials. It can be used either online or offline. Test types supported are multiple choice, true/false, matching, and essay. Exams can be randomized to reduce chances of cheating. Teamwork is also supported with teachers pooling resources and students able to receive both team and individual grades. Chat and drawing features add vital support for online learning environments.

Tom Snyder's *Essential Cloze Maker* <www.tomsnyder.com> allows teachers to enter their own text passages to create cloze practice in addition to passages provided in the software. In addition to being able to delete every *n*th word, you have options to omit all words of any particular type (e.g., verbs or nouns). You can leave the selected word but scramble its letters. A maze procedure cloze provides three words per blank to allow students to test each word in context (Johnson, 2002). *Word Link* (from teachertools.com) also creates and prints cloze activity sheets.

Advantages

A significant advantage of a test-generating program is the ability to produce alternate forms of a test with little effort. Once an item bank of sufficient size exists, the computer easily *could* prepare a unique test for each student in the class, although this may be practical only for online testing. You may be content to prepare one basic exam with alternative forms for each class section, for makeup exams, or for retesting.

Test generators often allow you to select specific items from the pool, with the program performing only the clerical service of arranging everything on the page in an appropriate layout. Items in the bank can be deleted, modified, and added easily, with the current pool always available for the next exam on the subject. Because the test-item bank is normally prepared with both questions and answers, most programs also provide a complete answer-key printout along with the test.

Even if you do not need multiple versions of a test, you may still find a test generator useful. The final printout will be free of typographical errors, if you proofed your items carefully when you created the item pool. The computer assists with matters of page layout so that the test is well formatted. You do the thinking; the computer handles the drudgery.

Additional Test-Related Applications

At Kildeer Countryside School in Long Grove, Illinois, fourth-grade teachers Mrs. Moses and Mrs. Habley have students select a topic to research, and then they create a web test about their topic (Figure 9.4). This approach adds meaning to the research assignment because students know other students will see and use their work to learn more themselves.

Along with creating tests, students can find assistance in test taking through technology. Houghton Mifflin offers test-taking assistance in mathematics (Figure 9.5) at <www.eduplace.com/kids/mhm/testquest/flash/4_1b_s.html>. Another site for test and general study skills is provided by a PBS television station in Kent, Ohio, at <www.pbs 4549.org/tstquest/intro.htm>.

Student Information Systems

Student information systems (SIS) are not new, but they are taking on new importance. Trefny (2002) commented that "(w)ith the No Child Left Behind Act coming into full swing . . . , school districts are scrambling to collect and disseminate data on student test results, achievement levels, graduation rates, and other information the government

Figure 9.4

Student research becomes "web tests" for others to learn from.

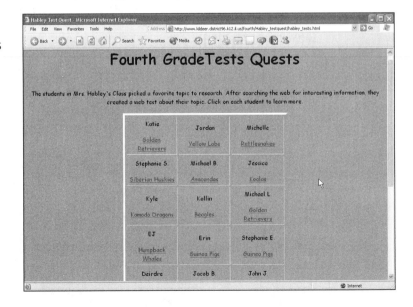

Figure 9.5
TEST-TAKING SKILLS
ADVICE OFFERED
ONLINE

requires in exchange for federal funding." An SIS is a school database that tracks basic demographic data, grades, and attendance. In the past, this was a central office application, but today many schools use a web-based SIS. Teachers can enter data at any time from the nearest computer or even using their handheld device, which you'll meet later in the chapter. Often parents can gain access to information for their own children. If you are interested in SIS details, please consult McIntire (2002).

Readability Analysis

Teachers should be interested in text readability level for many reasons. Perhaps a student or group of students is having difficulty with assigned material. The cause could be that the reading level is too high. When selecting material for a class, you should determine its *estimated* reading level as part of your selection process. You should also analyze the materials that *you* develop for students to be sure the reading level is appropriate.

Readability analysis is very straightforward but mechanical and time consuming and, thus, well suited to a computer. A typical stand-alone program requires the user to type in three passages of 100 words each. The software analyzes word frequency, syllabication, long words, numbers of sentences, and so on and then calculates readability using multiple formulas. This is beneficial because each formula follows different assumptions; results can vary significantly.

Word processors often provide at least some elements of readability analysis as part of spelling or grammar checking. For example, Microsoft *Word* can report word counts, several averages, the percentage of sentences written in passive voice as well as Flesch Reading Ease and Flesch–Kincaid Grade Level scores after grammar checking (Figure 9.6).

Figure 9.6

READABILITY ANALYSIS OF A DOCUMENT

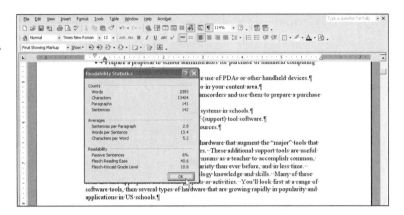

Some teachers approach creative writing assignments for older students by having them write stories for other readers, usually younger children. This is an excellent opportunity for use of readability analysis to assure that the materials are suitable for the intended audience. Writers will develop beneficial insight into language use through such exercises.

Statistical Analysis Software

Many teachers cringe at the thought of statistics; perhaps you do as well. If you haven't been exposed to statistics already, you probably will be within your remaining teacher preparation courses. Regardless of such exposure, we acknowledge that many teachers do not use statistical data analysis as part of their teaching. However, perhaps they should. The increased focus on accountability for learning outcomes, including legislation such as No Child Left Behind, may lead to requirements for more analysis of what we are achieving. There is also growing interest among teachers in what is called "action research," which focuses on your own classroom and your students. Succinctly, this approach to studying what we are doing unites research and classroom practice, rather than setting up special experiments. It involves taking some action, critically reflecting on it and its outcomes based on data, and then repeating the process in search of ever better ways to help students learn. See <www.scu.edu.au/schools/gcm/ar/arhome.html> for detailed information about action research. Roblyer (2003) also noted calls for teachers to become researchers in their own classrooms.

Any computer today is powerful enough to perform data analysis that required a mainframe not so very long ago. With relative ease you can perform the simplest of descriptive analyses (means and standard deviations) all the way to the most complex multivariate analyses, provided you know which analyses to use and how to interpret the results. For decades researchers relied on mainframe versions of SPSS and SAS software, which are available today in much more user-friendly versions for any PC. However, without buying any new software, you probably have all the statistical analysis power you need in the functions provided in your spreadsheet program (Figure 9.7).

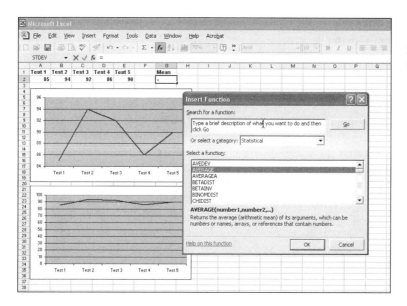

Figure 9.7

STATISTICAL ANALYSIS
USING A SPREADSHEET

Grade Books

Among the earliest of teacher-support tools to appear on the market was the electronic grade book. Although similar to an actual grade book on the surface, any grade-book software worth considering will have far greater flexibility and capability.

Typically, you begin by entering student names and the number of values (assignments) to be entered per student. Useful grade-book software then allows weighting of the individual assignments (e.g., tests are worth four times as much as quizzes) and provides alternative methods of dealing with missing values or late work. The weighting factors generally can be changed at any point, allowing great flexibility in overall grading with no modifications to the data.

Among representative products, *Grade Machine* <www.mistycity.com/grademachine> can manage 10 subject areas over 20 grading periods, each with up to 10 categories. You can define your own grading scales with curving options, create student progress graphs and class histograms, and import and export data across other applications. This program also offers photographic seating charts, attendance and behavior tracking, and support for progress reports in English, Spanish, French, German, or Russian. Any class can be a mix of regular grading systems and specialized ones, such as those for students with IEPs. Final reports may combine information from multiple parts of the record, which you can then email to students, parents, tutors, and others, using the built-in email support.

If some of the features that go well beyond a normal grade book appeal to you, then seek out the best grade-book software that you can find. A simple web search will lead you to many other electronic grade book programs, which you should compare before choosing one for yourself or your school. We provide links to several on the companion website. On the other hand, if what you really want is an automatic calculator of final grades that also allows experimentation with weights, you probably only need a spreadsheet as your grade book, as described in Chapter 7.

Research Bibliographic Aids

Anyone who has ever written a research paper knows the difficulty of keeping accurate track of research materials and specific citations, then formatting all in-text citations and the final references or bibliography correctly. Assignments in different subjects or courses may have required the use of different reference styles as well, whether APA, MLA, or Chicago, as examples. Software is available to assist with the research process.

EndNote allows you to enter and manipulate article abstracts and research and lab notes, then aids in compiling annotated bibliographies and reading lists. It even imports bibliographic data directly from online databases such as ERIC, OVID, or ProQuest. Once you create your database of references, *EndNote* formats in-text citations in whatever style you need (author, date, number, etc.) and compiles your bibliography in any of more than 200 common styles, including APA and MLA. *EndNote* integrates directly into *Word* to become readily accessible from the Tools menu. A product like this can be indispensable for students preparing term papers, theses, or dissertations. You can download a trial version of *EndNote* at <www.endnote.com>, and most college bookstores sell this valuable tool.

Portable Documents (PDF Files)

Have you ever received a computer file from someone else that you could not open on your own computer to view? The most probable cause of this all too common problem is that you do not have the software on your computer that created the file. Common examples include widely used, costly desktop publishing programs such as *Pagemaker*, whose files are not readable in most other software. This can lead to needless frustration.

One of the most popular solutions to the problem is to convert original files into Portable Document Format or PDF files. PDF files are the file format specified by Adobe as the output of its *Acrobat* software. *Acrobat* itself is somewhat costly, but the *Acrobat Reader* that allows you to open, display, and print PDF files is totally free. In fact, most computer makers install *Acrobat Reader* on all their computers at the factory. Thus, nearly anyone can read a PDF file, and if you do need the reader software, it's a free download from <www.adobe.com>.

Acrobat files are much more than just "universal." They also preserve the look and layout of the original file. This is significant in electronic publishing and graphics especially, where the original may use a font that you do not have and may have a page layout that you simply cannot duplicate with other software. The PDF version of the file will look virtually identical to the original. Forms can be created using any software and then converted to PDF format for electronic distribution. They can even be interactive, so that users can fill in the blanks at their own computer and print the completed form to submit. An enormous range of sources from the U.S. government to electronic magazines and journals uses the PDF format as the ideal way to distribute materials. You'll find links to some of them on the companion website.

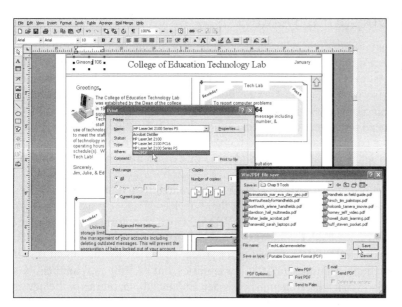

Figure 9.8

CREATING A PDF FILE FROM A DOCUMENT FILE

If you want to create your own PDF files, you can purchase the Adobe *Acrobat* software, which is the most powerful tool of this type. Alternately, you can download any of several different shareware products that also produce such files (see the companion website for links). Once you install PDF creation software on your computer, just prepare your materials as you ordinarily would. When you are ready to convert the file, follow the normal process for printing your document but don't select your regular printer. Instead, look in the list of installed printers for your PDF software. Figure 9.8 shows two choices—Adobe *Acrobat* and another called *Win2PDF.* Make your choice and then complete the printing process, as shown in the inset at the lower right of the figure. Some programs such as *Print Master* offer the option to save directly as a PDF file as well.

PDF files are an excellent choice for *electronic portfolios*, which are becoming increasingly common at all levels of education. The contents of an e-portfolio typically range across all the kinds of technologies you have been learning about and may pose many problems for potential reviewers of the portfolio. Some experts on portfolios, such as Helen Barrett at the University of Alaska, strongly recommend PDF files as the ideal format for all the contents of the portfolio, regardless of its original source (see <http://transition.alaska.edu/www/portfolios/sitepaper2001.html>). When everything has been burned onto a CD, you have as close to a universally viewable project as is possible.

Hardware Tools

Now that you have explored a broad range of software tools that support the teaching and learning process, it is time to meet several hardware tools as well—handheld computing systems, GPS/GIS systems, and digital video.

Handheld Computing Systems

One of the major concerns about educational technology throughout the world is how to provide sufficient quantities of technology hardware. It is hard to claim that technology is an integral part of any educational program if students have only a few minutes a day (or even per week) of computer or other technology access time (Wood, 2002). The dream of technology advocates is "ubiquitous computing," meaning that all students have access at all times or as close to that as possible (Dede, 2002; McAnear, 2002). Although prices for computers and related technologies continue to decline, they are still far too high to achieve a ratio of one student to one computer (the ultimate meaning of ubiquitous) in all but a very few schools.

Among the technologies that have substantial potential to achieve a much higher level of technology access are a variety of handheld devices. These devices are today's successor to early personal digital assistants, or PDAs, which were little more than electronic versions of pocket calendars and note pads. Early PDAs had much to offer adults, including teachers, but relatively little value for students. Today, the handheld is still far from, say, a notebook computer in broad capabilities, but exciting new applications are appearing regularly that educators must consider. Enhanced capabilities of the newer handhelds, new peripherals for them, and new software applications combine to create a powerful new tool for teaching and learning. The twin virtues of low price and portability bode well for educational acceptance of these devices and set them apart from most previous technologies.

Handheld Technologies

Obviously the name *handheld* carries some expectations with it, namely, of a device that is small enough to fit in your hand (more or less). Palm Computing and Handspring are among the major makers of such units, which use the Palm operating system. As discussed briefly in Chapter 2, users input information into their handhelds using a stylus (Figure 9.9) and a slightly stylized print format called Graffiti. Accessory keyboards are also available (Figure 9.10), some of which even fold for portability. Palm-powered handhelds are designed to synchronize their data with any type of computer through a

Figure 9.9
Input data into a handheld with a stylus.

Figure 9.10
HANDHELD WITH
KEYBOARD FOR
FASTER INPUT

charger/cradle or USB cable. In addition to duplicating the information in the PDA, the Palm desktop software allows normal keyboard input, which is easier for many users than printing in Graffiti (Figure 9.11). These devices can also share information among themselves and send output to a printer by "beaming" infrared signals. The least expensive models now sell for roughly the price of a modest graphing calculator, less than $100. This makes the dream of ubiquitous computing seem achievable.

The other major category of handheld is generally known as a Pocket PC. Numerous computer companies, including Hewlett-Packard and Toshiba, produce these devices that run a "pocket" version of Microsoft *Windows*. Pocket PCs run scaled-down

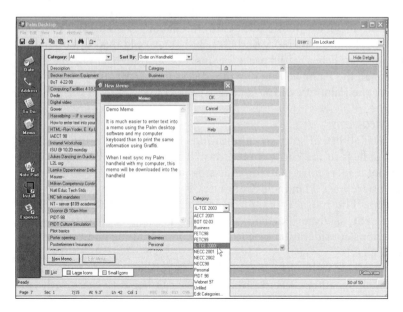

Figure 9.11
HANDHELD SOFTWARE ON
THE COMPUTER

versions of the Microsoft *Office* applications and have small built-in keyboards as well as handwriting input. They are more powerful than Palm OS devices but also larger and generally more expensive, making them somewhat less popular in schools.

Accessories can add greatly to the usefulness of either type of handheld device; we can mention only some of the most fascinating. Wireless network connectivity is possible using standard network protocols. Modems for wireless connectivity anywhere are also available, as are modules that turn the handheld into a digital camera. Some models include a cell phone, whereas some cell phones now have the computing functions of a handheld. The two technologies may be on a course to converge at some point in the future. For school uses, probes for measuring light, temperature, and so on offer exciting possibilities in the curriculum.

Handheld Software

All handhelds offer the basic PIM (personal information manager) applications of date and address book, to-do list, and some kind of note or memo pad (Figure 9.11). However, they are just the tip of the iceberg. The website K12 Handhelds <www.k12 handhelds.com> lists over 100 great educational applications, many of which rely on additional software.

At the forefront of developing such applications is the Center for Highly Interactive Computing in Education at the University of Michigan <www.handheld.hice-dev.org>, codirected by Elliott Soloway. Soloway devoted his career to artificial intelligence, hoping for an impact on education, but more recently concluded that "making children smarter was more interesting than making machines smarter" (Wood, 2002). He now develops and distributes free of charge unique educational applications for handheld computers. Among the products of HICE are *PicoMap*, a "mini-Inspiration" for concept mapping; *Cooties*, a simulation of how viruses spread that uses an electronic virus that spreads by beaming among handhelds; *BB Math*, which provides math drills for students who need extra practice; and *Sketchy*, a sketchpad with animation capabilities.

Other applications include e-Book reader software, enabling users to carry the complete text of many books in the memory of their handheld. Could this be the solution to the problem of excessively heavy backpacks for students? Although hardly all (or even primarily) educational, the Palm website provides access to over 10,000 pieces of software that run under the Palm OS <http://software.palm.com>.

Curriculum Applications

Beyond the very availability of software applications for handhelds is the far larger issue of how to use them in the curriculum. Pownell and Bailey (2002) argued persuasively that school leaders must plan for and assess handheld use if it is to be truly successful. They offered the Handheld Computer Implementation Rubric to help guide school leaders. The rubric is organized around 13 themes, including leadership, staff development, safety, ethics, and curriculum. We believe their recommendations deserve serious consideration by any school contemplating an investment in handheld technologies.

Even though handheld technology in schools is in its infancy, already far more fascinating curriculum applications have evolved than we can begin to share with you.

Hopefully our selections will stimulate your thinking and encourage you to dig into the published literature as well.

Tinker, Staudt, and Walton (2002) described the use of handhelds to collect and analyze field data anywhere, noting that students often fail to gain much concrete knowledge from field experiences because they lack the tools to record their experiences. Imagine students working in teams on an outdoor project. One team might rely on an observation checklist in their handheld. Another team might record specific data into a database they constructed in school prior to the excursion. Still others use sketchpad software to record the sites and their impressions. A digital map of the field area enables the students to record their data in geographic context. We encourage you to read the entire article, which offers a wealth of concrete ideas and applications. Also check the companion website for links to handheld software and other resources.

Would you think of using billiards to teach the mathematical concept of reflection? Perhaps—but using a handheld? Horton and Wiegert (2002) did exactly that. They programmed a carom billiards game using *The Geometer's Sketchpad* software for a Pocket PC. A significant part of the learning in their lesson plan comes from students creating their own billiards table using this software. They explained in detail how to build the table, set up the game, and then analyze the results. This is a powerful application in math.

Bell (2002) described a scenario in which students use handhelds with wireless web access to study the stars. Using downloaded star maps and satellite positioning (next section of this chapter), students were able to easily locate specific stars and constellations in the night sky as part of their homework.

Starting in 2002, a group of students at Tremont (Maine) Consolidated School pursued a project that addresses State of Maine Learning Results with state-of-the-art technology tools (Starr, 2003). The students counted clams in the area clam flats, which have been closed to fishing for some time. Their goal was to convince state officials to clean up the polluted flats and reopen them to area fishers, based on the number of harvestable clams they documented. Library teacher Tammy Crossman-Turner led the effort. Working at low tide, students picked a starting point on shore and used a GPS device to record the precise location coordinates. Following a prescribed pattern, they would dig in one area and count and measure every clam they found. Then they moved on and repeated the process to form a search grid. Students input their data into a handheld, recording such details as sediment type, any odor, plot number, coordinates, and the number of clams found. They also took digital photos of the site to document their work. Crossman-Turner believes the primary benefit of this project is that kids learn that they, too, can be scientists as they see that what they learn at school is both real and important.

Handhelds can also be assistive technology for students with special needs (Barfield, 2003). They can help with organization of projects by giving a tactile way to keep calendars and other information. In the year 2000 teachers in all 50 states had the opportunity to apply for a Palm Education Pioneers (PEP) grant <www.palmgrants.sri.com>. A New York teacher experimented with handhelds and keyboards for students with learning disabilities that made writing on paper a struggle. He reported a "significant decrease" in student frustration when writing using the handheld.

In Tony Vincent's fifth-grade class in Omaha, students have the use of handhelds and keyboards. Vincent has documented his experiences with the students extensively at <www.mpsomaha.org/willow/p5/handhelds> and we cannot begin to do justice to his work. He lists nearly 50 activities his students have done with the help of their hand-helds, among them keeping a reading journal (notebook), calculating inflation (calcu-lator), animating math algorithms and cell structures, recording and charting observations, and creating a database of famous Americans. There's even a video of stu-dents talking about their favorite activities. Vincent shares his solutions to such man-agement issues as how to teach Graffiti, how to store and charge the handhelds, how to handle distribution of the devices, and how to communicate with parents about the activities. There are also many student projects to review and a wide range of links to useful sites related to handhelds. Tony Vincent is modeling what will become common classroom practice in the near future.

The PEP program mentioned previously involved an extensive study of handheld applications in schools (Vahey & Crawford, 2002). Some 90 percent of the 100+ par-ticipating teachers reported a very positive experience that they would continue after the grant period ended. Elementary teachers were more positive about the experience than secondary teachers. Writing activities and science uses received the highest acclaim. Participants reported several key benefits to students: increased time using technology, increased motivation, and increased collaboration and communication. Difficulties encountered included inappropriate use (e.g., beaming), synchronization and other tech-nology management issues, problems with Graffiti for long text input, and the inevitable damage to equipment. Although he was not a participant in PEP, Tony Vincent addressed many of these problems on his class website (listed previously).

Although experience working with students and handheld devices is limited, the potential is enormous. Educators at all levels should be alert to further developments with this exciting technology.

GPS/GIS

Several of the curriculum applications described previously in this chapter involved the use of global positioning system (GPS) receivers. These small handheld devices use or-biting satellites to determine the exact latitude and longitude of their current location, anywhere on Earth. When these satellite data are combined with a digital map, it is lit-erally possible to chart your path with complete precision as you drive or walk. GPS is the basis of the navigation systems increasingly common in vehicles, including rental cars whose drivers are often unfamiliar with the area. Once an exotic technology, GPS devices are now available at very affordable prices (less than $200; see, for instance, the GPS Store at <www.thegpsstore.com/site>) and are beginning to find applications in education. A very understandable primer on GPS is available at <www.aero.org/publications/GPSPRIMER>.

A geographic information system (GIS) is a collection of computer hardware, soft-ware, and geographic data for capturing, storing, updating, manipulating, analyzing, and displaying all forms of geographically referenced information <www.michigan.gov/cgi/0,1607,7-158-14767-31861--F,00.html>. GIS answers the question "Where?" by matching the location of a place with its characteristics using common identifiers, for example, a street name <http://kangis.org/gps/multimedia/2>. A GPS receiver, then, is a data-gathering component of a GIS, which uses the information to generate maps and other geographic data. Interest in GIS/GPS is such that there are already dedicated K12 websites for these technologies such as <www.gis2gps.com> and <http://kangis.org/gps>. Both offer K12 lesson ideas that use GIS and/or GPS as well as useful links and some downloadable materials. Another comprehensive K12 resource site is provided by the Berrien County (Michigan) Intermediate School District at <www.remc11.k12.mi.us/bcisd/classres/gis.htm>.

Often a single GPS device or GPS accessory for a handheld could be shared by multiple classes through careful scheduling, making this a truly affordable new technology. Starr (2003) reported on the Maine clam project previously mentioned, in which students used GPS data to determine their precise location in the clam flats they were surveying. Any field application would benefit from a similar use. Ligon GT Magnet Middle School (North Carolina) offers an elective interdisciplinary science and technology course called Satellites, Computers, and Mapping <www.ncsu.edu/midlink/gis/gis_intro.htm>.

With the generally sad state of geography education in the United States, we can only hope that the increasing availability of GPS technology may help to stimulate both teaching and learning of geographic concepts. What was once considered a somewhat dull subject can come to life in the students' own hands.

Digital Video

Our final topic on hardware support tools is digital video. The use of moving pictures as an educational tool goes back decades to the early days of film. Students today are often unfamiliar with physical film, having grown up only with VCRs and tapes, which are now rapidly being supplanted by digital video such as DVDs. However, we are not concerned here with use of prerecorded material but rather with video that you or your students create. Camcorders and digital editing on a computer are revolutionizing the potential for this highly visual learning medium.

Video Applications

Think about all the video you have probably watched as a student. Why was the content presented in this way? Was it because there was some sort of motion inherent in that content, such as how to do something or perform some skill? Was it to give a better feel for some location or activity than a lecture might be able to do? Was the video more than a narrated lecture, perhaps something like a Ken Burns documentary?

Teachers use video for all kinds of reasons. However, we have found that in many cases, videos have a limited number of segments that are the real heart of the content, and they may not even be presented in the order that you, as the teacher, would prefer. You show the entire video to the class because it is too difficult to locate the individual segments you really want quickly and accurately using your VCR. It may even be that the "extraneous" content detracts from what you ideally would like to present. DVDs have potential for easier access to segments, but given the scarcity of real educational material on DVD and the fact that fast, accurate access depends on how the producer provided for "chapters" in the content, DVD is not yet the ideal technology, in our view, for the most effective use of video.

Our challenge to you, then, is to think of video in a new way; to focus on what really matters in the content, regardless of how little that might be of the entire video at hand; and equally importantly, to think of video as a possible tool in the hands of students to demonstrate their learning.

Creating Video

Even if you've never been in a TV studio, you've seen late night television shows and many others that make no effort to hide the huge cameras that are used and the fact that a set is just that, no matter what that window behind the host seems to be showing for a view. Some schools do have television studios on a somewhat smaller scale, but they are the exception. Still most teachers can expect to have some kind of access to video equipment today.

At the simplest level, digital still cameras (see Chapter 8) frequently include a video mode. Often they can take only a very short video because of limited memory. For instance, the Sony Mavica cameras that store everything onto floppy disks may record as little as 15 seconds of video. At first glance, that may seem like a uselessly short time. However, if you think of the *key* content that you might wish to convey by video, you will be surprised how often an easily managed 15-second clip can show just what you really need. It's a great exercise to analyze your content from this perspective.

If you use a still camera in "movie mode," the camera will save the video in its memory in a ready-to-use format. Take the floppy out of the camera and it contains a ready-to-use video. If your camera uses the more common memory card, then you connect the camera to the computer by cable, just as you do to retrieve still images. Again, the video will be in a ready-to-use format that you can play on the computer right away.

Chances are you will also have access to a camcorder in your school. It may be the traditional large VHS type, which records onto standard videotapes that you can play back using a VCR. However, more and more schools are purchasing new, small digital camcorders that fit in the palm of your hand—another type of "handheld"! Figure 9.12 shows a typical low-cost digital camcorder and the miniature DV tape that it uses. Apart

Figure 9.12

DIGITAL CAMCORDER
WITH DV TAPE AND
ANALOG CABLES

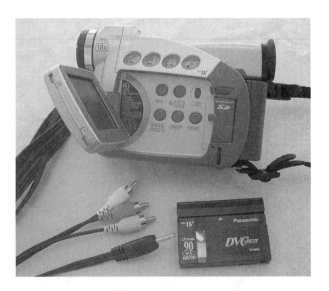

from size, digital camcorders produce a noticeably better-quality video image than VHS recorders. Digital camcorders offer educators vast new potential for incorporating video into the learning environment.

Because digital camcorders do not use regular videotape, playback of the video requires a different approach. Special cables (also shown in Figure 9.12) allow you to connect such a camcorder directly to a TV or video projector. You can also connect it to a VCR and *dub* or copy the video to a regular tape. However, that reduces the quality of the video back to the lower level inherent in VHS. An alternative that is becoming increasingly feasible and popular is to import the video into a computer for playback, with or without editing, which is the next topic.

Digital Video on Your Computer

The ability to import video into a computer for playback and editing is actually not new, but the hardware required to do so from any analog video source (VCR or laserdisc) was never common in schools. The digital camcorder is changing that because it is designed to connect to computers easily, most commonly using an IEEE 1394 connection, also known as Firewire or iLink. More and more computers, including notebooks, have these connections, which means you can have a mobile video production facility in your backpack today (Figure 9.13). If your computer lacks such a connection, it can be added for less than $100, including software to edit your video.

You'll learn more about working with digital video on your computer in Chapter 11. For now, just note that once you can easily import video into a computer, you can edit your video into clips of any desired length. Short clips may better focus student attention on the critical aspects of the content, whereas longer clips may be essential to comprehend the entire process being shown. With modestly priced hardware and even free software such as Apple's *iMovie* and Windows *MovieMaker,* you can produce just the video you really want and students have a powerful new learning tool in their hands.

Selecting a Digital Camcorder

In our experience, even the less expensive digital camcorders seem to work extremely well and give excellent results. You should be able to look at the lower end of the price

Figure 9.13

A PORTABLE VIDEO EDITING SYSTEM

range to find a DV camcorder for school (or personal) use. We suggest you take into account just a few basic points and that you go to an electronics store where you can actually hold and test various models.

First, does it fit you well? Many DV camcorders are very small, which means the controls are also very small. To fit so many things into such a small package, not all controls may be located where they make sense to you and are easy to reach and use. How does the camera turn on? Where is the zoom lens control located and is it easy to use while you are filming? Where are the playback controls located? How large is the viewing screen (most users try to ignore the much smaller viewfinder) and how bright is it in outdoor light?

Second, just as with a digital still camera, how powerful is the optical zoom of the lens? There will also be some astronomical total zoom ratio, like 500X, but a large part of that will be digital, which is less desirable.

Third, what is the tape format? The most common at this time is called MiniDV, but there are others that are incompatible. At the least, you want all camcorders in a school to use the same kind of tape.

Fourth, is there a still picture mode? If so, does the camera use some kind of memory card to store still pictures in addition to being able to do so on the tape? (A still on tape is typically a five-second recording of the one image.) Can you download stills with a USB cable, which nearly every computer can use, or do even the stills require a Firewire connection? If there is a memory card, is the card type compatible with any digital still camera you may have and with your printer, if you have the type that can read camera memory cards directly without a computer?

Fifth, most digital camcorders have some kind of electronic image stabilization. You may already realize that when you shoot video, any movement of your hands shows up as shake in the video. Because digital camcorders are so small, few users bother with a tripod for stability. The camera tries to compensate for your unintentional movements electronically. How well does this feature work? You can test this even in a store by intentionally not holding the camera as steady as you may well be able to do and then review the recording to see the effect.

Finally, make use of online hardware reviews to help you identify what to look for and which brands and models seem to offer you the most for your money. One resource that we depend on is ZDNet at <http://reviews-ZDNet.com.com>.

SUMMARY

This chapter pointed you toward a diverse range of software and hardware support tools, which can help to make your teaching and your students' learning more interesting, more effective, and more efficient. Nearly every teacher at some time makes use of worksheets. The days of laboriously making them by hand or settling for commercially prepared ones that didn't really fit your need are past. Today's teachers can use software on their own computers to create worksheets and puzzles or go online to any of several sites that create a wide range of worksheet types. The key to appropriate use of worksheets of any kind is to focus on their value for learning. They need to be more than just diversions from other class activities.

You also learned about software to help you construct and even administer the inevitable test. Statistical software may be very useful in better understanding the student outcomes in your classroom, which seems to be taking on new significance in light of increased emphasis at the national level of testing and accountability. For research assistance, you learned about tools that can manage your research note taking and documentation, then format the citations and references correctly in the research paper you write. High school students could benefit from this software as well.

Grade-book software may be useful to you, especially if you want more capabilities than you can easily create for yourself using a spreadsheet. You also explored PDF files, a way to enable others to view your documents just as you wanted them to look, even if they do not have the software you may use to create the document.

We then turned to three kinds of hardware tools that are growing rapidly in availability and use in schools. Handheld computing devices, sometimes called PDAs and pocket PCs, offer amazing potential in the hands of students and may offer our best hope of putting significant computing power into the hands of every student. At a cost not much different from a graphing calculator, class sets of handhelds are starting to appear in schools across the country and software to use on them is rapidly increasing as well. Best of all, some excellent software for PDAs is totally free.

Next we turned briefly to the lesser-known technology of GPS and GIS systems. We believe teachers will increasingly use these technologies in the next few years, so watch for more information in professional publications. Finally, you took a whirlwind look at digital video, the technology that can turn you into your very own video producer. At last you have potential, at remarkably low cost, to use just the video you really need in your teaching. Your students can also become video producers to demonstrate the depth and breadth of their learning in many subjects. We hope this introduction has whetted your appetite for the further treatment of digital video you'll find in Chapter 11.

chapter 9 activities

1. Create a range of sample worksheets appropriate for your teaching area. If possible, use both local software and online resources to compare their ease of use and capabilities.
2. Develop several lesson plans that include worksheets and/or puzzles.
3. Research and prepare a position on the merits of electronic test generators. Would they be useful to you? Why or why not?
4. What potential do you envision in statistical software and research aids for yourself and also for your students?
5. Convert materials that you have created in as many different software packages as possible into PDF format. If necessary, download and install shareware PDF software.
6. Research the specifications and capabilities of at least five different electronic gradebook software packages. Compare and contrast them and then make a recommendation

to your school concerning which one to purchase.

7. Research various brands and types of handheld computing devices, both Palm powered and Pocket PC. Compare their specifications and determine which ones you would most like to have as a set in your classroom.

8. Look for lesson plans on the Internet that incorporate handhelds. Modify several to fit your teaching or develop new ones based on what you learn.

9. Prepare a proposal to school administrators for the purchase of handheld computing devices with justification.

10. Investigate whether any applications of GPS or GIS exist in your school or other schools in your area.

11. Research GPS/GIS technologies and write a position paper on appropriate uses at your teaching level.

12. Visit an electronics store and examine the available digital camcorders. Write up a comparison of the models you find.

13. Investigate whether your school has computers available to you to which you can connect a digital camcorder. If not, ask appropriate individuals whether this technology will become available any time soon.

Companion Website

Visit the companion website at <www.ablongman.com/lockard6e> for more information about the topics discussed in this chapter.

---

expect the world®

The New York Times

nytimes.com

Themes of the Times

Expand your knowledge of the concepts discussed in this chapter by reading current and historical articles from the *New York Times* by visiting the Themes of the Times section of the companion website <www.ablongman.com/lockard6e>.

References

Barfield, D. F. "Addressing the Special Needs Student through Technology." *Technology & Learning*, January 1, 2003. Retrieved February 7, 2003, from <www.techlearning.com/db_area/archives/WCE/archives/dianesn1.html>

Bell, R. "A Fistful of Stars." *Learning & Leading with Technology*, May 2002, *29*(8), p. 16.

Dede, C. "Augmented Reality through Ubiquitous Computing." *Learning & Leading with Technology*, May 2002, *29*(8), p. 13.

Horton, B., and Wiegert, E. "Using Handhelds and Billiards to Teach Reflection." *Learning & Leading with Technology*, May 2002, *29*(8), pp. 32–35.

Johnson, J. M. "Summertime Software." *Learning & Leading with Technology*, May 2002, *29*(8), pp. 62–63.

McAnear, A. "Moving Toward Ubiquitous Computing." *Learning & Leading with Technology*, May 2002, *29*(8), pp. 4–5.

McIntire, T. "The Administator's Guide to Data-Driven Decision Making." *Technology & Learning*, June 15, 2002. Retrieved February 7, 2003, from <www.techlearning.com/db_area/archives/TL/2002/06/guide.html>

Pownell, D., and Bailey, G. D. "Assessing Handheld Readiness." *Learning & Leading with Technology*, October 2002, *30*(2), pp. 50–55.

Roblyer, M. D. *Integrating Educational Technology into Teaching*, 3rd ed. Columbus, OH: Merrill Prentice Hall, 2003.

Soloway, E., Luchini, K., Quintana, C., and Norris, C. "Which Scenario Is Better for Learning?" *Learning & Leading with Technology*, May 2002, *29*(8), pp. 14–15.

Starr, L. "Kids Count Clams to Spur Community Cleanup." *Education World*, January 6, 2003. Retrieved February 2, 2003, from <www.education-world.com/a_curr/profdev032.shtml>

Tinker, B., Staudt, C., and Walton, D. "The Handheld Computer as Field Guide." *Learning & Leading with Technology*, September 2002, *30*(1), pp. 36–41.

Trefny, B. "A Guide to Student Information Systems." *Technology & Learning*, September 15, 2002. Retrieved February 7, 2003, from <www.techlearning.com/db_area/archives/TL/2002/09/spotlight.html>

Vahey, P., and Crawford, V. *Palm™ Education Pioneers Program: Final Evaluation Report*. September 2002. Retrieved February 7, 2003, from <www.palmgrants.sri.com/PEP_Final_Report.pdf>

Wood, C. "Technology in America." *PC Magazine*, March 12, 2002. Retrieved February 7, 2003, from <www.pcmag.com/article2/0,4149,15154,00.asp>

Computer-Assisted Instruction Fundamentals

OBJECTIVES

After completing this chapter, you will be able to:

- Explain the nature of computer-assisted instruction (CAI) in terms of its three main characteristics.
- Briefly outline the historical development of CAI.
- Identify five major types of CAI, based on the traditional taxonomy.
- Develop appropriate applications of each type of software.

- Explain the issues surrounding each of the five software types.
- Discuss the basis for the Learner-Centered Taxonomy as an alternative to the traditional software classification scheme.
- Describe basic findings of research studies on the effects of CAI.
- Analyze the merits of new directions in CAI research.

Computers are just tools, but arguably the most versatile tools known to humans. Thus far, you have learned about their potential as a *personal productivity tool:* communications and information resource, word processor and publishing center, spreadsheet, database manager, and graphics and support system. This chapter introduces another major application area: the computer as an instructional tutor, a *tool for learning* specific things. You will study the nature and evolution of computer-assisted instruction, major types and primary characteristics of such software, their potential strengths and weaknesses, and research findings concerning the outcomes of computer-assisted instruction.

The Nature of Computer-Assisted Instruction

NETS
NOTES

NETS **S** 1
NETS **S** 4
NETS **S** 6
NETS **T** I-A
NETS **T** I-B
NETS **T** II-A
NETS **T** II-B
NETS **T** II-C
NETS **T** III-A
NETS **T** III-B
NETS **T** III-C
NETS **T** IV-C
NETS **T** VI-B
NETS **T** VI-C

Computer-assisted instruction (CAI) is the most common term for the interaction of a learner with a computer in a direct instructional role. CAI software provides instruction in some particular content in any of a variety of formats, with or even without any involvement of a human teacher. Much of CAI is "designed to make it easier, quicker, or otherwise more efficient to continue teaching the same things in the same ways we have always taught them" (Maddux, Johnson, & Willis, 1992, p. 23). Maddux, Johnson, and Willis called these Type I applications, and they are quick to note that their definition is not an indictment of CAI at all. There is a clear potential role for CAI within the total scope of educational computing. However, using computers *primarily* for CAI does not take full advantage of the technology. They, like we, believe that the software and tools presented in Chapters 3–9 of this book should be the main focus of computing in schools, with CAI playing a supporting role.

What, then, are the major characteristics of CAI?

Engaged Learning

In typical classroom group instruction, it is difficult at best for any teacher to keep all learners *actively* engaged in the learning process. With CAI, each learner interacts directly and continually with the computer, responding to prompts and questions, receiving feedback to whatever they do. The computer becomes a sort of private tutor. Computer-assisted instruction largely removes the potential for learners merely to observe without active participation.

Flexibility

Another appealing aspect of CAI is its flexibility to teach virtually anything from higher-order thought processes such as problem-solving skills to the relatively simple cognitive learning usually associated with B. F. Skinner's stimulus-response theory. Teachers use CAI for instruction that is integral to the ongoing curriculum, to enrich or supplement basic instruction, and for remediation.

Meeting Student Needs

Interaction and flexibility are key elements of meeting the diverse learning needs of individual students. Not all students learn at the same rate or in the same way, yet typical classroom instruction does little to account for this reality. In fact, schools are ill equipped to deal with individual differences. Children typically start school at about the same age, advance one grade per year, use the same textbooks, do the same assignments, follow the same curriculum, and are expected to attain essentially the same standards. As you may have experienced, one teacher with 30 students per class is unable to devote significant attention to just one student at a time. These conditions all *minimize* rather than capitalize on individual differences.

A teacher working one-to-one with a student adapts the instruction continuously based on the student's responses, both in method and in content. Computer-assisted instruction also can provide instruction adapted to the current user of the software, whose needs may vary greatly from those of the next user. As in one-to-one tutoring, CAI users can set their own pace through the material, taking as little or as much time as they need to achieve mastery. Based on student responses, the computer can make decisions to provide remediation or to advance to new topics or more difficult material, much as a tutor might. In addition, most CAI attempts to appeal to varied learning modalities by using text, graphics, and often animation and sound.

Evolution of Computer-Assisted Instruction

Computer-assisted instruction has evolved over a period of more than 50 years. Let's briefly trace the major developments.

The Early Years

In 1950, scientists at the Massachusetts Institute of Technology designed the first CAI, a flight simulator for training combat pilots, on a mainframe computer. This led to CAI for staff development and training in many industries. In 1959, IBM adapted its staff-development CAI technology for use with children. At about the same time, Florida State University developed and offered CAI courses in physics and statistics, and Dartmouth College researchers created the first simple CAI programming language—BASIC.

Researchers at the University of Illinois initiated the PLATO (Programmed Logic for Automatic Teaching Operations) project in 1960. Their goal was to demonstrate the technical feasibility, manageability, and economic viability of an extensive computer-based education network. High cost proved a significant barrier to adoption by other educational institutions.

At Stanford University in the mid-1960s, Patrick Suppes and his team developed a small tutorial system in mathematics and language arts, primarily for disadvantaged elementary school students. Parallel to this, the Stanford Drill and Practice System was introduced. The fundamental assumption of this mainframe system was that the teacher would first present the basic concepts, then the computer would provide *intensive* drill and practice at a level of difficulty tailored to each learner.

Computer technology advanced steadily during the 1960s. The precursor to today's computer monitors was the cathode-ray tube, which IBM introduced in 1964, followed in 1966 by the first computer system designed expressly for CAI—the IBM 1500. Late in 1971, Intel introduced the "computer on a chip," the technology that made possible low-cost microcomputers appropriate for instructional use.

Major Research and Development Efforts

Although early efforts led to much enthusiasm for the potential of CAI, cost was a serious deterrent to its application. Few schools had access to mainframe systems with terminals. Educational software was scarce and often of questionable quality. Such problems are typical of any new technology, of course.

Based on what prior research had demonstrated, in 1971 the National Science Foundation invested $10 million in two major CAI projects, the PLATO system described previously and TICCIT (Time-shared Interactive Computer Controlled Information Television). The aim of TICCIT was to demonstrate in community colleges that CAI could provide better instruction in mathematics and English at lower cost than traditional instruction could. TICCIT was based on an educational philosophy termed *Learner-Controlled Instruction (LCI)*, which stressed that students must be able to adapt the sequence of instruction to their own pace and learning style. A special keyboard made it easy to request additional examples, redisplay of rules, practice items, and so forth (Merrill, Schneider, & Fletcher, 1980).

Educational Testing Service evaluated both PLATO and TICCIT. In community colleges, PLATO lessons produced achievement gains in mathematics, chemistry, and biology. Teacher and student attitudes toward PLATO were positive. In grades 4, 5, and 6, PLATO math lessons also produced significant achievement gains and more positive attitudes toward the subject matter than among students in a traditional class. TICCIT also produced achievement gains among community college students in math and English, along with positive attitudes. See Steinberg (1991) for more details.

Thus, by the mid-1970s evidence supported the instructional potential of CAI in different settings using different instructional models and differing hardware technologies. The major remaining barrier to broad CAI viability in education—economics—began to fall in 1977 with the introduction of microcomputers by Radio Shack, Commodore, and Apple. Mass access to computers was becoming a reality.

A Taxonomy of CAI

Today a wide range of CAI is available, which has led to attempts to categorize and succinctly describe these software products. Certain labels are now common, including drill and practice, tutorials, simulations, games, and problem-solving software. However, not everything fits neatly into such categories.

Drill and Practice

Drill and practice has been the most common and best known form of instructional software. The name suggests its purpose—to help learners remember and use information they have *previously* been taught. Teachers assign students to use these programs for extensive repetitive work with selected skills or knowledge (Figure 10.1).

Do not assume, however, that drills apply only to low-level tasks. While this is often true, drill and practice also can develop skills that are vital to more complex tasks. For instance, work on subword and word recognition is important in the development of reading comprehension. Even what appears to be routine practice on arithmetic facts can be essential preparation for coping with more difficult skills at a later time.

Types of Drill and Practice

The least sophisticated drill and practice resembles traditional flash cards or programmed instruction. Every user of the program receives a fixed number of items. A student who has mastered the content must complete the same tasks before moving ahead as one who truly needs the additional work.

Slightly better is the program that uses an arbitrary mastery criterion, perhaps ten correct responses in a row. The best students should complete the exercise in just ten items, while a student needing more practice might require several times that number to achieve the criterion. Upon completion, the student is able to select the next level of drill.

The most highly adaptive program might assume "mastery" after relatively few responses and automatically increase the difficulty level, or even move on to the next topic, say from addition to multiplication. If performance falters, the difficulty is decreased or the content returns to the previous topic. Such continual adjustment seeks to assure mastery throughout, while neither boring the student with needless repetition nor causing frustration by demanding something beyond the student's capabilities.

Figure 10.1

DRILL AND PRACTICE ON VERBS
IN *GRAMMAR ROCK*

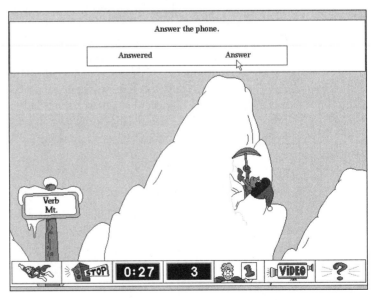

Examples of Drill and Practice

Mary Jones, a third-grade teacher, noticed that several of her students were still having trouble with basic math skills. She selected *Mental Math Games* to motivate and assist those students to master math operations and facts. Five separate games aim at speed and accuracy in all operations. For example, in "Tip-a-Duck," problems appear on figures in a carnival shooting gallery. To move through "Maze," learners must solve problems that appear on arrows pointing in the direction they wish to move. The scope of work ranges from single-digit addition to three-digit division. *Mental Math Games* received an Award of Excellence from *Technology & Learning* magazine.

For further help, Ms. Jones may have students use *Math Wizard*, a talking program that includes activities covering addition, subtraction, multiplication, fractions, decimals, and division. In language arts, she might choose *Punctuation* to help elementary-age students improve their punctuation skills. Learners are challenged to find a punctuation error in each sentence, then indicate which rule explains the error.

The Drill-and-Practice Controversy

Drill-and-practice programs have attracted considerable criticism. Critics claim that they are often boring, are very narrow in their pedagogical approach, drill all students the same way regardless of their ability or level of functioning, may interfere with desired remembering, and often provide undesirable negative feedback.

Proponents argue that drill and practice already exists as flash cards and worksheets in most classrooms. Software motivates students better and can effectively reduce the tedium of learning many skills that require extensive practice for retention or speed. Because feedback is immediate and errors are not allowed to compound, CAI avoids a major weakness of traditional worksheets and other independent work forms with which a student may actually "master" incorrect material. Also, the computer can target practice where it is most needed without dwelling on what the learner has mastered, something difficult, at best, with traditional methods.

Drill and practice as an element of learning is hardly subject to debate. Much of the criticism of such CAI is attributable to poorly conceived software, rather than computer-based drill and practice per se. Design flaws can lessen, even negate, the impact of a product that is sound in its basic concept. Useful drill-and-practice programs are available, and they may save teachers valuable time that would otherwise go into preparing and grading alternatives. Drill-and-practice CAI need not produce greater achievement than traditional instruction to be valuable. If it is "merely as good," it can give the teacher time to use more profitably, working with students directly.

Characteristics of Better Drill and Practice

Viable drill-and-practice programs possess certain characteristics. Summarizing a variety of sources (e.g., Geisert & Futrell, 2000; Roblyer, 2003; Salisbury, 1990), these characteristics typically include:

- Clear educational purpose/goals.
- Recognition of short-term memory limits (e.g., works with no more than seven items at once).
- Appropriate use of graphics, sound, and color.

- Inclusion of tutorial "help" options.
- Effective feedback for correct and incorrect responses.
- Control over the rate of presentation.
- Provision for reviewing directions or previous information.
- Random generation of items.
- Application of appropriate learning theory and pedagogy (e.g., spaced practice and spaced review).
- Presentation of accurate content with correct language.
- Ability to stop at will and resume at the same point later.

Integrating Drill-and-Practice Software in the Curriculum

Drill-and-practice CAI is not equally common for all areas of the curriculum. Not every subject fits the appropriate uses of this CAI format, nor do teachers of all subjects use drill and practice of any kind uniformly. Much of the available software is for elementary-level arithmetic and language arts, or for adult remedial learning. Basic arithmetic facts, spelling, and punctuation are fundamental learning for all and involve the kinds of learning tasks appropriate to drill and practice.

Essentially, drill-and-practice activities present a stimulus to the student, elicit a response, and provide immediate reinforcement. One appropriate use of drill-and-practice programs is when the learning objectives relate to multiple discrimination learning. This type of learning involves, first, perceiving differences among events and, second, attaching the proper label to each one. Discrimination learning emphasizes the ability to distinguish among members of a set of stimuli and to make an appropriate response to each.

Paired associate tasks are also appropriate for drill and practice. In these tasks, the computer helps to create meaningful links between related items or ideas. Overlearning is the goal, to enable the student to perform a task automatically with very little mental activity. Examples of this type of desired overlearning are addition and multiplication facts, sight vocabulary words, and correct spelling of commonly used words.

Your task as a teacher is to *evaluate* any software personally prior to using it in the classroom to determine its potential role and value. (In Chapter 12, you will learn about evaluation techniques.) You must determine that the software is compatible with your curriculum, then plan your lessons so that students will have adequate preparation before using the software. Drill and practice should not introduce new material; rather, it should provide needed work with already familiar content.

This need not mean teaching as usual. Rather, plan CAI into your lesson from the beginning, omitting what you would otherwise do that the software can do for you, changing aspects that can be done differently because of what the software should help students achieve. Integrate the computer work into the lesson; do not tack it on as an afterthought.

Beyond such integrated use, profitable ways to use drill-and-practice CAI include (1) to maintain a performance level previously reached, (2) to automatize skills, and (3) to review material prerequisite to a new lesson (Geisert & Futrell, 2000; Jonassen, 2000). Finally, Mann et al. (1999) confirmed that the more students worked with basic skills software, the greater the improvement in their standardized test scores.

Tutorials

Tutorials are designed to tutor, to instruct. They introduce and present new, unfamiliar material to the learner. They are often designed for stand-alone learning, for which other CAI forms are less suitable. Tutorials typically present content in chunks (Figure 10.2), then ask the learner questions to verify short-term learning. At various points in a lesson, including the end, larger units of content become the focus of the questioning. If the learner at any point fails to meet the program's criteria for achievement, the lesson may move to review and remediation before advancing to the next topic.

Types of Tutorials

There are two general types of tutorial CAI: *linear* and *branching* (Alessi & Trollip, 2001). Linear tutorials have a single path through the lesson for all students. Regardless of any performance differences, every learner must read and respond to the same content. The only individualization involved is that learners set their own pace. All learners experience the same instruction, however. Early tutorial CAI was mostly linear.

In branching tutorials, learners follow alternative paths through the lesson based on their responses to questions. During a pretest or at any point in the lesson, if the learner demonstrates mastery of the content, the lesson "branches" to the next topic or lesson. Some pattern of incorrect responses leads to remediation segments. It is always the learner's response that determines what happens next in the lesson. Branching tutorials reflect popular learning theory.

Examples of Tutorials

Tool software, such as a word processor, often includes online tutorials for new users. This is an ideal application for stand-alone CAI, because new users of complex software

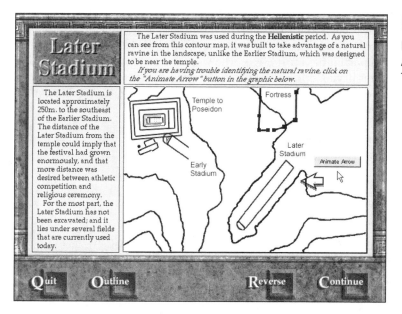

Figure 10.2

EXCAVATIONS AT ISTHMIA—
AN ARCHAEOLOGY/HISTORY
TUTORIAL

often have no other means of learning to use their new purchase. Do you know whether your word processor has a tutorial? If so, have you tried it?

Keyboarding and typing tutors are common "self-help" software aimed at the individual user working independently to master a skill. Such software illustrates the difficulty of using terms such as *tutorial*, because they are actually combinations. They clearly tutor the learner but also provide substantial drill and practice to help the learner achieve the automatic response patterns so essential to effective keyboard use.

Tutorials are also available for major content areas. Each lesson in *Verb Usage* teaches one verb that is commonly misused. Students must choose its correct form to complete a sentence and can put each alternative into the sentence to "try it" before giving their final answer. *Understanding Multiplication* begins with dot counting and patterns followed by successive addition, then addition of patterns and, finally, multiplication. *The Geometry Series for Macintosh* offers a potential two semesters' study, including tutorials in such topics as theorems, definitions and proofs, circles, area, and volume. Students can access introductions, examples, questions, and step-by-step help.

The Tutorial Controversy

Critics of tutorial software contend that, as with drill and practice, many of the programs are poorly written and deal primarily with "trivial" concepts. Tutorials are regarded as nothing more than electronic page-turners that force the student into a limited range of possible responses, thus severely restricting meaningful exploration of the concept.

Advocates of tutorials contend, however, that in some cases tutorials might teach material even better than a teacher. Tutorials provide a one-to-one teaching situation and afford learners an opportunity to proceed with the learning task at their own rate. An additional benefit is that learners respond to *every* question—not just a very few—as is the case in typical classroom instruction.

As with drills, many of the concerns about tutorials are really about poor design. Tutorial CAI is widely used in adult-learning situations, such as training in business and industry. It is well accepted as efficient and effective. Within K–12 education, tutorials may offer makeup opportunities for students who were absent, an alternative approach to a topic for a student having difficulty, or a way to offer instruction not possible otherwise. The quality of the software is, of course, critical, which underscores the need for evaluation prior to purchase and use.

Characteristics of Better Tutorials

Briefly summarized, an effective tutorial should include the following:

- Acceptable instructional methodology/strategy.
- Valid pretests and posttests.
- Internal questioning that measures progress toward criterion.
- Appropriate sequence and scope of content.
- High interest for the potential audience.
- Learner control over pacing.

- Ability to move backward for review.
- Automatic recordkeeping, so that the teacher can access class and individual performance data.

Integrating Tutorials in the Curriculum

Tutorials exist for most areas of the curriculum and for content ranging from simple factual information to higher-order problem-solving processes. They have been particularly effective in science and foreign-language learning, as well as for learning to use other software. Based on research (CEO Forum, 2001; Roblyer, 1985), using CAI to *supplement* teaching produces greater effects than replacing a teacher with CAI. Caution is in order when considering how to use a tutorial.

Assuming a sound rationale for using a tutorial, such as enrichment of the curriculum, your evaluation should include the program's match with your curriculum and completeness of topic treatment. As you plan a lesson for which a tutorial exists, determine exactly where and how you will incorporate it into the lesson, for example, to introduce or extend, to review or to remediate. Make it integral to the lesson from the start of your planning.

Simulations

A computer simulation is an interactive model of some "reality" such as an event, object, or phenomenon. Simulations offer learners the opportunity to manipulate variables that affect the outcomes of the experience. Often learners read or view a scenario, analyze it, and input decisions based on the data. The simulated environment then changes, based on the student decision, creating a revised situation with new decisions to be made. This type of activity continues until some predetermined solution is obtained, the learner runs out of time or enthusiasm, or the number of inappropriate decisions terminates the activity.

Simulations can be Type II applications, those that make possible new and better ways of teaching (Maddux, Johnson, & Willis, 1992) or exploration of things not possible in actuality. They offer some of the most exciting potential of CAI. No doubt, you realize immediately that simulations are complex to design and create. Designers must try to anticipate all reasonable responses at each point and account for the effects of each on their model (Figure 10.3).

Types of Simulations

Alessi and Trollip (2001) distinguish four categories of simulations. Although useful, their definitions are not mutually exclusive.

Physical simulations relate to some physical object, which the student may "use" or learn about. Appropriate content for such a simulation ranges from reading aircraft instruments to experiments in the physical sciences.

Procedural simulations teach a sequence of actions. The situation presented is not an end in itself (e.g., learning about the instruments in an airplane cockpit); rather, it is a means for developing the skills and activities needed to function in the situation

Figure 10.3

Exploring the Nardoo offers multiple ecology investigations.

(e.g., flying the aircraft). This category also includes diagnostic simulations, such as those used in medical education.

Situational simulations place the learner in a role within the scenario presented. Rather than explicitly teaching rules or procedures, situational simulations apply discovery-learning principles. The learner explores various responses to a situation and various roles through repetition of the simulation. The computer or other students may play other roles in the scenario.

In *iterative simulations*, the learner does not play a role but instead is an external experimenter. Initial decisions are made regarding parameters for one cycle or trial, then the simulation progresses to conclusion without further learner intervention. It is the result of the process that is of primary interest. This form of simulation changes the rate at which a process might occur to one more suited to learning. In the case of economic forecasting or genetic experimentation, time is compressed. In the study of physical phenomena, time may be extended to permit thorough observation of the outcome.

Examples of Simulations

The *Sim* series has been a commercial success as well as popular among educators. In *SimCity*, you take charge of a growing, evolving city. You can design your own model or pick from real cities. You must deal with budget, traffic, population, pollution, disasters, industrial growth, and so forth. *SimEarth* models our planet as a single interconnected organism. Everything you do affects the entire planet! If you'd rather be an ant out to conquer a suburban yard and house, try *SimAnt*, where you'll face such obstacles as rival ants, spiders, a dog, the lawnmower, water hoses, and of course, human feet. *SimFarm* challenges learners to build a small family farm into a profitable and responsible business while preserving the environmental integrity of the land.

Decisions, Decisions is a social studies simulation series for grades 5–12. Individual titles include *Violence in the Media, AIDS, Colonization, Revolutionary Wars, Immigration, Urbanization, Foreign Policy, Prejudice, The Environment, Substance Abuse, Drinking and Driving, Balancing the Budget*, and *The Campaign Trail.* In *Substance Abuse* a scenario involves seeing a friend buying drugs in school. As a teacher approaches, the friend flees, dropping the drugs at your feet. What would you do? The simulation provides a structured, nonthreatening situation in which learners can observe and practice positive actions in difficult circumstances. The hope is that they will internalize real-life skills. *Prejudice* has as its broad goals increasing awareness and identification of the processes that underlie and preserve prejudice. The simulation encourages students to work together to understand prejudice, racism, and discrimination in themselves and others.

The Simulation Controversy

Proponents see in simulation CAI much promise for learning higher-order skills—problem solving and decision making. Simulations allow students to explore environments that are too expensive, too dangerous, impractical by virtue of time or location requirements, or otherwise impossible to actually attempt. In a simulation, students may safely make errors and explore complex problems without fear of being wrong. Good simulations are highly motivating because they present options that are thought provoking and choices that are not easily made. They readily evoke higher-order thought processes such as reasoning and critical thinking.

Jonassen (2000) applauds the potential of simulations, especially those carried out among scattered participants via telecommunications. Critics complain, however, that it is often difficult to assess just what truly has been learned. Another concern is content accuracy. How can you assess the apparent realism of a scenario? What about the accuracy of the model underlying the simulation? Complex mathematical relationships are often involved. Can you be certain of their validity? Teachers may need to help students deal with these issues. However, in terms of desirable learning outcomes, perhaps only the *process* of working through the problem is critical.

Characteristics of Better Simulations

Better simulations exhibit certain qualities or features. They should:

- Be engaging to gain and hold user attention.
- Permit continuation from any stopping point over multiple sessions.
- Allow attainment of meaningful goals within a reasonable time.
- Be realistic or at least plausible.
- Have clearly defined learning goals that fit your curriculum.
- Be appropriately random and unpredictable.
- Focus on significant content, not trivial details.
- Include extensive support materials to guide integration into your lesson.
- Encourage socialization and collaboration over competition.
- Teach critical thinking as well as content (Alessi & Trollip, 2001; Geisert & Futrell, 2000; Roblyer, 2003).

Integrating Simulations in the Curriculum

The availability of simulations across the curriculum varies. Although there are few limits to what the creative software developer might conceive, most simulations are in the natural and social sciences. It is more difficult to imagine scenarios and situations in which the content of mathematics or language arts lends itself to simulation activities.

For maximum effectiveness, simulations require careful background preparation of students. Seldom are simulations designed to support a discovery-learning approach. Rather, the user must have mastered the content or procedural fundamentals to benefit from the simulation. Would you allow students to work in a chemistry lab or learn surgery with a discovery-learning approach?

Simulations are especially well suited to group work. Many products from Tom Snyder Productions were designed expressly for group use in a one-computer classroom. Others can be used readily in this way. Divide the class into teams that must reach consensus on each response. Establish specific tasks for each team member, such as recording decisions and their outcomes, researching the next decision, and so on. Class use of a simulation may be greatly enhanced with large-screen projection, so that students need not try to follow the activity on a small monitor.

To help in determining what has been learned as a result of a simulation activity, it is extremely beneficial to include teacher-directed "debriefings" after completion of the simulation. The teacher can help the group to focus on the desired learning outcomes and determine what in the simulation "worked" and what did not. Other questions to pose include: What might have been the situation in real life? How might that have differed from the simulated experience?

Contact other schools on the Internet to set up multischool simulation sessions as an extension of class groups. The debriefing can greatly enhance the experience, as each group explores why responses to the simulation differ among the participating groups. Distance simulations can support both content and interpersonal, even multicultural goals.

Instructional Games

Instructional games present content in a game format. The content and the game are integrated and inseparable, in contrast to a game that is a reward for performance within another form of CAI (such as a drill). In the latter, the game may be unrelated to the content, serving only to motivate. Instructional games have been designed to help teach or reinforce a wide range of instructional objectives.

Game Characteristics

Instructional games typically are governed by a clear set of rules, are competitive, and have a winner (and a loser) at the end. Games are designed to be entertaining and use color, sound, and graphics to capture and hold the student's interest.

In his classic study of children and their preferences regarding games, Malone (1981) reported three characteristics of intrinsically motivating environments: challenge, curiosity, and fantasy. In instructional games, there typically is a goal to achieve (challenge). The player anticipates what will happen (curiosity), but these anticipations are not always fulfilled because chance plays a role. Most games seem to be set in a military, space, or fantasy realm.

Types of Instructional Games

Instructional games fall into one of two categories on each of two dimensions. First, they may be derived from games already well known in other formats (e.g., Hangman), or they may be new creations for the computer. The second dimension is the nature of the competition involved. In some games, individual players compete against themselves, a time limit, or the computer. In others, players compete against each other, or even as teams.

Examples of Instructional Games

Hangman is one of the most ubiquitous of paper-and-pencil games and has been adapted to the computer for a wide range of subjects. Content is integrated with the game in that the player must correctly guess a letter contained in the "secret" word or have a body part added to the "victim." Hangman games have been criticized for their inherently morbid theme.

What began as an intriguing geography game became an unprecedented media phenomenon. The *Carmen Sandiego* series (Figure 10.4) challenges users to track the nefarious Carmen and her criminal gang, using reference tools to decipher clues. Individual geography games cover the United States and the world. History becomes vital in *Where in America's Past Is Carmen Sandiego*, as well as in *Where in Time Is Carmen Sandiego*. Like the SIM series of simulations, these programs have been commercial successes and are sold in most computer stores that carry software. There is also a complete line of Carmen Sandiego merchandise (mugs, shirts, etc.), and a television game show was based on the concept.

The Game Controversy

Proponents of instructional games stress that they provide yet another instructional strategy for the teacher, one that is a proven motivator. They have the flexibility to be used

Figure 10.4
Carmen Sandiego mysteries bring U.S. history to life.

effectively with simple drill-and-practice type activities or may be designed to foster higher-level cognitive processes such as analyzing relationships or synthesizing previous learning when faced with new situations. Such analysis and synthesis can greatly enhance retention of learning.

Opponents focus on the potential for abuse that exists when games are permitted in the classroom. While learning is the desired outcome, play may become the dominant goal for the student. This is especially true in situations where the game is a reward, rather than the essence of the activity, although we would not classify such games as instructional. Clearly, any game should be carefully scrutinized for its educational value, then used appropriately.

Problem Solving

Concern over student development of critical-thinking skills led to the creation of many CAI programs that are designed as problem-solving activities. There appear to be two distinct types of software in this category.

Types of Problem-Solving Software

The first and oldest type of problem-solving CAI is based on the premise that there are generic problem-solving skills that can be learned in one environment and then applied successfully in others. Examples include searching for patterns, alternative strategies, process of elimination, and trial and error. A second and more recently developed type is software that is itself a problem-solving tool focused on a specific domain and its unique requirements. Unlike the generic tool software you learned about previously, tool CAI is designed to focus your attention and thinking on the skills, concepts, and procedures needed to solve specific types of problems, as well as providing support for the mechanics of each (Figure 10.5).

Examples of Problem-Solving Software

The *Incredible Laboratory* illustrates the generic-skills development approach. The learner creates monsters in a "science" lab, using such chemicals as alien oil, yellow rind, and blue goo. Each chemical affects a different part of the monster, but all go into a beaker at the same time, after which the monster appears. The problem is to determine which chemical produces which variation in which body part. At higher levels of difficulty, the effects of a chemical change each time the program is run. The learner needs to use both trial-and-error and process-of-elimination skills to solve the problem. There is also a challenge mode in which players alternately add chemicals that each hopes the other has not investigated. Three monsters appear, one of which is the product of the combined chemicals. The players must determine which monster they produced.

Math Connections: Algebra II offers learners a wide array of tools and objects from which to build concrete representations of expressions, matrices, tables, graphs, or even conic sections. Then students connect objects into networks to visualize and explore relationships. Free exploration is encouraged, and instant results promote experimentation. *Technology & Learning* magazine honored this product with an Award of Excellence.

Figure 10.5

The Logical Journey of the Zoombinis promotes math and problem-solving skills.

The Problem-Solving Controversy

Educator interest in helping students acquire and develop problem-solving skills is high. Concerns over actual student problem-solving abilities figure prominently in many critiques of American education and in the education reform movement. Advocates of problem-solving software assert that it contributes to enhancing student skills.

Critics question whether problem-solving software can deliver on its promise. The assumption that any skills developed will indeed transfer is open to question. Maddux, Johnson, and Willis (1992, p. 37) suggested that automatic transfer is doubtful, but there may be general groups of problem-solving skills for which proper teaching strategies can facilitate transfer across applications.

Integrating Problem-Solving Software in the Curriculum

Most of the problem-solving tool CAI available to date is for various aspects of mathematics. Sunburst offers packages for algebra (*The Function Analyzer*), geometry (*Geometrix; The Geometric SuperSupposer*), graphing (*Green Blobs and Graphing Equations*), even trigonometry (*The Trigonometry Explorer*). For specific ideas, Horton and Wiegert (2002) and Weaver and Quinn (1999) detailed their use of *Geometer's Sketchpad*. If any of these is appropriate to your teaching, your first and foremost task is to master use of the software yourself. Once you understand its operation and capabilities, you will have little difficulty finding applications, whether for individual student use or to enhance group-learning experiences.

With all previous types of CAI, curriculum fit is largely a conscious effort of the teacher to integrate software use into lesson plans. Generic problem-solving CAI is obviously not curriculum specific, making it difficult to determine where, when, and how

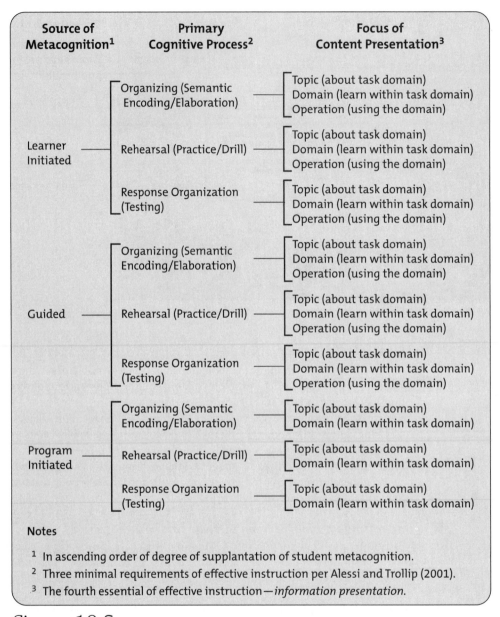

Source of Metacognition[1]	Primary Cognitive Process[2]	Focus of Content Presentation[3]
Learner Initiated	Organizing (Semantic Encoding/Elaboration)	Topic (about task domain) / Domain (learn within task domain) / Operation (using the domain)
	Rehearsal (Practice/Drill)	Topic (about task domain) / Domain (learn within task domain) / Operation (using the domain)
	Response Organization (Testing)	Topic (about task domain) / Domain (learn within task domain) / Operation (using the domain)
Guided	Organizing (Semantic Encoding/Elaboration)	Topic (about task domain) / Domain (learn within task domain) / Operation (using the domain)
	Rehearsal (Practice/Drill)	Topic (about task domain) / Domain (learn within task domain) / Operation (using the domain)
	Response Organization (Testing)	Topic (about task domain) / Domain (learn within task domain) / Operation (using the domain)
Program Initiated	Organizing (Semantic Encoding/Elaboration)	Topic (about task domain) / Domain (learn within task domain)
	Rehearsal (Practice/Drill)	Topic (about task domain) / Domain (learn within task domain)
	Response Organization (Testing)	Topic (about task domain) / Domain (learn within task domain)

Notes

[1] In ascending order of degree of supplantation of student metacognition.

[2] Three minimal requirements of effective instruction per Alessi and Trollip (2001).

[3] The fourth essential of effective instruction—*information presentation*.

Figure 10.6 THE LEARNER-CENTERED TAXONOMY OF INSTRUCTIONAL SOFTWARE, BASED ON CAPUTI (1991)

to integrate it into lessons. We question the value of this software if only an individual teacher will use it. Such software requires a commitment across grade levels and content areas to maximize its potential impact. General problem-solving skills do not develop quickly, nor are they limited to one field. To the extent that they can be taught at all, the task should be undertaken on a broad scale throughout the school district, at least K–8, if not K–12. A team of teachers should develop a scope and sequence for problem solving, then monitor and assist the classroom teachers who work with specific software.

An Alternative CAI Taxonomy

Thus far, a traditional taxonomy of CAI has guided your consideration of CAI formats. We noted at the outset that not all software is easy to classify.

Caputi (1991) was concerned with the labels so widely applied to CAI. Her experience convinced her that regardless of her own understanding of what, say, "tutorial" meant, there was no assurance that software producers used the term in the same way. In fact, she encountered numerous examples of mislabeled software, especially products that seemed best to fit the drill-and-practice type, yet were labeled otherwise, possibly because of the negative connotation of drill and practice.

In addition, Caputi believed that existing CAI labels reflected the behaviorist origins of CAI at a time when cognitivism has become the dominant view of learning. She set out to develop a new taxonomy for CAI, based not on the *external* form of the software, but rather the *underlying instructional strategy;* not the computer's activity, but the learner's. The result is the *Learner-Centered Taxonomy of Instructional Software.*

Briefly, this taxonomy classifies software according to the extent to which it supplants the learner's own mental processes (called *metacognition*). The metacognition dimension of the taxonomy has three levels: program initiated (the software is in control), guided (the software suggests, but does not require actions), and learner initiated (the learner directs and controls the interaction). Each may be divided according to the primary cognitive processes involved: organizing (semantic encoding and elaboration), rehearsal (practice), or response organization (assessment). Finally, the focus of the content presentation may be topic oriented, domain oriented, or operation oriented. Figure 10.6 illustrates this taxonomy.

The Learner-Centered Taxonomy is not widely known. One problem is its lack of simple terms, such as tutorial or game, to apply to the 24 possible categories. That sheer number of categories is also daunting compared with the traditional scheme. However, Caputi's arguments about the weaknesses of the dominant classification system are sound, and the goal of providing an identification system on which educators could better rely when selecting and evaluating CAI is laudable. This alternative taxonomy deserves further attention.

What the Research Shows

NETS
NOTES

NETS **S** 2
NETS **S** 5

Computer-assisted instruction has been used for more than 50 years. Although the emphasis in educational computing has shifted to application software tools, as presented in Chapters 3–9 of this book, CAI remains popular among educators. The number of available CAI packages is large, both for Macintosh and Windows computers. Because CAI use is widespread, it is vital that you consider what researchers have learned about its impact. According to Cradler, McNabb, Freeman, and Burchett (2002), "Evidence is mounting to support technology advocates' claims that 21st-century information and

NETS
NOTES

NETS **T** II-A
NETS **T** II-B
NETS **T** II-C
NETS **T** III-A
NETS **T** III-B
NETS **T** III-C
NETS **T** IV-C
NETS **T** V-B
NETS **T** VI-B

communication tools as well as more traditional computer-assisted instructional applications can positively influence student learning processes and outcomes" (p. 47). Their conclusions stem from the work of the Center for Applied Research in Educational Technology (CARET) and you are strongly urged to visit the CARET website <http://caret.iste.org> for much more detail than we can provide here. The following sections provide an overview of nearly three decades of research on learning with technology.

Subject-Matter Achievement

Numerous studies over many years have compared achievement scores of students using CAI with scores obtained in regular instruction. Typically, the results showed that CAI produces equal or greater achievement from lower grades through college level (e.g., Alderman, 1979; Baker, Gearhart, & Herman, 1994; Bayraktar, 2001–2002; Christmann & Badgett, 2000; Fisher, 1983; Glenn, 1988; Goode, 1988; Krein & Maholm, 1990; many studies by the Kuliks, and their colleagues; Mann et al., 1999; Sivin-Kachala, 1998; Swan et al., 1990; Wenglinsky, 1998).

Two studies from the 1980s provide a baseline. In an overall assessment of the research, Roblyer (1985, p. 20) concluded that "computer-based instruction achieves consistently higher effects than other instructional treatments to which it is compared in experimental situations, but the effects usually range from small to moderate in magnitude." Roblyer, Castine, and King (1988) conducted a meta-analysis of studies dated from 1980 on. Of the content areas reviewed, CAI appeared to have the greatest effect in science. Consistent with previous findings, mathematics skill learning appeared to profit most from CAI, while reading skills profited least.

Khalili and Shashaani (1994) also used the meta-analysis approach to review 36 published studies on CAI and students' academic achievement. They determined that the use of the computer as an instructional tool continued to be effective for achievement. These researchers also concluded that duration of computer use was a significant variable. Computer instruction lost effectiveness when used for less than three weeks or more than two months. The most effective duration appeared to be from four to seven weeks.

Kulik's meta-analysis (1994) showed that over all students who used CAI scored at the 64th percentile on achievement tests compared to the 50th percentile for students who did not use computers. Gains ranged from 9 percent in precollege science to 22 percent in special education. On the other hand, the high-tech *Apple Classrooms of Tomorrow* (Baker, Gearhart, & Herman, 1994) produced no gain on standardized tests.

Ester (1994–95) compared CAI with lecture instruction but also included student learning style among the variables. He found that abstract learners performed significantly better under the lecture method, while concrete learners performed equally well in either treatment.

Sivin-Kachala (1998) found increased achievement from preschool through higher education for both regular and special needs students. Extensive study of the statewide West Virginia Basic Skills/Computer Education initiative (Mann et al., 1999) showed very positive results. A cost-benefit analysis demonstrated that the program was more cost effective for improving student achievement than reducing class size from 35 to 20, increasing instructional time, or cross-age tutoring programs. Importantly, no gender differences in achievement were found.

Schacter (1999) pulled together the most current research on technology and achievement. Based on more than 700 studies, he concluded that students with access to CAI and other technologies show achievement gains, whether on researcher constructed tests, standardized tests, or national tests.

The CEO Forum (2001, pp. 6–7) cited extensive research conducted in Idaho and West Virginia, two states that have implemented technology across the curriculum. Both have seen impressive gains in test scores. For instance, West Virginia reported increases across the board in all areas of basic skills, 11 percent of which was directly related to the state Basic Skills/Computer Education (BS/CE) initiative. The BS/CE program also was found to be more cost-effective than other interventions.

Field studies of an algebra tutor showed student gains of 15 to 25 percent on standardized tests compared to control groups. Pinellas County (Florida) invested heavily in multimedia reading software and teacher professional development, longer instructional time, and smaller classes. Students entering tenth grade with a fourth-grade reading level gained one grade level each semester (CEO Forum, 2001, pp. 6–7).

Blok, Oostdam, Otter, and Overmaat (2002) conducted a meta-analysis of 42 studies of students ages 5–12 and the effectiveness of CAI on their acquisition of reading skills in both English and Dutch. They documented small positive effects (gains of 0.2 to 0.5 standard deviations), similar to the many previous studies of CAI. They found greater effects for students who were stronger readers at the start, which is the opposite of typical findings by other researchers. The fact that two languages were involved may partially explain the difference. Soe, Koki, and Chang (2000) also conducted a meta-analysis of studies of CAI and reading and reached similar conclusions. Boling, Martin, and Martin (2002) studied vocabulary development in first graders who used CAI as part of a balanced literacy program. Both the CAI and the control groups showed gains from pretest to posttest, but the CAI group's gains were much larger.

Learning Retention and Speed

In addition to positive achievement gains, Kulik, Bangert, and Williams (1983) found that CAI improved retention of learning. They reported that four of five studies investigating retention over a period of from two to six months showed greater retention by those students who used CAI. These differences were not, however, large enough to be statistically significant. Roblyer (1985, p. 24) concluded that "data lend little support to the belief that computer-based instruction enhances retention."

Computer-assisted instruction has often decreased the *time* that students require to learn material. Reports of the time saved range from 10 percent (Blaschke & Sweeney, 1977) to 25 percent (Krein & Maholm, 1990) to 40 percent (Fisher, 1983) to an incredible 88 percent (Lunetta, 1972). Kulik (1994) concluded that students learn more in less time when they use CAI.

Attitudes

In addition to investigating the impact of CAI on cognitive growth, researchers have studied its impact on affective outcomes. Kulik, Kulik, and Cohen (1980), Baer (1988), McLeod (1988), Hatfield (1991), Kulik (1994), Baker, Gearhart, and Herman (1994), and Sivin-Kachala (1998) all reported positive attitude gains toward the subject matter attributable to CAI.

Roblyer, Castine, and King (1988) also found generally positive attitudinal outcomes. They argued, however, that the attitudinal impact of CAI is greater toward the computer itself than toward learning the subject matter. In addition, they found little evidence that positive attitudes about computers contributed to better attitudes toward school and academic achievement. In a study outside the United States, Soyibo and Hudson (2000) found improved attitudes toward biology as well as CAI and increased achievement among eleventh-grade female science students in Jamaica.

Westrom and Shaban (1992) studied the intrinsic motivational effects of an instructional game compared with a noninstructional game. Although the motivation for the noninstructional game started out higher, it dropped significantly with experience, whereas that of the instructional game actually increased slightly. The researchers also found no gender differences, which supports the use of games to motivate all learners, contrary to some other gender studies. Westrom and Shaban suggested that CAI could be made more effective by greater attention to factors enhancing motivation.

Problem Solving

Field studies of an algebra tutor showed student gains of 50 to 100 percent on assessments of problem-solving ability compared to control groups (CEO Forum, 2001, p. 7). In Pittsburgh, researchers at Carnegie Mellon University created an intelligent tutoring system for algebra students (Keodinger, Anderson, Hadley, & Mark 1999). "Students in tutor-using classes outperformed students in comparison classes by 15 percent on standardized tests and 100 percent on tests that emphasized real-world problem solving and multiple mathematical representations" (p. 1).

Dudley-Marling and Owston (1988) critically assessed the potential of CAI to teach general thinking and problem-solving skills. The investigators wrote, "In the absence of any significant research literature evaluating the claims of the developers of problem-solving software, the CAI approach . . . can be evaluated only in terms of the general research and theory in problem solving. Based on this literature, it is highly unlikely that the use of CAI will lead to the development of generalizable problem-solving skills" (p. 29). They cautioned that this does not mean such software is useless, but rather that there are no simple solutions to developing higher-order skills. They did not test their views.

Funkhouser and Dennis (1992) studied the effects of software on the problem-solving skills of students in high school geometry and second-year algebra. They selected software from Sunburst (*Building Perspective* and *Blockers and Finders*) after extensive efforts to identify products that seemed most likely to produce the claimed effect. The control group had lab activities; the experimental group used the CAI. Grade-point average was used as a covariate to control for academic ability. On measures of problem-solving skills, the control group achieved significantly better results in solving word problems. When looking only at the geometry subgroup, the experimental group outperformed the control group in spatial ability. Both results were consistent with the skills most evident in the traditional instruction and software, respectively. The researchers also gathered data on all subjects from their regular tests that were written by the textbook publishers. The students who had used the CAI performed significantly better overall in their course than did the control-group students. Thus, time "taken" for problem solving actually enhanced the basic expected performance.

Duffield (1990) also assessed the outcomes of using popular software designated as problem solving, specifically Sunburst's *The King's Rule* and *Safari Search*. She concluded that the software was of limited value in developing problem-solving skills.

A meta-analysis of studies reporting cognitive performance (Liao, 1992) found that 23 of 31 studies favored the CAI group over a control group. Overall, "students who had CAI experiences scored about 18 percentile points higher on various cognitive ability tests than [students without CAI]" (p. 367). Of 29 variables examined, 6 contributed significantly to the outcome, showing that CAI had an impact beyond its specific content. Cognitive performance included such things as planning skills, reasoning, logical thinking, and transfer.

At-Risk and Special Needs Students

An eight-year longitudinal study by Bain and Ross (1999, 2000) focused on a school that developed an integrated technology curriculum. The researchers reported consistently significant gains on the SAT-1 test. Students with learning disabilities (LD) gained 84 points on the combined math and verbal scores over students in the traditional school program, whereas the gain for all students was 92 points. The subject school enrolls a larger than typical proportion of LD students. In addition, the private boarding school increased its student retention from 66 percent prior to implementing the technology program to 91 percent by the end of the eight-year study period.

In a small study using animations of social situations, Bernard-Opitz, Sriram, and Nakhoda-Sapuan (2001) found potential for CAI to teach problem-solving skills to children with autism. Williams, Wright, Callaghan, and Coughlan (2002) also studied autistic children's reading development and found that CAI increased time on task and produced clear achievements.

Ross, Smith, and Morrison (1991) studied at-risk seventh graders who had participated in grades 5 and 6 in intensive computer-based learning experiences in the Apple Classroom of Tomorrow (ACOT) program. Subjects were matched with others from the same elementary school who had not been part of ACOT. Treating the complex ACOT program as a whole, comparisons examined attitudes toward school, teacher evaluations, grades, computer skills, and standardized test scores. On the California Achievement Test, the ACOT group was significantly superior to the control group in mathematics, and their advantage in reading approached significance. Also, despite relatively little computer use in seventh grade, ACOT students seemed to retain their keyboarding skills.

Less encouraging was the finding that, over all, ACOT students were indistinguishable from others in their school when achievement was defined as the grades earned. There were also no attitudinal differences. The researchers concluded that the ACOT students remained at risk in the seventh grade, as did the controls. In a potentially significant finding for all schools that use computers, they noted that achievements during the ACOT period were rapidly lost by the lack of ongoing computer use and access after the two-year experiment. Continuity appears to be critical, suggesting need for an articulated curriculum.

Swan and Mitrani (1993), working with 135 at-risk high school students, found that there were greater student–teacher interactions when using the computer-based programs than in traditional classroom settings and that these interactions were much more student centered and individualized than in traditional classrooms.

Problems with Traditional Research

After more than 30 years of CAI, the broad picture of its value is relatively consistent (CEO Forum, 2001; Cradler et al., 2002; Schacter, 1999). However, problems continue to trouble many who read existing research.

Most serious is the question of thoroughness or, more broadly, methodology. Roblyer (1985, p. 22) wrote of two 1984 studies, "Descriptions of the study methods do not give sufficient information to determine if methodological flaws are present. And, perhaps because the reports themselves are so brief, the conclusions drawn by the researchers do not always seem supported by the results presented."

In their meta-analysis, Roblyer, Castine, and King (1988) reported that of some 200 studies initially reviewed for consideration, 38 studies and 44 dissertations were included in the analysis. The others were omitted because of insufficient data or methodological flaws. This is a serious indictment against the quality of research. Our observation is that much of what passes for research in CAI is anecdotal reports of experiences, not actual research. Clearly, there remains a need for better research into the outcomes of computer intervention in the instructional process.

Alternative Research Directions

The results of relatively traditional investigations into the effects of CAI on student learning have been mixed. Still, as you read previously, there is solid evidence that CAI can foster achievement gains and that it is at least as good as traditional instruction. CAI has a place in education alongside many other uses of the computer. The question is not whether to use computers in the schools, but how best to use them.

Given this perspective, the direction of research must change. Willis (1991) cogently discussed the "error" of the social-science research base, including the flaws of comparison studies. Salomon (in Polin, 1992) suggested a need to direct research attention to patterns of groups and interactions, making the classroom the unit of analysis, not individuals and variables. Important questions become: What are the most appropriate tactics/strategies/approaches, and so forth, for which types of CAI users, and under what circumstances? Studies may then compare, say, alternative CAI conditions to see which is more effective, rather than comparing the computer with traditional teaching.

Polin (1991) provided a fascinating introduction to what could become another research base—the theories of the Russian scholar Vygotsky (1896–1934), which contradict Piaget's developmental concepts. After finding disappointing results in transfer from CAI to concrete tasks based on a fairly typical CAI simulation, Russian researchers tried a different approach that permitted learners to work with a faulty model that reflected the students' own ideas. Attempts to apply the faulty model led to failure, but in over 60 percent of the cases, students quickly self-corrected their concepts. Where such investigations as this may lead is uncertain.

Some researchers suggest that it is time for an entire paradigm shift away from the objectivism of behavioral and cognitive psychology to constructivism. The latter holds that learning is a cumulative, intentional, goal-directed process of actively interpreting and constructing individual knowledge representations (Jonassen, 2000, pp. 8–15). This view partially may explain a shift in interest toward multimedia and hypermedia, which you will explore in Chapter 11.

A Sampler of Studies

Traditional CAI research was based largely on media-comparison studies comparing achievement gain, attitudes, and so forth for CAI versus standard classroom instruction. We can only give you a small taste of the newer approach to research that assumes potential effectiveness of CAI as a starting point.

Dalton and Goodrum (1991) investigated the effects of three pretesting strategies on learner motivation and achievement. Randomly assigned groups took either no pretest, a full-length pretest, or an adaptive pretest that ended as soon as it diagnosed nonmastery. Learners in the adaptive group scored significantly higher on the achievement posttest. The other two groups did not differ significantly. The full pretest group showed significantly lower motivation than either of the other groups, which themselves did not differ significantly.

In a study of computer simulations, Gorrell (1992) analyzed changes in learners' responses to various classroom-management situations presented as they tried to improve their performance over multiple tries. While results were positive, Gorrell concluded that the primary learning gains were "best understood as being associated with increased practice rather than with the development of integrated schematic knowledge" (p. 359). In other words, evidence of higher-order thinking skills development was lacking.

In a study of a small group of at-risk urban minority high school students, Signer (1991) found achievement gains on retests as well as increased motivation, self-confidence, and self-discipline. Contrary to other studies of female self-confidence with computers, this study found its female subjects were highly confident of their abilities to use a computer.

Morrison, Ross, and Baldwin (1992) investigated two adaptive CAI strategies that might have beneficial effects on motivation and cognition. One was the amount of instructional support provided in a lesson, and the other was a user-selectable context so that the material might better relate to student backgrounds and interests. The researchers hypothesized that elementary-age children would benefit in achievement from context choices, but would lack ability to make effective use of control over instructional support. As expected, students able to control the level of instructional support performed least well on the posttest. The expected benefits of context choice did not materialize, however. Subjects simply varied their choice of context across lessons rather than selecting those most relevant to them, as had been expected. Although achievement gains did not result from the flexibility provided, subjects reported positive attitudes about the strategies.

Hooper and Hannafin (1991) studied the effects of student ability, learning accountability, and cooperative work on achievement, interaction, and instructional efficiency using CAI. They were concerned that, although highly adaptive software is clearly desirable, it is hard to find because it is difficult and costly to create. The results of 185 studies on achievement under cooperative versus competitive conditions favored cooperation. The researchers assigned sixth- and seventh-grade students to heterogeneous or homogeneous pairs based on ability. The pairs were then designated as having either group or individual accountability for mastering the content. Results showed a significant positive correlation between cooperation and achievement for heterogeneous pairs. They also found that low-ability students interacted more in heterogeneous pairs but did not actually learn more. Students who collaborated on quizzes scored higher on the posttest than those who completed quizzes individually. The effect size was, however, rather small. In addition, the study found that high-ability student pairs learned most efficiently, while low-ability pairs were least efficient. In heterogeneous groups, the low-ability student benefited from, but slowed the progress of, the high-ability student.

Hooper and Hannafin considered their study to be preliminary and did not offer specific practical ramifications, nor shall we attempt to do so. Our purpose in detailing this study is only to show you how very different current research directions are from their predecessors. If you wish to obtain and read other studies, consider some of the following: Cardelle-Elawar and Wetzel (1995); Mattoon, Klein, and Thurman (1991); Pridemore and Klein (1991); Reglin (1990); Salerno (1995); and Tyler and Vasu (1995).

SUMMARY

Computer-assisted instruction has existed for over three decades. Its potential has been the subject of much speculation and prediction from the beginning. Early laboratory studies were sufficiently encouraging to keep interest alive until the microcomputer made CAI economically viable to use with large numbers of students. Today, CAI is used to teach a wide range of skills and knowledge, from relatively simple stimulus-response learning to complex forms of problem solving. CAI offers a higher level of interaction than group instruction, is inherently flexible, and may better meet individual student needs.

Traditionally, CAI has been classified into the categories of drill and practice, tutorials, simulations, instructional games, and problem solving. Drill-and-practice software has been the most widely available and used. Now, quality simulations and problem-solving software are available in greater quantity and have been well received. They appear to use the power of the computer more effectively and often permit instruction that was previously impractical or impossible, a Type II computer application (Maddux, Johnson, & Willis, 1992).

However, a major problem with our common labels for CAI is that there is no standard definition of each, nor is there any standard for applying them to specific software products. Mislabeling is common and may lead to inappropriate purchases or even misuse of the product. The Learner-Centered Taxonomy of Instructional Software classifies CAI based on the learner's metacognitive processing, rather than the activity of the computer itself. It may offer a more useful way to categorize CAI.

Research findings suggest that outcomes of CAI depend on many factors and have not been equal at all levels or in all fields, as was once widely hoped. Under the right circumstances, CAI has shown positive achievement gains, learning in shorter periods of time than traditional instruction, longer retention of content learned, and a more positive attitude on the part of the student toward the learning process. These results are encouraging and provide support for the use of CAI in our classrooms. Much research is still needed to learn how best to apply the computer to instruction.

Many of the research studies to date have been comparison studies, seeking to establish the value of CAI vis-à-vis traditional instructor-led classes. Newer studies generally assume that CAI is a viable learning medium and focus on alternative approaches or strategies. The goal is to investigate what approaches work best with which types of learners under what circumstances. Other new research directions rest on different theoretical bases, such as the non-Piagetian psychology of Vygotsky and constructivism in lieu of behaviorism or cognitive psychology.

The best advice available to those who wish to use CAI in their classrooms is to be cautious about expectations. CAI is not an automatic route to learning; it is not a stand-alone resource. Rather, teachers must devise ways to carefully *integrate* CAI into instruction. The CEO Forum's (2001, p. 2) review of a wide array of research led to the conclusion that the greatest impact will occur when technology is integrated into the curriculum to achieve specific, concrete objectives. It is through such support for the curriculum that technology maximizes learning for students. Of critical importance are "debriefing" strategies, including role playing, reaction papers, compare and contrast, visual summaries, panel discussions, software evaluation, and noncomputer simulation. All are means for integrating computers and instruction. Viewed in this way, as yet another learning tool, CAI can assume a vital role in our schools.

chapter 10 activities

1. For the grade level you teach or plan to teach, select *one* content area (e.g., the Civil War, second-grade science) and determine what CAI programs are available in your school. Review them to determine whether they are drill and practice, tutorials, simulations, games, or problem-solving programs. Create a database from your findings. What fields should it contain?

2. Review available drill-and-practice and tutorial programs, using the suggested characteristics of good software presented in this

chapter. Expand your database to include such information as objectives, appropriate grade level, and strengths and weaknesses of each program.

3. Examine the CAI products available to you and determine in what units of your curriculum you could best integrate the material. Add this information to your database.

4. As you examine various CAI products, try to categorize them using the new Learner-Centered Taxonomy. Does this cause you to see their potential differently?

5. Actually try a CAI drill-and-practice or tutorial program with a group of your students. How did it work for the slow learner? How about the gifted student? Discuss the software with the students to determine their feelings about its use. What did *they* see as strengths and weaknesses?

6. Work your way through any available computer simulation. Can you place it into one of the four types presented? How would you rate the simulation for motivation? For en-

tertainment? What would the student minimally have to know before use could be profitable? What learning outcomes would you expect? How would you determine if they have been achieved? Design a lesson plan for using a simulation.

7. Examine any available CAI package that claims to teach problem-solving skills. Begin by carefully examining the accompanying documentation. Where might the package "fit" in the curriculum? Does the producer encourage use of the package alone, or is there evidence of concern for the total context of problem-solving instruction? How would you determine if the package has met desired outcomes after using it with students?

8. Read at least five CAI research articles published since 1990. Which of the new directions in research do they exemplify, or do they set other directions themselves? Can you find a traditional "comparison" study in the recent literature?

Companion Website

Visit the companion website at <www.ablongman.com/lockard6e> for more information about the topics discussed in this chapter.

expect the world®

The New York Times
nytimes.com

Themes of the Times

Expand your knowledge of the concepts discussed in this chapter by reading current and historical articles from the *New York Times* by visiting the Themes of the Times section of the companion website <www.ablongman.com/lockard6e>.

References

Alderman, D. I. "Evaluation of the TICCIT Computer-assisted Instruction System in the Community College." *SIGCUE Bulletin*, 1979, *13*(3), pp. 5–17.

Alessi, S., and Trollip, A. *Multimedia for Learning: Methods and Development*, 3rd ed. Boston: Allyn and Bacon, 2001.

Baer, V. E. "Computers as Composition Tools: A Case Study." *Journal of Computer Based Instruction*, Fall 1988, *15*(4), pp. 144–148.

Bain, A., and Ross, K. "School Reengineering and SAT-1 Performance: A Case Study." *International Journal of Education Reform*, 1999, *9*(2), pp. 148–153.

Bain, A., and Smith, D. "Technology Enabling School Reform." *T.H.E. Journal*, October 2000, *28*(3), Retrieved February 15, 2003, from <www.thejournal.com/magazine/vault/A3130.cfm>

Baker, E. L., Gearhart, M., and Herman, J. L. "Evaluating the Apple Classrooms of Tomorrow." In E. L. Baker and H. F. O'Neil Jr., Eds. *Technology Assessment in Education and Training*. Hillsdale, NJ: Lawrence Erlbaum, 1994.

Bayraktar, S. "A Meta-Analysis of the Effectiveness of Computer-Assisted Instruction in Science Education." *Journal of Research on Technology in Education*, Winter 2001–2002, *34*(2), pp. 173–188.

Bernard-Opitz, V., Sriram, N., and Nakhoda-Sapuan, S. "Enhancing Social Problem Solving in Children with Autism and Normal Children through Computer-Assisted Instruction." *Journal of Autism & Developmental Disorders*, August 2001, *31*(4), pp. 377–384.

Blaschke, C. L., and Sweeney, J. "Implementing Cost-Effective Educational Technology: Some Reflections." *Educational Technology*, January 1977, *17*(1), pp. 13–18.

Blok, H., Oostdam, R., Otter, M., and Overmaat, M. "Computer-Assisted Instruction in Support of Beginning Reading Instruction: A Review." *Review of Educational Research*, 2002, *72*(1), pp. 1–130.

Boling, C., Martin, S. H., and Martin, M. A. "The Effects of Computer-Assisted Instruction on First Grade Students' Vocabulary Development." *Reading Improvement*, Summer 2002, *39*(2), pp. 79–88.

Caputi, L. J. "A Taxonomy of Instructional Software for Nursing Education." Unpublished doctoral dissertation, Northern Illinois University, DeKalb, 1991.

Cardelle-Elawar, M., and Wetzel, K. "Students and Computers as Partners in Developing Students' Problem-Solving Skills." *Journal of Research on Computing in Education*, Summer 1995, *27*(4), pp. 387–401.

CEO Forum. *Year 4 STaR Report*. 2001. Retrieved February 12, 2003, from <www.ceoforum.org/downloads/report4.pdf>

Christmann, E. P., and Badgett, J. L. "The Comparative Effectiveness of CAI on Collegiate Academic Performance." *Journal of Computing in Higher Education*, 2000, *11*(2), pp. 91–103.

Cradler, J., McNabb, M., Freeman, M., and Burchett, R. "How Does Technology Influence Student Learning?" *Learning & Leading with Technology*, May 2002, *29*(8), pp. 46–49.

Dalton, D. W., and Goodrum, D. A. "The Effects of Computer-based Pretesting Strategies on Learning and Continuing Motivation." *Journal of Research on Computing in Education*, Winter 1991, *24*(2), pp. 204–213.

Dudley-Marling, C., and Owston, R. D. "Using Microcomputers to Teach Problem Solving: A Critical Review." *Educational Technology*, July 1988, *28*(7), pp. 27–33.

Duffield, J. A. "Problem-Solving Software: What Does It Teach?" Paper presented at the Annual Meeting of the American Educational Research Association, Boston, April 16, 1990. (ERIC document ED 329 239.)

Ester, D. P. "CAI, Lecture, and Student Learning Style: The Differential Effects of Instructional Method." *Journal of Research on Computing in Education*, Winter 1994–95, *27*(2), pp. 129–140.

Fisher, G. "Where CAI Is Effective: A Summary of the Research." *Electronic Learning*, November/December 1983, *3*(3), pp. 82, 84.

Funkhouser, C., and Dennis, J. R. "The Effects of Problem-Solving Software on Problem-Solving Ability." *Journal of Research on Computing in Education*, Spring 1992, *24*(3), pp. 338–347.

Geisert, P., and Futrell, M. *Teachers, Computers, and Curriculum*, 3rd ed. Boston: Allyn and Bacon, 2000.

Glenn, C. "Results of Using CAI to Improve Performance in Basic Skills Areas." *T.H.E. Journal*, June 1988, *15*(11), pp. 61–64.

Goode, M. "Testing CAI Courseware in Fifth- and Sixth-Grade Math." *T.H.E. Journal*, October 1988, *16*(3), pp. 97–100.

Gorrell, J. "Outcomes of Using Computer Simulations." *Journal of Research on Computing in Education*, Spring 1992, *24*(3), pp. 359–366.

Gray, B. "Enhancing Learning through Debriefing." *The Computing Teacher*, June 1988, *15*(9), pp. 19–21.

Hatfield, M. M. "The Effect of Problem-Solving Software on Students' Beliefs About Mathematics: A Qualitative Study." *Computers in the Schools*, 1991, *8*(4), pp. 21–40.

Hooper, S., and Hannafin, M. J. "The Effects of Group Composition on Achievement, Interaction, and Learning Efficiency During Computer-Based Cooperative Instruction." *Educational Technology Research and Development*, 1991, *39*(3), pp. 27–40.

Horton, B., and Wiegert, E. "Using Handhelds and Billiards to Teach Reflection." *Learning & Leading with Technology*, May 2002, *29*(8), pp. 32–35.

Jonassen, D. H. *Computers as Mindtools for Schools: Engaging Critical Thinking*. Upper Saddle River, NJ: Merrill, 2000.

Khalili, A., and Shashaani, L. "The Effectiveness of Computer Applications: A Meta-analysis." *Journal of Research on Computing in Education*, Fall 1994, *27*(1), pp. 48–61.

Koedinger, K., Anderson, J., Hadley, W., and Mark, M. *Intelligent Tutoring Goes to School in the Big City*. Pittsburgh, PA: Carnegie Mellon University. Retrieved February 13, 2003, from <http://act.psy.cmu.edu/awpt/AlgebraPacket/kenPaper/paper.html>

Krein, T. J., and Maholm, T. R. "CBT Has the Edge in a Comparative Study." *Performance and Instruction*, August 1990, *29*(7), pp. 22–24.

Kulik, C. C., and Kulik, J. A. "Effectiveness of Computer-based Education in Colleges." *AEDS Journal*, Winter–Spring 1986, *19*(2–3), pp. 81–108.

Kulik, C. C., and Kulik, J. A. "Effectiveness of Computer-based Instruction: An Updated Analysis." *Computers in Human Behavior*, 1991, 7(1–2), pp. 75–94.

Kulik, J. A. "Synthesis of Research on Computer-based Instruction." *Educational Leadership*, September 1983, *41*(1), pp. 19–21.

Kulik, J. A. "Meta-analytic Studies of Findings on Computer-Based Instruction." In E. L. Baker and H. F. O'Neil Jr., Eds. *Technology Assessment in Education and Training*. Hillsdale, NJ: Lawrence Erlbaum, 1994.

Kulik, J. A., Bangert, R. L., and Williams, G. W. "Effects of Computer-based Teaching on Secondary School Students." *Journal of Educational Psychology*, February 1983, *75*(1), pp. 19–26.

Kulik, J. A., and Kulik, C. C. "Computer-based Instruction: What 200 Evaluations Say." Paper presented at the 1987 Annual Conference, Association for Educational Communications and Technology. Atlanta, GA, 1987. (ERIC Document ED 285 521.)

Kulik, J. A., and Kulik, C. C. "Review of Recent Research Literature on Computer-based Instruction." *Contemporary Educational Psychology*, July 1987, *12*(3), pp. 222–230.

Kulik, J. A., Kulik, C. C., and Bangert-Drowns, R. "Effectiveness of Computer-Based Education in Elementary Schools." *Computers in Human Behavior*, 1984, *1*(1), pp. 59–74.

Kulik, J. A., Kulik, C. C., and Cohen, P. A. "Effectiveness of Computer-based College Teaching: A Meta-analysis of Findings." *Review of Educational Research*, Winter 1980, *50*(4), pp. 525–544.

Kulik, J. A., Kulik, C. C., and Schwab, B. "The Effectiveness of Computer-based Adult Education: A Meta-analysis." *Journal of Educational Computing Research*, 1986, *2*(2), pp. 235–252.

Liao, Y-K. "Effects of Computer-assisted Instruction on Cognitive Outcomes: A Meta-analysis." *Journal of Research on Computing in Education*, Spring 1992, *24*(3), pp. 367–380.

Lunetta, V. N. "The Design and Evaluation of a Series of Computer Simulated Experiments for Use in

High School Physics." Dissertation, University of Connecticut, Storrs, 1972. *Dissertation Abstracts International 33*:2785A.

Maddux, C. D., Johnson, D. L., and Willis, J. W. *Educational Computing: Learning with Tomorrow's Technologies.* Boston: Allyn and Bacon, 1992.

Malone, T. W. "Toward a Theory of Intrinsically Motivating Instruction." *Cognitive Science*, 1981, *4*, pp. 333–369.

Mann, D., Shakeshaft, C., Becker, J., and Kottkamp, R. *West Virginia's Basic Skills/Computer Education Program: An Analysis of Student Achievement.* Santa Monica, CA: Milken Family Foundation, 1999.

Mattoon, J. S., Klein, J. D., and Thurman, R. A. "Learner Control Versus Computer Control in Instructional Simulation." Paper presented at the Annual Convention of the Association for Educational Communications and Technology, Orlando, FL, February 13–17, 1991. (ERIC document ED 334 995.)

McLeod, D. B. "Affective Issues in Mathematics Problem Solving: Some Theoretical Considerations." *Journal for Research in Mathematics Education*, March 1988, *19*(2), pp. 134–141.

Merrill, M. D., Schneider, E. W., and Fletcher, K. A. *TICCIT.* Englewood Cliffs, NJ: Educational Technology Publications, 1980.

Morrison, G. R., Ross, S. M., and Baldwin, W. "Learner Control of Context and Instructional Support in Learning Elementary School Mathematics." *Educational Technology Research and Development*, 1992, *40*(1), pp. 5–13.

Polin, L. "Vygotsky at the Computer: A Soviet View of 'Tools' for Learning. (Research Windows)." *The Computing Teacher*, August/September 1991, *19*(1), pp. 25–27.

Polin, L. "Looking for Love in All the Wrong Places. (Research Windows)." *The Computing Teacher*, October 1992, *20*(2), pp. 6–7.

Pridemore, D. R., and Klein, J. D. "Control of Feedback in Computer-assisted Instruction." *Educational Technology Research and Development*, 1991, *39*(4), pp. 27–32.

Reglin, G. L. "The Effects of Individualized and Cooperative Computer Assisted Instruction on Mathematics Achievement and Mathematics Anxiety for Prospective Teachers." *Journal of Research on Computing in Education*, Summer 1990, *22*(4), pp. 404–412.

Roblyer, M. D. *Measuring the Impact of Computers in Instruction: A Non-technical Review of Research for Educators.* Washington, DC: Association for Educational Data Systems, 1985.

Roblyer, M. D. *Integrating Educational Technology into Teaching*, 3rd ed. Columbus, OH: Merrill Prentice Hall, 2003.

Roblyer, M. D., Castine, W. H., and King, F. J. "Assessing the Impact of Computer Based Instruction: A Review of Recent Research." *Computers in the Schools*, 1988, *5*(3–4).

Ross, S. M., Smith, L. S., and Morrison, G. R. "The Longitudinal Influences of Computer-Intensive Learning Experiences on At-Risk Elementary Students." *Educational Technology Research and Development*, 1991, *39*(4), pp. 33–46.

Salerno, C. A. "The Effect of Time on Computer-assisted Instruction for At-Risk Students." *Journal of Research on Computing in Education*, Fall 1995, *28*(1), pp. 85–97.

Salisbury, D. F. "Cognitive Psychology and Its Implications for Designing Drill and Practice Programs for Computers." *Journal of Computer-based Instruction*, Winter 1990, *17*(1), pp. 23–30.

Schacter, J. *The Impact of Education Technology on Student Achievement. What the Most Current Research Has to Say.* Santa Monica, CA: Milken Family Foundation, 1999.

Signer, B. R. "CAI and At-Risk Minority Urban High School Students." *Journal of Research on Computing in Education*, Winter 1991, *24*(2), pp. 189–203.

Simonson, M. R., and Thompson, A. *Educational Computing Foundations*, 3rd ed. Upper Saddle River, NJ: Merrill, 1997.

Sivin-Kachala, J. *Report on the Effectiveness of Technology in Schools, 1990–1997.* Washington, DC: Software Publishers Association, 1998.

Soe, K., Koki, S., and Chang, J. M. *Effect of Computer-Assisted Instruction (CAI) on Reading Achievement: A Meta-Analysis.* Honolulu, HI: Pacific Resources for Education and Learning (PREL).

June 2000. Retrieved February 15, 2003, from <www.prel.org/products/products/Effect-CAI.pdf>

Soyibo, K., and Hudson, A. "Effects of Computer-Assisted Instruction (CAI) on 11th Graders' Attitudes to Biology and CAI and Understanding of Reproduction in Plants and Animals." *Research in Science & Technological Education*, November 2000, *18*(2), pp. 191–199.

Steinberg, E. R. *Computer-Assisted Instruction: A Synthesis of Theory, Practice and Technology*. Hillsdale, NJ: Lawrence Erlbaum, 1991.

Swan, K., Guerrero, F., Mitrani, M., and Schoener, J. "Honing in on the Target: Who Among the Educationally Disadvantaged Benefits Most from What CBI?" *Journal of Research on Computing in Education*, Summer 1990, *22*(4), pp. 381–403.

Swan, K., and Mitrani, M. "The Changing Nature of Teaching and Learning in Computer-based Classrooms." *Journal of Research on Computing in Education*, Fall 1993, *26*(1), pp. 40–54.

Tyler, D. K., and Vasu, E. S. "Locus of Control, Self-esteem, Achievement Motivation, and Problem-Solving Ability: *LogoWriter* and Simulations in the Fifth-Grade Classroom." *Journal of Research on Computing in Education*, Fall 1995, *28*(1), pp. 98–120.

Weaver, J. L., and Quinn, R. J. "Geometer's Sketchpad in Secondary Geometry." *Computers in the Schools*, 1999, *15*(2), pp. 83–95.

Wenglinsky, H. *Does It Compute? The Relationship Between Educational Technology and Student Achievement in Mathematics*. Princeton, NJ: Educational Testing Service Policy Information Center, 1998.

Westrom, M., and Shaban, A. "Intrinsic Motivation in Microcomputer Games." *Journal of Research on Computing in Education*, Summer 1992, *24*(4), pp. 433–445.

Williams, C., Wright, B., Callaghan, G., and Coughlan, B. "Do Children with Autism Learn to Read More Readily by Computer-Assisted Instruction or Traditional Book Methods?: A Pilot Study." *Autism: The International Journal of Research and Practice*, March 2002, *6*(1), pp. 71–91.

Willis, J. "Research and Instructional Technology: What We Have and What We Need." *Computers in the Schools*, 1991, *8*(4), pp. 115–133.

Multimedia for Learning

OBJECTIVES

After completing this chapter, you will be able to:

- Identify several major contributors to the evolution of hypermedia.
- Differentiate among hypertext, multimedia, and hypermedia.
- Discuss several technologies that support or enable hypermedia.
- Distinguish CD, CD-ROM, laserdisc, DVD, and digitizing technologies.
- List and briefly describe several hypermedia software tools.
- Describe several uses of interactive multimedia for content.

- Explain uses of interactive multimedia for presentations.
- Assess hypermedia development software as a student tool.
- Discuss at least two issues surrounding hypermedia.
- Describe several possible applications of hypermedia in your teaching area.
- Evaluate interactive multimedia based on available research.
- Develop a specific lesson plan that incorporates hypermedia.

This chapter focuses attention on a particularly exciting form of educational software, interactive multimedia (IMM), and common ways to create it. Although the concepts are not difficult to understand, there is considerable confusion over terminology, which we attempt to clarify. You will consider several hardware technologies that contribute to IMM applications. Software for IMM may be useful as you consider your own potential applications. Finally, consider with us some classroom applications of this new tool and what limited research findings tell educators about it.

Interactive Multimedia Environments

To begin consideration of interactive multimedia, let's explore its concepts and terminology in some detail.

NETS
NOTES

NETS **S** 1
NETS **S** 3
NETS **T** I-A
NETS **T** I-B
NETS **T** III-A
NETS **T** III-B
NETS **T** V-B

Limitations of Traditional Tools

From its beginning, computing has been largely sequential and linear. Computers carry out instructions one by one. Databases organize and store information in a largely linear fashion. Although books cannot restrict your approach to reading them, how often do you read a book other than beginning to end? Even if you take chapters out of sequence, do you also read pages or paragraphs out of sequence? Perhaps in reference works, but not generally.

Think of what it is like to look for information in encyclopedias and other reference works. What happens when your reading brings up a topic you'd like to pursue further? Assuming that the same book even contains this related topic, how easily can you find it? Linearity is limiting when compared with the way in which the human mind interconnects information.

Have you ever struggled to read a text because you encountered words that you did not know? Did you immediately look them up in a glossary or dictionary? Was a dictionary even at hand? Might it have helped if you had heard the words pronounced? Have you ever tried to understand a procedure or process based on a verbal description of it, perhaps accompanied by diagrams with arrows showing the action?

If you can relate to any of these limitations of traditional communications media, you will welcome the versatility and power of hyper environments.

Hyper Origins

In 1945, Vannevar Bush, an electrical engineer and science advisor to U.S. President Franklin D. Roosevelt, described a system that he called *memex* (Bush, 1945). Memex was "a hypothetical, mechanical device that predated computers and that would use state-of-the-art photographic technology to manipulate, display, and interconnect information on microfiche" (Locatis, Latourneau, & Banvard, 1989, pp. 66–67). Memex was to emulate the human mind, but it never got beyond the conceptual stage for lack of adequate technology.

In the early 1960s, Douglas Engelbart adapted Bush's concept to the computer. His oNLine System (NLS) provided a means to organize and retrieve text, as well as electronic mail and a teleconferencing facility. At about the same time, Ted Nelson created a literary system called Xanadu that allowed complex derivations of new material from existing text. It could trace the development of ideas by recording linkages and information transfers, and provide royalty payments to the original creators (Locatis, Latourneau, & Banvard, 1989). Nelson coined the term *hypertext* to describe his system. Wolf (1995) chronicled the Xanadu story into the mid-1990s.

Hyper What?

In our context, the term *hyper* means the potential to move about within an environment without linear, sequential restrictions. A hyper environment consists of information in *nodes*, which could be pages, notecards, computer screens, or even individual objects on a screen. Nodes are interrelated through *links*, as Figure 11.1 illustrates. You move about through a web of information by using these links.

Hypertext

If the information in nodes of a hyper environment is (predominantly) text, it is termed *hypertext*. Hypertext can be as simple as pages (or screens) of text, each of which is "linked" to one or more other pages. Nelson attempted to demonstrate this in print form with his book *Computer Lib/Dream Machines* (1987). The implementation is far more successful on a computer. Imagine an electronic encyclopedia or other reference work. A simple mouse click on an unfamiliar word takes you to a glossary entry, which itself contains links back to your starting point and on to other related items. If you assume the existence of *all* appropriate linkages, you should readily see the potential and power of such a system. Text need no longer be constrained by its basic, linear form, as Figure 11.2 illustrates. You have probably experienced hypertext on the Web.

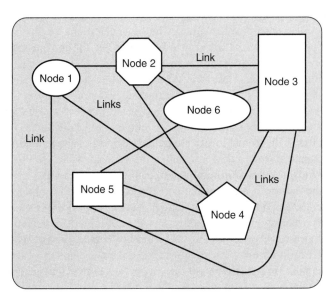

Figure 11.1
A HYPER ENVIRONMENT
OF INTERLINKED NODES

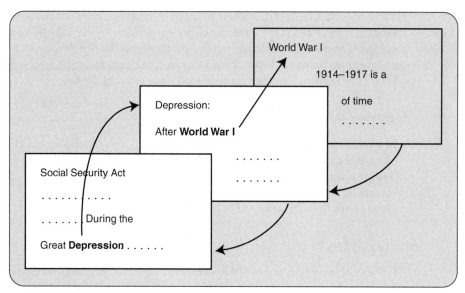

Figure 11.2 CONCEPT OF HYPERTEXT

Multimedia

Multimedia describes any system that unites two or more media into a single product or presentation. Probably the earliest multimedia system was the theater in which a pianist accompanied silent movies. From this evolved the "talkies" and eventually television. Educators long used sound filmstrips and slide-tape sets. All of these represent multimedia—materials that communicate through more than one sense.

What is *not* inherent in multimedia is the hyper element, or Bush's linkage concept. Multimedia can be just as linear as a book! Think about your experiences with filmstrips or slide sets if you are familiar with those older technologies. Have you ever seen either used in a nonlinear fashion? What happens if someone wants to see a previous frame or slide again? To back up (or jump ahead) requires going through the intervening frames, which may discourage users from doing so because it takes time and often disrupts the train of thought. Similarly, video is essentially linear. Its physical nature makes it difficult at best to locate particular segments. VCRs are *not* random access devices. Furthermore, linkages imply interactivity between the user and the environment, which is also not inherent in multimedia.

To clarify the nature of multimedia, consider an excellent example—*The Voyage of the Mimi*, created by the Bank Street College of Education. *Mimi* follows a research expedition to study whales. This multimedia package contains 13 video episodes that are adventures of the research party and 13 documentary videos of visits with scientists at work. Independent software modules deal with ecosystems, maps and navigation, whales and their environment, and the themes of the series. There are teacher and student guides, posters and wall charts, and even a *Mimi* newsletter. The parts of *Mimi* are integrated by the way in which the teacher uses them. The computer is just one element and provides typical computer-assisted instruction (CAI) that is related to the video lessons but with no hyper elements. The popularity of the first *Voyage of the Mimi* led to production of *Mimi II*, centered on archaeology and Mayan civilization. The *Mimi* series has been widely used in classrooms and many individuals have shared their resources on the Web, such as <www.amphi.com/~dgrimble/mimi.html>. A web search will locate many more.

As of early 2003, Bank Street College of Education was hoping to create the third *Voyage of the Mimi*, focusing on the Mississippi River. To learn more about the *Mimi* project, visit the *Mimi* website at <www.bankstreetcorner.com/voyages_of_mimi.shtml>.

Multimedia became a major buzzword in the 1990s, and it is often used interchangeably with hypermedia. However, there is a distinction. Read on!

Hypermedia/Interactive Multimedia

Hypermedia is the integration of a computer and multimedia to produce interactive, nonlinear hyper environments. The nodes of a hypermedia environment contain some combination of text, graphics, sound, and video, which are interlinked and associated nonlinearly by the computer, just as Bush envisioned. Imagine studying the civil rights movement at your computer. As you read a basic article on the movement, you come to a reference to Martin Luther King's "I Have a Dream" speech. A mouse click brings up the text of the speech, with hypertext links to written explanations of specific words or context. With another click you listen to Dr. King deliver the speech, or see that event as a video plays on your screen. You are experiencing the power of hypermedia.

Commercially, many hypermedia products are labeled simply multimedia. For example, *National Geographic* calls its *Mammals* "a multimedia encyclopedia." In fact, it is a hypermedia encyclopedia. However, the term *multimedia* probably seems somehow more approachable, less "techie," and, therefore, more marketable. Hypermedia is the more accurate term, but we are also comfortable with *interactive multimedia* or IMM, which many writers use. Interactive multimedia also can serve to differentiate these products from traditional television and other noninteractive, nonhyper multimedia environments.

The Technologies of Interactive Multimedia

NETS
NOTES
NETS S 1
NETS T I-A
NETS T I-B

Given our basic definition of interactive multimedia, next you should understand some of the technologies available, even needed, to create and support such a hypermedia environment (Figure 11.3). Current computer systems include multimedia playback capability, but creating IMM usually requires additional components.

Multimedia Hardware

Let's look at several potential hardware technologies for an IMM system: compact discs, laserdiscs and DVD, and digitizers for both audio and video.

Figure 11.3
INTERACTIVE MULTIMEDIA HARDWARE AND SOFTWARE

Compact Disc Technology

The audio compact disc (CD) has become a familiar medium, having led to the demise of the long-playing (LP) record and the rapid decline in popularity of cassette tapes. The second common CD format is CD-ROM, first introduced in 1985. A CD-ROM stores data in a spiral track of digital pits that would be three miles long if unrolled. A CD can store any digital data—text, sound and graphics, even movies—with equal ease. Compact disc players use a laser beam to "read" the digital data. Because only a light beam touches the disc, there is no wear and no loss of initial quality over time. Data can be accessed randomly, making highly interactive environments possible. Also, CD duplication is quick and easy, which helps to keep costs down.

One CD-ROM can store about 700MB of data, equivalent to some 300,000 pages of text, nearly 500 3.5" diskettes, or seven 100MB Zip disks! CDs are ideal for large databases, and because a duplicate disc costs little to produce, initial production investments can be recouped quickly from savings on paper copies. CDs are also beneficial for multimedia because digital audio and video files are huge.

CD-ROM drives are now part of all computer systems and the majority of new computers include CD-RW drives for creating your own CDs as standard components (Rojas, 2003). Many computers, especially notebooks, have combination drives that can play DVDs and also play and record CDs, so-called *combo drives.* You get the functionality of three separate types of devices in a single drive.

DVD and Laserdisc Technologies

The newest optical disc technology is, of course, the DVD. As we write, DVD drives are rapidly replacing CD-ROM drives in computer systems, as they can play all the same discs as a CD drive plus DVDs for very little additional cost. In Chapter 2 you learned that a typical DVD holds 4.7 GB of data per side, nearly seven times the capacity of a CD in the same physical size package. This makes DVDs ideal for multimedia, where file sizes are always large, but especially so for full-screen-size videos. The educational potential of DVD is still developing, as there are relatively few choices other than commercial movies. We expect this situation to change, as DVD has the same instructional potential that educators have had with *laserdiscs* (or laser videodiscs) for more than 20 years.

Although laserdisc (LD) technology is rapidly becoming obsolete, it will likely remain available in many schools for years to come, so you should have some basic knowledge of it. It also illustrates what we anticipate as part of the future of DVD. Laserdiscs are 12" discs that look like overgrown silvery CDs. They store multimedia content that the laserdisc player reads using a laser beam, much like CDs and DVDs. Movie connoisseurs favored LDs because they produce a higher-quality picture on a standard TV set than videotape and have higher-quality audio. Unlike tape, you can pause a laserdisc to look at a single image for as long as you like without damage, which has great educational potential. Imagine being able to show your students a video and freeze the image on the screen at will to discuss what they just saw or to call attention to detail in the image that students might easily overlook. Furthermore, imagine being able to find any location on the video almost instantly using your remote control. You could replay segments that students need to see more than once with ease. You could use only those segments of the video that you really need to make your point. These are very different uses of video from what we can do with videotape. They have unique potential to enhance learning by allowing you to focus on what matters most to you and your students.

We include this short explanation of laserdisc technology to encourage you to ask whether you have players and discs in your school and, if so, to explore what you can do with them. Our point is not the LD technology, but rather its potential as hypermedia, as interactive multimedia. In the 1980s and 1990s many truly interactive learning programs were sold that involved both discs and software. The laserdisc player was connected to the computer, and CAI software accessed the video on the disc as appropriate to the lesson. This approach to multimedia learning was never possible with videotape, which lacks the random accessibility. The large size and high cost of LD technology contributed to its relative unfamiliarity among teachers, and many educators who do have access to it are unfamiliar with the technology or how to use it. The potential, however, is great and soon to become more practical.

The future of interactive multimedia appears to be the DVD. Most laserdiscs were essentially educational movies in an interactive hardware format that involved large machines and large discs. And even then, one side of a laserdisc played only 30 or 60 minutes depending on format. Today, even better image and audio quality are available on the much smaller DVD that will play on your computer screen or TV. Random access of segments is possible, as is freeze frame, as you likely know well from watching movies on DVD. What you may not have considered is the educational potential of rapid access to the desired segment(s) and the use of freeze frame. When educational videos become available on DVD, educators will finally have the promise of laserdiscs in a much more desirable physical format.

Furthermore, think of the interactivity already available with movies, the ability to jump to specific scenes, to view additional materials provided on the disc, to change sound track language, even to view subtitles in more than one language. What is missing is, foremost, the educational content, but also the flexibility of laserdiscs to randomly access an exact frame. DVD movie instant access is based on menus provided by the producer, which is limiting. However, it is possible for CAI software to control the DVD player and to duplicate the interactive potential of laserdisc technology. We urge you to think carefully about how you could best use video in your classroom and imagine the potential of interactive video, which you could well have available by the time you read this.

In addition to the fact that DVD technology can duplicate the interactive advantages of laserdiscs in much smaller, cheaper hardware, it has one other major advantage. There was no possibility of recording your own laserdisc. The increasing availability of DVD recorders ("burners") in computers means it is now possible for educators to produce their own interactive DVD materials at affordable prices. And the process is becoming easier all the time. However, it requires both hardware and software that are not yet widely available. How you turn video into a format that at least could be recorded onto a CD or DVD is the next topic.

Digitizing Hardware

Interactive multimedia typically includes digital images, digital audio, and digital video. You learned about digital cameras and images in Chapter 8. Digital audio hardware is standard in today's computers, although most users are unaware of its existence beyond speakers and the ability to play audio CDs on the computer. Getting video into a digital form on a computer requires hardware that is not yet standard on most computers, but it is becoming more and more common and you surely will have access to it in the near future, if not already.

Audio on a computer must be converted from its original analog format to digital. Your computer is ready to do this in virtually any case. If you are not already aware of this, examine any computer in the area where the speakers or headphones plug in. You are almost certain to find additional jacks there as part of the sound system. One will be for a microphone, which you can purchase for less than $10 if you don't have one. The possibilities for recording audio through a microphone are endless. There is usually another jack to which you can connect any kind of audio device by cable—a cassette player or a record turntable is commonly used. You probably have access to such sound sources, but you may need a "patch cord" to connect one to your computer. Such connecting cables cost just a few dollars at your nearest electronics retailer, or even at Wal-Mart. Figure 11.4 shows how a microphone and cassette deck can be connected to a notebook computer to allow recording live sounds or digitizing content from an audio cassette. Beyond the hardware, you need audio software, which you'll learn about in the next section.

Unless your computer has an IEEE 1394 ("Firewire") connection, you probably lack video digitizing capabilities. If you do have such a connection, then you are ready to connect a digital camcorder and create digital videos, as you briefly learned in Chapter 9. You also can add Firewire economically to any computer. However, most of us have access primarily to video on standard VHS videotapes. For that you must have analog digitizing hardware. We have had good results from digitizers costing less than $200 so, again, the cost is not prohibitive. Both internal and external digitizers are readily available and there are even models that combine Firewire and analog capabilities

Figure 11.4
AUDIO CONNECTIONS
WITH A NOTEBOOK
COMPUTER

in a single unit. External devices usually attach to your computer through a USB port (Figure 11.5), and they can be used with both regular and notebook computers.

Digitizing hardware normally comes with all necessary software as well as connecting cables. In short, you buy a complete solution to your digitizing needs. However, don't forget that your digital still camera may well have a movie mode. If so, check it out, as you may be able to meet very basic video needs for multimedia with equipment you already have.

Multimedia Creation and Editing Software

Before you or your students can produce multimedia projects, you must have all the multimedia elements—images, sounds, video clips. You learned about digital images in Chapter 8. Next you will learn about actually creating digital audio and video.

Figure 11.5
VIDEO CAPTURE
(DIGITIZING) FROM
AN ANALOG SOURCE

Digital Audio

As previously mentioned, you probably have basic audio digitizing capabilities on your computer right now but are unaware of it. The principles are the same for both PC and Macintosh systems, although our illustrations are based on a Windows system.

Even before you consider connecting a microphone or external sound device to your computer, you have the capability to record sound from an audio CD. All the necessary connections exist inside the computer between the CD or DVD drive and the computer's sound hardware. The process is fundamentally as simple as putting an audio CD in your drive and running whatever audio recording software you have. Macintosh users favor Apple's *iTunes*. All versions of Windows include a rudimentary program called *Sound Recorder.* If you are unfamiliar with it, it should be located in the Start menu, Accessories folder, Entertainment subfolder. Use whatever software your computer has for playing the CD. You can then record simply by clicking the Record button (Figure 11.6) in *Sound Recorder* or comparable software.

For greater flexibility in recording audio, there are many software products on the market, including the popular *MusicMatch Jukebox* <www.musicmatch.com>, which is available in a functional free version (Basic) and an inexpensive Plus version that offers many additional features (Figure 11.7). You will have choices for the audio format you want (wav is common, but music files are very large; mp3; etc.) and, within flexible formats like mp3, select the quality level you need.

Figure 11.6
BASIC AUDIO DIGITIZING (RECORDING)

Figure 11.7
MORE FLEXIBLE SOFTWARE FOR AUDIO DIGITIZING

To edit audio to get exactly the starting and stopping points you want for your purpose, whether it's a voice or music recording, you can also use *iTunes* or *Sound Recorder*. Among the inexpensive products that we have used, *Sound Forge XP* from Sonic Foundry is easy to learn and rich in features (Figure 11.8). *Sound Forge* will, of course, perform the original recording functions as well as allow you to edit to your precise needs.

As you think about digital audio, don't overlook its potential in the hands of your students. What might a student project on oral history be like if the final product were a *PowerPoint* presentation with digital photos of the persons interviewed accompanied by digital audio clips edited from the interviews?

We would be remiss if we ended this section without reminding you that audio CDs and commercial tapes are copyrighted materials. Although you can do many things with them using your digital audio hardware and software, be sure not to violate copyright law in the process. You can learn more about copyright law in Chapter 15.

Digital Video

Both Macintosh and Windows XP users have basic video capture and editing software as part of their systems, namely, *iMovie* and *MovieMaker2*, respectively. Both are easy to use and adequate for many educational purposes. If you find their capabilities inadequate, more sophisticated products are available from companies such as Pinnacle <www.pinnaclesys.com> at reasonable cost.

It is far beyond the scope of this book to show you how to create digital video, but we do want you to have a basic sense of the process to understand that it is not very complicated. We are confident that you will add digital video to your technology tool kit in the near future, if you haven't already.

In Chapter 9 and previously in this chapter you learned about aspects of digital video. Assuming you have a computer with a Firewire connection, a simple cable between that

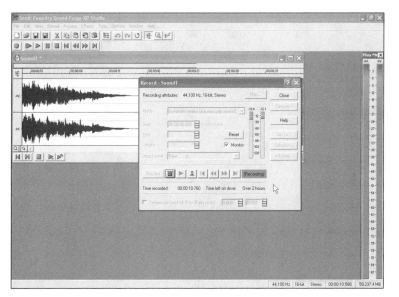

Figure 11.8

AUDIO DIGITIZING AND EDITING

connection and the comparable one on your digital camcorder is all that you need. The computer will receive both video and audio from your tape through that connection. This is somewhat simpler than the three cables required to connect analog equipment as shown in Figure 11.5—one each for the two audio channels of stereo sound and one for the video signal.

Using a Firewire connection, the computer senses that a digital camcorder is attached when you plug in the second end of the cable or when you turn on the camera that is already connected (Figure 11.9). It then loads the software and you make any prerecording settings that you need (Figure 11.10). Next use onscreen controls to view the video and select the point at which you want to begin recording (Figure 11.11). Click the Record button to start digitizing; click Stop when you have captured as much video as you want (Figure 11.12).

As the computer captures your video, the software automatically divides it into individual "scenes" based on when you stopped and started the camcorder during recording or based on changes in the content of the video itself (Figure 11.13). This can be a great time saver in the editing process, enabling you to find segments quickly and do any final editing (e.g., trimming the start and stop points). Drag the edited segments onto the timeline at the bottom of the screen in the desired order (which can be totally different from the order on the tape) and you have much of the work of creating an edited digital video completed. Most video editing software also provides many choices of transitions that you can insert between scenes as well as a full range of titling options with effects such as rolling the text from the bottom to create your credits (Figure 11.14).

When you have completed your editing, you then save the edited movie into one of a variety of digital video formats. Apple's *QuickTime* was the first popular format and it has been joined by such others as *Video for Windows* (AVI) and *MPEG* (the initials of

Figure 11.9

AUTOMATIC DETECTION
OF A DIGITAL VIDEO
CAMCORDER CONNECTION

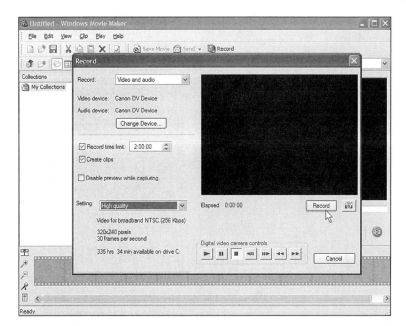

Figure 11.10
DIGITAL VIDEO RECORDING SETUP

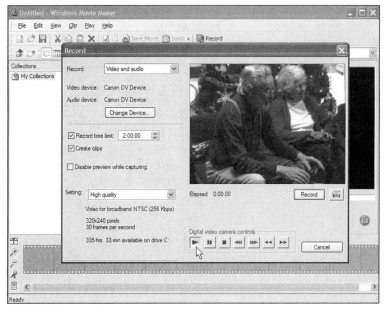

Figure 11.11
ONSCREEN CONTROLS FOR THE CAMCORDER

the Motion Picture Experts Group that devised the specifications for it). All rely on compression to reduce the enormous native size of a digital video file (roughly 10 MB per second!) to a more manageable size. However, this was inadequate once the Web became a major multimedia platform. Few individuals were willing to wait potentially for hours to download a massive video file before they could play it.

Figure 11.12
RECORDING (DIGITIZING)
FROM A DV CAMCORDER

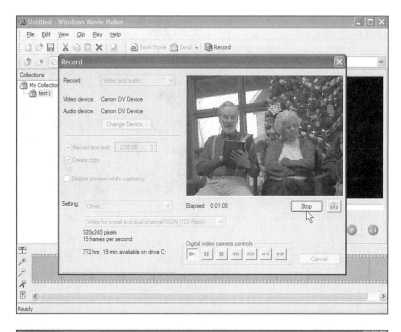

Figure 11.13
ASSEMBLING CLIPS ON A
TIMELINE

Streaming is the most common solution to web transmission of video (and also audio). Popularized by Real <www.real.com>, streaming media files are compressed even more and do not require a complete download before playback begins. Rather, the streaming player delays the start of playback only until its internal memory space, called a *buffer*, is filled. Playback then begins and empties the buffer slowly, while the buffer continues to fill via the Internet. Video quality is often relatively poor but at its highest quality is

Figure 11.14

ADDING TITLES AND
TRANSITIONS TO A
VIDEO CLIP

quite acceptable. Streaming video has become a popular advertising medium for Hollywood, which quickly puts short previews called *trailers* on the Web to promote movie products. The quality of these trailers is generally higher than the typical streaming video and represents the best the technology has to offer at this time. To remain competitive, Apple added streaming capabilities to *QuickTime* (both audio and video) and Microsoft responded with its Windows Media Formats (wma for audio and wmv for video). Whether any one format will ultimately "win" over the others is uncertain.

Multimedia Authoring Software

Once you have created your multimedia elements, it's time to put them together into an interactive multimedia extravaganza! There are multiple possible software products from which to choose for purposes of multimedia *authoring*, but we'll focus on just two that are most common in schools—presentation software such as *PowerPoint* and *HyperStudio*, a very popular hypermedia creation product.

Multimedia Presentations

In Chapter 8 you learned about software designed to make highly graphical presentations without huge amounts of work, the most popular of which is probably *PowerPoint*. The basic templates for presentations make it easy to include text, typically as bullet points, and basic graphics, from clip art to photographs. These products are also capable of producing interactive multimedia presentations, the focus of this chapter, which include digital audio and/or video on slides and add flexible navigation to get away from simple linear movement.

In *PowerPoint* use the Insert menu to add sound or a "movie" to a presentation. Figure 11.15 shows a composite view of the Insert menu to add a sound from an existing

Figure 11.15

ADDING SOUND FROM AN
AUDIO FILE

audio file and the Insert Sound dialog box that appears separately. After you select your sound, a small speaker icon appears on the screen, which you can relocate and resize as desired (see the lower right corner of the figure). You also choose whether the sound plays automatically when you reach this slide in the presentation or only when you click on the speaker icon. Adding a movie is a parallel procedure, as shown in Figure 11.16.

Flexible navigation is achieved by use of action buttons or hyperlinks. Select the desired button style, draw the button onscreen in the desired size and location, and se-

Figure 11.16

ADDING A MOVIE FROM A
VIDEO FILE

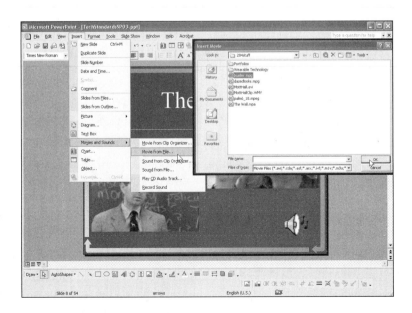

lect the slide to which the button will jump. Figure 11.17 is a composite image of the multiple steps involved. Sometimes buttons are not desirable as part of the screen design, so you can achieve the same flexibility with hyperlinks, as the composite image in Figure 11.18 illustrates. Either approach offers the same basic choices, including linking to another screen in the same presentation, to another presentation entirely, to some other program or file, or even to a URL on the Web. These simple options can turn the typical linear presentation into a truly interactive multimedia production.

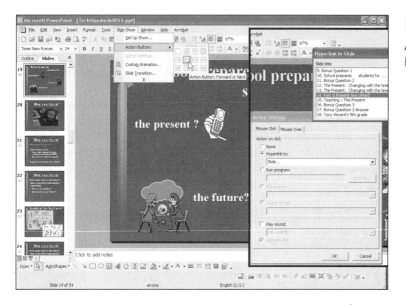

Figure 11.17
ADDING A NAVIGATION BUTTON

Figure 11.18
ADDING A HYPERLINK FOR NAVIGATION

Hypermedia

In 1987 Apple Computer introduced the first major software for hypermedia, *HyperCard* for the Macintosh. *HyperCard* projects were called *stacks* and consisted of a set of screens called *cards*. Cards were created one by one and were made up of *objects*, most basically fields (for text), pictures (for stills or movies), and buttons (to control actions and provide for navigation among the cards or to perform some action). Potentially, any object on any card could be linked with a button to any other card in the same or any other stack. *Hyper-Card* was promoted as an erector set, a type of software "Tinker Toys." The idea was that *HyperCard* was simple enough for anyone to learn to use to create hypermedia applications. *HyperCard* deserves much credit for triggering the explosive growth of hypermedia.

Because it was first on the market, the name *HyperCard* became somewhat synonymous with hypertext or hypermedia. However, just as *Kleenex* is only one brand of tissue, *HyperCard* was only one software product. It has since been superceded by *Hyper-Studio*, which is available for both Windows and Macintosh, and it is even simpler than *HyperCard*.

Following the pattern from *HyperCard*, with *HyperStudio* you build screens (also called cards) out of objects. Figure 11.19 illustrates the available objects in *HyperStudio*. Creating text fields and placing images onto a screen are trivial tasks. Just click a menu item, select options, then position the object on the card (Figure 11.20). A novice can easily create a series of screens after minimal instruction. Once you have two or more screens completed, button objects make things happen.

A button is a graphic image or some area on a screen to which the user can point with the mouse cursor and then click. The click causes something to occur, which depends on the action(s) associated with that button (Figure 11.21).

Figure 11.19

HYPERSTUDIO OBJECTS

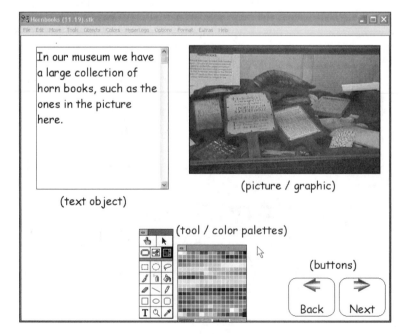

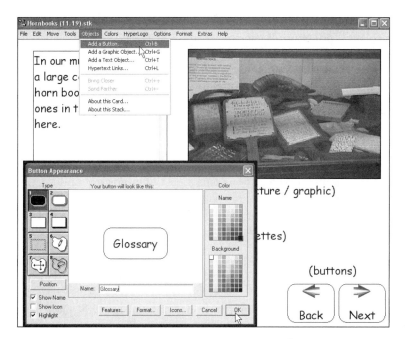

Figure 11.20

Point and click to create objects with the mouse.

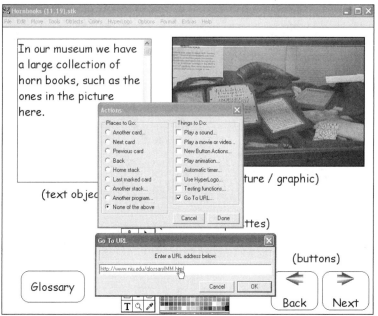

Figure 11.21

BUTTON ACTIONS IN *HYPERSTUDIO*

The simplicity of multimedia authoring software such as *PowerPoint* and *HyperStudio* has made them extremely popular among teachers and students alike. In many schools open house evenings have become showcases for student-created interactive multimedia, giving parents the opportunity to see their child's developing technology skills integrated with their content learning. Creating multimedia projects is an ideal activity in classrooms where teachers practice the principles of constructivism and engaged learning.

The impact of hypermedia tools in many schools has been substantial. Teachers who avoided computers completely have become advocates of student hypermedia products and have themselves learned enough about some software tool to work with students who are eager to use it. The International Society for Technology in Education organized a hypermedia SIG (Special Interest Group) to accommodate member interest. The American Association for Computing in Education launched the *Journal of Educational Multimedia and Hypermedia* in 1992, which is filled with practical ideas and research reports. Every conference we have attended in recent years has had a significant percentage of presentations and workshops on some aspect of interactive multimedia. It appears that *HyperCard* launched a software creation boom in schools.

The important point, of course, is not that students are developing hypermedia; rather, it is the educational benefits that are presumed to result. Hypermedia development creates a constructivist learning environment regardless of subject matter. Beichner (1994) observed students who took charge of their own work as never before because they saw a clear reason for what they were doing. The end product had personal meaning to them.

The future of hypermedia looks very bright indeed. Consider this 1989 quote from Sparks in light of today's reality:

> Our society will spend the next ten years learning how to produce and distribute high-quality hypermedia. Whole careers and new companies will emerge around it. But it will not be confined to computer professionals. This will be to the 1990s what hobbyist programming was to the late 70s, what word processing and spreadsheets were to the 80s. The difference will be that hypermedia will attract many, many more people who need to get their thoughts and ideas into better circulation. (p. 10)

Although not directed specifically to education, Sparks's projection certainly has been achieved in many classrooms. Hypermedia will continue to be one of the most exciting and beneficial computer Mindtools.

Learning with Interactive Multimedia

You only need to scan the contents of computer and professional education publications, starting about 1991, to see the attention being given to interactive multimedia. Clearly, many educators are fascinated by its potential as a learning tool. Let's look at some possible applications.

Interactive Multimedia for Content

One popular application of IMM is to provide flexible, nonlinear access to large amounts of information stored on CD-ROM. *On the Brink* (from Bytes of Learning) deals with endangered and threatened animals of North America through multimedia. *Compton's Interactive Encyclopedia, Grolier's New Multimedia Encyclopedia,* and *Microsoft Encarta* (Figure 11.22) are representative of the evolution of electronic reference works. These are

Figure 11.22

TYPICAL MULTIMEDIA REFERENCE PRODUCTS

multimedia resources, not just digitized text, complete with hyperlinks among articles that allow much more rapid location of related entries than do print encyclopedias. Furthermore, more users can copy information of interest directly from the CD into a word processor for report and other writing. CD encyclopedias include links to Internet resources for the very most current information. However, educators need to consider carefully the learning ramifications of this capability. Plagiarism remains an issue.

Another popular type of CD-ROM product is the children's storybook, pioneered by Discis. Typical is its *Tale of Benjamin Bunny*. This CD used images taken directly from the original book—one picture and one page from the story per screen. Similar in principle but more appealing to the students we've observed is the *Broderbund Living Books* series (Figure 11.23). Its first product, *Just Grandma and Me*, remains a favorite. The original Mercer Mayer pictures are animated, appropriate voices read the story aloud, and the computer highlights the corresponding words in the onscreen text. The characters even add short extra dialogues to extend the story. A child can "read" this story without adult assistance in a straight, linear fashion. The child can also click on any part of each picture to reveal a hidden animation with sound. If the child clicks the text, the appropriate character speaks the word or phrase. In yet another major departure from the book's limitations, the CD offers English, Spanish, or Japanese text and sound tracks. The Living Books collection includes several Dr. Seuss and Arthur stories as well.

Producers are also finding new home markets for learning materials. An example is *The Indian in the Cupboard*, a popular book among students that became a movie, then appeared as a CD-ROM called *The Indian in the Cupboard: A Magical Learning Experience*. Using the appeal of a popular story, the CD takes the learner on an adventure in the woods that requires problem-solving skills. There are also games on the CD, including one real Native American seed game, which could contribute to learning about native people. This CD is an interesting example of the potential synergy that can arise across various media.

Figure 11.23

Just Grandma and Me fascinated young and old alike.

Multimedia CAI and reference tools are typically installed on individual computers or on a network server. The World Wide Web also offers a multimedia environment but one that has been promoted more for its reference value. The Web is seeing explosive growth as an instructional medium, primarily at the postsecondary level, but the Virtual High School at <www.govhs.org> may be a preview of the future (Figure 11.24). Many software products such as BlackBoard, WebCT, and Learning Space have made creation of web-based courses feasible overnight.

Figure 11.24

The Virtual High School features interactive multimedia lessons.

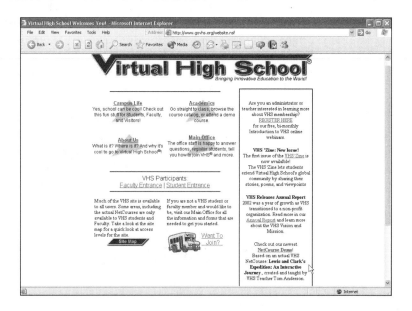

Much interest has focused on a computer language from Sun Microsystems called *Java*. Java effectively makes it possible to create and distribute software applications, including CAI, across the Internet. It is too early yet to gauge the ultimate role of Java in education, but if it works out as Sun projects, our whole notion of the mechanics of computer use may change drastically to an Internet-based approach. This would have a major impact on schools in all areas of computing, including interactive multimedia.

Interactive Multimedia in Presentations

Previously in this chapter you learned about creating multimedia elements such as audio and video clips. You also encountered multimedia tools such as *PowerPoint* and *Hyper-Studio*, which make it easy to incorporate them into a presentation. We needn't repeat that information here, but we do want to encourage you once more to consider both your own teaching applications for multimedia and especially the ways in which students might use interactive multimedia to demonstrate their learning. Lehrer, Erickson, and Connell (1994) studied students developing hypermedia on social studies topics. The goal was to create products for the school media center from which other students could learn. Student time off task declined to less than 3 percent late in the experience. At the end of the study students articulated gains that paralleled the researchers' goals. They saw the hypermedia experience as assisting them to define a problem and break it into chunks. Their research located new information, which they had to organize, evaluate, and structure in the end product. Testing with peers necessitated evaluating their design and revising. Hypermedia development clearly stimulated and supported higher-order thinking, a goal that is often elusive.

The first step in using hypermedia with students is to gain enough experience with it personally to be able to envision student uses that support the curriculum. Do not use hypermedia simply for its own sake. Within the curriculum, you would need a flexible project orientation in your teaching, one that goes beyond written assignments, drawing, physical model building, and other traditional learning projects. How might students demonstrate their learning by creating a hypermedia product? Here's just one example.

High school physics teacher Clarence Bakken got information from a nearby amusement park about how their rides work. Students then did library research and field study on the rides. The "Great America Sampler" became an elaborate hypermedia project on the physics of amusement rides (Piller, 1992). Today high schools all over Illinois send students to Physics Day at Six Flags Great America from which they return to complete projects at school.

Virtually any content in any subject has potential to be documented in a hypermedia product. You need only expand student options to include hypermedia and be willing to support students technically in their initial efforts. Once they get started, they may quickly surpass your skill with the software, so get out of their way!

Classroom Applications

According to Falk and Carlson (1992, p. 96), interactive multimedia is the best "single set of technologies to promote among teachers to improve the way they educate students." How, then, do creative teachers actually use IMM products or tools with students?

Royer and Royer (2002) provided much guidance to teachers wishing to assist students to gain the benefits of creating knowledge through multimedia development. A key concept is that the student project must ESCAPE the normal fact-based orientation of student work. Their acronym ESCAPE stands for:

- Explain critical concepts through original examples.
- Select appropriate content with purpose.
- Connect ideas.
- Apply new knowledge to previous knowledge.
- Provide analysis of key concepts.
- Express differing points of view.

The authors detail a ninth-grade science lesson on biomes that was designed from the start to require student multimedia development. They discuss important issues in classroom management and provide detailed guidance on project evaluation, including a complete rubric. The lesson concludes with the all-important student-guided reflection on what they have learned. This is an excellent article for anyone new to the idea of multimedia to demonstrate learning.

A different kind of interactive multimedia application is the Wazzu Widgets project <http://education.wsu.edu/widgets/>. Wazzu is Washington State University and widgets are "learning objects," or small learning activities. The focus is on a small, clearly defined learning goal or concept that could be applicable over a range of learning needs. Some of the widgets were developed for use by students with mental retardation. It is much more effective to experience the widgets than to read a description of them, so by all means, visit the site.

Marlene Boney, a 30-year veteran teacher, uses *HyperStudio* to teach K–6 basic skills. She has shared *HyperStudio* lessons and lesson plans on carnivores, herbivores, and omnivores and another on regions of the United States with any interested teacher. Her materials include the project itself, the lesson plan, the assessment rubric, and extension activities. Visit the *HyperStudio* Success Stories website <www.hyperstudio.com/showcase/stories.html> to access her materials and those of other teachers who share her enthusiasm for multimedia as a learning tool.

Poftak (1999) described both the rationale and concrete examples of the move to multimedia yearbooks and school newspapers. Student producers must learn more in-depth applications of multimedia, while exploring the luxury of more capacity to document events of interest during the school year.

Annually, the International Society for Technology in Education (ISTE) sponsors Multimedia Mania to promote "effective student use of multimedia in content-based projects" (Solomon, 1999). Projects "must be connected to the curriculum, be factual, and have documented resources." Among the 1999 winners was a project from an Ohio high school that focused on conflict in literature. Using multimedia, the students presented an overview of conflict, its three types, and their representations in literature. The project drew from novels common to high school literature curricula. Another winner from rural Illinois was the result of students exploring the history of the civil rights movement. The key point is that all submissions integrated interactive multimedia into the curriculum to evoke deeper understanding of the topic.

Taylor and Stuhlmann (1995) described Project KITES (Kids Interacting with Technology and Education Students). Education majors were paired with fourth-grade students; neither group had much experience with computers. Each pair read the same children's book and worked together to create a multimedia slide-show book report. The teachers for the class prepared a sample book report to illustrate the potential. *Kid Pix* was used because it not only could easily combine original pictures into a slide show, but it also supported transition effects between slides, sound, and digital movies, making it a basic multimedia tool. Taylor and Stuhlmann report that the project produced significant attitude changes in both the elementary and university students.

Native American students created illustrated versions of their own legends. The project stimulated the students' understanding of their heritage while applying a new software tool (Beekman, 1992). Groups of three or four students researched traditional legends and developed storyboards as part of their communications class, then created their stacks in computer class. All stacks included original artwork; many featured animation and sound. Project leaders stressed not only the skills development, but also the sense of accomplishment and mastery, which was uncommon for many disadvantaged students. How could you apply this idea to any student group?

Concern over lack of interest in math and science among young women led to a project at George Washington University (Baxter & Heller, 1992). Over a period of nine months, participants attended Saturday sessions during the school year and a ten-day residential program in the summer. Formal Saturday sessions developed participants' computer applications skills. Professional scientists made presentations to the young women in the afternoon. The summer focused on cooperative learning using hypermedia. Teams worked together to create and present a science project. Each team had to research their topic and prepare an outline. Next, they designed and created the presentation. After delivering the presentation, students revised it based on audience feedback. Anecdotal evidence suggests the program may meet its purpose of encouraging young women to consider careers in engineering.

Falk and Carlson (1992) offer a model of how educators use hypermedia products (Figure 11.25). One dimension of the model is the method of use, either *model T* as a teaching tool (in the hands of the teacher) or *model L* as a learning tool (in the hands of the learner). Either may involve any of five different instructional styles. *Video-enhanced didactic presentations* use IMM materials to enhance the teacher's presentation (model T) or as tutorial CAI. *Exploration* models allow teacher or learner to move about freely

Method of Use	Video-Enhanced Didactic	Exploration	Structured Observation	Simulated Personal Interaction	Assessment & Focused Instruction
Model T					
Model L					

Figure 11.25 HYPERMEDIA USAGE MODEL (FALK & CARLSON, 1992)

Figure 11.26

MODEL OF
HYPERMEDIA
APPLICATION
DEVELOPMENT
(BASED ON
TRAUTMAN, 1992)

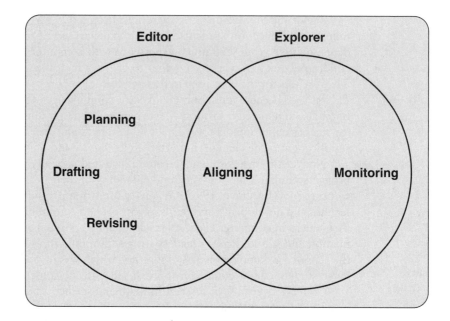

through the content. *Structured observation* requires students to attend to specific things as they use the lesson or see it presented in a group setting. *Simulated personal interaction* is a hypermedia simulation in which the learner assumes a role and interacts with the media. *Assessment and focused instruction* involve testing the learners' knowledge and directing them to appropriate instruction or remediation.

Trautman (1992) suggests that building a multimedia product is an active, creative effort to compose meaning, as are reading and writing. Every multimedia application has two operational modes: editing (creating or altering a product) and exploring (using, investigating). As editor, a teacher or student should progress through three distinct stages of creation. *Planning* involves preparation to undertake the project and goal setting. *Drafting* is the design phase. Trautman suggests working on large posterboard with sticky notes to create and modify a diagram of how the product will work. *Aligning* is making the product fit the intended audience. As editor, you try to keep the audience in mind as you create the product. When a preliminary version is complete, you mentally shift to the explorer mode to look at it from the audience's perspective. Group critiques can be helpful. If pieces are out of alignment, revising allows creators to fix the problem. The main explorer function is monitoring, being alert at all times to the success of or need for the other processes. Figure 11.26 illustrates the model.

Issues in Interactive Multimedia

One major issue when students create interactive multimedia is *copyright*. The potential to digitize virtually anything and incorporate the digital result in a software product raises numerous concerns among copyright holders. Although the legal issues are continually in flux, it is clear that digitizing materials for inclusion in new *commercial* products is not permissible, as this would deprive the copyright holder of justifiable income from the original, which is the essence of copyright protection. An excellent online resource for school use is provided by the Groton (Connecticut) schools at <http://groton.k12.ct.us/mts/cimhp01.htm>. You may also wish to follow the work of the Digital Future Coalition at <www.dfc.org> and the Electronic Frontier Foundation at <www.eff.org>.

Can content be made *too* easy? Two early CD-ROMs presented the lives of Stravinsky and Beethoven and their music. With products such as these, you can read a biography of the composer, view portraits and other illustrations, listen to the music, study the musical score, and even take a quiz on the content, all without leaving your computer (Figure 11.27). The creator of the CDs reported divergent reactions to the works. Music students and the general public liked them, but music professionals were disturbed that they were so attractive and easy to use that the technology made the subject *too* easy, *too* accessible. The creator of the products suggested such attitudes are a major reason for slow acceptance of IMM instructional materials (Greenberger, 1990).

There are *operational issues* with hyper environments as well. Let's look at wandering, disorientation, and cognitive overload.

The term *wandering*, or "unmotivated rambling," refers to the potential for the user of hypermedia to meander aimlessly through the vast available resources, potentially gaining little or nothing beyond enjoyment. This becomes an issue when the product is used specifically for learning. Traditional CAI, as presented in the previous chapter, is generally designed to all but ensure that some type of learning will occur. Its interaction types and control structures are notably absent from hypermedia products, such as ABC News Interactive's products *In the Holy Land* and *Martin Luther King* (to say

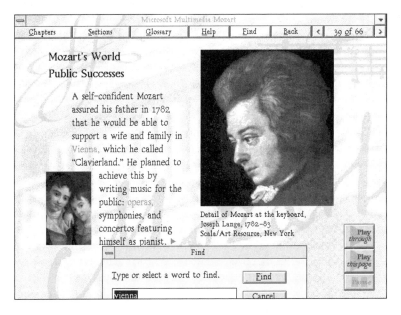

Figure 11.27

INTERACTIVE MULTIMEDIA ON THE LIFE, TIMES, AND MUSIC OF MOZART nothing of the Internet). Users have vast *potential* to learn but must make a definite effort on their own to do so.

How many learners in any given context are capable of profiting fully from the freedom hypermedia provides? Should the software include more traditional elements of instruction (frequent questions to answer, feedback and guidance, exit criteria, etc.), or is it the teacher's responsibility to prepare the learner for hypermedia and to set learning expectations outside of the software? Are such products equally beneficial to all types of learners? Only much further research will provide the answers.

Disorientation is another concern. When you have flexibility to move about in a hypermedia environment, you also have the potential to become "lost in hyperspace." As one idea leads to another and then another, you may no longer recall where your inquiry started, much less how to return to the screen from which the digression began. Good hypermedia products include maps of their organization that you can access at any time, clearly marked to show exactly where you currently are. Another approach is buttons that return you to some intermediate point, such as the menu level just above your current location. From there, you usually can reestablish your orientation.

The magnitude of the problem and the difficulty in effectively managing it may be proportional to the overall size of the environment. Displaying an understandable map of a large, complex system is itself difficult. The World Wide Web may well be the ultimate hypermedia environment, and navigating within it clearly illustrates the issue, for which solutions remain to be found. Stanton and Baber (1994) argue that the problem is not inherent in hyper environments, but rather an issue of poor interface design. Pay special attention to the interface, especially when working with large environments.

Because an interactive multimedia environment can—indeed, should—be rich in content, users may face *cognitive overload*, or a sense of inability to cope with and draw meaning from an overwhelming array of information (Stanton & Baber, 1992). This may lead to "flagging commitment" to pursue any goal (Heller, 1990). We have observed this phenomenon when students encounter *GTV: A Geographic Perspective on American History* with little guidance as to what they are supposed to do or learn. Do not expect novices to know how to effectively use something so radically different as IMM. Rather, expect to teach them the needed skills.

What the Research Shows

Given its comparative newness, research on interactive multimedia is not yet extensive. This section provides a sampling to illustrate some of the issues, approaches, and findings.

Johnson (2002) studied an inner-city school system with a predominantly African American student body. The goal was to increase academic achievement and the tools chosen were multimedia and multiple intelligences within the framework of the Baldridge Core Values and Criteria. Johnson found that the goal was attainable when students were coproducers of learning within schools that used aligned and coordinated curriculum approaches, which resulted from staff development including technology skills.

Is it really multimedia that matters? Lookatch (1997) and Clark (1983, 1985) maintained that it is the underlying instructional strategies that actually influence learning outcomes. Thus, instructional multimedia is useful or not, depending on the strategies within it. Kozma (1994) refuted these claims and stressed the uniqueness of the contributions that media can bring to the learning experience. Supporting Kozma, Bagui (1998) found unique capabilities in multimedia as a learning tool because both sensory stimulation and navigation in IMM parallel our natural ways of learning. Roblyer (1999) found that the multiple channels through which multimedia communicates to the learner seemed to be the source of its benefits. However, all of these researchers, like most who follow, focused on prepared multimedia learning materials, not on students preparing such products to demonstrate their newly constructed knowledge.

After students completed their first multimedia project in language arts and social studies, teachers reported significant increases in student research skills, organizational skills, interest in the course content, and ability to apply their learning in authentic situations (Cradler & Cradler, 1999). More research of this type is needed to document the perceptions of teachers that students learn more from multimedia projects.

Barba and Armstrong (1992) believed general research missed such important issues as which types of students benefit more from various learning systems. They compared student achievement gains from a *HyperCard* stack with those from the same stack enhanced with video from a laserdisc. They found no significant difference for the two treatments per se, but as expected, there was a significant difference among low-, average-, and high-verbal-ability students. They also found that students with low verbal ability benefited disproportionately from the interactive video instruction (IVI). High-verbal-ability students in the no-video treatment actually outperformed their counterparts in the IVI group, but the differences were not significant statistically.

Davidson-Shivers and colleagues (1999) studied fifth-grade student use of learning strategies, encoding processes, and navigation decisions in a hypermedia lesson. They found great variation in both the number and types of learning strategies used by students based on high, average, or low achievement scores. The groups also differed on navigational decisions and encoding processes. High-scoring students used more and more varied learning strategies and showed greater consistency in navigation. Low-scoring students made many errors in encoding the information.

Rasmussen and Davidson-Shivers (1998) found that learning style preference can enhance learner performance in conjunction with learner control. Learners who had a moderate level of learner control outperformed those with high and low levels of control on a delayed posttest, while those who tended toward abstractness as a learning preference outperformed those who tended toward concreteness. The researchers concluded that instructors can enhance the learning experience by developing lessons that accommodate learning style preferences.

Fitzgerald and Semrau (1998) explored a range of student characteristics, including field dependence/independence as an element of learning style, in the context of hypermedia case studies. Their results suggest that such case studies are equally effective as a learning environment among all learners.

European researchers Nuldén and Scheepers (1999) investigated ways to enhance experiential and problem-based learning (PBL) with interactive multimedia. They focused on ways to enhance the vignette, the story that presents the problem situation, using IMM. Using input from experienced PBL students and teachers, they developed a prototype that added significant dimensions to the learning experience. In another

European study involving novice learners in a case-based hypermedia environment, Demetriadis and Pombortsis (1999) found that hypermedia produced comparable results with linear materials for basic content learning. However, the students who experienced hypermedia performed significantly better on more complex problems and showed deeper understanding of the learning domain.

Szabo and Kanuka (1999) studied the effect of screen design on recall learning, learning time, and completion rate among adult learners. Subjects showed no difference in achievement whether using IMM that followed accepted screen design or a parallel version that violated common principles. However, those using the well-designed version completed their lessons in 21 percent less time. Their overall completion rate was 74 percent versus only 45 percent among the poor design group.

McDonald and Stevenson (1999) studied navigation aids and their impact on learning. Subjects whose hypermedia environment included spatial maps of the environment were able to navigate better than those who had access only to a content list or no aid at all. However, the two aids were indistinguishable in terms of learning produced. The no-aid group performed the worst. A second experiment confirmed that a spatial map best facilitated navigation, while a concept map produced greater learning.

Lai and Waugh (1995) investigated the effect of different forms of links in a hypermedia program. In essence, they compared traditional menus that were either hierarchical or associative and embedded associative menus. The latter are similar to the highlighted link words in World Wide Web documents, although this study used *HyperCard*. The researchers found that cross-reference links (associative menus) did little to improve search efficiency unless the search space was rather large. For small to medium-size content, hierarchies sufficed. If the search space grew or the goals were complex or vague, the value of associative links grew. This study appears to have considerable value for the design of future hypermedia systems, including instructional materials that may reside on the Web for delivery using a technology such as Java, as previously mentioned.

Chun and Plass (1995) developed and tested an IMM application for second-language learning. The software provided a digital video clip as an advance organizer for reading a passage in German. Hot words within the text linked to glosses that were text, graphics, video, or sound, offering multiple ways to facilitate and reinforce vocabulary acquisition. Based on two studies of the material, students were enthusiastic about the graphics and videos and chose those links over text links. Achievement and retention over time both increased. The researchers also found that students who were visualizers chose visual links, while verbalizers tended to choose text links, each reflecting their own cognitive styles. The software supported both styles well, a potentially valuable lesson for designers of future IMM products.

What can the computer offer individuals with special needs? In a most unusual article, Rieber (1995) related in considerable detail the "informal case study" of an 11-year-old's interaction with computers, including with interactive multimedia. The child, Thomas, was diagnosed with multiple learning disabilities resulting from Pervasive Developmental Disorder. Thomas could read only a few letters and sight words, count from one to five, and write only a few letters crudely. We cannot begin to recount Thomas's story here, for the article is lengthy. Instead we note Rieber's enthusiastic conclusion that this child "is learning and finding the computer to be an engaging medium" (p. 90).

He also notes the irony that a special needs child "finds comfort and confidence in a machine that threatens and intimidates other normally functioning adults." We highly recommend this article to you.

Heller (1990) summarized the work of many researchers who explored aspects of hyper environments. Among the more interesting findings was that users who browsed through a hyper environment grossly overestimated the amount of the total system they had actually seen. Further, high school students tended to browse using simple techniques, rather than developing effective search strategies. In summarizing the research on discovery learning, Heller suggested that the inherent flexibility of a hyper environment may be inappropriate for children below junior high age. She noted that research on hypermedia was comparatively scarce. Small and Ferreira (1994) also noted that some adults expressed frustration that they did not achieve closure with their hypermedia resources because they had no idea how much of the total system they had actually engaged, unlike a book.

In sum, there is continuing need for research concerning all the possible variations in learning materials that constitute interactive multimedia and their relationships to learner characteristics. As the boundaries between IMM and traditional CAI disappear, thanks both to market demand and the storage capacities of CD-ROM and DVD, the research needs of the two areas also are converging. Much remains to be determined about how to achieve the maximum learning potential of this medium.

SUMMARY

In this chapter, you learned about the nature of hyper environments. Linear computer applications seem very limited once you have experienced the flexibility and naturalness of hypermedia. There is tremendous intuitive appeal in the full sensory communication of computer-based multimedia. A critical element of worthwhile applications is interaction between user and computer. Hypermedia seems an appropriate term for this learning tool, but multimedia is already commonly used. We support *interactive multimedia* (IMM) to properly identify the key elements.

Interactive multimedia draws on the hardware technologies of compact disc, DVD, and digitizers. Software products, such as *HyperStudio*, provide software construction sets that are relatively easy to learn to use. Hardware and software technologies such as QuickTime and MPEG add digital video to IMM.

Interactive multimedia can provide easier access to vast multimedia resources. Teachers can use IMM tools to deliver more exciting presentations. Some of the most intriguing possibilities stem from students creating IMM projects as alternatives to traditional school assignments. Of course, there are areas of concern with this technology, as with all others. Copyright issues and acceptance by educators are common concerns. Operational issues include wandering through an IMM product, becoming disoriented, and dealing with cognitive overload.

Concerning the potential of IMM to enhance learning, findings to date are encouraging, but there is still a need for much research to determine what strategies are most appropriate for which learners under what circumstances.

Technologies like CD-ROM and DVD are extending access to interactive multimedia to users everywhere, while the multimedia capabilities of the Internet offer explosive growth potential for this unique tool. Perhaps the ultimate application of interactive multimedia is what is termed *virtual reality*, an interactive, computer-generated microworld. You'll learn about virtual reality in Chapter 16.

chapter 11 activities

1. Create a poster, bulletin board, or electronic presentation that explains and illustrates the differences among hypertext, multimedia, and hypermedia (or interactive multimedia).
2. Try out several different types of CD-ROM products, from text-only to hypermedia. Compare those that have hypermedia access systems, such as an encyclopedia, with those that do not.
3. Experiment with any video and audio digitizing hardware that you have access to.
4. Create a simple product using any hypermedia software. Develop a basic lesson outline for something you could teach with about four main points. Create and link support screens for each of the main points. The support screens may consist of further text, or they may call up other resources.
5. Plan an assignment for your students that would encourage them to develop an IMM product in lieu of more traditional projects.
6. Read any current research literature on interactive multimedia that you can find.
7. Keep a journal of your Internet surfing, making special note of hypermedia elements that you encounter and your assessment of their merit.

Companion Website

Visit the companion website at <www.ablongman.com/lockard6e> for more information about the topics discussed in this chapter.

expect the world®

The New York Times
nytimes.com

Themes of the Times

Expand your knowledge of the concepts discussed in this chapter by reading current and historical articles from the *New York Times* by visiting the Themes of the Times section of the companion website <www.ablongman.com/lockard6e>.

References

Bagui, S. "Reasons for Increased Learning Using Multimedia." *Journal of Educational Multimedia and Hypermedia*, 1998, 7(1), pp. 3–18.

Barba, R. H., and Armstrong, B. E. "The Effect of *HyperCard* and Interactive Video Instruction on Earth and Space Science Students' Achievement." *Journal of Educational Multimedia and Hypermedia*, 1992, 1(3), pp. 323–330.

Baxter, T., and Heller, S. "Getting Closer to Science: Experiences Using *HyperCard* to Interest Young Minority Women in Science." *Journal of HyperMedia and MultiMedia Studies*, Fall 1992, 3(1), pp. 8–11.

Beekman, G. "Recreating Native American Legends with *HyperCard*." *The Computing Teacher*, February 1992, 19(5), p. 31.

Beichner, R. J. "Multimedia Editing to Promote Science Learning." *Journal of Educational Multimedia and Hypermedia*, 1994, 3(1), pp. 55–70.

Bush, V. "As We May Think." *Atlantic Monthly*, July 1945. Retrieved February 15, 2003, from <www.theatlantic.com/unbound/flashbks/computer/bushf.htm>

Chun, D. M., and Plass, J.-L. "Project *CyberBuch:* A Hypermedia Approach to Computer-Assisted Language Learning." *Journal of Educational Multimedia and Hypermedia*, 1995, 4(1), pp. 95–116.

Clark, R. E. "Reconsidering Research on Learning from Media." *Review of Educational Research*, 1983, 53(4), pp. 445–459.

Clark, R. E. "Evidence for Confounding in Computer-Based Instruction Studies: Analyzing the Meta-Analyses." *ECTJ*, 1985, 33(4), pp. 249–262.

Cradler, R., and Cradler, J. *Just in Time: Technology Innovation Challenge Grant Year 2 Evaluation Report for Blackfoot School District No. 55*. San Mateo, CA: Educational Support Systems, 1999.

Davidson-Shivers, G. V., Shorter, L., Jordan, K., and Rasmussen, K. L. "Learning Strategies and Navigation Decisions of Children Using a Hypermedia Lesson." *Journal of Educational Multimedia and Hypermedia*, 1999, 8(2), pp. 175–188.

Demetriadis, S., and Pombortsis, A. "Novice Student Learning in Case Based Hypermedia Environment: A Quantitative Study." *Journal of Educational Multimedia and Hypermedia*, 1999, 8(2), pp. 241–269.

Falk, D. R., and Carlson, H. L. "Learning to Teach with Multimedia." *T.H.E. Journal*, September 1992, 20(2), pp. 96–100.

Fitzgerald, G. E., and Semrau, L. P. "The Effects of Learner Differences on Usage Patterns and Learning Outcomes with Hypermedia Case Studies." *Journal of Educational Multimedia and Hypermedia*, 1998, 7(4), pp. 309–331.

Greenberger, M., ed. *On Multimedia: Technologies for the 21st Century*. Santa Monica, CA: Voyager Company, 1990.

Heller, R. S. "The Role of Hypermedia in Education: A Look at the Research Issues." *Journal of Research on Computing in Education*, Summer 1990, 22(4), pp. 431–441.

Johnson, D. G. "Multimedia, Multiple Intelligences, and the Baldridge Core Values and Criteria." Presentation at the 2002 National Educational Computing Conference, June 19, 2002, San Antonio, TX.

Kozma, R. "A Reply: Media *and* Method." *Educational Technology Research and Development*, 1994, 42(3), pp. 11–14.

Kozma, R. "Will Media Influence Learning: Reframing the Debate." *Educational Technology Research and Development*, 1994, 42(2), pp. 7–19.

Lai, Y., and Waugh, M. L. "Effects of Three Different Hypertextual Menu designs on Various Information Searching Activities." *Journal of Educational Multimedia and Hypermedia*, 1995, 4(1), pp. 25–52.

Lehrer, R., Erickson, J., and Connell, T. "Learning by Designing Hypermedia Documents." *Computers in the Schools*, 1994, 10(1/2), pp. 227–254.

Locatis, C., Letourneau, G., and Banvard, R. "Hypermedia and Instruction." *Educational Technology Research and Development*, 1989, 37(4), pp. 65–77.

Lookatch, R. "Apples, Oranges, and the Type I Error." *Contemporary Education*, 1997, 68(2), pp. 110–113.

McDonald, S., and Stevenson, R. J. "Spatial Versus Conceptual Maps as Learning Tools in Hypertext."

Journal of Educational Multimedia and Hypermedia, 1999, *8*(1), pp. 43–64.

Nelson, T. *Computer Lib/Dream Machines.* Redmond, WA: Tempus Books (Microsoft Press), 1987.

Nuldén, U., and Scheepers, H. "Interactive Multimedia and Problem Based Learning: Experiencing Project Failure." *Journal of Educational Multimedia and Hypermedia,* 1999, *8*(2), pp. 189–215.

Piller, C. "Separate Realities." *MacWorld,* September 1992, pp. 218–230.

Poftak, A. "Reinventing Tradition: CD Yearbooks and Online Newspapers." *Technology & Learning,* August 1999, *20*(1), pp. 32–38.

Rasmussen, K. L., and Davidson-Shivers, G. V. "Hypermedia and Learning Styles: Can Performance Be Influenced?" *Journal of Educational Multimedia and Hypermedia,* 1998, 7(4), pp. 291–308.

Rieber, L. P. "Using Computer-based Microworlds with Children with Pervasive Developmental Disorders: An Informal Case Study." *Journal of Educational Multimedia and Hypermedia,* 1995, *4*(1), pp. 75–94.

Roblyer, M. D. "Our Multimedia Future: Recent Research on Multimedia's Impact on Education." *Learning & Leading with Technology,* March 1999, *26*(6), pp. 51–54.

Rojas, P. "Diskettes Squarely Keep Hold on Public." *Chicago Tribune,* February 15, 2003, Business Section, p. 3.

Royer, R., and Royer, J. "Developing Understanding with Multimedia." *Learning & Leading with Technology,* April 2002, *29*(7), pp. 40–45.

Small, R. V., and Ferreira, S. M. "Information Location and Use, Motivation, and Learning Patterns When Using Print or Multimedia Information Resources." *Journal of Educational Multimedia and Hypermedia,* 1994, *3*(3/4), pp. 251–273.

Solomon, G. "The Road to Success: Learning From the Winners." *Technology & Learning,* June 1999, *19*(10), pp. 33–40.

Sparks, D. G. "HyperStudio." *Call-A.P.P.L.E.,* March 1989, pp. 8–10.

Stanton, N., and Baber, C. "An Investigation of Styles and Strategies in Self-directed Learning." *Journal of Educational Multimedia and Hypermedia,* 1992, *1*(2), pp. 147–167.

Stanton, N., and Baber, C. "The Myth of Navigating in Hypertext: How a 'Bandwagon' Has Lost Its Course." *Journal of Educational Multimedia and Hypermedia,* 1994, *3*(3–4), pp. 235–249.

Szabo, M., and Kanuka, H. "Effects of Violating Screen Design Principles of Balance, Unity, and Focus on Recall Learning, Study Time, and Completion Rates." *Journal of Educational Multimedia and Hypermedia,* 1999, *8*(1), pp. 23–42.

Taylor, H. G., and Stuhlmann, J. M. "Creating Slide Show Book Reports." *Learning and Leading with Technology,* September 1995, *23*(1), pp. 8–10.

Trautman, P. "Reading, Writing, and Digitizing!" *The Computer Teacher,* April 1992, *19*(7), pp. 40–41.

Wolf, G. "The Curse of Xanadu." *Wired,* June 1995, pp. 137–152, 194–202.

Courseware
Evaluation

OBJECTIVES

After completing this chapter, you will be able to:

- Discuss the issue of courseware quality and suggest possible reasons that complaints about quality have been common.
- Explain why educators need to evaluate courseware for classroom use and who should be involved.
- Describe the three major phases in courseware evaluation.
- Explain the primary means of identifying courseware to evaluate.

- Discuss the purpose of and procedures for hands-on evaluation by educators.
- Assess the importance of student field-testing of courseware.
- Explain the significance of courseware's intended use as an element of evaluation.
- Discuss the merits of learning theory as an element of evaluation.
- Select five general instructional criteria that you believe are the most critical, then defend your choices.

- Identify at least four CAI-specific evaluation criteria and defend their importance.
- Explain which usability criteria are most significant to you.
- Use a software evaluation form to assess critically the learning potential of available CAI.
- Devise one or more courseware evaluation forms incorporating your most vital criteria.
- Assess the variations in evaluation criteria and procedures that might arise from different software formats, especially hypermedia and multimedia.

The tens of thousands of instructional software products on the market, the range of content they entail, the widely differing formats they employ, the cost involved in acquiring them for school use—these are the elements of a confusing, even overwhelming, situation for many educators. How can you know what is available, whether it is worth using, and how best to use it?

In this chapter you will consider selecting and evaluating instructional courseware for your students. The term *courseware* acknowledges that many instructional programs consist of more than just a CD. Software is computer files; courseware includes support materials such as documentation, teacher guides, and student manuals, which can be vital components of the total package.

This chapter first considers the issue of courseware quality, which leads directly to the need for evaluation and our suggested approach to it. You will learn about specific evaluation criteria in several categories, including those applicable to all educational materials, those unique to the computer, and those that contribute to usability. You will also consider the use of an evaluation form and how to create your own unique form.

The Issue of Quality

As you learned in Chapter 1, schools in the United States have invested billions of dollars in technology annually for more than a decade. This investment means there is a vast amount of computer hardware in U.S. schools. However, hardware is only one component of educational technology.

NETS
NOTES

NETS **S** 5
NETS **S** 6
NETS **T** I-A
NETS **T** I-B
NETS **T** II-A
NETS **T** II-C
NETS **T** III-A

Software—The Critical Component

Hardware is really just a bunch of electronic components. By itself, computer hardware is relatively useless—too large to make a good paperweight and too costly to serve as a boat anchor. A computer makes a nice conversation piece on someone's desk or in a classroom or a learning center. With the addition of software, hardware becomes truly useful (Figure 12.1).

Figure 12.1
Software brings life to a computer.

NETS
NOTES

NETS **T** III-B
NETS **T** III-C
NETS **T** IV-C
NETS **T** V-C
NETS **T** VI-B
NETS **T** VI-C

Because software brings life to a maze of electronics, that software actually is more critical than the hardware. The significance of hardware is its ability to run the software you need to perform a given task. Thus, it is vital to meeting your goals for your students to use high-quality software. Mediocre (or worse!) software only negates the computer's potential.

Quality Trails Quantity

In the computer industry, improvements in hardware are an all-but-daily phenomenon. Regrettably, the same cannot be said of courseware. For years, almost any gathering of educators with computer interests at some point prompted discussion of the quality of courseware on the market. The concern is not a reflection of naiveté on the part of educators with limited computer experience. When Neill and Neill (1993) examined reviews of more than 13,000 pieces of educational software, they found that fewer than 8 percent met their criteria for an "A" grade! Nearly a decade earlier, Alfred Bork, a major figure in educational computing, had commented on the rapid increase in software *quantity*, but not *quality:* "We know how to produce decent computer-based learning material at the present time. But most of the available programs have not been produced by any careful process, and few have undergone careful evaluative study. Our increased capabilities in producing materials have largely gone unused" (1984, p. 93). Remarkably, quality concerns remain today.

Why Quality Has Been Problematic

There are several possible explanations for less than ideal courseware quality.

Lack of a Theoretical Base

The field of learning theory offers many views concerning how we learn. Yet much courseware appears to reflect little effort to apply *any* theory (Hoffman & Lyons, 1997). Many courseware developers seem to require little more than a vague notion of content to begin production of a new package. Would it not be wiser to consider what we know about learning and include that in the design?

Technical Concerns Dominate

In the early days of educational software, errors in programming were common, even in commercial materials. Developers were still exploring the capabilities of then-new microcomputers and lacked sophistication. Complaints of amateurish results were common. Today, this has changed dramatically. Commercial materials are technically sound. Graphics are slick, sound and video are appealing, and concern for visual design is evident (Figure 12.2). Actual serious programming flaws are rare. In most cases, however, nothing resembling comparable attention to the instructional design of the program exists. We have reached a level of technical excellence and continue to ignore educational soundness. One can only wonder whether experienced educators have played a role in developing many of the products on the market.

Applying Old Models to a New Medium

Someone once observed that the passenger railroads sealed their doom by failing to realize that their business was transportation, not trains. The history of motion pictures contains something of a parallel. Early filmmakers viewed the new medium as a means of recording stage plays for posterity. Only after considerable time did the adventurous begin to break out of old patterns and begin to explore the new medium itself.

Figure 12.2

Technical quality is high in most software.

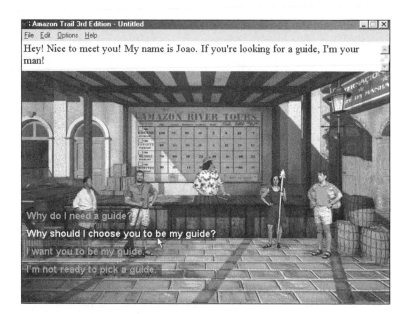

This echoes the concern of Maddux, Johnson, and Willis (1997) that far too much computer use in schools is Type I activity, that is, doing with a computer what educators and students have always done. Instead, educational computing takes on real value when it empowers students and teachers to do what they otherwise could not, that is, Type II applications. Much educational courseware is Type I, notably drill and practice, many games, and tutorials—the very computer uses found least effective for math learning in an ETS study (Wenglinsky, 1998). Simulations and today's interactive multimedia and hypermedia products offer real promise of Type II activities. Quality courseware goes beyond what other alternative learning approaches provide to create a niche of its own. That's not impossible, but is it the norm?

Educators Have Not Demanded Quality

Courseware production and sales are big business. Success is measured in gross sales and net profits. With hardware springing up like mushrooms and software necessary to make it useful, there was an initial rush to get courseware on the market. In the early 1980s, educators were too desperate for anything to use with their new tools to be fussy about quality. The new equipment dared not just sit there! Regrettably, the situation has changed less than you might expect.

The real evidence of courseware quality is *student learning*. We educators largely have failed to look at our results. In too many cases, we accept courseware based on its producer's claims of value. A catchy title, flashy graphics, and bold claims of applicability from kindergarten students through adults sell materials to uncritical consumers.

Indeed, software producers themselves appear to be little concerned about the effectiveness of their products. Have you ever seen a piece of instructional software that included field-test data? Zane and Frazer (1992) contacted 34 software producers whose products they were evaluating. Each was asked to provide "any evaluative data, research findings, or field-test results" in five areas, including documentation that students learn something from the software, evidence of generalization from the software to other contexts, and comparative data showing an advantage for the software over other independent learning materials, such as workbooks. Only 15 companies responded at all. Nine just sent more literature. Six admitted having no data. The researchers state: "It should not be the responsibility of computer software users to conduct initial validation evaluations of the effectiveness of a software program" (p. 416). Not only should producers assure basic effectiveness, but they also should determine the learner characteristics (gender, achievement level, etc.) most relevant to success with or efficient use of their product.

Improvements over Time

Roblyer (2003) points out that the many years of experience that schools now have had with instructional courseware have removed much of the early mystique from this use of computer technology. Developers have learned critical lessons over time and realize that just putting instructional materials into digital form is not enough. In fact, Roblyer contends, "Courseware producers have obviously learned much from their early errors and problems, and overall quality has improved considerably" (p. 106).

Although we agree that the technical problems of the past have largely disappeared, we are less convinced that typical instructional courseware is educationally sound. We are still unaware of substantive efforts by producers to test and verify the learning outcomes attained from use of their products. As tool applications have gained in popularity among educators, there is less concern about what to do with school computers and less perceived pressure to use whatever "instructional" products may be available, regardless of their value. Teachers can now focus on at least the potential for learning that they find in products available to them.

The Need for Evaluation

NETS
NOTES

NETS **T** I-A
NETS **T** II-C
NETS **T** IV-C
NETS **T** VI-C

Instructional courseware is not the ultimate justification for computers in schools, nor will computers disappear if schools fail to identify and obtain good CAI. The kinds of tool applications that you studied in Chapters 3–9 alone assure the future of computers in schools. However, CAI, carefully selected and used, can extend the usefulness of computers. Consider the elaborate efforts undertaken in schools for textbook selection. Committees invest countless hours assessing and comparing the latest offerings of publishers before adoption. Educational videos and other media under consideration for purchase are evaluated similarly. Snap decisions are unacceptable—too much is at stake. Does courseware deserve less attention?

Evaluating courseware is significantly different from examining other educational materials. Teachers involved in selecting textbooks and media tend to have years of experience teaching and learning from such materials. Far fewer educators have such experience to draw on for courseware evaluation. We believe educators are well aware of the need to evaluate courseware, but many are perplexed about procedures. Let's consider basic guidelines.

Who Should Evaluate Courseware?

There is no simple answer to the question of who should be involved in courseware evaluation. In most cases, the best approach is probably to begin in the same manner used to select textbooks. Clearly, the teachers who will use the materials must be involved. If these individuals have no role in selection, the likelihood of their using the materials is greatly reduced.

Because of the technical aspects of courseware, it seems likely that the school's computer "expert" should also be involved. This may be a designated coordinator, a resource specialist, or even an administrator. It should be someone with a greater understanding of computer materials than a typical classroom user is apt to have or need. This person's role might be to conduct a workshop for the selection committee on the process of courseware evaluation rather than to be involved actively in the entire process.

If school policy includes administrators or parents in selection of other materials, the same should be true of computer materials. It can, in fact, be advantageous to include parents in the process. Even those who are highly and vocally committed to bringing computers into the schools may have little knowledge themselves of the whys and wherefores. We can ill afford a repeat of the "new math" experience. That curriculum development failed in part because parents had not learned in such a manner in their school days and were unable to understand and support what their children were doing.

Parental support of technology in the schools is vital to a successful program. Efforts to involve parents and inform them about these tools can only help.

Phases of Courseware Evaluation

There are three distinct phases to courseware evaluation: identifying products of interest, hands-on evaluation by educators, and student field-testing.

Identifying Courseware to Evaluate

To identify courseware of potential interest, simply look through catalogs or visit nearby stores, ask the advice of professional colleagues, or consult published reviews.

Catalogs and Dealers

The quickest way to get a lead on software often is to look through producers' and distributors' catalogs. If you know of a company that is well regarded for courseware in your field of interest, be sure to get their latest literature. Otherwise, try the extensive product catalogs of distributors such as Educational Resources <www.edresources.com/ERHomePage.process>, Learning Services <www.learnserv.com>, and Technology Resource Center <http://gotrc.com>. Ideally you will find program descriptions, not just long lists of titles and/or technical specifications.

All dealers make choices about which products to carry and they may not carry every product from each producer. Once you identify courseware of interest or have actually tested and been pleased with a specific product, visit the website of the producer to explore other offerings. Although one quality product is no guarantee that all materials from that producer are equally good, it is a reasonable starting point for your broader search. Use your favorite search engine to locate producer websites, if your original source of information does not include the URL.

Finally, major software vendors routinely exhibit at national conferences (e.g., the National Educational Computing Conference) and also at those that are held in their region (e.g., the Illinois Technology Conference for Educators). Vendor exhibits are an excellent place to try out software of interest and to learn more about a company's products.

Most instructional software does not have the broad sales appeal that would place it on the shelves of a major software retailer. Some programs, however, do become popular well beyond schools. The *Carmen Sandiego* series, *Reader Rabbit*, and *The Oregon Trail* can be found in many retail stores. In addition, there are specialty firms that cater to the needs of educators for everything from bulletin-board materials to resource books and fancy chalk. Often such companies include computer products in their lines. If you have access to such a store, by all means visit it.

Advice of Colleagues

Another way to identify potentially appropriate courseware is to ask colleagues in other buildings or districts what their students are using and if they are satisfied with it. Do not rely on colleagues for much more than a pointer in the right direction, though, because what works for them may not be right for you. The key element must be effectiveness in promoting learning, and that is linked to curriculum. To what degree is your curriculum comparable to that of your colleague? Are your course objectives similar enough that you well might find the same courseware valuable? Does your colleague have any hard data on the educational value of the software? One of the most useful services your professional contacts can provide is to tell you which products to *avoid* rather than which ones you surely will want.

Published Reviews

At one time, it took some effort to locate software reviews. Today, professional journals and periodicals in most fields publish them, a reflection of the broad acceptance of computer-based learning. Start with the publications most relevant to your needs (e.g., *Arithmetic Teacher*), as any reviews that they publish will be for software in your broad area of interest. Computer-oriented educational publications such as *Learning and Leading with Technology* and *Technology & Learning* publish reviews of educational software in all content areas. Even consumer publications such as *PC Magazine* review educational products of particular note (e.g., *Carmen Sandiego*), although their real strength is thorough reviews and tests of hardware and tool software such as office suites and multimedia tools.

There are also many specialized resources to which educators can turn. *Educational Software Preview Guide* (Johnson, 2001) is an annual publication designed specifically to help educators identify materials worthy of preview. Products enter the guide only after passing stringent evaluations and remain from year to year only if they continue to receive high ratings. The Northwest Educational Technology Consortium <www.netc.org> provides easy access to many online review sources. Just select the Software Evaluation link. Among the resources is the California Instructional Technology Clearinghouse <http://clearinghouse.k12.ca.us>, a searchable database that allows the user to access reviews in the California Technology in the Curriculum Evaluations Database (Figure 12.3). K–12 math and science materials of all manner can be located through the Eisenhower National Clearinghouse at <www.enc.org/>. *Technology & Learning* magazine has a searchable database of its software reviews (Figure 12.4), which you can access at <www.techlearning.com/content/resources/product_guide>.

Of special note is the *Children's Software & New Media Review* (CSR), a bimonthly publication devoted to testing and reporting on learning materials for children. Each issue contains over 100 reviews. CSR prides itself on obtaining reviews only from educators, who are just as "picky" as you should be on behalf of your own students. When we last visited the site, it contained nearly 6,000 reviews. Check it out yourself at <www.childrenssoftware.com>.

Although reviews can be useful in identifying courseware for further evaluation, they are inadequate for making purchase decisions. One concern is the objectivity of the reviews. Look at several issues of the same review source, especially if it is one that carries producer advertising, to see whether only positive reviews are published. If so, can you determine whether this is because it is the best use of limited space in the publication, or just that this source likes everything? Who wrote the review? What are that individual's qualifications? Was the software actually tested with students? Could the review reflect only the producer's advertising campaign?

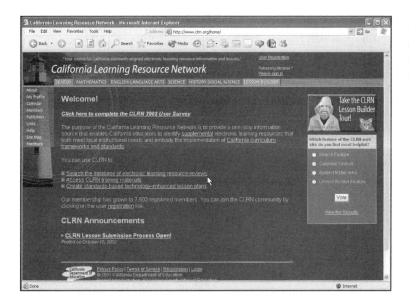

Figure 12.3

CALIFORNIA LEARNING
RESOURCE NETWORK
REVIEWS

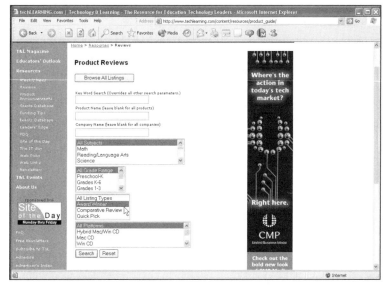

Figure 12.4

*TECHNOLOGY & LEARN-
ING'S* SEARCHABLE REVIEW
DATABASE

Another concern is the lack of accepted standards for reviews. Evaluation is not a science. For example, Jolicoeur and Berger (1986) found a low correlation between the overall ratings of two review services on the same 82 pieces of software. Most reviews are not based on actual student-performance achievement. Rather, they are one person's impression of the software and related materials. It is uncommon to find a review based on actual classroom testing or the experiences of multiple users of the package. Zahner et al. (1992) reported that software rated highly in *Only the Best* and *TESS* actually produced only modest learning gains when tested with students. Owston and Wideman (1987) found that trained evaluators rated software lower initially in about one-third of the cases than they did after field-testing the same software. Thus, objective testing with students may suggest different conclusions than initial subjective assessment.

Borton and Rossett (1989) found a major discrepancy between factors highly valued by teachers and those valued by software evaluators. Evaluators tended to focus on pedagogical concerns, such as content presentation, integration into curriculum, and how well the software uses the computer's capabilities. Teachers tended to value freedom from bugs and other operating difficulties above all, followed by content accuracy. The researchers believe this reflects the view of most teachers that the computer is strictly peripheral, meant to stand alone as a supplement or for enrichment. What, then, is the value of published reviews if they rest on factors other than those of most concern to teachers?

Hands-On Evaluation by Educators

Once you identify courseware of potential interest in your curriculum, you must actually try out the materials.

Obtain Courseware to Evaluate

Software producers develop products for one main reason—to earn a profit from sales. Because copying computer software is so simple, producers initially refused to allow previews and/or used software schemes to "copy protect" their products. Fortunately, most reputable software producers and distributors now understand that software must "fit" to be of use and that a bad purchase means a lost customer. Preview and return privileges, once rare, are now the norm. Educators must continue to insist on such access to courseware and refuse to buy what they have not seen in action. In turn, you must also scrupulously resist any temptation to copy software on loan or trial. (Software piracy is addressed in Chapter 15.)

Don't overlook the potential to review courseware yourself at a neighboring school where it is in use. A local community college, college, or university may have a courseware collection available to you. Some states support regional media or computer consortia with courseware collections for preview or loan. Become familiar with resources in your region.

Standardize the Evaluation

Once you obtain courseware to evaluate, you'll want to follow some guidelines in conducting the evaluation. This is especially true when multiple reviewers examine the same product and must compile their results. Evaluation forms, discussed in more detail later, serve this purpose.

Conduct the Evaluation

While the only real test of courseware is in the hands of students, initially you or a teacher committee should evaluate courseware to determine if it even merits testing with students. This can be very time consuming because of the number of criteria to consider and the fact that courseware is different from other educational materials. Educators have personal experience with most other educational materials, which provides a basis for judgments. Far fewer have used much instructional software. Furthermore, you cannot skim courseware as you would a textbook; rather, you must work your way through the content as a student would. You also need to examine any accompanying student and teacher guides, workbooks, activity sheets, and so on. The software review itself is the most time-consuming component, for which we recommend a three-step assessment.

First, go through the program as a high-achieving student might; that is, give relatively few incorrect responses along the way. This will demonstrate what the top students will experience and clearly show how the software treats correct responses. Keep track of how long it takes to complete the program in this way to approximate minimal student-use time.

Second, complete the lesson again, but as a low-achieving student might. This will demonstrate how the program handles incorrect responses and the branching provided. How much remediation is provided to a user having difficulty? Does the program just display the same screen again, or are there different approaches to the same content? What is the nature of the online help, if any? Record the time you spend with the program in this manner, which will be much longer than in the first trial.

Third, execute the lesson again, testing its ability to handle totally inappropriate responses. For instance, if the desired answer is numeric, enter letters or symbols, and vice versa. This must not cause the program to crash. What happens if you press just the "Enter" key without typing an answer? You should hear a beep or see a message to enter a valid response. This should never be accepted as a wrong answer. Can you find any "invisible" buttons that you can click to cause something unexpected to occur? It may seem trivial or absurd to test a program this way, but students delight in finding such "features" in software, which then detract from the learning experience. Good software handles accidental and malicious actions gracefully.

The next major section of this chapter reviews specific evaluation criteria.

Student Field-Testing: The Real Test

Most discussions of courseware evaluation stop at the "expert" review stage just described, assuming that such a subjective process will indeed identify appropriate products to purchase and use. However, if the ultimate criterion of quality is student learning, then only actual use with students can demonstrate the value of a product.

Reiser and Dick (1990) proposed a detailed model for software evaluation that focused primarily on student learning, not subjective judgments concerning content, accuracy, and so forth. It involved multiple levels of student testing and final ratings that depended on measured learning gains. In two pilot tests (see also Gill et al., 1992), the process proved impractical for teachers to use routinely, suggesting a need for a more efficient model. Zahner et al. (1992) reported on the simplified model, which reduced the time and number of students involved in the evaluation, but would it produce comparable results?

Two studies compared published ratings with ratings produced by the full model and the simplified model (Zahner et al., 1992). One used a tutorial selected from *Only the Best*, and the other used a tutorial that was highly rated in *TESS*. In the first case, the simplified model led to a different conclusion than the full model; in the second, the results were comparable. The researchers concluded they had yet to find a proven approach that was practical for the busy teacher, yet also accurate in its results. In neither study, however, did the software produce the high level of learning that one might expect from the glowing published reviews. Furthermore, Zahner et al. (1992) reported that teachers do not necessarily judge the value of software on learning achievement.

We believe student learning gains are the primary measure of worth in a software product. The process developed by Reiser, Dick, and their colleagues was idealistic but impractical. Instead, we suggest a simpler approach that summarizes this section of the chapter.

First, identify candidate software. Review it to determine whether it seems suitable. Then, if the software seems to have merit, try it out with your students. Assess what they have learned immediately and check retention after some delay. Also check student reactions to the program. Then make your decision about purchasing and using the product.

Evaluation Considerations

Perhaps the day will come when educators can turn to a review service that bases its evaluations on student learning outcomes. Better yet, producers should be accountable for the results their software produces. Evidence of effectiveness should be an expected part of each courseware product. For now at least, we must still rely on our own devices.

While traditional subjective evaluation has its flaws, many of the issues addressed by typical evaluations do have merit. They are not the final word on effectiveness, but neither should they be ignored. The following sections provide considerations for your own review phase or during student testing.

NETS
NOTES

NETS **T** I-A
NETS **T** I-B
NETS **T** II-A
NETS **T** II-C
NETS **T** III-A
NETS **T** IV-C
NETS **T** V-B
NETS **T** VI-C

Intended Use

A major aspect of identifying potential software is its match to your need. Although the same courseware may serve multiple goals, it may not be equally suited to all. Two teachers may evaluate the same courseware differently, based on different goals. What are the objectives for this part of your curriculum? Do you want courseware to address all of them? Do you really want something to help with those aspects that cause students the most trouble? Perhaps you want a supplement for students who are ready for more than you can offer the entire class. In other words, you determine what needs to be learned and then seek appropriate courseware.

Learning Theory

Theories of learning seek to explain how individuals learn or to identify factors that contribute to learning. You might evaluate courseware based on its inclusion of elements consistent with one or more learning theories. (See <http://tip.psychology.org> for a quick review of a large number of learning theories.)

The Nine Events of Instruction
One of the better-known learning theories is the classic nine events of instruction (Gagné and Briggs, 1974). Figure 12.5 adapts the nine events into a flowchart, showing how a

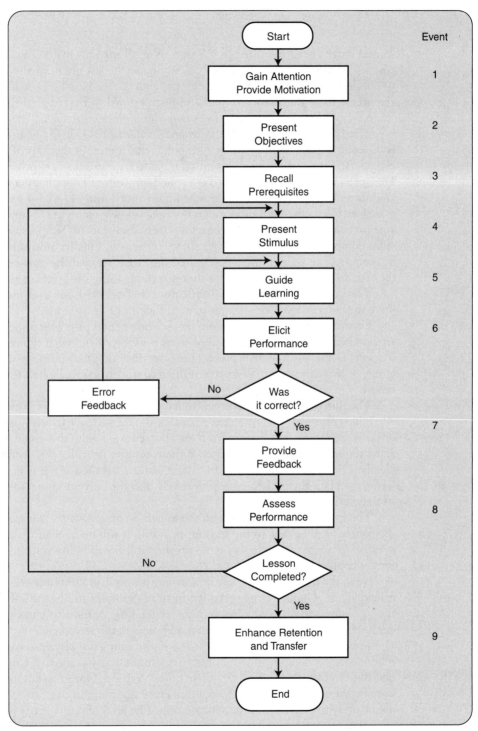

Figure 12.5 THE NINE EVENTS OF INSTRUCTION (BASED ON GAGNÉ AND BRIGGS, 1974)

learner might progress through a lesson. Not all nine events will be found in every courseware product, nor must they be. Some may be left intentionally for the teacher to develop with students before or after the courseware-based lesson. Keep the overall requirements of the lesson content and instructional format (e.g., drill, etc.) in mind when considering these criteria. Let's consider each one briefly.

The first event is to *gain attention and provide motivation*. One common approach is the colorful, animated graphics and sounds that appear at the start of most commercial courseware. Once student attention is gained, various features provide motivation. Having a *clear goal* to work toward is a sound motivator. Though not always appropriate, *competition* against the clock can be highly motivating. Look for a visual cue, such as a clock face, a digital display, or an hourglass slowly emptying. Many packages provide for competition against the computer or another student. Simple scorekeeping provides competition with oneself or against a criterion. Finally, motivation is enhanced by *challenge*, but only if effort is required (not too easy) yet the goal seems attainable (not too hard). Software may offer user-selectable difficulty levels or may adjust itself based on patterns of responses. If difficulty is self-selected, the user should be able to leave the current level for a less or more difficult one at any time.

Event two is to *present the objectives*. A fundamental principle of performance objectives is that the learner must know what is expected and what the result of the lesson will be. The software may present the objectives, they may be in the student learning guide, or perhaps you will just present them to students verbally before they begin the lesson.

The third event of instruction is to *recall prerequisite knowledge*. New learning usually builds on existing knowledge. Learners should review whatever prior knowledge or skills are required to benefit from the courseware. Again, this could be part of class activities before using the computer. If the computer provides this event, the software ideally should direct the learner to earlier materials if the learner is not ready for the lesson, or place the individual appropriately into the current lesson based on demonstrated mastery of components.

The lesson actually begins with the fourth event: *present the stimulus*. In a tutorial, the content will be new to the learner; in a drill, it will be familiar. A simulation must present the scenario. All lesson types must establish and follow a strategy appropriate for the content.

Next, the lesson should *guide the learning* (event five). Stimulus presentation alone is inadequate. Guidance may take the form of examples to illustrate the rule or concept, questions to probe the learner's understanding, or hints or clues available on request or provided automatically at certain points in the lesson.

The key aspect of interactivity is the sixth event: *elicit performance*. Books are excellent conveyors of information, but they cannot demand activity. Courseware poses questions frequently to which the learner must respond. One great advantage of courseware is that each learner must respond to every question, in contrast to the occasional opportunity to respond in group instruction. The level of interactivity is a critical benefit of courseware.

Event seven acknowledges that following a performance, any form of instruction should *provide feedback*. A major problem of typical homework assignments is that the student may not learn of errors until the next school day or even later. Courseware typically provides feedback to every question. You should consider carefully the quality of this feedback. Related to this is whether the learner is allowed multiple tries per question and, if so, whether the number permitted is appropriate. Courseware that traps the learner until a correct response is made is likely to destroy the motivation of a learner having difficulty with the lesson.

Though not an event in the model, *reinforcement* is closely related to feedback. Feedback entails knowing that a response was correct or incorrect, or its ramifications. Reinforcement takes two forms. One is to provide the correct answer for the learner. This should occur regardless of how the learner responded. Feedback and reinforcement often are combined in a form such as, "That's correct. A mammal nurses its young." The second form of reinforcement is to praise a job well done or encourage the learner to continue. Psychologists have studied various levels and schedules of reinforcement, but their findings often are ignored in courseware. Reinforcement tends either to be absent or appear for every item.

The eighth event is to *assess performance*. Learners need to know their progress toward the criterion as they study a lesson. This provides a feeling of accomplishment and adds to motivation. For a timed lesson, a timer onscreen may serve the purpose. A scoreboard showing the number of correct responses also works. To stress achievement, it may be best to report only the number of correct responses and wait until a final summation to list the number of errors or percentage correct. Other methods that provide some assessment, but also encourage the learner, are special displays at specific points in the lesson such as halfway, a periodic report of the number of items completed, or a countdown toward the end. Many students are encouraged more by knowing only 2 items remain than that they have completed 98!

The ninth and final event of instruction is to *promote retention and transfer*. Neither should be assumed in any lesson. Instead, explicit provision should exist to enhance both. Within the lesson, this might be user-selectable enrichment activities after mastering basic content or the option to request further practice. Simulations and newer interactive multimedia courseware often provide for concurrent on-computer and off-computer activities, such as data-recording forms to help students organize data, analyze results, and determine appropriate actions for the next session at the computer. Interactive multimedia courseware often includes directions to jot down points using an online notepad, which can be saved or printed for further study. In addition, do not overlook the need to promote retention and transfer after the computer lesson. Many products contain suggested follow-up activities. Modify or add to these lists as you deem appropriate. This is a vital element in integrating the computer into the curriculum, one often lacking in schools.

Specific Criteria

Beyond the general concerns of intended use and evidence of application of learning theory, a wide range of evaluation factors can and should be considered. There is no standard list of such factors, so we have combined ideas from various sources in three major categories: general instructional criteria, CAI-specific criteria, and usability.

General Instructional Criteria

This category covers broad concerns for *all* educational materials, whether print, traditional media, or computer format.

1. *Is the content accurate?* Obviously, errors in fact are unacceptable. Content accuracy, however, may be relative. For example, a simulation such as *SimEarth* or any of several based on elections may be difficult to assess in terms of accuracy. The purpose of such programs is less to convey content than to stimulate analysis of the context presented, to raise questions for discussion, and to allow testing of strategies. Adherence to "reality" is not crucial to these goals. Likewise, a simplified business simulation may not be "accurate" enough for older students, but it could suffice as an introduction to business principles for young children. "Accuracy" may vary with the learning objectives and student level in some cases.

2. *Is the instructional strategy pedagogically sound? Appropriate? Creative?* Would you use such a strategy yourself? Does it clearly enhance the lesson? Does it support your teaching approach?

3. *Is the material free of violent or aggressive behavior and all bias, including gender and race?* You might expect this to be a given, but in a scathing critique of the popular *Oregon Trail* software, Bigelow (1997) makes the case that it is sexist, racist, and culturally insensitive.

4. *Are the objectives clearly stated and reasonable?* With courseware, often no objectives are specified, or they are general and low level, perhaps a result of claims that some packages fit all users from preschool through adult!

5. *Are the objectives important to the curriculum?* If a courseware product does not fit the curriculum, does it offer so much that you would change the curriculum to fit it?

6. *Is the interest and readability level appropriate for your audience?* Do not rely on the publisher's claims for audience suitability. Test readability yourself.

7. *Is the material free of grammatical errors, typos, and misspellings?* The infallible image of the computer might well reinforce language errors as correct usage.

8. *Are instructions clear and correct?* Users should never wonder what's next.

9. *Is the overall difficulty level appropriate for your learners?*

10. *Does the software promote student creativity, higher-order thinking, and problem solving?*

11. *Does the package appear to offer good value for the price?* Important here may be the versatility of a given product. In how many different courses or grades could it be used? Will it fit only a brief period of instruction in one grade? Are there both remedial and enrichment applications that extend usability? A costly graphing program may find wider usage in mathematics than an inexpensive tutorial on a specific topic, for example. Price alone is an inadequate criterion.

12. *Does the software appropriately treat ethical, cultural, and social issues, including diversity?*

13. *Does this package support learning goals defined by local, state, and national standards for both content areas and technology?*

CAI-Specific Criteria

The unique qualities of courseware require evaluation criteria that are not applicable to other educational materials.

1. *Does the package take advantage of the computer's capabilities?* What does it offer that students could not previously do? (That is, is this a Type II application?)

2. *Is this a more effective or efficient approach to the content than any other?* Or is it really another case of print materials converted to the computer screen?

3. *Is the sequence of the presentation appropriate?* Is it compatible with your approach to the topic or are you willing to change? Remember, with a book or set of transparencies you can alter the sequence if you wish. There is often less potential to do so with computer materials.

4. *Does the learner control the pace and/or sequence of the presentation?* Is there a menu of choices or does the computer adjust the sequence to fit user response patterns? Can the user back up in the program to review? Are displays changed by user action or are they timed? The programmer should not presume to know how long an individual needs to read any screen.

5. *What is the level of interaction?* How much must the student read before making a more meaningful response than just pressing the space bar or clicking the mouse to continue? Do not accept "electronic page turners" that will not engage the learner.

6. *Can the student exit the program before the end is reached?* If so, are the directions for exiting clear and easy to remember? Better yet, are they given on the screen whenever it is possible to exit? Can the student later reenter the program at the point of exit, or is it necessary to start all over again?

7. *Is the program designed for only one student at a time, or does it encourage group activities?* Many persons are concerned that the computer could decrease student socialization if all activities are individual. Could you use this program as a group activity with only one computer?

8. *If there are pretests and posttests, do they appear to be valid?* Do all "tests" actually measure learning progress?

9. *Is feedback to responses appropriate?* Does the feedback help the learner to understand the cause of an error or just say it was wrong? Feedback should never demean or belittle the user, regardless of the error.

10. *Is feedback effective?* Some programs provide more attractive feedback for wrong answers than correct ones, especially in graphics. This may encourage students to give wrong answers just to see what happens.

11. *Are graphics supportive of the learning process?* Or are they merely window dressing? Graphics, including animation, can readily enhance the appeal of a program, but they should also provide visual learning.

12. *If sound or video is used, does it serve a helpful purpose?* Auditory cues when a user has made an error can be very helpful, but musical tunes can become an annoyance in a classroom or a lab. Can the sound be turned off? Is the video important or just entertaining? Does it play smoothly at an adequate viewing size or is it small and jerky?

13. *Do verbal responses require more than minimal typing?* If so, typing skill or spelling may be as much a key to success as knowledge or analytic thinking.

14. *Do all typed responses require clicking a button or pressing the "Enter" key when finished?* If not, users can become confused. When is a concrete response needed, and when is it not? Why the distinction?

15. *Is the program "bombproof"?* Can the user give responses that cause the program to crash? Students will find such problems if you do not.

Usability Criteria

Various factors make one product easier to use than another. Consider usability from both the teacher's and the learner's perspectives.

Teacher Perspective

1. *Can you integrate the courseware easily into your instruction?* What support materials are provided, including web links? How appropriate and useful do they appear to be? Are both teacher and student manuals available, if appropriate? Are there worksheets or study guides? Are suggested activities and references to related materials included? The more assistance is provided, the easier the package will be to incorporate into instruction. That is the difference between courseware and just software. Figure 12.6 shows examples.

2. *Is there a recordkeeping or management component?* If so, what does it record, and how complex is it to use?

3. *Can you (or students) modify the program?* Most teachers lack the time and knowledge to tamper with a program and make major changes. However, drill programs

Figure 12.6

Courseware should include ample support materials.

become more versatile if you are able to enter or change the content of the drill, altering, say, a weekly spelling list. This is usually achieved through a utility program provided with the package. If this option exists, how difficult is it to enter your material?

4. *How manageable is the program's flexibility?* This is an issue with interactive multimedia. How will you guide student usage for varying goals? How will you know what (or if) your students have learned?

Student Perspective

1. *Can the software be used with little or no teacher intervention?* Are all directions presented onscreen, or must the user keep a manual at hand for guidance? Manuals are not necessarily less effective, just more cumbersome. On the other hand, printed manuals allow skimming or bypassing information for quick access to what one is seeking. In classroom settings, wall charts of directions can also be effective. Preparing them could be a worthwhile student project.

2. *How difficult is it for a student to get started?* Some packages with management components require elaborate log-on procedures.

3. *Does the package require diskette handling or CD swapping?* Especially with younger students, it is desirable to avoid student contact with the software medium as much as possible. Networked software eliminates this potential problem.

4. *Is there provision for use of alternative input devices that could make the package more usable for special needs populations?*

5. *How helpful is the "HELP" function, if available at all?*

For other perspectives on courseware evaluation, we suggest the following resources: Bader (2000); Buckleitner (1999); Buckleitner, Orr, and Wolock (2002); Case and Truscott (1999); Childress, Lee, and Sherman (1999); Dolowy (2000); Gibbs, Graves, and Bernas (2001); Goyne, McDonough, and Padgett (2000); Hall and Martin (1999); Hosie and Schibeci (2001); Luckin (2001); Marshall and Hillman (2000); Nisanci (2000); Pan and Carroll (2002); Polonoli (2000); and Ruberg (2001).

Using and Creating Evaluation Forms

Courseware evaluation is multifaceted and complex. The time required simply to review a package to decide whether to test it with students can be significant. Any evaluation approach may fail to reveal some aspects of a program, especially a simulation or today's complex hypermedia. The more sophisticated the courseware, the less certainty there is that you will ever see all of it. How can you at least get a handle on your task?

| NETS
| NOTES

NETS **T** I-A
NETS **T** I-B
NETS **T** II-B
NETS **T** II-C
NETS **T** III-A
NETS **T** III-B

The most common answer is to use an evaluation form or rubric. Such a form assures some level of attention to key factors, as well as a common base for all evaluations that you undertake. Evaluation forms abound in the literature, with variations appearing regularly. Each form has its own predilections, revealing its creator's biases. Any given one may or may not suit your needs.

NETS
NOTES

NETS **T** IV-C

NETS **T** V-B

NETS **T** VI-B

NETS **T** VI-C

One Approach to Evaluation

Because evaluation is inherently specific to a given setting, we believe that you should ultimately develop an instrument that addresses your own major concerns. However, it may be useful to start with a sample evaluation form. This will give you some idea of the kind of approach that is commonly employed.

We suggest that there are minimally four aspects of any package that need to be included in an evaluation form. They are basic descriptive notes plus the three specific criteria areas previously discussed. Taken together, they can yield an instrument such as Figure 12.7. We show this in the common checklist format, which is often favored because of its simplicity and ease of use. When evaluating any instructional software, each reviewer completes one copy of the form for each product under review. The selection group compiles the completed forms, reviews the data and summary comments, then reaches a decision.

Although much of this form should be self-explanatory, some of the items in the Description section may not be, so here is what they mean. Most useful descriptive information comes directly from the resources you used to identify the package initially or from the product literature. The item CAI Format means the producer's *claim* that the package is a simulation, tutorial, or whatever. Distribution medium means whether the product is distributed on CD-ROM, DVD, or via Internet download. The producer's backup or replacement and upgrade policies usually are explained in the documentation or on the producer's website. It is critical to have a backup copy of any software, just as it is for your own personal files. It is also important to consider whether there will be a discounted price for current users when a new version is released or a new operating system renders your current version obsolete. This is the producer's upgrade policy.

Compatibility starts with whether the product is available for more than one type of computer. Even if your school has only one type currently, say Macintosh, this could change and you would likely want to acquire the same software for the new type. Record this information for possible future use. Also note which operating system versions are supported, whether there are specific hardware requirements (CPU speed, amount of RAM, and/or hard drive space), and whether the product can be run on a network. Is some other software required to use the product, such as a specific database or graphics package?

Finally, if you read one or more reviews of the product, note the sources for future reference or save a copy of the published review with your local reviews.

A more thorough (and complex) approach to evaluation is the software evaluation checklist used by the Kent (WA) school district <www.kent.k12.wa.us/KSD/IT/TSC/ITRC/tools/soft_eval_summary.pdf>, which is to be completed in conjunction with a very detailed rubric <www.kent.k12.wa.us/KSD/IT/TSC/ITRC/process/ITRCprocess.htm> that gives specific meaning to the various criteria and their ratings. Each listed criterion is described in terms unique to the item under the headings "makes an excellent (good or minimal) case for recommendation." The form has six sections: curriculum content, instructional design for learners, program design, assessment, instructional support materials, and technical support materials. The content of this rubric is among the most extensive we have ever seen for evaluating instructional software and reflects a major effort on the part of the district to take software selection very seriously. There

Courseware Evaluation Form

Date of Review _____ Name of Reviewer _____

Description

Product Name _____ CAI Format _____
Content Area _____ Age/Grade level _____
Producer _____
Distribution Medium _____
Backup Policy _____
Upgrade Policy _____
Compatibility _____
Available from (full contact information) _____
_____
Price (each, pack of N, etc.) _____
Reviewed in _____

	Rating	Superior (3 pts)	Adequate (2 pts)	Marginal (1 pt)	Inadequate (0 pts)
General Instructional Criteria					
Content accuracy					
Instructional strategies					
Appropriate treatment of diversity					
Free of language errors					
Clear instructions					
Appropriate difficulty level(s)					
Designed or adaptable for cooperative learning					
Correlates to desired standards					
CAI-Specific Criteria					
Takes good advantage of computer power					
Appropriate sequence of instruction					
High level of interactivity					
Effective learning guidance					
Multimedia elements support learning goals					
Works correctly without glitches or crashes					
Easy to use interface					
Usability Criteria					
Will fit curriculum easily					
Useful recordkeeping component					
Students will need minimal assistance to use					
Help function is useful					
Flexible but manageable					
Group or individual use potential					

Summary Comments _____
_____
_____
_____

Figure 12.7 SAMPLE COURSEWARE EVALUATION FORM

is even a sample form for students to complete to express their views on specific software. We encourage you to take a careful look at these materials.

Other evaluation instruments are available in abundance, should you care to review the widely varied approaches taken. An Internet search for software evaluation forms will yield many results. You may also wish to review sources such as Anderson and Speck (2001, pp. 112–113), Forcier and Descy (2002, pp. 122–130), Morrison and Lowther (2002, pp. 330–332), and Roblyer (2003, pp. 106–112). McVee and Dickson (2002) offer a rubric for primary literacy software.

Creating an Evaluation Form

The goal of an evaluation form is to organize the maze of factors and concerns in some coherent and manageable way. Otherwise, the task quickly becomes overwhelming. At the same time, there is a tendency to view a form as some relatively simple, highly quantifiable, and totally accurate wonder. Just make checks where a quality is observed, leave blank all others, tally the checks, and voilà: a good or bad product has been found.

The Kent School District combination of a summary form and a detailed rubric makes clear that evaluation is not a quick and dirty process if you are serious about making the best possible selection. This district shares our view that the most useful form is one that includes the primary concerns of the evaluator, be that an individual or a team. Therefore, we recommend that anyone setting out to evaluate courseware consider developing a personal, school, or district form for the purpose. The form should begin with basic descriptive information, followed by elements from each of the three broad categories. Exactly which elements are included will vary depending on your own needs and views, perhaps even the type of courseware. Figure 12.8 offers only an outline and leaves it to you, the user, to include as many elements as you choose from the suggestions in this chapter and other resources.

Description
Review the explanation of descriptive items provided along with the sample form in this chapter. They offer a starting point for gathering the most basic objective information about any product under consideration.

Category Criteria
Review the many criteria discussed previously in this chapter. Include as many in each of the three categories as you think important. Our skeletal form is not meant to suggest a specific number of criteria; rather, it allows the flexibility to use as few or as many as you wish. Add others from additional sources as desired.

Adding a Rating Scale
Once you have chosen your criteria, you have the basis of a simple checklist evaluation form. What is the meaning, however, of a series of checks? We suggest quantifying your assessment by using some scale. You might rate each item as Outstanding, Acceptable, or Unacceptable, assigning 3, 2, or 1 points, respectively. Devise a scale that you like. The verbal meaning need not be identical for every item, as long as the relative point values remain consistent. A sum of these values will quantify your assessment.

Courseware Evaluation Form

Date of Review _____ Name of Reviewer _____

<u>Description</u>

Product Name _____ CAI Format _____

Content Area _____ Age/Grade level _____

Producer _____

Distribution Medium _____

Backup Policy _____

Upgrade Policy _____

Compatibility _____

Available from (full contact information) _____

_____

Price (each, pack of N, etc.) _____

Reviewed in _____

<u>General Instructional Criteria</u>

Criterion	Rating	×	Weight	=	Total Pts.
_____	_____		_____		_____
_____	_____		_____		_____
_____	_____		_____		_____

<u>CAI Specific Criteria</u>

Criterion	Rating	×	Weight	=	Total Pts.
_____	_____		_____		_____
_____	_____		_____		_____
_____	_____		_____		_____

<u>Usability Criteria</u>

Criterion	Rating	×	Weight	=	Total Pts.
_____	_____		_____		_____
_____	_____		_____		_____
_____	_____		_____		_____

Grand total points for this package _____

<u>Overall Assessment</u>

Holistic reaction to the package: _____

_____

_____

Instructional strategy (from the Learner-Centered Taxonomy): Circle the appropriate item in each column.

<u>Metacognition Source</u>	<u>Primary Cognitive Processes</u>	<u>Content Presentation</u>
Program Initiated	Organizing	Domain Oriented
Guided	Rehearsal	Topic Oriented
Learner Initiated	Assessment (Response Organization)	Operation Oriented

Application Potential (circle one):   Type II   Type I only

Recommendation:
  Excellent. Purchase without field test
  Good. Proceed with field test
  Fair. Marginal, field-test only if no better alternative
  Poor. Insufficient merit to field-test

<u>Field-test data summary:</u>

Figure 12.8 TEMPLATE FOR A COURSEWARE EVALUATION FORM

Adding Weights

Going a step further, it is unlikely that all listed criteria are of equal importance to you. Weight each in some manner. In most cases, assigning a weight from 3 (most important) to 1 (least important) will suffice. Adding a numerical value to your rating categories and multiplying your assessment by the weight for that item yields a potential score of 9 (outstanding and most important) to 1 (unacceptable and least important). A final sum of these values yields an "objective" picture of the package's merits for your situation.

Overall Assessment

After completing the first parts of the evaluation form, briefly write your overall reaction to the courseware. Think about the merits of the product by classifying its instructional strategy according to the learner-centered taxonomy that you learned about in Chapter 10. The source of metacognition is particularly important. Is the program controlling the learning (program initiated), is the program guiding the learner (guided metacognition), or is the learner in control (learner initiated)?

Your final recommendation may be wholehearted endorsement without further ado, a decision to proceed with a student field test to determine instructional effectiveness, or rejection of the product as unsuited to your needs and interests.

Exactly how you go about a field test is up to you. The critical point is to measure the learning gain derived from the software. Record at least a summary of your field-test results right on your form to complete the record.

Using Your Form

In general, once you have created a form to your liking, using it for any specific product should pose no problems. To guard against overreliance on the quantifiable data, complete your narrative assessment and classification by the learner-centered taxonomy *before* you tally the rating numbers. Indicate whether the software clearly promotes a Type I or Type II experience. You may be willing to take more of a chance with Type II courseware than you can justify for Type I. Within each criteria category, do not reject a product based solely on concerns with one or a few items. Consider omissions or weaknesses in the total context of what the product provides and how well it fits your need. You should compare your holistic reaction with the "hard data" from the numbers and consider their respective merits. The more experience you develop in examining software and using it with your students, the more valid your subjective view is apt to be. Still, it is the field-test data that should be the final determiner of whether to use a product widely with your students.

SUMMARY

With appropriate and effective courseware, the computer can become an integral part of the learning process. It can assume a portion of the teaching responsibility, becoming a student's private tutor. In turn, this may free the teacher to spend more time with individual students. However, to achieve such a goal assumes the availability of excellent courseware.

The first step in courseware selection is identification of potentially useful products. Catalogs and dealers, colleagues, and published reviews are all useful at this stage. Next, you should do a hands-on evaluation of candidate courseware to determine whether it is worth testing with students. Some CAI software is of little or no instructional value, and you may be able to eliminate many packages through your own preliminary assessment. The ultimate value of instructional courseware, however, is the student learning to which it contributes. Evaluation of effectiveness requires student field-testing, something developers infrequently do.

During your own initial screening, as well as during field-testing, there are so many potential evaluation considerations that they may appear impossible to manage. An evaluation form can help to assure that no vital point is overlooked and to provide a common framework for the work of multiple reviewers. It seems best that individuals, schools, or districts develop a form that addresses their own major concerns, rather than simply adopt one that seeks to serve all. If you alone are responsible for evaluating software, you will find that you can make holistic judgments more readily and comfortably as you gain experience in evaluating courseware and in using it with students.

Despite efforts to streamline the process, courseware evaluation, if done conscientiously, will always be a time-consuming task, much more so than teachers are accustomed to in selecting other materials. If the computer, however, is to live up to its potential to contribute to learning, this task cannot be ignored or minimized. The quality of materials and curriculum fit will determine whether the computer achieves its potential as an indispensable element in the educational process or joins earlier technological marvels in the school storeroom.

chapter 12
activities

1. Locate several published reviews of courseware to which you have access. Without first reading the reviews, conduct your own evaluation of the package. Compare your findings with the reviews. What does this exercise suggest about the value of "professional" reviews?

2. Use the software evaluation form provided in Figure 12.7 to guide your review of at least five products. Based on that experience, what are the strengths and weaknesses of the form? How would you modify it to better suit your needs, experience, content field, and so on?

3. Starting with the outline model of an evaluation form shown in Figure 12.8, complete the form by adding the criteria most important to you, your school, or district. (Expand the space devoted to categories as you wish.) Try to balance a desire for thoroughness with concern for the time it will take to use your instrument.

4. Compare your evaluation form with those of your colleagues and classmates. Discuss the reasons you each selected different elements to include.

5. In groups of at least three persons, try to create a common form acceptable to all, much as a school or district committee would. What did you have to give up from *your* list of important elements to reach consensus while

avoiding a ten-page instrument? Did your negotiations cause you to rethink the merits of certain possible items?

6. Using your instrument, critically evaluate at least one courseware product in each of as many different categories (e.g., drill, simulation) as you can.

7. Using your instrument, evaluate three or more courseware products intended for the same or similar instructional use. Does your "objective" assessment agree with your holistic view of these packages? If not, why? Does your form require modification?

8. Organize a project to contact producers of the software to which you have access to request student field-test data. Compare your results with those of Zane and Frazer (1992) reported earlier in this chapter. If you do get a positive response, refer to Smith (1988) for guidance in evaluating claims.

9. Evaluate at least one courseware package solely on the basis of Gagné's events of instruction. From this theoretical perspective, does the package appear to be effective? If you could find no evidence of one or more events, is the omission justifiable in this case?

Companion Website

Visit the companion website at <www.ablongman.com/lockard6e> for more information about the topics discussed in this chapter.

expect the world®

The New York Times
nytimes.com

Themes of the Times

Expand your knowledge of the concepts discussed in this chapter by reading current and historical articles from the *New York Times* by visiting the Themes of the Times section of the companion website <www.ablongman.com/lockard6e>.

References

Anderson, R. S., and Speck, B. W. *Using Technology in K–8 Literacy Classrooms.* Upper Saddle River, NJ: Merrill Prentice Hall, 2001.

ASCD. *Only the Best: The Annual Guide to the Highest-Rated Educational Software and Multimedia.* ASCD 1999–2000. Association for Supervision and Curriculum References.

Bader, M. J. "Choosing CALL Software: Beginning the Evaluation Process." *TESOL Journal,* Summer 2000, *9*(2), pp. 18–22.

Bigelow, B. "On the Road to Cultural Bias: A Critique of 'The Oregon Trail' CD-ROM." *Language Arts,* February 1997, *74*(2), pp. 84–93.

Bork, A. "Education and Computers: The Situation Today and Some Possible Futures." *T.H.E. Journal,* October 1984, pp. 92–97.

Borton, W., and Rossett, A. "Educational Software and Published Reviews: Congruence of Teacher, Developer, and Evaluator Perceptions." *Education,* Summer 1989, *109*(4), pp. 434–444.

Buckleitner, W. "The State of Children's Software Evaluation—Yesterday, Today, and in the 21st Century." *Information Technology in Childhood Education Annual*, 1999, pp. 211–220.

Buckleitner, W., Orr, A., and Wolock, E. *Complete Sourcebook on Children's Interactive Media.* Logan Township, NJ: Association of Education Publishers, 2002.

Case, C., and Truscott, D. M. "The Lure of Bells and Whistles: Choosing the Best Software to Support Reading Instruction." *Reading & Writing Quarterly: Overcoming Learning Difficulties*, October–December 1999, *15*(4), pp. 361–369.

Childress, M. D., Lee, G., and Sherman, G. P. "Reviewing Software as a Means of Enhancing Instruction." *Information Technology in Childhood Education Annual*, 1999, pp. 255–261.

Dolowy, B. "Educators Share Ideas about Software for Children—Educational Tool or Inappropriate Activity." *Child Care Information Exchange*, November–December 2000, *136*, pp. 76–78.

Forcier, R. C., and Descy, D. E. *The Computer as an Educational Tool. Productivity and Problem Solving*, 3rd ed. Upper Saddle River, NJ: Merrill Prentice Hall, 2002.

Gagné, R. M., and Briggs, L. J. *Principles of Instructional Design.* New York: Holt, Rinehart, and Winston, 1974.

Gibbs, W., Graves, P. R., and Bernas, R. S. "Educational Guidelines for Multimedia Courseware." *Journal of Research on Technology in Education*, Fall 2001, *34*(1), pp. 2–17.

Gill, B., Dick, W., Reiser, R., and Zahner, J. E. "A New Model for Evaluating Instructional Software." *Educational Technology*, March 1992, *32*(3), pp. 39–44.

Goyne, J. S., McDonough, S. K., and Padgett, D. D. "Practical Guidelines for Evaluating Educational Software." *Clearing House*, July–August 2000, *73*(6), pp. 345–348.

Hall, V. G., and Martin, L. E. "Making Decisions about Software for Classroom Use." *Reading Research & Instruction*, Spring 1999, *38*(3), pp. 187–196.

Hoffman, J. L., and Lyons, D. J. "Evaluating Instructional Software." *Learning and Leading with Technology*, October 1997, *25*(2), pp. 52–56.

Hosie, P., and Schibeci, R. "Evaluating Courseware: A Need for More Context Bound Evaluations?" *Australian Educational Computing*, October 2001, *16*(2), pp. 18–26.

Johnson, J. M. "Evaluating Educational Technology Resources." *Learning and Leading with Technology*, April 1998, *25*(7), pp. 43–50.

Johnson, J. M., ed. *2001 Educational Software Preview Guide.* Eugene, OR: International Society for Technology in Education, 2001.

Jolicoeur, K., and Berger, D. E. "Do We Really Know What Makes Educational Software Effective? A Call for Empirical Research on Effectiveness." *Educational Technology*, December 1986, *26*(12), pp. 7–11.

Luckin, R. "Designing Children's Software to Ensure Productive Interactivity through Collaboration in the Zone of Proximal Development (ZPD)." *Information Technology in Childhood Education Annual*, 2001, pp. 57–85.

Maddux, C. D., Johnson, D. L., and Willis, J. W. *Educational Computing: Learning with Tomorrow's Technologies*, 2nd ed. Boston: Allyn and Bacon, 1997.

Marshall, J., and Hillman, M. *Effective Curricular Software Selection for K–12 Educators.* ERIC Document Reproduction Service, ED 444468, 2000.

McVee, M. B., and Dickson, B. A. "Creating a Rubric to Examine Literacy Software for the Primary Grades." *Reading Teacher*, April 2002, *55*(7), pp. 635–639.

Morrison, G. R., and Lowther, D. L. *Integrating Computer Technology into the Classroom*, 2nd ed. Upper Saddle River, NJ: Merrill Prentice Hall, 2002.

Neill, S. B., and Neill, G. W. *Only the Best, 1993: The Annual Guide to Highest-Rated Educational Software/Multimedia for Preschool–Grade 12.* Carmichael, CA: Educational News Service, 1993.

Nisanci, M. *Instructional Software Evaluation Criteria Used by the Teachers: Implications from Theory to Practice.* ERIC Document Reproduction Service, ED 444534, 2000.

Owston, R. D., and Wideman, H. H. "The Value of Supplemental Panel Software Reviews with Field Observation." *Canadian Journal of Educational Communication*, 1987, *16*, pp. 295–308.

Pan, A. C., and Carroll, S. Z. "Preservice Teachers Explore Instructional Software with Children." *Educational Forum*, Summer 2002, *66*(4), pp. 371–379.

Polonoli, K. E. "What Makes Educational Software Educational?" ERIC Document Reproduction Service, ED 453827, 2000.

Reiser, R., and Dick, W. "Evaluating Instructional Software." *Educational Technology Research and Development*, 1990, *38*(3), pp. 43–50.

Roblyer, M. D. *Integrating Educational Technology into Teaching*. Columbus, OH: Merrill Prentice Hall, 2003.

Ruberg, Laurie F. *Evaluation of Program Impact Based on Teacher Implementation and Student Performance*. ERIC Document Reproduction Service, ED 466208, 2001.

Smith, R. A. "Claims of Improved Academic Performance: The Questions You Should Ask." *The Computing Teacher*, May 1988, *15*(8), pp. 42–44, 61.

Wenglinsky, H. *Does It Compute? The Relationship Between Educational Technology and Student Achievement in Mathematics*. Princeton, NJ: Educational Testing Service, 1998. Available online at <www.ets.org/rsearch/pic/technolog.html>

Zahner, J. E., Reiser, R. A., Dick, W., and Gill, B. "Evaluating Instructional Software: A Simplified Model." *Educational Technology Research and Development*, 1992, *40*(3), pp. 55–62.

Zane, T., and Frazer, C. G. "The Extent to Which Software Developers Validate Their Claims." *Journal of Research on Computing in Education*, Spring 1992, *24*(3), pp. 410–419.

Beyond Computer Literacy: *Technology Integration and Curriculum Transformation*

OBJECTIVES

After completing this chapter, you will be able to:

- Outline common computer literacy models.
- Differentiate infusion from integration.
- Discuss computer integration concepts.
- Assess issues involved in considering significant curricular changes.
- Persuasively argue your own view concerning the proper model for computers in education.

The growth and acceptance of microcomputers in education has been little short of spectacular. It is both a cause and an effect: a result of new ideas for application and, in many cases, a stimulus for new ideas, as well as a prod to educators to find ways to use these devices. This is the Information Age, where computer technology pervades our lives, and the schools alone may be responsible for preventing generations of *techno-peasants*, a term coined many years ago by Collis (1988).

In the preceding chapters you learned about major uses of computers in education, the "what" of instructional computing. Now let's turn to the "why" and "how" to provide perspective on the evolution of computer use in schools (this chapter) and to explore practical concerns for implementation (Chapter 14) and some of the critical issues related to technology in education (Chapter 15).

Roblyer (2003) speaks of the need to develop a sound rationale for technology in our schools. This chapter chronicles the search for that rationale from the beginning.

You have learned about major uses of computers in earlier chapters. Now you will focus on the questions: "How can we actually deal with computers in our schools? What roles have educators defined for computers in the classroom?" Let's consider two major categories: *computer literacy* and *curriculum integration*.

Computer Literacy

NETS
NOTES

NETS **T** II–B
NETS **T** II–E
NETS **T** III–B
NETS **T** III–C
NETS **T** V–B

Computer literacy became a buzzword in education around 1980, and it has been a topic of controversy (Jonassen, 2000). Inherent in the idea is that some body of fundamental knowledge and skills regarding computers exists that *all* members of society should possess. A literate citizenry has long been an unquestioned goal; the computer is merely a new component. As Luehrmann (1983, p. 29) stated early on, "The ability to use computers is as basic and necessary to a person's formal education as reading, writing, and arithmetic." Disagreement about the meaning of "use" is the major concern, not whether there is a need for such literacy. Indeed, basic concern for computer literacy is worldwide and in some parts of the world, December 2 is designated as World Computer Literacy Day (see <www.worldcomputerliteracy.net>).

Central to the arguments has been the issue of computer programming. At one end of a continuum are those who have argued strongly that some programming skill is essential if an individual is to be considered computer literate. At the other end are those who view programming as completely unnecessary. Rather, one must be able to *use* computers and application software. In between come various compromises, and some definitions are all-encompassing. Regardless of the position on the continuum, we classify as computer literacy all models that *focus on the computer* rather than the curriculum.

The Programming Model

When the first microcomputers entered the schools in the late 1970s, there was practically no software available for them. Usually a science or math teacher was the first to attempt to use the new device, probably because those teachers were the most likely to have had some contact with computers during their teacher preparation. That contact nearly always meant programming. With such a background and no software, naturally the microcomputer was used for programming instruction.

Arthur Luehrmann, the father of computer literacy, was a vocal advocate of programming as the heart of computer literacy. Luehrmann (1982, p. 20) wrote, "To tell a computer what you want to do, you must be able to communicate with it. To do that, you will need to learn a language for writing your ideas down so that you can review them, show them to others, and improve them." He stressed that computer literacy meant the ability to do something constructive with a computer, not just possess a general awareness of computer capabilities. A computer-literate person can write and interpret a computer program, can select and operate software written by others, and knows from personal experience what a computer is and is not capable of doing. For many educators, literacy and programming became synonymous, which probably contributed to much teacher technophobia. By the way, Luehrmann went on to found Computer Literacy Press to publish materials related to computer literacy.

The Literacy Curriculum Model

Slowly the literacy definition broadened to become units or classes at all grade levels (Moersch, 1995), a K–12 curriculum for computer literacy instruction that included four components. Let's consider each one briefly.

Survival skills are skills that anyone must master to work effectively on a computer. They include knowing how to boot a computer, handle diskettes and optical disks, start up software packages, and use the keyboard and mouse. Such low-level skills are important for *all* persons who use a computer. These skills remain basic to the NETS standards today. They are analogous to such basic driving skills as inserting the key into the ignition, turning the key, checking mirrors, and so on.

Computer awareness pertains to knowledge and skills that help us better understand what a computer can and cannot do. Awareness of how computers are used in our society, the misuses of computers, and computer ethics are topics that should receive attention. Future trends and developments in computer technology could also be dealt with under this category. See <http://tdi.uregina.ca/~complit>, the Computer Literacy Repository, as a current resource example.

Application skills include word processing, the use of database management programs, and spreadsheets. This category emphasizes the use of *existing* programs that enable students to accomplish some desired task and provides considerable carryover value into later life needs.

Within the context of computer literacy, *programming* is seen as a skill to enhance the student's ability to function as a problem solver.

Implementing a Literacy Curriculum

A computer-literacy curriculum might be implemented across the existing curriculum or as new, separate courses at various grade levels.

Scope and sequence advocates recommended diffusing computer instruction throughout the K–12 curriculum. Teachers at all levels and in all fields should become "computer teachers," teaching the literacy units for that grade level. This approach requires a strong district commitment. It is appealing because the computer is encountered within the regular curriculum throughout the school years. However, there are also problems. Will all teachers really participate? Since that seems unlikely, what about the holes in the K–12 sequence that result? Are all teachers prepared to handle computer units? Given the demands of an already crowded curriculum, will teachers find the time (or inclination) to squeeze in new units on computers?

Luehrmann (1984) strongly advocated separate literacy courses. He suggested a junior-high-level class for all students, based on selected computer literacy goals. Such a class offers potential for carefully monitoring outcomes and may better ensure that a well-trained teacher is responsible for computer instruction. Of course, survival skills, including keyboarding, would be taught as needed in earlier grades so that students would be able to use the computer for appropriate activities.

Separate courses, then, offer the prospect of well-trained, specialist teachers delivering carefully constructed and sequenced content. Accountability should be greatly enhanced over a diffused approach. However, separate courses have been criticized for creating a new content area apart from the rest of the curriculum. The computer becomes just another subject to be learned and then forgotten as students move on to other unrelated subjects. Furthermore, teachers can view the computer as "someone else's problem" because it is removed from their domains, a "special subject" such as art, music, or physical education in lower grades. In addition, a separate course usually necessitates a lab facility, which may increase costs or preclude placing computers in individual classrooms.

The concept of a computer literacy curriculum is very much alive and well. A web search in mid 2003 found nearly 700 hits for that term, a large number of which were specific curricula posted by schools across the United States and around the globe.

The Problem-Solving Model

Norton (1988) identified problem solving as another model of computer literacy. Development of problem-solving ability is a universally accepted objective. Concerns parallel those presented for the literacy curriculum. Software aimed specifically at problem solving tends to be general, making it difficult to link to the curriculum. Time for problem-solving activities comes at the expense of something else. Unless a teacher is firmly convinced of the value of the activity *and* comfortable in presenting it, he or she is unlikely to voluntarily teach the activity. If coerced, however gently, effective presentation and use are unlikely.

The Tools/Applications Model

By the mid-1980s, even though computers were still new to many educators, the tide had begun to turn against programming as literacy. Literacy curricula proved more difficult to implement than anticipated, and whether computers could teach generic problem-solving skills was not clear. Educators were still seeking ways for computers to make an impact. They turned in many cases to the tool software presented in Chapters 3 through 9. By the end of the decade, Collis (August/September, 1988) had declared that applications had replaced programming as the most common model of computer literacy.

The reasoning was sound. Computers have become a part of our lives, and they will not go away. Schools prepare children for productive lives in society. The "real world" has embraced computer applications wholeheartedly. Therefore, students need to learn to use those tools in school.

In many cases, the implementation approach was to revamp existing computer-literacy courses. Out went programming, computer history, noncritical terminology, and other "marginal" topics. Survival skills became the precursors of word processing, databases, spreadsheets, and more. Students got excited, as did many teachers. The computer had become relevant.

Norton (1988), however, criticized the tool approach from two perspectives. First, tool courses tend to emphasize mechanics. Assignments are contrived to meet the needs of a stand-alone course. "Tool applications are worthwhile only when students are prepared to use them to solve problems which have meaning and applicability to their needs" (p. 8). Second, tools are typically treated as neutral, which they never really are. Students must study the *effects* of computers on themselves and society, not just how to use them efficiently (see Chapter 15).

Conclusion

A major problem in understanding computer literacy is that it is not a single, clearly defined concept. Rather, there have been and still are differing definitions and approaches to it. They may even represent a developmental hierarchy stretching from the programming model through applications. Each model has had its proponents and defenders, and all have their critics. The common thread through the criticism has been that these models basically treat the computer as subject matter, an end in itself.

Where do we turn next to capitalize on what the literacy experience has taught us? The following section offers one response.

Technology Integration

NETS
NOTES

NETS **T** II-A
NETS **T** II-B
NETS **T** II-E
NETS **T** III-A
NETS **T** III-B
NETS **T** III-C
NETS **T** V-B
NETS **T** VI-E

Technology integration moves well beyond just computer literacy. "Technology-based tools are integrated [into the curriculum] in a manner that provides a rich context for students' understanding of the pertinent concepts, themes, and processes. Technology . . . is perceived as a tool to identify and solve authentic problems" (Moersch, 1995, p. 42). This provides the essential context that makes learning to use a tool meaningful (Jonassen, 2000).

Do not confuse integration with infusion. *Infusion* means simply that computers are physically present in our schools. Hardware proliferation is not the key point of the "computer revolution." Statistics about the number of computers in schools and the ratio of computers to students or teachers are evidence of growing infusion. Once the hardware is in place, how can it become a vital tool for learning?

Integration means "the process of totally integrating the use of computers into the existing curriculum through learning activities that address the subject-area objectives" (Staff, 1988, p. 36). "[T]he true pioneers . . . are dealing systemically with all aspects of the curriculum in order to create well-integrated systems designed (1) to meet the needs of the students and (2) to be improved on the basis of feedback from those students" (Komoski, 1987, p. 22). Data on the extent of computer integration are far more difficult to identify than infusion statistics.

What Is the Scope?

Integration places the computer in the service of the curriculum. It capitalizes on the best from the literacy approaches that preceded it but starts with the curriculum, not the computer. It seeks to identify those places where the computer can increase learning effectiveness, enable learners to do what they otherwise could not (Type II applications as described by Maddux, Johnson, & Willis, 2001), or teach increasingly significant life skills. Integration is all-inclusive, but more importantly, all-pervasive. Let's consider the computer-literacy models in the context of integration.

Within curriculum integration, programming is appropriate whenever it reflects a specific need, such as in a data-processing curriculum. In other subjects, programming may be an appropriate technique for solving particular problems. For example, learning to create macros to automate procedures in applications such as spreadsheets (and many others) is programming, as is creating scripts to achieve more complex results in hypermedia programs such as *HyperStudio*. Many students are still learning to program, although they probably don't even realize it. Programming is not, however, a general skill for all students.

As for a literacy curriculum, it would be difficult to imagine any scope and sequence being more than a rough guide, since all curricula are determined locally in the United States. However, such a model could well contain elements that clearly support curriculum objectives and should be kept in the new plan. K–12 articulation is essential to success.

From the beginning, the problem-solving model suffered from lack of a curricular home. Everyone wants the result, but no one claims responsibility, nor wants to give up class time for it. The issue is not an integration model but how to handle problem solving at all. Research suggests that many views of learning problem solving have been too simplistic. Dudley-Marling and Owston (1988) reviewed a vast range of research and concluded that "while problem-solving skills within any particular domain can be taught, . . . transfer . . . across domains is difficult to achieve. . . . Therefore, it is likely that no single problem-solving program, Logo or CAI, will develop the wide range of problem-solving skills students need to survive in and out of school" (p. 31). However, the researchers did not suggest giving up the quest. Rather, they advised starting with the curriculum and then examining carefully the potential of any problem-solving approach to support curricular goals. Furthermore, don't expect unattainable results; be realistic.

Finally, there is the application software model, which has been our bias throughout this book. We believe that software tools are inherently useful; they offer powerful ways to improve learning with Type II activities, things previously not possible in education. Jonassen (2000, p. 9) formalized this thinking in his term *Mindtools:* "Mindtools are computer-based tools and learning environments that have been adapted or developed to function as intellectual partners with the learner in order to engage and facilitate critical thinking and higher order learning."

Technology integration simply means using tools, including computers, throughout the curriculum *wherever appropriate*, rather than relegating them to a separate course. Thus, students may begin to learn word processing whenever in the curriculum they need to write essays of sufficient length to justify the use of technology. Math lessons are enhanced at appropriate points with spreadsheet applications. Students in social studies may more readily comprehend important concepts by graphing data. The fine arts curriculum can introduce draw, paint, and music composition software. Assuming the appropriate level of curriculum articulation across the grades, teachers at each grade know what student skills they can expect and, thus, tailor new experiences at the appropriate level. Such integration has been our ideal throughout this book.

For a thorough discussion of integration, which is a cornerstone of the NETS projects, we recommend the NETS book *Connecting Curriculum and Technology* (ISTE, 2000), starting with the chapter "What Is Curriculum Integration?," which is available online <http://cnets.iste.org/students/pdf/curr_integration.pdf>. The entire book is devoted to providing examples of how to integrate technology into the curriculum and is an essential addition to your professional library.

Advantages over Literacy

Why is such an integration approach "better" than its predecessors? There are multiple clear improvements.

- Integration puts the emphasis squarely where it belongs: on the curriculum, not on the computer. This helps address Rhodes's point that "[t]echnology adds cost but not value unless it is part of the essential work that directly determines the quality of the organization's results" (1995, p. 35). Computer use is always in a meaningful context when it is integrated.

- There is no need to add new objectives to the school's curriculum specifically to deal with computers. Instead, existing objectives are enhanced with computer applications and, as new objectives enter the curriculum, technology applications to support them are included automatically. This minimizes, but may not totally dispel, the issue of "How do we make room for computer skills?"

- The computer becomes the teacher's partner, not a competitor. Any lingering fears that teachers may be displaced by computers can be vanquished. It is also the learner's intellectual partner (Jonassen, 2000).

- Integration treats the computer in a natural way, as one fundamental tool for learning and living. Was there ever a course in pencil? Perhaps for those who aspire to manufacture them. Does there need to be a course in computer? Outside of data processing instruction, we think not.

- Integration fosters invisibility. While chief scientist of Xerox and director of its Palo Alto Research Center (PARC), John Seely Brown (1998) wrote an article titled "To Dream the Invisible Dream." In it, Brown described the ultimate history of computers as follows: First, there were no computers, then there were computers, and then they disappeared. Not literally, of course, but from consciousness, meaning computers will become so simple and ubiquitous, so totally integrated into the fabric of life, that we will cease to notice them. That is hardly true today, but as our students make more and more integrated use of technology as they learn, they will continue to think less and less about the technology as they just use it (Regan, 2002). Computer technology is here for the duration and is becoming as invisible as pencil or calculator technology. By *not* separating it from normal routine, educators help technology become invisible, yet vital.

Beyond Integration: Curriculum Transformation

NETS
NOTES

NETS **T** II-A
NETS **T** II-B
NETS **T** III-A
NETS **T** III-B
NETS **T** III-C
NETS **T** V-B
NETS **T** VI-E

For some educators, curriculum integration is a step in the right direction, but not enough in and of itself. Norton (1988, p. 10) saw significant gains in the integration approach but found it insufficient nonetheless. "[I]ntegration carries with it a set of unspoken assumptions which fail to recognize the unique potentials of the computer. . . . [It] defines learning and education as content specific and content oriented and presupposes an existing curriculum that is best left unchallenged." Norton argued that it is not enough to bolster a curriculum that needs to be changed.

Johnson (1991) offered a provocative view of curriculum (see Figure 13.1), which we present here without targeting any specific content area. The relative sizes of the areas in the diagram do not imply corresponding amounts of content. Rather, the diagram simply presents relationships. Johnson suggests that part of what is now taught should not be, although it may once have had value (a view that is not new, as evidenced by Peddiwell's wonderful 1939 classic, *The Saber-Tooth Curriculum*—highly recommended reading). Furthermore, the computer can help teach some things that we do not now teach. However, computers also offer possibilities that exceed the bounds of what should be taught, while leaving untouched other areas of the content field. What does this suggest concerning whether integration is an end or merely a step toward a larger goal? Johnson has reminded us that the computer is no panacea, but a vital element of twenty-first-century curricula.

Schools seeking to create a constructivist learning environment using computers as Mindtools (Jonassen, 2000) find that the existing curriculum cannot remain static, a "saber-tooth curriculum." In *Connecting Curriculum and Technology*, ISTE (2000) noted in large

Figure 13.1
A MODEL OF TECHNOLOGY AND CURRICULUM CONTENT (ADAPTED FROM JOHNSON, 1991)

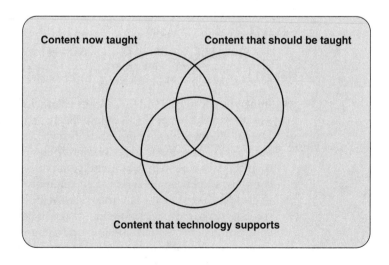

Content now taught   Content that should be taught

Content that technology supports

type that "Our educational system must produce technology-capable kids . . . (because) (t)ools are different, work is different, kids are different and learning is different" (pp. 2–3). The curriculum must change to meet the challenges of the future in which our students will live.

The issues involved in significant curricular transformation or reform are numerous and complex. Johnson (1991) urged educators to examine the role of the computer in their field based on its ability to help *teach*, *learn*, and *do* what is appropriate to the field. According to Wales (1995, p. 41), restructuring begins with integration. "How do you integrate computers into the content areas? Teachers recognize what works. . . . It works to use computers when the process of learning can be enhanced. . . . That is the road a teacher will travel to restructuring." Jonassen (2000) argues persuasively for sweeping changes in the role of computers in a new, constructivist curriculum. Whitfield and Latimer (2002–2003) provided a concrete model for making curriculum integration work, along with valuable tips for success in your own school. We urge you to read their works.

Views such as these deserve careful consideration. Rather than being radical, they offer a rational approach to deliberate change in a profession that is more accustomed to slow, "glacial" movement than upheaval. Someone once said that changing education is the only task more difficult than moving a cemetery. We accept that change will come slowly. Early in the twenty-first century, many educators have adopted the applications model, while others are well along the road to integration. Some are exploring dramatic school restructuring based on constructivism. All deserve recognition for their efforts, and encouragement and assistance as they apply new approaches and insights. We support Jonassen's goal to make far more use of the computer than integration necessarily does but believe such transformation is a long-term process that requires intermediate steps toward its attainment. Major implementation issues are considered in the next chapter.

SUMMARY

There is widespread agreement that knowledge and understanding of computers and those skills essential to computer use are legitimate educational goals. Computer literacy sought to meet such goals by treating the computer as something unique and special. The four broad models of computer literacy are programming, a literacy curriculum, problem solving, and application software or tools. All added new content to the curriculum.

Curriculum integration, in contrast, can incorporate all the literacy content, but it does so in direct support of the curriculum. Problems of "finding time for computers" largely vanish because there are no new curriculum objectives. Rather, the computer is the teacher's colleague and on the way to becoming as invisible as the pencil. Students learn with their technological partner what they need to know, when and in the context in which they need it—just like real-world computer use.

Some educators contend that integration is a step in the right direction but does not go far enough. No curriculum can be static; rather, it must change to capitalize on the unique potential of the computer to enhance critical thinking, to move into more Type II applications, experiences seldom before possible, which is also the essence of Mindtools. For the computer merely to support what already is retards the inevitable transformation of education that must occur to keep pace with societal changes.

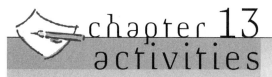

chapter 13 activities

1. Reflect on the models of computer literacy presented in this chapter. How do you view them from the perspective of a student in the twenty-first century? Justify your position.
2. Is programming skill (including macros and hypermedia development) essential for today's learners? Why or why not?
3. Discuss the respective merits of the separate class and the K–12 scope and sequence approaches to the literacy curriculum. Which is preferable? Why?
4. Is *computer literacy* a meaningful term? How can it assist or hinder the implementation of computers in our schools?
5. Contrast computer integration with computer literacy and infusion. Outline their essential characteristics.
6. Analyze literacy versus integration, focusing on strengths and weaknesses of each.
7. Determine the position of your state education authority on computers in education, both for K–12 students and for teachers. How has this changed in recent years? What further changes would you support, if any?
8. Argue for or against the view that technology integration is insufficient unless curriculum change also occurs.

Companion Website

Visit the companion website at <www.ablongman.com/lockard6e> for more information about the topics discussed in this chapter.

expect the world®

The New York Times
nytimes.com

Themes of the Times

Expand your knowledge of the concepts discussed in this chapter by reading current and historical articles from the *New York Times* by visiting the Themes of the Times section of the companion website <www.ablongman.com/lockard6e>.

References

Brown, J. S. "To Dream the Invisible Dream." *Red Herring,* July 1998. Retrieved March 7, 2003, from <www.redherring.com/mag/issue56/think.html>

Collis, B. *Computers, Curriculum, and Whole-Class Instruction.* Belmont, CA: Wadsworth, 1988.

Collis, B. "Research Windows." *The Computing Teacher,* August/September 1988, *16*(1), pp. 6–7.

Dudley-Marling, C., and Owston, R. D. "Using Microcomputers to Teach Problem Solving: A Critical Review." *Educational Technology*, July 1988, *28*(7), pp. 27–33.

I.S.T.E. *National Educational Technology Standards for Students—Connecting Curriculum and Technology*. Eugene, OR: International Society for Technology in Education, 2000.

Johnson, J. "Are Paradigms Worth More Than a Pair of Dimes?" *The Computing Teacher*, October 1991, *19*(2), pp. 38–40.

Jonassen, D. H. *Computers as Mindtools for Schools: Engaging Critical Thinking*. Upper Saddle River, NJ: Merrill, 2000.

Komoski, P. K. "Beyond Innovation: The Systemic Integration of Technology into the Curriculum." *Educational Technology*, September 1987, *27*(9), pp. 21–25.

Luehrmann, A. "Computer Literacy: What It Is, Why It Is Important." *Electronic Learning*, May/June 1982, *1*(8), pp. 20, 22.

Luehrmann, A. "Computer Illiteracy—A National Crisis and a Solution for It." In Harper, D. O., and Stewart, J. H. (eds.), *Run: Computer Education*. Monterey, CA: Brooks/Cole, 1983, pp. 29–32.

Luehrmann, A. "The Best Way to Teach Computer Literacy." *Electronic Learning*, April 1984, *3*(7), pp. 37–44.

Maddux, C. D., Johnson, D. L., and Willis, J. W. *Educational Computing: Learning with Tomorrow's Technologies*, 3rd ed. Boston: Allyn and Bacon, 2001.

Moersch, C. "Levels of Technology Implementation (LoTi): A Framework for Measuring Classroom Technology Use." *Learning and Leading with Technology*, November 1995, *23*(3), pp. 40–42.

Norton, P. "In Search of a Computer Curriculum." *Educational Technology*, March 1988, *28*(3), pp. 7–14.

Peddiwell, J. A. *The Saber-Tooth Curriculum*. New York: McGraw-Hill, 1939.

Regan, T. "Computer? What computer?" *Christian Science Monitor*, January 17, 2002. Retrieved March 10, 2003, from <www.csmonitor.com/2002/0117/p12s01-stct.htm>

Rhodes, L. A. "Technology-Driven Systemic Change." *Learning and Leading with Technology*, November 1995, *23*(3), pp. 35–37.

Roblyer, M. D. *Integrating Educational Technology into Teaching*, 3rd ed. Columbus, OH: Merrill Prentice Hall, 2003.

Staff. "One Hundred and One Things You Want to Know About Educational Technology." *Electronic Learning*, May/June 1988, *7*(8), pp. 32–48.

Wales, C. "Paving In-roads for Technology Integration: A Classroom Example." *Learning and Leading with Technology*, October 1995, *23*(2), pp. 41–42.

Whitfield, C. M., and Latimer, B. T. "A Model for Technology Integration." *Learning & Leading with Technology*, December/January 2002–2003, *30*(4), pp. 50–55.

Technology
Implementation

CHAPTER 14

OBJECTIVES

After completing this chapter, you will be able to:

- Outline the implementation goals and methods of the early 1980s.
- Analyze reasons that the so-called computer revolution has had limited impact.
- Discuss the concept of computer competence as it relates to computer literacy and curriculum integration.
- Compare the fundamental concepts of integration, reform, and restructuring.
- Assess reasons commonly given for why teachers do not employ technology.
- Explain the importance of a plan for technology in education.

- Describe and assess the role of a technology coordinator and the need for teacher involvement in technology planning and implementation.
- Discuss issues and ideals for staff development and articulation.
- Argue an appropriate position regarding hardware purchases for your specific situation, including needed peripherals.
- Analyze the merits of a lab, computers in classrooms, and mobile computers, based on your position on cooperative learning strategies.
- Outline potential applications in a one-computer classroom.

- Briefly discuss technology as it relates to special needs populations from both legal and applications standpoints.
- Propose and justify distribution of budget funds across categories of necessary expenditures.
- Outline approaches to stretching a limited budget.

Chapter 13 presented a theoretical consideration of the proper goal for computers in education—namely, invisible integration into the curriculum (Brown, 1998; Rhodes, 1995) and, ultimately, curriculum transformation and school restructuring (D'Ignazio & D'Ignazio, 1998; Dyrli & Kinnaman, 1995; Knapp & Glenn, 1996; Roblyer, 2003). This chapter presents a short history of the first 20 years of educational computing, including problems encountered by computing pioneers and reasons that a different approach may be required. Some of the critical implementation questions and issues, which require attention by any teacher committed to twenty-first century education using computer technology, are then surveyed.

The State of Computers in Education

It took education more than 300 years to fully take advantage of the technological revolution in movable type. And it was almost 100 years between the invention of the pencil and its wide use in schools. This is not so with microcomputers. Change has come quickly. Our challenge is to manage that change, and to put the new technology into the service of quality education. (Lengel, 1983, p. 18)

NETS
NOTES

NETS **T** I-A
NETS **T** I-B
NETS **T** II-E
NETS **T** V-B

Lengel wrote in the early years of computers in schools. Scarcely ten years later, former U.S. Secretary of Education Terrel Bell wrote:

The technological revolution that has greatly enhanced the efficiency of industry, business, and publishing has had little impact on the classrooms of America. . . . Teachers desperately need the advantages that today's technology offers to address the many diverse needs of students. . . . Neither educators nor students are trained or equipped to do their work; we send them to a 1950's model classroom and expect them to deliver a product ready to face the 21st Century. . . . American education truly is wobbling down the electronic avenue in an ox-cart. (Bell, 1992, p. 6)

Some observers saw little change in the 1990s. Rosenthal (1999) and Barksdale (1996) documented the lack of teacher preparation for using technology. D'Ignazio and D'Ignazio (1998, p. 56) commented, "There is a growing discrepancy between the words and dreams of educational technology leaders and the actual use of technology by most of our nation's schools." The entire NETS project <http://cnets.iste.org> is a reflection of the challenge as the various standards documents finally define the skills, competences, and outcomes to be expected of students, teachers, and administrators.

The contrast between Lengel and the more recent writings are stark and disturbing. The pace of change—at least in the sense of computer infusion—has been rapid, as Lengel noted, and there are outstanding examples of technology-enriched learning environments (e.g., every issue of *Learning & Leading with Technology* and *Technology & Learning*; Bozeman & Baumbach, 1995; Wilson, Hamilton, Teslow, & Cyr, 1994). However, looking at education broadly, the impact now appears to be far less than Lengel projected (D'Ignazio & D'Ignazio, 1998; Hayes & Bybee, 1995).

The CEO Forum was a unique cooperative effort among major corporations and educational organizations (e.g., Apple, AOL, IBM, the National Education Association, and the National School Boards Association) to assess and monitor "progress toward integrating technology in America's schools . . . to ensure that the nation's students will achieve higher academic standards and will be equipped with the skills they need to be contributing citizens and productive workers in the 21st century" (CEO Forum, 2001, p. 2). The CEO Forum functioned from 1996 to 2001. In one of its last reports, the following is noted:

> Over the past four years, schools, states and the federal government have made great strides in acquiring the critical technology infrastructure and training to support integrating technology into schools and school curriculum. . . . Initially our national focus had to be centered on preparing schools to harness technology. Now, we need to apply technology's powerful tools to change the way our students learn. (CEO Forum, 2001, p. 4)

In other words, education has made a major step forward but still does not show the essential impact on how students learn.

Why have we not "put the new technology into the service of quality education?" One possible explanation is that "revolutions have a way of mandating change while glossing over logistical details" (Roblyer, Castine, & King, 1988, p. 131). The dream is very much alive, but we must learn from the experiences that have contributed to the expressed concerns and move forward based on those experiences that have succeeded.

One View of Implementation History

NETS NOTES

NETS **T** I-A
NETS **T** I-B
NETS **T** II-B
NETS **T** III-B
NETS **T** V-B

From its initial availability, schools have embraced computer technology at a rate unprecedented for educational innovations. In 1983–84, the national average was 125 students per computer; in 1994–95, it was 12 to 1 (Hayes & Bybee, 1995) and has since fallen below 6 to 1 (NCES, September 2002), reaching a level considered to be adequate for effective use within the curriculum (President's Committee, 1997). In no other case in the history of American education has so much money been spent with so few questions asked, so little known about the implications, so little thought given to implementation, and ultimately, so little demanded in return. Computers flooded schools with less consideration than was given to ordering the year's supply of paper towels for the washrooms. Schools competed with one another to acquire greater *numbers* of computers, with little thought given to their actual use. There were exceptions, of course, but far too often the approach was just hopping on a moving train, destination unknown.

The Early 1980s: Getting Started

Idealists in the early 1980s proclaimed the need for *planning* (e.g., Klein & Strothers, 1983–1984; Lengel, 1983). The process could be neat and tidy. First, establish a planning committee to draft a school (district, state) philosophy concerning computers and get the appropriate authorities to endorse it. Extend the philosophy into policy statements. Develop a curriculum plan, even a scope and sequence, with clear objectives for all grade levels. Establish a computer budget, determine hardware and software to purchase, and plan staff-development activities. Draw up a facilities plan for placement of the computers. Order hardware and software. Implement staff development. All teachers will be inspired and will eagerly use computers throughout the schools. Learning magically will flower!

As with many generalizations, there is a thread of truth running through the preceding synopsis, however inaccurate it may be for specific cases. The longed-for magic did not occur broadly. Concerns arose within the first decade of educational computing, and a bibliography of commentators sounding much like Bell and D'Ignazio would be lengthy. What we *thought* would happen did not.

Into the 1990s: Assessment and Reflection

One significant explanation for lack of greater change is that educators took the "Field of Dreams" approach. We "built it," but often they did not come. We put all our faith in the technology and gave too little attention to the critical need for professional development for teachers (Doersch, 2002; Lever-Duffy, McDonald, & Mizell, 2003; Roblyer, 2003; Wetzel, 2001). It is this concern for teacher technology competence that has led to the NETS standards that frame each chapter in this book. Major problems remain to be solved in both pre-service and in-service teacher training, but NETS for Teachers (NETS-T) and its acceptance by most states and the National Council for Accreditation of Teacher Education demonstrate movement in the right direction as well as concrete goals toward which to work.

The issue, however, goes beyond professional development. Stieglitz and Costa (1988) found that an overwhelming majority of Rhode Island teachers opted *not* to continue beyond an introductory computer workshop, although six coordinated sessions were readily available. These researchers also noted that, despite positive attitudes, less than half the teachers reported using their classroom computer. Some teachers felt they had too little hardware available to attempt anything of consequence ("How can I teach word processing with one computer?"). Others were discouraged by the physical placement of computers in their schools or found computers too difficult to incorporate into their teaching (Solomon & Solomon, 1995). These may be training issues, but frankly, teaching *with* technology takes more time than without.

Coughlin (1999, p. 23) described observations in a school that was widely viewed as a role model for technology integration. He concluded, "Technology resources . . . are being inserted into classrooms on the basis of formulas describing students per computer rather than in support of specific learning solutions. . . . Teacher training, where it exists, is primarily . . . measured in hours of seat time—as if such training will prepare those teachers for the successful use of technology in support of learning."

Computer implementation may have had minimal impact because it has not been integrated tightly into the curriculum. In addition, many efforts to evoke change failed to take reality into account, notably that computers run counter to long-established teaching styles. During their own training, teachers generally lack role models of strategies for implementing and managing computers in the classroom (Barksdale, 1996; Knapp & Glenn, 1996).

We also believe that still more patience is required. The potential of computers to revolutionize education has been overstated, expectations have been raised to unreasonable levels, and the time to achieve such goals has been greatly underestimated. We need a more realistic view. In general, implementation succeeds or fails on the level of the individual teacher. The only thing you can count on in your school is what you are yourself ready, willing, and *able* to do! The sole purpose of this book is to provide you with the motivation and knowledge to implement computer technology productively so that its educational potential may finally be attained.

Implementation for the Twenty-First Century

NETS
NOTES

NETS **T** II-A
NETS **T** II-B
NETS **T** II-C
NETS **T** II-D
NETS **T** III-A
NETS **T** III-B
NETS **T** III-D
NETS **T** V-B
NETS **T** VI-B
NETS **T** VI-E

The history of education is littered with the artifacts of innovations that failed to deliver on their promises. Perhaps the preceding discussion suggests that computers are only the most recent such fad. If you have come this far with us and accept that view, then we have failed completely. By now, we hope you are so convinced of the potential of educational computing that you will let nothing stand in your way! Read on as we sketch some directions and offer resources for additional help.

The Goal: Computer Competence

The preceding chapter stressed that the overall goal for computers in education is integration into and restructuring of curriculum so that the computer plays an essential, invisible role in daily classroom activity. Your students must become not just computer literate but also *computer competent*—that is, able to use a computer productively, easily, and effectively whenever appropriate. To guide them, *you* must achieve computer competence as well, although what is appropriate for you as a teacher may differ from what your students should achieve. Still, *personal* competence will determine the extent to which *you* integrate technology into your teaching.

The very content and structure of this book support the view that the most promising uses of computers in education are:

- As tools of personal and professional productivity.
- As facilitators of higher-order thinking skills.
- As vehicles for creative expression.
- As facilitators of cooperative learning.
- As multiple-modality learning environments.
- As a means of empowerment. (Kelman, 1993)

Of course, each of these points is of fundamental importance to education per se. When computers are invisible within the curriculum, students will develop computer competence as they work to attain the broad goals defined by these key uses. That is twenty-first century education, and it stands in marked contrast to simply adding the computer to the curriculum as a special object of instruction.

Integration, Reform, Restructuring?

It is popular to proclaim that today's schools are in such bad shape that modest change is no longer viable. The concern leads to the contention that schools must be reformed, even totally restructured, to reclaim their significance. Restructuring is not necessarily physical change, but more critically, a fundamental change in the way students are taught and learn. In turn, many voices strongly contend that successful restructuring requires technology to play a central role in the "new" schools (e.g., Holland, 1996; Knapp & Glenn, 1996).

Although we applaud the ideals of the reform and restructuring movements, their potential to go beyond rhetoric into widespread adoption is not yet clear. The history of education suggests that radical change on a wide scale is uncommon. If technology integration is linked to total school restructuring, then educators in schools not yet committed to restructuring would appear to be helpless. We do not accept such an all-or-nothing position.

In school districts where teachers are committed to radical change, we support fully the rapid move to technology-rich learning environments. For others, significant technology integration is still possible, and it must begin with recognition of existing reality. Start where teachers and the curriculum currently are. Identify places where the computer has the potential to make a difference. Implement at those points in ways that are comfortable for teachers (Cuban, 1995). Provide appropriate conditions, and the curriculum itself will evolve. Bracey (1993, p. 8) reported results of an extensive study showing that technology first strengthens the existing curriculum, which gradually yields to "far more dynamic learning experiences for students."

Technology Planning

To work toward curriculum integration, a carefully developed plan is vital for many reasons. "If you fail to plan, you plan to fail" is a widely quoted maxim of uncertain origin. Developing that plan requires strategic planning to articulate the vision of the school district in a concrete way; plan development also sets a tone for budgets. "It must be directly connected to the educational aims of the school district, and it needs community-wide support and ownership" (Kinnaman, 1992). A district plan commands support at the building level and signals broad commitment. Regardless of a school's position on reform/restructuring, a plan should have three key elements: a long-term view, system-wide applications, and major involvement of teachers. Detailed planning resources are listed in the References section for this chapter. You may also find help in such web resources as the California Department of Education <www.cde.ca.gov/ctl/edtechplan.pdf>, the Texas Center for Educational Technology <www.tcet.unt.edu/tek-plan.htm>, Apple Computer <www.apple.com/education/planning>, and the National Center for

Technology Planning <www.nctp.com>. Bowman, Newman, and Masterson (2001) documented an in-depth three-year case study of a school district's adoption of an educational technology plan. The study highlighted many of the topics in this chapter, including technology planning and professional development training. Brush (1999) analyzed differences in technology planning and implementation among schools in the southeastern United States.

The Technology Coordinator

Early in the planning process, schools should address the issue of a *technology coordinator*. Successful change in education requires effective leadership. Computers represent a qualitatively different change from the influx of videocassette recorders (VCRs), for instance. Integrating computers throughout the curriculum for effective learning is an enormous task (Pearson, 1994). There are many issues to face, many decisions to make, and someone has to be in charge. An excellent beginning resource in this area is *The Technology Coordinator* (Moursund, 1992), despite its age. There are also countless online resources such as the Technology Coordinator's Resources site at <http://home.socal.rr.com/exworthy/tc.htm>. You may want to review the requirements to be a technology coordinator in states of interest (e.g., Wisconsin's list is at <www.dpi.state.wi.us/dpi/dlcl/imt/tekcordlic.html>).

Questions to address about coordination include the scope of responsibilities (district, building, both), extent of commitment (full- or part-time), and position type (administrator, teacher, or both). Top administrators must assume a vital leadership role in technology implementation (NETS-A, 2002), but district- and building-level coordinators are also vital. Another possibility is a building computer liaison, a full-time teacher or media specialist who takes on extra responsibilities, including serving on the planning committee, providing building leadership in technology applications, and conducting staff-development sessions. This could well become *your* role, one you should promote and then be prepared to accept.

Short of total restructuring of a school and major infusions of new hardware and software, technology integration is certain to be achieved only over some years. A shotgun approach to integration throughout the curriculum tends to spread the effort too thin for real effect. The maximum benefit is more likely to accrue from focusing resources on specific areas. Those teachers who are ready to move forward with technology will identify most of these. The coordinator's role is to help empower these teachers to achieve their goals.

Articulation across Grades

Regardless of exact implementation details, coordination across grade levels is vital. All teachers need to know what skills students have learned previously to plan effectively for their own grade level. Just as curriculum is articulated across grade levels, so must be computer integration to assure appropriateness. This is further justification for a technology coordinator. Inadequate attention to articulation is a common, serious flaw in technology planning.

Teacher Involvement

The real success of technology integration depends ultimately on the classroom teachers who develop and implement actual plans at the curriculum, class, and unit level. Teachers like you have already self-selected themselves to participate in the exciting new possibilities of technology. Most of the resources should be focused on this group of teachers.

Teachers who have not yet decided to adopt technology personally should continue to be exposed to the possibilities, gently encouraged, and offered support, but their participation cannot be forced. More will result from supporting the willing than from cajoling the reluctant. To try to interest skeptical colleagues, inquire as to the areas of their teaching that cause them the most difficulty. Explore the potential for technology intervention. If there is an acknowledged problem, that teacher may be more willing to consider a new approach. If not, try again next year.

Years of mandatory in-service training for all teachers have failed to persuade many teachers to join the technology movement (Cuban, 1995). It is time to concentrate on those of you who are convinced and to hope that the excitement generated in your classes will pique the interests of less adventuresome colleagues. Eventually, perhaps, the vast majority of teachers in a school will use technology broadly and effectively, but that is a long-term goal.

Staff Development

The level of support that a school invests in training teachers to use technology will directly affect the extent of its educational impact. Schools that invest in hardware and software, but not teacher training, make a serious mistake. Cradler, Freeman, Cradler, and McNabb (2002) noted that teacher surveys consistently show teachers are interested in technology, but their capacities to use it need much development. They cited research that shows a direct correlation between the amount of technology training teachers have had and their expressed comfort in working with technology. What, then, should characterize staff development?

One-shot institute days with guest speakers are hardly the answer. Rather, the identified needs of the teachers committed to technology must be addressed, needs that will vary greatly from one school to the next. Teachers vary in existing knowledge and interest in technology, making large-group sessions less likely than ever to be useful. The ever-increasing range of subject-specific materials also limits large-group potential. As skills and interest grow, technology users become ideal resources for miniconferences and institute days, in which they share their experiences with their colleagues and thus stimulate further interest among them.

Generic staff-development ideas include computer support groups (teachers sharing their experience and knowledge), some form of incentives for the time and effort invested, and setting annual school targets to work toward. Increased technical support has proven effective in enhancing computer use, as have increased salaries for "master teachers" who use technology, summer curriculum development assignments, extra preparation time in the daily schedule, and computer access at home and school.

Cradler et al. (2002) supported these ideas and provided other concrete approaches that work based on research. One of the most important in our experience is working with other educators who are experienced technology users in a mentoring relationship (e.g., see Doersch, 2002). Role modeling is one of the most powerful influences in the lives of teachers (Roblyer, 2003). Other key factors include ample time for collaboration and practice to gain confidence with technology, home computer access and use, ready access to technology, flexible scheduling for planning and teamwork, and long-term programs for curriculum redevelopment.

We have observed the growth in technology interest and use among teachers who have a home computer. In fact, the number of computers in teachers' homes may be more significant for what happens in a school than the number of computers in the school itself. Some schools have found the means in their budgets to assist teachers who want to purchase a home computer. We have witnessed plans that ranged from giving teachers a computer in exchange for participating in staff-development programs and developing classroom applications (e.g., see Crystal, 2001) to interest-free or reduced rate loans to cover the cost of purchasing a home computer. All such programs signal the strong support of the school for technology in the curriculum and send a powerful message to teachers about its importance, but most schools are unlikely to be able to afford such programs.

A no-cost approach is to send computers home with teachers on weekends, breaks, and over the summer. Obviously, a computer sitting unused in a school achieves nothing. That same computer with appropriate software sitting in a teacher's home might enlist a new technology recruit or support further advances by an existing trooper. We recommend that schools announce the availability of loaner computers but keep requests for them confidential. Some potential borrowers may prefer not to let their peers know of their explorations until they feel ready. In the early stages, anything that increases privacy and avoids the potential embarrassment of group training is useful.

Whatever the staff-development program, schools must demand technology skills of all candidates for teaching positions. This alone will reduce the need for lower-level staff development and permit redirection of funds and time to more sophisticated uses.

Hardware Platforms: Macintosh versus Windows

While detailed discussion of selecting specific computer models and peripheral hardware is beyond our scope, the issue of the major competing hardware platforms, Macintosh versus Windows, warrants comment. Although there were many incompatible microcomputers from which schools could choose in the late 1970s, Apple Computer quickly came to dominate the educational market with its Apple II series. The Apple II offered features important to educators, such as relative ease of setup and use, color, graphics, and even limited sound. Software developers embraced the Apple II immediately, and as the range of compatible educational software leaped far ahead of competitors, this computer's popularity continued to soar. Software availability drove the market. Apple II remained the most common machine in schools into the 1990s.

Inevitably, the fundamental technology of the Apple II became obsolete. Apple (and third-party companies) made many efforts to patch up the Apple II and extend its useful life, but technological obsolescence is a fact of life with computer technology. The Apple II will always hold a place of distinction in the history of educational computing.

Apple recognized the need for a different technology base and created the Macintosh, which abandoned the popular color feature. IBM entered the market rather late with its IBM-PC, but its dominance in large systems in business virtually assured the success of its PC. Furthermore, the decision of IBM to make its system specifications open to all stimulated not only third-party peripheral developers (as Apple had always done) but also direct competition with the computer itself, the so-called "Wintel" systems, computers based on Intel (and compatible) chips and running MS Windows operating systems. This spurred rapid advances in computers and drove prices steadily down. The enormous success of Microsoft Windows closed much of the gap with the Mac in operating style and ease, too. In contrast to IBM, Apple kept its Macintosh technology proprietary, prevented the development of clones, and kept prices inflated.

As purchasers started to turn away from the Apple II, software developers began to convert existing programs to run on other platforms, as well as to create more complex software that never could have run on an Apple II. Initially, developers assumed that schools would stick with Apple and migrate from the Apple II to Macintosh. Educational software for Intel-based PCs was more limited. However, a combination of marketing tactics and significant price advantages led more and more schools to adopt Wintel computers, and software developers quickly followed. Today's software offerings are comparable for both platforms for all common applications.

While sound advice in the early 1980s was to identify the software that met your needs and then buy whatever computer could run it, today there is little software that is unique to either hardware platform. The trend is clearly toward software for both major platforms that is as near identical in look, feel, operation, and capability as possible. Many major products no longer even have separate manuals for their Mac and Windows versions. Today, schools can buy the computers they prefer and then get the software they desire, at least in major application tools and popular CAI and utility packages. There will probably always be niche products that are unique to one platform or the other.

Where *does* this leave schools in the 2000s? What hardware platform should they purchase? That decision is more the personal preference of the decision maker than objective. Both Macintosh and Windows computers are highly desirable systems, and neither is clearly better than the other. Macintosh continues to hold a slight edge in ease of setup and use, whereas Windows systems often provide greater power and versatility at lower cost. According to the most current data at the time of writing, over two-thirds of the computers in schools are Wintel machines, the rest mostly Macintosh (QED, 2002). The balance seems likely to favor Wintel systems increasingly, as only 11 percent of school purchases in 2002 were Macintosh systems, down from 22 percent in 1998 (Yue, 2003).

In short, we find no compelling arguments for preferring either Macintosh or Windows systems. With perpetual school budgetary stress, price may well be the most important factor. Beyond that, intended use or instructional goals play a role. Many schools move older computers down to the elementary level as quickly as possible, where power requirements remain lower. At any grade level, for art and graphics work, Macintosh may offer some advantages. For high school business education, Windows makes the most sense, since businesses favor it overwhelmingly over Macintosh. However, students and teachers should learn to use both. Schools change preferences and teachers change schools. A computer today is essentially just another appliance like a microwave. You should be comfortable using whatever is available.

Essential Peripherals

Beyond the basic hardware platform, the heavy use of tool applications makes printers more important than in a primarily CAI environment. Schools should buy enough printers, even if it means purchasing fewer computers. To enhance group and cooperative learning experiences, projection is valuable, if not essential. Liquid crystal display (LCD) projectors have become economical. Every school should have several, even if it means cutting a computer or two from the purchase list. Similarly, each school should have a scanner, digital still camera and digital camcorder, video digitizing station, CD/DVD recorder, and DVD player to support multimedia project development.

Aiding Special Needs Learners

Technology can empower learners with special needs—those with mental or physical disabilities and also those with uncommon abilities, the talented and gifted or TAG students. For TAG students, technology offers endless opportunities to go beyond the basic curriculum, to explore more advanced topics, to make connections with experts, to pursue more challenging projects. Heward (2003) categorized these opportunities into three groups: electronic communities, database research, and interactive multimedia presentations. In short, the general approach for TAG is to guide students in more advanced uses of the full range of educational technologies.

Let's turn now to students with disabilities who are our primary focus here, given their prevalence within the school-age population and the many legal issues surrounding their education. The applications of technologies for students with special needs are the subject of entire books and courses (e.g., Bryant & Bryant, 2003; Hardy, 2002; King, 1999; Male, 2003; Woodward & Cuban, 2001). We can only highlight some of the key regulations and major applications. On the companion website you will find links to additional resources, including producers of adaptive technologies.

Legal Bases

Since the late 1980s, the U.S. Congress has established the rights of special needs individuals and increased the responsibilities of educational institutions for providing appropriate learning environments. One of the most important laws is the Americans with Disabilities Act (ADA) of 1990 (PL 101-336), which requires, among many things, accessible buildings and facilities as well as aids to communication. The 1988 Technology-Related Assistance Act for Individuals with Disabilities (PL 100-407) funds statewide agencies to provide assistive technology devices and services. IDEA (Individuals with Disabilities Education Act), which was reauthorized in 1997, requires educators to consider adaptive technologies as part of every individual education program (IEP). The core concept is that every student is entitled to free appropriate public education (FAPE). In its 23rd Annual Report to Congress, the most recent available, the U.S. Department of Education (2002) reported that under IDEA over 200,000 young children received early intervention services, nearly 600,000 preschoolers (5 percent of all preschoolers) received disability-related services, and over 5.5 million individuals ages 6–21 received such services.

For students with disabilities, technology can be a critical enabler. The potential of and need for technology in every classroom have increased with the growing practice of inclusion or "mainstreaming," which creates classrooms that are more diverse. Monahan (1999) detailed how a database project helped a mainstreamed student achieve important goals. Pratt (1999) maintained that technology can do "wonders" for students whose special needs go beyond the level at which inclusion works best. She described how using tools such as *KidPix* improved her students' development. Teachers more than ever need the broadest possible range of learning options to meet the needs of all students.

How, then, is technology being used to assist special needs learners? Let's briefly consider some of the major approaches by categories of disabilities.

Sensory Disabilities

Individuals who are deaf or hearing impaired may need little assistance to use computer technology, except when it is important to hear audio, whether as a message from the system or as the "soundtrack" of a multimedia piece. Technology cannot yet address this problem automatically, but designers can avoid providing any information solely in audio format. In a New York City junior high school for deaf students, the graphics arts teacher developed Fingerprints Press, a student-run business that used computers to produce sign-language products. Staff members were severely hearing impaired, and some had other disabilities as well. Through this venture, these students achieved success, overcame communication limitations, learned to work cooperatively, and gained valuable life experiences (Holzberg, 1993). The press evolved into "StreetSigns: A City Kid's Guide to American Sign Language," a CD-ROM developed to "record, archive and disseminate American Sign Language. It (was) created on-site at the New York City School for the Deaf, with more than 650 signs divided into 24 language categories" (Abdulezer, 1998). The project is an outstanding example of special needs students learning with and benefiting from technology.

For moderate vision impairments, software to enlarge the image on the screen may suffice. Persons who are blind or have very limited vision are aided by "reading machines," which are essentially scanners combined with speech synthesizers. A student can place any printed material on a device such as the Kurzweil 1000 <www.kurzweiledu.com/products.asp> or VERA system <www.freedomscientific.com> and learn as the machine reads the text aloud using voice synthesis. Screen readers such as *Jaws* from Freedom Scientific read the information on the monitor screen and present it to the user via speech synthesis. This company also produces "braille monitors," which are tactile systems that convert screen text into refreshable braille characters on a small device (Figure 14.1).

Accessibility of information on the Web is a significant issue, especially for the vision impaired. Imagine trying to navigate many of the web pages you are familiar with

Figure 14.1
A BRAILLE MONITOR FOR TACTILE OUTPUT

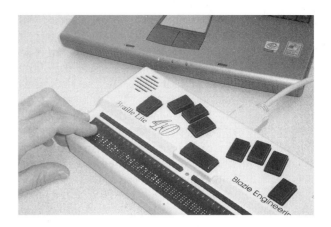

if you could not see. Anyone can check the accessibility of web pages through the Bobby service <http://bobby.watchfire.com>, which also provides detailed information about accessibility issues.

Motor Disabilities

Motor disabilities may result from such varied sources as cerebral palsy or paralysis following an accident. Adaptive technologies can enable individuals with these disabilities to benefit from technology, which might have been impossible otherwise. Example technologies include "sip and puff" switches <http://orin.com/>, such as Christopher Reeves used following his paralyzing accident, to large-size, single-button switches to switches activated by eyebrow movement to special pointing devices and alternative keyboards such as Intellikeys <www.intellitools.com>. All serve as alternative means to control a computer for individuals who cannot use the typical keyboard and/or mouse.

Mild Cognitive Disabilities

Mild disabilities include the full range of learning disabilities, emotional disabilities, and mild retardation. According to the U.S. Department of Education (2002), learning disabilities were the most prevalent disability among students ages 6–12, accounting for over half of students served under IDEA. Problems to be addressed with these students most commonly relate to attention, memory/retention of learning, reading, and to some extent, writing. Teachers have remarked to us that students give more attention to work that involves technology than to traditional class work, and schools are experimenting with PDAs to assist students in organizing their time and as memory aids. The Web can also be an effective tool with this population (Gardner & Wissick, 2002; Wissick & Gardner, 1998).

There are countless specialized software products aimed at reading and writing instruction for all populations. *Reader Rabbit* and the *JumpStart* series are widely used across all student populations, as are electronic books such as the Living Books series (e.g., *Just Grandma and Me*). It may be only the grade level or functional level that differs.

However, some students may be too distracted by the wide range of activities in, say, the Living Books. They may be better served by somewhat "simpler" software such as the *Start-To-Finish Books* from Don Johnston <www.donjohnston.com>, a company that specializes in "interventions" in early literacy, reading, writing, and math with a wide range of software products, including talking word processors (*Write:OutLoud*) and software that tries to complete words based in the first letters entered (*Co-Writer*), allowing students to write by selecting words rather than typing them in their entirety. Accessibility products are also available.

Moderate and Severe Cognitive Disabilities

This category includes developmental disabilities and the more severe instances of mental retardation. As for individuals with motor disabilities, assistive devices (switches, special keyboards, alternative pointing devices) are often effective for students with cognitive impairments. However, many severely disabled individuals require extensive assistance in learning basic living skills (money, cooking, shopping, getting around, personal care). Technology-based learning tools, including videos and CAI software, are showing promise in helping students with disabilities learn the basic skills that can give them a new level of independence (e.g., Wissick, 1996; Wissick & Gardner, 2000; Wissick, Gardner, & Langone, 1999).

Facilities

Is there an ideal physical arrangement for computers in a school? To start, every classroom teacher should have a telephone and computer on the desk. For students, there are pros and cons of computers as mobile stations, in classrooms, in labs, in libraries, and/or learning centers. Each configuration has merit, and many schools have more than one. Figure 14.2 presents selected points for the most common patterns.

Physical arrangement should support the goal of integrating computers into instruction. In many cases, that suggests computers in each classroom. Where better to integrate them into everyday activity? Consider the probable use of other media, including books, if they were available *only* in a lab or library versus on demand in a classroom. Classroom computers should be provided to those teachers who want them, rather than being placed automatically in every classroom, which may threaten and further turn off some teachers.

Labs are particularly important for keyboarding and word processing, vocational skills classes, and advanced computer courses. Internet use, database research, tutorials, and drill and practice all benefit from more machines but can be managed on a rotating "station" basis, just like other forms of group work.

The decline in cost of notebook computers and the advent of wireless networking have led to great interest in mobile carts of notebook computers (Figure 14.3). Although the cost per unit remains somewhat high, the flexibility more than justifies the purchase in many cases. A cart can be moved into any classroom or space with a network connection and, almost instantly, the classroom becomes a lab. It is not necessary to devote space exclusively to a lab and saves significant time as classes no longer need to leave their regular room to spend a period in a "lab." It is also less costly to install one

Factors	Permanent Lab	Mobile Workstations	In Classrooms
Usage Patterns and Potential	Individual or group	Individual or group	Individual without video projection
	Requires scheduling, decreasing flexibility	Same as a lab	Always available for maximum flexibility
	Curricular integration only if readily accessible, e.g., daily	May promote integration within the class if easily available	Constant availability supports integration
	Supports tool, tutor, learner functions	Roles supported depend on number of units	Tutor for enrichment and remediation; group work
	Can provide special hardware/interfacing	Added flexibility if wireless	
Personnel	Needs supervisory/operating staff	User responsibility	User responsibility
	May necessitate a computer specialist lacking content to help student users	Regular teacher with knowledge of content and students	Same as mobile
	Teachers need mostly software skills	Teachers need software and hardware skills	Same as mobile
Cost	Based on number of systems/peripherals	Number of systems plus mobile carts, etc.	Number of systems may be many or few
	Potential economies of networking	Moving may increase repairs	May require most copies of software
	Highest security	Moderate security outside school hours	Lowest security
Most Common Grade Level	Middle school or above	All levels	Elementary schools

Figure 14.2   CHARACTERISTICS OF COMMON COMPUTER CONFIGURATIONS

network connection in a room than to wire it for a full set of computers. We believe this approach will become increasingly popular with schools as they replace existing computers or add to their inventory.

The goal of "ubiquitous computing" requires that students have access to a computer at any time when it would be useful. The ideal, then, would be one computer per student and, especially if the computers were notebooks with wireless capabilities, every room could be a lab. However, that seems likely to remain an elusive goal for years to come, unless educators turn to alternative devices. For example, since it is

Figure 14.3
Wireless networking and mobile notebook computers move easily among classrooms.

hardly realistic to teach word processing or to use it regularly without easy access to hardware, many schools have turned to limited-purpose devices such as the products of AlphaSmart, Inc. <www.alphasmart.com>. The AlphaSmart 3000 is a low-cost device for writing, from which text can be sent to a computer for final formatting or to a printer. The Dana is a similar device that runs on the Palm operating system, making it compatible with the full range of Palm OS devices. Such devices merit consideration as alternatives to computers where appropriate.

Finally, recall the discussion about handheld devices or PDAs in Chapter 9. We believe the growing power of these small inexpensive tools will soon make them a highly competitive alternative to regular and even notebook computers for common applications. Just as many high school students long have been required to purchase a graphing calculator for their math classes, the next step is likely to be the PDA as a required learning tool. Ubiquitous computing may, in fact, be getting much closer.

The One-Computer Classroom

A single computer in a classroom is a common situation, even in schools with lab facilities or mobile systems. What can you do with just one computer? Clearly, the answer is not to require word-processed assignments from all students if there is no other computer facility. However, teachers do not expect more than one overhead projector or VCR. How is a computer different?

Visibility has been one problem. Most computer monitors are far too small for more than a few students to see, especially given the tiny text that is often displayed. However, LCD projectors for large-screen projection are no longer cost-prohibitive for schools. The issue is more creativity in using software with a student group than how the students can all see.

Much educational software was designed with a single user in mind, but other uses are possible. Typically, drill and practice, tutorials, and games are hard to use with groups. However, simulations and problem-solving software can be adapted easily to small-group or whole-class instruction. Some software producers, notably Tom Snyder Productions <www.tomsnyder.com>, emphasize group applications for their products.

Don't overlook the computer as a demonstration tool using application software. Database searching can be a group activity, applying strategies developed by the class, which then sees the result immediately. With spreadsheet software, a group easily can observe the effect of changes in data or how data are manipulated. The ideal in biology may be real dissection, but if that is not possible, or as preparation for the lab, you could project *Operation: Frog* for the group. How many students can actually see a live demonstration anyhow?

Finally, presentation graphics software was designed for a single computer and a group. It is an electronic overhead or slide projector without the physical media. You can teach with such software, and students can make their own presentations using it. The real key to effective use of one computer in a classroom is a creative teacher.

For a wide range of strategies for using one computer in a classroom, check out Linda Burkhart's suggestions at <www.lburkhart.com/elem/strat.htm>, those from Learning Solutions at <www.learnsol.com/onecompt.html>, the Berrien County (MI) Intermediate School District at <www.remc11.k12.mi.us/bcisd/classres/onecomp.htm>, or the Educational Technology Training Center of Middlesex County (New Jersey) at <www.techtrain.org/curriculum/1c_bmark.htm>. There are many overlapping suggestions, but each site offers some unique ideas. The companion website provides links to these and other resources for your convenience.

Cooperative versus Individual Learning

In the early 1970s, educational visionaries longed for the day of electronic calculators for every student. Skeptics scoffed, but the dream became reality rather quickly. Today's dream is of ubiquitous computing—one student, one computer. Even when it becomes true, educators must not lose sight of the value of cooperative learning.

In two studies, competitive environments revealed gender differences disadvantageous to females that did not exist in cooperative arrangements (Bracey, 1988). Both U.S. and British studies found superior gains from group work compared with individual work (Collis, 1988–89). Glasser (1989) found that students usually said they felt important only in extracurricular activities, which he attributed to the group or team nature of the activity. Becker (1994) found that exemplary technology-using teachers were more likely to use small-group activities than their peers.

Of course, cooperative learning means much more than just putting students together at a computer. Goal setting is a key to success. One student will often get or take more than a fair share of the time. For maximum effectiveness with pairs, for instance, always prepare two sets of activities and designate group members as A and B. Have each complete one set. Have students give each other challenges or tasks to perform. This can increase the practicality of their work. Consider designating clusters of two or three computers as mutual help groups. Students should seek assistance within their help group before asking you or a lab aide.

Finding and Spending Funds Wisely

The subject of money rears its ugly head. Of course, there is never enough of it. So what can a school do?

Funding

Beyond its own local resources, many schools now devote considerable effort to obtaining outside funding, that is, grants and donations. Grant writing is part art and part science and it is well beyond the scope of this book. However, there are many resources available to assist those who wish or need to pursue funding opportunities. We particularly recommend David Moursund's (2002) website that offers his entire book on the subject. It contains excellent advice from a very experienced technology advocate. *Technology & Learning* is another source for leads on potential funding sources and also tips on writing a proposal <www.techlearning.com/grants.html>. The E-Rate program <www.fcc.gov/learnnet> has also provided billions of dollars to schools for technology. Florida and Illinois, among other states, have made special funding available competitively to schools for technology. Other obvious resources include special educational categories and the No Child Left Behind programs, parent-teacher organizations, and local education foundations. Although far from plentiful, outside funding is sometimes possible. Companies often donate equipment, rather than cash, for innovative, creative applications.

Local businesses, area foundations, and district foundations have all assisted schools in acquiring educational technology. You'll never know what could be had unless you ask.

Allocating Available Funds

The technology plan should drive the budget in any school. It is important to avoid common errors of the past. In the absence of a sound plan, the computer budget has often been like personal savings, consisting of what, if any, funds are "left over." This is an inadequate approach even for the short term and clearly contrary to any long-term vision. More than a decade ago, Kinnaman (1992) proposed that schools allocate at least 5 percent of the total budget to technology support for the classroom. As he commented, "[F]ive percent is an awfully small price to pay for guaranteed school improvement" (p. 20). We still agree.

However the budget was set, many schools have spent virtually all their money on hardware. This is a serious error that ignores the essential need for software, staff development, maintenance, supplies, and even support materials such as computer books and relevant journals. Even a first-year budget should allocate *no more than 50 percent to hardware*, perhaps *20 percent to software*, and *at least 20 percent for staff development*. The remaining 10 percent may cover supplies and other items, excluding salaries. If major hardware purchases are made one year, other budget categories could well increase in the next. These figures are not absolutes, of course, just guidelines to emphasize the significance of nonhardware components, which are often overlooked.

Cradler, Freeman, Cradler, and McNabb (2002) note that the No Child Left Behind legislation stresses the need for staff development by requiring that 25 percent of technology funding be devoted to staff development that is research based. Pinellas County (Florida) spends one-third of its technology budget on teacher professional development (CEO Forum, 2001, p. 7). Both are exemplary approaches to appropriate budgeting.

Another common error has been to view the computer budget as a one-time or short-term allocation. In fact, computers in the curriculum mean serious financial commitments every year. Proportions may change, but there will be continuing needs for hardware repair and replacement, software updating and replacement, new peripherals, and so on. Morse (1995) reported a government estimate that initial hardware purchase is just 15–30 percent of the ultimate cost of using and supporting the system. To ignore the true "total cost of ownership" can doom any technology effort.

Stretching the Hardware Budget

Since all budgets are inadequate by definition, how can you get the most out of what you have? Shop smart! Always look for educational discounts. Even in the highly competitive price market today, schools should still be able to buy computers at slightly lower prices than the general public does. Teachers often can get school prices for personal purchases, too.

The widespread competition in the Windows market has led to competitive prices from all computer makers. Even Apple has had to drop Macintosh prices to compete. Desire for a low price need not preclude purchasing a name brand. Look at Dell and Gateway, and then compare their features with low-end products from any other makers. Demand at least a three-year warranty (more if possible). The power of today's computers should mean they will remain useful at least that long, and the cost of an initial warranty upgrade is much less than the potential repairs after three or four years of school use.

Since hardware purchases are part of a long-term plan, don't be shortsighted. It costs only slightly more to purchase computers with more RAM and larger-capacity hard drives than you think you need. Next year, you'll be glad you did, since upgrades later tend to cost more than initial enhancements. Finally, many vendors offer system bundles, adding peripherals or software at less than normal cost, which can be excellent buys for schools.

Beyond the basic budget, consider seeking hardware donations from businesses, which can afford to replace their computers more frequently than most schools. Many are still quite usable, but always evaluate any potential donation for its fit within the school's technology plan ("Donated," 1998).

Stretching the Software Budget

Competition is fierce for software sales as well as hardware. Unless a product is sold only by its producer, you should be able to buy it for 20 to 40 percent less than list price. Educational pricing exists for software as well as hardware. Some companies such as Microsoft, Corel (*WordPerfect*), and Apple offer very low prices, either directly or through dealers. A few companies specialize in heavy discounts to educators on major software products. The companion website has links to several such companies.

Shareware is software that its creator distributes on a "try it and pay me if you like it" basis. It is widely available to download from the Internet (e.g., <www.shareware.com>) and by mail from specialized companies such as Software of the Month Club at <www.somc.com>. The latter charge a service fee for distributing the software. Sometimes you get the full version and sometimes only a limited trial version. The developer requests a registration fee, often less than $50, which gets you the latest full version, more complete documentation in some cases, perhaps the next upgrade, and/or other benefits. There is a lot of good shareware that could meet some school needs at very low cost. Shareware vendors may also offer *public domain* software that you are free to use without further payment or registration.

There is also *freeware*, software that is offered to users free of charge, which may, however, be under copyright to the creator, unlike public domain software. Brunelle and Bruce (2002) make a strong case for the importance of free software as part of national efforts to achieve technology literacy and equity.

Another approach to economizing on software is to choose alternatives to the dominant Windows and Macintosh systems. Linux, a popular variant of the Unix operating system, has become a viable choice for some schools. It is very stable and the price is right—usually free, as are many other so-called "open source" software products (Gonsalves, 2003). There are clear disadvantages, such as lack of technical support, but for schools with capable IT staffs, the advantages may carry the day. We have yet to experiment with Linux, so we certainly offer no recommendation. However, in times of financial difficulty such as the early 2000s, it may be wise to explore all the options.

SUMMARY

This chapter considered one view of computer implementation history through the 1990s. The initial goal of quick mass participation by teachers in the computer revolution now appears naive. The impact of computers in schools has been less than anticipated for various reasons that you read about. The twenty-first century demands a new direction to retarget the educational benefits of computers.

The goal remains invisible integration of computers into the curriculum to achieve student competence to apply the computer to whatever tasks may be appropriate. From this, the curriculum will itself change. Only some teachers are now prepared to implement computers, and others may join them only slowly. Within that context, you considered issues and ideas for staff development, hardware, physical facilities, and budgets.

A more thorough consideration of implementation issues exceeds the scope of this book. It is also beyond the immediate need of someone relatively new to educational computing. As your involvement matures, this initial exposure to some of the issues will perhaps come to mind again and lead you into more extensive resources as needed.

Former Surgeon General Jocelyn Elders was quoted in the *Pittsburgh Post-Gazette* (Srikameswaran, 2003) as saying "You can't teach what you don't know, and you can't lead where you won't go." You are on the road to technology leadership. The future of education depends on technology; and it also depends on *you!*

1. Interview teachers and/or administrators who were involved early in their school's implementation of computers. How do their experiences compare to our "history"?

2. Contact local school districts to learn about their technology plans. Request copies of written plans and other documents (such as the district mission statement) that refer to computers. Visit the National Center for Technology Planning at <www.nctp.com> if you lack local resources. Analyze what you obtain.

3. State and defend a position on the question of whether *all* teachers should be involved in computer implementation.

4. Based on your knowledge, experience, and views, articulate the most compelling reasons that teachers do not use computers. Try to interview several teachers who are nonusers to explore their reasons.

5. Propose a staff-development plan congruent with activities 3 and 4.

6. Interview one or more technology coordinators to learn more about their job. Also talk with several technology users in each coordinator's school. Write a job description for a technology coordinator, including justification for the position.

7. Interview persons experienced with computer labs and mobile or room-based computers. Synthesize our commentary and their experiences into a recommendation for computer configuration(s) in a school.

8. Outline a plan for computer use in a one-computer classroom. Focus on collaborative learning activities.

9. Determine which adaptive or assistive devices are available in your school. Learn to use as many as possible and reflect on what these devices offer to individuals who need them.

10. Compile a list of shareware and/or public domain software that you would consider using with your students. If possible, obtain several of these products and learn to use them. How do they compare with commercial products that you may have also used?

11. Research possible funding opportunities appropriate to your teaching area.

Companion Website

Visit the companion website at <www.ablongman.com/lockard6e> for more information about the topics discussed in this chapter.

expect the world®

The New York Times
nytimes.com

Themes of the Times

Expand your knowledge of the concepts discussed in this chapter by reading current and historical articles from the *New York Times* by visiting the Themes of the Times section of the companion website <www.ablongman.com/lockard6e>.

References

Abdulezer, S. "Making Connections with a Hearing World." *Converge*, October 1998. Retrieved March 10, 2003, from <www.convergemag.com/Publications/CNVGOct98/specialed/specialed.shtm>

Barksdale, J. M. "New Teachers: Why Schools of Education Are Still Sending You Staff You'll Have to Train in Technology." *Electronic Learning*, March/April 1996, *15*(5), pp. 38–45.

Becker, H. J. "How Exemplary Computer-Using Teachers Differ from Other Teachers: Implications for Realizing the Potential of Computers in Schools." *Journal of Research on Computing in Education*, Spring 1994, *26*(3), pp. 291–321.

Bell, T. H. "Teaching and Technology (On Education)." *School and College*, November 1992, *31*(11), p. 6.

Bowman, J. Jr., Newman, D. L., and Masterson, J. "Adopting Educational Technology: Implications for Designing Interventions." *Journal of Educational Computing Research*, 2001, *25*(1), pp. 81–94.

Bozeman, W. C., and Baumbach, D. J. *Educational Technology: Best Practices from America's Schools.* Princeton Junction, NJ: Eye on Education, 1995.

Bracey, G. W. "Two Studies Show Students Gain When Teaming Up." *Electronic Learning*, January 1988, *7*(4), p. 19.

Bracey, G. W. "New Pathways: Technology's Empowering Influence on Teaching (Research)." *Electronic Learning*, April 1993 (Special Edition), *12*(7), pp. 8–9.

Brown, J. S. "To Dream the Invisible Dream." *Red Herring*, July 1998. Retrieved March 7, 2003, from <www.redherring.com/mag/issue56/think.html>

Brunelle, M. D., and Bruce, B. C. "Why Free Software Matters for Literacy Educators." *Journal of Adolescent & Adult Literacy*, March 2002, *45*(6), pp. 514–518.

Brush, T. A. "Technology Planning and Implementation in Public Schools: A Five-State Comparison." *Computers in the Schools*, 1999, *15*(2), pp. 11–23.

Bryant, D. P., and Bryant, B. R. *Assistive Technology for People with Disabilities.* Boston: Allyn and Bacon, 2003.

CEO Forum. *Education Technology Must Be Included in Comprehensive Education Legislation. A Policy Paper.* CEO Forum, March 2001. Retrieved March 10, 2003, from <www.ceoforum.org/downloads/forum3.pdf>

Collis, B. *Computers, Curriculum, and Whole-Class Instruction.* Belmont, CA: Wadsworth, 1988.

Collis, B. "Research Windows." *The Computer Teacher*, December/January 1988–89, *16*(4), p. 7.

Coughlin, E. "Professional Competencies for the Digital Age Classroom." *Learning and Leading with Technology*, November 1999, *27*(3), pp. 22–27. See also <www.milkenexchange.org/prooject/pcc/ME159.pdf>

Cradler, J., Freeman, M., Cradler, R., and McNabb, M. "Research Implications for Preparing Teachers to Use Technology." *Learning & Leading with Technology*, September 2002, *30*(1), pp. 50–52.

Crystal, J. "Building from Within: Two Professional Development Models That Work." *Technology & Learning*, September 15, 2001. Retrieved March 14, 2003, from <www.techlearning.com:8080/db_area/archives/TL/200109/building.html>

Cuban, L. "Déjà Vu All Over Again." *Electronic Learning*, October 1995, *15*(2), pp. 34–37, 61.

Dias, L. B. "Integrating Technology: Some Things You Should Know." *Learning and Leading with Technology*, November 1999, *27*(3), pp.10–13, 21.

D'Ignazio, F., and D'Ignazio, C. "Are We Missing the Boat? Reflecting on Educational Technology." *Learning and Leading with Technology*, March 1998, *25*(6), pp. 56–57.

Doersch, D. "Put Me In, Coach." *Learning & Leading with Technology*, November 2002, *30*(3), pp. 46–49.

"Donated Computers in K–12 Education." *Learning and Leading with Technology*, February 1998, *25*(5), pp. 52–56.

Dyrli, O., and Kinnaman, D. "What Every Teacher Needs to Know About Technology." *Technology & Learning*, January 1995, *15*(4), pp. 38–43.

Gardner, J. E., and Wissick, C. A. "Enhancing Thematic Units Using the World Wide Web: Tools and Strategies for Students with Mild

Disabilities." *Journal of Special Education Technology*, Winter 2002, *17*(1), pp. 27–38.

Glasser, W. "Quality: The Key to the Disciplines." *National Forum*, Winter 1989, *69*(1), pp. 36–38.

Gonsalves, A. "The Linux Alternative." *Technology & Learning*, March 2003, *23*(8), pp. 9–12.

Hardy, C. *Autism and ITC: A Guide for Teachers and Parents.* London: David Fulton, 2002.

Hayes, J., and Bybee, D. L. "Defining the Greatest Need for Educational Technology." *Learning and Leading with Technology*, October 1995, *23*(2), pp. 48–50.

Heward, W. *Exceptional Children: An Introduction to Special Education*, 7th ed. Upper Saddle River, NJ: Prentice Hall, 2003.

Holland, H. "Whither School Reform?" *Electronic Learning*, January/February 1996, *15*(4), pp. 34–42, 49, 55.

Holzberg, C. S. "Special Education Success Stories." *Technology & Learning*, January 1993, *13*(4), pp. 53–56.

Kelman, P. "Alternatives to Integrated Instructional Systems." In Cannings, T. R., and Finkel, L. (eds.), *The Technology Age Classroom.* Wilsonville, OR: Franklin, Beedle, 1993.

King, T. W. *Assistive Technology: Essential Human Factors.* Boston: Allyn and Bacon, 1999.

Kinnaman, D. E. "A Clear Vision and a Five-Percent Commitment." *School and College*, October 1992, *31*(10), pp. 19–20.

Kinnaman, D. E. "We Need Thinking Like That (The Leadership Role)." *Technology & Learning*, January 1996, *16*(4), p. 78.

Klein, K., and Strothers, D., eds. *Planning for Microcomputers in the Curriculum.* Bloomington, IN: Phi Delta Kappa, Hot Topics Series 1983–1984.

Knapp, L. R., and Glenn, A. D. *Restructuring Schools with Technology.* Boston: Allyn and Bacon, 1996.

Lengel, J. G. *Computer Considerations for Vermont Schools.* Burlington: Vermont Department of Education, 1983.

Lever-Duffy, J., McDonald, J. B., and Mizell, A. P. *Teaching and Learning with Technology.* Boston: Allyn and Bacon, 2003.

Male, M. *Technology for Inclusion. Meeting the Special Needs of All Students*, 4th ed. Boston: Allyn and Bacon, 2003.

Monahan, S. "Our Classmates." *Learning and Leading with Technology*, March 1999, *26*(6), pp. 10–13.

Morse, G. "Building the Foundation. Harnessing Technology for Schools and Communities." *Learning and Leading with Technology*, May 1995, *22*(8), pp. 53–55.

Moursund, D. *The Technology Coordinator.* Eugene, OR: ISTE, 1992.

Moursund, D. G. *Obtaining Resources for Technology in Education: A How-To Guide for Writing Proposals, Forming Partnerships, and Raising Funds.* Retrieved March 5, 2003, from <http://darkwing.uoregon.edu/~moursund/GrantWriting/index.htm>

NCES. U.S. Department of Education, National Center for Education Statistics. *Internet Access in U.S. Public Schools and Classrooms: 1994–2001.* Washington, DC: September 2002. NCES 2002-018. Retrieved December 20, 2002 from <http://nces.ed.gov/pubs2002/2002018.pdf>

NETS-A. *National Educational Technology Standards for Administrators.* Eugene, OR: ISTE, 2002. Retrieved March 14, 2003, from <http://cnets.iste.org/administrators/index.shtml>

Pearson, C. "Empowering Teachers for Technology." *The Computing Teacher*, September 1994, *22*(1), pp. 70–71.

Pratt, B. "Making It Work: Using Technology in a Classroom for Young Children with Multiple Disabilities." *Learning and Leading with Technology*, May 1999, *26*(8), pp. 28–31.

President's Committee of Advisors on Science and Technology, Panel on Educational Technology. *Report to the President on the Use of Technology to Strengthen K–12 Education in the United States.* 1997. <http://www.ostp.gov/PCAST/k-12ed.html>

QED. Quality Education Data. "Technology Spending in U.S. School Districts Holds at $7 Billion." Press Release November 15, 2002. Retrieved March 14, 2003, from <www.qeddata.com/combo_pr.htm>

Rhodes, L. A. "Technology-Driven Systemic Change." *Learning and Leading with Technology*, November 1995, *23*(3), pp. 35–37.

Roblyer, M. D. *Integrating Educational Technology into Teaching*, 3rd ed. Columbus, OH: Merrill Prentice Hall, 2003.

Roblyer, M. D., Castine, W. H., and King, F. J. "Assessing the Impact of Computer-Based Instruction." *Computers in the Schools*, 1988, *5*(3/4).

Rosenthal, I. G. "New Teachers and Technology: Are They Prepared?" *Technology & Learning*, April 1999, *19*(8), pp. 22–27.

Solomon, G., and Solomon, S. "Technology and Professional Development—10 Tips to Make It Better." *Learning and Leading with Technology*, November 1995, *23*(3), pp. 38–39, 71.

Srikameswaran, A. "UPMC Diabetes Initiative Gets Boost from Former Surgeon General." *Pittsburgh Post-Gazette*, January 30, 2003. Retrieved March 1, 2003, from <www.post-gazette.com/healthscience/20030130eldershea3.asp>

Stieglitz, E. L., and Costa, C. H. "A Statewide Teacher Training Program's Impact on Computer Usage in the Schools." *Computers in the Schools*, 1988, *5*(1/2), pp. 91–98.

U.S. Department of Education. *23rd Annual Report to Congress on the Implementation of the Individuals with Disabilities Education Act*. May 2002. Retrieved March 13, 2003, from <www.ed.gov/offices/OSERS/OSEP/Products/OSEP2001AnlRpt/>

Wetzel, K. "Preparing Teacher Leaders: A Partnership That Works, Part 2." *Learning & Leading with Technology*, November 2001, *29*(3), pp. 50–53.

Wilson, B. G., Hamilton, R., Teslow, J. L., and Cyr, T. A. *Technology Making a Difference: The Peakview Elementary School Study*. Syracuse, NY: ERIC Clearinghouse on Information and Technology, 1994.

Wissick, C. A. "Multimedia: Enhancing Instruction for Students with Learning Disabilities." *Journal of Learning Disabilities*, September 1996, *29*(5), pp. 494–503.

Wissick, C. A., and Gardner, J. E. "A Learner's Permit to the World Wide Web." *Teaching Exceptional Children*, May–June 1998, *30*(5), pp. 8–15.

Wissick, C. A., and Gardner, J. E. "Multimedia or Not to Multimedia." *Teaching Exceptional Children*, 2000, *32*(4), pp. 34–43.

Wissick, C. A., Gardner, J. E., and Langone, J. "Video-Based Simulations: Considerations for Teaching Students with Developmental Disabilities." *Career Development for Exceptional Individuals*, Fall 1999, *22*(2), pp. 233–249.

Woodward, J., and Cuban, L. *Technology, Curriculum, and Professional Development: Adapting Schools to Meet the Needs of Students with Disabilities*. Thousand Oaks, CA: Corwin, 2001.

Yue, L. "Biggest Apple at Home in Chicago." *Chicago Tribune*, June 26, 2003, Section 3, pp. 1, 9.

Issues and Implications

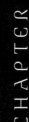

OBJECTIVES

After completing this chapter, you will be able to:

- Discuss ways in which computers are affecting the world of work.
- Synthesize issues related to computers and personal privacy.
- Explain four areas of concern related to ethics and discuss the role of teachers in addressing them.
- Evaluate the issues of gender and socioeconomic equity in computer access and propose responses to them.
- Explain and assess changes in the traditional educational roles of teachers, students, and parents due to technology.

Too often, discussions of computers in education are so glowingly positive as to be naive. Many educators seem content to blindly accept whatever fate technology brings to them, never questioning, never wondering. The bandwagon continues to roll and pick up passengers.

The computer does not deserve such blind devotion. Rather, the impact of computers on society and education should be closely scrutinized (e.g., see Healy, 1998; Oppenheimer, 1997; Stoll, 1999). It is difficult to argue against the claim that society is already so computerized that there is no turning back. By now it should also be obvious that we have no wish to turn back. However, greater attention to the impact of computers on our lives may serve to better guide future changes.

This chapter, then, is devoted to considering some of the key issues and implications raised by computers in society and, within it, education. It is critical that educators not neglect these issues as technology becomes ubiquitous. We do not claim to provide answers; rather, we seek to raise your awareness of the issues and of the need to consider them personally and with students. Each topic is a fertile opportunity for student research, discussion, and debate.

Social Issues

Within the broad category of social issues, we will look at the impact of computers on the world of work and on personal privacy. The underlying concern is what computers are doing to individuals and thus to society.

NETS
NOTES

NETS S 2
NETS T I-A
NETS T I-B
NETS T III-A
NETS T V-B
NETS T VI-A
NETS T VI-D
NETS T VI-E

Impact on Work

Best-sellers such as Naisbitt's *Megatrends* and *Powershift* popularized the idea that society has moved past the Industrial Age into the Information Age or the Information Society. Some believe the transformation has occurred; others see it as under way, but far from complete. These are mostly semantic differences. The major "product" of today's workforce is indeed information.

The Workforce

Consider some of the changes that occurred in the workforce in the twentieth century (Bureau of Labor Statistics, 2002; USDA, 2003). In 1900 there were over 13.5 million farm workers in America (roughly 35 percent of the workforce), but by 2000 the number had fallen to fewer than 3 million (less than 3 percent). The percentage of persons involved in production of goods fell to roughly 10 percent (it was over 50 percent in the 1950s). Of some 20 million new jobs created in the 1970s, nearly 90 percent were information or service related, a trend that has continued and accelerated. However, service jobs pay far less than disappearing manufacturing jobs. What are some of the important ramifications of these changes?

The labor movement developed from concerns over working conditions in industry. Traditional union strongholds, such as the automobile industry and mining, employ far fewer persons than at the peak of union strength. Membership is down accordingly; robots in factories are not potential union members.

What is the future of labor unions? What will be the rallying cries among information workers, if they become unionized? What are the new labor issues in the Information Age? Can there be such a thing as job security in an era when huge companies including IBM and AT&T have reduced their workforces by tens of thousands? What will become of persons displaced by technology? Technology may create more jobs than it destroys, but not for the same people, nor at comparable wage levels.

Perhaps retraining of workers is the answer. Some question whether the workforce, especially blue-collar workers, can be retrained for new responsibilities. Is there any incentive for industry to retrain older workers if younger people are available with the required skills? Is it possible that we are approaching an era when blue-collar workers in their 40s and 50s will become permanently unemployable or able to find only jobs near minimum wage?

Looking at projections for job growth from 2000 to 2010 (ACINET, 2003), eight of the top ten growth occupations relate directly to computers—software engineers and system administrators to desktop publishers. Projected growth rates range from 60 percent to 100 percent over the decade. Six of the eight require at least a bachelor's degree and will offer salaries in the top quartile of all occupations; the other two require at least some postsecondary education and will pay in the upper half of all salaries. The other two growth areas in the top ten are health related, require only on-the-job training, and pay the lowest wages. However, in terms of greatest numbers of jobs projected to be offered, the top four occupations (and 11 of the top 25) are all in the lowest wage categories of service industries—retail sales, food preparation and serving, cashiers, wait staff, cleaning personnel, and so on. Conversely, of the 25 occupations projected to lose the most jobs in this decade, 14 are occupations that pay wages in the upper half of all earnings. What are the implications of these trends for the students you will be teaching in the coming years?

Where One Works

Particularly in urban areas, it has become common for people to spend a great amount of time just getting to and from work. Expressway systems become parking lots at 7 A.M. and 4 P.M.; mass transit, where it exists, is crowded. For some years now, this waste of potentially productive human time has been of concern. It was clear in the age of factories that the worker had to go to the factory as most service workers still must. Is this still true in information industries?

Technologically, we have long had the potential for employees in certain kinds of jobs to work from their homes via telecommunications. A computer, modem or broadband connection, and fax can link a home office to the "physical" job site. What would it mean if large numbers of workers were no longer required to be physically "on the job?" What would this mean for family life at home? What would it mean for the real estate industry if huge office complexes were no longer needed? How would you like to work alone at home rather than with other people? Past experiments with working from home have tended to flounder on the lack of socialization with others. Is this likely to change?

Health/Safety Issues

Concerns over possible physical side effects of prolonged exposure to computers, particularly monitors, have arisen many times since the early days of computers. Eye fatigue, for instance, can result from poorly located monitors, inappropriate eyeglass prescriptions, and other factors. Radiation produced by electronic equipment may also have health implications that are as yet unclear. In the face of inconclusive medical evidence, the Swedish government imposed on computer monitors far stricter standards for emissions, for instance, than those of most other nations. Related are concerns over posture-induced back problems brought on by long hours seated at a computer (<www.cdc.gov/niosci1.html> and <www.cdc.gov/niosh/ergopage.html>).

Other issues include the toxicity of chemicals used in chip manufacturing, the problems of proper disposal of old equipment, even the trade-offs between the environmental impacts of, say, paper production and those of using computers to reduce or eliminate paper flow in businesses (Nichols & Welliver, 1991). Repetitive hand actions may lead to carpal tunnel syndrome (see <www.cdc.gov/niosh/ergosci1.html>). Students should be challenged to investigate and consider all sides of such concerns.

Personal Privacy

Computers have permitted corporations, government, and other groups to create databanks on a scale previously undreamed of. How wonderful it is to be able to make a purchase anywhere in the world by credit card, which the merchant can instantly verify. How nice to be able to write a personal check in a distant city because the store can quickly determine if the check will clear. For all the convenience, these things are possible only because somewhere a computer has a lot of information on file concerning you and your finances. How willingly would you share such information with strangers if they simply asked you for it?

According to one technology lawyer, "Hell is a loss of privacy and nothing brings us closer to hell than telecommunications technology. We will all end up consumers with no privacy in a technological world with no protections" ("Multimedia," 1995). Have we indeed passed the point where personal privacy can be maintained?

Do you consider the ramifications of filling out a credit card application? Of responding to information requested for a city directory? Of applying for a job? Of subscribing to a magazine or completing a "marketing survey" that comes in the mail or email? All of these things provide data about you to others. Of growing concern are so-called "smart cards" that store information about the user (Veverka, 1999). The information may be financial, medical, whatever. Whenever you use these cards, you leave behind a trail that one expert describes thusly: "In many ways, it's better than a diary" (p. 1). Theoretically, an insurance company might one day review your shopping habits to decide whether you are a good risk. Too much junk food, tobacco, or alcohol might doom your application. A potential employer might be able to review your medical history before deciding whether to hire you. If you keep a diary, do you share it with everyone with whom you do business? An alternative to credit and identification cards, smart cards are already in use in the military and on college campuses.

Another issue related to privacy is *spam*, the unwanted email messages sent by businesses and even individuals to persons whose email addresses they have obtained in a variety of ways. According to Krim (2003), "The flood of unsolicited email . . . is growing so fast that spam may soon account for half of all U.S. email traffic, making it . . . possibly a threat to the continued usefulness of the most successful tool of the computer age." He noted that spam accounted for only 8 percent of email in 2001 and that it is growing at a very rapid rate, leading to calls for federal legislation to regulate it. You may be inviting spam whenever you complete an electronic survey on the Web, when you make an online purchase, or when you register a product you have purchased. Any time you share your email address with someone you don't know, the potential exists for your address to reach unintended recipients.

Many spam messages have a "remove me from your list" link at the end, and in the most legitimate cases, using it will indeed stop the email from that source. However, it appears that in some cases, a reply merely confirms your electronic existence and leads to a still wider spread of your address among spammers. In short, just as you protect your personal information in face-to-face transactions, you should be very alert to how you are sharing your email address. Once spam starts to reach you, it is very difficult to stop (Coates, March 2003).

Are you aware of "cookie" files, which allow a web site that you access to store information about your visit on your own hard disk? Few web users have been conscious of this feature. Do you have personalized web access through a major portal such as Yahoo, Excite, or Microsoft Network? They are able to customize content to your own interests because of the information you provided, which they store on your computer. Did you realize you gave permission to access your computer when you enrolled for the service? Who actually looks at that information, if anyone? Is there such a thing as a secure computer system, where only those duly authorized and strictly supervised can gain access to your information? Evidence suggests there is not.

Other electronic wonders are creating trails of information on individuals as never before. Consider the use of automatic teller machines and other systems for electronically transferring funds. All transactions must be fully documented, which means a paper trail possibly open to misuse, though its intent is the opposite. As electronic mail has become commonplace, there is reason for concern for the privacy of your messages, since it is all but certain that electronic copies of everything you send and receive are stored in the backup tapes of the computers you use for mail. Old email has become a common target of subpoenas in legal proceedings including the collapse of Enron and Arthur Andersen. How does this compare to the potential of someone getting access to your normal mail? Consider the uproar over the Intel Pentium III chip when it was introduced in early 1999 because of its ability to identify itself (that is, *your* computer) by its serial number to other computers as it accesses them via the Internet (Coates, 1999). Intel was forced to deactivate the "feature."

It is not our desire to cause outbreaks of paranoia over privacy. We have yet to see evidence of problems so severe as to bring technology use into question. However, the issue is one that requires continual scrutiny, such as has been formalized in the Privacy Rights Clearinghouse in San Diego <www.privacyrights.org> and by the organization Americans for Computer Privacy <www.computerprivacy.org>. For links to many groups concerned with personal, medical, and consumer privacy in the Information Age, visit Computers and Privacy <http://special.northernlight.com/privacy> or the privacy resources of About.com at <http://search.about.com/fullsearch.htm?terms=privacy>.

The privacy and, ultimately, security of children are a major issue for schools, and the Internet especially presents challenges such as predators. Young (1998) referred to the Internet as an "electronic red-light district." Federal directives that schools and public libraries use filtering software to protect young users have been accepted widely by schools but attacked as infringing on the right of free speech by others. You should also become familiar with Kids Privacy <www.kidsprivacy.com>, a site cosponsored by the Federal Trade Commission, where you can learn about the Children's Online Privacy Protection Act among other topics. (See also the FTC information on complying with the act at <www.ftc.gov/bcp/conline/pubs/buspubs/coppa.htm>). Students must become aware of the situation and become part of a monitoring system to insist that necessary laws, standards, or policies are implemented to protect personal rights.

Ethics

NETS
NOTES

NETS **S** 2
NETS **T** I-A
NETS **T** I-B
NETS **T** III-A
NETS **T** III-C
NETS **T** IV-B
NETS **T** V-B
NETS **T** VI-A

Some two decades ago Hamilton (cited in Bitter, 1984, p. 293) wrote, "Today's computer is intellectually a moron, and morally permissive. Provided it is instructed in a language it understands and is programmed to receive the instructions, it will do as it is told whether this be right or wrong." Although computers are now vastly more capable machines, Hamilton's points remain just as valid as when he wrote them.

With the widespread availability of computers have come significant problems in ethical, and even legal, behavior. It is interesting to speculate on what permits individuals who otherwise might never cross the legal line beyond overtime parking to alter their behavior with computers. Is this somehow another effect of computers on individuals? What makes the situation sufficiently different from others to affect moral behavior? Let's consider four areas: academic dishonesty, software piracy, hacking, and viruses.

Academic Dishonesty/Plagiarism

While cheating in schools is hardly something new, the potential has reached new levels thanks to the Internet (Goot, 2002; Mayfield, 2001). The scope of the problem led to publication of the book *Student Cheating and Plagiarism in the Internet Era* (Lathrop & Foss, 2000). One widely reported issue is the easy availability of research papers that one can download from unscrupulous websites (e.g., schoolsucks.com). This may be just the latest variation on hiring someone else to do one's work or the legendary fraternity house "files," but it differs in that these "resources" are readily available to any student with web access. Teachers must be more vigilant than ever, and detection may be more difficult than when a more finite set of papers circulated among students. Addressing the issue through open discussions of academic dishonesty is probably the best approach. Think of an entire paper as the ultimate form of plagiarism, which has to be dealt with for Internet research just as for conventional research.

Research integrity was treated in greater detail in Chapter 4.

Software Piracy/Copyright

The cost of software development is enormous for high-quality, complex products. Copyright law seeks to protect the rights of software producers to profit from sales of their products. Few individuals seem inclined to violate copyright law by making copies of whole books or films, yet many think nothing of "pirating" copies of software for themselves or friends in violation of the law and the license agreement for the software.

While there can be some confusion because of differences in software licenses (Schwartz & Beichner, 1999), in general, you are entitled to use only a single copy of the software you purchase, while storing a backup copy for use in case the working copy is damaged. Any other use is illegal unless explicitly permitted by the license agreement. The Software & Information Industry Association (SIIA) provides much information about copyright definitions and educational use on its website at <www.siia.net/piracy/copyright>.

At the same time, efforts to control software copying can lead to undesired reactions. The makers of the popular income tax preparation software *TurboTax* created an enormous uproar when they included a copy protection scheme within the 2002 tax year edition of the product. The effort was in response to industry estimates that half the copies of *TurboTax* in use were pirated (Coates, February 2003). The system used in this case effectively limited use of the software to a single machine but did so by using a small program installed without the user's knowledge that checked the registration with the company each time the software was used. The furor stemmed in large part from users who believed that they should have been warned in advance of installation about this "spy" software and that the company violated users' rights because the spyware was not removed from the computer when the tax software itself was uninstalled. Predictions at the time were that *TurboTax* would lose its place as the most popular tax software because of the consumer revolts. The point is that the issue of piracy is not a simple one and neither is how best to deal with it.

Software piracy exists among very young computer users as well as adults. To some extent, it falls to teachers to deal with the issue, preferably as a matter of ethics and practical ramifications rather than as a major legal concern. The fact is that few casual pirates are apt to be prosecuted; apprehension is simply too unlikely. However, corporations and even schools have been targeted for prosecution. Many companies have paid substantial fines for not controlling software usage (e.g., *USA Today*, June 10, 2002). For the latest news on legal actions against software piracy, visit the antipiracy area of the Software & Information Industry Association's website at <www.siia.net/piracy> and of the Business Software Alliance (SBA) at <www.bsa.org/usa/antipiracy>, especially their news reports <www.bsa.org/usa/press>. You should also read about the education initiatives of the Software Publisher's Association (SPA) at <www.siia.net/piracy/policy/educate.asp>.

We believe that potential software pirates first must understand that their actions are in fact theft, just like shoplifting a candy bar. Many now attach no such stigma to copying software. As soon as children are old enough to learn to duplicate a diskette or install software from a CD, they should be taught the legal issues of copyright.

Second, computer users also must become aware of the magnitude of the piracy problem. The Business Software Alliance states that the global software piracy rate in 2001 was 40 percent (25 percent in the United States alone) at a cost to the software industry of nearly $11 billion. Small wonder the level of concern runs so high.

Third, educators must consider the by-products of piracy. Teachers have long had a less than pristine image among publishers because we have always been "borrowers" of materials. Perceptions of "fair use" have been extended to cover copying virtually anything. Software may appear to be just the latest source of "free" materials.

Obviously, school budgets are limited, while teacher demand for software grows daily. Limited school budgets cannot, however, justify piracy. Most producers now offer economical licensing deals to meet legitimate concerns of educators over the cost of the multiple software copies required to operate legally. In turn, educators must be role models for their students. There is no place for pirated software in a school. Budgets must allocate appropriate amounts for software as well as hardware.

Additional resources are in the chapter references and on the companion website.

Hacking

The Internet poses security risks that necessitate knowing something about the issues of hacking to avoid becoming a victim. At its simplest, *hacking* is gaining unauthorized access to any computer system. A *hacker* is typically a young person who is totally caught up in working with a computer, often to the exclusion of other activities, eventually becoming a very skilled programmer. With telecommunication access to computers around the world, hackers delight in finding ways around the security checks of systems so that they can just "browse" through a computer's files. One hacker website distinguishes *hackers*, whom they define as "builders" who apply "appropriate ingenuity" to create software, from *crackers* who are criminal hackers seeking to "break" things <www.happy hacker.org/define.shtml>. Detailed information about hacking can be found using the search term "hacking" at the website <www.about.com>. For a very different point of view, just browse the Happy Hacker website <www.happyhacker.org> that appears to aim its content at youthful hackers.

Some hacking can perhaps be viewed as youthful exuberance, a sense of power over mechanical objects. At least at the start, hackers are rarely malicious. Indeed, the Happy Hackers claim to provide a service by looking for security holes, then informing system owners so that they may take corrective action. However, hacking has led to unauthorized access to government and corporate computers and the theft, alteration, or destruction of data in them. A 20-year-old student at the University of Texas (UT) was charged in March 2003 with hacking into the UT computer system and allegedly stealing personal information including social security numbers from over 50,000 faculty, staff, and students ("Student charged," 2003). The student reportedly claimed he had no malicious intent. In Chicago, hackers broke into a restaurant's voice mail system and reprogrammed it to give an obscene message to callers (Van, 1996). Cases have been publicly reported of records being altered in hospital files, which could mean harm to patients. Thus what may have begun as play can become deadly serious.

Just as schools must bear some responsibility for educating youngsters about software piracy, so, too, must they address the issue of unauthorized entry into a computer system. Stoll (1989), Elliott (1990), and Markoff and Hafner (1991) provide fascinating looks into the subculture of hackers and other "cyberpunks" in their early days. An equally intriguing book is *The Hacking of America* (Schell & Dodge, 2002), which is easy reading on a complex topic. In addition to the Happy Hacker site mentioned previously, you'll also find a very prohacker stance at *2600 The Hacker Quarterly* <www.2600.com>.

Van Buren (2001) wrote of experiences in trying to educate school-age hackers away from destructive practices and toward ethical computing behavior. Her article is based on an ethnographic study of students at a California high school.

Viruses

Another element of computer security has arisen along with the Internet. Physicians may diagnose an illness as a virus—a submicroscopic agent that causes disease. A computer virus is a program "written specifically to disrupt computer operations and/or destroy data" (Lever-Duffy, McDonald, & Mizell, 2003, p. 419). Webopedia <www.webopedia.com/TERM/V/virus.html> notes that a virus is "loaded onto your computer without your knowledge and runs against your wishes." It remains undetected and inactive until a specific date or particular set of conditions occurs. At that point it is activated to begin its malicious task: perhaps denying access to users, deleting or altering files, even reformatting hard disks. "Worm" viruses reproduce themselves, taking up more and more memory and/or disk space until they cause the system to crash. Detailed information about viruses can be found at <www.cert.org/other_sources/viruses.html>. The first virus appeared in 1987 and attacked the ARPANET, precursor to the Internet <www.webopedia.com/TERM/V/virus.html>. In 1989, new viruses were appearing at a rate of four per year. By mid-1991, a new virus was detected every day ("A Virus Epidemic," 1991). Viruses may be on diskettes or even recorded onto CD-ROMs by mistake, where they can't be erased. They commonly travel across networks, especially the Internet, and have been found in software downloaded from shareware sites. They then pass from individual to individual as those files are shared, frequently as attachments to email messages. Many viruses spread through email and some of the nastier ones may be able to "read" your address book (especially if you use *MS Outlook* software) and send themselves on to all of the listed addresses, thus rapidly expanding their area of impact. Reputable download site operators routinely screen their files for viruses. However, even commercial vendors occasionally have distributed infected software through carelessness.

The best defense against viruses is "safe computing." Be cautious about the source of your software. Install and always use antivirus software, some of which is available free. Given the rate of appearance of new viruses, the latter cannot be perfect, even though many such products are updated frequently. Still, they seem to provide protection against the viruses most common in schools and among typical home computer users. For more information, visit McAfee Security (Figure 15.1) at <www.mcafee.com/anti-virus> or Symantec at <http://securityresponse.symantec.com>, both of which provide information about the latest viruses as well as solutions should you become infected. You should also be aware that there are many hoaxes, which are virus warnings that circulate via email but are not true. Sometimes they direct the recipient to delete files that are allegedly viruses but which may be part of the operating system or other software. Deleting them can have severe consequences, as intended by the creator, but the user has done it personally by reacting to the warning, not the virus. If you receive a virus warning, even from a friend, always check to see if it is a hoax before you take any action. Hoax information can be found at many sites, including McAfee and Symantec as previously listed.

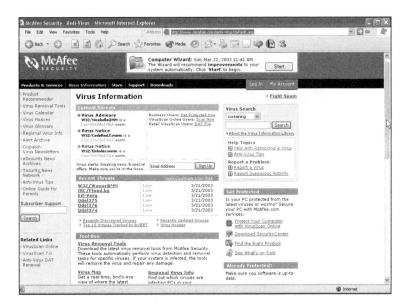

Figure 15.1

VIRUS INFORMATION
RESOURCE FROM MCAFEE
SECURITY

If you don't have antivirus software, some campuses provide such software free to faculty, staff, and students as a form of protection for their own infrastructure. There are also free, inexpensive, or limited-time trial versions of antivirus software available at major shareware sites, including <http://shareware.cnet.com>, which lists antivirus as one of its major links, and <www.jumbo.com/utilities> or <http://download.com.com>, which list antivirus software as a category of utility software. Symantec also offers a free on-line Security Check service at <http://security.symantec.com>. If you have a broadband connection to the Internet, you may need to consider installing firewall software to add protection to a connection that is constantly active, even if you are not there (Goldsborough, 2000). The security sites listed also offer firewall software.

Further information about issues of computer security is provided by Ekhaml (2001).

Equity

NETS
NOTES

NETS **S** 2
NETS **T** I-A
NETS **T** I-B
NETS **T** III-A

Although you have just considered some of the darker sides of computing, on balance computers have been highly beneficial and are today's basic tools of learning and work. However, equity of access to computers is an issue of grave concern. In 1984, Pantiel and Petersen wrote, "Probably the most critical question of the decade is whether computers are going to be available to everyone" (p. 170). That question remains unanswered nearly two decades later. Forcier (1999, p. 15) championed the educational benefits of computers but also noted, "We currently have a class of 'haves' and 'have nots,' those with good access to computers and those without." Let's consider two aspects of equity: gender and socioeconomics.

| NETS
| NOTES
NETS **T** III-C
NETS **T** IV-B
NETS **T** V-B
NETS **T** VI-A
NETS **T** VI-B
NETS **T** VI-C
NETS **T** VI-E

Gender

Many studies have documented that girls have not been involved in computing to an appropriate extent, given the importance of computers to their futures (Fiore, 1999). Girls are far less likely to participate in elective computer activities than boys, whether in courses, out of school, or at camps (McLester, 1998). Female interest begins to lag in middle school and continues from there. Girls exhibit greater anxiety about computers and less confidence; they are less likely to major in computer science in college. Yet when they do participate, girls perform as well as boys (see Milone & Salpeter, 1996; McGrath et al., 1992). Shashaani (1994) found "consistent, significant gender differences in computer interest, computer confidence, and gender-stereotyped views about computer users." She found the situation largely unchanged over time.

More recently, Poftak and Kennedy (2002) reported on a study commissioned by the Girl Scouts of America. Researchers confirmed what many teachers have observed, namely, that the Internet has been integrated into the basic communication strategies of teenage girls. Among girls surveyed, two-thirds reported going online two to three times a day, mostly to socialize with friends, and another 32 percent logged on at least a few times a week. Instant messaging plays a key role in this communication. "As for what they talk about, 52 percent of girls who chat online every day reported they prefer to express their emotions online rather than face-to-face, and 54 percent favor using email to fight with friends instead of in-person confrontations." However, Swain and Harvey (2002, p. 17) claimed that "while more girls are on the train, they aren't the ones driving" and Gilley (2002, p. 23) reported from her research that "girls may now be as capable with computer technology as boys, but they still either lack confidence or interest."

There are many possible explanations for this gender gap, all social or cultural. Shashaani (1994) found that parental attitudes and encouragement were highly significant. Both fathers and mothers tended to believe that computers were a male thing, a view that encouraged sons' but harmed daughters' interest, confidence, and views. Computers tend to be identified with math and science, both of which have been male dominated, rather than integrated throughout the curriculum (Forcier, 1999; Wiburg, 1994–95). According to Forcier (1999), females may be less confident with computers because of male dominance of computer labs, perceived irrelevance of school computer offerings to girls' interests, preference for cooperative rather than competitive work, and teachers who accept assumptions that girls are less interested and less capable than boys. Swain and Harvey (2002, p. 17) documented from multiple studies that "boys' aggressive and domineering behavior within the coeducational classroom" hinders girls' use of technology.

Carr-Chellman, Marra, and Roberts (2002) made a case that female aesthetics and sensibilities contribute to the problem. They explored "how gender has influenced the design of computer hardware . . . and how these gender-driven aesthetics may have worked to maintain, extend, or alter gender distinctions, roles, and stereotypes . . . " (p. 4). Clark (2002) offered many suggestions for engaging female students with technology. Among them are evaluating the curriculum for fairness, investigating girl-friendly projects, identifying role models, and structuring projects to integrate girls better. Swain and Harvey (2002) advocated computer classes for girls only as an effective strategy based on their research.

Fiore (1999) attributed much of the problem to a need for different kinds of software to entice girls to use technology and then described in detail approaches that address the issues raised. Visit her website (Figure 15.2) at <www.classroom.com/edsoasis/ Treasure/girls.html>, which contains links to many sites that are "girl friendly." Other such sites are accessible from the companion website.

Educators clearly must guard against gender inequities. Awareness of the issue is the essential starting point. As schools achieve full integration of technology into the curriculum at all grade levels, experiences should become more uniform for all students.

Socioeconomics and the Digital Divide

The term *digital divide* refers to the gap that separates the technology "haves" from the "have nots." There is much concern that the disparity in technology access among children today may widen the gap as those with access leap further ahead of those who lack it. Previously in this book you read about the massive infusion of computer technology into schools, but that is only a start on the problem. Access to technology is a function of several factors.

Family income is directly related to the presence of technology in the home. According to the National Telecommunications and Information Administration (NTIA, 2000), although more than half of all homes have a computer, more than two-thirds of families with annual incomes in excess of $50,000 have Internet access compared to only about 45 percent of households with incomes between $35,000 and $50,000. Differences in access exist by location (lower in rural areas) and by ethnicity (African Americans and Hispanics trailing other groups by a wide margin).

Are schools the solution to the digital divide? Clearly, they are a major potential contributor, and the impressive figures presented earlier in this book on the growth of

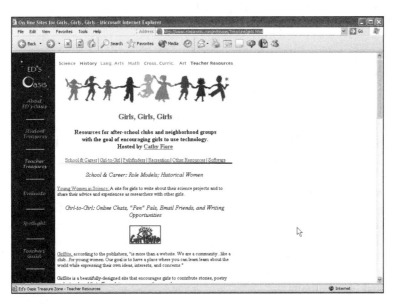

Figure 15.2

ONE OF MANY SITES AIMED AT INCREASING GIRLS' INVOLVEMENT WITH TECHNOLOGY

technology in schools seem to suggest movement in that direction. However, the broad numbers mask large differences among individual school districts. The issue has nothing to do with technology per se and everything to do with the way most schools are organized and funded. Technology only calls further attention to the fact that schools in the United States are anything but equal. For example, for the five years from 1995 to 1999, state appropriations for educational technology varied from $4 per student in Maine to $441 per student in Ohio (Milken, 1999). Inequities affect everything from basic supplies such as paper and pencils to library resources and even the quality of teachers. The computer era may focus attention on the problems; it did not create them.

Another resource of growing importance is public libraries, many of which offer public access to technology, even in small communities. However, neither schools nor public libraries offer the level of access available to students who have technology in the home.

Given the power and benefit of computers in education, how can equitable access be achieved? Or will computers only increase the separation of those who are adequately prepared to compete in the employment marketplace from those who are not? What does this do to the significance of public education? The Benton Foundation and various partners jointly sponsor the Digital Divide Network <www.digitaldividenetwork.org>, which offers a wealth of information and resources for combating technology equity problems. The Hispanic Research Center of Arizona State University offers important resources at <www.asu.edu/DigitalDivideSolutions>. There are also many resources on all equity issues at the International Society for Technology in Education <www.iste.org/resources/equity>. Malter and Wodarz (2000) and Yau (2000) offered many concrete suggestions for assisting students and families who lack technology access.

Equity is a major social issue, not just an educational issue. "It is in the best interest of both today's young people and the nation as a whole that *all* students have an opportunity to master the elements of technology they will need to have a productive future" (Milone & Salpeter, 1996, p. 39). A solution is far beyond the local teacher and school, but the equity issue must concern educators, however small their individual contribution toward a solution may be.

Changing Roles

Teachers

NETS
NOTES

NETS **S** 2
NETS **T** I-A
NETS **T** I-B
NETS **T** III-A
NETS **T** III-B
NETS **T** V-B
NETS **T** VI-A
NETS **T** VI-B

Chapter 14 presented some of the issues related to staff development. Teacher training is surely the single greatest obstacle to integration of computers into education. Teachers need to acquire new content knowledge and computing skills. How can this be achieved?

The widespread acceptance of the NETS standards for teacher preparation is the most encouraging sign to date that computer education is becoming part of all teacher-preparation curricula. New teachers like you will enter the profession with the needed skills. For the far larger number of teachers whose preparation did not include computer skills training, the only familiar option is continuing education. Further advances will take time, but there is already resistance from those who are unfamiliar with the educational potential of computers.

But what is the teacher's classroom role? This goes beyond knowledge and skills to altered behavior. As constructivism becomes the dominant view of learning, the role of the teacher must change from transmitter of knowledge to facilitator of the learning process, from "sage on the stage to guide on the side." Teachers must help students learn how to learn and how to use their electronic tools effectively. They need to become guides to and navigators through the vast resources available to their students. Some teachers question whether they are even doing their job when they adopt constructivism. They must be assured that they are (Sprague & Dede, 1999; Yau, 2000).

For the foreseeable future, many teachers will have to accept that some of their students know far more about technology than they do. This is difficult for many teachers to acknowledge, yet the problem is almost solely the teachers'. Few students are bothered if asked to help the teacher with something on the computer. Rather, it can be an interesting contribution to the student's emerging self-image to be able to do things that an adult can't.

In addition, teachers must recognize the time demands that arise from using computers. The time involved in selecting appropriate courseware was discussed in Chapter 12. Examining materials and planning lessons that utilize them takes more time than skimming a textbook chapter. Teachers may have to develop support materials, as well as ways to monitor and assess student progress. Such familiar activities will require teachers to spend time at the computer, rather than being able to mull work over at lunch or while driving. Teaching with technology is more demanding than traditional teaching. Are you ready to accept the challenge?

Students

The role of the student is also changing in the Information Age. The exponential growth of knowledge and information makes it impossible for students to "learn" everything they will need in their lives. Rather, they must learn how to obtain, manipulate, and assess the relevance of information from the multitude of resources at their disposal.

Today's students are growing up with computers as a natural part of their lives. They do not view them as something unusual but simply as a normal tool for daily living. The promise of computers for students is that they are being "acted upon" less by the educational process and becoming more active shapers of their own growth and development (Jonassen, Peck, & Wilson, 1999; Jonassen, 2000). This is well illustrated by the experiences of students with hypermedia, databases, and the Internet, to single out examples. Students are confronting their world differently than their parents did. They are becoming more sophisticated problem solvers and have new opportunities to develop thinking skills. These are essential life skills of the Information Age.

At the same time, educators dare not lose sight of the fact that living is more than just information management. Steve Case, former CEO of America Online, observed at an educator's conference that "information isn't knowledge any more than a bag of cement is the Washington Monument" (<http://pdonline.ascd.org/pd_demo/lesson.cfm?lnum=1&SID=38&jx=&ttl=8>). Students must be assisted in creating knowledge from the information that is now so readily available. Furthermore, no matter how sophisticated students become in using computers for the "mechanical" side of life, they must still develop interpersonal and social skills to cope with "human" concerns. A technology-rich educational system may be able to devote less time to traditional instructional concerns, but it dare not abdicate responsibility for assisting in the development of the complete human being. It is in this area that the personal touch will never be lost.

Parents

The traditional role of parents in educating children is also changing. This has been nearly the total responsibility of the schools in the past, with parents providing encouragement and perhaps some help with homework. Technology is altering this role, too.

To really allow the computer to become an effective partner in the educational process, not only must teachers become familiar with its effective use, but parents similarly should become familiar with educational computer usage. This need for parent education is an even more difficult problem than present or future teacher preparation, but it is nonetheless important if the computer is to reach its full potential in our educational system.

By early 1999, over half of American homes had a computer, opening up new possibilities for learning. More will follow in coming years as costs decline further. Parents who are themselves computer competent will be able to assist their children in new ways. They may, however, be unprepared for the task of selecting computer learning materials for home use, as material selection has long been a school responsibility. Educators should consider establishing ways of assisting parents in this task.

Even greater problems loom for parents who perceive a need for a computer at home but are strangers to the technology themselves. Just as the new math caused many difficulties for parents seeking to help their children, so may computers, probably to an even greater extent. Again, there is a role for the schools to play in developing computer competence in parents through adult education programs.

Computers in the home raise new concerns of educational equity, an issue touched on previously. Just as differences in school budgets are contributing to a potential widening of the gap between the haves and have nots, so may technology in the home. Some districts have addressed this issue by providing parents the opportunity to borrow computers for home use. This is an approach worthy of serious consideration.

SUMMARY

In this chapter we have sought to identify and provide perspective on issues arising from the spread of computers throughout society. Consideration of such issues is a critical component of any computer education program, however difficult it is to address.

The social impact of computers requires careful attention, lest we awaken too late to changes that profoundly affect our lives. Educators must guide students in thinking about all aspects of the computer's impact on where and how we work and on our personal privacy. Computers have come to pervade society today with little thought given to their effects on individuals. It is not too late to develop a critical stance.

Schools must take a leading role in developing understanding of ethics related to computers. The first concern is academic dishonesty, made easier than ever before with access to term papers via the Internet. Another obvious area of concern is software piracy. By example and by teaching, computer users must learn that software is property, which is protected both legally and ethically. Attention to this issue must begin in the early grades. Somewhat later, students should be exposed to concerns over abuse of computer systems, ranging from seemingly innocent "hacking" and the release of computer viruses to full-scale computer crime.

Issues of equity raise major concerns for education and society. While the computer as an educational tool offers genuine potential to benefit all students, economic reality suggests that not all may have access to it. How should this problem be approached? In addition, where computers are readily available, concerns exist over equitable use by both sexes. To the extent that computers are more of a male experience, what should and can be done to correct the imbalance?

Finally, the computer is having a significant effect on the educational roles of teachers, students, and parents. To produce the most positive outcome, these changes need to be confronted directly. Both teachers and parents require special help in adapting to their new roles, so that students gain maximum benefit from available technologies.

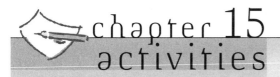

chapter 15
activities

1. Ask acquaintances in different kinds of jobs how computers have changed their work in the past few years. Summarize your findings.
2. If possible, talk with someone who works from home through telecommunications to gain direct insight into the benefits and the problems involved.
3. Identify several aspects of the effects of computers on personal privacy. How might privacy be better protected? Interview local police, credit bureaus, or banks about the kinds of information available in their databases, the importance of computers to them, and their perceptions of privacy issues.
4. What is your position on software duplication that goes *beyond* the copyright law? Is there such a thing as "fair use" of software? How should schools present this issue to students? Research copyright law applied to technology.

5. What, if anything, should be done if a student were to bring an illegal copy of a software product to school for class or lab use?
6. Should such ethical issues as hacking and viruses be considered in the curriculum? If so, where? How?
7. What do you see as the major equity issues of computing? How can schools contribute to solving these issues? Interview a school superintendent, board member, and community activist for their views.
8. Who is affected by the digital divide, and what are the potential consequences of this social problem? Research the issues and present your findings in a multimedia format.
9. For a look at technology efforts specifically directed at girls, explore several of the following websites: <www.cybergirl.com, www.girl tech.com, www.her-online.com, www.hygirls. com, www.girlsplace.com, www.girlzone.com, www.planetgirl.com, www.purple-moon.com,

www.lizzys.com>. Write a brief report discussing your perceptions of what the sites are attempting to achieve and whether you find merit in it.

10. Describe your perceptions of the changing roles of teachers, students, and parents. How can this change be managed? Interview teachers who use computers to learn of their experiences.

11. What are the legitimate roles of the schools relative to computers? What are the historical, philosophical, and/or sociological bases for these roles? Lead a discussion of these topics in your class.

Companion Website

Visit the companion website at <www.ablongman.com/lockard6e> for more information about the topics discussed in this chapter.

expect the world®

The New York Times
nytimes.com

Themes of the Times

Expand your knowledge of the concepts discussed in this chapter by reading current and historical articles from the *New York Times* by visiting the Themes of the Times section of the companion website <www.ablongman.com/lockard6e>.

References

ACINET. America's Career Information Network. "Fastest Growing Occupations." Retrieved March 13, 2003, from <www.acinet.org/acinet/oview1.asp?soccode=452093&stfips=&from=National&Level=Overall&x=24&y=11>

Bitter, G. G. *Computers in Today's World.* New York: Wiley, 1984.

Bureau of Labor Statistics (BLS). "The Employment Situation: February 2002." Retrieved March 14, 2003, from <www.bls.census.gov/cps/pub/empsit_feb2002.htm>

Carr-Chellman, A. A., Marra, R. M., and Roberts, S. L. "Round Girls in Square Computers: Feminist Perspectives on the Aesthetics of Computer Hardware." *TechTrends*, November–December 2002, *46*(6), pp. 4–10.

Clark, L. V. "Girls and Technology. Gender Equiry in the New Millennium." *Classroom Connect*, May 2002, *8*(8).

Coates, J. "Privacy Issue Just Catching Up With Computer Revolution." *Chicago Tribune*, 14 March 1999, Section 5, p. 5.

Coates, J. "E-Mail Address Should Be Kept Close to the Vest." *Chicago Tribune*, March 1, 2003. Retrieved March 20, 2003, from <www.chicagotribune.com/technology/columnists/chi-0303010143mar01,1,5629219.column>

Coates, J. "New TurboTax Edition Stirs Up a Hornet's Nest." *Chicago Tribune*, February 10, 2003. Retrieved March 22, 2003, from <www.chicagotribune.com/business/columnists/chi-0302100015feb10,1,4044792.column>

Ekhaml, L. "Computer Security—Risks, Threats, and Safeguards." *School Library Media Activities Monthly*, November 2001, *18*(3), pp. 35–36.

Elliott, L. "Hunt for the Hacker Spy." *Readers Digest*, April 1990, pp. 185–232.

Fiore, C. "Awakening the Tech Bug in Girls." *Learning and Leading with Technology*, February 1999, *26*(5), pp. 10–17.

Forcier, R. *The Computer as an Educational Tool.* Upper Saddle River, NJ: Merrill, 1999.

Gilley, J. "Gender and Technology Awareness Training in Preservice Teacher Education." *TechTrends*, November–December 2002, *46*(6), pp. 21–26.

Goldsborough, R. "Keeping Hackers Away with Personal Firewalls." *School Planning & Management*, December 2000, *39*(12), pp. 57–58.

Goot, D. "Thin Line Splits Cheating, Smarts." *Wired News*, September 10, 2002. Retrieved March 22, 2003, from <www.wired.com/news/school/0,1383,54963,00.html>

Healy, J. *Failure to Connect: How Computers Affect Our Children's Minds—For Better or Worse.* New York: Simon and Schuster, 1998.

Jonassen, D. *Computers as Mindtools for Schools*, 2nd ed. Upper Saddle River, NJ: Merrill, 2000.

Jonassen, D. H., Peck, K. L., and Wilson, B. G. *Learning with Technology: A Constructivist Perspective.* Upper Saddle River, NJ: Merrill, 1999.

Krim, J. "Flood of Spam May Be Threat to Email." *Chicago Tribune*, March 22, 2003. Retrieved March 22, 2003, from <www.chicagotribune.com/business/chi-0303220092mar22,1,4818318.story?coll=chi%2Dbusiness%2Dhed>

Lathrop, A., and Foss, K. *Student Cheating and Plagiarism in the Internet Era.* Westport, CT: Libraries Unlimited, 2000.

Lever-Duffy, J., McDonald, J. B., and Mizell, A. P. *Teaching and Learning with Technology.* Boston: Allyn and Bacon, 2003.

Malter, A., and Wodarz, N. "Technology Equity. Closing the Digital Divide." *School Business Affairs*, August 2000, *66*(8), pp. 92–94.

Markoff, J., and Hafner, K. *CyberPunk. Hackers and Outlaws on the Computer Frontier.* New York: Simon and Schuster, 1991.

Mayfield, K. "Cheating's Never Been Easier." *Wired News*, September 4, 2001. Retrieved March 22, 2003, from <www.wired.com/news/school/0,1383,45803,00.html>

McGrath, D., Thurston, L. P., McLellan, H., Stone, D., and Tischhauser, M. "Sex Differences in Computer Attitudes and Beliefs Among Rural Middle School Children After a Teacher Training Intervention." *Journal of Research on Computing in Education*, Summer 1992, *24*(4), pp. 468–485.

McLester, S. "Girls and Technology. What's the Story?" *Technology & Learning*, October 1998, pp. 18–26.

Milken Exchange on Education Technology. "State Appropriations for Education Technology." Retrieved March 9, 1999, from <http://206.117.127.97/ statepolicy/ compcharts.taf?chart=2>

Milone, M. N., Jr., and Salpeter, J. "Technology and Equity Issues." *Technology & Learning*, January 1996, *16*(4), pp. 38–47.

"Multimedia Era May Spark Anarchy." *Chicago Tribune*, 15 September 1995, Section 1, p. 14.

Nichols, R. G., and Welliver, P. W. "Computers: Issues of Health and Safety." *Tech Trends*, 1991, *36*(3), p. 52.

NTIA. *Falling Through the Net: Toward Digital Inclusion.* Retrieved March 22, 2003, from <http://search.ntia.doc.gov/pdf/fttn00.pdf>

Oppenheimer, T. "The Computer Delusion." *Atlantic Monthly*, 1997, *280*(1), pp. 45–62. Retrieved March 10, 2003, from <www.theatlantic.com/issues/97jul/computer.htm>

Pantiel, M., and Petersen, B. *Kids, Teachers, and Computers.* Englewood Cliffs, NJ: Prentice-Hall, 1984.

Poftak, A., and Kennedy, K. "The Back Page: Girls Take to the Web." *Technology & Learning*, April

2002. Retrieved March 22, 2003, from <www.techlearning.com/db_area/archives/TL/2002/04/backpage.html>

Schell, B. H., and Dodge, J. L. *The Hacking of America. Who's Doing It, Why, and How.* Westport, CT: Quorum Books, 2002.

Schwartz, J. E., and Beichner, R. J. *Essentials of Educational Technology.* Boston: Allyn and Bacon, 1999.

Shashaani, L. "Socioeconomic Status, Parents' Sex-Role Stereotypes, and the Gender Gap in Computing." *Journal of Research on Computing in Education,* Summer 1994, *26*(4), pp. 433–451.

Sprague, D., and Dede, C. "If I Teach This Way, Am I Doing My Job?" *Learning and Leading with Technology,* September 1999, *27*(1), pp. 6–9, 16–17.

Stoll, C. *The Cuckoo's Egg: Tracking a Spy Through the Maze of Computer Espionage.* New York: Doubleday, 1989.

Stoll, C. *High-Tech Heretic: Why Computers Don't Belong in the Classroom and Other Reflections by a Computer Contrarian.* New York: Doubleday, 1999.

"Student Charged in Hacking, Theft of University Records." *Chicago Tribune,* March 15, 2003, Section 1, p. 12.

Swain, S. L., and Harvey, D. M. "Single-Sex Computer Classes: An Effective Alternative." *TechTrends,* November–December 2002, *46*(6), pp. 17–20.

U.S. Department of Agriculture. National Agricultural Statistics Service. *Agricultural Charts and Maps.* Retrieved March 14, 2003, from <www.usda.gov/nass/aggraphs/graphics.htm>

USA Today. "Report: Software Piracy a Growing Problem." Retrieved March 22, 2003, from <www.usatoday.com/tech/news/2002/06/10/software-piracy.htm>

Van, J. "Vandals Give Frontera Grill a High-Tech Fright." *Chicago Tribune,* 17 February 1996, Section 2, p. 1.

Van Buren, C. "Teaching Hackers: School Computing Culture and the Future of Cyber-Rights." *Journal of Information Ethics,* Spring 2001, *10*(1), pp. 51–72.

Veverka, A. "Dumb Idea?" *Chicago Tribune,* 8 March 1999, Section 6, pp. 1, 7–9.

"A Virus Epidemic." *Data Training,* June 1991, pp. 8–9.

Wiburg, K. "Gender Issues, Personal Characteristics, and Computing (Research Windows)." *The Computing Teacher,* December/January 1994–95, *22*(4), pp. 7–10.

Yau, R. "Technology and Equity." *Principal Leadership,* December 2000, *1*(4), pp. 54–55.

Young, J. "Techno-Realists Hope to Enrich Debate over Policy Issues in Cyberspace." *Chronicle of Higher Education,* March 23, 1998. Retrieved June 27, 2003, from <http://chronicle.com/colloquy/98/technoreal/background.htm>

Today and Tomorrow:

What May Lie Ahead

OBJECTIVES

After completing this chapter, you will be able to:

- List and briefly describe at least three trends in computer hardware that seem likely to continue.
- Discuss some possible future directions in software, including multimedia.
- Describe the concept and potential applications of virtual reality (VR).

- Synthesize your knowledge and experiences into your own scenario for the future of computers in education.
- Define and critically evaluate the role you foresee for yourself as an educator in the twenty-first century.

This chapter provides a brief recap of what you have accomplished. Then it considers what the future may hold for technology and its applications in education. The future of hardware is considered in terms of microprocessor chips, memory, physical size, mass storage, ease of use and versatility, telecommunications and networking, cost, and compatibility. Considerations for the future of software include selection, complexity, cost, software for learning, multimedia, and virtual reality. The future of technology in education is related to the potential for computers to empower teachers and learners in the twenty-first century. The chapter concludes with reflections on your journey toward the technology-rich educational environments essential to the new millennium.

Looking Back

By this point, you've journeyed through an extensive survey of educational computer hardware, software, and applications. Let's summarize that journey before pondering what the future may hold.

| NETS
| NOTES
NETS **S** 1
NETS **T** I-A
NETS **T** I-B
NETS **T** V-B

Getting Started

Your journey began with our effort to provide a context for the remainder of this book. The first chapter gave an overview of the place of computers and technology in education, including successful efforts to establish technology standards for teachers and students. The second chapter traced the gradual development of early computing equipment, starting with the abacus. Greater attention was focused on the past hundred years, from early census tools to the first modern mainframe computers and the evolution of the personal computer.

From this brief history, the basic terminology and operating concepts of computers were explored. The fundamentals of hardware and how a computer system is controlled completed the section.

The Computer as Tool

Chapters 3–9 provided extensive treatment of the most common computer applications. The largest and most popular category of software consists of tool applications, which are those programs that help teachers and students (or any computer user) to perform common tasks more efficiently and effectively and that often enable us to perform tasks previously impossible.

First, you explored the vast scope of the Internet and the World Wide Web. The Internet has made the "Global Village" a reality in countless schools, homes, and businesses. After learning about the Internet itself, you moved on to its most familiar manifestation, the World Wide Web. Following the basic concepts of the Web and how it works, you considered some of the problems of students using the Web as a learning tool and a special approach to making web use meaningful and productive—the WebQuest. Sections of Chapter 4 dealt with how to create WebQuests and more general web pages, with attention to issues of accessibility for individuals with various disabilities. Many issues related to web use were presented, notably research integrity and how to cite web resources in research papers, acceptable use policies in schools, and personal safety of students who use the Web.

Then you turned to word processing and related programs for writing and publishing with computers. The Internet and word processing account for the majority of computer use. Next, you studied information management through databases, followed by number manipulation and presentation with spreadsheets. Graphics, multimedia, and support-tool software enable computer users to communicate more effectively.

The Computer as Tutor

Even before most tool software had been imagined, educators began to experiment with computers as learning tools. In Chapters 10–12, you first studied the traditional forms of computer-assisted instruction (CAI) and some of the research that supports the educational potential of CAI. Today's interactive multimedia brings the entire range of media materials to the personal computer, turning the text- and graphics-based CAI of the past into far more exciting materials that can compete for learner attention in the media age.

Of course, all instructional materials require evaluation before they are purchased and used. We presented a framework for evaluating educational software that is practical and can be tailored to varying needs.

Computers in Education

After such extensive treatment of the individual aspects of computers in education, you considered, in Chapters 13–15, how they might fit together in an educational context. We suggested that the concept of computer literacy has become outmoded, replaced by the far more important effort to integrate computers throughout the curriculum. Integration recognizes that the computer has become just another tool for teachers and students, no different in principle from a pencil or chalk. We educators need to develop a high level of competence in computer use, so that we benefit fully from technology, rather than being limited by a lack of knowledge about and skills to use it.

However lofty the goal, achievement comes down to the details concerning how to actually go about it. We attempted to suggest some critical factors in implementation, ranging from issues of school reform and restructuring to practical considerations of budget and benefits for individuals with special needs. Chapter 15 was devoted to some major concerns and social issues that arise from the spread of computers in society.

Looking Ahead

This final chapter offers some speculation about the future. The discussion is divided into sections on hardware, software, and computers in education. Predicting the future is difficult and risky, and we claim no crystal ball. As Naisbitt (1982) wrote in *Megatrends,* "The gee-whiz futurists are always wrong because they believe technological innovation travels in a straight line. It doesn't. It weaves and bobs and lurches and sputters" (p. 41). Furthermore, we agree with Naisbitt that "The most reliable way to anticipate the future is by understanding the present" (p. 2). Let's look at current trends.

NETS
NOTES

NETS **S** 1

NETS **S** 5

NETS
NOTES

NETS **T** I-A
NETS **T** I-B
NETS **T** II-C
NETS **T** III-B
NETS **T** V-B

The Future of Computer Hardware

All indications are that the directions of hardware development over the last 15 years will continue and, in some cases, accelerate.

Microprocessors (CPUs) and Connectivity

The processing speed of computers will continue to increase rapidly. From the Apple II and original IBM-PCXT with processors operating at 1MHz (megahertz), speeds of 3GHz (3,000MHz) and greater were available in 2003, with no end to further increases in sight. In daily use, speed increases are not always very noticeable. Could you tell the difference between spell checking this chapter in 2 seconds or 1? However, speed is very significant when it permits a computer to execute more complex software than ever before, such as advanced graphics and digital video demand. This, in turn, makes defining the differences among computers based on factors other than physical size increasingly difficult. Today's personal computer is yesterday's mainframe, enhanced significantly and placed on the desktop.

Another area of microprocessor development that is advancing rapidly is special chips for portable computers. Processors in desktop machines can use as much current as necessary and generate whatever heat results, both problematic in a notebook computer. In March 2003, the first notebooks using the new Intel Centrino mobile technology appeared on the market. This technology combines a processor designed for mobile computing with technology to dramatically increase battery life and with integrated wireless networking technology (see <www.intel.com/products/mobiletechnology/centrino>). Further integration of technologies can be expected along these lines as wireless connectivity rapidly expands.

Memory

Faster computers require more and more random access memory (RAM). The Apple II eventually reached 128K of RAM. A typical Macintosh or Windows computer now features at least 128MB of RAM, which already is inadequate for some applications. Maximum RAM configurations of 2GB are possible today and seem certain to go even higher. For most uses, memory beyond 256MB primarily improves the performance of the computer when running multiple applications simultaneously, called *multitasking*. However, multimedia creation software often performs much better with additional memory. If you will be working with digital video, you probably should have 512MB as the minimum. Memory prices fluctuate significantly, so it's somewhat of an economic decision as to how much to buy. A good rule of thumb is, buy as much as you can reasonably afford today because you may well need more tomorrow. Be sure your computer has memory expansion space for future needs.

Displays

The familiar computer monitor (CRT) is a close relative of the television set, using a similar type of display tube technology. Laptop computers have long used LCD displays, which have been noted for their high cost and occasional fragility. Now, the CRT on the desktop is being replaced rapidly by flat-screen LCD technology as display sizes increase and prices fall steadily because of increased sales and manufacturing efficiencies (Miller, 2003). In fact, LCD televisions are also growing in popularity for their thin profile, potential for mounting directly on the wall, and brilliant, easy-to-view images. We are confident that the days of the CRT are numbered for all but some highly specialized uses. We have met no one who did not prefer an LCD monitor, once they had a chance actually to experience using one.

A write-on display is the heart of Tablet PCs, which may alter our thinking about how best to interact with a computer. The handwriting recognition accuracy of even the early Tablet PCs was impressive, but whether this is what users really want remains to be seen. Inevitable price cuts may help promote this technology.

We are intrigued more, however, by *smart displays* (see <www.microsoft.com/ windows/smartdisplay/evaluation/overviews/default.asp>), which seem to offer the best technologies all together. A smart display is a touchscreen monitor that connects to the computer using standard wireless technology. There is no need to remain near the computer to use it. Take just the display wherever you go within the range of the wireless system. Interact with the computer by touching the screen with a stylus or using the onscreen keyboard, which is very similar to a PDA in concept. Although these systems also support a normal wireless keyboard and/or mouse, this means carrying more components around and thus, is somewhat inappropriate to the concept. The display also features a writing pad and handwriting recognition, similar to a Tablet PC. Smart display technology is far too new to assess at this time, but the possibilities are truly awesome, especially for the home or office.

Physical Size

As electrical engineers find new ways to achieve the same goals in ever-smaller packages, the physical size and weight of computers has fallen. From the desktop computer evolved the portable, then the battery-powered laptop, and finally notebook and subnotebook computers (and printers!) small enough to fit inside a standard briefcase. Regardless of further miniaturization potential, today's subnotebooks are about as small as seems feasible without creating unusable keyboards and marginal viewing screens. Attention has shifted to packing still more power into the current-size packages, larger displays with brilliant color, and adding wireless networking and multimedia support. The best notebook computers today rival desktop systems in almost every way.

Apart from such refinements, there is also a move toward still-smaller devices that serve more specific purposes. One type is the personal digital assistant (PDA), which may have no keyboard or only a tiny one on screen. The user can just write on the screen, and the computer recognizes the handwriting. Slightly larger is the so-called Pocket PC that runs scaled-down versions of typical office tool software but still has only a rather small screen and tiny "thumb" keyboard. Just where all of this will lead we cannot guess with any confidence. This is an area of true "zig-zag" developments in technologies. However, the director of the Media Lab at MIT predicted more than a decade ago that the computer of the future will be worn like a watch (Bane, 1990). You may well see it in the near future, perhaps as an enhanced cellular phone.

Mass Storage

As programs and multimedia files grow ever larger, so must the storage devices that hold them. The original 5.25" magnetic diskette holding about 100K of data was replaced by high-density 3.5" diskettes that hold 1.44MB. By early 2003 it was becoming increasingly common to find both notebook and desktop computers for which a floppy drive was an option, not standard equipment. However, some form of removable storage is essential for nearly all users. Removable cartridge systems such as the Iomega Zip store 100–750MB per diskette-sized "cartridge," but the cost of the cartridges has cooled enthusiasm for these devices.

The floppy disk alternative of choice at this time is the mini USB drive, available under a host of different brand names (Figure 16.1). These drives fit in your pocket or on your key chain and basically are just a memory chip in a plastic case with a USB connector. Plug one into a USB port on any PC or Macintosh and you have instant storage ranging in mid 2003 from 32MB to 2GB (equivalent to about 24 to nearly 1400 floppy diskettes!). We anticipate much further development of miniature solid-state storage devices as a truly viable means of moving files easily from one computer to another.

Optical discs in the form of CDs and DVDs also have become popular storage devices because of their substantial capacity. The CD recorder, or CD-RW drive, is rapidly becoming standard equipment on both desktop and notebook computers, sometimes in a combination drive that also reads DVDs. A drive that can only read CD-ROM discs is not flexible enough for today's users and we do not expect to see such drives on the market much longer. Data-retrieval speeds of optical drives remain slower than hard disks, although drive speeds continue to improve. This means that accessing data on a CD or DVD is not as quick and smooth as from a hard drive, but the difference is not noticeable in most common applications.

The next step is already under way, and that is the growing availability of DVD "burners." We have seen prices fall already to very affordable levels as more and more "multimedia" computers come equipped with these drives. Whether one DVD standard (–R/RW versus +R/RW, as explained in Chapter 2) will dominate is unclear. However, the issue may be less than critical, as some drives can read and write both formats as well as CD-R and CD-RW discs. In short, such a DVD drive handles every common form of optical media. Since DVD technology is so very similar to CD technology, we antic-

Figure 16.1
MINI USB DRIVE (128MB),
EQUIVALENT TO MORE
THAN 85 FLOPPY DISKETTES

ipate the end of both the CD burner and the CD-ROM drive, as multiformat DVD burners become the norm. Initially this is occurring in higher-cost multimedia computers, but it will eventually spread to more basic models and notebooks as well.

For basic storage on any computer, hard drives under 20GB (1GB = 1,000MB) have become rare as much larger units become the norm. Drives holding 30–60GB and more are common, even in notebook computers. Our latest multimedia production PCs have twin 200GB hard drives to support ever larger applications (e.g., Macromedia *Studio MX* requires over 500MB for a full installation, MS *Office XP* even more) and enormous audio and video multimedia files.

Miller (2003) reports on a new technology still under development called *nanopatterned* data storage media that can hold up to 500GB per square inch. Toshiba engineers project a target date of 2006 for products using this technology. Moore's Law posits that, since the beginning of chip technology, "data density" of chips of all kinds roughly doubles every 18 to 24 months, a geometric increase in capacity, and the end is nowhere in sight (see <www.webopedia.com/TERM/M/Moores_Law.html>). If nanopatterned storage does not become the future technology, there will be something even better.

Ease of Use/Versatility/Convergence

The overwhelming acceptance of Microsoft Windows and the Macintosh is clear evidence that the vision of first Xerox, then Apple of how a computer should operate has gained the upper hand. Typing arcane commands at a blinking cursor prompt is unsatisfactory to most computer users. This is less a battle between two hardware platforms than evidence of the significance of ergonomics. Ease of use is important to consumers. But is a graphical user interface enough?

The underlying issue is simply how much the user must conform to the limits of a machine and how much the machine should be able to accommodate the user. Artificial intelligence researchers are working toward the next widespread level of adaptation of computers to users. Keyboard use, already reduced by the mouse, should decline further. Touch screens are one possibility, but not the most likely in our view. *Pointing devices* (the generic term for a mouse or any comparable device) and scanning may improve and become still easier or more effective.

However, the real leap will be into voice technologies. Computers that respond to voice commands became available in mid-1993, but even in 2003 the technology remains imperfect and in need of further development. Voice-synthesized output could reduce some of our dependence on monitors. At the same time, larger flat-screen LCD displays with ever-higher resolution are making the screen more appealing and richer in information than ever before, while taking up less space in one's work area. All-in-one computers like the *iMac* and its imitators take us back to the earliest days of Macintosh. They are growing in popularity in Asia (Miller, 2003) but have yet to capture the fancy of most U.S. consumers. However, as the capabilities of all-in-ones continue to increase, the advantages of larger cases (such as expandability) seem destined to fade. Their benefit in maximizing space utilization in labs is already clear (Figure 16.2). We believe the convenience of these compact, integrated systems will eventually win out. In fact, these are the systems most likely to bring the computer out of the home office into the actual living areas of the home, once screen sizes increase just a little, television tuners are built

Figure 16.2

All-in-one computers are space efficient for labs.

in, and wireless broadband Internet access becomes more common. Such devices will achieve the long predicted convergence of computing and entertainment.

Telecommunications and Networking

The classroom of the very near future will be "wired," if it isn't already. The high cost of wiring existing buildings for Internet and local area network access has been addressed by the rapid increases in less-costly wireless networking capabilities, which make access very affordable and installation much faster. Network connections will link all computers within the school to one another to share data and peripherals, and to other computer systems around the world via the Internet. Fast, efficient, and inexpensive exchange of information with other sites is becoming ubiquitous. Educators have access to large-scale data repositories, somewhat analogous to those serving the medical and legal professions. The Internet is quickly providing an efficient vehicle to make this all possible.

The day has arrived when students of all ages can routinely communicate with peers, adults, and field specialists by email without regard to geographic location or time zones. The broadest possible range of information has become available in a "virtual library," in which access to information is not limited by physical ownership of materials. The problem of obsolete data in textbooks has been replaced by the still greater challenge of identifying in volumes of data never before known those items of greatest relevance and importance to the issue at hand. The only foreseeable change will be in speed and ease of access to ever increasing data stores, perhaps with intelligent agents to aid searching.

While telecommunications and networking benefit all, they have particular significance in rural areas, where they are likely to be the most cost-effective solution to distance education needs. One's educational opportunities need not depend on the number or proximity of other learners.

Cost

From the beginning, electronic hardware costs have gone downward routinely despite general trends toward higher prices for most goods. This is partially due to manufacturing efficiencies and economies of scale from growing demand. It also is due to intense competition in the marketplace. Even without direct competitors, Macintosh prices have been forced downward as Apple acknowledged that brand loyalty is limited by economic reality. While would-be owners will pay more to get just what they want, many will not pay much more.

Obviously, prices cannot fall indefinitely, since there must be a minimal price level at which a product will be improved for the same price rather than sold for less. It appears that this plateau is at about $500 to $1,000 per computer system. For several years, it has been possible to purchase a complete entry-level computer system for that price. Over the years, what you get at the base level has evolved from an Apple II or basic PC clone to a basic iMac or Wintel system—either one a far more powerful and desirable computer than its predecessors. We expect this trend to continue. New chip technology beyond the Intel Pentium 4 and Apple G5 will cause today's top-of-the-line models (or features) to become the entry-level product six months from now.

Similarly, desirable peripherals also continue to decline in price. Even color laser printers are now affordable. CD and DVD drives and quality stereo sound are now standard equipment. Displays are significantly better today and growing larger. Computer hardware offers genuine value.

Given the apparent stability of the $500–$1,000 price level, there is less justification than ever for schools to delay purchasing computer hardware. Each delay carries with it significant "opportunity cost," that is, lost opportunity to enhance education. Furthermore, the technological life of a computer seems to be three years maximum, too short to justify waiting for a "better deal."

Compatibility

We can only hope that over time the problems caused by two camps based on operating system (*Mac OS* and *Windows*) will be overcome. It was encouraging when in 1991 Apple and IBM jointly created Kaleida Labs to work toward applying the best that each had to offer to products that neither could produce alone. Regrettably, the effort of these rivals to cooperate did not last (see <www.businessweek.com/1995/49/b345362.htm>). Education would benefit greatly from no longer having to choose between Macintosh and Windows. The continued rivalry of the two systems has benefited neither educators nor students.

The Future of Software

Historically, advances in hardware have far outpaced progress in software development. The high-performance hardware readily available today has little software that truly capitalizes on its power. The *MacOS X* and *Windows XP* operating systems demand a high-powered system, but as much for its brute strength as for its sophistication. Software will continue to evolve, and while possibly closing this gap somewhat, it seems unlikely to catch up with hardware.

Selection

The vast number of computer users has created a demand for software, and the market responds to profit potential. New products for personal productivity flood the market. Developers are refining high-quality products in popular market segments such as word processing, while constantly searching for additional applications for which little, if any, software now exists. This is consistent with the view of computers as a Swiss army knife, an all-in-one tool. No one knows what the next *Netscape* will be, but you can be confident there will be continued breakthroughs with "killer apps" that nearly every computer user will want and benefit from.

Complexity

Refinements in word processors, databases, and spreadsheets are vivid testimony to market economics and increased computer power. These packages do far more with less user effort than ever before. Programs are becoming increasingly comprehensive in scope. Freed from the constraints of underpowered hardware, developers can achieve a new level of sophistication.

Perhaps more important to educators than increased power is increased ease of use, often through enhanced human-machine interfaces. Some gains come from the strong emphasis on GUIs (graphical *u*ser *i*nterfaces) and WIMP (*w*indows, *i*cons, *m*enus, *p*ointer) interfaces first created by Xerox researchers, popularized by the Macintosh, and made nearly universal by Windows. Further gains may come from advances in artificial intelligence (AI) research. For instance, *neural networks* seek to model the human mind (see <www.webopedia.com/TERM/n/neural_network.html>). Rather than "programming" a neural network, one "teaches" it by example to recognize patterns and reach decisions. Neural nets actually learn from their experiences. When such technology becomes part of software applications, programs will be able to customize themselves to the user's needs and working style. This will create a whole new generation of "intelligent" software.

Cost

Significant reductions in prices for educational software seem unlikely. The market is already sensitive to school budgets, with CAI and utility products generally priced around $50 per copy. Heavily discounted multiuser lab packs and network versions leave little room for further reductions. Although major tool software tends to carry prices in the range of $100 per copy and higher, "academic prices," software bundles, and office suites often cost much less, making such products very affordable. Features pioneered in leading products tend over time to filter down into less expensive ones as well. We foresee little likelihood of major declines in prices. It is mostly specialized graphics and multimedia development software that remains quite expensive for schools.

Software for Learning

As both the theory and application of computer teaching and learning evolve, new generations of educational software should appear. This software will take greater advantage of the hardware's capabilities to interact with learners in more sophisticated ways, perhaps using AI. It will achieve greater impact on learning, while offering greater ease of use and more assistance to teachers.

As traditional publishers move more heavily into the software industry, expect more and more stand-alone software and web support as part of a complete set of teaching materials to accompany text series and individual books. Books accompanied by web-sites are becoming increasingly common as this book exemplifies. Perhaps the day will come when every textbook sold to schools will have correlated multimedia software available via the Internet. All it will take is one highly successful experiment by a publisher, and others will follow quickly.

Home use of educational software and the Internet has increased to supplement school educational programs. Education will be more fluid, with both home and school contributing significantly to the overall result. This is especially important in what it does to integrate these two realms for the benefit of learners.

Interactive Multimedia/Hypermedia

The scope and realism of computer courseware will grow with further developments in interactive video technologies, some pioneered by game developers. Using still and motion sequences, simulations will take on new levels of realism and electronic "virtual tours" will allow learners to explore environments they cannot experience physically. Multiple stereo sound tracks will serve varied purposes, including bilingual and foreign language instruction as well as permitting narration on multiple difficulty levels to enable use of the same multimedia resources for different audiences. These capabilities existed initially with laserdiscs and are available now in DVD technology, but DVD has not been exploited yet to any significant extent for educational purposes. We eagerly anticipate the software catching up with the hardware in the area of multimedia courseware.

Books versus E-Books

Despite the resources of the Internet, books are unlikely to disappear from our schools, although their role in rapidly changing content areas such as science and world affairs is already diminishing. Still, there are huge differences between reading large amounts of material from a computer display and from a book in your hands. As several acquaintances have commented, it is difficult to curl up in bed with your notebook computer to read. Books are the ultimate in transportable information resources, requiring no electricity.

PDAs can store increasing amounts of text, but the screen size makes them unsuitable to most eyes for extended reading times. Several companies have promoted the electronic book or e-book, a specially formatted version of written materials. Larger than a PDA but smaller than a notebook computer, dedicated e-book readers are specialty devices designed just for easy access to text materials. A reader can store the entire text of many printed volumes at one time, and the contents can be changed at any time as you finish with a particular book or just need to have access to another. The range of content available in e-book format might surprise you. NetLibrary claimed over 37,000 titles in March 2003 (see <www.netlibrary.com/reading_room/index.asp>). NetLibrary offers several titles to try using your computer, offering a chance to experience the text searching and embedded dictionary features of its subscription-based materials. Also look at the massive Project Gutenberg at <http://promo.net/pg>, which focuses on "famous and important texts." Project Gutenberg offers over 6,000 titles as we write. To learn more about e-book technology, visit <http://e-books.org/>, a website that labels itself a "resource for reading appliance research." As the site notes, with appropriate reader software you can read e-book formatted materials on many PDAs as well as on Tablet PCs.

Whether e-books will truly succeed as a technology and as a learning tool is unclear. However, the potential is fascinating. E-books could address the issue of students carrying far too much weight around in their backpacks. Publishers could save the enormous expense of physically printing books and could update information or correct errors at any time, offering the new and improved version for download. Schools could likely update their "textbooks" more frequently than is now the case. We know of students whose interest in reading has improved markedly since their parents acquired an e-book reader, but we cannot claim broad evidence of such improvements, though they would be clearly desirable. At this time, we believe that the technology has promise and merits watching in the coming years.

Virtual Environments

A microworld is an environment which children can explore and experiment on their own terms. One advanced form of microworld is *virtual reality (VR)*, the ultimate multimedia interface. Commonly, the VR user blocks out the physical world by donning a helmet with small monitors before the eyes and speakers over the ears (Figure 16.3).

Figure 16.3
A TYPICAL VIRTUAL REALITY (VR) SETUP WITH HEAD-MOUNTED DISPLAY

A computer generates a virtual, that is, simulated, environment through the monitors and speakers. The user interacts with that environment through some set of controls, often a control stick or special high-tech glove. It is possible to move around in an environment and touch and examine elements of it. (We've seen one VR demonstration in which the user could wander through a house, pause and raise a hand to a bookshelf and remove a book, plunge into a swimming pool and swim among the fish, and so forth.)

No doubt you can see from this brief description that VR offers potential to become the ultimate simulation. Medical educators are excited by the possibilities for learning. Most fields of study offer intriguing opportunities to immerse students in active simulations of events, principles, or whatever. We do not foresee K–12 applications in the next few years and believe that VR is more likely fantasy than practical for schools at this time. Furthermore, there are potentially serious issues of physical side effects that have not been addressed (Strauss, 1995; Van, 1995). Still, the potential of VR is such that educators should remain alert to developments. (For an outstanding history of VR, see Rheingold, 1991.)

Among public VR applications, entertainment is the goal. Opportunities to experience VR exist in cities around the world, including major entertainment centers such as Las Vegas. If you want to know what is available in your area or an area that you plan to visit, check out the list of VR entertainment centers worldwide at <http://vr-atlantis.com/lbe.html>.

Computers in Education

Whatever exciting developments occur in hardware and software, their ultimate significance to educators lies in their application in schools. Just as software advances trail hardware, education's ability to use what is already available trails that of business and other sectors. More than a decade ago, one popular computer publication called education "the final frontier" and proclaimed that "computers will ultimately have their greatest impact on education" (Zachmann, 1991, p. 97). Education has made progress in computer use since the late 1970s, yet it is painfully apparent that far less has happened than computer advocates expected. The obstacles to widespread, effective computer use in schools have been far greater than most "experts" imagined.

One major concern is the vast amount of overzealous evangelism that has accompanied the computer education movement. Predictions were made that computers quickly would transform and save education, inaccuracies that reflect Naisbitt's "danger of the technofix mentality" (1982, p. 52). We can think of few more certain ways to undermine a dream than to oversell it. Realists do not see computer technology as the answer to all of education's ills.

Perhaps the greatest single factor that should prevent failure of the computer movement is that much of its support comes from outside the schools. Unlike, say, the new math, about which few people outside of schools cared, advocates for computers in the schools are found everywhere. Too many people have a stake in this to let it fail.

In most cases, the glowing scenarios from the early 1980s of an education revolution have yet to be achieved. Will they ever be? In many cases, we believe the answer is no. In fact, Dede (1987) argued that we really have no idea yet how best to use computers in education. His points largely remain valid today. There is still much need for experimentation to determine how to maximize the value of computers in education, but we think we are on the right road. The trend toward developing computer competence through integration of computers into the curriculum is encouraging. It will indeed make the computer a tool of empowerment for students and teachers—its ultimate value.

The Internet

One aspect of technology in education of which we are certain is that use of the Internet will continue to grow, probably exponentially. This is a result of many factors, including the rapid increase in access in schools (including building networking), the increasing awareness of educators of the potential value of the Web, and the wide scale use of the Internet in homes. Children are very likely to be aware of the Internet, perhaps even to have used it in some way, before they enter our schools. We do not believe they will be willing to leave their experiences at the schoolhouse door. Nor should they have to.

From classroom research to distance education and online learning, the Internet has already had a profound effect on learners and the process of learning. Educators will become increasingly sophisticated in using it and, we trust, educationally sound resources will continue to appear, resources developed for our students, in addition to all the materials that we can appropriate for educational purposes. The Internet is a powerful tool for students working to attain most of the basic goals of education and it can be a dramatic means of achieving greater understanding among the peoples of the world. Never before in human history has such an opportunity, and such an obligation, presented itself to educators.

Empowerment for the Twenty-First Century

For the computer to empower teachers and students, computers in education must attain a level of *invisible integration*. They must become such an essential part of education that no one notices them or thinks about them as something more remarkable than a book or chalk. A computer has unique power and capabilities, but it is fundamentally still a tool in the service of learning and living. Children now are expected to learn to read, write, calculate, spell, and behave in school. They will come to experience the computer as a tool, a resource, not something as uncommon as a field trip.

However, it would be unfortunate if computer integration meant only support of the existing school curriculum and structure, however beneficial that might be. Teachers empowered by computer technology see the nature of teaching differently. The "sage on the stage" must yield to the "guide on the side." There is little need for a dispenser of information. Teaching can focus on individuals and their development, on motivation, thinking, and creativity, not on bodies of content to present or absorb. Students become investigators, builders of their own knowledge, and not just recipients of information. Teachers pose problems, help learners identify problems, and assist learners in finding solutions to problems. Information resources are explored and used as needed and are not divided into small components to be committed to memory. The ultimate test is whether students can locate, analyze, assess, synthesize, and evaluate information to create personal knowledge. This demonstrates the skills of a lifetime, not just the short-term memory that gets you through the next test. Life skills are inherently empowering.

Reflections

A vision of computers as tools of empowerment is filled with possibility, not certainty. To the extent that empowerment occurs, and it is in many schools already, teachers and students are richly rewarded. However appealing the vision, we do not believe it represents the dominant reality today. The computer competence required to become empowered as a teacher is far greater than most teachers possess. We see no viable means of changing that situation quickly or widely, as a true revolution in education would require. Rather, we foresee an evolution in that direction that will take much more time.

Is there an alternative to patience? We cannot be certain. Private initiatives such as Whittle Communication's Edison Project at <www.edisonproject.com> seemed to offer one, but they remain controversial (e.g., <http://mathforum.org/epigone/mathed-news/yermbolsai>). Instead, we hope that those teachers who have experienced the power of computer technology in their teaching will become catalysts for change among their peers. In addition, national standards movements, such as NETS, are pointing in the right direction, in our view.

All this makes you, a teacher on the way to computer competence, critical to the future. You have a vision of what computers can mean in education, and you have at least begun to develop your skills to pursue that vision. With even one computer in your classroom, you can accomplish more than many schools have with quantities of unused computers. Your example and enthusiasm can encourage others to explore the possibilities. Your willingness to share your knowledge and skills can ease the transformation of a reluctant, skeptical, or technophobic colleague into a hesitant, then comfortable, then competent computer educator. *You* are the key to the future of computers in education.

CHARGE TO READERS

This book has attempted to present an overview of the evolving field of educational computing. This field has quickly become important to all educators concerned about the future of our children. Technology cannot be ignored; it will become increasingly important in the educational process. You already have made a commitment to become a more knowledgeable user of computer technology and a better teacher by empowering students to use technology. In this way, you will contribute to the evolution of education from a nineteenth-century model to one worthy of the twenty-first century. Accept the challenge, and help transform education!

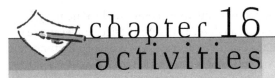

chapter 16 activities

1. Which trends in hardware development do you believe will be most significant for education? Why?

2. What developments in software would you most like to see? What, if any, evidence offers promise that these may occur?

3. Develop and justify your own vision of the future. What contributions do you foresee making personally to that vision?

Companion Website

Visit the companion website at <www.ablongman.com/lockard6e> for more information about the topics discussed in this chapter.

expect the world®

The New York Times
nytimes.com

Themes of the Times

Expand your knowledge of the concepts discussed in this chapter by reading current and historical articles from the *New York Times* by visiting the Themes of the Times section of the companion website <www.ablongman.com/lockard6e>.

References

Bane, M. "Lippman Says, Try This Computer on for Size." *Chicago Tribune*, 18 November 1990, Section 19, pp. 11, 24.

Dede, C. "Empowering Environments, Hypermedia, and Microworlds." *The Computing Teacher*, November 1987, *15*(3), pp. 20–24, 61.

Levin, C. "Flash Forward to 2005." *PC Magazine*, 16 November 1999, *18*(20), p. 36.

Miller, M. J. "Forward Thinking." *PC Magazine*, March 25, 2003, p. 7.

Naisbitt, J. *Megatrends*. New York: Warner, 1982.

Rheingold, H. *Virtual Reality*. New York: Summit Books (Simon and Schuster), 1991.

Strauss, S. "Cybersickness: Virtual Reality's Dark Side." *Chicago Tribune*, 11 August 1995, Section 7, pp. 47–48.

Van, J. "Actual Side Effects from Virtual Reality. " *Chicago Tribune*, 14 August 1995, Section 4, pp. 1, 3.

Zachmann, W. F. "Education: The Final Frontier." *PC Magazine*, August 1991, *10*(14), pp. 97–98.

Glossary

Abacus: An ancient computing device consisting of several rods that represent columns and small beads that move on these columns to represent digits.

Ada: Computer language named for Lady Ada Augusta Lovelace, colleague of Charles Babbage and daughter of the British poet Lord Byron.

Adaptive technologies: Hardware and/or software designed to compensate to some degree for user handicaps.

Algorithm: Step-by-step procedure for obtaining a specific result.

Alignment: A straight margin in a document, as in left alignment (right margin is ragged) and right alignment (left margin is ragged). See also *Justified*.

ALU (arithmetic logic unit): That part of the CPU that performs calculations and logical functions. See also *Control unit, CPU*.

Analog: Electronic signals that vary continuously over a range in the form of wave patterns. (Cf. *Digital*)

Analog computer: A computer that represents values by continuously changing physical variables, such as amount of electrical current. (Cf. *Digital computer*)

Animated GIF: Graphic file in GIF format, consisting of several related views of the subject matter. Browsers and some other software display the individual views in rapid succession, creating the appearance of movement. Commonly found on web pages.

Applications software: Computer programs designed and written to perform certain major tasks, especially spreadsheets, databases, and word processors.

Arithmetic logic unit: See *ALU*.

Articulation: Agreement as to what is taught at each grade level and therefore can be assumed at succeeding levels.

Artificial intelligence: A specialty area of computer science concerned with the development of machines and programs capable of functions that, in humans, appear to require consciousness or intelligence.

ASCII: *A*merican *S*tandards *C*ode for *I*nformation *I*nterchange. A standardized format for representing numbers, letters, and special characters.

Assembler language: Low-level language that uses mnemonics to represent machine-language instructions. Assembler language source code must be translated into executable machine code by an appropriate assembler program.

Asynchronous: Not occurring at the same time. Describes email because the sender and receiver need not be online simultaneously. (Cf. *Real time*)

Authoring: The process of creating instructional software (CAI) using specialized software development tools.

Authoring language: A specialized high-level language that allows the user to write limited types of CAI without extensive programming knowledge or experience.

Authoring system: Software designed to allow nonprogrammers to create computer-based learning materials by responding to prompts or completing simple forms.

Automatic recalculation: Changes in the value in a worksheet cell resulting from a change in the value in another cell, e.g., changes in a total when a single entry is modified. Also called *automatic updating.*

Back up: To make a copy of data files to guard against loss of the original.

Backup: Duplicate files created to guard against loss of the original.

Bandwidth: The relative ability of cables to carry information. Fiber optic cables offer much greater bandwidth than traditional copper wires.

BASIC (Beginners All-purpose Symbolic Instruction Code): A comparatively easy to learn and use high-level programming language.

Baud: The speed of a modem. Roughly ten times the number of characters being transmitted; e.g., 56K baud is about 5,600 characters per second.

BBS (bulletin board system): Computer system set up for posting and exchanging messages and software. See also *RBBS.*

Bézier splines: Basis of technique used for handwriting recognition by Tablet PCs based on curves defined by mathematical formulas.

Binary: Any system composed of only two alternate states, such as zero and one, or on and off.

Bit (binary digit): The smallest unit of information meaningful to a computer, usually represented as zero or one. (Cf. *Byte*)

Bitmap: A graphic image saved as a pattern of dots, or a computer file containing such an image.

Boot/Boot up: To start up a computer so that it is ready for normal operations.

Branching tutorial: CAI in which learners follow alternative paths through the tutorial lesson based on their responses to questions.

Broadband: Term used to describe any high-speed Internet connection because of the increased bandwidth provided. Examples include Ethernet, DSL, and cable modems.

Browser: Internet client/server software such as *Netscape* that can display documents on the World Wide Web.

Buffer: Area of memory used to temporarily store data.

Bug: An error within a computer program.

Burn: To record an optical disc, e.g., CD or DVD. So called because the recording is done by a laser beam that "burns" information into the surface of the disc.

Button: An area on a computer screen that causes some action to occur when the user places the cursor over it with the mouse and then clicks.

Byte: A series of bits, usually seven or eight, that together represent an individual letter, number, or other character. See also *Giga, K, Mega.*

C: A highly structured computer language developed by Bell Labs, originally for the Unix operating system. Variations such as *C++* are widely used to develop applications software.

Cable modem: Modem-like circuitry or add-in board for connecting a computer to a cable television network for high-speed Internet access.

CAI (computer-assisted instruction): Interaction of a learner with a computer that is playing a direct instructional role. Also the instructional software itself. (Cf. *CMI*)

Card: A single screen in a hypermedia product such as *HyperStudio:* Called a page in *SuperLink* and *ToolBook.* Similar to a database record.

CAV (constant angular velocity): Laserdisc format that provides up to 54,000 individually viewable images (or 30 minutes of motion video) per side. (Cf. *CLV*)

CD-R (CD-recordable): Designation for a CD that can be recorded on, but from which data cannot be erased and the used space cannot be recorded on again.

CD-ROM (compact disc–read only memory): An optical disc technology with large storage capability. Blank CDs for recording may be CD-R (record only) or CD-RW (read/write).

CD-RW (CD read/write): Designation for a CD "burner" or recorder, as well as CDs that can be recorded on, then erased and recorded on again.

Cell: The space that is the intersection of one row and one column in a worksheet. See also *Spreadsheet.*

Cell pointer: Indicates current cell within a worksheet; a cursor.

Chip: A small piece of semiconducting material such as silicon on which electrical circuits are etched.

Classroom publishing: Use of inexpensive software to approximate desktop publishing.

Client: Software that calls on server software for resources within a client/server context. Also, the computer running the client software. See also *Client/server, File server.*

Client/server: A model for network computing in which two computers share resources. The client requests services from the server. Many Internet functions, including Gopher and World Wide Web browsers, are client/server applications.

Clip art: Professionally drawn graphics obtained specifically for use in one's own products, such as computer screens or desktop-publishing materials, in lieu of producing original artwork.

Clipboard: An area of memory used to temporarily store data cut or copied from a file prior to pasting it into another file. Enables easy movement of text and graphics among applications.

Clone: A computer functionally equivalent to another that is itself a standard, e.g., those based on Intel chips, but manufactured by other than a "major" company such as IBM or Compaq.

CLV (constant linear velocity): Laserdisc format for extended play. Provides up to 60 minutes of full-motion video per side, but without individual frames that can be viewed independently. (Cf. *CAV*)

CMC (computer-mediated communication): A form of electronic distance education in which communication among learners, who may never meet as a group, occurs through computers. May range from email to video conferencing.

CMI (computer-managed instruction): Use of a computer in the organization and management of instruction and classroom activities. (Cf. *CAI*)

COBOL (*common business oriented language*): A high-level language for business applications that uses common English words and phrases as *Commands.*

Code: Instructions to a computer. Usually modified to indicate the nature of the code, e.g., machine code, source code, COBOL code. Also, the act of converting an algorithm into the specific statements and syntax of the programming language being used to develop software.

Combo Drive: An optical computer drive that combines the functions of two or more drives into a single unit. For example, a DVD-ROM/CD-RW drive can play DVDs and CDs (audio and data) and also record or "burn" CDs.

Command: An instruction to a computer system to perform a specified input, processing, or output task.

Commercial network: See *Information service.*

Communication: The process of one computer transferring data to and from another computer through channels such as telephone lines.

Compiler: Program that translates an entire program in a high-level language into machine code prior to execution. (Cf. *Interpreter*)

Computer-assisted instruction: See *CAI.*

Computer awareness: Intellectual knowledge of computers, with no implication of any specific ability to actually use the computer.

Computer competence: Knowledge sufficient to recognize when computer use would be advantageous, combined with the necessary skills to use a computer effectively and efficiently for such identified tasks. (Cf. *Computer literacy*)

Computer conferencing: Real-time communication between two or more parties via computer. Requires participants to be online simultaneously, in contrast to email.

Computer literacy: The knowledge and skills required to function in an environment that utilizes computer and information technologies. Less knowledge and skill than computer competence. (Cf. *Computer competence*)

Computer-managed instruction: See *CMI*.

Computer-mediated communication: See *CMC*.

Computer network: Any of several distinct ways in which groups of computers (and users) are connected together to share information and peripheral devices. (Cf. *LAN*, *WAN*, *Workgroup*)

Conferencing: See *Computer conferencing*.

Connect time: In telecommunications, the time spent online from signing on to signing off the host system.

Control unit: That part of the CPU that directs and manages all system components. See also *ALU*, *CPU*.

Courseware: Instructional computer programs and related support materials designed to enhance the teaching potential of the product.

CPU (central processing unit): A microprocessor chip that is the "brain" of a computer system. Consists of the control, arithmetic, logic, and primary memory circuits where processing is actually performed.

Crop: To remove parts of an image to improve the composition, such as eliminating distracting backgrounds.

Curriculum integration: Use of computers to support and enhance curriculum goals and objectives in all content areas and in any appropriate manner so that the computer is no longer viewed as something special or unusual.

Cursor: A movable shape that indicates current location on a computer monitor; most commonly an arrowhead, hourglass, or hand, or a blinking underscore or lighted box.

Data: Pieces of information, especially information used by a computer.

Data manager: See *Filing system*.

Data processing: Manipulating pieces of information to produce a desired result.

Data redundancy: Data duplicated in multiple database files for the purpose of identifying related records across the files.

Database: Information stored in an organized system of electronically accessible files, e.g., information on all students in a school.

Database management system (DBMS): Application software for creating and manipulating databases.

Debug: To identify and correct errors in a program.

Deductive shell: An expert system shell that requires the system developer to write the rules that constitute the system's knowledge base.

Desktop presentations: Electronic presentations created and delivered onscreen using presentation graphics software such as *PowerPoint*.

Desktop publishing: Use of sophisticated (and sometimes costly) software to compose text and graphics into near-typeset-quality pages.

Digital: Electronic signals consisting solely of on and off. (Cf. *Analog*)

Digital computer: Computer in which all data are represented digitally as on or off states. (Cf. *Analog computer*)

Digital subscriber line (DSL): Very high speed dedicated Internet connection through the local telephone company, using existing phone lines that simultaneously carry voice. Can approach LAN speeds/bandwidth.

Digital versatile disc (DVD): Optical disc format similar to CD-ROM, but with much greater storage capacity. Uses MPEG format for digital video to achieve full screen, full motion video similar to laserdiscs. Originally called *dig-*

ital video disc. Popular alternative to videotape for movie viewing.

Digital zoom: Zoom-like effect created by digital cameras by manipulating the pixels of an image. Resulting quality is generally much poorer than *optical zoom,* frequently showing the blocks that are the actual pixels.

Disc: A data storage medium from which the computer can read, but to which it normally cannot write, e.g., compact disc, laser disc. (Cf. *Disk*)

Disk: A data storage medium with both read and write capability, e.g., hard disk, floppy disk. (Cf. *Disc*)

Diskette: A small, flexible disk with limited storage capacity that is inserted into a drive and removed as needed, e.g., a floppy disk.

Disorientation: Losing your place in a hyper environment so as not to know where you are or how to return to some starting point. "Lost in hyperspace."

Distance learning: Any instructional situation in which some or all learners are physically separated from one another. Includes audio and video conferencing, computer-mediated communication (CMC), and web-based instruction.

Documentation: The manuals and accompanying materials that explain the functioning, use, and possible applications of computer hardware and software.

Document camera: A television camera mounted to a post and pointed downward at a platform. The camera picks up the image of any object, flat or 3-D, laid on the platform. Used widely in schools to project large images of real objects and printed materials for class viewing. Modern replacement for opaque projectors of the past.

DOS (disk operating system): See *Operating system.*

Dot matrix printer: A printer whose characters are patterns of dots formed by small pins striking an inked ribbon.

Download: To transfer data from a remote computer to your own computer. (Cf. *Upload*)

Drag-and-drop: To move part of a document by selecting it, then dragging the selection to a new location. Comparable to Cut followed by Paste.

Drill and practice: A form of CAI that provides repetitive opportunities for a student to respond to items concerning already-learned content and to receive feedback from the computer (Cf. *Tutorial*)

Drive bay: Mounting location in a computer case for a floppy drive, hard disk drive, optical drive, etc.

Driver: Small program (software) that enables a computer to communicate with a peripheral device such as a printer or scanner.

DSL: See *Digital subscriber line.*

Dub: To make a copy of an audio or video product, such as a cassette, CD, or DVD.

DVD: See *Digital versatile disc.*

E-commerce: Business conducted on the World Wide Web. Examples include Amazon.com and e-Bay.

E-journal: An academic journal that exists only in electronic form on the World Wide Web. Offers very fast publication compared to traditional printed journals and is thus typically more current in content.

Electronic mail: See *Email.*

Electronic portfolio: Increasingly common means of collecting one's work over time in an easily stored medium. Contents are selected to be representative of the preparer's work and are accompanied by the individual's reflection on the significance of each item (often called *artifacts*).

Email: Transmission and receipt of files, typically messages, among users of a computer network.

Ergonomic: Designed for user comfort and healthy use; tailored to human needs. Used to describe specialty office furniture, curved keyboards, etc., intended to combat carpel tunnel syndrome and other work-related injuries.

Ethernet: A standard specification for high-speed LAN connections. Also the most common type of LAN connection.

Expert system: Computer program that performs some task at the level of an expert. Consists minimally of a knowledge base, an inference engine to manipulate it, and a user interface.

Expert system shell: An expert system development tool consisting of user interfaces, an *inference engine*, and a structure for handling the *knowledge base*, but which is empty. Analogous to spreadsheet software.

Export: Save a file in a format other than that which is normal for the application software, thus requiring format translation. See also *Filter*. (Cf. *Import*)

Field: In hypermedia, an area on a screen that can contain text. In data management, the smallest meaningful unit of information, such as zip code or last name. See also *File, Record*.

File: A group of related database records, such as an inventory. Also, any digital data saved onto a hard disk or diskette. See also *Field, Record*.

File server: The "master" computer of a LAN on which may reside a common copy of application software as well as shared data files. Peripherals attached to the server are available to all work stations on the LAN.

Filing system: Data management software suitable for simple, single-file applications, but lacking many features of database software. Also termed *data manager*.

Filter: 1. Software that enables import and export of data in file formats not native to the application in use, such as importing a graphic into a word processor. 2. To search for specific types of records in a database by specifying criteria. 3. To attempt to block access to Internet sites that may be offensive or otherwise inappropriate for some users.

Firewire: Very high speed interface port on newer computers. Used to connect digital camcorders to computers for nonlinear video editing on the computer. Also known as the IEEE1394 standard. See also *Parallel, Serial, USB*.

Floppy disk: See *Diskette*.

Flowchart: A graphic representation of an algorithm or program; a visual algorithm.

Focal length: Describes the area that is captured by a camera lens. Fixed focal length lenses have only one setting; zoom lenses can be varied over a specific range of focal lengths.

Formula: An expression of calculations to be performed or relationships among cells in a worksheet.

FORTRAN (*formula translator*): A high-level language particularly suited to mathematical and scientific applications.

Forum: A discussion group on an information service such as CompuServe. Similar to a conference or a list on the Internet, but charges may apply.

Frames: 1. In desktop publishing, areas of varied size and shape on a page, each designated for text, a graphic image, a photo, or other content. Useful in creating a specific look for a document, independent of the actual frame contents. 2. On the Web, specific areas of a web page which can change independently of other areas.

Freeware: Software distributed at no more than duplication cost.

Function: In spreadsheet software, a predefined formula.

Fuzzy logic: The basis of decision making in an expert system, using confidence levels to indicate the strength of a judgment that is hoped to be "usable" rather than the only correct outcome.

Giga: Prefix that represents one billion (1,000 million). Hard disk drive capacities are given in gigabytes (GB).

GIS (geographic information system): A collection of computer hardware, software, and geographic data for capturing, storing, updating, manipulating, analyzing, and displaying all forms of geographically referenced information.

Gopher: Internet client/server software used to organize and locate information anywhere on the Internet.

GPS (Global Positioning System): Technology that allows precise determination of one's geographic location via satellite signals.

Graffiti: Stylized printing used to write on Palm OS PDAs, which convert characters to computer text.

Graphical user interface (GUI): Popularized by Apple's Macintosh computer, a GUI enables users to perform many computer operations by pointing a cursor to graphics (icons) and clicking the pointing device's button(s). See also *WIMP.*

Graphics: Computer output in the form of images, pictures, charts, graphs, etc., as opposed to alphanumeric characters.

Graphics pad/tablet: An input device on which the user can draw with a stylus or other device to create images on the computer screen.

GUI: See *Graphical user interface.*

Hacker: An individual who accesses and uses a computer system without authorization.

Handwriting recognition: Technology that allows a user to write on a screen with a stylus, then converts the handwriting into computer characters. Very different technologies are used in PDAs and tablet PCs primarily. See also *Graffiti, Bezier splines.*

Hard copy: Printed computer output.

Hard disk: A large-capacity, high-speed data storage device with multiple magnetic disks that are generally not removable. (Cf. *Diskette*)

Hardware: The physical components of a computer system.

High-level language: A programming language whose instructions resemble English statements more than computer codes. These instructions must be converted into machine code by an interpreter or compiler before the computer can execute them. (Cf. *Low-level language*)

Home page: An HTML file that displays a page intended as the initial point of access to resources on the World Wide Web.

Host: The computer that controls a telecommunications network, to which you log in or sign on after calling from your computer. A server on a WAN.

HTML: See *Hypertext Markup Language.*

HTTP (hypertext transport protocol): The communications protocol for accessing HTML documents.

Hub: Device for connecting multiple devices to one port. Examples include Ethernet hubs for sharing network connections and USB hubs that add more USB ports to a computer.

Hyper: As used in hypertext or hypermedia, nonlinear or nonsequential.

Hypermedia: Software that interconnects nodes containing differing data formats in a nonlinear fashion. Text, graphics, sound, animation, and laser or compact disc segments all can be interrelated in a web or network of information.

Hypertext: Text with cross-reference links among words that allow for nonsequential reading. Ted Nelson is credited with coining the term.

Hypertext Markup Language (HTML): The standard language used to create pages for the World Wide Web. HTML files are interpreted and displayed by a browser. See also *Page, Tag.*

Icons: Graphics used to represent actions, functions, or components of a computer system. Generically, any symbol. See also *Graphical user interface.*

ILS: See *Integrated learning systems.*

Import: Load a file in a format other than that which is normal for the application, e.g., load a WordPerfect file into Word. Necessitates translation of file formats. See also *Filter.* (Cf. *Export*)

Individualized instruction: Instruction tailored to the specific needs of each student, in contrast to group instruction.

Inductive shell: An expert system shell that derives its rules from examples provided by the system developer, requiring little or no programming.

Inference engine: The logic or reasoning component of an expert system.

Information service: National or international network offering access to a vast and diverse array of resources. Major services include

America Online, CompuServe, Microsoft Network, and Prodigy. Also called *information utility* or *commercial network*.

Information utility: See *Information service.*

Infusion: The physical presence of significant numbers of computers in a school or district, apart from their actual use.

Ink jet printer: Printer whose characters are formed by spraying tiny droplets of ink onto paper.

Input: Data received by a computer system. Also the process of entering data.

Input device: Any device that transmits data to a computer. Examples include keyboard, mouse, disk drive, and modem.

Instant messaging: Communicating synchronously via the Internet, in contrast to email.

Instructional game: CAI that integrates content into a game format.

Integrated circuit (IC): A complete, complex electronic circuit etched onto a single piece of semiconducting material, usually silicon.

Integrated learning systems (ILS): Hardware and software systems, usually provided by a single vendor, that provide CAI for most or all of the curriculum and CMI for administration.

Integrated software: A single computer program that performs the functions of more than one major application and is capable of transferring data easily among its applications.

Intelligent CAI (ICAI): Any form of CAI in which branching decisions are made by program components based on artificial intelligence.

Intelligent tutoring system (ITS): Complex CAI that attempts to replicate a Socratic tutorial. The system teaches, then queries the learner, seeks to identify misconceptions, and remediates appropriately.

Interactive multimedia: Software that incorporates media, such as digitized video, still photos, sound, and text in a nonlinear environment. Also called *hypermedia.*

Interactive video instruction (IVI): Multimedia CAI in which a computer controls a videodisc or DVD player to display graphics, sound, and/or motion segments.

Interface: Circuits that connect separate parts of a computer system, such as a disk drive or printer controller, or even separate computers. Also, the means whereby humans and machines interact. See *Graphical user interface.*

Interface method: How electronic devices connect to one another. Common methods include serial, parallel, USB, and Firewire.

Internet Relay Chat (IRC): Real time, multi-user global communication system on the Internet. IRC software uses the client/server model.

Internet service provider (ISP): Any company that sells accounts for access to its Internet host computer.

Interpreter: A program that translates and executes, one instruction at a time, another program written in a high-level language. (Cf. *Compiler*)

Intranet: A LAN or WAN that is completely private and available only to authorized users within an organization.

I/O: Input/output. See *Input, Output.*

ISDN (integrated services digital network): An international digital communications–network architecture that integrates voice and data over a single line. ISDN has significantly greater bandwidth than standard telephone lines and thus can carry digital video and other high volume data types. (Cf. *DSL*)

ISP: See *Internet service provider.*

Iteration: Repeated execution of one or more statements in a program. See also *Loop.*

Joystick: An input device that moves the screen cursor in correspondence with your movement of a vertical stick or lever. Used primarily for games.

Justified: Text that is both left and right aligned, i.e., both margins are straight.

K (kilo): A prefix used to represent 1,000. Technically, in computing K means 2^{10} or 1,024. Used to measure memory or disk capacity in bytes. See also *Giga, Mega.*

Keyboard: The most common input device, consisting of an arrangement of keys resembling those of a typewriter with additional function and cursor-movement keys.

Keyboarding: Use of a computer keyboard efficiently, without need to look at your hand movements. Differs from touch-typing in that keyboarding does not involve page layout concerns and is integral to all computer use, not only word processing.

Keypals: Penpals via email.

Knowledge base: A set of rules that contain the subject matter content and interrelationships in an expert system.

Knowledge engineering: The analysis of a problem domain to determine the factors, procedures, and information that an expert considers in reaching a conclusion. The basis for an expert system.

Labels: Alphanumeric or alphabetic data entered into a worksheet cell.

LAN (local area network): An interconnected group of computers that share applications, data files, and peripherals through a centralized file server. Bus, ring, and star configurations are common.

Language: A set of words, syntax, and rules that allows humans to communicate with, and direct, a computer.

Laptop computer: See *Notebook computer.*

Laserdisc: Optical disc containing digital data that is read by a laser beam. Includes compact discs (CDs), digital versatile discs (DVDs), and analog videodiscs.

Laser printer: Printer whose characters are formed using technology similar to photocopiers. Produces the highest-quality output among printers.

LCD projector: Liquid crystal display device that connects to video output of a computer to project computer images onto a large screen for group viewing.

Light pen: Input device resembling a ballpoint pen that is used to select from choices on a screen by touching it to the screen.

Linear tutorial: Tutorial software with only a single path through the lesson for all students.

Links: Connections among nodes in a hyper environment.

LISP (LISt Processor): The dominant logic language used in artificial intelligence applications in the United States, from which Logo is derived. (Cf. *PROLOG*)

List: On the Internet, an email discussion group. Participants must subscribe to send and receive messages, but there is rarely any subscription charge.

List processing: Text manipulation in Logo; manipulation of symbols rather than numbers in logic programming such as using LISP.

Listserv: Software that automatically operates Internet discussion groups (lists). Listproc and Majordomo are comparable software.

Local area network: See *LAN.*

Logical constructs: Structural elements of a computer program, such as sequence, selection, and iteration.

Logo: A high-level language and computer environment based on the theories of Swiss psychologist Jean Piaget and derived from the artificial intelligence language LISP. Created by an MIT team headed by Seymour Papert. Emphasizes learning by discovery in a computer-based microworld.

Loop: A sequence of operations repeated within a program. See also *iteration.*

Low-level language: Computer language closely related to a specific computer type, e.g., machine language, assembler language.

Lumens: Unit of measurement of the brightness of a light source. One of the key characteristics of video projectors. The higher the lumens, the brighter the projected image and the less need for room darkening.

Lurking: Reading the messages you receive from a list but not entering into the discussion.

Machine language: Binary coded instructions that a computer can process without any form of translation.

Mainframe computer: A large-scale, multi-processor computer system capable of operating at extremely fast speeds, handling large volumes of data, and servicing many users simultaneously.

Marginalia: Elements of a publication that appear in the margins of a page, e.g., marginal glosses, headers, page numbering.

Mark sense scanner: An input device that "reads" data into a computer by scanning specially prepared sheets marked with pencil in designated areas, such as test answer sheets.

Mastery learning: The educational premise that all students can achieve to a high level under the right conditions.

Mega: Prefix that represents one million. Disk capacities are given in megabytes (MB).

Megapixels: Millions of pixels. Defines the resolution of digital cameras.

Meta search engine: A web search engine that simultaneously searches other search engines to yield a broader range of results.

Memex: Vannevar Bush's hypothetical "memory extender" that was the conceptual precursor of interactive multimedia systems.

Memory: A computer's capacity to store data as patterns of ones and zeros. Also the chips and storage devices that contain the data.

Microcomputer: A computer system usually containing only a single microprocessor and intended for individual use. Now commonly referred to simply as *computer* or *personal computer*.

Microelectronics: Miniaturized electronic components, such as the chips used in computers.

Microprocessor: See *CPU*.

Microworld: A self-contained, fully functional simulated environment in which one can explore freely and learn by discovery.

Middle-level language: A language such as C that offers the advantages of both low- and high-level languages while minimizing their disadvantages.

Mindtool: A computer application program used to engage learners in constructive, critical, higher-order thinking about whatever they are studying.

Modem: Computer peripheral that *MO*dulates/*DEM*odulates information, enabling computers to communicate over telephone lines.

Monitor: Output device that displays text and graphics on a screen, similar to a high-quality TV.

MOO (MUD object oriented): A small form of MUD. See also *Multi-user dialog*.

Motherboard: The main circuit board of a computer, to which other components attach.

Mouse: A handheld input device that is moved on a flat surface to position the screen cursor and to select what is beneath the cursor with a button click. See also *Touchpad, Trackball*.

MPEG: Standard for digital video compression and decompression that offers larger better quality images than *QuickTime* or *Video for Windows*: Developed by the Motion Picture Experts Group (MPEG) working under the International Standards Organization (ISO).

Multimedia: Any system that combines two or more media into a single product or presentation, e.g., sound filmstrips, videos, motion pictures, TV. There is no inherent computer component.

Multimedia CAI: See *Interactive multimedia*.

Multitasking: Doing more than one task at a time. Used to describe running multiple programs simultaneously on a computer. Also describes individuals who read the paper while carrying on a conversation on a cell phone while driving their car, etc.

Multi-user dialog (MUD): Internet talk or chat involving multiple individuals simultaneously, specifically to play fantasy games. Also called *multi-user dungeon*.

Multi-user simulation environment (MUSE): Variation on *multi-user dialog*.

Network: See *Computer network*.

Network interface card (NIC): Circuitry, often on a separate board, to connect a computer to a LAN.

Neural network: A type of artificial intelligence program that is patterned after the human brain and that "learns" from its experiences, rather than requiring programming of its knowledge base.

Newsreader: Software for accessing Usenet newsgroups on the Internet.

Node: Basic organizational unit of hyper environments. In typical interactive multimedia/hypermedia, equivalent to a single screen.

Nonvolatile: Term applied to memory chips that are permanently programmed and thus do not lose their contents when the computer is turned off.

Notebook computer: Lightweight, portable personal computer small enough to fit into most briefcases, much like a notebook. Can be as powerful as any other personal computer.

Object: Any component used to construct screens in interactive multimedia environments, most commonly text fields, graphics, and buttons.

Object code: Machine-language output of a compiler.

Object-oriented software: Software in which each screen consists of discrete objects, such as areas of text and graphics, that can be created and edited independently of one another, e.g., most hypermedia software.

OCR (optical character recognition): The process by which specialized software attempts to convert the graphic image of text created by a scanner into a true text file or word processor document for manipulation. Also the software itself.

Online: Ability of a user to gain immediate access to data through a computer system; also the state of being connected to a remote computer system such as through an information service.

Operating system (OS): Software that controls and manages a computer system and its various peripheral devices. Examples include *Linux*, *MacOS*, and *Windows*.

Optical character recognition: See *OCR*.

Optical disc: Any disc format from which data are read by laser beam, e.g., CD, CD-ROM, DVD, laser videodisc, photo CD.

Optical scanner: An input device that "reads" pages of text and graphics and converts them into computer files.

Optical zoom: Zoom capability of a camera made possible by the lens itself. Quality remains relatively constant throughout the range. (Cf. *Digital zoom*)

Output: Information sent by the CPU after processing to any peripheral device.

Output device: Any peripheral capable of receiving output from a computer, e.g., monitor, printer, disk drive, modem.

Overlay card: Computer circuit boards that can display full-motion digital video on a computer monitor simultaneously with computer text and graphics.

Page: A file written in HTML for display by browser software on the World Wide Web. Often much more than just one screen full, requiring scrolling.

Parallel: Mode of data transmission in which multiple bits are transmitted simultaneously through sets of lines, such as from computer to printer. (Cf. *Firewire*, *Serial*, *USB*)

Pascal: A high-level language known for features that promote structured programming. Popular in computer science instruction. Named for seventeenth-century French mathematician Blaise Pascal.

PDA: See *Personal digital assistant*

Peer network: See *Workgroup*.

Performance support system: A combination of an expert system and other software applications to assist a human on the job, when and where aid is needed, in the most useful form possible. Also called *electronic performance support system* (EPSS).

Peripheral: Any piece of auxiliary hardware, such as a printer, modem, or scanner.

Personal computer: A computer system usually containing only a single microprocessor and intended for individual use. Also called *micro-computer* or simply *computer*.

Personal digital assistant (PDA): Handheld electronic data organizer, exemplified by products of the Palm and Handspring companies among many others.

Piracy: Making or using copies of software beyond those that the specific software license agreement permits.

Pitch: Number of characters per inch of printed text.

Pixel: Picture element; a dot on a computer screen that can be independently controlled, i.e., turned off or on in a specified color. The basis for computer displays.

Pointing device: Any input device used to move the cursor on the screen, such as a mouse, trackball, or touch pad.

Points: Unit of measure for the height of type-face characters, one point being approximately 1/72 of an inch.

Port: External connector on a computer. Examples include keyboard and mouse ports, USB ports, printer port, and Firewire port.

Portal: Websites intended to be one's initial access point to the Web; typically can be customized to address specific interests of the user.

Power supply: Transformer in a computer that turns house current into the voltages specifically required by electronic components. A cooling fan is often integrated into the power supply.

Presentation graphics: Software for production of graphics screens combining text and images which may then be printed or, more commonly, projected on a screen as an alternative to traditional overhead transparencies.

Prewriting: Activities that precede the actual start of composition that are intended to stimulate the writer's creativity.

Primitive: Any word that the Logo language understands under all circumstances, such as FORWARD; the fundamental Logo vocabulary.

Printer: Output device that produces hard copy on paper or transparency plastic.

Print graphics: Software for production of hard copy graphics, e.g., *Print Shop*.

Problem-solving software: CAI intended to help learners to develop their critical thinking skills in hopes of transfer to other contexts.

Procedure: Commands in a programming language, such as Logo primitives, that are grouped together and given a name. Together they cause a complete action to occur, such as drawing a box, when the name is used as a command.

Process approach: A method of teaching writing that addresses the total act of writing, from prewriting through completion, rather than only the final document.

Program: A series of instructions that direct and control a computer to perform a desired task.

Programmer: Person who writes computer programs.

Programming: Planning and creating a new computer program using some language or software development tool.

Programming language: The words, structure, and syntax used to communicate intelligible instructions to a computer.

PROLOG: *Pro*gramming in *Log*ic. A language popular in Europe and Japan for work in artificial intelligence. See also *LISP, Logo*.

Prompt: A symbol on the monitor screen that informs the user that the computer is ready for further input.

Prompt area: That location within a spreadsheet's display where your current typing is displayed.

Public domain: Not copyrighted. Software legally copiable by anyone.

Query: To search a database for specific information. Also, the search itself.

RAM (random-access memory): Memory chips in a computer system that accept and retain data temporarily but lose their contents when the power is cut off. See also *Volatile*. (Cf. *ROM*)

RBBS (remote bulletin board system): Computer system set up for posting and exchanging messages and software among its users.

Real time: Processing of data instantly as it is available, as in digitizing video at full running speed. In telecommunications, connection to other users who are themselves currently on-line on the network, as opposed to email, which does not require an active recipient. (Cf. *Asynchronous*)

Rebus: A story in which some words are replaced by images of the item, e.g., replace "cow" with a graphic of a cow.

Record: A group of related fields containing information that is a logical unit, e.g., all data on Jane Doe. See also *Field, File*.

Recursion: The ability to use a procedure as part of its own definition.

Relational: Database software that can link multiple files together based on a common "key."

Research network: National or international network linking researchers and other users, such as Internet and ARPANET.

Restructuring: Reorganizing schools at a deeper, more fundamental level than just typical curriculum changes, so that the organization better serves the needs of learners. Goes beyond just "school reform."

Right alignment: Text formatting that creates a straight margin down the right side of a page or column.

ROM (read-only memory): Nonvolatile memory chips that are programmed by the manufacturer. The computer system can read their contents but cannot write to them. (Cf. *RAM*)

Sans serif: A plain typeface lacking ornamentation at the ends of the lines of the characters, e.g., Arial. (Cf. *Serif*)

Scan converter: Electronic device that converts computer output to TV standard so that the computer's image can be shown on a TV. Frequently used in schools as an alternative to video projectors, but a poor substitute at best due to reduced image quality and much smaller viewable image.

Scanner: An input device that "reads" existing materials such as pages of text or pictures and creates computer files from them. Also called *optical scanner*.

Script: Instructions that determine the action of a hypermedia button.

Serial: Mode of data transmission in which data are transferred one bit at a time in sequence. Also known as the RS-232 standard. (Cf. *Firewire, Parallel, USB*)

Serif: A typeface with extra lines or curves at the end of the essential lines of each character, e.g., Times Roman. (Cf. *Sans serif*)

Server: See *File server*.

Shareware: Software distributed on a pay-if-you-like-it basis.

Simulation: Form of CAI in which the learner assumes a role to play within a structured environment that is an interactive model of some "reality."

Slot: Connector on a motherboard for expansion cards.

Smart display: A touch screen computer display that connects to the computer wirelessly, allowing the user to roam within the wireless range and still use the computer without the need for a keyboard or mouse.

Sneaker net: Carrying files on diskette from one computer to another in the absence of a LAN.

Software: The programs that cause a computer system to perform desired tasks.

Software suites: Sets of programs that have been designed to work together in an integrated fashion and to share data easily, such as *Microsoft Office*.

Source code: Computer instructions written in some language.

Spam: Unwanted email. Electronic equivalent of junk mail. Not wanted and difficult to stop.

Special characters: Characters on a keyboard that are neither numbers nor letters, e.g., punctuation marks.

Spreadsheet: An electronic tabular workspace that is used to enter and manipulate data, especially numeric data, in rows and columns.

SQL (structured query language): An interface in advanced database software that permits access to data on differing computer types with common commands.

Stack: Collection of related screens ("cards") in *HyperStudio* among which the user can move about in a non-linear manner. Called a *book* in *ToolBook* and a *folder* in *SuperLink:* Similar to a database file.

Statements: The basic vocabulary items of a programming language.

Step wise refinement: See *Top-down design.*

Storage devices: Floppy, optical, and hard disk drives that provide large amounts of data storage external to the CPU, RAM, and ROM.

Stored program control: The concept that a computer should be general-purpose and that a program, not its wiring pattern, should control it.

Storyboards: Sketches of visual content. Used to plan video productions, graphical presentations (e.g., *PowerPoint*), and websites.

Streaming: Method of transmitting audio and/or video signals over the Internet that does not require the receiver to wait until the entire file has arrived before playing it. Streaming is essential to online audio and video because their file sizes are otherwise so large as to require an unacceptably long time to download completely using any connection other than very high speed, e.g., Ethernet. Even then, streaming may be preferable, although quality is often mediocre to poor.

Structured programming: Programming using a limited set of logical constructs, minimal branching, modularity, and thorough documentation.

Style: In typography, variations in the appearance of a character without changing typeface or points, e.g., **bold,** *italic.*

Suites: See *Software suites.*

Support tools: Special-purpose software that assists the user to do some task more efficiently than by traditional means, e.g., puzzle and test generators.

Surf: To wander about the World Wide Web, following links of interest but without focus on a specific goal, as when one encounters and follows interesting links while searching that are unrelated to the original search intent.

Survival skills: Those basic computer skills that students must gain to begin to use a computer, such as booting, diskette formatting, and cursor movement.

Syntax: The required form or structure for the statements of a computer language; the rules governing use of a language.

Sysop: The *sy*stem *ope*rator of a remote bulletin board system (RBBS).

Tag: Special marker such as <H1> in an HTML file that tells a browser how to display text or where to locate resources such as image files.

Tape drive: An external storage device that writes to and reads from magnetic tape similar to audio tape. Used for backup of large volumes of data.

TCP/IP: *T*ransmission *c*ontrol *p*rotocol/*I*nternet *p*rotocol, the standards that allow diverse computer types to communicate using the Internet.

Technology-competent: Able to take full advantage of computers and other technologies to expand and enhance learning opportunities, teaching methods, and ultimately daily living.

Technology coordinator: Individual in an organization designated as responsible for overseeing technology usage and assisting current and potential users to meet their own needs.

Telecommunications: Communication by telephone lines that does not necessarily involve computers and modems.

Telecomputing: Telecommunications specifically connecting computers over telephone lines, including all exchanges between them.

Template: A reusable master plan for a word-processor document, worksheet, presentation graphics screen, or desktop-published material.

Text editor: Computer program for editing text, but with much more limited functions than a word processor.

Thread: All messages on the same topic within an Internet discussion group.

TLD (top level domain): The part of a URL that indicates, to some extent, the nature of the website. Examples include .com (commercial), .edu (educational), and .org (non-profit organization).

Tool software: See *Applications software*.

Top-down design: Development of a program starting with the overall goal and refining it into subparts until each part at the lowest level is trivial to program.

Touchpad: Cursor control device similar to a trackball in which the ball is replaced by a touch sensitive pad over which the user moves a finger.

Touch screen: A special monitor that allows the user to input information by touching designated areas on the screen.

Trackball: An inverted, stationary mouse; users rotate the ball with their thumb to guide the cursor. See also *Mouse, Touchpad*.

Transfer protocols: Standards for how computers exchange data.

Turtlegraphics: Graphics created by a robotic or cybernetic turtle, as implemented in the Logo environment.

Tutorial: A form of CAI in which the computer initiates and carries on a dialogue with the learner, presenting information, posing questions, and providing feedback. (Cf. *Drill and practice*)

Typeface: In typography and desktop publishing, the unique shape of the letters that comprise any given character set, e.g., Courier, Times Roman.

Typeface family: See *Style*.

Uniform resource locator (URL): Standardized form for giving the location of any resource accessible using the World Wide Web.

Unit record: Data specific to one instance, such as the census data for an individual. Also the cards developed by Herman Hollerith to record such data in the early days of automated data processing.

Universal serial bus (USB): High-speed interface port on newer computers that can replace serial and parallel ports with better performance and greater ease of connection. See also *Firewire, Parallel, Serial*.

Unix: Operating system originally for minicomputers, now available on personal computers. Noted for ability to execute multiple tasks simultaneously, hence popular for servers.

Upload: To transfer information from your own computer to a remote computer. (Cf. *Download*)

URL: See *Uniform resource locator*.

USB: See *Universal serial bus*.

Usenet: A conferencing system encompassing thousands of discussion and news groups. Acessible from most Internet accounts.

UXGA: High resolution setting of a computer display; 1600 × 1200 pixels.

Values: Numbers entered into a worksheet cell; numeric data.

VGA: Low resolution setting of a computer display; 640 × 480 pixels.

Videodisc: A laser disc that stores video in analog format.

Virtual reality (VR): Any computer-generated microworld with which a user may interact as if it were real. Often requires special viewing helmets (head-mounted displays, or HMDs) and controls such as a wired glove.

Virtual University: An institution of higher education that delivers courses entirely via the World Wide Web, especially one that offers entire degree programs online. There are also Virtual High Schools that offer high school courses and completion to graduation.

Virus: A program planned and written to cause mischief or damage to a computer system. Spread through computer networks, bulletin board systems, and infected diskettes.

Visual cues: Design elements (such as lines and bullets) in desktop publishing to help the reader locate and distinguish elements of the page.

Voice recognition: Ability of a computer to respond to spoken commands.

Voice synthesizer: Output device that converts computer output into intelligible speech; especially useful for the visually impaired.

Volatile: Term applied to memory chips that retain data only so long as the system is turned on, e.g., RAM.

VR: See *Virtual reality.*

WAN (wide area network): A network that spans a large area, necessitating connections through dedicated telephone lines rather than direct cabling. (Cf. *LAN*)

Wandering: Meandering aimlessly through a hyper environment. Often raised as a potential weakness of hypermedia as a learning tool.

Web-based instruction (WBI): Instruction that is delivered primarily or entirely via the World Wide Web. A common form of distance learning.

Web page: Any single file written in the HTML web programming language.

Website: A set of web pages that together constitute a complete web entity. Also used synonymously with *home page* to designate where one first enters a web entity.

WebQuest: An inquiry-based learning experience built around an engaging task which requires use of teacher-selected web sites. Provides focus and better time utilization online than common "surfing."

Wide area network: See *WAN.*

WIMP: Term sometimes applied to graphical user interfaces, denoting the major components of a GUI, namely *w*indows, *i*cons, *m*enus, and *p*ointer.

Window: A portion of the computer screen, used for a different purpose than other parts of the screen, such as a help window or a space in which to work in a different application within integrated software.

Wintel: Combination of *Windows* and *Intel*, reflecting the fact that computers that run the Windows operating system are based on chips pioneered by the Intel corporation, though it is no longer the sole supplier of such chips.

Word processing: The act of using a word processor to generate written materials.

Word processor: Software for writing, editing, revising, formatting, and printing text. Also a computer running such software, or a skilled user of such a system.

Word wrap: In word processing, the automatic arrangement of text to fit within the margins established for the document, such as moving a word that is too long for the line on which it began to a new line.

Workgroup: A type of computer network in which each computer is connected to the group by cable but is also fully functional as an independent work station. Files are not stored centrally on a file server. (Cf. *LAN*)

Worksheet: A specific application of a spreadsheet, such as the student records for one class or one specific budget. Often used as a synonym for spreadsheet.

World Wide Web: A system for accessing hypermedia documents stored anywhere on the Internet. Documents are called pages and are written using HTML. Usually called simply the Web.

Writing aids: Software such as spelling checkers, thesauruses, and grammar or style analysts, which extend the composition assistance provided by a word processor.

WWW: See *World Wide Web.*

WYSIWYG: Acronym for *what you see is what you get*. Refers to the ability of software to display a document on the screen just as it will look when printed, including graphics, special layouts, and text effects.

XGA: High resolution setting of a computer display; 1024 × 768 pixels.

Index

Q

R

Photo Credits

p. 1, Comstock Royalty Free Division; p. 14, Corbis; p. 64, Brian Smith; p. 99, David Young-Wolff/PhotoEdit; p. 190, Zigy Kaluzny/Getty Images Inc.–Stone Allstock; p. 221, Michael Newman/PhotoEdit; p. 244, Nancy Sheehan; p. 275, David Young-Wolff/PhotoEdit; p. 337, Comstock Royalty Free Division; p. 348, Will Faller; p. 372, Bill Aron/PhotoEdit; p. 391, Hironori Miyata/FDB/Getty Images Inc.–Liaison